Research Methods for Criminal Justice and Criminology

This book explains and illustrates criminal justice research topics, including ethics in research, research design, causation, operationalization of variables, sampling, methods of data collection (including surveys), reliance on existing data, validity, and reliability. For each approach, the book addresses the procedures and issues involved, the method's strengths and drawbacks, and examples of actual research using that method. Every section begins with a brief summary of the research method. Introductory essays set the stage for students regarding the who, what, when, where, and why of each research example, and relevant discussion questions and exercises direct students to focus on the important concepts.

Research Methods for Criminal Justice and Criminology: A Text and Reader features interesting and relevant articles from leading journals, which have been expertly edited (second edition) to highlight research design issues. The text offers instructors a well-rounded and convenient collection that eliminates the need to sift through journals to find articles that illustrate important precepts. The author has included new material on ethical issues, researcher safety during field work, and tips on how to communicate what works in criminal justice to the public. Articles in the second edition address issues relevant to the field today, such as crime and policing during the COVID-19 pandemic, online extremism, sextortion, mass murder, problem-solving courts, the death penalty, saturation enforcement, drug use, victimization among the LGBT community, perceptions of immigration and crime, correctional interventions, measuring theft, perceptions of safety, bullying and hate crimes, correctional staff training and attitudes, social media exposure and opinions about law enforcement, and crisis intervention team training. Ensuring a rich array, additional articles are downloadable at the Support Material tab.

The book encourages classroom discussion and critical thinking and is an essential tool for undergraduate and graduate research methods courses in criminal justice, criminology, and related fields.

Christine Tartaro is a Distinguished Professor of Criminal Justice at Stockton University. She is an expert in corrections, suicide in correctional facilities, jail design, police contact with people with mental illness, correctional treatment of individuals with mental illness, and criminal justice education. Dr. Tartaro has been teaching research methods for over 20 years, including at both the undergraduate and the graduate level. Prior to joining Stockton University, she worked at the New Jersey Department of Corrections, where she evaluated state residential community release programs. She is also the author of *Suicide and Self-Harm in Prisons and Jails*, 2nd edition (Lexington Books) and dozens of articles in several journals, including *The Prison Journal, Criminal Justice Policy Review*, *Corrections: Policy, Practice, and Research*, and the *Journal of Criminal Justice Education.* Dr. Tartaro earned her BA in history from the College of New Jersey and her MA and PhD in criminal justice from Rutgers University.

Research Methods for Criminal Justice and Criminology

A Text and Reader

Second Edition

Christine Tartaro

Routledge
Taylor & Francis Group
NEW YORK AND LONDON

Designed cover image: Getty Images

Second edition published 2026
by Routledge
605 Third Avenue, New York, NY 10158

and by Routledge
4 Park Square, Milton Park, Abingdon, Oxon, OX14 4RN

Routledge is an imprint of the Taylor & Francis Group, an informa business

First edition published by Routledge 2021

ISBN: 978-1-041-11755-1 (hbk)
ISBN: 978-1-041-11754-4 (pbk)
ISBN: 978-1-003-66151-1 (ebk)

DOI: 10.4324/9781003661511

Typeset in Times New Roman
by Newgen Publishing UK

Access the Support Material at www.routledge.com/9781041117551

To my parents, and to Jen, Dena, and Abbi

Contents

Online Articles

Operationalization/measurement

4.A Crittenden, C.A., Gateley, H.C., Policastro, C.N., & McGuffee, K. (2022). Exploring how gender and sex are measured in criminology and victimology: Are we measuring what we say we are measuring? *Women & Criminal Justice, 32*(1–2), 205–218. https://doi.org/10.1080/08974454.2020.1826388

Validity and Reliability

4.B Ceccato, V. (2019). Fieldwork protocol as a safety inventory tool in public places. *Criminal Justice Studies, 32*(2), 165–188. https://doi.org/10.1080/09589236.2019.1601367

Classical experiment

6.A Ferdik, F., Smith, H.P., & Cochran, T.J. (2025). Testing the effects of a servant leadership intervention using a cluster randomized experiment. *Justice Quarterly*, 1–24. https://doi.org/10.1080/07418825.2025.2451316

One group before-after

7.A Simpson, R., Frewing, Q., & Bayer, J. (2023). The effects of saturation enforcement on speed(ing) along a highway corridor: Results from a police-directed field study. *Justice Evaluation Journal, 6*(1), 20–31. https://doi.org/10.1080/24751979.2022.2106882

Cross-sectional

7.B Lee, Y.-J., & Santiago, L. (2023). Race, class, and gender identity: Implications for transgender people's police help seeking. *Police Practice and Research, 24*(1), 17–31. https://doi.org/10.1080/15614263.2022.2085102

Impact of sampling on results

8.A Maeder, E.M., Yamamoto, S., & McManus, L.A. (2018). Methodology matters: Comparing sample types and data collection methods in a juror decision-making study on the influence of defendant race. *Psychology, Crime, & Law, 24*(7), 687–702. https://doi.org/10.1080/1068316X.2017.1409895

Paper/pencil surveys/self-reports and Survey items

9.A Abderhalden, F.P. (2024). Environmental and psychological correlates of self-injurious thoughts and behaviors among jail detainees. *Corrections, 9*(2), 127–150. https://doi.org/10.1080/23774657.2021.2023339

Ethics and field research

10.A Goode, E. (1999). Sex with Informants as deviant behavior: An account and commentary. *Deviant Behavior, 20,* 301–324. https://doi.org/10.1080/016396299266416

Content analysis

11.A Barranco, R.E., & May, D.C. (2023). Theft by any other name is still theft: Examining "looting" during the COVID-19 pandemic. *Deviant Behavior, 44*(9), 1320–1333. https://doi.org/10.1080/01639625.2023.2182657

Existing records

11.B Willis, T., Kern, L.J., Hedden, B.J., Nelson, V., Comartin, E., & Kubiak, S. (2023). The impact of Crisis Intervention Team (CIT) training on police use of force. *Journal of Offender Rehabilitation, 62*(3), 157–173. https://doi.org/10.1080/10509674.2023.2182863

Secondary data

11.C Outlaw, M., Teasdale, B., Bradley, M.S., & Ménard, K.S. (2023). Risk and danger among the "invisible": Bisexual IPV victimization, lifestyle factors, and feelings of marginalization. *Victims & Offenders, 18*(1), 122–140. https://doi.org/10.1080/15564886.2022.2137612

12.A Kierkus, C.A., Johnson, B.R., Hoffman, H., & Parks, J. (2023). DWI courts in Michigan: An examination of the interlock effect on drunk driving recidivism. *Justice Evaluation Journal, 6*(2), 201–218. https://doi.org/10.1080/24751979.2023.2251558

Preface

Why Use This Book?

I have been teaching research methods for over 20 years, and have experience working with both undergraduate and graduate research methods students. I believe that students at all levels learn best when they read empirical research to reinforce the lessons included in research methods textbooks. They need to see the principles of research in action to understand the strengths and weaknesses of each method.

When I started this project, I had three goals. First, I wanted to provide everything necessary for teaching research methods to criminal justice and criminology students in one book. As a professor at a state university, I am mindful of the cost of tuition, fees, and textbooks, and I wanted to offer a cost-effective option. My goal was to save students money by providing everything in one book while saving professors time by giving them both a textbook and timely articles illustrating a variety of research designs. Second, I wanted the reader portion of the book to cover an array of topics in criminal justice so that students could learn about their field while simultaneously improving their ability to read and understand empirical research. The articles that I selected include a mixture of topics, including police, courts, corrections, and victimization. I specifically chose articles that address some trending subjects, such as immigration and crime, the impact of COVID-19 on crime and the criminal justice system, public perceptions of the police, harm reduction, characteristics of mass murderers, and problem-solving courts. Third, I wanted to make assignments more manageable by editing some of the longer articles so that they are shorter while still including the essential elements of research.

I hope that you enjoy the book.

Acknowledgments

I am very grateful for the help and support of my friend, Ellen Boyne of Routledge, as I don't think I would have completed either edition of this book without her. Being a sole author can be a lonely experience at times, but while working on this project, I knew I could always lean on Ellen for help and support. Kate Taylor was vital to the production of the first edition and was very helpful getting the second edition moving in the right direction. Maia Berliner of Routledge jumped in to see this project to completion. Leigh Westerfield and Suriya Rajasekar were very helpful with moving this project to completion. This was a tough project to complete while teaching full-time, but the Routledge staff did everything they could to make it as painless as possible.

I am lucky to have some great teacher friends who have proven to be great sounding boards over the years. Deeanna Button and I have had so many conversations about teaching research methods. The reading exercises sheet that I included in the instructor materials was mostly derived from my paper and test grading checklists, but I did adopt a few of her questions. I've also spent lots of time talking about the best ways to help students learn with Kimberley Schanz and Jess Bonnan-White. Those conversations helped as I worked on finding ways to explain difficult concepts in this book.

Any time I take on a project this size, my poor family and friends have to hear about it. I know that listening to someone talk about writing a book is not exactly the most exciting way to spend one's day, but they have all done their best to be patient with me. My parents, sisters Jennifer and Dena Tartaro, niece Abbi, and friends Christopher and Lindsay DeSantis have all heard about the ups and downs of this project for the past few years. Of course, some of the best support came from my pets, who sat next to me and even occasionally jumped on my keyboard while I worked on this. Thank you, RayRay, Scruffy, Petey, Todd, and Scooter. While working on this, I had to say goodbye to Sully and Winston, and I miss both of them terribly.

Credits

Reading 3.1

Source: Conway, M. (2021). Online extremism and terrorism research ethics: Researcher safety, informed consent, and the need for Tailored Guidelines. *Terrorism and Political Violence.* http://doi/abs/10.1080/09546553.2021.1880235

Reading 4.1

Source: Hadi, S.T., & Tartaro, C. (2024). "Do immigrants cause higher crime rates?" A cumulative cross-sectional general social survey data analysis. *Journal of Ethnicity in Criminal Justice, 22*(4), 357–378. https://doi.org/10.1080/15377938.2024.2415955

Reading 4.2

Source: Stauss, K., Sparks, L., & Gallagher, J.M. (2023). Extending a letter-writing intervention developed for incarcerated mothers to incarcerated fathers: A mixed methods study. *Corrections, 8*(3), 166–186. https://doi.org/10.1080/23774657.2020.1850219

Reading 5.1

Source: Rash, J., Scott, T., Clements, P., & Strom, K. (2023). Stealing tires or copper wires? How the national incident-based reporting system changed how the Arlington, Texas, Police Department addresses larceny-thefts. *International Journal of Comparative and Applied Criminal Justice, 47*(4), 417–429. https://doi.org/10.1080/01924036.2022.2059535

Reading 5.2

Source: Boehme, H.M., Burrow, J.D., & Jung, S. (2024). An exploratory analysis examining the relationship between protective and risk factors of bullying and hate crime victimization within schools. *Journal of School Violence, 23*(3), 348–362. https://doi.org/10.1080/15388220.2023.2299974

Reading 6.1

Source: Rodriguez, N., & Usman, H. (2023). An examination of prison-based programming and recommitment to prison. *Justice Evaluation Journal, 6*(2), 219–244. https://doi.org/10.1080/24751979.2023.2170262

Reading 6.2

Source: Harmon, T., Taylor, D., Schoepflin, T., Henning, C., & Falco, D. (2024). Does depth of information matter? An empirical test of the Marshall hypothesis. *Criminal Justice Studies, 37*(3), 241–254. https://doi.org/10.1080/1478601X.2024.2392227

Reading 7.1

Source: Najman, J.M., Farrington, D.P., Bor, W., Clavarino, A.M., McGee, T.R., Scott, J.G., Williams, G.M., & McKetin, R. (2022). Do cannabis and amphetamine use in adolescence predict adult life success: A longitudinal study. *Addiction Research & Theory*. https://doi/abs/10.1080/16066359.2022.2032679

Reading 7.2

Source: Patterson, C., Hogan, L., & Cox, M. (2019). A comparison between two retrospective alcohol consumption measures and the daily drinking diary method with university students. *The American Journal of Drug and Alcohol Abuse, 45*(3), 248–253. https://doi.org/10/1080/00952990.2018.1514617

Reading 8.1

Source: Jossie, M.L., Lane, J., & Cook, C.L. (2023). Attitudes about rehabilitation among jail correctional officers. *Victims & Offenders, 18*(8), 1521–1541. https://doi.org/10.1080/15564886.2023.2181250

Reading 8.2

Source: Cross, A.R., & Fine, A.D. (2022). Police-related social media exposure and adolescents' interest in becoming a police officer. *Police Practice and Research, 23*(5), 553–568. https://doi.org/10.1080/15614263.2021.2017932

Reading 8.3

Source: Webster, J.M., Dickson, M.F., Tillson, M., & Staton, M. (2024). Impaired driving and other risky drug use and sex behaviors: A cross-sectional examination of high-risk rural women incarcerated in jail. *Journal of Addictive Diseases, 42*(1), 45–54. https://doi.org/10.1080/10550887.2022.2138701

Reading 8.4

Source: Gezinski, L.B., & Gonzalez-Pons, K.M. (2022). Legal barriers and re-victimization for survivors of intimate partner violence navigating courts in Utah, United States. *Women & Criminal Justice, 32*(5), 454–466. https://doi.org/10.1080/08974454.2021.1900991

Reading 9.1

Eaton, A.A., Ramjee, D., & Saunders, J.F. (2023). The relationship between sextortion during COVID-19 and pre-pandemic intimate partner violence: A large study of victimization among diverse U.S men and women. *Victims & Offenders, 18*(2), 338–355. https://doi.org/10.1080/15564886.2021.2022057

Reading 9.2

Source: Tierney, H.R., Ma, Y., Bacchetti, P., Adimora, A.A., Chandran, A., Kempf, M.-C., Collins, L.F., DeHovitz, J., DiClemente, R.J., French, A.L., Jones, D.L., Sharma, A., Spence, A.B., Hahn, J.A., Price, J.C., & Tien, P.C. (2024). Pivoting from in-person to phone survey assessment of alcohol and substance use: Effects on representativeness in a United States prospective cohort of women living with and without HIV. *The American Journal of Drug and Alcohol Abuse, 50*(1), 54–63. https://doi.org/10.1080/00952990.2023.2267745

Reading 9.3

Source: Smylie, C., Duxbury, L., & Bennell, C. (2024). Community policing during the pandemic. *Police Practice and Research, 25*(2), 230–243. https://doi.org/10.1080/15614263.2023.2222869

Reading 10.1

Source: Santelices, C., Matsumoto, A., Boulad, M., & Stopka, T. J. (2023). Evaluating technologies to identify fentanyl and adulterants in street drug paraphernalia: Qualitative perspectives of service providers and their clientele. *Substance Use & Misuse*. https://doi/abs/10.1080/10826084.2023.2231067

Reading 10.2

Source: Brougham, P.L., Uttley, C.M., & Haley, T.M. (2023). Researcher safety: Studying social deviance or criminal behavior. *Journal of Criminal Justice Education, 34*(1), 53–70. https://doi.org/10.1080/10511253.2022.2137540

Reading 11.1

Source: Brucato, G., Hesson, H., Dishy, G., Lee, K., Pia, T., Syed, F., Villalobos, A., Rogers, R.T., Corbeil, T., Stone, M.H., Lieberman, J.A., Appelbaum, P.S., & Girgis, R.R. (2023). An analysis of motivating factors in 1,725 worldwide cases of mass murder between 1900–2019. *The Journal of Forensic Psychiatry & Psychology, 34*(2), 261–274. https://doi.org/10.1080/14789949.2023.2208570

Reading 11.2

Source: Nee, C., White. M., Woolford, K., Pascu, T., Barker, L., & Wainwright, L. (2015). New methods for examining expertise in burglars in natural and simulated environments: Preliminary findings. *Psychology, Crime & Law, 21*(5), 507–513. https://doi.org/10.1080/1068316X.2014.989849

Reading 11.3

Source: Jalain, C.I., Lucas, P.A., & Higgins, G.E. (2024). Assessing the effectiveness of mental health courts in reducing recidivism: A systematic review with meta-analysis. *Justice Evaluation Journal, 7*(2), 212–230 https://doi-org/10.1080/24751979.2024.2373245

Reading 12.1

Source: Cheesman II, F.L., Marlowe, D.B., & Genthon, K.J. (2023). Racial differences in drug court referral, admission, and graduation rates: Findings from two states and eight counties. *Journal of Ethnicity in Criminal Ju*stice, *21*(1), 80–102. https://doi.org/10.1080/15377938.2023.2193952

Reading 12.2

Source: Borseth, J.L., Myer, A.J., & Makarios, M.D. (2023). Superficial adherence to EBP: An example of low fidelity to the RNR model using a halfway house. *Corrections, 8*(5), 371–390. https://doi.org/10.1080/23774657.2021.1886888

1 Introduction

If you are reading this, you are probably enrolled in a research methods course. You also probably aren't thrilled about it, but it will be okay. A common knock on academics is that it lacks practical application to real life. After all, how many of us regularly use the trigonometry that we learned in high school or even in college? Don't get me wrong. I believe that there is value in trigonometry, because it challenges us with higher-order thinking. Plus, I like certain types of math, but I can respect those who do not. While it might not seem so now, this class is something that you can use in your life. Knowing about research can truly help you be a better criminal justice professional and be in a stronger position to judge evidence that people use to support their arguments.

I have had enough experience working with students that I am well aware that many dread research methods and statistics courses, and the only reason why they take them is because they are mandatory. I understand the apprehension because of how challenging the classes can be. What I find frustrating is when students fail to appreciate what they stand to gain. While you might not realize it now, this class has tons of practical application to all criminal justice jobs and life outside of work. This class will help you sort through what is real and what is pseudoscience, "fake news," or a fad lacking any evidence of effectiveness. This is of vital importance to your careers. You might start out in a low-level position, such as a police officer on a regular beat or a case worker for a social service agency, but you are going to want to move up in the ranks and become someone who has a hand in making decisions. When that happens, you can either move the field of criminal justice in the right direction, using evidence to inform your decisions, or you can try to use what people think of as "common sense" and advocate for something that is probably ineffective. The "common sense" approach to criminal justice policy has brought us such failures as Scared Straight, D.A.R.E., mandatory sentences for drug possession, and correctional boot camps.

Fortunately, our field is moving in the direction of **evidence-based practice** (EBP). Gies et al. (2020) define EBP as "the use of best available scientific evidence on the effectiveness of programs, practices, and policies, to guide the decision-making process" (p. 156). What this means for criminal justice is that there is a push to learn about what types of interventions work, to implement only programs that work, and to discard those that are ineffective. As implausible as it may seem, this is *not* how criminal justice has operated for decades. While lamenting misguided efforts in the field of corrections, Latessa, Cullen, and Gendreau (2011) argued that what we have been doing qualifies as **quackery**, meaning the use of interventions that are *not* based on our knowledge of what causes crime or what we know is effective in changing behavior. Our use of ineffective programs based on flawed premises has cost us billions of dollars and has harmed victims, communities, and even people serving sentences for criminal behavior. EBP became a priority for criminal justice in 1996, when Congress required the US Attorney General to produce an "independent, comprehensive, and scientific review" of crime prevention programs funded by the Department of Justice (Gies et al., 2020, p. 156).

EBP specifically focuses on empirical research and prioritizes that over professional experience. Researchers contribute to EBP by producing methodologically rigorous program

DOI: 10.4324/9781003661511-1

evaluations. Practitioners and policymakers will hopefully then use this information to guide their decisions about which policies and programs to keep, which to modify, and which to jettison (National Institute of Corrections, n.d.). Notice that this is a two-step process that requires work from both researchers and practitioners. Many students approach research methods classes with the attitude of "I am not going to be a researcher, so I don't need this." But that is not true. It might have been the case back when your parents or grandparents got jobs in this field, but not anymore. You are probably in this class because you either want to be a researcher (less likely) or a criminal justice practitioner (more likely). Either way, for evidence-based practice to work in our field, you need to be part of it. To do that, you don't have to be a researcher, but you must at least have a basic understanding of research and how to distinguish between good and bad information.

This book will also help you with life outside work. We have access to more information than previous generations could have ever imagined. That is a blessing, but it is also a curse. With this proliferation of information comes the creation of and dissemination of misinformation. Two of today's most prominent examples of how damaging misinformation can be are vaccines and climate change. An MIT professor in geochemistry reviewed 11,602 scientific articles about climate change and found that, among those articles, there was near 100% agreement that global warming is not only real but is a product of human activity (Powell, 2017). And yet, there are people, some in high-ranking positions in government and industry, who dismiss the science and insist that climate change is a hoax. This has profound implications for policy.

Given the strength of corporations, lobbyists, and politicians who promote certain industries, it is likely that climate change denial would continue to exist even without the availability of the internet to spread misinformation. The internet, however, has been vital to the spread of misinformation, leading some people to believe that vaccines cause autism (Larson, 2018). The only research conducted by an actual scientist that linked vaccines to autism was published in 1998, but the study had to be retracted due to fraud. The lead researcher took numerous steps throughout the study to make sure that the research team would find the exact results that he was seeking in order to financially benefit himself (Sathyanarayana & Andrade, 2011). Since that retraction, there has been no research conducted by any actual professional researcher that supports the autism-vaccine link. Despite the overwhelming lack of evidence, this kind of misinformation continues to spread, largely through the internet. That fraudulent autism study has been cited 1,650 times, with 940 of those citations coming *after* the misconduct was uncovered (Retraction Watch, 2023). The creation and spread of misinformation, however, is not solely the work of unethical researchers. Anyone can make a website and post claims that have no basis in fact. Sadly, "news" organizations also purposefully spread misinformation for the sake of stoking outrage, as they have learned that this leads to higher ratings and increased revenue (Shapiro et al., 2023). Additionally, the internet has empowered everyone to become "researchers," and those who are unable to differentiate good sources from bad can be easily convinced with incorrect information, especially if the misinformation feeds into their existing beliefs.

With the help of this book and your professor, you should leave this class having a much better sense of what constitutes actual research. You will also learn that all research is *not* created equal, and we must always consider how the research was conducted as we try to make sense of the findings. This will help you as you hear not only about research in criminal justice but work on all subject matters. Research methods classes for all disciplines are remarkably similar. The ethics precautions that are necessary for each discipline vary. For example, in your class, you will not be reviewing the necessary steps to ethically care for lab rats or chimpanzees, as you would in biology or even psychology. The research designs and sampling considerations, however, are the same no matter the discipline. So, once you start to feel more comfortable understanding the basics of criminal justice research, you should feel more confident in being able to judge the quality of work elsewhere. That will make you a better consumer of information in all corners of life.

The Scientific Method

I am sure that you have already conducted some research on something. You had to do research to figure out which laptop or car you should buy. You probably did a good amount of research to choose a college. You have also done research to write papers for other classes. All of that is good. You are better off knowing that one of your top choices of cars got an excellent crash test rating, while your other choice decapitated the crash-test dummy. Reading consumer magazines and comparing laptops at a store do not involve scientific research, though. This book and your class will teach you about a more systematic way of learning.

The research that is the subject of this course is based on the **scientific method**. What sets this apart from the research you did to shop for a computer is that the scientific method requires adherence to a strict set of rules. Just as with your computer or car-buying research, we make observations, but with the scientific method we do so in a very systematic way, with the goal of generating an *unbiased* image of the world rather than an individual's personal image of it (Haig, 2018; Wallace, 1971). In his classic work on the scientific method, Wallace (1971) visualized the research process as a wheel, including theory formulation, hypothesis construction, observations, and then generalization of findings (Figure 1.1). The use of a wheel as an illustration is important here, as wheels lack a clear starting point. For research, the start- and end-points vary depending on the method the researcher adopts. The two most common approaches in criminal justice research are deductive and inductive. When determining which method you want to use, ask yourself if you want to test a current theory or see if a program works. If so, you are using the deductive approach. This method has been the favored set of steps in the natural sciences for decades, and it is commonly used in criminal justice research.

The **deductive reasoning** approach starts with theory. A **theory** is an attempt to construct a plausible explanation of reality (Hagan, 2007). Researchers then use logical deduction to take theories and write **hypotheses**, or predictions of relationships between variables based on our understanding of theory (Maxfield & Babbie, 2012; Wallace, 1971). Only after the steps for exploration of theory and development of hypotheses are completed does the researcher determine how to test the hypotheses and conduct observations. These observations must follow specific protocols to reduce the potential for bias. Once data have been collected, it is time to test the hypotheses. Based on the rigor of the research design, it may or may not be appropriate to generalize the findings to the wider population. Researchers using deductive reasoning would start at the top of the research wheel in Figure 1.1 and move clockwise.

If you are more focused on making observations and then using that experience to generate a theory, you want an **inductive reasoning** approach. Research based on inductive reasoning has a different starting point, at the bottom of the wheel and moving clockwise. Rather than beginning with a theory and then moving on to hypothesis testing, researchers taking the inductive approach use observations as their starting point. They seek to observe facts without any particular theory in mind. Those observations can be used to draw conclusions and then generate a theory based on the findings. These theories are known as **grounded theories**, since they are based on data that are grounded in researchers' observations (Glaser & Strauss, 1967; Maxwell, 1996). Researchers can then take that newly formed theory, generate hypotheses based on it, and go around the wheel again but with the deductive approach this time.

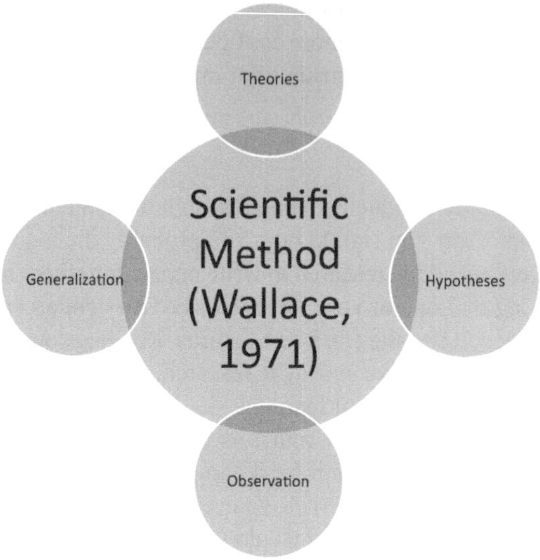

Figure 1.1 The scientific method
Source: Wallace, W. (1971). *The logic of science in sociology.* Chicago: Aldine. P. 18

Qualitative and Quantitative Research

The decision of whether to approach research with inductive or deductive reasoning might be related to the kind of study the researcher is planning. Criminal justice as an academic discipline has benefited from both quantitative and qualitative research. Quantitative research is the more common approach in criminal justice in the United States. Quantitative work tends to start with a deductive approach, with researchers using knowledge of theory to write and then test hypotheses. The primary distinguishing characteristics of quantitative research are the use of numerical values to represent concepts and the quantification of results, often involving statistical procedures. Due to the rules governing statistical analysis, quantitative studies rely on large sample sizes, but to get the necessary sample size, researchers often forego the opportunity to interact much, if at all, with potential research participants. In fact, a popular trend in criminal justice research today is to obtain access to large datasets with information collected by other researchers or practitioners, with many current researchers performing sophisticated statistical analysis but never meeting or interacting with any of the humans who were the subject of data collection.

Qualitative research largely involves observation and long interviews of smaller groups with the goal of generating a more complete understanding of a group or subculture. Qualitative research in criminal justice draws from the work of urban anthropologists and sociologists who spend extensive amounts of time and sometimes even live among those they are studying. Qualitative work could start from either the inductive or the deductive approach. Unlike quantitative studies that involve testing a specific hypothesis, some qualitative studies entail collecting data first and then focusing on theory generation based on the conclusions drawn from the observations. While quantitative research follows strict data collection plans with interview schedules or data collection checklists written out and pretested prior to data collection, qualitative researchers might begin their observations while lacking any research questions (Hagan, 2007; Maxfield & Babbie, 2012).

Both qualitative and quantitative research have helped our discipline grow, and both will be necessary to help us continue to learn why people commit crime and what we can do to stop it.

There are, unfortunately, professional rivalries that develop, and there are occasionally debates about the merits of both the qualitative and the quantitative approach. As I noted earlier, quantitative methods are more frequently used in criminal justice research in the United States, but there have been calls to increase the number of studies involving both qualitative and quantitative methods (Rodriguez, 2024). Quantitative approaches, with deductive reasoning, are synonymous with **positivism**, or the natural sciences approach to research. In its more extreme form, researchers who identify as positivists can endorse scientism and be skeptical about the value of qualitative research. Specifically, **scientism** suggests that the only research worth doing consists of concepts that are measurable, frowning upon the lack of quantitative orientation in qualitative work (Hagan, 2007; Hartley, 2011). At the other end of the research spectrum are researchers who view knowledge through the lens of **historicism**, meaning that they consider all social events as unique and as warranting chronicling. That approach avoids the quantitative practice of trying to draw generalizations from research findings and, as such, is unscientific (Hagan, 2007).

Basic and Applied Research

There are two additional categories of social science research—basic and applied. This distinction is a carryover from the natural sciences (Hammersly, 2000). **Basic research**, also known as pure research, involves seeking information for the sake of advancing theory or our knowledge base. **Applied research** aims to solve practical problems and can be divided into two categories—program evaluation and policy analysis. Applied research, according to Maxfield and Babbie (2012), seeks links between justice policy and problems. Common types of applied research involve evaluations of criminal justice programs and policies to see what kind of impact, if any, they had on the problems that they were designed to alleviate. **Program evaluation** tends to be more focused on the past in that it answers the question of what impact the program or policy had on the problem. **Policy analysis** is more forward-looking and seeks to identify possible solutions to current and future problems and then to choose the best or most feasible option. Hammersly (2000) correctly noted that basic and applied research are not necessarily mutually exclusive. There have been numerous occasions where basic research has led to practical applications, while applied research has been relevant to theory development.

Hammersly (2000) suggested that we move away from the basic/applied distinction and move toward considering social science research as either scientific or practical. Scientific inquiry, according to Hammersly,

> refers to research that is designed to contribute to a body of academic knowledge, where the immediate audience is fellow researchers—though the ultimate aim is to produce knowledge that will be a resource for anyone with interest in the relevant topic (Hammersly, pp. 223–224).

Those engaging in scientific research rely more on the research community to evaluate the validity of their research, usually resulting in slower processes of production and dissemination of knowledge. Practical research is

> geared directly to providing information that is needed to deal with some practical problem, so that here the immediate audience for research reports is people with a practical interest in the issue; notably, but not exclusively, policymakers and occupational practitioners of the relevant kinds (Hammersly, p. 224).

Practical research places an emphasis on the direct relevance of their work to current policy and practical concerns.

Whether we use the basic/applied or scientific/practical categories, it is important to appreciate the value that both types of research bring to our field and to humanity in general. Basic research may not appear to the layperson to have relevance and may be subject to criticism for appearing to be a pointless academic exercise. In fact, the late US Senator William Proxmire used to mock scientists whose research he deemed to lack relevance to the world by declaring them to be winners of the Golden Fleece award for what was, in his opinion, a waste of federal money. The negative publicity that came from Proxmire's criticism prompted some agencies to pull their grant funding from important research that Proxmire just did not understand. For example, he criticized Ohio State University researchers' work on a six-legged robot and the National Institute on Alcohol Abuse and Alcoholism's study on alcohol aggression in animals. The robotics research eventually led to the invention of computer-controlled knee joints. As for alcohol and aggression in animals, the researchers studied animals because they could not ethically ask humans to get drunk and fight (Irion, 1988). So, while you might hear about a science project that appears to have no practical value, keep in mind that we use basic research to develop theory and learn about the world, and it is that knowledge that is the basis for development of scientific advances and social programs that benefit society. Once those advances and programs are implemented, applied or practical research can assess their effectiveness.

Steps of the Research Process

When I introduced the scientific method, I presented the wheel of research with four steps: theory, hypotheses, observations, and generalization. Now that you know a bit more about research, it is time to break down the process into more detail. I am going to do this in the order that we would follow using the deductive method.

Theory: Theories are plausible explanations of reality. Criminal justice draws on theories from multiple disciplines, including criminology, sociology, psychology, economics, biology, and business, when working to explain human behavior and the way that organizations function. Theories are used to speculate about why some people commit crime while others lead law-abiding lives, why some people desist from crime as they grow older while others remain active in crime, and why some organizations are more efficient and effective at achieving their goals than others. Theories often form the basis of researchers' ideas for what they wish to study.

I want to emphasize the importance of theory as the starting point for research. In criminology, we have an abundance of theories as possible explanations for why people engage in criminal behavior (Bernard & Engel, 2001; Cooper & Worrall, 2012; Kraska, 2006). Theories for why the branches of the criminal justice system and agencies within operate the way they do are not nearly as plentiful (Bernard & Engel, 2001; Kraska, 2006), but it is important for us to seek an understanding of why something should or should not be expected to work before we set out to understand whether it does work. There's a strong argument that can be made that conducting this exercise when we initially propose any criminal justice policy or program would save us a lot of time and hardship by allowing us to discontinue work on programs that really should not be expected to be effective. Correctional boot camps, which were very popular in the 1980s and 1990s, are a good example of the failure to consider theory before implementing a program. The idea was that we would have corrections officers act like boot camp drill sergeants, but let's think about why we should have expected this to work. When confronted with the lack of a theoretical foundation, supporters argued that it was just "common sense" that the boot camps would reduce recidivism (Cullen et al., 2005; Morash & Rucker, 1990). By the time the correctional boot camps appeared, the aspects of the military model adopted by corrections departments had already been phased out of the military (Morash & Rucker, 1990). Additionally, while many of us know someone whose life was changed by joining the military, the correctional version of boot camp graduation did not lead to job security, housing, clothing, healthcare, a full pension, and the respect of community members that came with military service. Contrast that with correctional boot camp graduates going back to the same, mostly impoverished, neighborhoods with no paycheck, housing, healthcare, or admiration from the community but with a criminal record that they needed to disclose to potential employers. There really was no theoretical justification for why correctional boot camps *should* serve as a form of rehabilitation (Latessa et al., 2020; Morash & Rucker, 1990), and the evaluation results showed that they were not associated with positive outcomes (Cullen et al., 2005; Mackenzie et al., 2001; Wilson et al., 2005). More careful consideration of the lack of viable theories for why we should have expected the boot camps to work might have prevented their proliferation.

Hypotheses: A hypothesis is a clear, measurable statement that predicts a relationship between variables. Hypotheses are usually generated based on the theory that is being used as the foundation of a particular study. Someone interested in the routine activities approach, for example, might hypothesize that the proliferation of doorbell cameras and other video security devices will reduce the incidence of porch theft. A researcher studying important events in juveniles' and young adults' lives would likely base their hypothesis about desistance from crime on life course criminological theory.

Concepts/operationalization/measurement: Researchers begin by thinking of concepts they want to study. **Concepts** tend to be rather abstract, such as "crime," "punishment," or "recidivism." All those words can have a wide variety of meanings. While they are a good starting point for determining one's research agenda, researchers need to be much more specific as they get closer to collecting the data. "Punishment" can mean a lot of different things. Do you mean legal sanctions? If so, just criminal sanctions, or do traffic violations count too? Would you prefer only to focus on the types of punishment that constitute a loss of liberty, such as incarceration? If your focus is on the loss of liberty, what about home confinement with electronic monitoring? Research that might look pretty simple at first glance tends to become much more complex when we have to move on from concepts and determine what we will actually measure. Take recidivism as an example. Recidivism is generally defined as reoffending, but it can be measured several different ways. It could be based on individuals' self-reported reoffending, but in that case are you concerned with just one specific crime type or reoffending in general? Reoffending could also mean rearrest, reconviction, and/or reincarceration. It might be helpful to measure recidivism multiple different ways. Research on the relationship between sex offender registration and offending often finds that registration is *not* associated with sex offending recidivism, but there is often a slight relationship between registration and general offending (Letourneau et al., 2010; Tewksbury et al., 2012; Zgoba et al., 2018; Zgoba & Mitchell, 2023), so you can see why it was important for the researchers to differentiate between different types of offending. In some of my own research, I found that diversion and reentry service participation for individuals with mental illness was not related to the chances of someone being reincarcerated within a certain time frame, but program participation was associated with staying in the community for longer periods of time before reincarceration (Tartaro, 2015). If you use data that already exist, you may be constrained in your choices for measurement, as you are going to have to use what is there. If you are collecting your own data, you will have to make a lot of decisions about your exact plans for measuring concepts. This process is referred to as **operationalization**, which is the development of operational definitions to specify how concepts will be measured (Maxfield & Babbie, 2012). We operationalize concepts to make them variables that are measurable.

Choice of research method and data collection plan: There are a number of ways to approach social science research. The question you must ask yourself is, what are you trying to learn by doing this? If you want to look at the effectiveness of an anti-truancy program, you might want to compare students who are in the new program to students subjected to the old program's rules. You might also want to compare the students and their truancy levels before and after they participated. Research methods can involve looking at one group or organization at one period in time, at multiple groups at one time, or at one or multiple groups over time.

How will you collect data necessary to test the hypotheses? There are a wide variety of options for data collection in criminal justice. Before you decide on a data collection plan, you must first choose your **unit of analysis**. The unit of analysis is who or what you plan to study, such as individuals or organizations. Knowing that will help guide your decision about what kind of data to collect and from whom. Researchers have conducted observations, interviewed victims and offenders in person, mailed surveys to homes, called people at home, stationed themselves in public locations and asked people to participate in interviews, or visited prisons, jails, homes, or had people come to university offices for interviews or to take surveys. Computers can aid in data collection through deployment of internet-based surveys or the use of computer-assisted survey equipment that takes the place of human interviewers. Research can involve no human contact at all, through collection of records from criminal justice organizations, businesses, or social service agencies, or the acquisition of publicly available data. One can even collect data by logging onto a streaming service and analyzing the content of criminal justice documentaries and dramas. At the other end of the spectrum, research plans can involve extensive contact and interaction with research participants, through long interviews and periods spent observing their behavior.

Collecting the data: Once proper ethical safeguards are in place, the next step is collecting the data. This could be as easy as downloading a preexisting dataset for secondary data analysis, or it could involve months or even years of observations and interviews. If you are collecting data by doing observations or surveys in the field, this could be time-consuming, expensive, and even dangerous work.

Analysis: The necessary analysis will depend on the measurement and data collection decisions. Analysis of quantitative data will involve some statistics, but the level of sophistication will depend on the data and what is necessary to properly test the hypotheses. For qualitative projects, the focus of data analysis will likely involve coding the data into different theoretical categories and/or contextualizing the data to understand the findings in context (Maxwell, 1996).

Dissemination and application of findings: Now that the research is finished, it is time to share the results with others. If the research was conducted at the request of an agency, you will most likely provide them with a report of your findings. They may choose to use the results to make changes to their operations. Others might benefit from seeing these results, so you should consider appropriate outlets for your work. Where you share the work will depend on your preferred audience. If you would like fellow researchers to see the findings, publication in an academic journal would be the best option. If you are hoping for criminal justice practitioners to benefit from your work, then a magazine or newsletter that targets professionals might be more appropriate.

Summary

We have all done some type of research in our lives, but not all types of research are equal. Understanding what makes some types of research good and valid, and other types suspect is a powerful tool that can help you in so many aspects of life. This book is about research guided by the scientific method. Unlike research that you might do to figure out which restaurant to go to this weekend, the scientific method requires that researchers follow specific protocols to generate objective results. Researchers draw on theory to generate hypotheses and follow very specific procedures to generate observations in a manner that aims to reduce bias and allow for generalization of the findings to a larger group. There are multiple types of social science research, including quantitative work that seeks to find trends among large samples. Qualitative research usually aims to take an in-depth look at a small number of individuals or one group or organization. Qualitative research is less concerned with patterns and generalizations than it is with fully understanding a unique set of circumstances. Research can also be divided into basic/pure versus applied categories, with the former generating knowledge for the furtherance of the discipline. Applied research consists of program evaluation and policy analysis and focuses on a specific problem or program that needs to be studied.

The exact steps one takes as part of the research process might differ depending on whether one is taking the deductive or the inductive approach. With inductive, researchers begin with observations and then use that to generate theory that can later be tested using a deductive approach. Deductive reasoning begins with theory and then moves to hypothesis generation. Following the development of hypotheses, researchers must determine who or what they are going to study and begin by turning vague concepts into items that can be measured. Researchers must also devise a research design and a data collection plan (including a sampling plan). Once we collect the data, it is time for analysis. Finally, we draw conclusions and disseminate results. The rest of this book will address exactly how to take each step in the research process.

Key Terms

Evidence-based practice	Quackery	Scientific method
Deductive reasoning	Theory	Hypothesis
Inductive reasoning	Grounded theory	Positivism
Scientism	Historicism	Basic research
Applied research	Program evaluation	Policy analysis
Concept	Operationalization	Unit of analysis

Discussion Questions

1. What are the steps of the scientific method? If someone is taking an inductive approach to research, what would the starting point be for that research process?
2. What are the differences between qualitative and quantitative research?
3. How can basic or scientific research ultimately impact the lives of everyday people?
4. Think of three topics in criminal justice that need more research. For those topics, come up with a question for each that you would like to answer through research.

References

Bernard, T. J. & Engel, R. S. (2001). Conceptualizing criminal justice theory. *Justice Quarterly, 18*(1), 1–30.

Cooper, J. A. & Worrall, J. L. (2012). Theorizing criminal justice evaluation and research. *Criminal Justice Review, 37*(3), 384–397. https://doi.org/10.1177/0734016812442940

Cullen, F. T., Blevins, K. R., Trager, J. S., & Gendreau, P. (2005). The rise and fall of boot camps: A case study in common-sense corrections. *Journal of Offender Rehabilitation, 40*(3–4), 53–70. https://doi.org/10.1300/J076v40n03_03

Gies, S. V., Healy, E., & Stephenson. R. (2020). The evidence of effectiveness: Beyond the methodological standards, *Justice Evaluation Journal, 3*(2), 155–177. https://doi.org/10.1080/24751979.2020.1727296

Glaser, B. G., & Strauss, A. (1967). *The discovery of grounded theory: Strategies for qualitative research.* Aldine Publishing Co.

Hagan, F. (2007). *Essentials of research methods in criminal justice and criminology* (2nd ed.). Pearson.

Haig, B. D. (2018). The importance of scientific method for psychological science *Psychology, Crime, & Law, 25*(6), 527–541. https://doi.org/10.1080/1068316X.2018.1557181

Hammersly, M. (2000). Varieties of social research: A typology. *International Journal of Social Research Methodology, 3*, 221–229. https://doi.org/10.1080/13645570050083706

Hartley, R. D. (Ed.) (2011). *Snapshots of research.* Sage Publications.
Irion, R. (1988). What Proxmire's Golden Fleece did for – and to – science. *The Scientist.* www.the-scientist.com/profession/what-proxmires-golden-fleece-did-for--and-to--science-62408
Kraska, P. B. (2006). Criminal justice theory: Toward legitimacy and an infrastructure. *Justice Quarterly, 23*(2), 167–185. https://doi.org/10.1080/07418820600688735
Larson, H. J. (2018). The biggest pandemic risk? Viral misinformation. *Nature, 562*, 309. https://doi.org/10.1038/d41586-018-07034-4
Latessa, E. J., Cullen F. T., & Gendreau, P. (2011). Beyond correctional quackery: Professionalism and the possibility of effective treatment. In E. J. Latessa & A. M. Holsinger (Eds.), *Correctional contexts* (4th ed., pp. 290–300). Oxford University Press.
Latessa, E. J., Johnson, S. L., & Koetzle, D. (2020). *What works (and doesn't) in reducing recidivism* (2nd ed.). Routledge.
Letourneau, E., Levinson, J., Armstrong, K., & Zgoba, K. M. (2010). Failure to register as a sex offender: Is it associated with recidivism? *Justice Quarterly, 27*(3), 305–331. https://doi.org/10.1080/07418820902972399
Mackenzie, D. L., Wilson, D. B., & Kider, S. B. (2001). Effects of correctional boot camps on offending. *The ANNALS of the American Academy of Political and Social Science, 578*(1), 126–143. https://doi.org//10.1177/000271620157800108
Maxfield, M. G., & Babbie, E. (2012). *Basics of research methods for criminal justice and criminology* (3rd ed.). Thomson Wadsworth.
Maxwell, J. A. (1996). *Qualitative research design: An interactive approach.* Applied Social Research Methods Series (Vol 41). Sage Publications.
Morash, M., & Rucker, L. (1990). A critical look at the idea of boot camp as a correctional reform. *Crime & Delinquency, 36*, 204–222.
National Institute of Corrections. (n.d.). *Evidence-based practices (EBP).* United States Department of Justice, National Institute of Corrections. https://nicic.gov/evidence-based-practices-ebp
Powell, J. (2017). Scientists reach 100% consensus on anthropogenic global warming. *Bulletin of Science, Technology & Society, 37*(4), 183–184. https://doi.org/10.1177%2F0270467619886266
Retraction Watch. (2023). The 10 most highly cited retracted papers. Retraction Watch ("powered" by Word Press). https://retractionwatch.com/the-retraction-watch-leaderboard/top-10-most-highly-cited-retracted-papers/
Rodriguez, N. (2024). Addressing the data gap to advance prison safety and why it matters for correctional policy. *The Criminologist, 50*(5), 1–7.
Sathyanarayana, R., & Adrande, C. (2011). The MMR vaccine and autism: Sensation, refutation, retraction, and fraud. *Indian Journal of Psychiatry, 53*(2), 95–96. https://doi.org/10.4103/0019-5545.82529
Shapiro, A., Simon, J., Jingnan, H., Folkenflik, D., & Retting, A. (2023). People working on climate solutions are facing a big obstacle: Conspiracy theories. *NPR.* www.npr.org/2023/10/05/1203893268/climate-change-conspiracies-disinformation
Tartaro, C. (2015). An evaluation of the effects of jail diversion and reentry for mentally ill offenders. *Journal of Offender Rehabilitation 54*(2), 85–102. https://doi.org/10.1080/10509674.2015.1009966
Tewksbury, R., Jennings, W. G., & Zgoba, K. M. (2012). A longitudinal examination of sex offender recidivism prior to and following the implementation of SORN. *Behavioral Sciences and the Law, 30*, 308–328. https://doi.org/10.1002/bsl.1009
Wallace, W. (1971). *The logic of science in sociology.* Aldine.
Wilson, D. B., MacKenzie, D. L., & Mitchell, F. N. (2005). Effects of correctional boot camps on offending. *A Campbell Collaboration Systematic Review*, 1(1), 1–9. www.aic.gov.au/campbellcj/reviews/titles.html
Zgoba, K. M., Jennings, W. G., & Salerno, L. M. (2018). Megan's law 20 years later: An empirical analysis and policy review. *Criminal Justice and Behavior, 45*(7), 1028–1046. https://doi-org.ezproxy.stockton.edu/10.1177/0093854818771409
Zgoba, K. M., & Mitchell, M. M. (2023). The effectiveness of sex offender registration and notification: A meta-analysis of 25 years of findings. *Journal of Experimental Criminology, 19*, 71–96. https://doi.org/10.1007/s11292-021-09480-z

2 Reading and Understanding Research

Sources of Information

We have access to so many different sources of information, but not every source is equal in its quality, accuracy, and even veracity. Knowing how to evaluate sources is a powerful tool that can help you not only learn more and excel in your classes, but it can also make you better equipped to succeed in your job and make informed decisions about other aspects of your life. Believe me when I tell you that the saying "knowledge is power" has some truth to it.

This chapter is devoted to the types of information that we might use to make decisions and the merits of each. Let me spoil it for you and tell you how it ends—research done in accordance with the scientific method is often the best source of information. This might be disappointing, because research articles can be intimidating. They seem to be written in some special language, often referred to as "researchese," include confusing statistical procedures, and have complicated tables. I will admit that they can also be a bit boring sometimes. The good news is that this book and your professor will teach you how to understand research.

Individual and Vicarious Experiences

None of us are blank slates, so we all acquire information based on personal experiences throughout our lives. Some of those experiences involve contact with actors in the criminal justice system, including police, court personnel, corrections staff, and even people who have committed crimes. Those can be powerful experiences that help to shape our perceptions. For example, you thought that the campus police were rude that time they broke up the party you were attending, so based on your experience, you have concluded that police, or at least those working on campus, are disrespectful. Additionally, our views are shaped by the experiences of other people in our lives. Research has revealed that even vicarious encounters with criminal justice professionals can have a powerful impact on our opinions (Cross & Fine, 2022; Wu et al., 2009), including hearing about friends' interactions with the police or seeing viral videos of police appearing to act rudely or otherwise improperly.

What is important to understand is that these stories and individual incidents comprise what is known as **anecdotal evidence**, or personal stories and observations. The stories may be true, but they might be quite unique and not reflective of what tends to happen in a given situation. Let's use stop-and-frisk police tactics as an example. Stop-and-frisk became popular because police hoped that it would help to remove guns from the street, plus they would be able to find and arrest people with existing warrants. You might have a friend or relative who is a police officer who was involved in some stops where police did find and arrest people with weapons. So, based on your friend's or relative's experience, you might be tempted to conclude that stop-and-frisk works. To do so, however, would mean that we are dismissing ample empirical evidence. **Empirical evidence** is derived from experimentation and the scientific method process. Stop-and-frisk has been found to be unconstitutional, because in its application, racial minorities were being stopped at a much

DOI: 10.4324/9781003661511-2

greater frequency than Whites (Meares, 2014). Specifically, young Black males were stopped in 77 of every 100 stops in New York City in 2006 (Geller & Fagan, 2010). Police departments using this tactic were not able to put up an "ends justifies the means" argument in court, because research indicates that the program was not effective in achieving its goals. Out of 506,000 police stops conducted by the NYPD in 2006, fewer than 1 percent resulted in confiscation of a weapon (Geller & Fagan, 2010). The most frequent arrest resulting from stop-and-frisk was marijuana possession (Geller & Fagan, 2010) and, given that more states are legalizing or decriminalizing marijuana each year, it is difficult to justify continued infringements on rights to confiscate small amounts of marijuana. What this means is that, overall, stop-and-frisk in New York City was not successful at doing what it was intended to do.

The empirical evidence here involved analysis of over half a million of these stops to see, overall, what are the results of these police-resident interactions, whereas your friend's or relative's experiences might consist of a few arrests after some stop-and-frisk encounters. Surely, we should give more weight to the review of 500,000 incidents than stories of a handful of arrests. Your friend's or relative's experience with stop-and-frisk was atypical and not in line with what the research revealed citywide.

Media

Crime investigation, courtroom drama, and even life in prison are among the favorite subjects of television and movie directors and producers. As a criminal justice professor, I am grateful in that it generates interest in my field and encourages people to study criminal justice in college. I also find it frustrating, though, as fictitious shows often take great amounts of creative liberty, and even the nonfiction shows and documentaries can be quite misleading.

Even when the media retelling of a crime incident is correct, it could still be problematic, because the coverage of crime is not proportionate to how often it occurs. Homicides receive a disproportionate amount of media coverage, and they also get different amounts of coverage depending on the race and gender, and sometimes the age of the victim (Schildkraut & Donley, 2012; White et al., 2021). Even true crime books, while nonfiction accounts of actual crimes, are not accurate depictions of crime in society. These books focus on specific types of victims (White and affluent), usually involving unusual murder weapons (Durham, Elrod, & Kinkade, 1995), while the typical crime victim in the United States is a young, Black male, and the most common murder weapon is a gun. The media must sell content and get clicks, so they are motivated to give the most coverage to what they consider to be compelling stories for their audiences. The result is that the general public gets a very distorted view of crime, as the least common crimes tend to get the most coverage, while the most common receive little or no publicity.

The combination of reliance on anecdotal experiences and media portrayals of crime and criminal justice interventions can give people a sense that they understand crime and the criminal justice system when they actually do not. The same rarely happens in occupations such as astrophysics or molecular biology. If you have ever had the experience of telling someone at a party what you are studying, my guess is that you were on the receiving end of some unsolicited advice for reducing crime. These opinions are formulated and shared regardless of how much people know about our field. One of my most amusing professional memories was being told by a career-long toilet paper salesman that I was wrong about criminal justice reform, but not to worry because he had a three-part plan that was sure to fix the system! I cannot imagine that same person telling a rocket scientist that her planned trajectory for tomorrow's launch was incorrect and that, based on his toilet paper career, the rocket should be launched another way.

Unlike rocket science, solutions in our field often appear to be "common sense." People imagine themselves standing in a prison with a large incarcerated person yelling threats at them, and they are sure that it would "scare them straight," so that must mean that the programs that place at-risk teens in prison as a scare tactic work. Plus, they've seen it work on television, not realizing of course, that the footage was edited, that there was no comparison group to see if any crime desistance was a part of the natural maturation process for the teens, and that many who were portrayed in those shows admitted to continuing with criminal behavior (Maahs & Pratt, 2017). Blomberg and Lucken (2010) used the term **illusion of knowledge** to explain the problem of people not being aware of how their *lack* of knowledge about a subject is interfering with their ability to come up with good solutions. Fortunately, there is lots of information out there obtained through solid research. The two challenges that we face are being able to interpret research and then to evaluate the quality of information.

Evaluating Sources of Information

Beyond what we personally know and what people around us are saying, we can search for other sources of information. The internet, cable television, streaming video services, and satellite radio have made the dissemination of information easier than ever. The quality and veracity of sources vary tremendously, so we all need to exercise caution and consider where and how we gather information. We can rank sources on their potential usefulness when we are conducting research.

First, we have sources created by an individual or individuals. The quality of these can vary tremendously. Anyone can create their own website, blog, or podcast. Keep in mind, just because someone wrote something and posted it on the internet, that doesn't mean that it has any credibility. I can wake up tomorrow and decide to start a blog on rocket science, even though I never took a physics course. Consider the author's credentials, including academic, work, and life experience. If you are doing a research paper on treatment for a specific cancer and you come across a blog written by an MD who has worked as the chief oncologist for a prestigious hospital and has a strong record of research, this could be a good source of information. I say "could" because it would be better to go with sources that were published using a process that has some quality control, and individual websites lack these safeguards. A blog or website that an individual sets up might not reveal any potential conflicts of interest that the author has, such as owning stock in the company that makes a particular drug. If the blog post is touting the effectiveness of that drug, one must ask if the author's desire to increase the stock prices is influencing their objectivity. So, the information found there might or might not be valuable. I suggest you search the name of the doctor who wrote the blog to see if you could find research they published in sources with checks and balances and use those articles instead, as many academic journals consider conflicts of interest in their publication decisions. While you might find some interesting blogs written by people who have decent credentials, you will also encounter ones written by people who have no business dispensing advice to other humans. If you find a medical blog written by someone with no formal degree in medicine and, therefore, no medical license, and this person's medical experience consists of internet research and their own personal attempt at curing a disease using sauerkraut tossed in a blender (yes, this really happened!) (Gander, 2018; Morris, 2018), you might want to think twice about following any "medical" advice that you get from there. Your digestive system will thank you for it.

Next, there are media outlets. Criminal justice issues are covered by hundreds, if not thousands, of media sources throughout the globe every day. Unfortunately, all have differing levels of bias and commitment to truthful and accurate reporting. In recent years, we have witnessed the proliferation of outlets designed to cater to certain groups by publishing biased and very inaccurate stories, and some that frequently peddle in conspiracy theories with a complete disregard for evidence. You can, and should, look to see if multiple sources are reporting on the same story. If only one or two sources have picked up what seems like very important news, you should be suspicious. There are also great websites that allow you to check the level of bias as well as the accuracy found in many media outlets. I strongly suggest you visit those sites. Figure 2.1 includes helpful suggestions for evaluating types of web sources, including those run by the media.

Is your web source credible?

Pay attention to the web domain. This can tell you where your source originated.

- Colleges and universities (.edu): These are usually reliable, with attention paid to validity and reliability of the published information.
- Government or military (.gov or .mil): These are generally reliable, but there are instances of these sites pushing certain political agendas. Examples are the federal government's insistence on equating marijuana with much more serious drugs and the government's scrubbing federal websites of climate change evidence.
- Company website (.com): There is a potential for bias here, as companies obviously have an interest in promoting their own products and services.
- Special interest (.org): These are mixed. Some are objective and reliable, while others seek to further their own agendas. Be careful and use some of the tips provided in this section.
- Other web domains (.com.co): Be suspicious of these. Some of these belong to satirical sites or ones that provide false information.

Consider the source.

- There are wonderful websites that check for bias of overall sites. Just search for media bias or fact-check sites, and you will find plenty. You should do that with all media sources that you are using for the first time. You will quickly learn which to avoid. These sites often provide information on both the level and type of bias of each source and the source's commitment to accurate reporting.
- Avoid *Wikipedia*. It is free and online, so it is convenient. It is also written entirely by volunteers, and not necessarily qualified ones. A page covering a person or topic might be credible one day, but a prankster or someone with an ulterior motive could easily go in and change what is written at any time.

Be mindful of headlines and content.

- Be concerned when you see headlines in all capital letters. How professional does that look to you?
- Beware of inflammatory headlines that try to emotionally arouse readers. Headlines that attempt to produce anger are likely attached to stories that lack objectivity and might even be factually incorrect.
- Memes are not news! You can do better than that. If something in a meme seems intriguing, research it. Try to find corroborating information on at least two different credible websites. Never, ever rely on memes for news.
- Does the article or headline appear to be purposefully misleading?
- Can you find at least two credible sources that are reporting the same story?
- Can you find this information on fact-check websites? What are those sites reporting?
- Does the article you are reading back up its assertions with either footnotes or links to supporting articles or original documents? This is very important. Credible sources include notes and hyperlinks so readers can see evidence for themselves.

Figure 2.1 Is your web source credible?

Sources: University of Maryland Global Campus (2020). *Is my source credible?* Baltimore, MD: University of Maryland Global Campus Library. https://sites.umgc.edu/library/libhow/credibility.cfm

University of Pittsburgh (2025). *Have you P.R.O.V.E.N. That this source is a good choice?* Pittsburgh, PA: University of Pittsburgh Library. https://pitt.libguides.com/ld.php?content_id=38775321

Trade publications can provide a window into some of the latest topics being discussed in various disciplines. Good examples of these in criminal justice are the *FBI Law Enforcement Bulletin* published by the FBI, *American Jails* by the American Jail Association, and *Corrections Today* by the American Correctional Association. These magazines focus on articles that are of interest to criminal justice practitioners. Readers can get information about new programs and the latest trends and controversies in the field. While there are occasional pieces written by professional researchers, most of the articles are written by practitioners, for practitioners. A drawback to these publications is their lack of peer review. Potential authors submit manuscripts to the editorial boards of these magazines, so there are checks and balances not found on websites, blogs, and podcasts run by individuals, but the articles do not undergo a rigorous review of the methods used to come up with the findings. Practitioners working for an organization that put together a new program might be motivated to highlight the good aspects of that program and ignore any drawbacks in their article. Since these magazines generally don't carefully critique the research plans that produced the results, these articles might be presenting biased findings.

Agency and government websites and reports can be an important source of information, particularly statistics to help measure the scope of a problem. Good examples are the FBI's National Incident-Based Reporting System, the Bureau of Justice Statistics, the Substance Abuse and Mental Health Services Administration, and the Office of Juvenile Justice and Delinquency Prevention. These sources are always excellent starting points for students and professional researchers. Some agency websites are also good sources of evaluations, policy pieces, and summaries of recent government activities. A few that come to mind are the Vera Institute of Justice, the Sentencing Project, the RAND Corporation, the Urban Institute, and the Pew Research Center. All these agencies employ professional researchers and provide information about the methods they used to collect their data.

Researchers often put their findings in book form or use the space allotted in books to review a large portion of existing research on a particular subject. Books can be very good, but books take a long time to write and publish. The latest research findings are less likely to appear in books than they are in peer-reviewed journal articles.

In the research world, the preferred source of information is **peer-reviewed** articles. Peer-reviewed journals, also known as refereed journals, are publications that use independent reviewers to assist the editor in determining whether a manuscript is appropriate for publication. Authors wishing to have their work considered submit their manuscripts to the journal editor. The editor typically conducts a quick review to confirm that the paper topic seems like it could be appropriate for that journal and does a cursory review of the research design before requesting assistance from peer reviewers, sometimes also called referees (Locke et al., 2009).

Editors have multiple ways of finding and choosing referees. First, journal editors are generally familiar with existing research and, therefore, know people who might be good judges of new work in that discipline. Second, editors could look to the bibliographies of the manuscripts submitted and reach out to researchers cited in the paper. A third, more recent option, is that the authors themselves are asked to identify experts in the field who would be appropriate reviewers. The editor typically contacts two researchers and asks them to review a manuscript. If the reviewers agree to provide feedback, the editor sends them a copy, frequently with the authors' names removed from the manuscript. This **blind peer-review** process is supposed to help reviewers make an unbiased judgment solely on the merits of the research rather than their opinions of the authors. Editors and reviewers might be willing to give a manuscript written by a well-regarded scholar the benefit of the doubt and accept an otherwise borderline or unacceptable paper. On the other hand, a manuscript written by a new scholar or someone who lacks a reputation might seem less attractive, even if it is of good quality.

Peer reviewers are expected to read the manuscript and then answer a few standard questions generated by the journal. These questions usually involve whether the paper topic is appropriate for the journal, whether the introduction and literature review are adequate, whether the decisions made in the research methods and statistics sections appear to be appropriate, whether the results and discussion sections add something to our knowledge base, and whether publication of this paper would provide a meaningful contribution to the discipline. Reviewers then have the following options for recommendations: accept manuscript as-is for publication, accept with minor revisions, have authors revise manuscript and resubmit it for an additional review, or reject the manuscript. The editor then considers the recommendations of the two reviewers and renders a decision. If the authors are invited to revise their manuscript and resubmit it, the editor will send the newly revised manuscript to the same reviewers, provided they are willing to review it again.

The peer-review process is designed to serve as a quality control measure to prevent substantially flawed articles from being published. Not all peer-reviewed journals are equally selective, though. Readers should be mindful of the fact that the peer-review process is no guarantee that poorly written and methodologically flawed articles will be flagged and denied publication. So, while peer review is an extra step in the attempt at quality control, it is far from perfect. There is a web page called Retraction Watch that reports on retractions of journal articles in a variety of fields. In Chapter 1, I mentioned an article that started the autism-vaccine scare and had to be retracted due to fraud. That article originally appeared in a highly regarded, peer-reviewed journal. *Criminology*, the flagship journal of the American Society of Criminology and one of the most highly regarded journals in criminal justice, was beset by controversy when one author from a multiauthored study requested that the journal retract one of his own articles, because he suspected that a coauthor manipulated the findings. The entire research team eventually agreed to ask *Criminology* to retract the article, and other highly regarded journals in the social sciences that published work from the same authors using the same dataset retracted articles (Chawla, 2019).

The point is that bad research does make its way to publication, even in journals that require peer review. While you would need to be very proficient in statistics to detect flaws in a few of these articles, a basic understanding of research methods will go a long way toward you being able to distinguish good research from bad. The good news is that most research results are obtained honestly and in an ethical manner, and peer-reviewed articles are considered the most appropriate sources to use when students and professionals are conducting literature reviews of their research topics.

There are steps that you can take to gauge the quality of the sources from which you are obtaining information. Locke et al. (2009) named four things to consider: journal selectivity, sources of funding, research or professional organization sponsorship, and reputation of the authors.

Journal Selectivity

Publishing is a requirement for most academic jobs and some professional research positions. Even if faculty secure tenure, they often need to continue to publish to be promoted and be eligible for grant money and other opportunities. The term "publish or perish" describes the pressure that researchers feel to have their work seen, preferably in the most prestigious journals possible, with the goal of promoting or even saving one's career. Since so many people want or even need to publish their work, there has been a proliferation of journals as potential outlets for research. Unfortunately, while there have been some very good journals developed by reputable publishing companies and researchers, not all journals are of equal quality, nor are all designed to be outlets to further science. Some journals are predatory.

According to 43 scholars who formed a working group to formulate a definition, **predatory journals** and publishers are "entities that prioritize self-interest at the expense of scholarship and are characterized by false or misleading information, deviation from best editorial and publication practices, a lack of transparency, and/or the use of aggressive and indiscriminate solicitation practices" (Grudniewicz et al., 2019, p. 211). The term "predatory publishers" was coined in 2010, and scholars have published checklists to encourage researchers to avoid predatory journals. These journals pose a danger because they look like legitimate scientific journals but lack quality checks. That means that false and misleading information may appear in what looks like a peer-reviewed scholarly journal but is not. Grudniewicz and colleagues were inspired to research predatory journals because an author's mother-in-law was fighting cancer, and the standard treatments were no longer effective. Relatives desperately looked for a way for her to keep fighting the disease and were hopeful when they found an article about a promising treatment. That hope faded once the author realized that the evaluation of the treatment was published in a predatory journal. That means that the article was likely published without anyone vetting the quality of the work and screening for conflicts of interest.

If there are so many reputable journals available, why would researchers publish their work in a predatory journal? One possibility is that they are unaware that the journal is predatory. Researchers get emails with invitations to submit manuscripts to journals every day, and many of these journals certainly have names that make them sound reputable, such as *Advances in Biomedicine and Pharmacy*, *British Journal of Science*, and the *International Journal of Advanced Research in Applied Science and Technology* (Scholarly Open Access, 2017). Scholars have a duty to do their homework before submitting, so not knowing that a journal is or is likely predatory is not an adequate excuse. The second reason why an author might publish in a predatory journal is because they are under such pressure to have their work published, they turn to journals that will quickly publish anything for a fee. Really, some of these journals will publish any combination of words that are submitted to them. Researchers with a sense of humor have demonstrated the lack of vetting that occurs in these predatory journals by conducting "stings" with absurd papers. One scientist wrote papers that made repeated references to *Star Wars* and The Force and had them accepted for publication in four "journals" that were supposed to focus on the natural sciences, not film reviews (Predatory Journals …, 2017). A few authors wrote the sentence "Get me off your f------- mailing list" over and over again to make a 10-page paper fit, with figures and tables containing nothing but those same seven words. The "paper" was accepted and published by the *International Journal of Advanced Computer Technology* (Stromberg, 2014). Clearly, you should not trust work published in a predatory journal to be valid or reliable, as the previous stories provide evidence that some will publish absolutely anything. How can you tell if a journal is predatory? Do a simple internet search for "predatory journal list." There are a number of lists out there, including one compiled by Yale University. If you are not already familiar with a journal's reputation, check these lists first. Another option is to do an internet search of the journal name. Journals that are affiliated with established publishing companies are not predatory. Just a few examples of reputable publishers in criminal justice are Taylor & Francis, Sage, Springer, Elsevier, and Wiley.

Elmore and Weston (2020) provided a list of warning signs that an email solicitation might be from a predatory journal, including grammatical errors, aggressive targeting of authors, requirements for authors to sign away their copyright of the article, and unclear review process, among others. Another very important warning sign is that publication is contingent on the author paying the journal a significant sum of money. I had my first paper accepted for publication in 1998. There was one time I had to pay a $10 fee to a journal as part of the review process, but that is the only time I ever put out any amount of money to have my work seen. I was comfortable with that, because it was a small amount, and the journal had an excellent reputation. If a journal is seeking hundreds or even a thousand dollars, that is a big red flag.

While information in predatory journals should always be considered suspect, articles in very prestigious journals may be of poor quality, and articles in less popular journals might be very strong and ultimately carry great weight in the field. One reason why is that the large, mainstream journals may lack interest in particular topics. A great example of this is terrorism. Prior to 9/11, terrorism was considered the domain of political scientists, so little work on terrorism was being published in mainstream criminal justice journals. Another reason is that a new idea might seem too controversial or far-fetched and be rejected by the larger journals. A mentor of mine is the father of a major crime theory. The article that proposed the new theory, which has now been cited thousands of times, was initially rejected by some of the top journals.

Sources of Funding

Researchers are expected to be unbiased and focused on advancing science. Of course, since we are also human, there are times when other priorities threaten the objectivity of work. **Conflicts of interest** are "personal, financial, professional, political, or legal interests that have a significant chance of interfering with the performance of his/her ethical or legal duties" (Resnik, 2017, p. 2). Resnik argues that conflicts of interest are concerning for two reasons. First, they have the potential to impact the integrity of research. Second, they can undermine the public's trust in science.

In the medical field, two studies from the late 1990s provided good illustrations of how conflicts of interest can harm research. Earlier in this book, I mentioned that the only scientific work to ever claim to have found evidence of a link between vaccines and autism was published in 1998 by Andrew Wakefield, MD, and colleagues. During an investigation that led to the article's retraction, it was revealed that Wakefield was secretly accepting payments from personal injury lawyers whose clients were suing the pharmaceutical companies and had an interest in generating research finding a link between vaccines and autism ("A case of junk science," 2008). During another study in 1999, a young man died during a gene therapy experiment at the University of Pennsylvania. Upon investigation, the Food and Drug Administration found that the research team withheld vital information from patients, including the risks associated with the study and the researchers' and university's financial interest in the results. The principal investigator of the study owned 30% of the gene therapy company's stock, and that same company paid the university $4 million per year. The university also owned stock in the company (Resnik, 2017).

The field of criminal justice is not immune to conflicts of interest in research. Geis, Mobley, and Shichor (1999) chronicled the work of Charles Thomas, PhD, from the University of Florida. Thomas became very closely affiliated with private corrections companies, particularly the Corrections Corporation of America (CCA). Dr. Thomas was frequently quoted in newspapers as an expert on private corrections, and he published articles in peer-reviewed journals on the success of private prisons. In his interviews and publications, Dr. Thomas failed to disclose his affiliation with a research center that received $400,000 from private prison companies. He also failed to disclose that he was a paid consultant for the Florida Correctional Privatization Commission or that he was being paid millions by CCA. Geis and colleagues concluded their paper with a recommendation that journals require authors to disclose any potential conflicts of interest. It is now customary for authors submitting manuscripts to peer-reviewed journals to have to disclose any funding that they received to conduct the research and to describe any type of possible conflict of interest. This information can then be used to make informed publication decisions.

Research or Professional Organization Sponsorship

Occasionally, a research or professional organization will choose to provide support for academic research. When I planned to survey all jails in the United States that were built using a certain design, I contacted the American Jail Association (AJA). While there had been some small studies done on these jails, my plan was to include hundreds of facilities in my analysis. After explaining my proposal to the president of the AJA, he agreed to write a cover letter to my survey to endorse the work. This was very valuable, since I was asking jail administrators to take time out of their busy schedules to do a favor for someone they had never met. I have no doubt that the AJA's support of my study helped boost my credibility among jail administrators and increased the response rate to my survey. Given that the AJA is a professional organization that has little involvement in research, their endorsement probably did not improve the prestige of my work in the research and academic communities. Sponsorship or support of research and professional organizations, such as the American Medical Association and American Bar Association, can help to bolster the reputation of research in the scholarly community.

Reputation of Authors

Earlier, I mentioned that the reputations of authors might influence journal editors' decisions whether to accept a manuscript for publication. I want to caution against becoming too preoccupied with the names on the paper. New scholars who have not had enough years in the field to become "names" are producing excellent work every year. The most important consideration should be whether that individual's work has previously been flagged or retracted for ethical issues, such as conflicts of interest, whether there have been questions about their objectivity, and whether there have been legitimate questions about their data collection and analysis.

Steps That Editorials Boards Are Taking to Improve Research Quality

Individual researchers have a responsibility to only put forth results that are legitimate and the product of ethically and methodologically sound work. Unfortunately, between the pressure to publish and some individuals' carelessness at best and lack of a moral compass at worst, journals have recognized the need to establish rules to protect their publications against unwittingly disseminating bad research. Earlier, I mentioned an incident involving *Criminology* and other top-tier journals publishing work that at least one of the coauthors later believed to be the product of data fabrication/manipulation. In the wake of that, the editorial board for *Criminology* announced that the journal was joining the Committee on Publication Ethics (COPE) (Sweeten et al., 2024). COPE is an organization that provides guidance to editorial boards and research institutes to encourage ethical practices in publishing culture (COPE, 2024). COPE offers best practices for journals looking to establish a solid peer-review process, and they also provide guidance to member editorial boards investigating and responding to allegations of research misconduct. *Criminology* is also encouraging all authors to share not only their datasets but the specific steps that they followed to produce their results so that anyone can confirm their findings.

Elements of Published Research

Now that you know a little bit about how to judge the quality of sources, it is time to discuss what is in a typical published piece of research.

Abstract

The abstract is a very brief synopsis of the article. These are typically 100 to 300 words, depending on the rules governing the journal. This is a short summary of the article and is a good way for readers to see whether the article matches the reader's interests and whether it would be worthwhile reading the entire article. Typical abstracts are usually a paragraph, but some journals require authors to write structured abstracts. Structured abstracts are longer and include headings for each section of the paper (research background, research procedure, findings, and conclusions). An example of a structured abstract can be found in Reading 7.2 of this book.

Introduction

The introduction is the authors' opportunity to introduce the topic to the reader. This section usually includes some statistics to give readers an understanding of the scope of the topic. For example, an article about children's separation from their incarcerated parents would likely begin with a review of the number of people in the United States who are incarcerated, the number of those people who have children under the age of 18, and estimates of how many children in the community have incarcerated parents. In this section, it is important to communicate to the reader why the topic needs to be studied. The writer should never exaggerate the extent of the problem, though. I have received several student papers where the authors seemed to believe that the only way their papers would be relevant is if they made it appear that their topic was a "growing problem" regardless of whether it actually was. This is a typical "rookie" mistake when learning to write about research. In just about all these instances, the students relied on hyperbole and assumptions instead of consulting and citing reputable sources of information.

Literature Review

In this section, the authors might discuss some theories related to the topic. Keeping with the example of children of incarcerated parents, it might be helpful to frame how incarceration could be detrimental to children's future. A number of sociological and psychological theories could be used as the theoretical framework of the research.

The literature review is an opportunity for the authors to present readers with a summary of the available research on this topic. This informs the reader about what is already known and allows the authors to highlight gaps in our current state of knowledge. After a discussion of the limitations of previous research, the authors can use the last few sentences of this section to explain the goals of their study.

Research Methods

If the research is exploratory in nature, the authors might not present any hypotheses. If the study involves hypothesis testing, the hypotheses will either appear at the end of the literature review or at the beginning of the research methods section.

Authors of research articles are expected to describe every step that they took to collect data. This includes how the sample was selected, how the concepts were operationalized to create measurable variables, the type of data collection plan, and the time frame used to collect the data. Readers should be able to understand what transpired during the data collection process, including the original plan and any issues that arose during data collection that impacted what data were ultimately available for analysis. For example, when researchers conduct surveys, they might get 1,000 responses, but once they review them, they discover that many respondents dropped out halfway through the survey, and a handful wrote sarcastic or unbelievable responses, so the number of usable surveys is actually 750. It is the author's responsibility to explain all of this to the readers so that they understand why there were 1,000 survey responses but only 750 usable for data analysis. Researchers conducting data collection inside a prison might initially believe that they will be able to ask for volunteers from all units but later discover that they cannot access those residing in the infirmary and that another unit is inaccessible due to lockdown. The methods section is where the researchers explain these challenges.

Results

Either at the end of the research methods section or at the start of results, the researchers will explain the characteristics of the sample. If researchers sent the link to an internet survey to every chief of police in cities with at least 200,000 residents, the results section would begin by providing information about the respondents. If the unit of analysis (who or what you are studying) is the police chiefs themselves, the results section would likely begin with their demographic information, such as age, gender, education, and years of experience of the responding chiefs. If the study's unit of analysis is the organization, and researchers sent the surveys to chiefs as representatives of the organizations, then the results section might start out with a description of the agencies, such as the number of sworn staff, demographics of staff members, and number of officers who work each shift. Next, the authors would discuss whether statistical tests revealed support for their hypotheses. Here, they could either have found the type of relationship between their independent and dependent variables that they predicted, no relationship between the variables, or a relationship between them but in the opposite direction than expected.

The results section of quantitative studies usually includes tables as well as narratives to explain what is in the tables. Depending on your understanding of statistics, you might find the tables to be helpful or confusing. The more comfortable you become with statistics, the greater your appreciation will be for tables, as they are a quick way to read the findings.

Discussion/Conclusion

The results section is simply a brief presentation of the results. It is in the discussion or conclusion sections where the authors try to explain why they found what they found. In instances where the findings are the opposite of what was expected, the discussion section is where authors will have the chance to reflect on whether they think this was a product of how they framed the research question, collected the data, and analyzed the results, or whether the findings are due to some aspect of the topic that they had not previously considered. Discussion sections summarize the findings but then also try to link this work to the research conducted in this area to date. The authors will usually tie the discussion back to topics mentioned in the introduction and literature review to place the current findings into the proper context. The authors' emphasis on criminological theory and policy implications will vary depending on the journal's focus.

Researchers often summarize the limitations of their study either in the discussion section or in the research methods section. Acknowledging the study's drawbacks is an essential part of any piece of research for three reasons. First, authors' full disclosure of the strengths and drawbacks of their work is a demonstration of scientific integrity. Second, this information can help readers understand the results in the proper context. Third, future researchers can design studies that will address these limitations.

References

Authors need to cite (give credit to) all the sources of information that they used to write the article. The reference page can be very useful to readers because they can look up and read the articles that comprised the literature review.

How to Read/Take Notes

I have observed that one of the biggest difficulties my students experience is making sense of research articles after reading them. I want to provide some suggestions for how to take notes for two reasons. First, it will help if you can go back to your notes to see a quick summary of what you read rather than rereading the article. Second, as you spend more time studying criminal justice topics, you will amass more and more readings. How do you keep track of all of it? Here's what I do.

I have separate documents for each general subject that I study. So, if you take an introductory policing course and read articles for that, you can put your article notes in a "policing" document. Later in your academic career, you might have to revisit that subject in a more advanced class. It would be helpful to have a synopsis of what you have already read, as this will save you a lot of time. Then, as you read more, you can add it to this same document. This is how I have managed to keep track of notes for books, reports, and articles that I read over a decade ago.

Once you set up the document, I suggest that you start your notes by putting the full American Psychological Association (APA) citation of whatever you read as the first line. Next, use headings similar to what I provided in the previous section to make sure you handle information properly should you ever need it for a research paper. Remember that information provided in the introduction and literature review sections of the articles came from research written by people other than the authors of the current article. So, if you want to write down anything interesting from the introduction or literature review, I suggest that you have it under an "intro/lit review" heading in your notes and then put a citation of the original source in your notes. That way, if you ever want to use that information, you can go look it up in the original source and cite it properly. That's important, as you do not want to incorrectly attribute research findings to the wrong people. You might not think it's a big deal, but believe me, it is. People want to be accurately credited for their life's work, and they also do not want to be wrongly associated with less-than-stellar research that they did not do. Plus, it hurts your credibility when someone who knows the existing research reads your work and sees you mixing up study findings and the authors who reported them.

Next, under "methodology" write a few notes about what, exactly, the researchers did. This will serve as a good reminder later after your memory fades, and it will help you understand the results. In the results section, use bullet points to jot down a quick summary of the findings. For discussion, you can note interesting ideas that the researchers had as they attempted to explain their findings. Finally, remember to take notes on the limitations of their study. You are going to want this later, especially if you are thinking about proposing a study yourself for this class or some other course. You will want to remember how the limitations may have impacted the results, and you will want to see if you can design a study that addresses those drawbacks. If you find something particularly problematic in the article, you might want to make a very visible note to yourself. I like to put my own thoughts inside double parentheses or in all caps. Remember how I cautioned that poorly designed research gets published sometimes? I have read a few articles where I think that the limitations are so substantial that they really call into question the results. I still take notes on those articles so that I have a record of having read them (so I don't forget and then read them again some other time), and then I put a note to myself about my misgivings upon reading it.

You might look at this and think that it is a waste of time, but if you wind up studying a topic over a period of semesters or years, taking notes this way will be very valuable to you. Have you ever looked at a bibliography for an article or a book and wondered how the author could possibly keep all that information organized? Well, this is one way to do it.

Summary

We are incredibly fortunate that more information than ever is accessible. We should all be grateful for this development, but with it comes the proliferation of sources that are biased, inaccurate, and sometimes outright deceptive. It is our responsibility, as educated individuals, to learn to be able to see through that, determine the quality of a source, and only use valid pieces of information to draw conclusions. In this chapter, I reviewed different types of sources and outlined the advantages and disadvantages of each. There are steps that we can take, such as being suspicious of outrageous stories being reported by only one or two outlets, researching the reputation of sources before using them, and considering potential conflicts of interest. When searching for sources to use in research, remember that there is a hierarchy, with peer-reviewed journal articles offering the best, but not foolproof, outlet for objective, quality-controlled research.

In this chapter, I provided an overview of how research papers are designed and what types of information are available in each section of the articles. Research articles can be intimidating, with their specialized language, mathematical formulas, and complicated tables. The key to understanding is to break the article down by section and understand what you should gain by reading each part. It will take practice, but you should become more comfortable understanding these articles, and taking notes on them, throughout the class.

Key Terms

Anecdotal evidence	Empirical evidence	Illusion of knowledge
Peer-review	Blind peer review	Predatory journals

Discussion Questions

1. Why is research in peer-reviewed journals considered among the strongest sources of information?
2. What are some of the ways that we can evaluate a story that we find in the media?
3. What are predatory journals, and why would anyone publish in them?
4. Go grab a media article. Then analyze it and provide reasons why it is credible or why it is suspect.

References

A case of junk science, conflict and hype [Editorial]. (2008). Nature Immunology *9*, 1317. https://doi.org/10.1038/ni1208-1317

Blomberg, T. G., & Lucken, K. (2010). *American penology: A history of control* (2nd ed.). Transaction Publishers.

Chawla, D. S. (2019). Quintet of study retractions rocks criminology community. *Science*. www.sciencemag.org/news/2019/11/quintet-study-retractions-rocks-criminology-community

Committee on Publication Ethics (COPE). (2024). About COPE. https://publicationethics.org/about/our-organisation

Cross, A. R., & Fine, A. D. (2022). Police-related social media exposure and adolescents' interest in becoming a police officer. *Police Practice and Research*, *23*(5), 553–568. https://doi.org/10.1080/15614263.2021.2017932

Durham, A. M., Elrod, H. P., & Kinkade, P. T. (1995). Images of crime and justice: Murder and the "true crime" genre. *Journal of Criminal Justice, 23*(2), 143–152.

Elmore, S. A., & Weston, E. H. (2020). Predatory journals: what they are and how to avoid them. *Toxicologic Pathology*, *48*(4), 607–610. https://doi.org/10.1177/0192623320920209

Gander, K. (2018). Woman who claims cabbage juice "cures" autism and can regrow limbs to be probed by officials. *Newsweek*. www.newsweek.com/jillian-mai-thi-epperly-claims-cabbage-juice-cures-autism-homosexuality-and-909737

Geis, G., Mobley, A., & Shichor, D. (1999). Private prisons, criminological research, and conflict of interest: A case study. *Crime & Delinquency, 45*(3), 372–388. https://doi.org/10.1177/0011128799045003005
Geller, A., & Fagan, J. (2010). Pot as pretext: Marijuana, race, and the new disorder in New York city street policing. *Journal of Empirical Legal Studies*, 7, 591–633. https://doi.org/10.1111/j.1740-1461.2010.01190.x
Grudniewicz, A., Moher, D., Cobey, K. D., Bryson, G. L., Cukier, S., Allen, K., Ardern, C., Balcom, L., Barros, T., Berger, M., Ciro, J. B., Cugusi, L., Donaldson, M. R., Egger, M., Graham, I. D., Hodgkinson, M., Khan, K. M., Mabizela, M., Manca, A., … Lalu, M. M. (2019). Predatory journals: No definition, no defence. *Nature, 576*, 210–212. https://doi.org/10.1038/d41586-019-03759-y
Locke, L. F., Silverman, S. J., & Spirduso, W. W. (2009). *Reading and understanding research* (3rd ed.). Sage Publications.
Maahs, J., & Pratt, T. C. (2017). "I Hate These Little Turds!": Science, entertainment, and the enduring popularity of scared straight programs. *Deviant Behavior, 38*(1), 47–60. https://doi.org/10.1080/01639625.2016.1190619
Meares, T. L. (2014). The law and social science of stop and frisk. *Annual Review of Law and Social Sciences, 10*, 335–352. https://doi.org/10/1146/annurev-lawsocsci-102612-134043
Morris, M. (2018). Jilly Juice recipe creator claims her concoction can regrow limbs, cure homosexuality. *Metro*. www.metro.us/body-and-mind/health/jilly-juice-recipe-jillian-epperly
Predatory journals hit by "Star Wars" sting. (2017). *Discover.* www.discovermagazine.com/mind/predatory-journals-hit-by-star-wars-sting
Resnik, D. B. (2017). Conflicts of interest in scientific research related to regulation or litigation. *The Journal of Philosophy, Science, & Law*, *16*(7), 1. https://doi.org/10.1080/23294515.2018.1510859
Schildkraut, J., & Donley, A. M. (2012). Murder in black: A media distortion analysis of homicides in Baltimore in 2010. *Homicide Studies, 16*(2), 175–196. https://doi.org/10.1177/1088767912438712
Scholarly Open Access. (2017). *List of standalone journals: Potential, possible, or probably predatory scholarly open-access journals.* https://web.archive.org/web/20170111172309; https://scholarlyoa.com/individual-journals/
Stromberg, J. (2014). "Get me off your fucking mailing list" is an actual science paper accepted by a journal. *Vox*. www.vox.com/2014/11/21/7259207/scientific-paper-scam
Sweeten, G., Topalli, V., Loughran, T., Haynie, D., & Tseloni, A. (2024). Data transparency at *Criminology. The Criminologist, 50*(1), 9–11.
University of Maryland Global Campus. (2020). *Is my source credible?* University of Maryland Global Campus Library. https://sites.umgc.edu/library/libhow/credibility.cfm
University of Pittsburgh (2025). *Have you P.R.O.V.E.N. That this source is a good choice?*. Pittsburgh, PA: University of Pittsburgh Library. https://pitt.libguides.com/ld.php?content id=38775321
White, K., Stuart, F., & Morrissey, S. L. (2021). Whose lives matter? Race, space, and the devaluation of homicide victims in minority communities. *Sociology of Race and Ethnicity*, *7*(3), 333–349.
Wu, Y., Sun, I. Y., & Triplett, R. A. (2009). Race, class or neighborhood context: Which matters more in measuring satisfaction with police? *Justice Quarterly, 26*, 125–156. https://doi.org/10.1080/07418820802119950

3 Ethics in Criminal Justice Research

As the allied countries moved through Europe and defeated the Nazis in 1945, soldiers discovered the horrors of the concentration camps. The primary purpose of the camps was to carry out the "Final Solution," of murdering people deemed genetically inferior and a threat to the "Aryan race." A secondary purpose of the camps was to serve as a laboratory for horrific science experiments, using non-consenting children and adults as research subjects. The research was cruel and often resulted in slow and painful deaths. Following the war, the International Military Tribunal convened trials at Nuremburg to bring those responsible to justice. One of the defenses employed by the Nazis came as a shock to ordinary Americans—the Nazis were doing what the Americans had been doing for years (Cohen, 2016; Hornblum, 1998; Mitford, 1973; Peterson, 2024).

As stunning at that defense may sound, it was true. The United States has a long history of performing dangerous experiments on vulnerable populations, including incarcerated people and children with special needs, without adequate protections. In 1915, a doctor in Mississippi infected several men serving prison sentences with pellagra, an extremely painful and potentially deadly disease (Hornblum, 1998; Oshinsky, 1996). During the American occupation of the Philippines in the early 1900s, doctors infected incarcerated persons with cholera, killing 13 people and compensating survivors with cigars. When the United States entered World War II, incarcerated individuals in the US were enrolled in medical experiments involving malaria (Hornblum, 1998). In Iowa, people in prison were given and then cured of scurvy in the late 1960s for reasons that are unclear, since scientists were already aware of the cause and cure for that disease (Mitford, 1973).

Despite the Nazis' attempt to shift the focus to the Allies' dangerous and unethical behavior, doctors who carried out the Nazi experiments were convicted and sentenced for their crimes. Outrage stemming from the Holocaust prompted government entities and some in the scientific community to take steps to prevent unethical medical experiments from being permitted in the future. The result was the **Nuremberg Code**, consisting of 10 elements to protect human participants in research. A summary of the elements are as follows:

1. Voluntary consent of participants is absolutely essential.
2. The results of any experiment must be for the greater good of society.
3. Human experimentation should be based on previous animal experimentation and only after there is knowledge of the natural history of the disease.
4. Experimental procedures should avoid unnecessary physical or mental suffering.
5. No experiments should be conducted if there is reason to believe it will cause death or disability.
6. Risks taken should never be greater than the humanitarian importance of the problem to be solved.
7. Adequate facilities should be used to protect subjects.
8. Only qualified scientists should conduct experiments.

DOI: 10.4324/9781003661511-3

9. Subjects should be able to end their participation at any time.
10. The scientist in charge must be prepared to terminate the experiment when injury, disability, or death is likely to occur (Jarmusik, 2019).

Following the development of the Nuremburg Code, the World Medical Association established the **Declaration of Helsinki** in 1964. This statement outlined ethical principles for medical research involving human subjects. As with the Nuremburg Code, the writers emphasized concern for the safety of individuals and the rights of participants to receive informed consent. Section 26 of the Declaration states:

> In medical research involving human subjects capable of giving informed consent, each potential subject must be adequately informed of the aims, methods, sources of funding, any possible conflicts of interest, institutional affiliations of the researcher, the anticipated benefits and potential risks of the study and the discomfort it may entail, post-study provisions and any other relevant aspects of the study. The potential subject must be informed of the right to refuse to participate in the study or to withdraw consent to participate at any time without reprisal. Special attention should be given to the specific information needs of individual potential subjects as well as to the methods used to deliver the information (World Medical Association, 2019).

Given the medical community's apparent commitment to adopting protections for people, one might think that harmful experiments involving humans would have ceased after publication of the Nuremburg Code and Helsinki Declaration. The problem was that neither of those were legally binding in the United States (Peterson, 2024). Harmful and unethical medical experiments continued in a few different settings, including prisons and jails. One of the longest-running and most notorious cases of using the incarcerated for human experimentation was chronicled by Allen Hornblum (1998) in his book *Acres of Skin.* Albert Kligman, a dermatologist with the University of Pennsylvania, set up a lab in Holmesburg Prison and ran dozens of medical experiments on incarcerated men for two decades. Holmesburg Prison was an overcrowded, violent county jail in Pennsylvania that held both sentenced individuals and those who were still awaiting trial. Kligman originally entered the prison at the request of the facility's pharmacist, who was seeking advice on how to deal with an athlete's foot outbreak in the facility. Once there, Kligman quickly saw an opportunity, as he was always in search of human subjects to test new dermatology products. He quickly began to recruit participants. Unfortunately for the recruits, it appears that Kligman did not necessarily view them as humans deserving of the protections outlined in the Nuremburg and Helsinki statements. Kligman explained his reaction the first time he entered Holmesburg: "All I saw before me were acres of skin. It was like a farmer seeing a fertile field for the first time" (p. 37).

But why go through the trouble of setting up a laboratory in a jail (Yes, I realize it was called Holmesburg *Prison*, but it largely held pretrial detainees, so a more apt description of the facility is jail)? The answer is simple. Just about all of us in free society would not have willingly participated in his research. The side effects ranged from skin irritation to permanent organ damage. Since Kligman had found a seemingly endless source of human subjects, private and government entities were eager to offer him funding to conduct more and more risky experiments, even if it meant branching out to fields of medicine where he was not qualified to practice. Kligman could not force anyone to participate, so he needed to find a group of people who were so desperate for money that they would tolerate pain and discomfort in exchange for a small reward and would refrain from asking questions about the dangers of the research. The people incarcerated in Holmesburg had the choice of making $0.15 per hour on a work detail, or they could do the experiments for $300 to $400 per month. Remember, most were awaiting trial, so they could use that income to post bail or to hire a private attorney. People who were already convicted could use the money for commissary or to send money home to support their families. People who were already sentenced might participate in the medical experiments with the hope of being seen as cooperative when it came time for parole consideration. Another potential benefit to participation was that they might be moved from the general population to a special medical experimentation wing. Some who feared for their safety in the notoriously violent facility saw the experiments as a lesser of the evils, since some of the studies allowed them to stay in safer areas of the jail. This was a population that was desperate for money, fearful for their safety, eager to be seen as cooperative, and saw no other options to earn money or freedom. Still, the research ethics rules called for informed consent. Participants later reported that they really did not know what kind of chemicals were involved in the studies, nor did they have an idea of the dangers and the potential short- and long-term health ramifications. When called to testify before Congress, one of the Holmesburg research participants explained that trying to give consent forms with medical terminology to incarcerated people and expecting them to read them was the equivalent of asking them to read hieroglyphics. To make things worse, there were allegations that race played a role in selection of participants, with minorities being given the less desirable and lower-paying projects. The Philadelphia prison system's Board of Trustees shut down Kligman's program in January 1974, but some of his test subjects experienced a lifetime of health problems as a result of his work (Hornblum, 1998).

Kligman's work was not an exception, as doctors around the United States used prison populations for pools of human research subjects willing to take big risks for little compensation. As an example of the cost savings associated with using incarcerated human research subjects, Mitford (1973) interviewed a biomedical researcher who paid incarcerated research participants $12.50 to $15 per month. Had the researchers asked financially strapped, but free, people to participate in that same research, the cost would have been $100 per month. Another doctor told Mitford that incarcerated research participants were cheaper than chimpanzees, so they were especially attractive for this type of scientific research.

Kligman's actions, and those of other biomedical researchers in prisons and jails, are examples of why the US government found the need to act on behalf of human research participants in the 1970s. Around the same time that Kligman's work was being exposed to the public, Americans learned about another extremely unethical study that had been in progress for decades. In 1932, the Public Health Service and the Tuskegee Institute recruited 600 Black men, 399 of whom had syphilis, for a study to chronicle the natural progression of the disease. While the original plan was to observe participants for six months, it continued for 40 years. During that time, researchers concealed the diagnosis from participants, mostly out of fear that they would seek treatment once it became available, thereby disrupting the natural progression of the illness. Instead, participants were left to suffer and die from something that became treatable decades before the study ended. The study continued until the project was exposed by the media in 1972 (Centers for Disease Control and Prevention, 2015). Additional unethical medical procedures exposed in the 1960s and early 1970s included sterilizations of Black, Latina, and Native American women without their consent. These were so common in the South that they were nicknamed "Mississippi appendectomies" (Peterson, 2024).

In the wake of these stories, Congress passed the National Research Act, and President Richard Nixon signed it into law in 1974. This law created the National Commission for the Protection of Human Subjects of Biomedical and Behavioral Research run by the Department of Health, Education, and Welfare (HEW) (Department of Health, Education, and Welfare, 1979). The Commission worked to consider specific types of research and establish ethical guidelines for them. One of their most important documents was published in 1979 and is known as the *Belmont Report*. The ***Belmont Report*** provided researchers with a useful summary of the basic ethical principles that should guide all research involving human subjects. The first principle is **respect for persons**, meaning research participants must be treated as autonomous agents. In the case of a person having diminished autonomy, there must be protection. Autonomous persons are able to consider whether to engage in research and make decisions to protect themselves without being coerced. The second principle is **beneficence**. Researchers must avoid harming human research participants while maximizing benefits and minimizing any possible harms. Finally, there is justice. The question of **justice** involves determining who should reap the benefits of research and who should have to bear the burdens of that work. These benefits and burdens must be equally distributed throughout society.

Harm in Social Science Research

So far, I have only discussed medical experiments, so you might be thinking to yourself right now, "That's terrible, but criminologists don't do medical experiments. We can't possibly harm people in that way." Very true. However, social scientists can still hurt people or put them in harm's way with research, and there are numerous examples as evidence.

While there is still stigma and discrimination surrounding homosexuality, we have come a long way since the 1970s, when Laud Humphreys (1970) embarked on his fieldwork to learn about anonymous male-male sexual encounters, mostly involving men who lived publicly as heterosexuals. Humphreys served as a "watch queen" in bathrooms, meaning he would guard the door in exchange for being permitted to watch the men in the bathroom having sex. While there, he would secretly write down their license plates, look up their information, and then visit their houses (this time with an altered physical appearance) to administer a survey on social health (a combination of socioeconomic and health factors with questions about marital relations and sex) (Humphreys, 1970). These men were unaware that they were selected for the health study due to their involvement in homosexual relations, nor were they informed or given the option to opt out of the part of the study that involved their sexual encounters. Being outed as a homosexual in the late 1960s and early 1970s would almost certainly ruin careers, livelihoods, marriages, and social standing. Humphreys published his research in a book titled the ***Tearoom Trade***. Critics argued that Humphreys put these men at risk without informing them of the risks and giving them the freedom to decline participation.

The **Stanford Prison Experiment** is one of the most famous psychology studies in US history. Philip Zimbardo, the researcher behind the experiment, has been criticized for several aspects of the study. Some of the problems with the research go well beyond the scope of this chapter. Of concern here are the ethical questions that surround the work. Zimbardo gathered college-age male volunteers to be randomly selected to adopt the roles of either incarcerated people or corrections officers in a simulated prison. The basement of one of the academic buildings at Stanford became the "prison," and the plan was to study dynamics between the officers and the incarcerated for two weeks. Instead, Zimbardo ended the study after six days out of concern for the participants' psychological well-being. He became worried that the "guards" were becoming so abusive and that the "prison" had become so real for the "prisoners" that continuation might produce psychological harm. Later, evidence emerged showing Zimbardo encouraging the aggressiveness exhibited by the "guards." This means that Zimbardo artificially generated what he characterized as organically occurring abusive behavior that was driving the "prisoners" to the breaking point (Blum, 2018). By now, generations of psychology and criminal justice students have seen or heard the most famous video clip of the study: a participant screaming about how he is losing it and needs to get out right now. The student who had that "breakdown" later reported that he did not want to participate in the research anymore but could not find any other way to be let out of the "prison." His request to be removed was denied, so he feigned distress to frighten Zimbardo into letting him go home. Zimbardo later claimed that he would have let any participant go home if they stated, "I quit the experiment," but no such instructions appeared on the informed consent page outlining the participants' rights (Perlstadt, 2018). As we already learned in this chapter, by today's standards, there must be a mechanism to allow participants to withdraw from research at any time, yet multiple "prisoners" were told that they could not exit the study over the six days.

More recently, a professor of organizational behavior wanted to watch how restaurants would respond to an allegation of food poisoning from a customer. Frank Flynn, a professor at Columbia University, sent letters to 240 restaurants claiming that his wedding anniversary dinner was marred by a case of food poisoning (Kifner, 2001). Restaurant owners and managers reported feeling distraught, they berated and retrained staff, and some even fired employees over the alleged mishandling of food (Frumkin, 2002). Once they realized that this was all part of research, two dozen filed suit against both the university and the professor (Fried, 2004).

My point in providing these examples is that social science research might not harm people in the same fashion as medical research, but the potential for harm does exist. When we study crime, we observe people, with or without their knowledge, conduct interviews, and review criminal case files. Some of this work can be harmless. A student who observes a four-way intersection and counts the number of cars that do or do not come to a full stop at the stop sign can be confident that no individual driving that day will be harmed by their "participation" in that research. People who are asked in interviews or written surveys to recount past victimization or the harm their drug addiction caused their family and friends may experience emotional harm. A researcher who collects data on sensitive topics, such as criminal offending or noncriminal deviant behavior, can cost participants their jobs and reputations if the data are not properly safeguarded.

Social science researchers have just as much responsibility as our colleagues in the medical field to respect others, keep them from harm, maximize the individual and societal benefits of our research, and ensure that the risks and benefits are distributed equally across participants. There are a few steps that we can take to safeguard individuals.

Informed Consent

Informed consent is a key element in maintaining the safety of potential research participants. People should have the right to choose to be part of research, but they cannot make an informed decision without appropriate disclosure from the research team. By engaging with research participants in the informed consent process, researchers help to ensure that potential participants maintain their autonomy and can deliberate and make their own decisions (Shahnazarian et al., 2013). The authors of the *Belmont Report* identified three elements of the consent process: information, comprehension, and voluntariness (Department of Health, Education, and Welfare, 1979).

Information

In most instances, individuals are to be informed about several elements of the research process before they are asked to consent to involvement. Standard information to be shared includes the identity of the researcher(s) and their professional affiliation(s), the research procedure itself, any information about potential risks and benefits, the voluntariness of the project, the length of the project, and confirmation that the individuals are permitted to withdraw at any time. They should also be given the chance to ask questions. There are times, however, when disclosure of some of the aforementioned elements could actually damage the validity of the research. Only then should one consider deviating from the standard consent rules. The Department of Health, Education, and Welfare (1979) identified three criteria that must be present to justify a deviation from common informed consent:

(1) Incomplete disclosure is truly necessary to accomplish the goals of the research, (2) there are no undisclosed risks to subjects that are more than minimal, and (3) there is an adequate plan for debriefing subjects, when appropriate, and for dissemination of research results to them (Department of Health, Education, and Welfare, 1979, p. 7).

Comprehension

Including all the necessary elements seems like a straightforward enough task, but the target population for a particular study may complicate matters. In criminal justice, we study people from all walks of life, including highly educated judges, attorneys, and criminal justice administrators. Setting up informed consent for these individuals is easy in that there are no concerns about their ability to understand verbal or written information. The same cannot be said for potential research participants who are justice-involved, incarcerated individuals, or people experiencing homelessness. It is the researcher's responsibility to frame informed consent in a way that they can understand. If the researcher is using a consent form, then it needs to be written to match the reading and comprehension level of the participant. In the case of people involved in the justice system, that is usually a fourth- to sixth-grade reading level. Another potential concern is whether the participants speak or read English and, if so, how well? If potential respondents speak and read in other languages, you will need to be able to communicate the consent information in the appropriate language. What if there is a severe developmental or psychological impairment? It may be appropriate to designate a third party, such as a social worker, to act as an advocate, observe the research, and help individuals who may have difficulty comprehending informed consent (Department of Health, Education, and Welfare, 1979).

Voluntariness

Are the people being asked to consent truly free to give it? HEW (1979) identified two different elements that can hinder voluntary consent. The first is coercion, meaning that there is a threat of harm for failure to comply. In the early 2010s, journalists reported that California was performing sterilizations of females incarcerated in a state prison. While some women were pleased to have gotten this medical procedure while in prison, others reported feeling violated and argued that they were coerced into consenting. Some complained that their status while incarcerated made it difficult for them to say no to any request or recommendation coming from those holding positions of authority. Others claimed that they were only asked for consent after being sedated (Chappell, 2013). The second threat to voluntariness is undue influence. This involves the offer of an excessive or improper reward or some other overture to encourage compliance. The reward might seem appropriate at first glance, but if the population happens to be especially vulnerable, viewed in that light, it could be inappropriate. As I noted earlier, people in Holmesburg Prison were frequent research participants because the financial rewards were too small to induce anyone from the general public to participate. How much money would it take to convince you to have a fingernail removed? Incarcerated men in Holmesburg did it for $50 (Hornblum, 1998). With inflation, that would be about $400 today. My guess is that no one reading this book would be willing to endure that for $400, but it is unlikely that any of us are in as desperate a situation as the inhabitants of Holmesburg Prison. Today, the United Nations Office of High Commissioner for Human Rights (OHCHR) cautions that incarcerated persons should not be offered "overwhelmingly attractive inducements" to engage in activities that can put their lives at risk while researchers make little to no effort to mitigate these risks. The OHCHR referred to such harmful behavior as "extrajudicial execution" (Office of High Commissioner for Human Rights, 2023).

In criminal justice, we frequently encounter individuals whose ability to consent is questionable. For example, juveniles are legally incapable of consenting on their own. Research involving juveniles must include consent from a parent or guardian in most cases. In the juvenile corrections setting, consent can come from someone from the administration who is designated as the person responsible. For homeless juveniles or those who are from homes where it does not seem feasible to be able to contact and communicate with a parent, an advocate such as a social worker can be assigned to consider the children's best interest. Juveniles are usually asked for their assent to participate in research. Research involving juveniles and the protocols necessary to protect them, are determined on a case-by-case basis by ethics review committees called Institutional Review Boards (IRBs). IRBs consider the risks of the research, the potential of the research to help children, and the ages and maturity of the particular individuals who are going to be involved in the study (United States Department of Health and Human Services, 2018). Both incarcerated people and juveniles are considered vulnerable populations that require extra protections when they are asked to participate in research.

The Informed Consent Process

Researchers can communicate the elements of informed consent in a variety of ways. One of the most common is to put this information in writing for people to consider. Participants can communicate their consent on written forms in a few different ways. One option is to leave a space for the individual to check "yes" or "no" and then provide a signature. There will be times, however, when the consent form is part of an anonymous survey, so a signature would run counter to the promise of anonymity. In that case, participants might be asked to check a box indicating "yes" or "no," or the instructions might state that they should fill out the survey if they consent or refrain from starting if they do not consent. If the research is being conducted over the phone or with a population that might have difficulty reading, then the researcher can deliver the consent information orally and ask for verbal consent.

Shahnazarian et al. (2013) describe informed consent as a process that must be considered throughout the study. Research participants may have second thoughts after providing consent. People may begin to participate in the research but then become anxious, fearful, sad, or even bored, and decide to terminate involvement. Everyone must always feel that they are free to withdraw from participation at any time.

Consent is not necessary for every social science research project. If a researcher is counting cars at a four-way intersection, that person would certainly not be expected to knock on the car windows and ask for permission to watch the car go through the intersection. If you are working with the local police station and agree to analyze their recent calls-for-service or arrest data, you are not expected to track down the people who called the police or got arrested to get their consent. Instructors who survey their classes as part of the course's educational process do not need to get student consent unless the survey is going to be used later in published research.

Institutional Review Boards

Institutional Review Boards (IRBs) were created in response to unethical research practices in both the biomedical and the behavioral fields. IRBs exist not only in the United States but in over 80 other countries. The boards typically consist of people with research backgrounds who are expected to independently evaluate research proposals to safeguard human subjects. IRB review is mandatory for funding proposals submitted to several federal agencies, including the Department of Health and Human Services (DHHS) (Grady, 2015). Colleges and universities typically have their own IRBs, since professors are often active in research and apply for funding from federal agencies that require IRB review.

All research that involves human subjects is expected to go through some level of IRB review, either exempt, expedited, or full review. Exempt proposals involving humans should still go through the IRB so the board can confirm that the research should be exempt from review. How do researchers decide whether something should go through the IRB? The DHHS Office for Human Research Protections has very useful flowcharts on their website to guide researchers in decision-making (Office for Human Research Protections, 2020). Research that involves obtaining information about living individuals, has an intervention or degree of interaction with people, and includes private information should generally be reviewed by an IRB. The proposal must receive some level of review if it is eligible for DHHS funding.

Examples of exempt research are teacher activities that include collecting data from students as part of the educational process, use of certain types of already existing data, use of publicly available data, and research that involves no harm to individuals should disclosure of the data become public. A colleague and I did a study to see whether there were any changes in patterns of mental health calls for service to a police department in one city before and during the COVID-19 pandemic. We had the dates and times police were either dispatched to a call presumed to involve someone experiencing a mental health problem, or police-initiated contact with someone appearing to be struggling with mental health. The dataset did not include any identifying information for any individuals, and we had no contact with any humans who were part of those calls (Tartaro & Lu, 2024). This is an example of research that was eligible for exemption.

Research proposals that have already been approved by an IRB and have continued past their expiration date are generally eligible for expedited review, as are previously approved proposals that require minor changes (Office for Human Research Protections, 2019). Other projects could be eligible for expedited review if there is going to be data collected directly from humans but the potential for harm is low. Research that involves collection of sensitive data that, if disclosed, could be harmful to people, requires a full board review. Any research that has the potential to physically or mentally harm someone, even if that harm means having to relive bad memories, needs full IRB review.

Some Ethical Dilemmas

Confidentiality or Anonymity

People who choose to participate in research deserve protection. Fortunately, we do not have the concerns that medical researchers have about causing physical harm. We do, however, use agency records to look up criminal records and drug treatment participation, and we ask people to self-report their victimizations and even their own illegal activities. Their willingness to assist researchers by participating in a study should never come back to harm them. One of the ways that we provide protection is through the promise of either anonymity or confidentiality. These are two very different concepts. **Anonymity** means that no one, including the researcher, will be able to look at the data and identify the individuals attached to that information. Anonymity can be achieved through distributing surveys and expressly asking for people to refrain from including their names or any other unique identifiers, such as a student identification number. For research involving agency or organizational records, the agency could deidentify cases before sending the dataset to the researcher by removing names and any other identifying information. **Confidentiality** is different, in that the research team has access to information that allows them to connect surveys or other information to individuals. When researchers promise that information will remain confidential, they mean that they will not show anyone copies of the surveys with the names still attached, share the dataset with identifying information still included, or write reports that identify any individuals.

While it is extremely rare, law enforcement can request or demand to see a researcher's notes and other files pertaining to a project. When this happens, the researcher seldom has any type of protection. Researchers are not provided the same protection as attorneys and members of clergy, who are exempt from having to provide information on clients and parishioners. The only protection available for researchers is a **Certificate of Confidentiality** (COC) available through the federal government. The COC is available only for select projects funded through the National Institutes of Health or the DHHS or non-federally funded projects at the discretion of these agencies (National Institutes of Health, 2019). Most researchers lack these certificates. This means that, if they are doing research and are promising confidentiality, there might come a time when they are faced with having to break that promise and cooperate with law enforcement, or keep the promise and face legal repercussions. Again, this is rare, but it is something that researchers need to consider before they embark on data collection.

During the data collection process, researchers must make sure that data are being collected and handled in a way that allows them to maintain whatever protections they promised the participants. If the promise was anonymity, then no identifying information should appear with the data. For confidentiality, interviews must occur in a setting that provides a degree of privacy. If people are being asked to fill out a survey that needs to remain confidential, respondents must be given instructions for how to return it to the researcher safely. If the researcher is not physically present to collect surveys upon completion, one option is for respondents to place their completed forms in envelopes, seal them, and then sign their names over the seal to deter tampering. Another option is for the researcher to leave a locked box in a location, such as a police station for a policing survey, where officers can drop off their completed forms. The forms will remain secure in the box since the researcher is the only person with the key. If the survey is distributed over the internet, and respondents are promised confidentiality, the researchers must take precautions to make sure that no one other than the research staff ever sees the full data with identifying information.

Data containing confidential information must remain secure and out of reach of others. IRBs require researchers to explain how they will handle sensitive information once they receive it. Paper copies that have identifying information and sensitive items must be kept under two sets of lock and key at all times. In my case, that means I have a filing cabinet in my office, and I have the only key to it. The custodial staff and campus police can get into my locked office at any time, but the files are still protected, because they are in the locked filing cabinet. If there are sensitive files with identifying information on a computer, the computer must be password protected. Whenever possible, researchers should work to de-identify datasets, meaning that as soon as individual names and any corresponding identification numbers are no longer needed, they should be removed. Failure to take these steps after data have been collected could result in researchers breaking their promise to protect respondents.

Compensating Participants

Another potential ethical dilemma pertains to offering to pay research participants for their time. If someone has ever asked you to fill out a survey or do an interview, your first thought was likely how much time this was going to take and what an inconvenience this would be. In addition to that, if the research involves collection of sensitive information, such as someone's drug use or criminal offending, people may be reluctant to participate simply because they would be taking a risk by divulging this information to a stranger who may or may not safeguard the data. To encourage people to participate and thank them for their time, researchers will sometimes provide some form of remuneration, such as a gift card or cash, in exchange for participation. There are a few ethical concerns here. First, we want to make sure that we are not tempting people so much with a reward that they become willing to take on a serious risk. Remember that the individuals housed in Holmesburg Prison were so desperate to make bail or earn money to hire an attorney that they were willing to engage in painful medical experiments for a small fraction of what it would have taken to convince a free adult to do the same. While it is acceptable to provide participants with remuneration, the money should not be so much that it would have undue influence on decision-making. The money should be enough to adequately express the researcher's appreciation and show respect for the individual's time. Second, given the populations that we often interact with in criminal justice, there is worry about what the participants will do with that money. One common concern is that the money will go toward buying drugs and alcohol. A possible way around this is to provide gift cards instead of cash. When I conducted interviews of family and friends of incarcerated people in the lobbies of two different jails, I wanted to provide some remuneration to encourage participation and thank people for their time. In order to avoid the two ethical concerns listed here, I used my grant to purchase several small gift cards for a local convenience store chain. The jails were in New Jersey, where convenience stores are prohibited from selling alcohol, so the worst that could happen would be that the cards would be used to purchase tobacco or caffeine.

Researchers may also try to show their appreciation and respect for participants by informally doing small favors. This is different from the financial remuneration that I discussed in the previous paragraph, as that type of compensation is much more formal and spelled out as researchers are obtaining consent. Researchers have provided transportation to people who needed a ride and helped people fill out job applications (Wright et al., 1992). Others have allowed people to use their phones (Adler, 1993) and done other small, but legal, favors. When I was conducting interviews in the lobby of a jail, family and friends would often approach a machine that allowed them to put money on their loved ones' commissary accounts. Older, less technologically savvy people often found it confusing, so whenever I was not in the middle of an interview, I always got up to help people use the machine. There have also been times when I have conducted interviews in prisons and let the conversation go on a bit longer even after I collected all the information I wanted when I sensed that the individual just wanted to chat with someone from the outside for a few minutes. I decided that, out of respect for the time that they just gave me, I could spare a little bit of my time and make some friendly conversation.

Plagiarism

This entire chapter has focused on ethical issues that may pose risks to human research participants (I always feel uncomfortable calling them "subjects"), but in research there is one more ethical concern that we need to consider. This one could arise regardless of whether the project involves human participants, and it can be problematic even with work that does not adhere to the scientific method. **Plagiarism** consists of passing someone else's work off as one's own and is considered a very serious offense among academics and writers. Plagiarism is considered problematic because it consists of two offenses: theft and fraud. It is theft because you are taking work from someone else (human or artificial intelligence [AI]), and it is fraud because you are claiming to be the author of such work. Let me explain why this is a big deal. Whether it is in a college class or at your job, if you are expected to produce some sort of report or brief, you are going to be evaluated on the quality of that product. Professors will want to grade you on not just the quality of the thoughts/facts but also on the clarity of the writing. The same goes for your work supervisor. If you take a sentence that someone else wrote and then put it into your own work without properly attributing that work, you are stealing from the original author and letting everyone assume that you took the time and effort to construct that sentence yourself.

You might be thinking that you can ignore this section, because you are very ethical and would never do something like this. What you need to understand is that plagiarism can take many forms, and it is very easy to do without even realizing it. The problem is that "I did not realize I was doing something wrong" stopped becoming an adequate excuse back in high school, because we teach you, at multiple points in time, how to avoid plagiarism in college. Let this serve as one more of those teaching moments.

The primary tools to protect you against plagiarism are paraphrasing and proper citations. I will revisit these after I discuss types of plagiarism.
Examples of intentional plagiarism:

- Purchasing a paper from a paper mill
- Taking a friend/relative's work and handing it in as your own
- Using AI to generate your paper or parts of it without acknowledging the parts that were written for you. You should always check with your professor or supervisor, as they may prohibit any use of AI.
- Copying and pasting statements/sentences/paragraphs from websites, articles, books, or any other source that you did not write

Examples of unintentional plagiarism:

- Copying entire statements/sentences from sources and then failing to properly cite them and use quotation marks to indicate those are not your words
- Using any idea or fact from another source and then failing to cite it

Here are some important rules to remember:

- *There is a difference between a quotation and plagiarism*: I have had students say to me, "well, I just used the sentences from the sources I read, because they stated it so well that I just could not think of a better way to write it." Unless your professor forbids it, it is usually acceptable to have a few (very few) quotations in your paper. There might, indeed, be something that would best be communicated in the words of the original author, and you will see a few examples of me quoting other authors in this book. Those quotations are acceptable because I am citing them properly and acknowledging that they are not my words. Whenever I take the exact words of others, I put quotation marks around them, and I either introduce or end the sentence by attributing them to the proper authors. Since we are in the social sciences, we like to use the American Psychological Association (APA) citation standards, which calls for (1) identification of the authors, (2) year of publication, and (3) page numbers when available for every quotation. Failure to include the quotation marks along with a proper citation turns a quotation into plagiarism. One other way that quotations could be problematic and detrimental to your grade or job performance is if you use them excessively. Remember, you are being judged on *your* writing, not your ability to copy and paste other people's work and insert quotation marks. If you turn in sentences written by others, how can anyone evaluate your writing?
- *Paraphrase*: Since we just established that only small amounts of quotations are acceptable, that means that you must learn to paraphrase others' work. You read sources to learn about the topic for your paper, and then you have to communicate your newly acquired knowledge in your paper in your own words. One good suggestion would be to read a section of an article,

put it down, and then type up a quick summary, in your own words, of what you just read. That way, your notes that you use to write your paper will already be in your own words. This will prevent you from taking someone else's sentences and attributing them to your own work.

- *Remember to cite what you paraphrase*: Putting notes into your own words is an excellent first step. That does not mean, however, that you now own that information. You learned new facts, and you might have gotten a few ideas that are not yours. Any time you are going to write about something that is not common knowledge and that you just took from something you read (or even saw or heard, because you have to cite videos and audio recordings too), you must properly cite it in your paper, or else it is plagiarism. For paraphrased items, APA style requires us to note the authors' last names and the publication year in the paragraph where you are using the information.

There is much more to learn about the specifics of when, where, and how to cite sources, and that is beyond the scope of this book. Your college or university's website is likely an excellent resource for learning about plagiarism and how to avoid it. There are very good books that also show students how to not only cite properly but how to navigate all the tricky aspects of writing, such as grammar and punctuation. Let me be clear that, given your level of education, it is now your responsibility to understand plagiarism and how to avoid it. Of course, see your professor, a librarian, or a writing tutor with specific questions.

Summary

It is unfortunate that the history of research has been marred by horrific events. The lack of ethical standards and sheer disrespect for fellow humans prompted people to commit acts of unbelievable cruelty in the name of science. After decades of disturbing examples of harmful medical research, several countries' governments and even international groups established regulations to police the research community. In the United States, the *Belmont Report* helped to provide general standards for protection of human subject. Universities, hospitals, and other institutions that often sponsor research have created their own Institutional Review Boards that are responsible for oversight of their employees' research involving humans.

In the social sciences, we do study aspects of people's lives that can prove harmful. We are interested in deviant behavior, criminal offending, and victimization. This research can be harmful in multiple ways. First, asking people to recall some of the darkest moments of their lives can make people relive the emotions, including guilt, shame, and sadness, that are associated with that time. Second, if others were to find out about the research participants' criminal record, drug use behavior, transactions with sex workers, stealing from employers, or any other illegal or unethical behavior that we are measuring, the consequences could be very severe. People can lose their jobs and even get into legal trouble just because they were willing to help a researcher. For these reasons, we must make protection of our participants a top priority.

Key Terms

Nuremberg Code	Declaration of Helsinki	*Belmont Report*
Respect for persons	Beneficence	Justice
Tearoom Trade	Stanford Prison Experiment	Informed Consent
Institutional Review Board (IRB)	Anonymity	Confidentiality
Certificate of Confidentiality	Plagiarism	

Discussion Questions

1. Consider the Holmesburg Prison experiments. In what ways did the researchers violate the principles in the *Belmont Report*, the Nuremburg Code, and the Helsinki Declaration?
2. What steps could Zimbardo have taken to make the Stanford Prison Experiment more ethically viable by today's research standards?
3. Imagine that you are going to give your fellow students a survey about their participation in off-campus parties where alcohol and/or illegal drugs are served.

   a. What elements need to be in the consent form for this?
   b. What are the potential risks to participants?
   c. Devise a plan for how you will distribute, collect, and store the data in a way that will be acceptable to your school's IRB.

References

Adler, P. A. (1993). *Wheeling & dealing: An ethnography of upper-level drug dealing and smuggling community* (2nd ed.). Columbia University Press.

Blum, B. (2018). The lifespan of a lie. *Medium*. https://medium.com/s/trustissues/the-lifespan-of-a-lie-d869212b1f62

Centers for Disease Control and Prevention. (2015). *U.S. public health service syphilis study at Tuskegee*. www.cdc.gov/tuskegee/timeline.htm

Chappell, B. (2013). California's prison sterilizations reportedly echo eugenics era. *NPR*. www.npr.org/sections/thetwo-way/2013/07/09/200444613/californias-prison-sterilizations-reportedly-echoes-eugenics-era.

Cohen, A. (2016). *Imbeciles*. Penguin Press.

Department of Health, Education, and Welfare. (1979). *The Belmont report: Ethical principles and guidelines for the protection of human subjects of research*. The National Commission for the Protection of Human Subjects of Biomedical and Behavioral Research.

Fried, J. P. (2004). No stomach pills, but many legal bills. *New York Times*. www.nytimes.com/2004/02/08/nyregion/following-up.html

Frumkin, P. (2002). Ten operators sue Columbia U., professor over letters. *Nation's Restaurant News, 36*(2), 1.

Grady, C. (2015). Institutional review boards: Purpose and challenges. *CHEST, 148*(5), 1148–1155.

Hornblum, A. M. (1998). *Acres of skin*. Routledge.

Humphreys, L. (1970). *Tearoom trade: Interpersonal sex in public places*. Aldine Publishing Company.

Jarmusik, N. (2019). *The Nuremberg code and its impact on clinical research*. IMARC Research, Inc. www.imarcresearch.com/blog/bid/359393/nuremberg-code-1947

Kifner, J. (2001). Scholar sets off gastronomic false alarm. *New York Times*. www.nytimes.com/2001/09/08/nyregion/scholar-sets-off-gastronomic-false-alarm.html

Mitford, J. (1973). *Kind and usual punishment: The prison business*. Alfred A. Knopf.

National Institutes of Health. (2019). *Certificates of Confidentiality (CoC) – human subjects*. U.S. Department of Health and Human Services.

Office for Human Research Protections. (2019). *Expedited review procedures guidance*, 2003. United States Department of Health and Human Services, Office for Human Research Protections. www.hhs.gov/ohrp/regulations-and-policy/guidance/guidance-on-expedited-review-procedures/index.html

Office for Human Research Protections. (2020). *Human subjects regulations decision charts: 2018 requirements*. United States Department of Health and Human Services, Office for Human Research Protections. www.hhs.gov/ohrp/regulations-and-policy/decision-charts-2018/index.html

Office of High Commissioner for Human Rights. (2023). *A/HRC/53/29: Deaths in prisons report of the special rapporteur on extrajudicial, summary or arbitrary executions, Morris Tidball-Binz*. OHCHR. www.ohchr.org/en/documents/thematic-reports/ahrc5329-deaths-prisons-report-special-rapporteur-extrajudicial-summary

Oshinsky, D. M. (1996). *Worse than slavery: Parchman farm and the ordeal of Jim Crow justice*. Simon and Schuster.

Perlstadt, H. (2018). How to get out of the Stanford prison experiment: Revisiting social science research ethics. *Current Research Journal of Social Sciences and Humanities, 1*, 45–59.

Peterson, E. L. (2024). *The shortest history of eugenics.* The Experiment.
Shahnazarian, D., Hagemann, J., Aburto, M., & Rose, S. (2013). *Informed consent in human subjects research.* University of Southern California Office for the Protection of Research Subjects.
Tartaro, C., & Lu, R. (2024). The impact of the COVID-19 pandemic on police involvement in mental health calls for service. *Criminal Justice Policy Review, 36*(1–2), 3–21. https://doi.org/10.1177/0887403424 1303024
United States Department of Health and Human Services. (2018). *Electronic code of federal regulations part 46 – protection of human subjects.* www.ecfr.gov/cgi-bin/retrieveECFR?gp=&SID=83cd09e1c0f5c 6937cd9d7513160fc3f&pitd=20180719&n=pt45.1.46&r=PART&ty=HTML#se45.1.46_1408
World Medical Association. (2019). *WMA declaration of Helsinki – ethical principles for medical research involving human subjects.* www.wma.net/policies-post/wma-declaration-of-helsinki-ethical-principles-for-medical-research-involving-human-subjects/
Wright, R., Decker, S. H., Redfern, A. K., & Smith, D. L. (1992). A snowball's chance in hell: Doing field-work with active residential burglars. *Journal of Research in Crime and Delinquency, 29*, 148–161. https://doi.org/10.1177/0022427892029002003

Reading 3.1 Online Extremism and Terrorism Research Ethics

Most writing on research ethics addresses protection of research participants, so there is little scholarship available about the risks faced by the researchers themselves. What literature there is on researcher safety focuses primarily on the dangers of field research with potentially dangerous environments that could expose the researcher to people who might harm them. Perhaps the most neglected area of the research ethics literature is the topic of researcher safety when data collection is limited to online interactions with research participants. Additionally, since online data collection has only been an option for a few decades, the questions of how and when to require informed consent and whether researchers should be allowed to deceive people about their reasons for engaging in online forums still need to be addressed. I thought that one part of Conway's (2021) article was particularly important, and that was a reminder that people who find it too emotionally difficult to work on a project should move on to another topic. That advice should be remembered by everyone in criminal justice, not just researchers.

Online Extremism and Terrorism Research Ethics: Researcher Safety, Informed Consent, and the Need for Tailored Guidelines

Maura Conway

Introduction

The study of extremism and terrorism raises significant ethical issues in their own rights as, separately, does online research; the combination of these poses particular ethical quandaries. Not having a problem-solving purpose *per se*, this article reflects on two core issues of human subjects' research ethics and how they play out for extremism and terrorism researchers in the Internet age. At the center of medical research ethics, on which social science research ethics are based, is the protection of research subjects from harm. This is appropriate given both the history of egregious violations of persons for purposes of medical research and the inherently risky nature of medical experimentation on humans overall. There is global consensus that the surest way to guarantee the protection of human subjects in medical research is via obtaining their full and free consent to their participation in any such research. In universities, this and other research ethics requirements are overseen by what are generally termed Research Ethics Committees (REC), Institutional Review Boards (IRBs), or similar, which govern not just medical research, but the ethics aspects of all research taking place within their institutions. The protection of research subjects via obtaining informed consent is thus now also a central pillar of social science research ethics as governed by RECs/IRBs.

Explored herein are two of the ways in which these, at first glance eminently reasonable, ethical requirements are complicated when applied in a specific non-medical research setting. The article reflects first on the domination of discussion around protection and harms by the potential for harm to research subjects to, in many cases, the almost total exclusion of potential harms to researchers. Concerns for researcher welfare are an important missing factor in contemporary research ethics governance it is argued herein, which have been gaining greater attention among online extremism and terrorism researchers since approximately 2018, and warrant much closer attention from

RECs/IRBs than they have received to-date. Second, if researcher safety is all-but-missing from research ethics discussions, the same cannot be said as regards informed consent and related issues, which dominate contemporary research ethics approval processes. A wide variety of issues complicate the fulfillment of this requirement by online extremism and terrorism researchers, however. Chief amongst these is researchers' desire to engage in incognito data collection for primarily safety, but also other reasons, which raises issues around the ethical permissibility of deception or even just concealment in our sub-field.

This article addresses a series of core and interconnected ethics issues within online extremism and terrorism research, namely researcher safety, informed consent and the closely related matter of harm to subjects, and, stemming from these discussions, the need for ethics guidelines tailored not just to terrorism studies—though these would doubtless be beneficial—but to our specific sub-field. The article is divided into three sections. The first and second sections take up researcher safety in "online field" research and the interrelated issues of informed consent, deception, and protection of research subjects respectively. Section three addresses the pros and cons of the currently available guidelines for engaging in ethically informed online research and advocates for the development of ethics guidelines tailored to our sub-field. In the conclusion, a case is made for committing our ethical thinking and decision-making to paper to a much greater extent than we have done to-date.

Researcher Safety in Online "Field Research"

Numerous texts supply guidance to security researchers on *Danger in the Field*, *Surviving Field Research*, and *Conducting Terrorism Field Research*,[1] but with most of these having little-to-nothing to say about the Internet. For online extremism and terrorism researchers, the Internet *is* the "field," however.[2] Per Barratt and Maddox therefore, "the safety of researchers working in digital spaces needs to be properly considered and safeguarded with the same care as is applied to conventional research engagements."[3] While texts solely concerned with online extremism and terrorism research ethics are still relatively rare,[4] articles and reports that include some reflection on ethics issues in online extremism and terrorism research are increasing in number.[5] A hallmark of this emergent literature is an emphasis on researcher welfare, especially researchers' mental and emotional wellbeing.[6] Many of these analyses mirror discussions that had begun to appear in media at about the same time regarding wellbeing issues among social media companies' content moderator workforce,[7] which may have laid the groundwork for researchers to relate their experiences.

Fortunately for Western scholars, "[t]o date, jihadist extremists have not systematically targeted researchers for potential violence outside of conflict zones. Indeed, groups such as al Qaeda have often sought to benefit from adversary research."[8] But as also pointed out, "[a]s research increases on rightwing movements with a larger and more diffuse presence, researchers may need to be more conscious of potential [physical] threats closer to home."[9] Aside from posing physical dangers to researchers, both jihadist and right-wing extremists have been known to engage in networked forms of abuse, some of which also has the potential to spill over into "real world" settings. Researcher online harassment and other forms of networked abuse can take a variety of forms, including "doxxing" (i.e. posting individuals' private information online oftentimes accompanied by implicit or explicit requests to use it for online and/or "real world" harassment), "brigading" (i.e. a group of users coordinating to "pile on" another user for harassment purposes), and "swatting" (i.e. making a hoax telephone call to emergency services in an attempt to have them dispatch heavily armed police—in the US, a "SWAT team"—to a particular address), which may also be used in combination. In fact, the extreme right has a long history of this type of behavior, having carried out "perhaps the world's first instance of doxxing" in the 1980s,[10] and employing swatting in their much more recent online harassment campaign against women in computer gaming known as "Gamergate."[11] Unfortunately, there is no way when researching online extremism and terrorism, to definitively avoid becoming the subject of such harassment and abuse. This may occur whether in the course of your research you identify yourself as a researcher, or engage in anonymous participant or non-participant online observation and are "outed" by research subjects or others, or arising from publication of your research findings.

While mental and emotional distress arising from exposure to certain types of online content might very well be "softer" than the challenges raised by being directly targeted by extremist and terrorist actors or those adjacent to them, "it is nonetheless far more frequent and should therefore be taken seriously" too.[12] From 2014, IS's online propaganda increased in both volume and goriness, with videos depicting beheadings and other atrocities delivered in a steady high definition content stream for maximum impact. It was arising from repeated and prolonged consumption of this content that some researchers began to reflect on its potential negative effects on them.[13] Winter was the first online terrorism researcher to comment in writing on the potential damage to researchers of a steady diet of hateful and often violent content:

> Jihadist propaganda can be extremely distressing, as its intent is to upset viewers. However, even the most violent materials are in need of consideration by researchers, because they not only help us understand what drives terrorism at an organizational and individual level, but also contain valuable intelligence insights on jihadist activities. The potential harm inflicted upon practitioners working on issues associated with violent extremism—those employed by law enforcement agencies or technology companies—are increasingly well-known. However, there is less awareness of how those same issues are or could be affecting academic researchers psychologically.[14]

Other researchers concurred in their comments to NPR journalist Hannah Allam whose piece on the topic included comments such as "You look at violent imagery all day, and it gets to you. And you want to tell yourself it doesn't, but it does" and "I look at my colleagues and myself, and I see slightly angrier, more cynical people than I saw a year ago or two years ago, and that makes me sad … And I think a lot of that is to do with having to, day in and day out, face up to the worst of humanity."[15]

Very welcome, in this context, is the emphasis in the 2020 iteration of the Association of Internet Researchers' (AoIR) ethics guidelines on "the growing need for ***protecting the researchers***, as well as our subjects and informants" [emphasis in original].[16] Interestingly, the bulk of the paragraph-long section is addressed to extremism and terrorism research, with "Gamergate" referred to and "simply reviewing and curating, e.g., videos of beheadings and other forms of extreme violence" described as potentially having "serious consequences for researchers' psychological health and well-being …"[17] While such acknowledgment in these globally respected guidelines is certainly positive, elsewhere it is pointed out that whereas others professionally tasked in relation to online extremism and terrorism content "benefit from a certain level of welfare," academia is increasingly lagging behind in this respect, with one interviewee observing the following to Mahlouly:

> Researcher welfare is an important thing that I personally spend a lot of time thinking about. I know that other people spending their time looking at propaganda think about [it] as well. Especially in this area, because you have exposure to law enforcement, government and military people, social media corporations … All of us doing kind of the same sort of thing. We are all looking at propaganda a lot. But there is a sliding scale of welfare for these people. So, at the top of that you get social media people that get flexible hours, free yoga (literally free yoga [laugh]) and 24-hour therapy, all that stuff. Then you have law enforcement and they don't have free yoga, but they have flexible hours to a degree, football on Thursdays, that kind of thing … And then academia, where you have nothing.[18]

Agreed upon by virtually all contributors on researcher safety issues in this space is thus the necessity for additional knowledge generation around the issues, dedicated resources to mitigate some of the potential risks and harms, and increased training for all researchers (and decisionmakers, such as REC/IRB members, funders, etc.) active in our sub-field.[19]

Cross-Cutting Identity-Related Issues

Unfortunately, certain online extremism and terrorism researchers' identities can cause both the negative security and privacy implications and mental and emotional wellbeing issues associated with their research to be exacerbated. Drawing attention to this is emphatically not for purposes of burdening certain researchers with additional responsibilities on the basis of their identities but highlighting instead, as already widely recognized,[20] that researcher safety issues are not uniform. While nobody is *a priori* exempt, depending on the online extremist or terrorist community they are focused upon, researchers with certain identity markers are more likely to be the targets of online hate and harassment than others.[21] For example, sections of the extreme right evince hatred for various people of color, including particularly black people, Jewish people, Muslims, immigrants, refugees, LGBTQI+ individuals, and women. In general, a researcher that is publicly identifiable as falling into one or more of these categories is likely to prove a more attractive and persistent target for extreme right online harassment than those who do not. In addition, a tactic of online harassers is to communicate false or private information about their targets, which could negatively impact researchers reputations and/or careers, to their employers. While, again, this could be unpleasant for established scholars, it could have profoundly negative consequences for those Massanari describes, in a slightly different context, as "untenured, and/or a member of a marginalized community, and/or facing a precarious professional situation (such as being an adjunct, a graduate student, on the job market, or in a university where their research was not valued)."[22]

Winter makes a number of useful suggestions for how online terrorism researchers may maintain their mental and emotional wellbeing, one of which is that "researchers should try to keep grounded when handling [online terrorist] materials, even if this means actively trying to remain detached from them." He goes on to say that "[w]hile a researcher's empathy is important, so too is their ability to separate themselves from the subject of study; it means they remain analysts and avoid becoming participants."[23] Prolonged and repeated exposure to content that denigrates or otherwise egregiously offends one or more of researchers' core identity characteristics renders detachment effectively out of the hands of some researchers, however; they are always already "participants." Examples of this could include female researchers doing work on incel forums or black, Jewish, LGBTQI+, or Muslim researchers focused on extreme right online activity. Having more than one of these characteristics may also be expected to intensify the negativity of the experience (e.g. exiled Iraqi or Syrian Muslim researchers consuming IS content, black female researchers consuming increasingly racist incel content, etc.). Another upshot of this is that researcher crossover from a focus on one type of online extremism or terrorism, say violent jihadism, to another, say white supremacism, may be experienced vastly differently by the same researcher. On the other hand, for many people who fit into one or more of the discussed identity categories, it is precisely these aspects of their identities that impels them to do this work and "keeps them going." The potential for identity characteristics to compound the negative effects of researching online extremism and terrorism is worth paying attention to nonetheless.

As regards privacy and security, the degree of any particular researcher's vulnerability will depend on the appropriateness and effectiveness of the preparations they have made before entering the "field," including the level of security they have implemented to reduce risks. According to Mertus, "[e]ach researcher should decide for themselves how far they are willing to go in protecting themselves and the threshold of acceptable risk."[24] In fact, what constitute appropriate protections and acceptable risks should ideally be discussed and agreed with experienced and well-informed RECs/IRBs; in the absence of this, careful risk assessment on the part of researchers, based on the nature of the online space(s) they plan on entering, their level of research experience, and similar, is warranted. In terms of researchers' maintenance of their mental and emotional wellbeing, this too varies from person to person. And while identity markers may affect the level and nature of some types of harassment, it does not necessarily determine how it is received. Some researchers' life and/or professional experience may have prepared them for these negative externalities while others have not. Ultimately, it is for each individual to continually evaluate their own positioning, identity, experience, and other factors, ideally in consultation with colleagues, others close to them, and/or relevant professionals—as sometimes individuals have difficulty identifying their own struggles with coping—in order to determine the best course for them at any given time. Finally, it is worth pointing out, in closing this section, that "[i]f your experiences become too difficult, give yourself permission to move on to other projects."[25] Ultimately, we are all of us, as individuals, more important than our research.

Informed Consent, Deception, and Harm to Subjects

One of the ways in which online extremism and terrorism researchers seek to protect their safety "in the field" and limit potential harms to themselves from their research subjects is not to request consent, but instead to lurk in extremist and terrorist online spaces for data collection purposes. Concerns about the attitudes of RECs/IRBs to these types of practices prompted Baele and colleagues to layout "An Ethics Framework for Contemporary Security Studies" in 2018 to seek to "prevent the kind of incongruous situations produced by the blind application of generic ethics rules (e.g., obtaining participants' written informed consent, avoiding deception) to research projects in which these commandments appear impossible or even dangerous to implement."[26] This section is divided into four sub-sections that address some of these "generic ethics rules"—"public" versus "private" online data collection, challenges around informed consent requirements in data-intensive online research, the ethical permissibility of deception and concealment, and the "do no harm" principle—and their application to online extremism and terrorism research.

The "Public" versus "Private" Data Debate

One of the first questions that often arises in discussions of online data collection is whether the content is "public" or "private." Why? Because this is a way of determining whether it is necessary for researchers to obtain the consent of the data's creators or not.[27] This question is much more difficult to answer than it may first appear, however. It is regularly argued that content posted in wholly open online settings, such as non-passworded discussion forums or unlocked Twitter accounts, is in the public domain and thus comparable to, say, a letter in a newspaper. This is because a letter in a newspaper is viewed as text and not thereby subject to the same ethical considerations as human subjects research. The use of such content by researchers poses minimal risk for the posters, on this view, because—like the newspaper letter writer—they are assumed to have an awareness that their content is public, which is underlined by users' ability to conceal their identities online to varying extents via the employment of pseudonymous screen and/or user names, which many do, and in the case of Twitter, the option to easily make their tweets private, which most do not.[28]

A more nuanced approach to this discussion seeks to dispense with public-private distinctions and determine instead whether the research subjects' are likely to expect that their consent will be requested before their data is collected. But nor is this approach without its challenges:

> Researchers ... may not be equipped to determine the expectations for privacy of individuals participating in these forums, and not all individuals will share the same expectation of privacy. The question is then to determine whether researchers should set the bar according to the most open or the most private individual.[29]

Rosenberg makes a useful suggestion in this respect however, pointing researchers to the norms of the online community being studied for guidance.[30] Décary-Hétu and Aldridge explain, for example, that it is routine for users of illegal cryptomarkets, to "explicitly espouse 'crypto-anarchist' and radical libertarian principles," leading Décary-Hétu and Aldridge and other researchers to determine that those particular online communities viewed their content as usable without consent.[31] Some online spaces in which, especially, varieties of the extreme right are active share this libertarian orientation. Having said all this, the only type of extremist and terrorist content that is uncontestably public is that which, like branded extremist and terrorist group propaganda, is produced and circulated online with the express purpose that it be widely disseminated, copied, downloaded, and similar. This segues with Article 9.2(e) of the EU's General Data Protection Regulation (GDPR), one of the bases on which it allows processing of what it terms "special categories of personal data" being that these have been "manifestly made public by the data subject."

Determining the Necessity of Informed Consent in Data-Intensive Online Research

Additional issues arise around informed consent in online "big data" research. The first such issue is the practicability of seeking consent from all research subjects in a large to very large to, potentially, massive dataset. This would require not just disproportionate efforts, due to the number of subjects, but the very act itself could, secondly, increase potential harm to subjects. The overwhelming majority of online spaces in which extremists and terrorists are currently active do not have "real name" policies, which means that most posters are pseudonymous but not anonymous. In some spaces, such as 4chan and 8kun however, posts are overwhelmingly anonymous (i.e. the platforms do not allow users to create unique usernames). In either case, potential harms, including firstly invasion of privacy, would stem directly from researchers' efforts to contact individual research subjects for the purposes of acquiring consent. Not all the online spaces in which extremists and terrorists are currently active have administrator and/or moderator roles, but some do, including the latter two spaces. A suggested compromise, in the absence of being able to obtain the informed consent of all users of a particular forum or board, might therefore be for researchers to obtain consent for a data crawl or the use of other data collection methods from the appropriate administrator or moderator.[32] Any online radicalization research based on open sources has the potential to be biased by a requirement that the subjects of such research, including administrators or moderators, be provided with such information however, even absent consideration of the likelihood of such permission being forthcoming. Outreach to research subjects for informed consent purposes in large-scale online research is thus oftentimes not in the interests of either the research subjects or the research.

Deception and Concealment

There is a spectrum of revelation possible online, including by online researchers. This ranges from full formal disclosure by researchers of their identities and research purposes on one end to wholesale deception as to one's identity and purposes on the other. The former approach is generally accompanied by the receipt of full informed consent from these researchers' subjects, in the latter case the research subjects generally remain fully in the dark that any research is taking place and, in fact, are often led to believe that the researcher is a fellow traveler of whatever variety (e.g. a right-wing extremist, jihadi, drug dealer, etc.).

The work of Barratt and Maddox is an example of the former and Ebner—a non-university-based researcher—of the latter.[33] While online interviews and interview-like interactions in which researchers fully disclose their identities and research purposes to their research subjects are not wholly unknown in extremism and terrorism studies,[34] much more commonplace in our sub-field is the collection of medium to large to very large or even massive—the latter generally using (semi-)automated means—of digital trace data and/or extremist and terrorist propaganda materials, which generally requires a measure of deception. Is this ethically permissible? There are, very broadly, two schools of thought on the ethical permissibility of deception in online research: one that takes a benign view when researching hostile or dangerous communities and another that views it as largely impermissible regardless of the nature of the online communities being researched.

Safety is the chief reason that deception is generally employed by online extremism and terrorism researchers. The most common way in which this occurs is researchers concealing their identities in online spaces via the use of a pseudonym, oftentimes a *Kunya* in online jihadi circles, and sometimes also the use of a profile picture communicating familiarity with whatever ideology dominates in the community they are researching. This is more ethically defensible than it may first appear as the use of "real names" is uncommon in these spaces, so a pseudonym is expected and it is usually possible to employ both a relatively neutral pseudonym and profile picture without raising alarms. A *kunya*, for example, is an honorific utilized in the Arab world, which is composed of either the term *abu* (i.e. father) or *umm* (i.e. mother) plus commonly the name of the user's eldest son or sometimes daughter (e.g. Umm Layth) and/or place of origin (e.g. Abu Talha al-Almani). In terms of profile pictures, it is increasingly common for these to be mundane in order to avoid the attention of content moderators. Ebner gives the example of a female Indonesian IS supporter: "I told my fellow Indonesian IS supporters to change or delete their IS profile pics and change their account names to something funny."[35]

A requirement of gaining ethical approval for research utilizing such concealment practices however, is commonly a commitment to non-engagement with research subjects; that is permission to "lurk" only. As far back as 2015, Décary-Hétu and Aldridge discussed Russian-language online hacker communities requiring potential members to prove their Russian origin by answering questions that only those deeply familiar with Russia could be expected to know.[36] Display of knowledge of the Koran and Sunnah has also been requested for purposes of admittance to some jihadi online spaces, while Ebner too discusses an instance in which users on a neo-Nazi online forum were requested to "send a hand or wrist photograph with a piece of paper reading MAtR—your username—timestamp" to verify their whiteness.[37] The ethical permissibility of these types of engagements are more difficult to construe than concealment—or even low-level deception?—and warrant further discussion and debate.

While it is possible to present in a gender-neutral fashion online, gender-switching (i.e. deceiving other users as to whether one is male or female) is easy and thus commonplace, including amongst online extremists and terrorists.[38] But what of its ethicality amongst researchers? In a previous article on the role of the internet in extremism and terrorism, I wrote that:

> ... in the past jihadi online forums were often segregated on the basis of gender. Anecdotal evidence collected by the author suggests that female researchers accessing extremist forums of various sorts are wont to adopt male personae, including screen names and avatar images, in those settings, but that male researchers retain male identities in the same circumstances. This is a potentially interesting phenomenon facilitated by the Internet that could mean that female users are more influential in extremist cyberspaces than previously thought. (Switching in the other direction is a possibility too, of course, and also has the potential for interesting findings).[39]

This points implicitly or explicitly to at least three reasons for online gender switching amongst extremism and terrorism researchers, the first is safety, the second is access, and the third is for research into online gender dynamics. As regards safety, many female researchers represent themselves as male in not just jihadi but also extreme right online spaces in order to avoid the gendered harassment common in both types of online locales, but that is especially severe in extreme right online settings. Second, regarding access to especially jihadi online spaces, many of the channels, groups, and chats in messaging and other services currently in use by IS supporters and others are gender segregated, with many more spaces accessible to users representing as males than females. Female-only extreme right online spaces, although much less numerous, are also inaccessible to researchers representing as male. Third, empirical research into the similarities and differences in the experiences of users representing as male versus those representing as female in extremist and terrorist cyberspaces may also require deception in this regard (e.g. an individual PhD student carrying out an online ethnographic study of the experiences of male versus female users).

Alternatively, Barratt and Maddox provide strong reasons supporting their commitment to conducting active participatory digital research, including:

> ... that active engagement through digital ethnography with hidden populations online forms an integral complement to digital trace analyses, for both methodological and ethical reasons. Active engagement adds richness, context and an opportunity for deliberate research participation by members of the community of interest, with which we can better interpret the findings of studies based solely on the analyses of their digital traces.[40]

While empowerment of extremists and terrorists may strike us as generally unwarranted, richer and more accurate analyses would certainly be welcome and could, eventually, be expected to feed into the development of more effective responses to online extremism and terrorism. As opposed to deception, Barratt and Maddox's research, and other similar studies,[41] illustrate that full disclosure by researchers as regards who they are and what they want is possible even in hostile online spaces. Full disclosure may moreover ensure a degree of legal protection in the event of a researcher's online activity falling within the ambit of the authorities.[42] It's worth pointing out too that the widespread use of fake accounts is likely to skew metrics, especially in smaller or newer forums, channels, chats, and the like (i.e. giving the impression to other researchers, law enforcement, or journalists that a channel or group has a greater following than it does), which may in itself be considered an ethical—in addition to a methodological—issue.[43] Thus "the decision to use fake identities for safety reasons needs to be carefully justified and weighted against the epistemic value of the research," say Eppert *et al.*[44]

"Do No Harm": Parsing Harm to Subjects in Online Extremism and Terrorism Research

Easily the most commonly acknowledged issue in the literature on the ethical dimensions of "real world" conflict and security field research is potential harm to research subjects. Neither the impracticability nor inadvisability of seeking consent for much online extremism and terrorism research nor the researchers' role as a non-participant observer in extremist and terrorist online spaces removes researcher's ethical responsibilities to their research subjects and, some might say, increases them. For the avoidance of doubt, requirements to avoid harm to research subjects do not, in most jurisdictions, extend to information obtained about past or present illegal activity. In many EU member states, for example, it is a criminal offense not to report planned crimes, which includes terrorist attack plotting.

The identification of individual users as extremists (or even terrorists) or as being popular, or even influential among extremists, or otherwise online extremist-adjacent raises significant ethical issues, which are alluded to by numerous authors, but most comprehensively treated by Berger.[45] Such identification is almost never necessary, but when might it be useful and ethically allowable? The two main reasons forwarded by Berger for identifying users are the:

> obvious value for replication of social media studies and more broadly for a public understanding of the drivers of extremism—the individuals who are influential or popular within an extremist network shed light on many aspects of a movement, including its key issues and important leaders.[46]

The potential harms to those so identified can be significant, however. Media coverage of online extremism and terrorism research, which is increasingly prevalent, "may be sensationalized or politicized, omitting nuance or misrepresenting facts."[47] A related problem is when analyses and subsequently media identify users as extremists, including just via online pseudonyms, who are not public figures and who may, as a result face serious harms (e.g. unemployment, loss of social media access).[48] Of course, some users relish being identified as it raises their profile within the extremist movement and more widely; Berger referred to this in his alt-right Twitter census: "... after a past study of white nationalist activity on Twitter by the author, users identified as being influential subsequently exploited their rankings for self-promotion."[49] The way to avoid all of this is simply not to publish usernames or any personally identifying information. Is this always and without exception the best route to take however, or are there instances in which it might be ethically permissible to publish such details?

There is a general feeling that public figures should be open to identification and scrutiny. So, Berger explains, for example, that as regards identifying users in his alt-right Twitter census:

> One exception was made, based on the fact that the user's connection to the alt-right is extremely public and uncontroversial, and whose ranking is unsurprising. The most influential user in the dataset was @richardb-spencer, the Twitter account of Richard Spencer, founder of the now-defunct website, alternativeright.com, which gave the alt-right its name. Spencer is the primary public face of the alt-right movement ... .[50]

In fact, the term "public figure" is usually used in the context of legal actions for libel and defamation to refer to persons known to the general public, such as politicians, actors, or sportspeople. Outside of "famous" people, publicness can be quite difficult to empirically discern however, especially on the Internet. We are probably all agreed that a Twitter user with 10 followers is not a public figure, but how about 10,000 followers? Or is publicness only reached with 10 million followers? What is the appropriate rubric, in other words, or can such even be determined, and is this instead a decision best taken on a case-by-case basis? Might it not be the case that a "real life" public figure only has, for whatever reason, 10 Twitter followers; must that account then be anonymised? If this matter is truly context-dependent, which it may very well be, an important factor to keep in mind for extremism and terrorism researchers is avoidance of harm to research subjects to the extent possible.

A research cohort that scholars are held to owe an increased level of responsibility to are children and minors (i.e. individuals below the age of legal responsibility). Some researchers oppose identification in research of any Internet users who have not given their explicit consent, except public figures already known to us in "real life," due to the possibility that any other users may be minors. This is not an outlandish concern even in online extremism and terrorism research. In July 2020, Feuerkrieg Division (FKD) became the sixth extreme right group to be banned in the UK. The now-dissolved heavily online group was allegedly established by a 13-year-old Estonian boy and had other teenage adherents too.[51] Even younger children featured prominently in IS propaganda materials,[52] which showed some of them carrying out atrocities that they had no capacity to consent to. While visual ethics remains a considerably underdeveloped area,[53] researchers should be mindful of sharing unblurred pictures of so-called "cubs of the Caliphate," which may contribute to their revictimization. Nor, I would submit, is the already wide circulation of these unblurred images online and in mass media an ethically defensible reason for their continued circulation.

Where Do We Go from Here? The Need for Tailored Guidelines

No code of ethics for terrorism research has yet been developed, despite calls for same dating back over at least a decade, and probably much longer.[54] There are however, a number of useful guidelines and codes of practice for undertaking ethically informed Internet research. The most well-known and widely relied upon documents are the aforementioned AoIR ethics guidelines, the third and most recent version of which, "Ethical Decision-making and Internet Research," appeared in 2019, but which should be consulted in conjunction with their first (2002) and second (2012) iterations.[55] Other well-regarded guidelines, and both now appearing in their second editions, are the British Psychological Association's *Ethics Guidelines for Internet-mediated Research* (2017) and the Norwegian National Research Ethics Committee's *A Guide to Internet Research* (2019).[56] Also worth mentioning, given the focus herein on both researcher safety and tailored advice, is Data & Society's *Best Practices for Conducting Risky Research and Protecting Yourself from Online Harassment*.[57]

A problem, such as it is, with generalized internet research ethics codes is that they are difficult to devise due to, among other things, the very fast changing nature of the online ecosystem they are developed to "govern" and the wide variety of types of research they are expected to cover, even when they are discipline-specific. This requires, in effect, that Internet research ethics guidelines focus on core ethical commitments—what AoIR refers to as "a basic ethical approach"[58]—while leaving enough room to account for new types of online spaces, data collection and other tools and methods, research topics, and so on. This, unsurprisingly, has both positives and negatives. Some scholars view the open-ended nature of various guidelines as vital given "a research and ethical landscape that continues to change and transform, often in dramatic ways, over a very short period of time"[59] (e.g. Facebook's pivot to private groups; extremist and terrorists forced migration from social media platforms to messaging applications). Nor does this type of "researcher-led, case-by-case approach"[60] make "*a priori* judgements whether some research per se is unethical"[61] and can be viewed as an opportunity for scholars to develop context-specific ethics practices and inform RECs/IRBs as to the appropriateness of these in scholars' particular (sub-) disciplinary context. Such non-prescriptive approaches are viewed as "less than adequate" by other researchers however.[62] This is due to the adoption in many available guidelines of a bottom-up rather than a top-down approach, which entails acknowledgment of "the messiness and complexity" of Internet research, description and discussion of the ethical issues thereby arising, and suggested ethical questions for researchers to ask themselves, but little to no instruction as to "how to act."[63] This caused many of the UK-based researchers, from a variety of disciplines, interviewed by Samuel, Derrick, and van Leeuwen to view such guidelines as "vague and unhelpful" and thereby placing too great a burden for ethical decision-making on individual researchers.[64]

Ultimately, Samuel, Derrick, and van Leeuwen's interviewees advocated for a discipline or analysis-specific approach to Internet research ethics as "a better way to ensure that, rather than having all encompassing guidelines useful to no-one ... having more, but more specific guidelines useful to everyone."[65] I too am inclined to favor the development and deployment of sub-discipline and analysis-specific guidelines. Marwick, Blackwell, and Lo's best practice document for conducting research likely to attract online harassment illustrates the utility of narrowly tailored advice albeit on a topic, researcher online safety, that is much less divisive than some others. How are we to arrive at guidelines that grapple with more contested issues? The best avenue is probably via the process-based bottom-up approach advocated by AoIR, which is:

> ... first of all *reflective and dialogical* as it begins with reflection on [one's] own research practices and associated risks and is continuously discussed against the accumulated experience and ethical reflections of researchers in the field and existing studies carried out. This further means an emphasis on the fine-grained contexts and distinctive details of each specific ethical challenges [*sic*] [italics in original].[66]

There is no fast or easy way to arrive at even a basic agreed level of prescription, in other words. Ultimately, "the best we can do is develop 'guidelines, not recipes' ... the issues raised by Internet research are *ethical* problems precisely because they evoke more than one ethically defensible response to a specific dilemma or problem. *Ambiguity, uncertainty, and disagreement are inevitable*" (emphasis in the original).[67] While some of the more obvious ethics issues pertaining to online extremism and terrorism research are treated herein, ongoing and systematic identification of and intensive discussion around the whole range of ethical ambiguities, uncertainties, and disagreements arising in our particular sub-field are, I submit, vital next steps if we're eventually to develop tailored guidelines that respect RECs/IRBs functions and criteria, but shaped to more closely correspond to and improve online extremism and terrorism scholars' research practice, which should, in turn, result in more thorough and considered REC/IRB evaluations and decisions.[68]

Conclusion(s)

There are myriad ethical issues facing extremism and terrorism researchers who undertake online "fieldwork." Two of the most important of these were treated herein, researcher safety, which is oftentimes overlooked in discussions of ethics, and informed consent, which is generally at the core of ethics discussions, but can be complicated not just in online settings, but particularly when it comes to hostile or dangerous (online) communities. What should certainly be clear at this stage is that these issues are certainly not new but have not been systematically discussed in our sub-field to-date. While colleagues in a variety of other fields—including directly related ones, such as internet studies—have engaged publicly with ethics issues for many years, (online) extremism and terrorism researchers have, when we have done so at all, more often discussed such matters informally among ourselves. This has to change; our nascent formal discussions on these issues must continue and develop. AoIR's most recent ethics guidelines are eloquent on the necessity for dialogue, including that "one of the most important ethical techniques to be recommended is one of the simplest: talk things over with colleagues and friends."[69] I want to go a step further, however; both informal and formal "talks" are crucial but not enough; we must, as individual researchers and research groups, commit our ethical decisions and decision-making processes to writing more often and fully than we have to-date so that a store of usable knowledge is built up over time that is then usable by us in our own and others' decision-making, including especially that of RECs/IRBs. Perhaps the greatest contribution this article can make therefore is the spurring of more discussion, the contribution of further written analyses, of both ethical successes and mistakes, and maybe ultimately, if appropriate, a formal set of ethics guidelines tailored for online extremism and terrorism research.

Disclosure Statement

The author reports no conflicts of interest. The author alone was responsible for the content and writing of the article.

Funding

This work was supported by the European Union's Framework Programme 7 (EU FP7) under Grant 312827 (i.e. VOXPol)and Swansea University's Legal Innovation Lab Wales, which is part-funded by the European Regional Development Fund through the Welsh government under Grant 82123.

Discussion Questions

1. Under what circumstances might it be okay for the researcher to fail to reveal their purpose for being on extremists' sites? When, if ever, might it be okay for researchers to be dishonest about their role (researcher, extremist, curious person) or their own characteristics (gender, race, etc)?
2. Discuss some things that researchers can do to keep themselves safe and maintain their well-being when engaging in online research of extremists.
3. Why might getting informed consent be difficult when doing online research of extremists? What issues complicate the question of whether informed consent is necessary?

Notes

1. Geraldine Lee-Treweek and Stephanie Linkogle (Eds.), *Danger in the Field: Risk and Ethics in Social Research* (London and New York: Routledge, 2000); Chandra Lekha Sriram, John C. King, Julie A. Mertus, Olga Martin-Ortega and Johanna Herman (Eds.), *Surviving Field Research: Working in Violent and Difficult Situations* (London and New York: Routledge, 2009); Adam Dolnik (Ed.), *Conducting Terrorism Field Research: A Guide* (London and New York: Routledge, 2013).
2. Maura Conway, "Determining the Role of the Internet in Violent Extremism and Terrorism: Six Suggestions for Progressing Research," *Studies in Conflict & Terrorism* 40, no. 1 (2017): 86; see also, Stephane J. Baele, David Lewis, Anke Hoeffler, Oliver C. Sterck, and Thibaut Slingeneyer, "The Ethics of Security Research: An Ethics Framework for Contemporary Security Studies," *International Studies Perspectives* 19, no. 2 (2018): 112.
3. Monica J. Barratt and Alexia Maddox, "Active Engagement with Stigmatised Communities Through Digital Ethnography," *Qualitative Research* 16, no. 6 (2016): 711–2.
4. Ted Reynolds, "Ethical and Legal Issues Surrounding Academic Research into Online Radicalisation: A UK Experience," *Critical Studies on Terrorism* 5, no. 3 (2012): 499–513; Elizabeth Buchanan, "Considering the Ethics of Big Data Research: A Case of Twitter and ISIS/ISIL," *PLoS ONE* 12, no. 12 (2017); Adrienne L. Massanari, "Rethinking Research Ethics, Power, and the Risk of Visibility in the Era of the 'Alt-Right' Gaze," *Social Media + Society* 4, no. 2 (2018): 7; Dounia Mahlouly, *Reconciling Impact and Ethics: An Ethnography of Research in Violent Online Political Extremism* (Dublin: VOX-Pol, 2019).
5. Baele et al., "The Ethics of Security Research"; J. M. Berger, *Researching Violent Extremism: The State of Play* (Washington DC: RESOLVE Network, 2019); Simon Cottee and Jack Cunliffe, "Watching ISIS: How Young Adults Engage with Official English-Language ISIS Videos," *Studies in Conflict & Terrorism* 43, no. 3 (2020): 183–207; Kerstin Eppert, Lena Frischlich, Nicole Bögelein, Nadine Jukschat, Melanie Reddig, and Anja Schmidt-Kleinert, *Navigating a Rugged Coastline: Ethics in Empirical (De-)Radicalization Research* (Bonn: CoRE—Connecting Research on Extremism in North Rhine-Westphalia, 2020); Joe Whittaker, *Building Secondary Source Databases on Violent Extremism: Reflections and Suggestions* (Washington DC: RESOLVE Network, 2019).
6. Baele et al., "The Ethics of Security Research"; Peter King, "Building Resilience for Terrorism Researchers," *VOX-Pol Blog*, 19 September 2018; Michael Krona, "Vicarious Trauma from Online Extremism Research: A Call to Action," *GNET Insights*, 27 March 2020; Massanari, "Rethinking Research Ethics"; Whittaker, *Building Secondary Source Databases*; Charlie Winter, *Researching Jihadist Propaganda: Access, Interpretation, and Trauma* (Washington DC: RESOLVE Network, 2019).
7. See, for example, Isaac Chotiner, "The Underworld of Online Content Moderation," *The New Yorker*, 5 July 2019; Casey Newton, "The Trauma Floor: The Secret Lives of Facebook Moderators in America," *The Verge*, 25 February 2019; Benjamin Powers, "The Human Cost of Monitoring the Internet," *RollingStone*, 9 September 2017. See also Ellen Silver, "Hard Questions: Who Reviews Objectionable Content on Facebook—And Is the Company Doing Enough to Support Them?" *Facebook Newsroom*, 26 July 2018. In fact, the "unseen toll" of online extremism and terrorism researchers' work has itself attracted journalistic coverage; see Hannah Allam, ""It Gets to You." Extremism Researchers Confront the Unseen Toll of Their Work,' *NPR*, 20 September 2019; Paris Martineau, "The Existential Crisis

Plaguing Online Extremism Researchers," *Wired*, 2 May 2019.
8. Berger, *Researching Violent Extremism*, 9.
9. *Ibid.*
10. Maura Conway, Ryan Scrivens, and Logan McNair, *Right-Wing Extremists' Persistent Online Presence: History and Contemporary Trends* (The Hague: ICCT, 2019), 3.
11. Svana M. Calabro, "From the Message Board to the Front Door: Addressing the Offline Consequences of Race-and Gender-Based Doxxing and Swatting," *Suffolk University Law Review* 51, no. 1 (2018): 55–75.
12. Baele et al., "The Ethics of Security Research," 115.
13. King, "Building Resilience for Terrorism Researchers"; Krona, "Vicarious Trauma from Online Extremism Research."
14. Winter, *Researching Jihadist Propaganda*, 3.
15. Allam, "It Gets to You"; see also Krona, "Vicarious Trauma from Online Extremism Research."
16. Aline shakti franzke, Anja Bechmann, Michael Zimmer, and Charles M. Ess, *Internet Research: Ethical Guidelines* 3.0 (AoIR, 2019), 11.
17. *Ibid.*
18. Interviewee quoted in Mahlouly, *Reconciling Impact and Ethics*, 24; see also Zoey Reeve, "Repeated and Extensive Exposure to Online Terrorist Content: Counter-terrorism Internet Referral Unit Perceived Stresses and Strategies," *Studies in Conflict & Terrorism*, [Online First], 14.
19. Allam, "It Gets to You"; Berger, *Researching Violent Extremism*, 9–10; Krona, "Vicarious Trauma from Online Extremism Research."
20. Stephen Brown, "Dilemmas of Self-representation and Conduct in the Field," in *Surviving Field Research*, eds. Sriram et al.; Julie A. Mertus, "Maintenance of Personal Security: Ethical and Operational Issues," in *Surviving Field Research*, eds. Sriram et al., 172. See also Reeve, "Repeated and Extensive Exposure to Online Terrorist Content," 19; Chaseedaw Giles, "Op-Ed: I'm a Black Social Media Manager in the Age of George Floyd. Each Day is a New Trauma," *Los Angeles Times*, 23 June 2020.
21. Franzke et al., *Internet Research: Ethical Guidelines 3.0*, 11.
22. Massanari, "Rethinking Research Ethics," 3.
23. Winter, *Researching Jihadist Propaganda*, 11–2.
24. Mertus, "Maintenance of Personal Security," 172.
25. Alice Marwick, Lindsay Blackwell, and Katherine Lo, *Best Practices for Conducting Risky Research and Protecting Yourself from Online Harassment* (New York: Data & Society Research Institute, 2016), 6.
26. Baele et al., "The Ethics of Security Research," 107.
27. Annette Markham and Elizabeth Buchanan, *Ethical Decision-Making and Internet Research (Version 2.0)* (AoIR, 2012), 6–10.
28. David Décary-Hétu and Judith Aldridge, "Sifting Through the Net: Monitoring of Online Offenders by Researchers," *The European Review of Organised Crime* 2, no. 2 (2015): 132.
29. Décary-Hétu and Aldridge, "Sifting Through the Net," 133.
30. Åsa Rosenberg, "Virtual World Research Ethics and the Private/Public Distinction," *International Journal of Internet Research Ethics* 3, (2010): 23–36; see also, Robert W Gehl, "Power/Freedom on the Dark Web: A Digital Ethnography of the Dark Web Social Network," *New Media & Society* 18, no. 7 (2016): 1221.
31. Décary-Hétu and Aldridge, "Sifting Through the Net," 133.
32. Décary-Hétu and Aldridge, "Sifting Through the Net," 133–4.
33. Barratt and Maddox, "Active Engagement with Stigmatised Communities"; Julia Ebner, *Going Dark: The Secret Social Lives of Extremists* (London: Bloomsbury). It should be noted that the combination of activity undertaken by Ebner—online and offline deception and engagement with extremists—is unlikely to be permitted by any university REC/IRB.
34. Aysha Navest, Martijn de Koning, and Annelies Moors, "Chatting About Marriage with Female Migrants to Syria," *Anthropology Today*, 32 no. 2 (2016): 22–25; Lorne L. Dawson and Amarnath Amarasingam, "Talking to Foreign Fighters: Insights into the Motivations for Hijrah to Syria and Iraq," *Studies in Conflict & Terrorism* 40, no. 3 (2017): 192.
35. Ebner, *Going Dark*, 81.
36. Décary-Hétu and Aldridge, "Sifting Through the Net," 134.
37. Ebner, *Going Dark*, 9. See also, Lorraine Bowman-Grieve and Maura Conway, "Exploring the Form and Function of Dissident Irish Republican Online Discourses," *Media, War & Conflict* 5, no. 1 (2012): 75.
38. Lizzie Dearden, "Safiyya Shaikh: How an Unemployed London Mother Ran an International ISIS Propaganda Network," *Independent* (UK), 3 July 2020; Meili Criezis, "Online Deceptions: Renegotiating Gender Boundaries on ISIS Telegram," *Perspectives on Terrorism* 14, no. 1 (2020): 67–73. See also, Adam Bermingham, Maura Conway, Lisa McInerney, Neil O'Hare, Alan F. Smeaton, "Combining Social Network Analysis and Sentiment Analysis to Explore the Potential for Online Radicalisation," in *ASONAM 2009: Advances*

in Social Networks Analysis and Mining (IEEE Computer Society: Digital Library, 2009), 234–5.
39. Conway, "Determining the Role of the Internet in Violent Extremism and Terrorism," 91.
40. Barratt and Maddox, "Active Engagement with Stigmatised Communities," 715.
41. Navest et al., "Chatting About Marriage"; Dawson and Amarasingam, "Talking to Foreign Fighters."
42. Universities UK, *Oversight of Security-Sensitive Research Material in UK Universities: Guidance* (London: Universities UK, 2019).
43. Eppert et al., *Navigating a Rugged Coastline*, 9.
44. *Ibid.*
45. Berger, *Researching Violent Extremism.*
46. *Ibid.*, 6.
47. *Ibid.*, 7.
48. *Ibid.*
49. J. M. Berger, *The Alt-Right Twitter Census: Defining and Describing the Audience for Alt-Right Content on Twitter* (Dublin: VOX-Pol, 2018), 21; see also, Carolyn Gallaher, "Researching Repellent Groups: Some Methodological Considerations on How to Represent Militants, Radicals, and Other Belligerents," in *Surviving Field Research*, eds. Sriram et al., 128.
50. Berger, *The Alt-Right Twitter Census*, 22.
51. Daniel de Simone, "Neo-Nazi Group Led by 13-year-old Boy to be Banned," *BBC News*, 13 July 2020; see also Ebner, *Going Dark*, 10.
52. Amy-Louise Watkin and Seán Looney, "The Lions of Tomorrow": A News Value Analysis of Child Images in Jihadi Magazines," *Studies in Conflict & Terrorism* 42, no. 1–2 (2019): 102–40.
53. Franzke et al., *Internet Research: Ethical Guidelines 3.0*, 23.
54. Tora K. Bikson, Ricky N. Bluthenthal, Rick Eden, and Patrick P. Gunn (Eds.), *Ethical Principles in Social-Behavioral Research on Terrorism: Probing the Parameters* (California: RAND, 2007).
55. Franzke et al., *Internet Research: Ethical Guidelines 3.0*; Markham and Buchanan, *Ethical Decision-Making and Internet Research (Version 2.0)*; Charles Ess, *Ethical Decision-making and Internet Research* (AoIR, 2002). Links to all versions of the guidelines are available on the AoIR website at https://aoir.org/ethics/.
56. British Psychological Society, *Ethics Guidelines for Internet-mediated Research* (Leicester: British Psychological Society, 2017); National Committee for Research Ethics in the Social Sciences and the Humanities (NESH), *A Guide to Internet Research Ethics* (Oslo: NESH, 2019). For listings of additional relevant guidelines, see Franzke et al., *Internet Research: Ethical Guidelines 3.0*, 12–14; Massanari, "Rethinking Research Ethics," 7; Gabrielle Samuel, Gemma E. Derrick, and Thed van Leeuwen, "The Ethics Ecosystem: Personal Ethics, Network Governance and Regulating Actors Governing the Use of Social Media Research Data," *Minerva* 57, no. 3 (2019): 324.
57. Marwick, Blackwell, and Lo, *Best Practices for Conducting Risky Research.*
58. Franzke et al., *Internet Research: Ethical Guidelines 3.0*, 3.
59. *Ibid.*
60. Samuel, Derrick, and van Leeuwen, "The Ethics Ecosystem," 329.
61. Franzke et al., *Internet Research: Ethical Guidelines 3.0*, 4.
62. Samuel, Derrick, and van Leeuwen, "The Ethics Ecosystem," 325.
63. *Ibid.*, 329.
64. *Ibid.*, 338.
65. *Ibid.*, 339.
66. Franzke et al., *Internet Research: Ethical Guidelines 3.0*, 4.
67. *Ibid.*, 6.
68. Baele et al., "The Ethics of Security Research," 123.
69. *Ibid.*

4 Measurement, Validity, and Reliability

What is it about criminal justice and criminology that interests you? Personally, I have always had an interest in how we deal with people who get caught committing crimes. I am bringing this up because if you are going to embark on research, willingly or because you must for a class, you need to come up with ideas for what to study. You will start with concepts but will need to get more specific as you develop your plan.

Operationalization and measurement are, in my opinion, some of the more challenging aspects of research design. The reason is that we must be very careful how we ask questions, because different people can visualize the same concept in different ways. This variety of interpretation can impact our results, so it is necessary to make sure that we move forward with clear definitions of what we are trying to study. In this chapter, we are going to discuss the process of defining our concepts. Next, we will discuss types of variables and how they are measured. Finally, we will review validity and reliability.

From Concepts to Measurements

Let's take an initial step for our research project and think of possible topics to study. "Corporate crime," "rehabilitation," and "problem gambling" are examples of concepts, as they are all rather vague mental images that can easily mean different things to different people. At the mention of corporate crime, one person might picture Bernie Madoff, the disgraced financier who pleaded guilty to running a multibillion-dollar Ponzi scheme. Others might think of the collapse of Enron, where the executives sold their own stocks while illegally concealing the company's massive debts, resulting in devastating losses to investors and lower-level employees. Or you might be picturing a company that saves money by illegally dumping waste into our rivers and streams. All are types of corporate crime, and you can choose to study all of them or be more specific and focus just on one type. Pretend that you have decided to limit your work to examining just one type of corporate crime, such as stock manipulation. You would have to operationalize exactly what you mean by this specific type of corporate crime before you work on other aspects of the study. Your data collection plan could involve your doing a systematic literature review where you look up instances of the specific type of offense that you identified, or you could survey individuals to get their opinions about how appropriate penalties are for such a crime. Either way, you are going to need to determine exactly what you mean by corporate crime before going any further.

Operationalization is the process of taking concepts and more concretely defining them. The end product should be measurable items that can be used for data collection. While working on operationalization, it might be useful to consider different dimensions of what you want to study. Maxfield and Babbie (2012) define **dimensions** as a specifiable aspect of a concept. Going back to the example of corporate crime, Unnever, Benson, and Cullen (2008) observed that corporate crime can cause a wide range of harms to society, including financial impacts, environmental hazards (illegal dumping), and physical harm (lax adherence to building regulations that lead to structural failures). While there are multiple possible harm dimensions for corporate crime, the

DOI: 10.4324/9781003661511-4

authors chose to measure corporate crime only as financial fraud for their study of public opinion of sentences for corporate criminals.

As another example of dimensions of a concept, consider prison violence. Nancy Rodriguez, former director of the National Institute of Justice, discovered a problem with the government's attempts to capture national statistics on prison violence—states use different definitions. One dimension of prison violence is the nature of the act itself, but what constitutes a violent act? We would all likely agree that punching someone in the face is a violent act. What about tossing bodily fluids? Another dimension is the extent of the injury. What constitutes a serious injury? Some states would consider needing something more than basic first aid to be a serious injury, while other prison systems would only classify injuries requiring off-site medical care as serious. These differences have made it difficult to compare the extent of prison violence from state to state.

Since this is such an important, and often hard to understand topic, I want to provide one more example that I think everyone reading this book can appreciate. Let's say, you did not do well on an exam, and you want to go talk to the professor about what you can do to improve in the class. If I'm the professor, my first question to you is, "Did you go into the exam prepared?" How do we properly operationalize "prepared?" There are a few ways. One is the class engagement dimension. How many of the classes did you attend prior to the exam? On a scale of 1 to 10, with one meaning you were mentally someplace else and 10 meaning you were 100% locked into what your professor was saying, how well did you pay attention in class? Did you take notes? I'm always fascinated by the students who sit in class, arms crossed, just staring at me for the entire period. Unless you are the rare individual with hyperthymesia, which is a condition where you remember every single thing a person says, the folded arms/glaring at the professor strategy is a recipe for failure. Another dimension here is out-of-class work. How much of the readings did you do? Did you take notes on the readings? Did you study your class notes and your reading notes before the exam? How much time did you take to study? How much of that study time was truly studying, and how much of it was playing on your phone because your favorite game just gave you a bunch of free minutes?

Variables

As we operationalize concepts, we make them measurable by creating variables. **Variables** are simply logical groupings of attributes that vary from case to case. **Attributes** are characteristics that describe something (Maxfield & Babbie, 2012). If I were to survey my students, gender would be a variable since it describes individuals' attributes that vary from person to person. Something that does not change on a case-by-case basis in our study would be called a **constant**. For example, if I am surveying my students at the end of a class session, and those are the only people I am surveying, I do not need to ask them if they are college students. That would be a constant, since 100% of those being surveyed would respond affirmatively to that question. What would likely be a variable in that same survey is their year in college (freshman, sophomore, junior, senior), provided that I am not teaching either a freshman or senior seminar. Another variable in that class would be the number of credits each student is currently attempting. Figure 4.1 includes some examples of moving from concepts to variables.

Independent variables are predictors that are thought to contribute to change in the value of the **dependent variable**. Other words that might be used to describe the independent variable are "predictor" or "cause," although we must be very careful with "cause," since it is extremely rare that we would be able to establish causation in social science research. The dependent variable is something that we think will change depending on the value of the independent variable and is also known as the "outcome" or "effect." For example, a safe prediction would be that alcohol use

Concept	*Operationalization*	*Variable(s)*
Recidivism	Reincarceration within one year of release	Individuals were reincarcerated within 365 days of being released from custody (yes/no).
Recidivism	Rearrest within one year of release.	Individuals were rearrested within 365 days of being released from custody (yes/no). Number of times individuals were rearrested within 365 days of release from custody.
Education level	Highest level of education completed	Please indicate the highest level of education completed: Less than high school High school/GED Some college AA/AS degree BA/BS degree MA/MS degree Doctorate (including MD, PhD, JD, EdD, PsyD)

Figure 4.1 Operationalization of concepts

Source: Author

(the independent variable) would predict driving performance (the dependent variable). Another type of variable is a **control variable**, which is a potential alternative explanation for the outcome but is not of central interest to the current study (Jennings & Reingle Gonzalez, 2019). If we were to look at the impact of number of prior convictions on sentence severity for people convicted of burglary, our independent variable would be number of prior convictions, and the dependent variable would be incarceration sentence in months. Of course, we know that number of prior convictions is not the only factor taken into consideration for sentence length. We would want to think about the possible impact of some other factors, such as whether the person was subject to pretrial detention or the dollar value of what was stolen. Sentencing researchers have also found that extralegal factors, such as personal characteristics of defendants, may impact sentence length as well (Bielen et al., 2021; Holmes & D'Amato, 2019; Spohn & Holleran, 2000; Steffensmeier, Ulmer, & Kramer, 1998; Tartaro & Sedelmaier, 2009). Since human behavior is so complex, most studies today involve multivariate statistical analysis that allows researchers to test the relationship between the independent and dependent variables while also accounting for the influence of control variables.

Variables can be structured to collect data in a variety of ways. There are **open-ended questions** or items. These are either fill-in-the-blank, short answer or long answer questions where the survey respondent or data collector who is making observations can express their thoughts using their own words. These open-ended options help in the collecting of qualitative data. **Close-ended questions** are items that have answer options included. These allow researchers to capture quantitative data and are helpful when the goal is to input data into a spreadsheet or database for quantitative analysis. The close-ended items allow researchers to quickly handle **coding**, meaning that they are assigning numerical values to items. Coding facilitates data entry and analysis.

Close-ended items should be both mutually exclusive and exhaustive. **Mutually exclusive** items give respondents one, and only one, appropriate answer option. So, for a question about income, the question might be written as follows:

What is your yearly household income?

1. 0 to $24,999
2. $25,000 to $49,999
3. $50,000 to $74,999
4. $75,000 to $99,999
5. $100,000+

The above answer options are mutually exclusive, because there is no overlap in categories. A respondent could correctly circle only one of the above responses. The categories are also **exhaustive**, because there is an option for every possible answer. No one can earn less than $0.00 each year. As for the upper range, we can continue to add categories, and if we know the groups we are surveying well enough, we can list enough categories to include the top income of all our respondents. The other option is to do just what I did above and write an open-ended category that allows for even multimillionaires to provide an accurate response.

One area where social science researchers have largely failed to write exhaustive survey questions is regarding gender identity. Valcore and Pfeffer (2018) analyzed the content of 1,629 articles published in highly regarded criminal justice and criminology journals from 2010 through 2015 and found that none provided attributes of transgender or nonbinary in their gender variables. One reason for this lack of inclusion is that criminologists often rely on preexisting data gathered by government agencies that have not been collecting such detailed information. At the federal level, this changed in 2015 with a federal working group researching how to measure both gender identity and sexual orientation (Office of Management and Budget, 2023) and then with the National Crime Victimization Survey (NCVS) including questions about both sexual orientation and gender identity for the first time shortly thereafter (Davies & Beckley, 2023). The NCVS data illustrate why exhaustive survey answer options are so important. NCVS reported that transgender individuals experienced violent victimization at a rate 2.5 times than that of cisgender people (Truman & Morgan, 2022). Additionally, lesbian or gay persons had twice the violent victimization rates of heterosexual individuals. These findings have important policy implications for violence prevention and response. In January 2025, the federal government reversed its stance and ordered all federal agencies, including the US Census Bureau that runs the NCVS data collection program, to use only the binary male/female categories for sex and gender (White House, 2025).

Answers to survey questions can be either **discrete**, having a finite, specific number of values, or **continuous**, meaning that they can take on any value (Kranzler, 2018). You will have to give careful consideration to this decision, as it will have implications for your data analysis options later. In order to understand why, we need to discuss levels of measurement.

Levels of Measurement

There are four levels of measurement for variables, starting with **nominal**. Nominal level is the most basic level of measurement where any numbers assigned to variable attributes are for labeling purposes only. For example, if I had a survey item asking for a respondent's favorite professional sport, I might code the answer options this way:

What is your favorite professional sport?

(1) Soccer (2) Baseball (3) Basketball (4) Football
(5) Golf (6) Tennis (7) Other

The numbers next to the sports do not rank them by level of importance, international popularity, television ratings, or anything else. They are simply for coding purposes, so when this information is input into a statistical package, such as SPSS, Mini Tab, Stata, or SAS, we can use the numbers for analysis. That is necessary, as statistical software will not run any tests when the variable attributes are input as words. Variables with two options, such as yes/no or pass/fail, are known as dichotomous variables and are also considered a nominal level of measurement. For those, we would likely code the responses as either yes = 1 and no = 0, or yes = 1 or no = 2.

The next level is **ordinal**. Unlike nominal, ordinal-level data are rank-ordered, so coding associated with items provide more information than for nominal-level variables. One drawback to ordinal ranks, however, is that they do not distinguish the precise magnitude of the difference between ranks. For example, runners who win a race are assigned first place, second place, and so on. What ordinal does not tell us is how close the second-place finisher was to the winner, and how far behind the third-place runner was. In other words, the units of measurement here (1st, 2nd, 3rd) are not necessarily equal (Kranzler, 2018). To put this in terms of class achievement, an ordinal ranking of class grades into A, B, C, D, or F for each student gives us more information than a nominal pass/fail variable. We have no way of knowing, however, if that A is a 90 or a 99, so we have no idea how close two students who got an A and a B are to each other in class achievement. There might be a one-point difference between them (89 and 90) or a 20-point difference (80 and 100). To get more detailed information, it is necessary to look at interval and ratio-level data.

Interval-level data have equal levels of measurement, a key characteristic that is lacking with ordinal ranks. Revisiting the example of runners completing a race, if we had the times that each runner crossed the finish line, we would not only know their rank order, but we would be able to tell the exact distance between the winner, second place, third place, and so on. There would be no question whether the battle for first or second was a photo finish or whether the winner easily defeated the field. We could compare the times, so we would know precisely how much faster the winner was compared to the competition. Interval-level data can go below zero, so a good example of data at this level would be the air temperature.

Ratio is the final level of measurement, and the only difference between interval and ratio is that interval lacks a true zero point (Kranzler, 2018). Ratio-level data can never go below zero. An example of this is the exact numerical grade that students received on the exam instead of the ordinal A–F categories. In other words, ratio-level of measurement would give us your exact number grade on the exam, such as an 89 or a 90. An exam grade is considered ratio instead of interval because, try as one might, it is impossible to get below a zero on an exam.

The highest levels of measurement (interval and ratio) are the most informative. Revisiting our running example, if you are a race organizer and are looking to give out finisher medals, all you need is nominal-level data (runners either crossed the finish line or they did not). If you are looking to give out medals for first place, second, and third, you need to collect ordinal-level data. If these race times are being used to determine qualifications for a future race, then we need ratio-level data of the exact times that people finished.

Which type of data should you collect if you aren't positive what you will be doing with it later? One can take interval and ratio-level variables and then turn them into ordinal or nominal. At this point, we don't know whether the race you are organizing will be used as a qualifier for a future race. To be safe, go with ratio. If we have the times for everyone who completed the race, we can either use those exact times for future qualifications, just use the rank orders (first, second, third) for the medals, or just label runners as having "completed the run or not" by seeing which people have finish times associated with their participation. In other words, we can take that ratio-level measure and then use it as ordinal or nominal. We cannot do that in reverse, though. If the race volunteer sitting at the finish line only tallied who crossed the line and who did not, race organizers would not be able to use that information to award medals to the top three runners, nor would they be able to provide exact finish times for future race qualifications.

When constructing variables, it is often advisable to collect as much specific information as possible, provided that doing so would not inconvenience the research respondents and decrease the chances of completing data collection. For example, if I were sending a survey to local jails and asking the administrator to provide an estimate of the percentage of incarcerated who were Latinx by checking an answer option such as 0–24%, 25–49%, and so on, someone as familiar with the jail population as the warden would likely be able to answer that without having to take the time to look up the daily census. If I asked for the exact percentage of Latinx incarcerated people, however, this would likely necessitate the respondents having to look up the information and would be more of a burden to the respondent. Besides convenience for the research participants, one other reason why researchers might request less specific, nominal or ordinal data would be to protect anonymity of respondents. I once supervised a student thesis on drug use in college. My student originally submitted a plan to the university's IRB to distribute an anonymous survey with some ratio-level variables, including age and college GPA, to a few criminal justice classes. The IRB required her to change the GPA question from ratio ("please provide your exact GPA on a 4-point scale") to ordinal ("please indicate if you have a GPA of 3.5 to 4.0, 3.0 to 3.49," etc.). The IRB's reasoning was that someone who knew which college courses received the survey could use the students' sex, age, and GPA answers to learn respondents' identities. For example, if there was only one 22-year-old female with a 3.97 GPA in that particular class, someone with access to the university database could determine who filled out that survey. Unmasking respondents would be much more difficult to do if the GPA variable was less specific, and the IRB determined that the risk to the participants was not worth the benefits of collecting such specific GPA information.

Scales and Indexes

Composite measures, or the combination of individual items, allow us to better measure some concepts. We can create an **index** by summing responses to items on a survey (Jennings & Reingle Gonzalez, 2019). When Costello, Ruckus, and Hawdon (2019) sought to study individuals' exposure to online hate, they needed to measure the extent of survey respondents' social media usage. The authors listed 22 different social media, game, photo-sharing, and instant message platforms on their survey, and asked participants to check all that they used. Before analyzing the data, the researchers totaled all individual items to generate a social media usage index.

In the social sciences, we often use scales to measure items. Scaling allows us to increase the level of measurement, usually from nominal to ordinal. We could ask someone if they approve of the job performed by the current governor and get a yes/no response, but we could find out more about what people think about the governor by framing the responses on a **scale**. A commonly used scale in social science is the **Likert scale**, which typically includes five to seven answer options that indicate a range of approval. Typical answer item responses are strongly disagree, disagree, neutral, agree, or strongly agree. For the example of the governor's job rating, we could use strongly approve, approve, neutral, disapprove, or strongly disapprove. Scales allow us to use either the five different points of approval for data analysis, or we could collapse categories to a dichotomous response with "strongly approve or approve" versus "disapprove or strongly disapprove," or add a third category of "neutral." You obviously could not, however, poll people and ask for just a yes/no or approve/disapprove response and then try to divide the responses into more detailed categories later.

Another possibility is to develop a scale with multiple survey items to capture a greater scope of content. This is important, because there are some concepts that cannot be properly operationalized with just one survey question. Mental illness and the stigma surrounding it is a good example of this. There are a number of reasons why some people hold negative perceptions of individuals with mental illness including, but not limited to, negative stereotypes about hygiene, perceptions that it would be too difficult to carry on a meaningful relationship, and pessimism about the treatability of the illness. It would be impossible to capture all aspects of stigma with just one question, so Day,

Edgren, and Eshleman (2007) created a 28-item Mental Illness Stigma Scale to capture the three aforementioned domains plus four others relating to mental illness stigma. Such composite items can serve to increase the validity of your measures, plus they make statistical analysis much easier.

Validity

Operationalization and precise measurements of variables are essential parts of data collection, as the consistency and accuracy of your measures obviously have direct bearing on the quality of your results. **Validity** refers to accuracy or the extent to which one is measuring what was intended, and there are four ways to measure this. First, and the least complicated, is **face validity**, or how well it appears that we are measuring items correctly. Simply put, regarding face value, does our survey or data collection checklist look appropriate? Measuring face validity tends to be an exercise in common sense (Hartley, 2011).

Content validity concerns whether the selected measurements capture the full range and meaning of the concepts in question (Hartley, 2011). Earlier in this chapter, I noted that, during the operationalization process, we might purposefully choose to measure a concept in a way that we select just one dimension of a broader topic. For example, we might choose to study only instances of corporate crime that involve financial fraud and leave environmental and physical damage out of this project. We would then construct questions related to just financial fraud. But, if our intention was to study all types of corporate crime and we then proceeded with a survey that covered only financial fraud, that survey would lack content validity. Remember my example of stigma surrounding mental illness? Stigma has multiple dimensions, so it is important to utilize a survey that includes items about all of the dimensions.

Criterion validity involves comparison of our measure of choice with some external item to see whether the two are similar. The criterion can be something measured at the same time (**concurrent validity**) such as a self-report survey of current drug use and then a urine test immediately thereafter. Another example of concurrent validity would be comparison of multiple suicide screening tools that are administered simultaneously. **Predictive validity** assesses how well a measure predicts future performance. The SATs, GREs, LSATs, and MCATs are used by colleges and graduate schools because they help to predict students' future academic performance. In corrections, researchers have found that the Correctional Program Checklist has good predictive validity for identifying which correctional programs will reduce recidivism (Makarios et al., 2019).

Construct validity refers to how accurately our measure reflects the theory and philosophy of what the researchers are attempting to measure (Hartley, 2011). The **Kansas City Preventive Patrol Experiment** is a classic study in criminal justice, and it was designed to see whether different types of police patrols impacted crime rates. Researchers divided parts of the city into areas designated for extra police patrols (proactive beat section), routine patrols (control beats section), or no patrols and only police presence in a response to a problem (reactive beats section). The researchers hypothesized that enhanced officer presence would reduce crime. Researchers encountered challenges in testing this this due to police officers using their discretion to go into and remain in the reactive beat locations, possibly because of their belief that police presence was so important for crime control (Kelling et al., 1974). This deviation from the research protocol posed a threat to construct validity, because the purpose of the study was to measure the impact of different police tactics, but evidence suggests that the beats were not as different as the researchers planned for them to be.

The Kansas City Preventive Patrol Experiment is just one of many studies that have struggled with construct validity. Fallik (2019) conducted an extensive review of research measuring racial profiling. The review revealed that some of the earlier studies either included irrelevant variables in their analysis or omitted potentially important ones. This limited the usefulness of these studies in helping to understand the extent to which racial profiling occurs due to weak construct validity.

Reliability

Whereas validity is concerned with the accuracy of various measures, **reliability** addresses their consistency or stability. A good example of reliability is a bathroom scale that is consistent. Ceccato (2019) notes that it is possible to consider reliability in three different ways: across time, across different observers, and across items. Regarding reliability across time, reliable measures would produce the same results when applied to the same variables, even over time. Ceccato used the example of noise estimates for subway stations during rush hour, as the noise levels during those times should remain fairly constant from one day to another at a particular station.

For survey and interview items, the **test-retest method** can check for reliability. For example, if researchers are studying behavior among college students and plan to survey first-time freshmen during welcome week and again at the end of the fall semester, it might be a good idea to find out about the students' behavior in high school. It would make sense that misbehavior in high school would predict future misbehavior in college. A helpful reliability check would be to ask students the number of times they were suspended from high school. That is likely to be a fairly memorable incident for individuals, and the number of suspensions rather than the number of days suspended is likely easier to remember. This question can be repeated during the second survey, as there is no reason for the answer to change now that the students are out of high school. Test-retest can be difficult to do, as you do not want to annoy your respondents by asking them too many identical questions multiple times.

Maintaining reliability can become problematic whenever someone's subjectivity enters into measurement and can become even more challenging when multiple observers are involved. When multiple individuals are involved in observing, interviewing, and/or coding responses, the interrater reliability, also known as inter-observer reliability, must be monitored, as it is certainly possible that different people would interpret the same observation or response differently. The two best ways to ensure a high degree of **interrater reliability** are to conduct training and maintain good communication between researchers. When I was a graduate student at Rutgers University, I worked as a field researcher with the Police Foundation on a study of crime and disorder in Jersey City, NJ. One of my duties was to conduct physical observations of street segments and fill out a data collection form that captured the amount of litter, broken glass, and drug paraphernalia in each area. Our response options were "none" "a little," "some," or "a lot," but what is "some" or "a lot" of litter? To decide, the research team had to work together, sometimes by emptying wastebaskets onto the floor to simulate litter so that all researchers would interpret things similarly. Drug paraphernalia was a bit easier. After a discussion, the research team decided that we would consider one empty drug bag, crack vial, or crack vial cap on a street segment to be "a little," two to three would be "some," and four or more would be "a lot." To keep ourselves in sync, we would start our observation days by doing one street segment together, followed by a discussion to reconcile any coding differences. After that warm-up, we would go our separate ways to collect data. Every few hours, we would do another segment together to test our interrater reliability.

If we are distributing surveys, how do we ensure a high degree of reliability of our survey items? The first step is to work very carefully on the question-writing phase of research. Good operationalization is key. Every item should be worded in a way that minimizes ambiguity so that all respondents understand what is being asked. A good way to do this is to pretest whatever data collection instrument (a fancy word for survey) that you plan to use with a small group of people who are similar to the target population. If it is not a survey but a fieldwork protocol sheet, ask a few fellow researchers to test it and see what they think. Pretesting does not take much time, but it can be a tremendous help and cut down on both validity and reliability problems. If you plan on collecting data from a very large group of people, it might even be a good idea to first do a small pilot test of your study to try a few different ways of measuring your variables of interest for the best validity and reliability results. Once you are satisfied with the performance of your measures, then you can take the next step and reach out to your target population (Sullivan & McGloin, 2014).

To test reliability across items, the **split-half method** is useful. This is a typical way of testing for reliability. If you have ever taken a survey in a psychology course or one that was administered by someone studying psychology, you might have noticed how it appeared that the researchers were asking you the same thing over and over again. That is because they were conducting a reliability check. The split-half technique involves surveying opinions or some other construct, splitting the survey in half (first half versus second half or even-numbered items versus odd-numbered), and then testing for internal consistency of the items designed to measure the same construct.

Mixed-Methods Approaches to Address Validity and Reliability

Working to ensure reliability is important, but remember that just because something is reliable does not mean that it is necessarily valid, and vice versa. Take the example of the reliable bathroom scale. It could be consistent in that it is reliably off by three pounds every time you use it. It is much less common for something to be valid while not also being reliable, but it is possible. Researchers must take steps to make sure that their measures are both valid and reliable. One way to do that is to do validity and reliability checks by using multiple methods to measure the same construct. For example, research involving self-reports could be supplemented by consulting official records. If we were surveying high school students about their behavior, self-report surveys would be really the only way to capture the things that they did without getting caught by the school system or police. The downside, however, is that we don't know whether to trust those results. One way that we can get an idea of how honest people are being is by asking them about the number of suspensions or detentions that they have received in the past year and then also consulting the school's disciplinary records to see if they were being truthful and/or were recalling at least some incidents correctly. A match between the two different sets of data would indicate reliability, and it would also bolster the validity of the results. Approaching data collection in multiple ways to increase validity and reliability is known as **triangulation.**

The work of Weisburd, Wycoff et al. (2006) provides a great example of multiple methods used to triangulate. The authors studied crime and disorder in two neighborhoods subject to intensive police interventions and compared them to adjacent neighborhoods that did not receive extra police attention. The goal was to not only observe the impact of the policing intervention in the target neighborhoods but to see if it would then lead to spatial, temporal, or tactical displacement of offending. In other words, would people committing crimes just do it at different times of the day, in different locations, or use different tactics in response to the police activity? Instead of relying exclusively on police reports and calls for service data to detect changes in offending patterns, the research team devised a plan to measure offending in several different ways. For community members' perspectives on crime in the neighborhoods, they did victimization surveys via random household telephone interviews and face-to-face interviews with shopkeepers and employees who worked in the neighborhoods. Researchers went to the police stations and county jail to interview people recently arrested, to ask about their offending patterns. Researchers were also stationed on randomly selected streets every day to observe individuals' behavior. The research team became such a fixture in the neighborhoods that sex workers and drug dealers became comfortable engaging with customers in their presence. To detect possible changes in the cleanliness of the neighborhoods, including the presence of indicators of disorder (discarded condoms, drug paraphernalia), researchers conducted physical observations of street segments before and during the police interventions. The police data, community surveys, social observations, and physical observations provided evidence that crime decreased in the target areas without displacing to adjacent neighborhoods. To understand why people did not just move to other locations to commit crimes, researchers relied on data from the jail and police station interviews. The use of so many different data collection methods to study neighborhood crime substantially enhanced the validity and reliability of the data.

Stauss et al. (2018) evaluated a program that aimed to help incarcerated mothers work on their communication skills while also improving the bonds with their children. A state prison for women offered a voluntary letter-writing program for mothers who had minor children. They adopted a mixed-methods approach for data collection by both conducting interviews with the mothers and administering a previously validated structured survey to measure parenting stress. The interviews addressed the drawback of structured surveys in that they fail to give respondents the opportunity to explain issues in their own words, while the surveys helped the researchers collect quantitative data using an instrument known to be valid and reliable. Both the interviews and the structured surveys provided evidence that the parenting program helped to reduce participants' negative emotions while increasing their confidence as parents and enhancing their communication skills.

Summary

Operationalizing concepts to produce measurable variables is a difficult process. If I am interested in criminological theory and want to study how levels of self-control may be related to juvenile delinquency, I must decide what I mean, precisely, by self-control. Also, what kind of delinquency do I want to study? Am I just worried about violent crimes? Do I want to include behaviors that are only illegal when people are juveniles, such as drinking alcohol, smoking/vaping, or breaking curfew? For almost all types of studies, we will need to make these decisions now so that we know what kind of data we need to collect.

We need to give thought to what kind of variables we need for our study and consider how we hope to collect data. Do you envision collecting data via interviews or written surveys? If so, do you want open-ended questions, close-ended questions, or both? Do you need multiple questions/items to measure a particular construct? Are you going out into the field to do observations and need a fieldwork protocol to complete? Even if you plan to collect data from existing sources, you might have to write up your own data collection form so that you can be consistent with the information you collect from each source. If you are working on the wording of any type of survey or data collection tool now, I suggest that you skip ahead to Chapter 9, since that chapter is an extension of this type of work. There are a number of already constructed and validated surveys available, so it might be possible for you to use an existing instrument or adapt one for your needs (with permission/acknowledgment of the original authors, of course).

We must make sure that we word items for surveys and other data collection protocol in a precise manner, as this will go a long way toward avoiding problems with validity and reliability. Validity reflects how accurately we are measuring what we hope to measure, while reliability is defined as the consistency or stability of an item or set of items. Just because an item or set of items have been found to be reliable, that is no guarantee that they are valid. Using a mixed-methods approach involving multiple ways of collecting data on the same construct is an effective way of addressing validity and reliability concerns.

Key Terms

Dimension	Variable	Attribute
Constant	Independent variable	Dependent variable
Control variable	Open-ended questions	Close-ended questions
Coding	Mutually exclusive	Exhaustive
Discrete variables	Continuous variables	Nominal level
Ordinal level	Interval level	Ratio level
Index	Scale	Likert Scale
Validity	Face validity	Content validity
Criterion validity	Concurrent validity	Predictive validity
Construct validity	Kansas City Preventive Patrol Experiment	Reliability
Test-retest method	Interrater reliability	Split-half method
Triangulation		

Discussion Questions

1. When deciding on levels of measurement for data collection, why is it usually wise to go with the higher levels of measurement?
2. Consider the concept "recidivism." Come up with five different ways that you could operationalize it.
3. What steps can researchers take to prevent reliability problems and/or to be in a position to check for reliability as they are designing a survey?

References

Bielen, S., Grajzl, P., & Marneffe, W. (2021). Blame based on one's name? Extralegal disparities in criminal conviction and sentencing. *European Journal of Law and Economics, 51*, 469–521. https://doi.org/10.1007/s10657-020-09670-6

Ceccato, V. (2019). Fieldwork protocol as a safety inventory tool in public places. *Criminal Justice Studies, 32*(2), 165–188. https://doi.org/10.1080/09589236.2019.1601367

Costello, M., Rukus, J., & Hawdon, J. (2019). We don't like your type around here: Regional and residential differences in exposure to online hate material targeting sexuality. *Deviant Behavior, 40*(3), 385–401. https://doi.org/10.1080/01639625.2018.1426266

Davies, A., & Beckley, A. (2023). Advances in measurement of sex, gender identify, and sexual orientation in surveys. *ACJS Today, 51*(4), 9–14.

Day, E. N., Edgren, K., & Eshleman, A. (2007). Measuring stigma toward mental illness: Development and application of the mental illness stigma scale. *Journal of Applied Social Psychology, 37*(10), 2191 2219. https://doi.org/10.1111/j.1559-1816.2007.00255.x

Fallik, S. W. (2019). The methodological struggles of racial profiling research: A causal question that automobile stop data has yet to answer. *Criminal Justice Studies, 32*(1), 32–49. https://doi.org/10.1080/1478601X.2018.1558057. Reprinted with permission from Taylor & Francis.

Hartley, R. D. (Ed.) (2011). *Snapshots of research.* Sage Publications.

Holmes, B., & D'Amato, C. (2019). Judicial and prosecutorial decision-making: Assessing the effects of race, gender, and age on federal downward sentencing departures, 2013–2016. *Journal of Crime and Justice, 43*(4), 449–466. https://doi.org/10.1080/0735648X.2019.1704838

Jennings, W. G., & Reingle Gonzalez, J. M. (2019). *Criminological and criminal justice research methods.* Wolters Kluwer.

Kelling, G. L., Pate, T., Diekman, D., & Brown, C. E. (1974). *The Kansas City preventive patrol experiment.* The Police Foundation.

Kranzler, J. H. (2018). *Statistics for the terrified.* Rowman & Littlefield.

Makarios, M., Lovins, L. B., Myer, A. J., & Latessa, E. (2019). Treatment integrity and recidivism among sex offenders: The relationship between CPC scores and program effectiveness. *Corrections, 4*(2), 112–125. https://doi.org/10.1080/23774657.2017.1389318

Maxfield, M. G., & Babbie, E. (2012). *Basics of research methods for criminal justice and criminology* (3rd ed.). Thomson Wadsworth.

Office of Management and Budget. (2023). *Recommendations on the best practices for the collection of sexual orientation and gender identify data on federal statistical surveys.* Office of Management and Budget. www.whitehouse.gov/wp-content/uploads/2023/01/SOGI-best-practices.pdf

Spohn, C., & Holleran, D. (2000). The imprisonment penalty paid by young, unemployed black and Hispanic male offenders. *Criminology, 38*(1), 281–306. https://doi.org/10.1111/j.1745-9125.2000.tb00891.x

Stauss, K., Sparks, L., Thomas, J., & Grant, K. (2018). Letters to children: Findings of a program to enhance communication of incarcerated mothers and their children. *Corrections, 3*(4), 225–247, https://doi.org/10.1080/23774657.2017.1381054

Steffensmeier, D., Ulmer, J., & Kramer, J. (1998). The interaction of race, gender, and age in criminal sentencing: The punishment cost of being young, black, and male. *Criminology, 36*(1), 763–797. https://doi.org/10.1111/j.1745-9125.1998.tb01265.x

Sullivan, C. J., & McGloin, J. M. (2014). Looking back to move forward: Some thoughts on measuring crime and delinquency over the past 50 years. *Journal of Research in Crime & Delinquency, 51*(4), 445–466. https://doi.org/10.1177/0022427813520446

Tartaro, C., & Sedelmaier, C. (2009). A tale of two counties: The impact of pretrial detention on later court processing decisions. *Criminal Justice Studies: A Critical Journal of Crime, Law & Society, 22*(2), 203–221. https://doi.org/10.1080/14786010902975507

Truman, J. L., & Morgan, R. (2022). Violent victimization by sexual orientation and gender identity, 2017–2020. United States Department of Justice, Bureau of Justice Statistics. https://bjs.ojp.gov/content/pub/pdf/vvsogi1720.pdf

Unnever, J. D., Benson, M. L., & Cullen, F. T. (2008). Public support for getting tough on corporate crime: Racial and political divides. *Journal of Research in Crime & Delinquency, 45*(2), 163–190. https://doi.org/10.1177/0022427807313707

Valcore, J. L., & Pfeffer, R. (2018). Systemic error: Measuring gender in criminological research. *Criminal Justice Studies, 31*(4), 333–351. https://doi.org/10.1080/1478601X.2018.1499022.

Weisburd, D., Wyckoff, L. A., Ready, J., Eck, J. J., Hinkle, J. C., & Gajewski, F. (2006). Does crime just move around the corner? A controlled study of spatial displacement and diffusion of crime control benefits. *Criminology, 44*(3), 549–592. https://doi.org/10.1111/j.1745-9125.2006.00057.x

White House. (2025). *Defending women from gender ideology extremism and restoring biological truth to the federal government.* The White House. www.whitehouse.gov/presidential-actions/2025/01/defending-women-from-gender-ideology-extremism-and-restoring-biological-truth-to-the-federal-government/

Reading 4.1 "Do Immigrants Cause Higher Crime Rates?"

The issue of immigration and crime has been a concern of Americans for 150 years. While there are certainly instances of immigrants committing crime, researchers have examined this subject in a variety of different ways using the scientific method and have yet to come up with evidence that immigrants (documented or otherwise) are disproportionately involved in crime. Despite this lack of evidence, we have seen politicians and media outlets stoke the fears of potential voters by seizing on individual crime stories or fabricating crime trends to fit their narrative. One way that we gauge the success of these tactics is by conducting opinion polls, but one important thing that we learned in Chapter 4 is that how we ask questions matters. Hadi and Tartaro (2024) illustrate this point with their analysis of General Social Survey (GSS) data. The GSS generally asked about respondents' concerns regarding immigration and crime the same way during each data collection period from 1996 through 2022, except for one year: 2000. For some reason, researchers changed the wording of their question that year, providing Hadi and Tartaro with an opportunity to assess the impact of slightly different wording on survey responses.

"Do Immigrants Cause Higher Crime Rates?" A Cumulative Cross-Sectional General Social Survey Data Analysis

Syeda T. Hadi and Christine Tartaro

Introduction

In the United States, public attitudes toward immigrants have been swayed by the fear that undocumented immigrants are increasing crime and violence (Pew Research Center, 2024; Simes & Waters, 2014). Politicization of immigration and racializing immigrant bodies played a pivotal role in constructing anti-immigrant sentiments (Agnew, 2019). Despite evidence to the contrary (see Adelman et al., 2017; Green, 2016; Harris et al., 2023; Mears, 2002; Sonnier & Haake, 2024), political discourse has highlighted the nexus between immigrants and crime, often as a campaign strategy (Adelman et al., 2017). In his most recent presidential campaign, while visiting the southern border in Texas, Donald Trump claimed, "what's happening with crime is it's through the roof, and it's called 'migrant'... They (immigrants) beat up police officers. You've seen that they go in, they stab people, hurt people, shoot people. It's a whole new form, and they have gangs now that are making our gangs look like small potatoes" (Sonnier & Haake, 2024, para. 2). This rhetoric represents a continuation of what Trump used to launch his successful 2016 presidential campaign.

While empirical research in the U.S. has debunked the longstanding stereotypical image of immigrants as criminals time and time again (Adelman et al., 2017; Green, 2016; Harris et al., 2023; Mears, 2002), Americans have held onto their prejudices (Pew Research Center, 2024; Simes & Waters, 2014). These prejudiced beliefs have resulted in real consequences for immigrant communities in America. Groups like the Tea Party have mobilized to support local ordinances seeking to criminalize undocumented people, dramatically increasing deportations (Simes & Waters, 2014). Trends suggest that immigrants and asylum seekers are increasingly being detained, including children, pregnant and nursing mothers, members of the LGBTQ community, and those with disabilities (Hadi, 2023). In immigrant detention centers, asylum seekers are often treated as prisoners, and extreme violations of their human rights have been reported (Hadi, 2023). The political and media rhetoric aimed at immigrants has also fueled an increase in hate crimes against racial and ethnic minorities (Linares & Telemundo, 2023; Santia et al., 2022).

Given the persistent nature, researchers have examined factors predicting anti-immigrant sentiments in the U.S. that support restrictive and punitive policies toward immigrants. Many of these studies utilized nationally representative cross-sectional General Social Survey (GSS) datasets examining respondents' beliefs on whether immigrants cause increases in crime. However, there are gaps in analyzing the GSS variable "Immigrants cause higher crime rates in the U.S." and the various predictors of this belief over the years. First, most GSS-based studies have analyzed cross-sectional data focusing on a single year rather than utilizing cumulative cross-sectional data collected between 1996 and 2022. Second, the GSS variable that measures respondents' beliefs about whether immigrants are causing crime rates to increase has not been consistent over the years (Simes & Waters, 2014). This article delves deeper into understanding the beliefs of Americans regarding the nexus between immigrants and crime using cumulative cross-sectional GSS data, gauging the changes over time, and identifying possible methodological limitations in analyzing this longstanding and persistent belief.

Background

Lack of Empirical Evidence to Support Immigrant Criminality

Empirical research and government investigations have failed to establish the connection between immigrants and crime time and time again. Mears (2002) characterized conclusions from government reports of early 20th century presidential commissions as paradoxical as they are "counter to conventional wisdom," (p. 284) that immigrants cause crime. Adelman et al. (2017) studied crime in the United States metropolitan areas over 40 years, between 1970 and 2010, and found an inverse relationship between immigration and crime. Areas with higher proportions of immigrants tended to experience decreases in both violent and property crime over the study period (Adelman et al., 2017). Harris et al. (2023) analyzed data from 2015 to study the impact of immigration on crime in the United States. Like Adelman et al. (2017), they observed that immigration tended to be negatively associated with both violent and property crime. In a more recent study, NBC News researchers (Sonnier & Haake, 2024) analyzed 2024 crime data on cities targeted by Texas's "Operation Lone Star," which buses migrants from the border to major cities. The analysis revealed an overall reduction of crime levels in cities that received the most migrants (Sonnier & Haake, 2024).

A common refrain among proponents of the theory that immigration leads to increased crime is that undocumented immigrants are the culprits of illegal behavior. Green (2016) distinguished documented versus undocumented immigration populations to test the "Trump hypothesis" that illegal immigration leads to crime in the United States. Since the speech that Trump made in 2015 to initiate his successful 2016 presidential bid focused on illegal immigration, specifically from Mexico, Green focused on Mexican immigrants and undocumented individuals. There was no relationship between violent or drug-related crimes and immigration from Mexico. While there was a small, positive relationship between undocumented immigration and drug-related crime, these results did not provide empirical evidence to support the anti-immigration rhetoric used in the 2016 presidential campaign.

Longstanding American Belief in the Nexus between Immigrants and Crime

Research examining the belief that immigrants contribute to higher crime rates (Pew Research Center, 2024; Simes & Waters, 2014) has revealed that a substantial number of Americans hold immigrants responsible for the rise in crime. Simes and Waters (2014), analyzing polling data by Gallup, indicated that respondents who believed that immigrants would exacerbate crime problems in the United States ranged from 50% in 2001 (pre-9/11) to 58% in 2007. Simes and Waters also examined GSS 1996, 2000, and 2004 data on responses to the question "Do immigrants cause crime to increase?" According to the analysis, in 1996, a third of the respondents, around 33%, "Strongly Agreed" or "Agreed" that immigrants cause crime compared to 2004, where a total of 27% respondents agreed. Simes and Waters (2014) claimed that the timing of the GSS survey administration in 1996, at the height of the Clinton administration's anti-immigrant legislation, resulted in higher proportions of respondents agreeing that immigrants cause crime.

Simes and Waters (2014) also pointed out an important measurement issue in the GSS data. The 2000 question on immigrants and crime was phrased differently, "Do more immigrants cause *higher* crime rates?," with response options ranging from "Very Likely" to "Not Likely" on a 4-point scale. This time, the GSS data resulted in a substantial proportion of respondents expressing concern about immigrants causing crime, with 72% of the respondents believing that the addition of immigrants was either "Likely" or "Very Likely" to cause higher crime rates. Simes and Waters speculated that the phrasing of the question in 2000 may have led to this difference compared to other years, stating:

> It is not the mere existence of immigrants, but the notion of the increase of immigrants that presents the criminal threat to respondents. The flow of immigrants through the metaphorical floodgates often discussed in political discourse conjures greater fear than the already settled immigrant groups (Simes & Waters, 2014, p. 464).

A recent Pew Research Center poll (2024), which adopted the same approach to measure Americans' fear of immigrants as the GSS 2000 data, found 57% of Americans expressed concerns that the large number of migrants seeking to enter the country leads to more crime. Moreover, many of these respondents were specifically concerned about crimes, such as terrorism (10%) and drugs (3%).

Consequences of Prejudices against Immigrants

The longstanding and consistent trend of Americans linking immigrants to crime has resulted in increasingly restrictive and punitive policies toward immigrants as well as hate crimes against them. A study by McCann and Boateng (2022) found that being an immigrant or non-citizen was associated with an increase in the odds of being the victim of a hate crime. Linares and Telemundo (2023), based on a study by the Center for the Study of Hate and Extremism at California State University, emphasized that, in 2022, the ten largest cities in the U.S. reported an average increase of 22% in hate crimes. This increase was observed despite underreporting of hate crimes against immigrants, since police departments do not consistently record victims' racial and ethnic information. Linares and Telemundo (2023) also noted that hate crimes associated with anti-immigrant sentiments can be racialized, targeting specific groups at a given time. One of the predictors of increased hate crimes, especially against Latinos, is extensive negative media coverage of migrants pouring into America. Politicians' use of bigoted rhetoric about increased border crossings by migrants is associated with negative publicity and serves to contribute to moral panics about crime.

Similarly, the Asian community in the United States experienced a wave of anti-Asian racism, which began in early 2020 after the news that the COVID-19 virus originated in Wuhan, China (Santia et al., 2022). More than 11,000 incidents of verbal harassment, physical assaults, and hate crimes were reported against Asian Americans. Like Linares and Telemundo (2023), Santia et al. (2022) observed that negative media and political rhetoric fueled anti-immigrant attitudes and, consequently, hate crimes against the Asian community.

The Current Study

A majority of the GSS-based studies (Chandler & Tsai, 2001; Jach & Gloeckner, 2020; Jeong, 2013; Pryce, 2018) have utilized cross-sectional datasets, focusing on single years, 1994, 2004 and 2014, broadly examining pro- and anti-immigrant attitudes. Opinions about immigrants and crime were not a focus for these studies. However, given the populist political discourse that both echo and ignite public perception about immigrants causing crime, there is a need to examine the GSS variable that measures opinions on "Immigrants cause higher crime rates in the U.S." over time from cumulative cross-sectional GSS datasets. Thus, the purpose of this study is to examine responses to the immigration and crime questions included in the GSS survey in 1996, 2000, 2004, 2014, and 2022.

While the question wording in the 1996, 2004, 2014, and 2022 surveys was the same, the 2000 survey question wording may have introduced some bias (Simes & Waters, 2014). Additionally, response options for 1996, 2004, 2014, and 2022 were on a 5-point Likert scale from "Strongly Agree" to "Strongly Disagree" with a "Neither Agree nor Disagree" option. The 2000 response options on the other hand lacked a "Neither Agree nor Disagree" category, with 4-point scale response categories from "Very Likely" to "Not Likely," thereby forcing respondents to take a stance on this topic. While examining public attitudes, studies have warned that a social desirability factor, where respondents conceal views on highly debated issues such as immigration, may impact responses (Janus, 2010; Rinken et al., 2021). Previous research indicates that respondents who are restrictionists or possess prejudiced attitudes toward a certain group were likely to hide their socially unacceptable attitude behind "don't know" or non-reactive "neutral" responses (Janus, 2010; Rinken et al., 2021). So, another purpose of this current paper is to examine characteristics of respondents that are associated with variations in opinions about immigration and crime with a focus on those who selected the neutral position.

The researchers searched the cross-sectional GSS datasets (Davern et al., n.d.) for independent variables previously highlighted in the literature (Chandler & Tsai, 2001; Jach & Gloeckner, 2020; Jeong, 2013; Macdonald, 2021; Pryce, 2018) as being predictors of opinions about immigrants. Race, ethnicity, age, income, sex, education, and political affiliation were selected. Though anti-immigrant attitudes were related to factors including ethnocentrism, social and cultural concerns, Hainmueller and Hopkins's (2014) study indicated, that higher education predicted lower levels of ethnocentrism, higher support for cultural diversity, and more pro-immigrant sentiments. Thus, in this study, researchers focused on respondents' education with the assumption that those with higher education will be more pro-immigrant and less likely to believe that immigrants cause crime. While examining these variables, this study also aims to highlight analytical limitations arising from inconsistent measurement approaches between 2000 and other years.

Data Analysis

The researchers analyzed a dataset in SPSS that included GSS data from 1996, 2000, 2004, 2014 and 2022. Univariate, bivariate, and multivariate analyses were conducted on the selected variables. For both bivariate and multivariate analyses, we recoded and condensed the response categories of the dependent variables to clearly distinguish between two groups: those who agreed versus disagreed, and those who expressed neutrality instead of agreeing or disagreeing. The 2000 immigration question response categories were condensed from four to two categories ("Somewhat Unlikely or Not Likely at All" = 0 and "Very Likely or Somewhat Likely" = 1). The dependent variable for 1996, 2004, 2014, and 2022, was condensed from having five response options to three ("Somewhat or Strongly Disagree" = 0, "Neither Agree nor Disagree" = 1, and "Somewhat or Strongly Agree" = 2).

Bivariate analysis consisted of Chi-squared tests to compare dependent variable categories across responses for the categorical variables of "Sex" and "Race." For the continuous independent variables of "Age," "Income," "Education" and "Political Party Affiliation", bivariate Pearson Correlation was utilized. The GSS Political Party Affiliation variable (PARTYID) scale included seven points, with one through six ranging from 1 = "Strongly Democrat" to 6 = "Strongly Republican." There was a seventh category which was not along the Democrat to Republican spectrum, so those responses were coded as missing for this analysis.

Multivariate analysis consisted of a binomial logistic regression model for the recoded 2000 dependent variable with two response categories and multinomial regression models for the remaining years. Multinomial regression allowed for the isolation of the neutral, "Neither Agree nor Disagree," response for 1996, 2004, 2014, and 2022, permitting direct comparisons of characteristics of respondents who utilized the neutral category rather than the agree or disagree options.

Univariate Analysis

Sample Description

Frequency distributions for predictor variables are displayed in Table 1. The majority of respondents, between 72 to 80%, were "White," compared to 13 to 16% "Black", and 5 to 12% "Other" races. The sample comprised a slightly higher percentage of female respondents, between 54 to 56%, compared to 44 to 46% males. On average, respondents were middle-aged individuals, 44 to 49 years old, with an average of 13 years of education. There were more Democrat-leaning respondents in the sample than Republican-leaning individuals. On average, respondents earned "$25000 or More" from 1996 to 2022.

Immigrants vs. "More" Immigrants Causing Higher Crime Rates

Table 2 shows that a substantially higher percentage of respondents, around 73%, agreed that "more" immigrants cause higher crime rates by selecting "Very Likely" or "Somewhat Likely" in 2000. In the remaining years only about a third of the respondents chose "Strongly Agree" or "Agree," with 33% in 1996, 27% in 2004, 21% in 2014, and 24% in 2022. It is likely that the potentially biased phrasing of the year-2000 question, in addition to not providing respondents the option to be neutral, yielded higher support toward anti-immigrant sentiment compared to other years. Around 25 to 31% of respondents in 1996, 2004, 2014, and 2022 chose the "Neither Agree nor Disagree" option. As Janus (2010) highlighted, it is possible that some these respondents were concealing their true, socially undesirable, opinions about immigrants causing higher crime by choosing the "neutral" option.

Bivariate Analysis

The Chi-squared analysis of the 2000 dependent variable "More immigrants cause higher crime rates" and the independent variables sex and race did not show significant variation between groups. Most respondents, around 73%, agreed that more immigrants coming into the U.S. causes higher crime rates, and this finding did not differ by respondent sex or race. Even 63% of the respondents who identified as "Other" race, who might have represented immigrant communities themselves, agreed that immigrants cause higher crime rates.

For the variable "Immigrants cause higher crime rates," in 1996, both White and Black respondents were slightly more likely to agree (χ^2=19.202, $p < 0.001$) compared to "Other" races. In 2004, both "Sex" and "Race" had significant association with dependent variable. Male (χ^2=14.273, $p < 0.001$) and White (χ^2=16.525, $p < 0.002$) respondents were more likely to agree that immigrants cause higher crime rates. In 2022, once again, male (χ^2= 8.766, $p = 0.012$) and White respondents (χ^2= 37.71, $p < 0.001$) were significantly more likely to agreeing more than other groups that immigrants cause crime (see Table 3). Neither sex nor race had a significant impact in 2014.

The Bivariate Pearson Correlations shows that "Age" had a statistically significant linear

Table 1 Descriptives for independent variables

	1996 N (%)	*2000 N (%)*	*2004 N (%)*	*2014 N (%)*	*2022 N (%)*
Race					
White	2349 (80.90%)	2213 (78.60%)	2234 (79.40%)	1890 (74.50%)	2514 (72.00%)
Black	402 (13.80%)	429 (15.20%)	377 (13.40%)	386 (15.20%)	565 (16.20%)
Other	153 (5.30%)	175 (6.20%)	201 (7.10%)	262 (10.30%)	412 (11.80%)
Total	2904	2817	2812	2538	3491
Sex					
Male	1285 (44.20%)	1229 (43.60%)	1280 (45.50%)	1141 (45.00%)	1627 (46.20%)
Female	1619 (55.80%)	1588 (56.40%)	1532 (54.50%)	1397 (55.00%)	1897 (53.80%)
Total	2904	2817	2812	2538	3524
Education (0–20 years)	*Mean (SD)*	*Mean (SD)*	*Mean (SD)*	*Mean (SD)*	*Mean (SD)*
	13.36 (2.929)	13.26 (2.869)	13.7 (2.889)	13.7 (3.071)	14.11 (2.894)
Total	2895	2808	2810	2537	3524
Income*					
	9.86 (2.99)	10.05 (2.92)	10.28 (2.90)	10.38 (2.90)	10.86 (2.46)
Total	1947	1818	1688	1523	1990
Age (18–99)	44.78 (16.868)	46.02 (17.366)	45.96 (16.804)	49.01 (17.412)	49.18 (17.974)
Total	2898	2809	2803	2529	3336
Party affiliation**					
	2.81 (1.98)	2.76 (1.94)	2.86 (2.07)	2.66 (1.92)	2.78 (1.98)
Total	2855	2757	2771	2450	3403

*Income (RINCOME) measured as 1 = $1,000 to $2,999 to 12 = $25,000 or more

**Party affiliation (PARTYID) measured on a scale of 1 = strongly Democrat to 6 = Strongly Republican.

relationship, with weak correlations ($r = 0.077$ and 0.111) for 2014 and 2022 respectively. The direction of the relationship was positive, meaning older respondents were more likely to "Strongly Agree" or "Agree" that immigrants cause higher crime. Education was significantly associated with the dependent variables in all of the study years. However, the strength of association was somewhat weak ("r" ranging from -0.128 to -0.252). Respondents with higher years of education were more likely to select "Strongly Disagree" or "Disagree." Party affiliation was significantly correlated with weak strength of association in 2004 ($r = 0.091$, $p = 0.007$) and 2014 ($r = 0.091$, $p = 0.002$). By 2022, political affiliation had the

Table 2 "Immigrants increase crime rates" vs. "more immigrants cause higher crime rates" by year

"More" immigrants cause higher crime rates			*Immigrants increase crime rates?*								
	2000			*1996*		*2004*		*2014*		*2022*	
Very likely	332	(25.20%)	Agree strongly	95	(7.50%)	83	(7.00%)	50	(4.10%)	107	(4.60%)
Somewhat likely	629	(47.80%)	Agree	328	(25.90%)	235	(19.80%)	202	(16.50%)	323	(14.00%)
–		-	Neither agree nor disagree	368	(29.10%)	345	(29.10%)	311	(25.40%)	734	(31.70%)
Not too likely	305	(23.20%)	Disagree	388	(30.70%)	437	(36.90%)	519	(42.40%)	777	(33.60%)
Not likely at all	51	(3.90%)	Disagree strongly	86	(6.80%)	84	(7.10%)	142	(11.60%)	372	(16.10%)
Total		1317			1265		1184		1224	2313	

strongest correlation with the dependent variable ($r = 0.414, p < 0.001$) (see Table 4). The direction of the relationship was positive, meaning that Republicans were more likely to "Strongly Agree" or "Agree" compared to Democrats. Respondents' income was associated with the dependent variable in 2004 only, with a weak negative correlation ($r = -0.072, p < 0.05$).

Multivariate Analysis

Binomial Logistic Regression for 2000 Data

The researchers developed a binomial logistic regression model for the 2000 data, with the dependent variable dichotomized into "Somewhat Unlikely" or "Not Likely at All" = 0 and "Very Likely" or "Somewhat Likely" = 1 (see Table 3). The overall model was statistically significant (χ^2=60.014, df = 7, $p < 0.001$, Nagelkerke R^2 = .099). Two individual variables were statistically significant—"Race-White" and "Highest year of school completed." White respondents were nearly twice as likely to believe that it was somewhat or very likely that a consequence of letting more immigrants into the country was higher crime rates (Odds Ration [OR] = 1.910, p = 0.036) when compared to respondents who selected "Other" as their race. Individuals with higher levels of education were slightly less likely to endorse the immigrants and crime myth (OR = 0.810, $p < 0.001$).

Multinomial Regression Analysis—1996, 2004, 2014, and 2022

Multinomial regression models for each of the remaining years in the study are displayed in Tables 4, 5, and 6. The five-point dependent variable on "Immigrants cause higher crime rates" was condensed into three categories: "Somewhat or Strongly Disagree," "Neither Agree nor Disagree," and "Somewhat or Strongly Agree." "Somewhat or Strongly Disagree" was used as the reference category for Models 1 and 2 (Tables 4 and 5, respectively), while "Somewhat or Strongly Agree" was used as the reference category for the third model (Table 6).

For all models, the –2 log likelihood tests were statistically significant, meaning that the addition of the independent variables provided a better explanation for the outcome than the null, and all goodness of fit tests were non-significant.

Table 3 Logistic regression analysis—year 2000

	B	*SE*	*OR*
Age	0.009	0.006	0.991
Sex	-0.087	0.165	0.917
Race – White	0.647	0.308	1.910*
Race – Black	0.687	0.373	1.987
Income	0.048	0.030	1.049
Highest year of school completed	-0.222	0.032	0.801***
Political party affiliation	0.040	0.044	1.041

*$p < 0.05$; **$p < 0.01$; ***$p < 0.001$.

Respondents Selecting "Agree" over "Disagree"

In Model 1 (see Table 4), respondents' age had a weak association with opinions on immigrants in 1996, and there was a slight change over time. After controlling for other potential predictors, age was initially negatively related to respondents' opinions about immigrants increasing crime, meaning older adults were slightly more likely to disagree or strongly disagree rather than agree. By 2014, that changed and older adults were slightly more likely to agree that immigrants increased crime, and this finding continued into 2022. Race was strongly associated with opinions about immigration in all years but 2014, with White respondents two to three times as likely as people who identified as a race other than White or Black (the reference category) to express a level of agreement that immigration increases crime. Black respondents in 1996 and 2022 were 2.5 times more likely than individuals who were not White or Black to also believe that immigration leads to increased crime. In 1996 and 2004, White respondents were almost three times more likely (OR = 2.925 and 2.719, respectively) to express agreement that immigration leads to increased crime compared to people who were not Black or White. In 2022, the relationship weakened a bit to OR = 2.111. In 1996 and 2004, females were almost half as likely (OR .619 and .623 respectively) as male respondents to agree that immigration was positively related to crime. Both education and political party affiliation were not associated with agreeing or disagreeing with immigration causing crime in 1996, but by 2004, they were associated with respondents' opinions about immigrants and remained so for 2014 and 2022. During these years, more educated individuals were slightly less likely to believe the myth of immigrants causing crime. The relationship between political party affiliation and having an opinion about immigrants strengthened gradually from 2004 to 2022. By 2022, respondents more aligned with the Republican Party were nearly twice as likely (OR = 1.872) than those identifying as Democrats to "Agree" or "Strongly Agree" that immigration increased crime.

Respondents Selecting "Neutral" over "Disagree"

Table 5 shows a comparison of respondents who chose "Neither Agree nor Disagree" and remained neutral rather than expressing that they "Disagreed or Strongly Disagreed" with the idea that immigrants increase crime. In 1996, older individuals were slightly more likely to check the neutral option than disagree compared to younger respondents. However, this changed in 2022, with older respondents slightly more likely to disagree compared to staying neutral. In 1996 and 2014, both White and Black respondents were likely to choose the neutral category over disagreeing compared to people of other races. White respondents were 3.6 times more likely and Blacks 4 times more likely than those of other races to choose the neutral category in 1996. In 2014, both White and Black respondents were more than 2.5 times more likely than people of other races to choose the neutral option rather than expressing a level of disagreement when responding to the question

In 1996 and 2022, people who were Republican leaning were also slightly more likely to choose neutral over disagreeing with

Table 4 Multinomial regression analysis—1996, 2004, 2014, and 2022 "agree/strongly agree" vs. reference category "disagree/strongly disagree" (Model 1)

	1996			2004			2014			2022		
	B	*SE*	*OR*	*B*	*SE*	*OR*	*B*	*SE*	*OR*	*B*	*SE*	*OR*
Age	-0.016	0.007	0.984*	0.002	0.007	1.002	0.016	0.008	1.016*	0.014	0.006	1.014*
Race (White)	1.073	0.405	2.925*	1.000	0.441	2.719*	0.446	0.358	1.561	0.747	0.331	2.111*
Race (Black)	0.951	0.460	2.588*	0.590	0.506	1.803	0.492	0.439	1.635	0.956	0.403	2.602*
Sex	-0.480	0.180	0.619**	-0.473	0.192	0.623*	-0.340	0.213	0.712	-0.229	0.181	0.795
Income	-0.010	0.030	0.991	-0.058	0.033	0.944	-0.023	0.039	0.977	0.029	0.037	1.030
Highest year of school completed	-0.230	0.036	1.019	-0.150	0.037	0.860***	-0.091	0.034	0.913**	-0.156	0.032	0.855***
Political party affiliation	0.019	0.047	1.019	0.125	0.047	1.133**	0.152	0.058	1.165**	0.627	0.053	1.872***

*$p < 0.05$; **$p < 0.01$; ***$p < .001$.

Table 5 *Multinomial regression analysis—1996, 2004, 2014, and 2022 "neither agree/disagree" vs. reference category "disagree/strongly disagree" (Model 2)*

	1996			2004			2014			2022		
	B	*SE*	*OR*	*B*	*SE*	*OR*	*B*	*SE*	*OR*	*B*	*SE*	*OR*
Age	-0.016	0.007	0.984*	-0.010	0.007	0.990	0.003	0.007	1.003	0.011	0.055	1.011*
Race (White)	1.289	0.440	3.628**	0.331	0.344	1.393	0.984	0.363	2.675**	-0.044	0.213	0.956
Race (Black)	1.415	0.490	4.118**	0.488	0.394	1.629	0.953	0.417	2.592*	0.468	0.259	1.596
Sex	0.005	0.175	1.005	0.002	0.183	1.002	0.013	0.181	1.013	0.111	0.144	1.118
Income	0.019	0.031	1.019	-0.015	0.033	0.985	-0.002	0.034	0.998	-0.004	0.028	0.996
Highest year of school completed	-0.094	0.034	0.910**	-0.107	0.036	0.899**	-0.011	0.032	0.989	-0.061	0.026	0.941*
Political party affiliation	0.123	0.045	1.131**	0.039	0.045	1.040	0.065	0.049	1.067	0.392	0.040	1.481***

$^{*}p < 0.05$; $^{**}p < 0.01$; $^{***}p < 0.001$.

the supposed link between immigrants and crime. In contrast, more educated people were less inclined to express neutrality and more likely to choose the "Disagree or Strongly Disagree" options in 1996, 2004 and 2022. In 2004, education was the only significant predictor in Model 2, with less educated people being slightly more likely to choose neutral rather than disagree (OR = 0.899).

Respondents Selecting "Neutral" over "Agree"

When comparing those who chose to be neutral over agreeing that immigrants cause higher crime (Table 6), four variables had significant associations during at least one of the study years – race, sex, education and political affiliation. Race had a significant impact in 2022 only, with White respondents less likely to stay neutral than agree (OR = 0.453) compared to people who identified as something other than White or Black. Sex had significant impact in 1996 and 2004, with female respondents 60% more likely than males to express neutrality rather than agreeing that immigration causes crime (OR = 1.6 in both years). Education yielded a significant association in 2004, 2014 and 2022, with higher educated individuals more likely to stay neutral than agreeing. Party affiliation had contrasting impact in 1996 and 2022. Republicans were significantly more likely to be neutral in 1996 (OR = 1.109), which reversed in 2022, with Republicans less likely to stay neutral than agree (OR = 0.791).

Discussion

The results of this article showed notable variations in Americans' beliefs regarding the nexus between immigrants and crime and its predictors. Americans' beliefs varied depending on which year the data were collected, between 1996 and 2022, and what measure was used to collect data. The nuanced nature of the anti-immigrant sentiment and how its predictors varied over time, strengthened and complemented some of the previous GSS-based studies (Chandler & Tsai, 2001; Jach & Gloeckner, 2020; Jeong, 2013; Macdonald, 2021; Pryce, 2018) that examined one year at a time. For the years 1996 and 2004, a third of the respondents agreed that immigrants cause higher crime rates. By 2014 and 2022, GSS data indicated that fewer people in the United States were endorsing the idea that immigration leads to increased crime, with only 21% in 2014 and 19% in 2022 responding "Strongly Agree or Agree." A quarter of respondents in 2014 were in the "Neither Agree nor Disagree" category, with this increasing to 31.7% of respondents by 2022. Even if all of the individuals in the neutral category for 2014 and 2022 chose "Strongly Agree or Agree" had they been faced with a four-option set of responses similar to what was used by GSS in 2000, this would still not bring us close to the 73% of respondents indicating that they believed immigration was linked to higher crime, as the GSS found in 2000.

A Wording Issue: 2000 Question Bias

A look back at 1996, 2000, and 2004 does not help to provide justifications for why anti-immigrant sentiment would be so much higher in 2000 compared to the 4 years before and after. In 1996, the political climate was defined by the infamous Illegal Immigration Reform and Immigrant Responsibility Act (IIRIRA) enacted by the Clinton administration. This act was a bundle of provisions that increased penalties on both unauthorized and legal immigrants who had violated US law in some way (Lind, 2016). The IIRIRA was responsible for dramatic increase in deportation and increase in illegal immigrants, as various provision within the Act made legal routes to citizenship practically impossible. However, by 2000, Democrats were mostly siding with immigration advocates (Lind, 2016). The shift started just 1 year after IIRIRA's passage. Congress passed a law protecting some Central American asylum-seekers from deportation in 1997 and, in 2000, it passed a law making it easier for people to immigrate legally to the US to be with relatives (Lind, 2016). Thus, if anything, in 2000, public sentiment should have been less anti-immigrant compared to 1996.

Table 6 *Multinomial regression analysis—1996, 2004, 2014, and 2022 "neither agree/disagree" vs. reference category "agree/strongly agree" (model 3)*

	1996			2004			2014			2022		
	B	*SE*	*OR*	*B*	*SE*	*OR*	*B*	*SE*	*OR*	*B*	*SE*	*OR*
Age	0	0.007	1	-0.012	0.008	0.988	-0.012	0.009	0.988	-0.003	0.006	0.997
Race (White)	0.215	0.516	1.240	-0.669	0.483	0.512	0.538	0.462	1.713	-0.792	0.338	0.453*
Race (Black)	0.464	0.562	1.591	-0.101	0.546	0.904	0.461	0.543	1.585	-0.489	0.41	0.613
Sex	0.485	0.187	1.625**	0.475	0.210	1.608*	0.353	0.239	1.424	0.341	0.181	1.406
Income	0.029	0.032	1.029	0.043	0.036	1.044	0.021	0.045	1.021	-0.033	0.037	0.968
Highest year of school completed	0.136	0.037	1.146***	0.043	0.04	1.044	0.081	0.04	1.084*	0.096	0.032	1.1**
Political party affiliation	0.104	0.049	1.109*	-0.086	0.052	0.918	-0.088	0.065	0.916	-0.234	0.052	0.791***

*$p < 0.05$; **$p < 0.01$; ***$p < 0.001$.

However, in the aftermath of September 11, 2001, terrorist attacks, immigration control became the primary tool in the "War on Terror" and preserving national security (Chishti & Bolter, 2021). Pre-2004, the United States was involved in the Second Gulf War and had experienced a complete overhaul of the nation's homeland security program. Some notable actions included, the enactment of the Patriot Act, creation of the Department of Homeland Security, and enormous authority bestowed on the U.S. Customs and Border Protection (CBP) to manage border security, and U.S. Immigration and Customs Enforcement (ICE), to enforce immigration laws in the interior of the country (Chishti & Bolter, 2021). These steps and the overall political climate, post-9/11, shaped media discourse and public sentiments against immigrants for decades after. Thus, once again, the sudden spike in anti-immigrant sentiment in 2000, between IIRIRA and pre-9/11, cannot be attributed to the political context.

To understand why the results for 2000 differed so much compared to the other years, we should look at how the 2000 question was worded compared to the other years. In 2000, the wording included "more immigrants" and, as Simes and Waters (2014) noted, invoked the picture of borders being overrun with immigrants. This wording could also explain the discrepancy between the more recent GSS findings of 2022 and the Pew research findings from 2024. The Pew study used similar wording as the 2000 GSS survey and asked about large numbers of migrants entering the country leading to more crime. The Pew study found that a majority of Americans (57%) shared these concerns. The GSS 2022, similar to earlier years excluding 2000, immigration and crime question did not insinuate that a large number or "more" immigrants entering to the United States are causing higher crime. These years, a smaller percentage of respondents, roughly less than a quarter, agreed that immigration is associated with increased crime. The contrasting results of the 2000 GSS survey and the Pew 2024 findings compared to the 1996, 2004, 2014, and 2022 datasets provide evidence of the impact of question wording on responses regarding immigration and crime.

Being Neutral vs. Agreeing or Disagreeing

In addition to the question phrasing, the 2000 question differed from other years of the GSS in that it did not provide respondents the option to be neutral with the statement that immigrants cause higher crime rates. To understand how not having the "Neither Agree nor Disagree" option impacted the outcomes in 2000, multinomial regression was computed on the remaining years, allowing identification of groups who chose to express neutrality on the immigration question.

The use of the "Neither Agree nor Disagree" option varied by race, with Black and White respondents 2.5 to 4 times more likely than those identifying as "Other" to choose neutrality rather than express disagreement with the alleged immigration and crime link in 1996 and 2014. For the model comparing the usage of the "Neither Agree nor Disagree" to "Agree," race was significant only in 2022. White respondents were half as likely as those in the "Other" race category to choose neutrality over agreement, suggesting that Whites held more negative views of immigrants than other groups. When the neutral option was unavailable in 2000, both White and Black respondents were significantly more likely than people of other races to agree that immigrants cause crime. While these findings support that of an earlier study (Simes & Waters, 2014) which claimed that race has a significant impact, it contradicts the Chandler and Tsai (2001) results finding no relationship between race and attitudes about immigration.

Political affiliation was significant in both 1996 and 2022 when it came to utilization of the neutral category. In 1996, more conservative individuals tended to choose the neutral option over agreeing or disagreeing that immigrants cause crime. However, by 2022, Republicans were more likely to choose agree over disagree, neutral over disagree, and agree over neutral, meaning that they provided the most anti-immigrant responses in every model. Similarly, in 1996, older respondents were somewhat more inclined to disagree than to agree or remain neutral on the statement that immigrants cause crime. However, by 2022, this trend had reversed. This can be explained by what Washington Post researchers (Newman et al., 2020) called the "emboldening impact." According to the Newman study, "When prominent political figures like Trump make racially charged statements, it can indeed let ordinary Americans feel that they can freely express their own bias" (Newman et al., 2020, para. 14).

The impact of education on opinions of immigration and crime was consistent over the years and in line with past research (Pew Research Center, 2024; Jach & Gloeckner, 2020; Jeong, 2013). Respondents with higher education consistently expressed pro-immigration sentiments. Similarly, in line with Jach and Gloeckner (2020) study findings, female respondents appeared more pro-immigrant compared to their male counterparts

Limitations and Recommendations

There were multiple limitations to this analysis. First, a wide range of predictors can influence anti-immigrant beliefs, but this article only focused on specific demographic variables frequently flagged by earlier studies. We were unable to include additional variables that might have helped to better explain variation in respondents' views of immigration. For example, using 2012–2014 GSS panel data, Macdonald (2021) found that lack of confidence in government was related to anti-immigrant attitudes. For the current study, the researchers attempted to run regression models including the variable "Confidence in Executive Branch of government" (CONFED), but the 2004 regression model could not be generated due to "insufficient" data. The limited number of variables available to us across the years of GSS data collection likely explains the low Nagelkerke R^2 statistics across the years (1996: 0.110; 2000: 0.099; 2004: 0.083; 2014: 0.052; 2022: 0.252). Since this study models consisted of demographic variables, future studies should generate models with variables related to perceived sociotropic or social and cultural concerns that are better predictors of attitudes toward immigrants, as Hainmueller and Hopkins's (2014) study claimed. These models might have stronger predictive capabilities.

Another limitation to this study was our inability to examine the impact of different data collection methods on likelihood to express anti-immigrant sentiments. Previous research (Janus, 2010; Rinken et al., 2021) observed that differences in responses may vary given direct measures versus indirect ways of asking about sensitive issues. Future studies could explore diverse direct and indirect measures to collect data on American's attitudes toward immigration and crime to study the extent that different data collection modalities impact findings.

The current article noted the possible insinuation of the 2000 GSS question, that the U.S. is dealing with an unprecedented number of undocumented/illegal immigrants flooding the borders and increasing crime. Nevertheless, future survey questionnaire should be specific about the categories of immigrants. We are essentially looking at a diverse group – immigrants, who came to the U.S. for mainly economic reasons, refugees, who move because of wars and fear of persecution, asylees, those who arrive at ports of entry to apply for asylum, and asylum seekers, whose claim as refugees are pending (Agnew, 2019; Hadi, 2023). Unless this distinction is clarified before the survey and in the question, we cannot be sure of the true attitudes of respondents about specific groups of immigrants and the extent to which Americans believe each group contributes to crime.

Conclusion

Despite the limitations, this article stressed the importance of examining anti-immigrant perspective not just within a single year, but a comparative analysis over the years. Opinions regarding the alleged link between immigration and crime varied over time, as did demographic characteristics of those who believed immigration to be harmful. This paper also demonstrated the impact of even slight wording changes to questions and answer options on survey results, as is evidenced by the negative views of immigrants visible in the 2000 GSS and 2022 Pew Research results compared to the more balanced findings offered by the 1996, 2004, 2014, and 2022 GSS studies.

Disclosure Statement

No potential conflict of interest was reported by the author(s).

Discussion Questions

1. In what ways did the 2000 GSS question about immigration and crime differ from the other years? According to the results of the analysis, how does the wording appear to have impacted results?
2. How were education, race, and political affiliation associated with fear of immigration and crime over the study period?
3. Hadi and Tartaro were limited in the number of variables they could use to try to explain individuals' fear of immigration and crime, because they could only utilize variables that were included in each of the years' data collection activities. Ideally, what other variables should have been included in this analysis?

References

Adelman, R., Reid, L. W., Markle, G., Weiss, S., & Jaret, C. (2017). Urban crime rates and the changing face of immigration: Evidence across four decades. *Journal of Ethnicity in Criminal Justice*, *15*(1), 52–77. https://doi.org/10.1080/15377938.2016.1261057

Agnew, J. (2019). The asymmetric border: The United States' place in the world and the refugee panic of 2018. *Geographical Review*, *109*(4), 507–526. https://doi.org/10.1111/gere.12333

Chandler, C. R., & Tsai, Y. (2001). Social factors influencing immigration attitudes: An analysis of data from the General Social Survey. *The Social Science Journal (Fort Collins)*, *38*(2), 177–188. https://doi.org/10.1016/S0362-3319(01)00106-9

Chishti, M., & Bolter, J. (2021). *Two decades after 9/11, national security focus still dominates U.S. immigration system*. www.migrationpolicy.org/article/two-decades-after-sept-11-immigration-national-security

Davern, M., Bautista, R., Freese, J., Herd, P., Morgan, S. L., Bautista, R., … Morgan, S. L., NORC. ed. (n.d). *General social survey 1972–2024* [Machine-readable data file]. Principal Investigator, Michael Davern; Co-Principal Investigators Sponsored by the National Science Foundation. NORC, 2024: NORC at the University of Chicago.gssdataexplorer.norc.org.

Green, D. (2016). The Trump hypothesis: Testing immigrant populations as a determinant of violent and drug-related crime in the United States. *Social Science Quarterly*, *97*(3), 506–524. https://doi.org/10.1111/ssqu.12300

Hadi, S. T. (2023). Female asylum seekers and refugees in detention: An exploratory review of research. *International Criminology*, *3*(3), 239–252. https://doi.org/10.1007/s43576-023-00097-y

Hainmueller, J., & Hopkins, D. J. (2014). Public attitudes toward immigration. *Annual Review of Political Science*, *17*(1), 225–249. https://doi.org/10.1146/annurev-polisci-102512-194818

Harris, C. T., Mutimer, A., & Thomas, S. (2023). From both near and far: Examining the diverse regions of origin for immigration and its relationship with crime across United States communities, 2015. *Justice Quarterly*, *40*(1), 51–74. https://doi.org/10.1080/07418825.2021.2013932

Jach, E., & Gloeckner, G. (2020). Attributes associated with postdoctoral fellows and views of immigration: A preliminary analysis using the general social survey. *Journal of Critical Thought & Praxis*, *9*(1), 1–21. https://doi.org/10.31274/jctp.9571

Janus, A. L. (2010). The influence of social desirability pressures on expressed immigration attitudes. *Social Science Quarterly*, *91*(4), 928–946. https://doi.org/10.1111/j.1540-6237.2010.00742.x

Jeong, H. O. (2013). Do national feelings influence public attitudes towards immigration? *Journal of Ethnic and Migration Studies*, *39*(9), 1461–1477. https://doi.org/10.1080/1369183X.2013.815428

Linares, A., & Telemundo, N. (2023). Rise in hate crimes includes a 'significant increase' against Latinos. *NBC News*. www.nbcnews.com/news/latino/hate-crimes-latinos-see-significant-increase-rcna123211

Lind, D. (2016). The disastrous, forgotten 1996 law that created today's immigration problem. *Vox*. www.vox.com/2016/4/28/11515132/iirira-clinton-immigration

Macdonald, D. (2021). Political trust and support for immigration in the American mass public. *British Journal of Political Science*, *51*(4), 1402–1420. https://doi.org/10.1017/S0007123419000668

McCann, W. S., & Boateng, F. D. (2022). An analysis of hate crime victimization amongst immigrants. *American Journal of Criminal Justice*, *47*(5), 795–817. https://doi.org/10.1007/s12103-021-09616-x

Mears, D. P. (2002). Immigration and crime: What's the connection? *Federal Sentencing Reporter*, *14*(5), 284–288. https://doi.org/10.1525/fsr.2002.14.5.284

Newman, B., Merolla, J., Shah, S., Collingwood, L., & Ramakrishnan, K. (2020). *Trump's Rhetoric does encourage open prejudice and bias*. We checked. www.washingtonpost.com/politics/2020/03/11/trumps-rhetoric-does-encourage-open-prejudice-bias-we-checked/

NORC. (2021). *The general social survey*. https://gss.norc.org/About-The-GSS

Pew Research Center. (2024). *How Americans view the situation at the U.S.-Mexico border, its causes and consequences*. www.pewresearch.org/politics/2024/02/15/how-americans-view-the-situation-at-the-u-s-mexico-border-its-causes-and-consequences/

Pryce, D. K. (2018). U.S. citizens' current attitudes toward immigrants and immigration: A study from the General Social Survey. *Social Science Quarterly*, *99*(4), 1467–1483. https://doi.org/10.1111/ssqu.12514

Rinken, S., Pasadas-del-Amo, S., Rueda, M., & Cobo, B. (2021). No magic bullet: Estimating anti-immigrant sentiment and social desirability bias with the item-count technique. *Quality & Quantity*, *55*(6), 2139–2159. https://doi.org/10.1007/s11135-021-01098-7

Santia, M., Oden, A., Kim, S.-W., Pingree, R. J., Wyers, J., & Bryanov, K. (2022). The other side of the pandemic: Effects of racialized news coverage on attitudes toward Asians and immigrants. *International Journal of Communication (Online)*, *16*, 5717.

Simes, J. T., & Waters, M. C. (2014). The politics of immigration and crime. In S. M. Bucerius & M. H. Tonry (Eds.), *The Oxford handbook of ethnicity, crime, and immigration* (pp. 457–483). Oxford University Press.

Solodoch, O. (2021). Do sociotropic concerns mask prejudice? Experimental evidence on the sources of public opposition to immigration. *Political Studies*, *69*(4), 1009–1032. https://doi.org/10.1177/0032321720946163

Sonnier, O., & Haake, G. (2024). Trump's claims of a migrant crime wave are not supported by national data. *NBC News*. www.nbcnews.com/politics/2024-election/trumps-claims-migrant-crime-wave-are-not-supported-national-data-rcna140896

Reading 4.2 Extending a Letter-Writing Intervention Developed for Incarcerated Mothers to Incarcerated Fathers

Quantitative research tends to be most common in criminal justice research in the United States, but if we seek more detailed information, it helps to include some qualitative aspects to a study. Strauss, Sparks, and Gallagher (2023) expanded their work implementing a letter writing campaign for female incarcerated individuals with a sample of males. When it came time to evaluate the program, the researchers chose a mixed-methods approach and combined quantitative pre- and posttests with participant focus groups. As you will see, the qualitative research provided some important context as the authors sought to explain the impact of the letter writing classes on the participants.

Extending A Letter-Writing Intervention Developed for Incarcerated Mothers to Incarcerated Fathers: A Mixed Methods Study

Kimberly Stauss, Leigh Sparks, and John M. Gallagher

Introduction

By the end of 2016, there were approximately 1.5 million prisoners in the U.S., that total down 7% from 2009 (Carson, 2018). Despite the decline, the rate of incarceration in the U.S. remains the highest in the world (World Prison Brief, 2020). In addition, in 2007, the country's total number of incarcerated parents with minor children was over 800,000 (approximately 750,000 fathers and 66,000 mothers), that total having risen 79% from 1991 (Glaze & Maruschak, 2010). In 2011, over 5 million American children had lived through some form of parental incarceration (The Annie E. Casey Foundation, 2016).

Parents tend to suffer more than non-parents during incarceration; limited child contact and the risk of foster care, among other issues, are particularly upsetting to mothers and fathers (Roxburgh & Fitch, 2014). While maternal distress is a significant problem that calls for gender-specific parenting programs in women's prisons (Arditti & Few, 2008), imprisoned fathers face their own distinct, and equally troubling, challenges to communicating with their children during incarceration and/or after they are released (Bushfield, 2004; Magaletta & Herbst, 2001; Pierce, 2015). Obstacles to father-child communication include but are not limited to the expense of calling home, complicated relationships with the children's caregivers, long distances between prisons and the children's residences, and inherent hurdles of prison visitation processes (Pierce, 2015; Zuckerman & Wright, 2010). As a result, many incarcerated fathers struggle to maintain, if not begin, relationships with their children and to reinforce their parental roles in their children's lives (Loper & Tuerk, 2006). Further, many children are negatively affected by the imprisonment of a father or mother (Martin, 2017; Murphey & Cooper, 2015; Murray et al., 2012; The Annie E. Casey Foundation, 2016).

Offering innovative and gender-specific programs for incarcerated fathers could reduce some of the long-standing obstacles to father-child contact and bonding within the U.S. prison system (Bushfield, 2004; Kjellstrand et al., 2012). Historically, programming for incarcerated fathers has taken the form of traditional parenting classes (Pierce, 2015). Not to minimize these opportunities, but often these classes limit activities to conjectural scenarios, and the participants struggle to apply much of what is learned upon being released (Bushfield, 2004). There is also scant outcome research on parenting programs for incarcerated fathers, particularly those programs applying innovative strategies to facilitate positive father-child communication and promote healthy father-child relationships.

This manuscript helps to address this gap. Following a review of the literature on parenting programs for incarcerated fathers, we report on the first delivery of the Letters to Children (LTC) program with male inmates. The LTC was designed, implemented and initially evaluated with a focus on incarcerated mothers (Sparks, Stauss, & Grant, 2017). Subsequently, the intervention was offered to incarcerated fathers. We used mixed methods to evaluate (1) the effectiveness of the intervention with men and (2) the way that participants perceived the target problems and the intervention. Within the discussion, we use these data to consider the potential need to make gender-responsive modifications in the LTC program.

Review of Literature

While parenting programs are currently available to both fathers and mothers in prison, the number of programs and level of participation vary based upon gender (Crittenden & Koons-Witt, 2017; Glaze & Maruschak, 2010), and the effectiveness of such programs can be questionable without follow-up evaluations (Hoffmann et al., 2010). Bushfield (2004) encouraged more research on incarcerated fathers' particular struggles with parenting issues like "problems related to empathy and child development" that may be "less amenable to change through classes which do not involve a behavioral component" (p. 114). If face-to-face contact between incarcerated fathers and their children is limited by administrative rules or the distance between prison and home, resulting in fewer opportunities for direct parenting (Loper & Tuerk, 2006), and if fathers are less likely to attend traditional parenting programs than mothers (Glaze & Maruschak, 2010), innovative programs that recruit more participants, allow for more active application of parenting principles, and encourage greater awareness of incarcerated fathers' specific needs should be offered within men's prisons.

Pierce (2015) recommended a number of alternative strategies for strengthening the connection between imprisoned parents and their families, including bringing down the high expense of calls and visits; locating prisoners so that they serve time closer to home; enhancing prisoner-family contact by making the visitation room more welcoming; revising strict sentencing policies, especially for nonviolent offenders; and supporting forms of parent-child contact like "letter writing, phone calls, video visits, and other forms of communication" (p. 386). Pierce (2015) also argued strongly for new forms of parenting programs that help inmate fathers stay in contact with their families, especially their children, since traditional parenting classes for fathers can be "limited" in how often they are available and how much they cover. Pierce recommended new parenting instruction for incarcerated fathers that covers "child development, communication, stress management, and discipline," as well as "the stresses of incarceration on the family unit" (p. 386).

The research, therefore, suggests that incarcerated fathers should be provided more comprehensive content within more innovative parenting classes (Pierce, 2015; Zuckerman & Wright, 2010). Such content responds to the importance of reducing conflict and building positive relationships within families in the Risk-Need-Responsivity (R-N-R) model (Andrews & Bonta, 2017). Likewise, prisons and jails have been encouraged to find ways to allow incarcerated fathers more opportunities for face-to-face contact with their children as well as alternative forms of direct contact like phone calls (Loper & Tuerk, 2006; Visher, 2013) and even e-mail (Zuckerman & Wright, 2010). However, if these forms of direct contact are not an option for incarcerated fathers, letter writing could potentially benefit a large number of them (Loper & Tuerk, 2006; Visher, 2013).

Promoting letter writing in men's prisons could help fathers in a number of ways (Loper et al., 2009). Letter writing remains a relatively accessible form of contact for both male and female inmates (Andrews & Dowden, 2007), though there has been some risk of letter writing being restricted in certain correctional facilities (Frost, 2016). In addition, writing has the potential to provide a more active understanding of what it means to be a father than what may be realized by those attending traditional prison parenting classes (Geraci, 2000; Magaletta & Herbst, 2001; Muth et al., 2013).

Further, writing and discussing letters in a group of one's peers has the potential to reinforce positive parenting roles and identities in a uniquely effective way. Group work has been recommended for incarcerated parents in general (Loper & Tuerk, 2006) and incarcerated fathers in particular (Zuckerman & Wright, 2010): "Just as becoming involved with the wrong crowd most likely played a large part in their arrest, inmates must be surrounded by supportive peers to maintain the right path. Housing fathers with other fathers is a programming measure that is mentioned often in the literature" (p. 32). Although not tied to a change in associates, this observation resonates with the R-N-R model's emphasis on increasing noncriminal identities (Andrews & Dowden, 2007) as a way to reduce antisocial cognition. While the writing process may be an individual activity, drafting a document is easily also a collaborative one. Likewise, writing groups for parents in prison allow participants to compose and read their documents–even those addressed to their children–so as to be first heard and commented upon by a sympathetic and often empathetic cohort of other incarcerated parents who can understand the writer's experiences of parent-child separation better than outside facilitators (Boudin, 1998). Discussing a writing workshop for women inmates, Jacobi (2009) argued that this form of group activity can "become an informal space for processing the distance between family members" (p. 53) and "provide space for challenging traditional classroom (and carceral) hierarchies by presenting opportunities for collaborative learning and leadership" (p. 54). While Jacobi (2009) emphasized how the format is uniquely beneficial to women, the structure appears flexible enough to meet, as well, the specific needs of men, especially incarcerated fathers.

Research has already confirmed reduced stress among incarcerated mothers participating in at least one prison letter-writing group (Stauss et al., 2018). More research is needed to measure the range of benefits that can be experienced by fathers when they choose to participate in their own letter-writing groups.

The Letters to Children Program

The Letters to Children (LTC) program was developed approximately three years ago using a feminist model of collaboration, support, and recognition of women's voices and stories (BLINDED). Core components of the intervention include: (1) a focus on participant strengths and self-determination, (2) peer-to-peer support and cooperative feedback within a group facilitated by two trained volunteers, (3) an emphasis on the safe expression of emotions within the group, (4) a focus on healthy parent-child bonding and communication, (5) writing prompts and activities geared toward deep communication, and (6) strategies to help the participants model communicative strategies to increase the likelihood of reciprocity from their children.

Initially, the intervention contained six weekly sessions and was tested with women in a correctional facility (Sparks, Stauss, & Grant, 2017). Although this model appeared to work well with the women, following the first 6-week session provided to men, the facilitators and unit staff suggested that an additional two weeks would allow the men greater time to complete two particularly challenging program letter prompts focusing upon parent-child relationship and reason for incarceration. Since this time, the LTC curriculum been expanded to eight weeks for women and men.

Purpose of the Study

The present study used a mixed methods design to explore the following broad topic: how male inmates responded to the first delivery of a parenting intervention developed for incarcerated mothers. The study had five related objectives. The first two were explored via focus groups and attempted to answer the following research questions: (1) how do incarcerated fathers perceive their relationships and communication with their children; and (2) how do incarcerated fathers perceive the LTC program? The final three objectives were explored using a single-sample, pre-post design. We hypothesized that LTC participants would experience statistically significant (3) decrease in parental stress, (4) increase in self-perceived communication skills, and (5) increase in perceived relationships with the caregivers of their children.

Methods

Setting, Recruitment, and Sample Description

Letters to Children was presented at the REMOVED FOR BLIND REVIEW. This institution currently houses approximately 200 low-risk, nonviolent male offenders. Most of the crimes committed by these men are drug-related offenses and their sentences range between 6 months and 2 years. Representatives of the research team visited the facility on four occasions between October 2017 and October 2018 for recruitment during evening meetings of all inmates. During all but the first outreach visit, research team members were joined by prior LTC participants who shared their experiences in the groups. During these meetings, research team members presented the purpose of the group, requirements of participation, and the voluntary nature of involvement. That is, eligible individuals had the right to participate in the intervention or not. Further, individuals had the right to participate in LTC, but not in the research component. Interested participants were required to sign up with their counselor. Criteria included: their having a child between the ages of three and 18 whom they were not legally barred from contacting and their expecting to remain in the institution for at least the next 12 weeks to allow group completion. At the start of the first group session, a representative of the research team provided participants with the informed consent document, answered any questions, and collected signed copies of the consent documents. All the data collection procedures were approved by the university's IRB and the facility's administration.

Fifty-three men began the intervention and completed the baseline survey. Posttests were completed by 62% of the participants. We have presented the characteristics of the completers and non-completers[1] in Table 1. As can be seen, the groups did not differ at a statistically significant level on any of the background characteristics we assessed. Additionally, we conducted a series of Mann-Whitney U tests to evaluate if the groups differed on pretest values on any of the dependent variables; they did not.

Table 1 Characteristics of full sample

Characteristic	*Completers (n = 33)*	*Non-completers (n = 20)*	*Test of difference*
Age (mean)	33	32	t (51) = -0.74, p = .461
White, non-Hispanic	76%	65%	p = .531 (FET)
Contact with child	79%	60%	p = .209 (FET)
Parent incarcerated	29%	30%	p = 1.00 (FET)

Note. FET = Fisher's Exact Test.

Data Collection and Instrumentation

To enhance the overall rigor of the study, we utilized a mixed methods approach. Through conducting focus groups with rich participant discussions and administering quantitative instruments, we were able to use triangulation of data. All data were collected by members of the research team during visits to the facility. Specifically, data were collected on the following schedule. During the first session, participants completed a survey which included background demographic information and the quantitative pretest. A member of the research team administered the quantitative posttest and facilitated qualitative focus-groups shortly after the final group session.

Qualitative Data

To measure the participants' perceptions of the program, focus groups were completed with all participants still involved at the end of the 8-week sessions. Each focus group lasted approximately 90–120 minutes and was digitally recorded. Semi-structured questions were used to explore the participants' perceptions of (1) communication barriers with their children and (2) the LTC program.

Quantitative Data

During the baseline survey, each participant was asked to self-report their age, racial and ethnic identification, if one of their parents were incarcerated during the participant's childhood, and their level of contact with their children during the current incarceration. For reporting, we created binary variables for (1) parental contact (none or any) and (2) race/ethnicity (White, non-Hispanic or minority).

To assess participant outcomes, we administered a modified version of an established instrument and administered 7 additional items. We discuss each category in turn.

We administered by a modified version of the Parental Stress Index, Short (PSI-4-SF) (Abidin, 1995). The PSI-4-SF is a well-validated and frequently used instrument that contains 36 items. It produces an overall measure as well as three theoretically informed sub-scales: competence, attachment, and depression (a measure of affective disturbance tied to parental stress, not a clinical measure). We modified the instrument by removing items that were not germane to incarcerated parents. Our version contains 16 items, including items from all sub-scales with higher scores indicating higher perceived stress. In the present study, the full scale demonstrated solid internal consistency with Cronbach's alpha values of .83 and .84 on the pre- and posttests, respectively. The reliability of the three sub-scales in the present study were mixed with pre- and posttest Cronbach's alpha values as follows: competence: .77 and .79; attachment: .53 and .48; and depression: .72 and 79.

Six additional items were developed by two members of the research team (Stauss et al., 2018), focusing on communication within the context of parenting and incarceration. They are presented in the Appendix. We used five of these items to form the communication scale based on logical coherence and solid internal consistency. Cronbach's alpha values for this scale on the pre- and posttests were .71 and .84, respectively. We are using one item alone due to its isolated – but important – focus on each inmate's relationships with their children's caregiver. For both measures, higher scores are associated with higher perceived problems regarding communication and relationship with caretakers. Finally, we decided to exclude one item from analysis due to ambiguous wording.

Data Analytic Plan

The focus group recordings were transcribed verbatim by a graduate assistant. Then, each of the three researchers immersed themselves in the data by reading the complete transcripts separately. After this initial analysis, the research team collaborated by discussing the emerging themes each researcher found. This collaboration and discussion are essential in the crystallization process described by Janesick (2000). Crystallization also enhances the credibility of findings by exploring the emerging themes from different perspectives. Qualitative rigor was further increased by using researchers from two different disciplines (social work and English) as well as providing rich descriptions of the themes presented.

Quantitative data analysis was conducted using SPSS, version 24. Prior to conducting tests, missing data analysis and imputation were undertaken. The rate of missing data for the 22 items used in the study was low (0.5% on pretest and 0.2% on posttest items) and the data are assumed to be missing at random. To capitalize on correlations between items within scales as well as those across scales, the three-step approach to item-level imputation developed by Little and Colleagues and described by Enders (2010) was utilized. The expectation-maximization (EM) algorithm was used to impute missing values.

Pre-to-post tests of difference were conducted on the three PSI-4-SF sub-scales, the communication scale, and the single item regarding relationship with children's caregivers. Owing to the non-normal distribution of the data, all tests were conducted using the Wilcoxon Signed Rank test. To measure effect size, *r* was calculated by dividing the test statistics' *z*-scores by the square root of the combined number of observations as suggested by Field (2013, p. 227).

Findings

Qualitative Findings

Several themes emerged through the analysis of the focus group data. We organize them in three clusters. The first two flow directly from the open questions used during the focus groups regarding barriers to parent-child communication and perceptions of the LTC program. The third cluster emerged organically and centers on perceived changes in the fathers, secondary to LTC participation

Cluster 1: Barriers to Father-Child Communication

LTC participants were asked what the main obstacles were to their communicating with their children. Four themes emerged; three are general while the last is focused on incarceration.

Repetition, Empty Promises, Nowhere to Begin

Fathers who had been in communication with their children reported several obstacles to productive dialogue. One father observed that he would say the same things over and over to his eleven-year-old daughter. "[E]very letter I wrote … just seemed like I was just repeating myself." Another problem in prior father-child communication was offering "empty promises" to the child.

Other fathers had difficulty knowing how to begin productive communication with their children. Describing how hard it had been to communicate with his daughter, one participant admitted, "All the way from my daughter being three to now, I've been lost. I didn't know what to do, what to tell her, how to even begin to tell her." Another father advised that he signed up for LTC because he was "dumbfounded on how to approach a 12-year-old girl after 8 years of not being in her life."

Hidden and Negative Emotions

Perhaps an even greater challenge to father-child communication was the suppression or interference of strong emotions. One father described how expressing emotions toward his sons, rather than his daughters, was particularly difficult due to his attempting to model what he considered to be masculine behavior: "I talked to [my sons] like, tough love … to show them that we are men, and we can be kind by not showing too much emotion … ." Another father credited the LTC program with helping him to "open up and access a part of [his] emotion[s] that [he had] never been able to kind of get in touch with."

Negative emotions that dominated positive emotions have also been challenging to some fathers. One member said his motivation for participating in LTC was a desire to get past his guilt for being absent from his daughter's life in hopes of reestablishing communication.

> I was in jail when she was 4 and some things happened to her, and I carry around that guilt and shame for her because I feel like I should have been there to prevent those things … . But, you know, I've come to realize that a lot of problems I have … today [are] because I've never faced my fears of getting in contact with my daughter.

Addressing Child as a Friend

Several participants discussed struggling with relating to their children as a parent as opposed to a friend. "The challenges I felt that I had," said one LTC participant, "was talking to my kid like he was my child instead of a friend, [I would talk to him] like a homeboy you know." Another father said he had "forgot[ten] how to talk to [his children] in a proper manner as a child."

Explaining Incarceration

Another significant challenge that can interfere with incarcerated fathers' attempts to communicate with their children is the topic of why and how the fathers came to be in prison. One LTC father expressed concern over sharing such information with a child due to the child's age: "My youngest she knows that I'm locked up but she don't really know for what or any of that and it's hard to tell a 7-year-old that." Another father, when asked which LTC writing prompt was hardest, responded,

> Like, telling them why I was here, and telling them not to do the same things I've done, but it's hard to tell your child, to elaborate on something when you've made mistakes; how do you tell them that it's not okay to make mistakes because you learn from mistakes? … Like my middle daughter she, she went down the same road I'm going down here.

Cluster 2: Perceptions of Letters to Children

Participants were asked open questions regarding the LTC program. Four themes emerged in this cluster. One focused on program content and three on its structure.

Children-Focused Content

In this facility, the men received ongoing programming, with a focus on the treatment of substance use disorders. Faith-based and 12-step programs were also offered and encouraged. During focus groups, participants unanimously reported that LTC's focus on parent-child communication was an important addition to their rehabilitation. Examples of these comments are included below:

> I've been here almost 9 months and it has been one of the better classes since I have been in here. It deals with something that we all have a problem with besides addiction. I mean, we get addiction classes 3 and 4 hours a day at least every day, and then we get our church or our AA … .but we don't get a parenting class or a class that deals with something that's real to us like our children.
>
> I've taken a lot of classes here but I'm going to have to say that I've got the most out of this because it's connected me with my daughters. I was already connected with them. I was already getting letters but like I said they were the same. This is by far one of the best things that has ever happened to me as far as getting close to my daughters.

Beyond seeing parenting-oriented content as having an independent value, a sub-set of participants saw it as adjunctive to the work they complete with the center's counselors. One participant reflected,

> Because [LTC] focuses on some of the things that not necessarily caused my addiction, but things that led me to the depression and the parts that [I] fed with addiction. So, it kind of got me to release some of those emotions.

Even more directly, this father describes how LTC participation impacted his work in counseling.

> It took me doing this, trying to contact my daughter to realize that it was really hurting me. It was really causing me to … it was just almost subconscious. I would physically stop myself thinking about my little girl. When I started down that path, I would cut it off. I'd stop. Change my thoughts because I didn't want to face it. I never would admit that before I wrote these letters. I told my counselor how much the letters have helped me with counseling.

Writing: Prompts, Process and Parenting

In reflection, the men consistently stated that the structure of LTC supported their attempts to grow closer to their children. They appreciated the general guidelines and the specific prompts for letters each week. The fathers found these topics to be helpful, giving them ideas for how to begin or continue conversing with their children. One father stated,

> The letters have gotten more detailed; it's really helped me… . The prompts are excellent. They actually give you a list of things and there was plenty of things to talk about, not just one or two. I mean there were numerous choices … you could write a 2-page letter.

Another father listed several specific changes he made in his writing style to communicate more effectively with his daughter:

> I have a hard time reading and writing and all that, but instead of just writing a quarter of a page or a couple of paragraphs to her, **I was writing a full-page, page-and-a-half letters to her**, and I was opening–like you were saying–**opening** … **my mind up to more things to talk about**. So like I was, like instead of the first time I said it, **I wasn't repeating over and over and over to express my feelings**. [Instead, I was] **expressing how things are going around here, different things I was into**, and then **I was asking her about her stuff that she was doing and asking her to reply**. And I told her about this thing–the Letters to Children–and she really did reply on that. Actually, she–**I sent one of the, I think it was, one of the little prompts**. I think it was one through six [of the prompts] to her, and I told her, **"Why don't you write a letter about this and then send it back to me?"** She never did, though. [Emphasis added via bold text.]

Note how the failure of the daughter to respond to the request is not the primary focus in the father's comments. Instead, he focused on lessons learned regarding letter writing and his approach to communication more broadly.

Beyond helping fathers who previously struggled with identifying any topic for communication, others discussed a further benefit. That is, they felt that the structure of the prompts and group process helped them avoid inappropriate topics. One father stated:

> When I first started my letters, I was writing to my daughter, but in a way at the same time I was trying to get aggravation out between my ex-wife–saying, like you said, saying negative thoughts that was on my mind to our daughter. But then I think a few [other participants and the facilitator] were like, "Hey, next class we are going to make a goal for you. Let's see [whether you can] come with just a letter [focused upon] you and your daughter." And that first one I wrote, everyone was just like, "Whoa!" Compared to how I was writing from then, it was just like, I kind of shocked myself too because it took me like three days to write, but it really helped, so.

It emerged during the focus groups that these prompts encouraged or reinforced healthy perspectives on parenting and increased the potential for stronger father-child relationships to be realized in the future. One incarcerated father described his process of writing to his children as "like starting new memories with them." Another father explained how, inspired by the actions of an LTC peer, he actually sent the letter prompts to his own children to communicate to them, more directly, what he had been doing in prison and also the extent to which he was trying to become a good father:

> He [an LTC peer] wrote his daughter and he sent the prompt home with them so that they could [see] that he was going to the class. He put in there, he was coming to the class to improve, and he put the prompt in there so they could see what the class told him to write about. So that gave me [the] idea to do the same, to let [my children] know that I'm making an effort, a conscious effort, to try to do better in my communication skills to them. And you know, because I have none right now, and I don't know where to start. Or I didn't know where to start. Now I've got some real good ideas on … how I've got to go about building a relationship back with them–some things that I can talk to them about to, just not what I would have [talked to them about] before.

Finally, participants occasionally drew direct lines between the process of writing and future communication with their children regardless of format. The following passage from a father who never received any communication from his child illustrates this well.

> So what I did was I chronicled my life and journaled like my feelings, thoughts, everything I could remember. I just poured my heart into it so when I finally do get contact with her I'm going to show her this. Maybe it will help explain to her why I wasn't there. Why I did some of the things I've done. I just really wanted to get my thoughts in order for when I talk to her.

Facilitators

Spontaneously, the fathers reflected on how the presence and interventions of the facilitators further strengthened the program. For the three groups involved in the focus groups, the facilitators of the weekly sessions were two females who came with many years of experience as social workers. This seemed to be a strong advantage according to the participants. For instance, one individual stated,

> One of the things that we would be missing is a woman's point of view on how to write our children. I thought that was awesome. I think you should keep the facilitators women when you do it again because we respect a mother/women's point of view so much. It is unreal. We probably got a lot farther in our group with it being women facilitators than men because a lot of the guys who come up here, I can't say for AA, but church groups–I got a lot of respect for them [the men], but it is all one-sided. We are in here with men 24/7 … so having a normal woman tell us how to go about writing normal letters and get off our criminal thinking was a major help.

Along with comments about the facilitators being female, the participants universally commented on how the facilitators were essential to the positive process. Some of the comments include: "She kind of kept the balance;" "If someone would get carried away and get off subject, she would kind of get on to them … 'Hey, let's stay on subject. Let's give everybody a time to share';" and "I don't know anything about them, but I know that they were trustworthy. They were genuine. They cared and a lot of times we went over, and they weren't in no rush to get out of here. They let everybody finish." Lastly, one participant summed up his perception of the facilitators. He reflected,

> Those ladies are great. I don't know where y'all found them but them women, I just got chills. But them women really cared and they made it real easy to sit in here as a grown man, a stranger, and them not know anything about me … and me being able to share anything about my two children with total strangers. I didn't feel the need to hold back … I feel I could have trusted them with any piece of information, and they genuinely cared. I mean, they would tear up when, I mean … they cared.

Peer Support and Bond

Since its inception, co-facilitation with the participants has been a key part of LTC's structure and has been encouraged by the facilitators. The participants, in turn, perceived that the collaboration and feedback they received from the other men was a strength of the program. Two participants shared the following thoughts on this topic.

> It kind of opened each one of us up, you know, for us to sit and listen to him talk, and for us to be able to give him feedback, either good or what was negative about it. It just helped us. I just feel like each of us helped each other, because after we read it, after we would read a letter, we got to sit back and each one of us would say what could have been better. I feel like that was a good part of it.
>
> We started learning from each other and taking constructive criticism. Like him [pointing to a peer], he took his constructive criticism very well and his letters started changing. After two or three letters, his letters got exactly to what the facilitators pointed out to him and what us other men pointed out. His letters got so, well, so beautiful. I mean there was a noticeable change. That in itself helped build my self-confidence to write a better letter seeing that. I was hoping for constructive criticism.

Interestingly, the participants of LTC reported the development of bonds that extended beyond the weekly sessions. One framed it as a "brotherhood of dads." Consistently, the participants perceived that the LTC process enhanced and developed a closeness and safety within their group of incarcerated fathers, and this experience was maintained during the day-to-day prison community life. An example of this can be seen in one participant's comments.

> I noticed one thing in just the group here, not everyone in this facility, but just this group. It kind of opened us up more as a person, more happiness kind of came out to each other. More talkative to each other, you know, coming up to each other. I try to tell them when I see them, like in the morning I'll say something and he will say something back, and it kind of makes me feel good. I'll have someone walk way over on the other side who says 'Hey! What's up?' This group has opened us up.

Another participant advised,

> It brings people together too, being in here with other grown men who might not want to open up and be as talkative, but being in here makes you feel like a family. Especially when you're talking about your kids, everyone here has a care for you. It draws you closer to people. It makes you want to be a better man for your children.

Cluster 3: Perceived Changes in Self

The final cluster centers on participant perceptions of changes following LTC participation. Four themes emerged. As will be explored in the discussion, many of the responses here resonate with barriers discussed in the first cluster and LTC approaches from the second cluster.

Accessing, Expressing, and Controlling Emotions

The first theme in this cluster centers on participants' emotions. Specifically, they discussed increases in their awareness that their emotions can pose barriers to effective communication as well as their ability to overcome such obstacles. "So now because of this program, I have opened my heart," one man said. "I have opened my feelings. I've got a lot of stress off of me." Another LTC participant again brought up the challenge of having anger at the mother distract him from showing love in his efforts to communicate with his child. He explained how the program helped him to go from "talking about paying child support and how she got me in court" to "talking about bubbles with my son, bubbles flying everywhere, a bubble bath, hearing those giggles and stuff." When other fathers were at risk of being overwhelmed by "sadness and depress[ion]," one LTC participant described how the two group facilitators aimed to "keep it positive–to keep [the men] on the right track."

Additionally, one participant analyzed in depth how he consciously manipulated his writing process in order to control his emotional state. By relying heavily on the free-writing opportunities, or "brain dumps," recommended by the facilitators, he was able to sustain his communication efforts–even discuss and receive feedback on his letter drafts in the group–without being stalled, in the writing process, by feelings of sadness:

> [W]hat I do is I go ahead and write it out, what I'm thinking, versus allowing emotion to get in my way if that makes sense. Because I could just start crying thinking about it, you know? I have this absolute assurance that God will [make things okay] and everything will [be] okay and before I start letting myself get upset and stuff, I just start writing down what is in my heart on paper, and then these guys in the group, I have been able to come to them and say, "Hey, what do you think about this?" and not shed a tear at all and then come down here to group and present it, and when I present it in front of everyone and kind of get the emotion and the "ooohhs and ahhs" and "I think you should do this," and that is when the emotion really starts setting in is when I am getting other people's opinions. When I am able to just go to another man and he is able to read it to me and he is like, "That is really good!" And I am just like, "Oh, this is just the rough draft, maybe I should just leave it at that." So not allowing myself to feel my feelings and kind of just–you know y'all did that pre-write at the beginning where we come in and just kind of freestyle and we just kind of write what is on our heart, that is kind of ... the approach I take when I am writing. I don't allow my emotion to get in the way if that makes sense. For me, personally, I could just allow emotions to overwhelm me.

Similarly, rebuilding a damaged relationship–or, for some, building a relationship with a child for the first time–can be a slow process, requiring great patience and respect for the children's emotions, not just the emotions of the fathers. The LTC participants, by the end of the program, seemed well aware of that fact. Looking ahead to being reunited with his son, one father said he would be "taking the small steps, kind of putting one foot in front of the other, and allowing [his son] to see I'm present and allowing him to build trust back in me [...]." Another father sagely observed that it would be unfair to his children for him to seek a quick reunion with them after he had been responsible, through his criminal behavior, for the current separation from them. Note how the father acknowledges the legitimacy of negative feelings from his children if those emotions exist:

> One of the things I've learned about my children is that I do not need to expect them to just jump back into a relationship with me, because I've done this–they wanted me to be around and I chose to do something else and it's my fault, and they probably have some resentment towards me for that.

Forgiveness of Self

Universally, the LTC participants reported shame and guilt around their children and what they believed their children endured because of their absence. These self-perceptions often kept them from reaching out to their family or other supports. According to the LTC participants, the encouragement of the facilitators and other men during the sessions helped them reframe their initial negative view of themselves. One participant stated,

> The [challenge] I faced before this class was being able to forgive myself for what I had done to even begin to start a conversation with my son ... I always tended to ask, "Please forgive me. Please understand." ... The thing that I broke through with writing these letters, was

> learning how to concentrate on the good things, not just concentrating on all the bad. Some of the letters were to write about memories we have had. So instead of concentrating on what times I have missed out on, ... going back to a time when we were happy and focusing on that.

Another participant described how LTC helped him deal with his previous self-hatred. He stated,

> If I wouldn't have taken this class, I would have still had all of them feelings that I never let out. I screwed up so bad I literally hated myself, but I can't do nothing about it. The only thing I can do now is to learn from my mistakes and do something different. Start making better choices.

Even if someone received a negative response from his child or no response at all, the participants were encouraged to stay positive with regard to how they saw themselves and the work they were doing within the LTC sessions. In the following comment you can see the participant's thought process after his letter came back unopened.

> Just trying made me feel so much better about myself. When the first letter came back, I did kind of get in that [negative] thought for a minute. But then I got to thinking about how much better I feel about myself because I'm not just sitting back and crying, pitying myself anymore. I'm actually putting forth the effort, I'm actually coming to this group. For me, I feel better about myself just doing it. It doesn't so much hinge on responses or progress or stuff like that. I'm doing this as much for me now as anything else. I'm amazed at how much it has helped me. I mean, it's crazy really. Even my counselor, I talked to her about this group, and she's, between our first session and our last session, she's seen a lot of growth in me and I think [LTC] has a lot to do with it. I mean, I got over the guilt, and got over the fear. That's amazing to me that I made that much more progress ... even without getting a response.

More Courage (Less Fear)

Many of the participants discussed their fear of contacting their children, due to a fear of rejection or having anger directed at them. As one father explained, "Sometimes people need a little push to have more courage in situations because they are scared or they're fearful of the situation at hand, the reaction they could get. A person doesn't want to be hurt, especially by their child. That's someone that means the world to them." Consistently, the participants reflected that the LTC process gave them the motivation needed to move beyond this fear even though their child's initial response may be anger. The participants perceived they could work through it together, as a group. One father stated,

> I've come to realize that a lot of problems I have today is because I've never faced my fears of getting in contact with my daughter. Even though she didn't write back [and] my letters came back. It still is a huge step forward for me because I'm not afraid of it anymore. You know what I mean. If she says the worst thing ever to me, I can take that as progress because at least she is talking to me.

Another participant described his fear of rejection and how LTC changed his perspective:

> I mean this class has really helped me get the courage to write them and tell them about where I'm at and what's going on because that was my biggest fear. You know, I didn't want them to not like me for what I did. And not being there for them right now.

Improved Identity as a Father

The men participating in LTC frequently discussed submerging or negatively valuing their identities as fathers. Some even felt that society in general did not value their roles as fathers. After participating in the groups, several of the men discussed a reemergence of their father identity and an excitement in reconnecting with that part of their lives. One participant stated,

> Before I didn't think there was any hope of being a father. I couldn't make a marriage work and couldn't make [my] being a parent work. I felt like my life … was over. Through [LTC I am becoming] able to express and talk, knowing that these guys have been through similar situations, and how they have gotten over it, and how we all have to go back out and face this thing. It has helped me deal with overcoming and getting back to what I want—I can still be a father. It's not too late.

After participants began to realize that it was not too late to "be a father," there emerged an excitement in the opportunities and possibilities regarding fatherhood. One participant described his goals clearly by stating,

> This class reminded me that I need to wake the hell up. I got more kids out there. I got more responsibilities; you know what I'm talking about? Be a man to your kids. This class inspired me a whole lot.

Quantitative Findings

As can be seen in Table 2, the participants did not experience a statistically significant change in any of the three PSI-4-SF sub-scales. Additionally, for two of the three sub-scales, the non-significant change was an increase in parental stress.

In contrast, participants reported statistically significant improvements in communication generally and in their relationships with the caregivers of their children. These changes were of small and medium magnitudes respectively based on Cohen's effect size conventions (Cohen, 1988).

Discussion

This mixed method study effectively explored several related objectives regarding the initial delivery to male inmates of a parenting intervention developed for incarcerated mothers. The qualitative component uncovered important themes regarding (1) barriers to parent-child communication, (2) perceptions of the LTC intervention, and (3) perceived self-change due to LTC participation. The quantitative component evaluated hypothesized changes among participants following participation. The first hypothesis that participation would decrease parental stress was rejected. However, participants did experience improvements in perceived communication and relationships with the caregivers of their children as hypothesized. Together, the results offer important insights for the delivery of LTC and similar interventions with incarcerated parents.

Table 2 Pre-to-post tests of difference on outcome variables

Measure	*Items*	*M, pretest (n = 53)*	*M, posttest (n = 33)*	*T*	*p*	*r*
Parental Stress Index						
Competence	6	2.23	2.27	234.00	.975	.04
Attachment	6	2.09	1.94	105.00	.119	.19
Depression	4	2.94	2.96	265.00	.500	.08
Original items						
Communication	5	2.24	2.01	296.50	.032	.26
Relationship with caregiver	1	2.53	2.00	6.50	.003	.37

Note. Although the Wilcoxon Signed Rank test is based on median scores, we are presenting mean values as they are more intuitively interpreted. *M* = mean; *T* = Wilcoxon Signed Rank test statistic

Barriers to Parent-Child Communication

The researchers initially asked the participants to describe their relationships with their children before they received the intervention. For the fathers in this study, the relationships with their children were often inconsistent if they had contact at all. According to the participants, some of this disengagement was a result of an inability to communicate effectively without responding with "empty promises," or the emotions they experienced when thinking about contacting their child were often difficult to overcome. Coming up with added content or developing ideas of what to say was an ongoing problem for these fathers. Similar repetitive content and "empty promises" challenges were described in another study with incarcerated mothers seeking to connect with their children through letters (Stauss et al., 2018). Both sets of participants confirmed that these barriers limited their motivation and ability to connect with their child(ren).

Additionally, fathers reflected that a bigger challenge of reconnecting was getting through their intense emotions or the subsequent suppression of these emotions when it came to initiate that first contact with their child(ren). Consistently, the participants reflected fear of rejection or dealing with their feelings as a barrier to connecting. Interestingly, in Stauss et al. (2018), incarcerated mothers expressed the same emotional turmoil of shame and guilt, but they did not share the need to suppress these emotions. Many of the fathers in this study, however, openly discussed the need or desire to suppress these emotions, perhaps related to the perceived gender norm of hiding their emotions.

Perceptions of the Letters to Children Intervention

Participants identified several strengths of the LTC intervention, many of which resonated with barriers they experienced in communicating with their children. Perhaps the clearest connection concerns the writing prompts. As was seen in the qualitative findings, many participants struggled with how to communicate with their children, falling into common traps such as making unrealistic promises and avoiding challenging topics. Yet, the writing prompts offered the men starting points and structure. They also endorsed the value of facilitators in helping them to take advantage of the prompts.

Moreover, the peer support between men in LTC built upon the above components. As discussed in the findings, the participants were able to open up and share often painful memories, guilt, and shame with their fellow inmates throughout the process. By going through this disclosure and subsequent feedback, the participants became connected on a deeper level, particularly with the men in the group, and they believed the culture within the facility changed–so much so, they began referring to their LTC peers as "the brotherhood of dads." The authors are unsure whether this culture change was maintained, but this change was noted following the end of the group.

Participant Changes Following Participation

In this sub-section we address changes shared by participants during focus groups as well as those measured by the quantitative instruments. We begin with the failure to observe a significant decrease in parental stress among the men. Interestingly, the initial scores for parenting stress were much lower than those observed in our prior research with incarcerated women (BLINDED). Parental stress has been shown in the literature to be particularly salient among women who are more likely than men to have lived with children prior to incarceration (Boudin, 1998; Kazura, 2001). Thus, it is possible that parental stress is less important of a construct with incarcerated fathers or that the approach to measurement should be modified.

Although the intervention did not reduce parental stress with the men as hypothesized, we found other forms of positive change. Qualitative findings showed that because of their participation, fathers were able to begin dealing with their fears and processing through their guilt and shame. Likewise, Jacobi (2009) espoused that writing groups for incarcerated women enable participants a space to work through their emotional struggles and the challenges of incarceration with others who have similar lived experiences.

There was a clear connection between going through the LTC writing process and enhancing communication skills. This is evident in the perceived impacts presented by the participants. For instance, the emotions the fathers often withheld became an obstacle to communication. The writing process allowed them to tap into those feelings of anger and sadness, subsequently giving them greater control and awareness. There was also an apparent relationship between the process of writing and revising the letters, and discussing that process with others, and an increased level of consciousness in one's parenting. By becoming more aware of what they were doing in their writing and why, the fathers appeared to become more aware, in general, of the strategies they could use to communicate differently with their children. Some of the changes in strategies included: 1) engaging the children by asking them questions about themselves; 2) focusing on the children's needs, instead of appealing to or targeting the caregiver through these conversations; and 3) reflecting on positive memories and future activities. These qualitative findings were reflected in the quantitative findings as well.

For the fathers who participated, significant change was seen in general communication and the overall relationship with the caregiver. Enhanced parent-child communication is important to note because prior studies found that children are negatively affected by this disconnect (Martin, 2017; The Annie E. Casey Foundation, 2016). Literature points to the fact that children of incarcerated fathers often reside with the mother and that this often complicates that relationship (Turney, 2014). Consistent with the importance of family relationships in the R-N-R model (Andrews & Bonta, 2017), previous studies have also reported that a complex relationship with the child's caregiver results in challenges for incarcerated fathers maintaining a positive parent-child communication (Pierce, 2015; Zuckerman & Wright, 2010).

The participants consistently agreed that society often downplayed their roles as fathers; therefore, they struggled to project their own worth to their children, particularly since they were incarcerated. Arditti et al. (2005) relayed that how a father defines himself is often influenced by what he can or cannot do for his child. Subsequently, redefining these roles and addressing this stigma while in prison will help the incarcerated father with his relationship with his child (Geller, 2013). Along with changes in self-identity, the participants reflected they were excited about their future as "fathers." This reframe opened new possibilities for them and the importance of increasing their level of involvement. It would also seem to have the potential to offer a pro-social identity as a buffer against criminal cognition. Those who were in contact with their children were hopeful about starting new memories with them. The fathers who were not currently in contact with their children saw the letters they wrote as evidence of their dedication to "fatherhood," and a chance to reconnect later. In the meantime, they could focus on their emotions around this disconnect. Consistently, the participants perceived these hidden or unconscious feelings as often a precursor to their addiction or substance-abusing lifestyle.

Study Limitations

Although these results are promising, there are important limitations to consider. Generalizability of the findings is limited by the voluntary nature of participation, the relative lack of racial and ethnic diversity, and the low-risk and treatment-oriented nature of the study setting. Additional limits include the inability to control for pre-incarceration level of contact, the lack of a comparison group and reliance on only the perceptions of the fathers as opposed to their children and caregivers.

Implications

Despite these important limitations, the present study offers implications for practice and future research. Methodologically, it will be important to test the LTC intervention with samples that are more diverse, include higher-risk offenders, and drawn from multiple institutions. Additionally, the introduction of a comparison group and random assignment would allow for the testing of causality.

Considering the lack of significant change regarding parental stress and qualitative themes in which participants emphasized changes in their identities as fathers and their emotional responses, future research should incorporate broader and more gender-responsive intermediate outcomes and examine their ability to affect criminological metrics. For example, increases in a positive social identity have been shown to increase cooperation with laws and legal authorities (Murphy et al., 2016; Tyler & Huo, 2002). Drawing on different psychological mechanisms, relationships have been found between emotional intelligence and recidivism (Stephens & Nel, 2014; Willis, 2019). Taken together, future research on the LTC and similar interventions would do well to measure social identity focused on parenthood and emotional intelligence to explore if LTC participation can affect those constructs and, subsequently, decrease institutional discipline and recidivism.

Fathers who have been incarcerated and have strong relationships with their children tend to have higher rates of success in the areas of employment, substance use, and criminal behavior (Maley, 2014; Petersilia, 2003; Visher et al., 2010). Therefore, encouraging these relationships during incarceration will result in more successful outcomes. Secondly, a study conducted by the U.S. Department of Health and Human Services (2016) found that incarcerated fathers with higher frequency of contact with their children by means of letters, telephone calls, and visits were more likely to live with their children following incarceration, and for those fathers who do not live with their children, they were more likely to actively spend time with their children than those fathers with low frequency of contact. Thus, a program like Letters to Children, which helps parents strengthen and rebuild relationships with their children, has promising possibilities. Viewed from the R-N-R perspective (Andrews & Bonta, 2017), the intervention directly targets one of the central eight criminogenic risk factors (family/marital) and has the ability to support change in another (antisocial cognition) through increasing a prosocial and non-criminal social identity: parent.

Programmatically, the intervention is inexpensive and has been effectively implemented in four different correctional facilities (although not yet published, it has been administered in state prison units for men and women). The strong and positive responses participants in the present study gave regarding the outside facilitators as well as peer-to-peer based support in the present study suggest possible modifications based on institutional resources and realities and may introduce further avenues for research.

Conclusion

Taken together, this mixed methods study suggests LTC's potential effectiveness in meeting the needs of incarcerated fathers. It provides an example of a low-cost and short-term model that can be incorporated into correctional institutions to help incarcerated fathers reconnect with their children. Our participants clearly noted the need for content focused on their children. The results also confirm that parenting programs should incorporate a strong emphasis upon peer support, as well as facilitator-participant collaboration, that provides a safe space for incarcerated participants to reflect and begin to get in touch with their emotions around their disconnection from their children. As many stated, they often worked very hard to protect themselves from these negative, sad feelings. Encouraging the reemerging of these emotions may allow them to see the importance of their roles as fathers, something that our society in general has minimized.

Disclosure Statement

No potential conflict of interest was reported by the authors.

Discussion Questions

1. How/where did the researchers get all their questions for the quantitative aspect of the study?
2. How did the eligibility rules for who could participate in the program potentially impact the results?
3. In what ways did the program seem to help the participants? In what ways did it seem to not have any impact?

Note

1. Although we refer to the 20 individuals who did not complete the posttest as non-completers, this is not entirely accurate. Some of these individuals completed the intervention but failed to return to a follow-up session during which the posttests were administered. Of those who did not complete the program, some withdrew while still incarcerated and others were actively participating at the time of their release to the community. Unfortunately, we are unable to distinguish between these groups. For the purposes of the evaluation, we treat them as a group.

References

Note: Two sources have been removed to facilitate blind review.

Abidin, R. R. (1995). *Parenting stress index professional manual* (3rd ed.). Psychological Assessment Resources, Inc.

Andrews, D. A., & Bonta, J. (2017). *The psychology of criminal conduct* (6th ed.). Routledge.

Andrews, D. A., & Dowden, C. (2007). The risk-need-responsivity model of assessment and human service in prevention and corrections: Crime-prevention jurisprudence. *Canadian Journal of Criminology and Criminal Justice, 49*(4), 439–464. https://doi.org/10.3138/cjccj.49.4.439

Arditti, J., & Few, A. (2008). Maternal distress and women's reentry into family and community life. *Family Process, 47*(3), 303–321. https://doi.org/10.1111/j.1545-5300.2008.00255.x

Arditti, J., Smock, S., & Parkman, T. (2005). "It's been hard to be a father.": A qualitative exploration of incarcerated fatherhood. *Fathering: A Journal of Theory, Research, and Practice about Men as Fathers, 3*(3), 267–288. https://psycnet.apa.org/doi/10.3149/fth.0303.267

Boudin, K. (1998). Lessons from a mother's program in prison: A psychosocial approach supports women and their children. *Women & Therapy, 21*(1), 103–125. https://doi.org/10.1300/J015v21n01_01

Bushfield, S. (2004). Fathers in prison: Impact of parenting education. *Journal of Correctional Education, 55*(2), 104–116. www.jstor.org/stable/23292156

Carson, A. (2018). *Prisoners in 2018 (NCJ 253516)*. Bureau of Justice Statistics, U.S. Department of Justice. www.bjs.gov/content/pub/pdf/p18.pdf

Cohen, J. (1988). *Statistical power analysis for the behavioral sciences* (2nd ed.). Lawrence Erlbaum Associates.

Crittenden, C. A., & Koons-Witt, B. A. (2017). Gender and programming: A comparison of program availability and participation in U.S. prisons. *International Journal of Offender Therapy and Comparative Criminology, 61*(6), 611–644. https://doi.org/10.1177/0306624X15601432.

Enders, C. K. (2010). *Applied missing data analysis*. Guilford Press.

Field, A. (2013). *Discovering statistics using IBM SPSS Statistics* (4th ed.). Sage.

Frost, C. (2016). *Protecting written family communication in jails: A 50-state survey*. Prison Policy Initiative. www.prisonpolicy.org/postcards/50states.html

Geller, A. (2013). Parental incarceration and father-child contact in fragile families. *Journal of Marriage and Family, 75*(5), 1288–1303. https://doi.org/10.1111/jomf.12056

Geraci, P. M. (2000). Reaching out the write way. *Journal of Adolescent & Adult Literacy, 43*(7), 632–634.

Glaze, L. E., & Maruschak, L. M. (2010). *Parents in prison and their minor children (NCJ 222984)*. Bureau of Justice Statistics, U.S. Department of Justice. www.bjs.gov/content/pub/pdf/pptmc.pdf

Hoffmann, H. C., Byrd, A. L., & Kightlinger, A. M. (2010). Prison programs and services for incarcerated parents and their underage children: Results from a national survey of correctional facilities. *The Prison Journal, 90*(4), 397–416. https://doi.org/10.1177/0032885510382087

Jacobi, T. (2009). Writing workshops as alternative literacy education for incarcerated women. *Corrections Today, 71*, 52–53, 55, 57.

Janesick, V. (2000). The choreography of qualitative research design. In N. A. Denzin & Y. S. Lincoln (Eds.), *Handbook of Qualitative Research* (2nd ed., pp. 379–399. Sage.

Kazura, K. (2001). Family programming for incarcerated parents: A needs assessment among inmates. *Journal of Offender Rehabilitation, 32*(4), 67–83. https://doi.org/10.1300/J076v32n04_05

Kjellstrand, J. M., Cearley, J., Eddy, J. M., Foney, D., & Martinez, C. R. (2012). Characteristics of incarcerated fathers and mothers: Implications for preventive interventions targeting children and families. *Children and Youth Services Review*, *34*(12), 2409–2415. https://doi.org/10.1016/j.childyouth.2012.08.008.

Loper, A. B., Carlson, L. W., Levitt, L., & Scheffel, K. (2009). Parenting stress, alliance, child contact, and adjustment of imprisoned mothers and fathers. *Journal of Offender Rehabilitation*, *48*(6), 483–503. https://doi.org/10.1080/10509670903081300

Loper, A. B., & Tuerk, E. H. (2006). Parenting programs for incarcerated parents: Current research and future directions. *Criminal Justice Policy Review*, *17*(4), 407–427.

Magaletta, P. R., & Herbst, D. P. (2001). Fathering from prison: Common struggles and successful solutions. *Psychotherapy: Theory, Research, Practice, Training*, *38*(1), 88–96. https://doi.org/10.1037/0033-3204.38.1.88

Maley, L. A. (2014). *The fatherhood factor: The impact of the father-child relationship on the social, interpersonal, and recidivism risk factors of previously incarcerated men (Publication No. 3620328)*. [Doctoral dissertation, Seaton Hall University]. ProQuest Dissertations and Theses Global.

Martin, E. (2017, May). Hidden consequences: The impact of incarceration on dependent children. *NIJ Journal*, *278*, 1–7. www.ncjrs.gov/pdffiles1/nij/250349.pdf

Murphey, D., & Cooper, P. M. (2015). *Parents behind bars. What happens to their children?* Child Trends. www.childtrends.org/publications/parents-behind-bars-what-happens-to-their-children

Murphy, K., Bradford, B., & Jackson, J. (2016). Motivating compliance behavior among offenders: Procedural justice or deterrence? *Criminal Justice and Behavior*, *43*(1), 102–118. https://doi.org/10.1177/0093854815611166

Murray, J., Farrington, D. P., & Sekol, I. (2012). Children's antisocial behavior, mental health, drug use, and educational performance after parental incarceration: A systematic review and meta-analysis. *Psychological Bulletin*, *138*(2), 175. https://doi.org/10.1037/a0026407

Muth, W., Walker, G., & F. A., M. (2013). Looking up: The temporal horizons of a father in prison. *Fathering*, *11*(3), 292–305. https://doi.org/10.3149/fth.1103.292

Petersilia, J. (2003). *When prisoners come home: Parole and prisoner reentry*. Oxford University Press.

Pierce, M. B. (2015). Male inmate perceptions of the visitation experience: Suggestions on how prisons can promote inmate-family relationships. *The Prison Journal*, *95*(3), 370–386. https://doi.org/10.1177/0032885515587471

Roxburgh, S., & Fitch, C. (2014). Parental status, child contact, and well-being among incarcerated men and women. *Journal of Family Issues*, *35*(10), 1394–1412. https://doi.org/10.1177/0192513X13498593

Stephens, O. A., & Nel, N. M. (2014). Recidivism and emotional intelligence of male recidivists in Lagos State, Nigeria. *Journal of Psychology*, *5*(2), 115–124.

The Annie E. Casey Foundation. (2016, April). *A shared sentence: The devastating toll of parental incarceration on kids, families and communities*. www.aecf.org/m/resourcedoc/aecf-asharedsentence-2016.pdf

Turney, K. (2014). Stress proliferation across generations? Examining the relationship between parental incarceration and childhood health. *Journal of Health and Social Behavior*, *55*(3), 302–319. https://doi.org/10.1177/0022146514544173

Tyler, T. R., & Huo, Y. J. (2002). *Trust in the law: Encouraging public cooperation with the police and courts*. Russell Sage Foundation.

U.S. Department of Health and Human Services. (2016). *Multi-site family study on incarceration, parenting, and partnering: Program impacts technical report*. Office of Planning, Research and Evaluation, Administration for Children and Families, U.S. Department of Health and Human Services. https://aspe.hhs.gov/system/files/pdf/257881/MFSIPImpactReport.pdf

Visher, C., Yahner, J., & La Vigne, N. (2010, May). *Life after prison: Tracking the experiences of male prisoners returning to Chicago, Cleveland, and Houston*. Urban Institute, Justice Policy Center. www.urban.org/sites/default/files/publication/28671/412100-Life-after-Prison-Tracking-the-Experiences-of-Male-Prisoners-Returning-to-Chicago-Cleveland-and-Houston.PDF

Visher, C. A. (2013). Incarcerated fathers: Pathways from prison to home. *Criminal Justice Policy Review*, *24*(1), 9. https://doi.org/10.1177/0887403411418105

Willis, J. (2019). *The relationship between emotional intelligence and recidivism among female offenders*. (Publication No. 13428576) [Doctoral dissertation, Northcentral University]. ProQuest Dissertations and Theses Global.

World Prison Brief. (2020). *Highest to lowest: Prison population rate*. Institute for Crime & Justice Policy Research, July 28, 2020. www.prisonstudies.org/highest-to-lowest/prison_population_rate?field_region_taxonomy_tid=All

Zuckerman, S., & Wright, D. (2010). Learning how to father effectively through jail programming. *American Jails*, *24*(3), 26–29, 31–33. https://search.proquest.com/docview/742498680?accountid=8361

5 Measuring Crime

The UCR, NIBRS, and NCVS

There are numerous data collection initiatives that provide us with valuable information about crime, victimization, criminal case processing, and the corrections system. It is not possible to review all of them in this book, although I do touch on a few in later chapters. For now, I want to cover some of the largest and most commonly used measures of crime in the United States: The Uniform Crime Report (UCR) Program, the National Incident-Based Reporting System (NIBRS), and the National Crime Victimization Survey (NCVS).

Uniform Crime Report and Police-Generated Crime Data

The FBI started the **Uniform Crime Report (UCR)** Program in 1930 as an effort to collect aggregate statistics for crime reported to the police. Aggregate, or summary-based statistics, provide us with the number of each type of crime that occurred in a geographic area but no details about each individual offense. Over 18,000 federal, state, county, city, tribal, and college/university law enforcement agencies provided yearly data for this voluntary reporting program until it was retired in 2021. While not every agency in the United States participated, most did. In 2010, agencies with jurisdiction over 300 million people in the United States contributed to the UCR, covering over 97% of the nation's population (Federal Bureau of Investigation, 2010a). States had to demonstrate that their reporting programs complied with the UCR program standards and that they maintained quality control procedures before they were permitted to participate (Federal Bureau of Investigation, 2010b). The UCR was divided into two types of crimes—Part I and Part II. Part I crimes were called index offenses and originally consisted of serious crimes such as criminal homicide (including murder and nonnegligent manslaughter), robbery, aggravated assault, burglary, larceny, motor vehicle theft, and arson. In later years, UCR added human trafficking/involuntary servitude, and human trafficking/commercial sex acts to the list of Part I crimes (Federal Bureau of Investigation, 2019a; Wormeli, 2022). Participating agencies sent data on the number of Part I offenses known to the police in their jurisdictions to the UCR each month, along with the number of those crimes cleared by arrest or other means. For Part II offenses, jurisdictions only shared data for crimes that ended in arrests (Federal Bureau of Investigation, 2019a). A full list of Part I and Part II offenses is shown in Figure 5.1.

The UCR produced two sets of statistics—raw numbers of crimes and crime rates. These two statistics tend to be what are used in the media in stories about crime trends. The raw numbers of Part I crimes, for example, told us how many of each type of crime was reported to the police in a particular area, such as the entire nation, state, county, city, tribal territory, or college or university. The crime rate differs from raw numbers in that rates take into account the size of the population for that jurisdiction. This goes a long way in helping us understand crime in different areas. It is difficult to compare crime in cities and states with different populations. By calculating rates, we can make the numbers much more comparable across both jurisdictions and time.

Table 5.1 shows violent crime and homicide data from 2024 for several cities of different sizes and in different regions of the United States. These numbers actually come from the UCR's

DOI: 10.4324/9781003661511-5

Part I	*Part II*
Criminal homicide	Other assaults (simple)
Forcible rape	Forgery and counterfeiting
Robbery	Fraud
Aggravated assault	Embezzlement
Burglary	Stolen property
Larceny	Vandalism
Motor vehicle theft	Weapons
Arson	Prostitution and commercialized vice
Human trafficking/commercial sex acts	Sex offenses (except forcible rape, prostitution, and commercialized vice)
Human trafficking/involuntary servitude	Drug abuse violations
	Gambling
	Offense against the family children
	Driving under the influence
	Liquor laws
	Drunkenness
	Disorderly conduct
	Vagrancy
	All other offenses (except traffic violations)
	Suspicion—arrested for no specific offense and release without formal charges
	Curfew and loitering laws (persons under 18)

Figure 5.1 UCR Part I and Part II offenses

Source: Federal Bureau of Investigation (2019a). *Crime in the United States Offense Definitions*. United States Department of Justice, Federal Bureau of Investigation

Table 5.1 2024 crime data for multiple US cities

	Population	*Violent crimes*	*Violent crime rate*	*Murder and nonnegligent manslaughter*	*Murder and nonnegligent manslaughter rate*
Little Rock, AK	204,247	3,415	1,672	36	18
San Francisco, CA	802,856	4,789	596	35	4
Chicago, IL	2,638,698	14,245	540	461	17
New York, NY	8,299,271	55,690	671	325	4
Portland, OR	623,066	4,487	720	67	11
Dallas, TX	1,321,502	8,698	658	180	14
Houston, TX	2,319,160	26,628	1,148	320	14

Source: Federal Bureau of Investigation (2025)

Table 5.2 Comparison of 2018 and 2023 crime data for Detroit, Michigan

	Population	*Violent crimes*	*Violent crime rate*	*Murder and nonnegligent manslaughter*	*Murder and nonnegligent manslaughter rate*
2018	671,275	13,478	2,007.82	261	38.88
2023	615,501	12,631	2,052.15	250	40.62

Source: Federal Bureau of Investigation (2019b, 2024)

successor, NIBRS, which we will discuss shortly. For now, our focus is on understanding the difference between raw crime statistics and crime rates. These cities vary in population from New York's more than eight million residents to just 200,000 in Little Rock. If we only look at the raw crime statistics, we would believe that New York is the most dangerous in terms of violent crimes, since it has twice the number of violent crimes (55,690) compared to the next city, Houston (26,628). For murders and nonnegligent manslaughter, Chicago's raw crime statistics are the worst, with 461, and New York comes in second with 325. The crime rates, however, tell us a very different, but much more accurate, story. New York has one of the lowest crime rates among the selected cities (671 per 100,000 residents). Compare that to Little Rock's 1,672 per 100,000 and Houston's 1,148 per 100,000. For homicides and nonnegligent manslaughter, Little Rock has the worst homicide rate of the cities (18 per 100,000 residents), with Chicago slightly behind at 17 per 100,000. New York and San Francisco are tied for the lowest homicide rates among the seven cities (4 per 100,000) (Federal Bureau of Investigation, 2025).

Calculating rates can also help us understand how crime changes over time, because it accounts for any changes in population statistics. Detroit, Michigan, is a good example good to use when considering the differences between raw crime statistics and crime rates, because the city recently experienced a substantial population change. When looking at the years 2018 and 2023, Detroit had about 850 fewer violent crimes and 11 fewer homicides. Initially, that appears encouraging. Unfortunately, during this same time, Detroit lost about 8 percent of its population. While the raw numbers for violent crime show a 6 percent decrease, once we take the population change into account, the violent crime rate increased 2 percent from 2,007 per 100,000 people in 2018 to 2,052 per 100,000 in 2023. Fewer murders and nonnegligent manslaughter incidents occurred in 2023 than in 2018, but once we account for the drop in the number of people living in Detroit, the murder and nonnegligent manslaughter rate increased slightly from 38.88 per 100,000 people in 2018 to 40.62 per 100,000 people in 2023 (Federal Bureau of Investigation, 2019b, 2024). Raw crime statistics really give us an incomplete story, which is why it is important to rely on crime rates instead.

In addition to data on Part I and Part II offenses, the UCR also collected data on the age, sex, and race of people arrested; law enforcement officers killed or assaulted; and on estimates of reported hate crimes (Federal Bureau of Investigation, 2011). The UCR also included the *Supplemental Homicide Report*, which provided detailed information about murders and nonnegligent manslaughters as well as the victims and perpetrators involved in those crimes.

While the UCR served an important purpose for almost 100 years, it had a number of drawbacks as a measure of crime. As a summary-based report, the UCR only presented data aggregated by jurisdiction. We could obtain data about crime rates in our own cities, but we could not then disaggregate the data to focus on more specific locations, such as neighborhoods, streets, or census tracts. With the exception of homicides, the UCR lacked detailed data about each crime incident. Additionally, the UCR required jurisdictions to use the hierarchy rule when recording offenses.

The rule "requires that when more than one Part I offense is classified, the law enforcement agency must locate the offense that is highest on the hierarchy list and score that offense involved and not the other offense(s) in the multiple-offense situation" (Federal Bureau of Investigation, 2004, p. 10). The result of the hierarchy rule was an undercounting of crimes known to the police. Imagine a scenario where someone robs a convenience store, murders the clerk, carjacks someone outside, and then eludes the police and resists arrest. Only the murder of the clerk would make its way into the UCR. The exception to the hierarchy rule was incidents that involved multiple crimes including arson. In that case, arson plus the other most serious offense were both counted (Federal Bureau of Investigation, 2004). The UCR also did not include some important categories of offenses, such as white-collar or financial crimes or any computer-based offenses, so the UCR was not aging well.

Additional weaknesses of the UCR stemmed from the use of police records. Using police-generated data to measure "**victimless crimes**," such as drug dealing, drug use, sex work, and gambling, is problematic. Think about how crimes come to the attention of police. The police will occasionally observe crime themselves or even participate in undercover operations to try to catch people, but most crime comes to the attention of police through victims and witnesses calling the police for help. For offenses where both parties are willing participants, it is very unlikely that either will call the police, so these "victimless crimes" are likely to go underreported whenever police data are the source of information. Whether police-generated data have lots of these crimes in their system is more a representation of the departments' enforcement priorities than actual levels of these crimes. If the police decide to prioritize drug dealing, there will be a lot of drug busts and the appearance that drug dealing is a significant problem in that jurisdiction. If they choose not to target drug dealing, the police-reported crime statistics for these types of offenses will be low.

Even when we consider crimes where there are clear victims, there is no certainty that people will report them to the police. Several steps must take place for a crime to wind up in the UCR. An individual must notice that something happened and interpret that incident to be a crime. I might notice my wallet is missing, but I could assume that I was careless and lost it when, in fact, it was stolen. Assuming that I recognize that a crime was committed, I must decide whether it is worthwhile to contact the police. There are a number of reasons why people would be hesitant or unwilling to do so. One possibility is that people might not think that the harm was worth police involvement, or they may think that calling the police is a waste of time since the individual is unlikely to be caught. Regarding the example of my wallet, if I do think it was stolen, I still might not report it if I have no idea who might have taken it. If I do know who took it, I might not call if I suspect it was a friend or relative, as I might hesitate to get that person in trouble. Other reasons for not calling the police are distrust of law enforcement, fear of reprisals for "snitching," and the need to keep one's own criminal involvement secret. Additionally, marginalized populations who have historically experienced poor treatment at the hands of police, such as racial minorities, LGBT individuals, and undocumented immigrants, might fear interacting with the police (Langton, Planty, & Lynch, 2017). If I do call the police, the dispatcher will interpret what happened, based on my description, and give it a code. After that, the police will determine whether there is evidence of a crime and decide whether to file a report. Based on what I just described, you can see how lots of incidents will not be recorded and, therefore, never make it into data based on police reports, such as the UCR or its successor, NIBRS. This is why police-based reporting systems must always be viewed with caution, as reports to the police miss what is called the **dark figure of crime**, or crimes not known to the police.

Crimes that tend to have the fewest problems with civilian non-reporting are homicides and motor vehicle theft. The reasons for this are simple. Homicide is the most serious offense, and with offense seriousness comes less discretion exercised among individuals about whether to call the police, and among police regarding whether to write a report. Not only that, as I always tell my students, if there is a dead body lying around, we are all going to be motivated to call someone about it. For motor vehicle thefts, auto insurance companies require a police report in order for anyone to file a claim, making it much more likely that people will file a police report.

One final problem with using police data as a measure of crime is that those statistics are subject to manipulation. There are members of police departments whose jobs or promotions depend on being able to produce good numbers and demonstrate that they are effective at reducing crime. Police who are also attempting to convince the mayor or governor's office to provide them with more funding might even be tempted to artificially inflate crime statistics to make it seem as though crime is worse than it actually is. In 2009, an officer with the New York City Police Department revealed that his fellow officers were purposefully downgrading felonies, neglecting to fill out reports, and even discouraging victims from filing complaints to give the appearance that crime was decreasing in their jurisdiction (Francescani, 2012). Rape statistics are particularly susceptible to manipulation, and police departments in St. Louis, Philadelphia, New Orleans, and Baltimore, were found to have manipulated rape statistics to make it appear as though crime was dropping or that the police were doing an exceptional job of solving crimes (Yung, 2014). Throughout the 1990s, the St. Paul (Minnesota) Police Department claimed to have a 90 to 100 percent clearance rate for rape cases. By 1999, they were claiming to have "cleared" 108% of the city's rapes, which is obviously impossible (Fazlollah, 2001).

The Philadelphia Police Department submitted highly inaccurate crime statistics to the UCR during the 1990s, and these figures were only corrected after a new police commissioner ordered a thorough audit of crime reporting. Commissioner John Timoney was immediately suspicious of Philadelphia's statistics, as they appeared to be too low for such a large city. Upon investigation, it became evident that the police had been doing what they called "going down with crime." For example, following an incident when a woman with a knife chased an elderly man into his apartment bathroom and stole items from his house, this crime, initially written up as a robbery, was later reclassified as a disturbance. This is important, as robbery was a UCR Part I offense that would have required UCR reporting, so this downgrade essentially made the crime disappear from Philadelphia's major crime statistics. Police also routinely wrote up burglaries as "lost property" and rapes as "investigate persons," meaning that neither of these types of crimes were making it to the UCR. Several other offenses were downgraded from Part I to Part II (Fazlollah, Matza, & McCoy, 1998).

Commanders of individual precincts and even police chiefs can feel pressure to lower crime rates and be tempted to help their officers, and their own careers, by tampering with statistics. At other times, they may be motivated to make it appear as if crime is increasing so that they can secure more funding. Unfortunately, the public is often at the mercy of those collecting the data, and we have to rely on them to be honest. Luckily, there are people like the commissioner who questioned the Philadelphia statistics, and members of the media who monitor irregularities and expose them when they do occur. Even statisticians and non-law enforcement crime experts can be of assistance. Jan Chaiken, then-director of the Bureau of Justice Statistics, noted that he and others who reviewed the Philadelphia crime data from the 1990s were suspicious partially because of one major irregularity. As I mentioned earlier, homicide data are generally reliable, because those numbers are too difficult to manipulate. Cities typically report 50 aggravated assaults for every single homicide, yet Philadelphia was reporting only about 15 aggravated assaults for every homicide, and that made some crime experts suspicious that the department was downgrading their aggravated assaults to less serious offenses (Fazlollah et al., 1998).

National Incident-Based Reporting System

The **National Incident-Based Reporting Program (NIBRS**, pronounced NIBERS**),** introduced by the FBI in the mid-1980s, is a more comprehensive reporting system and expands on the country's crime data collection efforts. After decades of rolling out the new system, the FBI finally transitioned from the UCR to NIBRS in January 2021. Progress was slow because of what a substantial undertaking NIBRS is compared to the UCR. Like the UCR, NIBRS is a measure of crimes known to the police. As of 2014, 44% of the country's 17,429 agencies were providing NIBRS data to the FBI (Federal Bureau of Investigation, 2020). By May 2024, all 50 states and the District of Columbia were certified to report their crime data to NIBRS, and the NIBRS-certified law enforcement agencies covered 82% of the US population. The large police departments nationwide have made significant progress. By May 2024, 125 of the 154 departments in cities and counties with populations of at least 250,000 were reporting to NIBRS (United States Bureau of Justice Statistics, 2024). These numbers are expected to continue to improve in the coming years.

Unlike the UCR, NIBRS is an incident-based reporting system. As a summary measure, the UCR required departments to provide numbers of how many crimes occurred each month. The only crimes that were treated as incident-based in the UCR were murder and nonnegligent manslaughter, since those data also appeared in the UCR's *Supplemental Homicide Report*. For homicides, agencies reported not only how many murders and nonnegligent manslaughters they responded to each month but also victim and offender demographics, murder weapon, victim-offender relationship, and other circumstances surrounding the crime (e.g., gang-related, robbery, argument, etc.) (United States Bureau of Justice Statistics, 2014). For all other offenses, the UCR served as a simple count of crimes reported for Part I offenses and arrests for Part II offenses.

Not only does NIBRS require more details about each crime, but it also includes more crimes than the UCR. Instead of Part I and Part II offenses, NIBRS has Groups A and B. Group A consists of 52 specific crimes lumped into 24 crime categories (see Figure 5.2). Law enforcement agencies

Group A offenses		*Group B offenses*	
Animal cruelty	Homicide offenses		
Arson	Human trafficking offenses	Bad checks	Family offenses, nonviolent
Assaults (aggravated, simple, intimidation)	Kidnapping/abduction	Curfew/loitering/vagrancy	Liquor law violations
Bribery	Larceny/theft offenses	Disorderly conduct	Peeping Tom
Burglary/breaking & entering	Motor vehicle theft	Driving under the influence	Trespass of real property
Counterfeiting/forgery	Pornography/Obscene material	Drunkenness	All other offenses
Destruction/damage/vandalism of property	Prostitution offenses		
Drug/narcotic offenses	Robbery		
Embezzlement	Sex offenses, forcible		
Extortion/blackmail	Sex offenses, nonforcible		
Fraud offenses (including identity theft and hacking)	Stolen property offenses		
Gambling	Weapons law violations		

Figure 5.2 NIBRS offenses

Source: Federal Bureau of Investigation (n.d.). *NIBRS Quick Facts*. Washington, DC: United States Department of Justice, Federal Bureau of Investigation are required to provide information about all these crimes that are reported to the police. Group B includes 10 offense categories that are only reported to NIBRS if an arrest is made. NIBRS also classifies offenses by their type of harm, specifically to society, to other persons, or to property. Crimes against society are what are typically thought of as "victimless" crimes, such as drug offenses, gambling, and sex work. For each crime, NIBRS collects information about several characteristics of the crime, each of which is referred to as a data element. There are currently 58 different data elements contained in six data segments: administrative, offense, victim, property, offender, and arrest report that need to be collected for each reported crime (Federal Bureau of Investigation, n.d.). Since there are both a wider range of offenses and more detailed data collection requirements for NIBRS compared to the UCR, it is easy to see how much more work needs to be put into NIBRS reporting.

Since NIBRS is incident-based, it does not use the hierarchy rule. This means that up to 10 offense types can be recorded within one incident. Regarding the example of a convenience store robbery that turned into a murder, followed by a carjacking, eluding the police, and then resisting arrest, all these crimes would be eligible to be counted by NIBRS, unlike with the UCR. Additionally, the NIBRS definitions tend to be more encompassing, so intimidation is now recorded under assaults, and specific forcible and non-forcible sex offenses are included, instead of just rape as in the UCR. NIBRS also makes the distinction between attempted and completed crimes. Victimless crimes, or crimes against society, are included in Group A for NIBRS, meaning that all police reports of those crimes appear in NIBRS reports, whereas they were Part II UCR crimes and would only be reported in the event of an arrest. NIBRS also allows for data collection concerning whether a computer was used in the process of committing a crime, something that the UCR did not do. While NIBRS is a substantial improvement over the UCR, we must remember that it is still subject to all the reporting problems inherent in the use of police data. NIBRS is still largely reliant on people reporting crimes to the police and on the police accurately recording each incident. While NIBRS expands what we know about crime, it will still not reveal the dark figure of crimes not reported to the police.

National Crime Victimization Survey

The limitations of crime reports generated by the police have been clear for decades, and there is a need to approach collection of crime data from a different angle, specifically going straight to crime victims. The **National Crime Victimization Survey (NCVS)** is a panel study conducted by the US Census Bureau with a nationally representative sample of households in the United States. Once selected, every member of the household who is at least 12 years old participates in an in-person interview using computer-assisted personal interview software, followed by six additional interviews spaced six months apart, most of which occur over telephone using computer-assisted telephone interviewing software. After 3.5 years, households rotate out of the sample. Samples typically consist of about 240,000 people from 150,000 households (Morgan & Oudekerk, 2019). If household residents move away during the 3.5 years that the house is designated to be in the sample, the new residents will be interviewed for the remaining follow-up periods (United States Bureau of Justice Statistics, 2022). The NCVS also collects data from individuals living in group quarters, including dormitories, rooming houses, and religious group dwellings (United States Bureau of Justice Statistics, 2009, 2017).

The purpose of the NCVS is to capture data on victimization (threatened, attempted, and completed crimes) against the individuals interviewed or their households, including incidents that were reported to the police and those that were not. The NCVS collects detailed information about each reported victimization by screening respondents about their recent victimization history and then asking detailed questions about any incidents. When an individual reports violent victimization, interviewers seek information about the victim's demographic characteristics, victim-offender relationship, type of crime, whether a weapon was involved, whether the offense was reported to the police, type of injuries, and where the incident occurred. For property crimes against the household, NCVS includes information about the household itself, including house size, household income, region, location of residence, and type of crime. NCVS also includes a School Crime Supplement (SCS) administered to participants 12 to 18 years of age who have attended primary or secondary school in the previous six months (Boehme et al., 2024).

The NCVS provides three different types of victimization measurements—victimization, incidents, and prevalence. For victimizations, researchers calculate the **victimization rate** by dividing the number of victimizations during a time period by the number of persons in that population and multiplying that by 1,000. In the event of a property crime, the denominator for the equation becomes the number of households rather than the number of people. Incidents differ from victimizations in that the former counts the number of specific criminal acts. Since **incidents** can have more than one victim involved, incident estimates are adjusted to account for the possibility of multiple victims reporting one incident. Finally, **prevalence** rates count the number of unique persons or households experiencing at least one victimization during a period of time. Prevalence rates are the number of victims or households experiencing victimization during a given time period over the total number of persons or households, multiplied by 100. In the calculation of incidents, a person being robbed twice during an interview period would count as two incidents but as one victim in the prevalence rate calculation. The prevalence rate gives us an estimate of the percentage of the population that was victimized at least once during a specified period of time (Morgan & Oudekerk, 2019).

The NCVS faces multiple challenges, including those related to relying on respondents' memories, to correctly recall incidents. One issue that researchers face is **telescoping**, or people recalling victimizations but placing them into incorrect time periods. NCVS researchers work to reduce telescoping by **bounding**. They do the initial interview with respondents and then, for the subsequent interview, ask "since the last interview…" to give respondents a frame of reference. While placing incidents into the wrong time period is one problem, another is completely forgetting about victimizations that occurred. This is one reason why people might underreport. Another reason for underreporting might be that people sometimes frame victimization at the hands of friends and family as something other than criminal behavior. People also might be too ashamed or embarrassed to report some incidents.

Since NCVS began in 1973, researchers have worked and reworked the survey so that the questions will trigger participants' memories and make them feel comfortable about answering questions. The most recent redesign began in 2016, with the new version of the survey being used with all NCVS participants in 2025. The redesign process began with a comprehensive examination of the survey to detect any potentially problematic language and find areas where it could include better prompts to encourage full reporting of crimes. The surveys were revised and then pilot tested, with some of the NCVS participants answering the previous version of the survey and some getting the new one. Analysis revealed that the updated version helped researchers gather more information on victimization (Truman & Brotsos, 2022). Offense reporting most impacted by the design changes included rape/sexual assault, robbery, burglary, simple assault, and household theft of lower-value items (Edwards et al., 2023). Figure 5.3 includes a comparison between the old survey prompts and the new ones for unwanted sexual contact. As you can see, the new version includes more detailed prompts. Note that the previous version asked about unwanted sexual acts that resulted from coercion, but the updated version goes into greater detail, such as threats to loved ones. The updated version also specifically requests information about incidents that occurred while the victim was unable to consent due to intoxication (Truman & Brotsos, 2022).

Measuring series victimization is always a challenge in victimization surveys. The NCVS defines **series victimization** as crimes that are "similar in type to one another but occur with

Old cues	*Redesign cues*
43a. Incidents involving forced or unwanted sexual acts are often difficult to talk about. (Other than any incidents already mentioned,) have you been forced or coerced to engage in unwanted sexual activity by… Someone you didn't know A casual acquaintance OR Someone you know well?	S-07A. The next questions are about any sexual contact in the past 12 months that you DID NOT CONSENT TO and that YOU DID NOT WANT to happen. The information you provide is confidential. {Sexual contact includes touching of your sexual body parts, or any type of sexual penetration with a body part or object. It also includes making you touch or penetrate someone else. This could have been done by someone you knew well, someone you casually knew, or a stranger and can happen to both men and women. Sexual contact includes someone touching your private parts, unwanted sex, or making you do these kinds of things to them. This could have been done by someone you know well, someone you casually know, or a stranger and can happen to both boys and girls.} {Other than the unwanted sexual contact you have already mentioned,} in the past 12 months… 1) Did anyone touch, grab, or kiss your {sexual body parts against your will/private parts when you didn't want them to}—or TRY to do this? (2) Did anyone force you to have sexual contact by holding you down with his or her body, pinning your arms, hitting or kicking you, or using some other type of force—or TRY or THREATEN to do this? (3) Did anyone threaten to physically hurt you or someone close to you if you did not have sexual contact? (4) Did anyone have sexual contact with you—or try to have sexual contact with you—while you were passed out, unconscious, asleep, or unable to consent because you were drunk or high?

Figure 5.3 Changes to NCVS victimization screener cues

Source: Edwards, W. S., Cantor, D., Yan, T., Sun, H., & Giambo, P. (2023). *National Crime Victimization Survey redesign letter and incentive experiment report.* Westat. www.ojp.gov/pdffiles1/bjs/grants/306158.pdf

such frequency that a victim is unable to recall each individual event or describe each event in detail" (Morgan & Oudekerk, 2019, p. 22). These types of victimizations accounted for 1.5% of all victimizations recorded by the NCVS in 2018. Excluding or counting these as one victimization would undercount the number of victimizations that actually occurred, but that has traditionally been the practice of victimization surveys. Series victimizations tend to be problematic, as victims must estimate how many incidents occurred, and they do not always recall details of each incident. During the initial stages of the NCVS, formerly called the National Crime Survey (NCS), series victimization was defined as at least three incidents of the same general type of crime, but researchers discovered that victims were better able to remember details of incidents within series that involved at least six criminal incidents. This discovery prompted the NCVS to change their series victimization criteria to at least six incidents during the data collection period. The NCVS caps the number of incidents in one series at ten, as researchers found that the reliability of series reporting began to suffer in series with more than 10 incidents. If respondents report that the series included at least six victimizations but are unsure of the exact number of incidents, for reliability purposes, those series are coded as including six incidents (Lauritsen et al., 2012).

In the 2010s, the NCVS expanded its data collection to include items beyond personal and household victimization. They added two survey topics—police performance and perceptions of community safety. Not only do these new survey items provide valuable information about residents' feelings about their communities and perceptions of police, but the hope is that inclusion of these will help to reduce participant attrition. Household members who do not have any victimization to report tend to be more likely than recent crime victims to decline to participate in the NCVS follow-up surveys, because they do not believe it is worthwhile to sit for an interview when they have nothing to say (Langton et al., 2017; Truman & Brostos, 2022).

While the NCVS and other victimization surveys are important to our understanding of crime, particularly those not reported to the police, they do have their weaknesses. One is that murder and manslaughter are excluded for the obvious reason that it is not possible to interview someone who is deceased. Another drawback is the lack of information on victimization of children 11 and under, since they are not included in the survey plan. Since the NCVS targets households and asks for information about property crime and personal victimization, many crimes are excluded from measurement. Bank robberies; crimes against businesses such as shoplifting, vandalism, and breaking and entering of an office; and white-collar offenses such as insider trading and embezzlement are currently excluded. The use of households for sampling also excludes crimes committed against nonresident visitors to the country, individuals experiencing homelessness, armed forces personnel residing in military barracks, crew members of maritime vessels, and institutionalized populations including people incarcerated in prisons and jails. These exclusions are problematic, given that some of these groups tend to be at a higher risk for victimization than people living in households. The NCVS also does not include victimizations that occurred outside the United States (Morgan & Oudekerk, 2019; United States Bureau of Justice Statistics, 2017). Like the UCR and NIBRS, the NCVS is also weak when measuring victimless crimes, referred to as crimes against society in NIBRS, such as sex for payment, drug dealing, drug use, and gambling.

The NCVS originated as a survey aggregated at the national level. In other words, it was not possible to do state-to-state or city-to-city crime comparisons as we could with the UCR or NIBRS. In 2016, the NCVS began collecting data that could be measured at the state level and even for some metropolitan areas within those states. The first NCVS publication to include state-level criminal victimization was published in 2023, but only the 22 most populous states and some of their metropolitan areas were included (Kena & Morgan, 2023).

A Warning about Crime Clocks

We all love nice graphics to explain potentially complicated topics. A popular type of graphic for crime was the **crime clock**. Crime clocks display how many crimes happen in a geographic area each hour, minute, or second. The FBI introduced crime clocks in their 1960 UCR report, and they were quite popular with the media. Some newspapers printed pictures of the crime clocks, and while the illustration of the clock is no longer used, the FBI continues to publish "crime clock statistics." I am sure that, at some point, you heard something along the lines of "every five minutes, somebody falls victim to [insert a crime]." That is a crime clock statistic. Unfortunately, this is not a helpful way of illustrating crime. Crime clocks lack an important function, and that is the ability to account for the size of the population being discussed. As I noted when explaining the difference between raw crime statistics and crime rates, raw data do not give us enough information to understand how much crime there is in an area. To put crime data in perspective, we need to account for the population of the location in question or changes in that population over time. Best (2022) explained that, if there were 10,000 murders and a population of 100 million at Time 1, and then 10,000 murders but with a population rising to 200 million at Time 2, the crime rate would have dropped from 10 murders per 100,000 people to 5 per 100,000 from Time 1 to Time 2. That is a substantial drop and something that should be cause for celebration, but not if we are looking at crime clocks. At both time points, the clock would show one murder every 53 minutes. Crime clocks can even give us the impression that crime is rising while it is actually falling. Using Best's (2022) research again, the United States experienced a tremendous decline in burglaries from 458 per 100,000 in 1960 to 341 per 100,000 in 2019. That is a 26% reduction in burglaries! What did the crime clock tell us about this change over time? The clock gave us the impression that burglaries were happening more often, with a burglary every 39 seconds in 1960 and one every 28 seconds in 2019. Next time you see or hear a source purporting to measure crime, drug overdoses, suicides, or diagnoses of diseases occurring every few seconds or minutes, remember what you learned here. Also, do not use crime clock data in any reports or presentations. Using rates is the way to go.

Summary

The UCR/NIBRS and the NCVS provide the United States with important crime data, but each offers very different types of information. As a summary measure, the UCR provided figures for selected serious crimes known to the police. The data were aggregated at the university level, tribal area level, and city, state, or national level. The UCR contained rules limiting the data's usefulness, including the hierarchy rule prohibiting more than one offense in a crime incident from being reported. Additionally, the UCR was restrictive in that it only provided information on a very limited number of crimes. The incident-based NIBRS replaced the UCR as the primary measure of crime statistics in the United States in 2021. Unlike the UCR, NIBRS collects information about the victim, offender, crime circumstances, and arrest for criminal incidents. NIBRS also collects data on a wider variety of crimes than the UCR. Since both measures are generated from police reports, both the UCR and NIBRS are vulnerable to some of the same limitations. Not all crime comes to the attention of the police. Some offenses, particularly those without a clear victim, are especially difficult for the police to detect, resulting in a substantial proportion of those crimes going unreported in the UCR and NIBRS. Police are often reliant on civilians to report crimes, but there are several reasons why someone would choose not to notify the police. Finally, police data are susceptible to manipulation by individuals whose job performance is being measured by the numbers.

The NCVS approaches crime not through police data but by sampling households and then interviewing all residents who are at least 12 years old about personal and household victimization. While NCVS reports more crime than what is known to the police, there are still reasons why people underreport victimizations during the interviews. People might not consider what happened to them to be a crime, especially if the perpetrator was someone they knew. Individuals may have forgotten about relatively minor offenses, and they might be too ashamed or embarrassed to report more serious incidents. The NCVS also misses some important types of crime and crime victims. For example, since this is a household-based survey, crimes against businesses are excluded, as are crime victims who live in military barracks, prisons, or lack housing.

Key Terms

Uniform Crime Report (UCR)
National Incident-Based Reporting System (NIBRS)
Incidents
Bounding
Victimless crimes
National Crime Victimization Survey (NCVS)
Prevalence
Series victimization
Dark figure of crime
Victimization rate
Telescoping
Crime clock

Discussion Questions

1. Go over all the ways that the information about a crime, from the moment the crime is committed, might fail to wind up being reported in NIBRS or the NCVS.
2. What types of crime are better measured with the UCR/NIBRS than the NCVS?
3. What types of crime are better measured with the NCVS rather than UCR/NIBRS?

References

Best, J. (2022). Considering what counts: On the clock. *Numeracy, 15*(2), Art. 7. https://doi.org/10.5038/1936-4660.15.2.1407

Boehme, H. M., Burrow, J. D., & Jung, S. (2024). An exploratory analysis examining the relationship between protective and risk factors of bullying and hate crime victimization within schools. *Journal of School Violence, 23*(3), 348–362. https://doi.org/10.1080/15388220.2023.2299974

Edwards, W. S., Cantor, D., Yan, T., Sun, H., & Giambo, P. (2023). *National Crime Victimization Survey redesign letter and incentive experiment report.* Westat. www.ojp.gov/pdffiles1/bjs/grants/306158.pdf

Fazlollah, M. (2001). City, national rape statistics highly suspect. *We News.* https://womensenews.org/2001/01/city-national-rape-statistics-highly-suspect/

Fazlollah, M., Matza, M., & McCoy, C. R. (1998). How to cut city's crime rate: Don't report it. *Philadelphia Inquirer.* A1. www.michaelmatza.com/down-with-crime

Federal Bureau of Investigation. (n.d.). *NIBRS quick facts.* United States Department of Justice, Federal Bureau of Investigation.

Federal Bureau of Investigation. (2004). *Uniform Crime Reporting handbook.* United States Department of Justice, Federal Bureau of Investigation.

Federal Bureau of Investigation. (2010a). *Crime in the United States: About the Uniform Crime Reporting (UCR) program.* United States Department of Justice, Federal Bureau of Investigation.

Federal Bureau of Investigation. (2010b). *Crime in the United States: Methodology.* United States Department of Justice, Federal Bureau of Investigation.

Federal Bureau of Investigation. (2011). *A guide to understanding NIBRS.* United States Department of Justice, Federal Bureau of Investigation.

Federal Bureau of Investigation. (2019a). *Crime in the United States offense definitions.* United States Department of Justice, Federal Bureau of Investigation.

Federal Bureau of Investigation. (2019b). *Crime in the United States.* United States Department of Justice, Federal Bureau of Investigation.

Federal Bureau of Investigation. (2020). *National incident based reporting system.* United States Department of Justice, Federal Bureau of Investigation.

Federal Bureau of Investigation. (2024). *Crime in the United States, 2023.* United States Department of Justice, Federal Bureau of Investigation.

Federal Bureau of Investigation. (2025). *2024 reported violent and property crime: City agency.* United States Department of Justice, Federal Bureau of Investigation. https://cde.ucr.cjis.gov/LATEST/webapp/#/pages/home

Francescani, C. (2012). NYPD report confirms manipulation of crime stats. *Reuters.* www.reuters.com/article/us-crime-newyork-statistics/nypd-report-confirms-manipulation-of-crime-stats-idUSBRE82818620120309

Kena, G., & Morgan, R. E. (2023). *Criminal victimization in the 22 largest U.S. states, 2017–2019.* United States Department of Justice, Bureau of Justice Statistics.

Langton, L., Planty, M., & Lynch, J. P. (2017). Second major redesign of the National Crime Victimization Survey (NCVS). *Criminology & Public Policy, 16*(1), 1049–1074. https://doi.org/10.1111/1745-9133.12335

Lauritsen, J. T., Owens, J. G., Planty, M., Rand, M. R., & Truman, J. L. (2012). *Methods for counting high-frequency repeat victimizations in the National Crime Victimization Survey.* United States Department of Justice, Bureau of Justice Statistics.

Morgan, R. E., & Oudekerk, B. A. (2019). *Criminal victimization, 2018.* United States Department of Justice, Bureau of Justice Statistics.

Truman, J. L., & Brotsos, H. (2022). *Update on the NCVS instrument redesign.* United States Bureau of Justice Statistics.

United States Bureau of Justice Statistics. (2009). *National Crime Victimization Survey.* United States Department of Justice Bureau of Justice Statistics. https://bjs.ojp.gov/data-collection/ncvs

United States Bureau of Justice Statistics. (2014). *The nation's two measures of homicide.* United States Department of Justice, Bureau of Justice Statistics.

United States Bureau of Justice Statistics. (2017). *National Crime Victimization Survey, 2016 technical documentation.* United States Department of Justice Bureau of Justice Statistics. https://bjs.ojp.gov/sites/g/files/xyckuh236/files/media/document/ncvstd16.pdf

United States Bureau of Justice Statistics. (2022). *NCVS sample design and redesign.* United States Department of Justice Bureau of Justice Statistics. https://bjs.ojp.gov/ncvs-sample-design

United States Bureau of Justice Statistics. (2024). *National Incident-Based Reporting System (NIBRS).* United States Department of Justice Bureau of Justice Statistics. https://bjs.ojp.gov/national-incident-based-reporting-system-nibrs

Wormeli, P. (2022). Counting crimes: An obsolete paradigm. *The Criminologist, 47*(1), 7–9.

Reading 5.1 Stealing Tires or Copper Wires?

As I explained in Chapter 5, the transition from UCR to NIBRS was a big deal in many ways. It required changes to the way police departments went about collecting data and sharing it with the FBI, but this new way of operating has its rewards. Rasch, Scott, Clements, and Strom (2023) take us through the Arlington, Texas Police Department's experience with crime analysis both before and after their adoption of NIBRS utilizing the example of larceny-theft. Larceny-theft was coded as a very general crime with few categories in the UCR's summary reporting system but developed into something much more detailed in NIBRS. The department found that the descriptive nature of NIBRS helped officers learn about the type of thefts occurring at specific places and times, and this information allowed for the officers to work with communities on problem-oriented-policing and situational crime prevention tactics. The more detailed crime data offered by NIBRS has the potential to help police reduce crime.

Stealing Tires or Copper Wires? How the National Incident-Based Reporting System Changed How the Arlington, Texas, Police Department Addresses Larceny-Thefts

Jason Rash, Thomas Scott, Patina Clements, and Kevin Strom

Introduction

In the 1920s, police leaders across the U.S. worked to establish a standardised crime reporting system that could provide an index of crime in the nation. Their desire to understand crime levels, combined with the limited resources available to law enforcement agencies (LEAs), led them to determine that a basic count of offences and arrests for a specific set of offence types would serve as a satisfactory crime monitoring system. In 1930, the Federal Bureau of Investigation (FBI) began collecting these basic crime and arrest counts through the Uniform Crime Reporting (UCR) Program via voluntary submissions by agencies to the UCR Summary Reporting System (SRS). In 1989, the FBI's UCR Program introduced the National Incident-Based Reporting System (NIBRS), established as a next generation crime reporting system. NIBRS differs from SRS in many ways, including that it collects detailed crime incident data rather than just simple crime counts, and that it records information on a greater number of crime types than SRS. Specifically, NIBRS currently records detailed information on 52 offences and information on arrests for an additional 10 offences; SRS records counts of reported crimes for just 10 distinct crime types and counts of persons arrested for an additional 29 crimes.

The amount of detail recorded in NIBRS is the feature that most demarcates it from SRS. For each criminal incident, defined as "one or more offenses committed by the same offender, or group of offenders acting in concert, at the same time and place" (Federal Bureau of Investigation, 2021, p. 5), NIBRS records information about the incident such as when and where it occurred and whether it was cleared (i.e., solved), including details about each offence (e.g., number and type of offences), victim (e.g., demographics and type of injury), offender (e.g., demographics), arrestee (e.g., demographics and type of arrest), and property (e.g., type and value of property) involved. This is compared to SRS, which only records 1) monthly counts of the most serious offences in criminal incidents for 10 offence types,

2) counts of offences cleared by arrest or exceptional means and counts of unfounded offences for these 10 offence types, and 3) monthly counts of persons arrested for an additional 29 offence types (Federal Bureau of Investigation, 2013).[1]

SRS also provides less information than NIBRS because it uses the hierarchy rule for counting offences, which rank orders the 10 offence types and directs LEAs to only report a count for the most serious offence in criminal incidents that involve more than 1 of the 10 offence types (Federal Bureau of Investigation, 2013, pp. 23–6). NIBRS, on the other hand, records information about every type of offence in multiple offence criminal incidents. Finally, NIBRS records 42 additional offence types than SRS. [2] Clearly, NIBRS provides much more information about crime in the U.S. than SRS does. The greater amount of information recorded in NIBRS is valuable to LEAs, because they can use it to better understand crime in their jurisdiction, including understanding its most common contexts, victims, offenders, circumstances, and outcomes. The goal of this article is to use the Arlington (TX) police department's (APD) experience transitioning to NIBRS as a case study of how the additional information in NIBRS can improve how an LEA understands and responds to crime in their area.

In this article, we use the police response to larceny-theft as an example. Larceny-theft is the "unlawful taking, carrying, leading, or riding away of property from the possession or constructive possession of another" (Federal Bureau of Investigation, 2018). The category of "larceny-theft" is heterogeneous. For example, the definition lumps together incidents of stealing tires with those involving stealing copper wires, despite the difference in how these two crimes occur. The broad categorisation of larceny-theft appears to satisfy the original purpose of the UCR, which was to index general crime levels. It is less beneficial for understanding larceny-theft from a police operational perspective. Here, NIBRS data are more valuable than SRS data, because larceny-theft is disaggregated into eight precise offence types with detailed incident data for each type. These offence types include pocket-picking, purse-snatching, shoplifting, theft from building, theft from coin-operated machine or device, theft from motor vehicle, theft of motor vehicle parts or accessories, and all other larceny (Federal Bureau of Investigation, 2011).

The added information collected in NIBRS offers multiple benefits to local LEAs, the public, and policymakers. For instance, the greater number of offences and crime details recorded in NIBRS can improve the ability of LEAs to identify the specific factors driving changes in crime. For larceny-theft, for example, NIBRS can reveal whether an increase in crime is driven by an increase in purse-snatchings or an increase in thefts from motor vehicles. Additionally, with SRS data, a LEA can identify only whether the frequency of a reported crime type changed in an area. NIBRS data allow the agency to examine whether a change in crime is general or specific to certain circumstances (e.g., gang conflict, commercial buildings, or crimes involving intimate partners). Regarding the public, if citizens can obtain information about the frequency of a given crime by time of day and crime location type, they can be informed about the conditions that most increase their risk of victimisation.

Despite the benefits that NIBRS offers over SRS, LEAs have been slow to transition from SRS due to NIBRS's more substantial reporting requirements. As of 2020, approximately 57% of LEAs that participated in the UCR Program submitted incident-based crime data through NIBRS (Federal Bureau of Investigation, n.d.). As of FY2020, the Bureau of Justice Statistics and the FBI have provided more than $100 million through the National Crime Statistics Exchange to support state and local agencies in their transition from SRS to NIBRS. The move to NIBRS is important, because as of January 2021, the FBI sunset the SRS and transitioned exclusively to NIBRS for crime reporting (Federal Bureau of Investigation, 2016).

The Arlington Police Department's Transition to NIBRS

In 2017, APD transitioned from SRS to NIBRS. At the same time, they implemented a new records management system (RMS). APD's previous RMS was almost 30 years old and was not robust in the data analytics that could be extracted. The RMS transition was not motivated solely because of APD's move to NIBRS reporting, but the agency did make the transition with an eye towards developing a new reporting standard, and, once the NIBRS standard was set, the new system was incorporated quickly to accommodate it. Personnel within APD felt that the largest benefit of the new RMS was its dashboard options since they allowed for closer to real time analyses, and the largest benefit of NIBRS reporting was that it allowed for a more detailed examination of crime within their recurring crime control strategy meetings.

The move to NIBRS presented more internal challenges than anticipated and required a comprehensive shift in how crime data were reviewed. Switching to NIBRS at the same time as installing a new RMS caused tension among APD's records staff and criminal investigations division. Additionally, implementation overlap of the new RMS and NIBRS made comparing current data and previous data problematic. The comparison of previous SRS data to previous NIBRS data indicated a significant increase in some crime categories (for example, larceny-thefts) due to SRS's hierarchy rule, which does not apply in NIBRS.[3] In SRS, the hierarchy rule requires recording only the most serious offence committed in the incident; in NIBRS, each individual offence contained in the incident is recorded separately. The change required comprehensive training to ensure quality data reporting throughout the organisation.

Before transitioning to NIBRS, a designated APD employee manually counted offences and reviewed all reported offences to ensure proper categorisation and reporting. A paper reporting document was subsequently mailed to the state Department of Public Safety (DPS) in Austin, Texas, allowing for complete departmental control over crime reporting. Monthly and yearly internal checks were easy to complete and correct, if necessary. Along with the transition to NIBRS and its more robust data-collection methods came a higher degree of scrutiny. The new RMS, fulfiling the demands of NIBRS reporting, now generates an automated report shared directly with the DPS. DPS then uses a vendor to convert NIBRS data back to an SRS report for public release. As several intermediate entities are involved, the reporting agency no longer retains sole control over its crime reporting.

APD has monthly crime reporting staff meetings in which the command staff and geographically-assigned lieutenants and sergeants discuss recent crime occurrences, short-term trends, the direction and allocation of resources, and the results of said allocation. Before the APD's transition to NIBRS, these officers reviewed crime data using broad offence categorisations that analysts would pull from SRS data. Now, analysts compile NIBRS data for these meetings, which has allowed for more detailed discussions of crime trends and crime prevention strategies. Table 1 demonstrates how the larceny-theft subcategorizations that APD used in these meetings changed after APD's transition to NIBRS.[4] Although the granular detail of NIBRS reports was initially overwhelming, APD quickly began to use it to better allocate

Table 1 APD's larceny-theft coding schemes using the summary reporting system and the National Incident-Based Reporting System

SRS	*NIBRS*
Burglary – vehicle	Pocket-picking
Shoplifting	Purse-snatching
Theft	Shoplifting
Vehicle theft – other	Theft from building
–	Theft – coin-operated
–	Theft from motor vehicle
–	Theft – vehicle parts/ accessories
–	All other theft

resources and customise crime responses. Overall, APD has found that the benefits of switching to NIBRS have far outweighed both the initial challenges they experienced and its learning curve.

The Impact of NIBRS on APD's Larceny-Theft Response

Before APD's NIBRS transition, larceny-theft offences were broken down into four categories, with "Other" capturing anything not included in the other three. This made it difficult to determine when trends and patterns were beginning to emerge. In addition to only disaggregating larceny-theft into four categories, APD applied the hierarchy rule in its crime reporting, and therefore did not record larceny-theft offences that were a lesser crime in a multiple offence criminal incident. When analysts mapped the larceny-thefts, they did not disaggregate offence types, and thus hot spots had limited use for formulating crime prevention strategies (see Figure 1).

With their transition to NIBRS, APD began counting, reporting, and including in a map all incidents of larceny-theft (whether or not they are the most serious offence in a criminal incident) to get a more accurate depiction of where larceny-theft hot spots are and when patterns are present (see, Figure 2). Because NIBRS data include precise subtypes of larceny-theft, APD analysts began mapping each subtype separately. This has allowed for greater transparency about the types of larceny-thefts that are occurring and a more focused approach when deploying resources to target a specific hot spot area or an emerging crime trend. Additionally, with the implementation of NIBRS and a new RMS system, the department now uses a dashboard system that is accessible to anyone in the department to see how crime in each of the offence categories and subcategories is changing daily. This allows for a more timely and focused police response to crimes in Arlington.

The operational effect of transitioning to NIBRS is best demonstrated when looking at APD's South Retail District Unit, which patrols and works with APD's retail partners in the Parks Mall and Highlands shopping districts (located on the corner of S Cooper St and W Bardin Rd in Figures 1 and 2). SRS crime counts provided only the total number of larceny-thefts that occurred in these areas. Using NIBRS counts, APD can look at how different types of larceny-theft are geographically distributed and what types of larceny-theft offences are driving trends in each area. Knowing whether spikes in larceny-theft are due to an increase in shoplifting or an increase in thefts from motor vehicles, for example, helps APD to direct resources and develop strategies to effectively and efficiently reduce crime. APD has leveraged the more detailed larceny-theft groupings available in NIBRS to improve its crime prevention efforts including the more appropriate use of camera trailers to prevent and investigate thefts from motor vehicles, foot patrols near shopliftings hotspots, and high patrol car visibility around the areas of greater vehicle theft offences. The empirical evidence on problem-oriented policing (Hinkle et al., 2020; Weisburd et al., 2010) and larceny-theft prevention (Clarke, 1997; Farrington & Welsh, 2002; Hayes & Downs, 2011) suggests that these more tailored crime responses should have prevented larceny-thefts in our jurisdiction. Although we do not have a research design appropriate to determine what effect APD's NIBRS transition has had on its ability to prevent and solve larceny-thefts, future research may be able to identify the impact of transitioning to NIBRS on changes in LEA policing tactics and crime and clearance rates.

Anticipated Effect of a More Detailed Understanding of Reported Larceny-Thefts

Although we do not evaluate the impact of APD's NIBRS transition on crime or agency outcomes, research suggests that its impact on how the agency practices situational crime prevention (SCP) and problem-oriented policing (POP) in responding to larceny-thefts should mediate a crime reduction. SCP is the perspective that crime is best prevented by focusing on

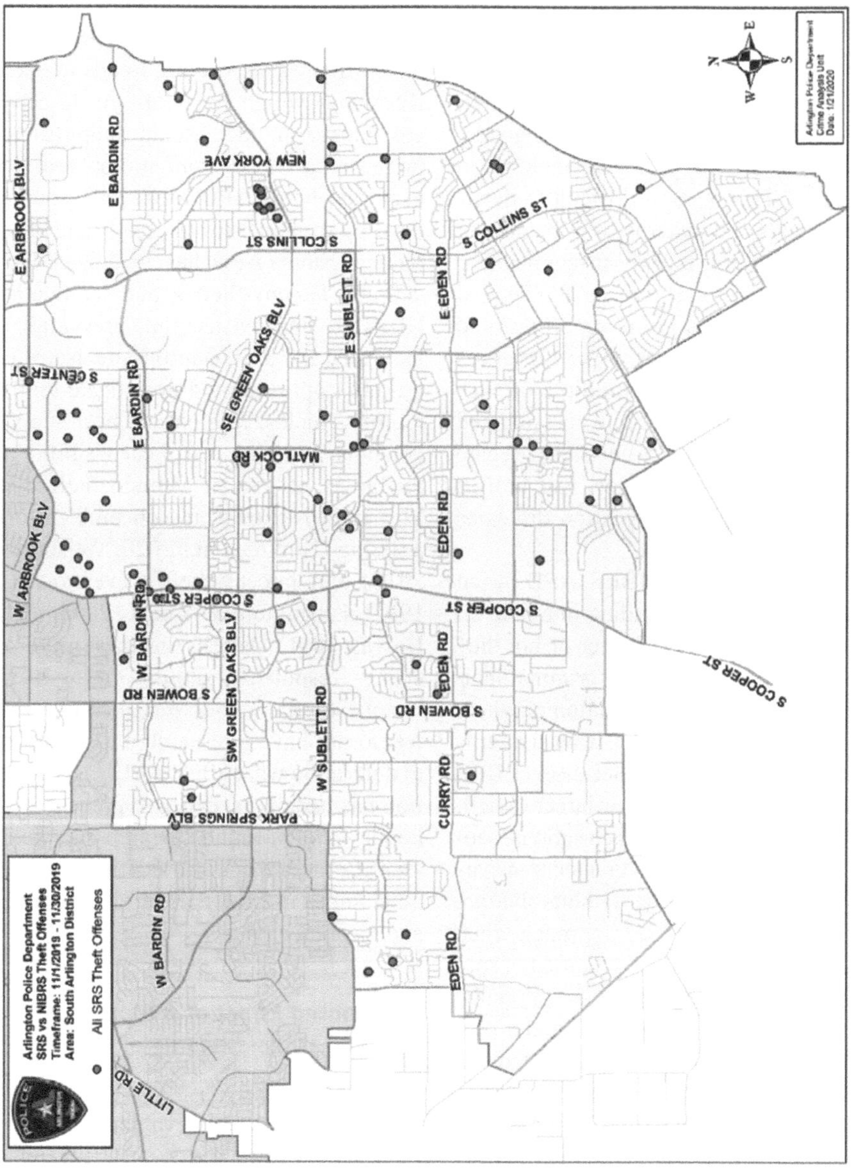

Figure 1 Crime map using SRS data

Figure 2 Crime map using NIBRS data

situations rather than offenders. Other crime prevention perspectives focus on individual characteristics (like a lack of education or poverty), social characteristics (like the availability of firearms or perceived legitimacy of the police in a community), and other aetiological factors. SCP directs attention to the settings surrounding potential crime opportunities, such as the lack of adequate lighting or parking attendants in a parking lot. According to Ronald Clarke (1997), one of the lead researchers into SCP,

> Situational prevention comprises opportunity-reducing measures that (1) are directed at highly specific forms of crime, (2) involve the management, design or manipulation of the immediate environment in as systematic and permanent way as possible, (3) make crime more difficult and risky, or less rewarding and excusable as judged by a wide range of offenders.

Through multiple case studies, Clarke demonstrated quick and easy solutions to crime problems that worked to prevent crime and can be used in conjunction with more challenging and time-consuming efforts to address the individual and societal causes of crime (Clarke, 1997).

POP is a method of policing that applies the SCP perspective. Spelman and Eck define POP as policing operations that target the problems that precede crime, involve a well-thought-out strategy for ameliorating those problems, and involve frequent communication with residents (Spelman & Eck, 1987). With POP, the targeted problems are often highly specific forms of crime or disorder; the policing strategies used in POP typically involve managing or manipulating the environment and making crime and deviance riskier.

The theory and logic behind POP have been translated to LEAs through crime response methods like SARA and CHEERS. SARA instructs LEAs to first *scan* their jurisdiction for crime problems or patterns, then to collect and *analyse* data on the problem, then to work with community partners to develop and implement a *response* or solution, and finally to evaluate or *assess* the impact of the response (Spelman & Eck, 1987). CHEERS, which stands for community, harm, expectations, events, recurring, and similarity offers a method for understanding crime problems in terms of these components (Clarke & Eck, 2003). Using these tools, officers across the U.S. apply SCP thinking and methods to implement POP each year. In fact, according to data from the 2,328 LEAs in the 2016 Law Enforcement Management and Administrative Statistics survey who reported the data, approximately 40% (159,482.4/406,000.2) of all full-time sworn personnel with primary responsibility for patrol are encouraged to engage in SARA-type problem solving projects (author's own analysis). Of course, what POP looks like differs greatly across LEAs. The current article shows how NIBRS data can be used to implement POP in ways SRS data cannot.

Research on POP has shown that it is an effective method of policing. In their comprehensive report on proactive policing, Weisburd and colleagues asserted that research studies "consistently show that problem-oriented policing programs lead to short-term reductions in crime" (National Academies of Sciences, Engineering and Medicine, 2018). In a recent meta-analysis of 49 high quality evaluations of POP, Hinkle et al. (2020) found that POP reduced crime and related outcomes by 34%, on average, and was cost effective. To help LEAs implement POP, the Arizona State University Center for Problem-Oriented Policing provides problem guides for several crime problems. Each guide includes a description of the problem and examples of response strategies. The Center's section on burglary and theft has problem guides for 18 unique offences, including shoplifting, thefts of and from cars in parking facilities, and thefts of and from cars on residential streets and driveways (Arizona State University, n.d.).

In summary, with APD's transition from SRS to NIBRS, the department began using more specific crime codes for larceny-thefts. In doing so, APD's leadership could determine which types of larceny-thefts were driving changes in crime and how different types of larceny-thefts were distributed around the city.

This simple change allowed APD to apply more direct forms of SCP in its POP, which evidence suggests will have a crime-reducing effect on larceny-thefts in Arlington. Moreover, when greater crime details are communicated to the public, residents can take more educated steps to avoid victimisation, which should prevent crime. In addition to these advancements, NIBRS contains more information that APD could leverage in their crime strategy meetings to better understand crime patterns and develop even more effective responses to crime. In the next section, the authors analyse APD's NIBRS data to demonstrate the value of using several additional data elements available in NIBRS and not SRS to inform LEA responses to larceny-theft. Notably, NIBRS contains as much or more information on person offences as it does on property offences compared to SRS. Therefore, LEAs should consider the value of this approach for improving responses to all crime types, not just larceny-thefts.

Looking Forward: Getting More Out of NIBRS to Improve Crime Responses

The disaggregation of larceny-theft (and other offence types) into narrower offence subcategories is an important benefit of NIBRS over SRS, but it only scratches the surface of NIBRS's value for informing POP strategies and resource allocations. Below, we analyse APD's NIBRS data for 2017 and 2018 to examine additional features of larceny-theft offences that occurred during these years. LEAs could use analyses like these to better understand larceny-theft (or other crime) trends in their jurisdictions and to develop better-informed crime responses. Before describing the results of our analyses, we briefly discuss our data, measures, and analyses.

Methods

Data. For the following analyses, we downloaded the year 2017 and 2018 NIBRS master files from the FBI's Crime Data Explorer website (FBI, n.d.) and kept the crime incident data for APD. A NIBRS master file includes all the crime incident data reported to NIBRS for a given year, which is split into 6 unique segments: administrative, offence, property, victim, offender, and arrestee. Each segment has a unique segment identifier and an incident identifier so that all segments can be linked to their respective crime incident. Some segments also have identifiers for other segments so that segments can be linked to each other, like in the case of victims and offenders to determine victim-offender relationships. We conducted all analyses using the linked incident, offence, and property segments. Table 2 shows the number of larceny-theft offences that came to the attention of APD in 2017 and 2018, by offence type. Immediately, one can see the value of disaggregating larceny-theft

Table 2 Number of larceny-thefts in Arlington, TX, by offence type, 2017 and 2018

Measure	*2017*	*2018*	*Total N*	*Total %*
Total larceny-thefts	9,846	9,319	19,165	100.0
Pocket-picking	27	17	44	0.2
Purse-snatching	29	28	57	0.3
Shoplifting	1,542	1,541	3,083	16.1
Theft from building	209	162	371	1.9
Theft from coin-operated machine or device	30	22	52	0.3
Theft from motor vehicle	3,402	2,973	6,375	33.3
Theft of motor vehicle parts or accessories	73	66	139	0.7
All other larceny	4,534	4,510	9,044	47.2

into specific offence types, as Table 2 shows that the overall decrease in these offences was caused by a decrease in the frequency of thefts from motor vehicles (and, to a lesser extent, thefts from buildings); the other forms of larceny-theft stayed relatively constant. Importantly, there is much more information recorded in NIBRS that can provide equally valuable knowledge about crime circumstances and patterns in an LEA's jurisdiction that we explore next.

Measures and Analyses. From APD's 2017–18 NIBRS data, we extracted information on the date and time of the incident, the offence types in the incident for which we dropped all incidents that did not involve a larceny/theft offence, the location/premise type where the offence occurred (e.g., parking lot; liquor store; residence/home), and the value of stolen property in dollars. We use crosstabs and heat plots to analyse these data. A crosstab is a table that uses numbers like counts or percentages to show the relationship between two or more variables. A heat plot is a graph or table that uses colour gradients to show the relationship between two or more variables. Often, these types of descriptive statistics are all that is needed for an LEA to perform POP effectively. Their value increases greatly with the detail of the data involved. The authors perform these analyses to answer the following 3 questions: when and where are different larceny-theft offences most likely to occur, and which types of larceny-thefts should APD prioritise addressing?

Results

When are different larceny-theft offences most likely to occur? NIBRS allows LEAs to answer this question since it collects multiple details of every recorded crime incident, including information on each offence, victim, and offender. In larceny-theft offences, among other details NIBRS records the time of day the crime was committed and what property was stolen, which LEAs can use to customise their crime responses: thefts of vehicle parts at night may require a different police response than thefts from buildings during the day. Using APD's NIBRS data for 2017–18, we generated a heat map to show the distribution of theft of motor vehicle parts or accessories offences and the distribution of theft from building offences, by the time of the offence. The map shows that most thefts from buildings occur in the afternoon, whereas most thefts of motor vehicle parts or accessories occur at night. LEAs could incorporate this information into their crime responses by tailoring elements of officer trainings to the offences that officers are most likely to encounter during their shifts. LEAs could also re-create this plot for different days of the week or months of the year to look for additional trends and could generate unique plots for different geographical areas to formulate even more targeted crime responses.

Where are different larceny-theft offences most likely to occur? Another benefit of NIBRS over SRS is that it records the location/premise type of each offence. LEAs often already have geocoded crime data that are useful for developing geographically targeted crime responses, but more effective crime responses would also factor in the location type of the offence, such as in a parking garage, on the street, in a commercial office building, or in a restaurant. NIBRS records 58 potential location types that LEAs can examine alone or in combination with additional crime features like offence dates and times and victim and offender characteristics (Federal Bureau of Investigation, 2021). We consolidated these location types into 6 categories and plotted the distribution of each larceny-theft offence across location types using a heat map. The aggregation of 58 location types to 6 was necessary because of space constraints, but we emphasise that LEAs could use the more detailed location types in NIBRS in their POP strategies to better apply SCP principles. Even our broad location categories provide useful information, showing some obvious findings like that most shoplifting occurs in retail locations, but also some less obvious things, like that relatively few purse-snatchings occur in transportation areas or other public locations.

Table 3 Location type of "all larceny theft" offence code in Arlington, TX, by 50th percentile of lost property value distribution

Low Property Value		*High Property Value*	
Location Type	*% of Incidents*	*Location Type*	*% of Incidents*
Residence/home	36	Residence/home	33
Other/unknown	9	Amusement park	11
Parking/drop lot/garage	7	Other/unknown	11
School—elementary/secondary	6	Parking/drop lot/garage	6
Grocery/supermarket	5	School – elementary/secondary	4
Department/discount store	5	Speciality store	3
Restaurant	5	Department/discount store	3
Amusement park	4	Restaurant	3
Shopping mall	3	Hotel/motel	3
Speciality store	2	Grocery/supermarket	3

Which types of larceny-theft offences should LEAs prioritise? LEAs can go beyond the offence codes in NIBRS to better understand and respond to larceny-thefts. In Arlington, the "all other larceny" NIBRS offence code made up 47% of all larceny-theft offences in 2017–18. This broad offence categorisation is not as useful for the development of problem-oriented crime responses as more specific offence codes, as discussed above. Fortunately, NIBRS has additional information that an LEA can use to break down this crime category and develop more informed response tactics. In 92% of crime incidents that involved an "all other larceny" offence in Arlington, the larceny-theft was the only offence in the incident. This suggests these crimes are distinct.

For incidents that involved this offence type, the average value of lost property was $2,061, the 25th percentile was $97, the 50th percentile (i.e., median) was $400, and the 75th percentile was $1,000. Under resourced LEAs may want to direct resources to investigating larceny-thefts involving a large value of lost property. We separated incidents involving an "all other larceny" offence into property value deciles and compared the distribution of location types for all other larceny offences in the top 50% of the property value distribution, where the mean value of lost property was at least $500, to offences in the bottom 50% of the property value distribution. Table 3 shows the 10 most common location types for each half of the property value distribution. Regardless of lost property value, most of these larceny-theft offences occurred at a residence, and the remaining most common location types are similar across the property value distribution. The point here is that the more LEAs can disaggregate this offence type using additional crime incident characteristics, the more problem oriented their larceny-theft responses will become. NIBRS data provide for these types of detailed analyses whereas the SRS-method of recording crime counts does not.

Conclusion

In conclusion, APD's transition to NIBRS was not without challenges, but the detailed crime incident data and new RMS proved valuable for improving APD's responses to larceny-theft offenses. NIBRS has many more features that APD can use to further inform its larceny-theft response strategy. Moreover, NIBRS is even more beneficial for analysing person crimes, for which LEAs can use the same information demonstrated here but also information on victims, offenders, their relationships, weapons used, and more to develop detailed, data-driven crime response strategies. As an example, for assault offences, LEAs could use information on the age of the victim and offender and their relationship to each other to analyse the circumstances of assaults at various times of the day and week. Finding that assaults during the week are most likely to occur among youth in the afternoon and among family members and intimate partners at night could be used to strategically set patrol assignments for officers with certain traits or skills. NIBRS can also be used to inform officers of the experiences they are likely to encounter when responding to certain types of incidents (c.f., Nix et al., 2021; Rennison & Addington, 2015), to understand how one's agency performs compared to similarly situated agencies (c.f., Scott et al., forthcoming), to guide decision-making and resource allocation within an LEA (c.f., Gardner et al., 2021), and more.

This article demonstrates the value to LEAs of NIBRS over SRS for developing more effective and efficient crime response strategies, with a focus on larceny-theft. In doing so, it adds to other recent work with similar motivations (Drawve et al., 2021; Gardner et al., 2021; Haberman et al., forthcoming; Scott et al., forthcoming) as well as work on the value of NIBRS for improving society's understanding of crime and its circumstances (Addington, 2006, 2019; Lantz, forthcoming; Roberts, 2009). The possible uses of NIBRS for improving LEA operations appear endless. With the growing number of LEAs transitioning from SRS to NIBRS reporting, it will be exciting to hear the experiences of other agencies that are using NIBRS data to inform and improve their crime response and prevention efforts. We hope efforts are made to evaluate both the impact of transitioning to NIBRS and the innovative uses of NIBRS data on changes in crime levels and other relevant outcomes.

Disclosure Statement

No potential conflict of interest was reported by the author(s).

Discussion Questions

1. In what ways are NIBRS data on larceny-theft more detailed compared to UCR data?
2. In what ways were transitioning from the SRS UCR data to NIBRS data challenging for the police department?
3. How did transitioning from UCR to NIBRS improve what the Arlington Police Department was able to do with the larceny-theft data to address crime?

Notes

1 Other UCR datasets contain additional information on crimes, arrests, and LEAs in the U.S. (Kaplan, 2021).

2 See, Strom and Smith (2017) for a deeper discussion of the differences between SRS and NIBRS.

3 In the case that several different offences occur in the same crime incident, the hierarchy rule specifies which offence LEAs are to record in SRS (Uniform Crime Reporting Program (UCR), 2004). Because five offence types are higher on the hierarchy rule than larceny-theft, all larceny-thefts that occur in multiple-offence crime incidents involving either a homicide, rape, robbery, aggravated assault, and/or burglary are missing from SRS.

4 Geographic coordinates are not recorded in NIBRS and were recorded separately in both APD's old and new RMSs.

References

Addington, L. A. (2006). Using national incident-based reporting system murder data to evaluate clearance predictors: A research note. *Homicide Studies*, *10*(2), 140–152. https://doi.org/10.1177/1088767905285439

Addington, L. A. (2009). Studying the crime problem with NIBRS data: Current uses and future trends. In Marvin D. Krohn, Alan J. Lizotte, & Gina Penly Hall (Eds.), *Handbook on crime and deviance* (pp. 23–42). Springer.

Addington, L. A. (2019). NIBRS as the new normal: What fully incident-based crime data mean for researchers. In Marvin D. Krohn, Nicole Hendrix, Gina Penly Hall, and Alan J. Lizotte (Eds.), *Handbook on crime and deviance* (pp. 21–33). Springer.

Arizona State University. (n.d.). *ASU center for problem-oriented policing*. https://popcenter.asu.edu/

Barrick, K., Strom, K. J., & Richardson, N. (2018). Individual and situational influences on injurious assaults against the police. *Policing: An International Journal*, *41*(2), 202–214. https://doi.org/10.1108/PIJPSM-09-2016-0144

Clarke, R. V. (1997). *Situational crime prevention: Successful case studies* (2nd ed.). Harrow and Heston.

Clarke, R. V., & Eck, J. (2003). *Become a problem solving crime analyst in 55 small steps*. Jill Dando Institute of Crime Science, University of College London.

Drawve, G., Harris, C. T., Thomas, S. A., Datta, J., & Cothren, J. (2021). Current and new frontiers: Exploring how place matters through Arkansas NIBRS reporting practices. *Crime & Delinquency*, *67*(6–7), 941–969. https://doi.org/10.1177/0011128720974317

Farrington, D. P., & Welsh, B. C. (2002). Improved street lighting and crime prevention. *Justice Quarterly*, *19*(2), 313–342. https://doi.org/10.1080/07418820200095261

Federal Bureau of Investigation. (2011). *NIBRS offense codes* https://ucr.fbi.gov/nibrs/2011/resources/nibrs-offense-codes

Federal Bureau of Investigation. (2013). *Summary Reporting System (SRS) user manual*. www.fbi.gov/file-repository/ucr/ucr-srs-user-manual-v1.pdf/view

Federal Bureau of Investigation. (2016, June 10). *The FBI's transition to a National Incident-Based Reporting System (NIBRS)-only data collection. Memorandum to state Uniform Crime Reporting (UCR) program managers*. www.bjs.gov/content/pub/pdf/nibrs.pdf

Federal Bureau of Investigation. (2018). *Crime in the United States, 2018*. U.S. Department of Justice. https://ucr.fbi.gov/crime-in-the-u.s/2018/crime-in-the-u.s.-2018

Federal Bureau of Investigation. (2021). *2021.1 National incident-based reporting system user manual*. www.fbi.gov/file-repository/ucr/ucr-2019-1-nibrs-user-manua-093020.pdf/view

Federal Bureau of Investigation. (n.d.). *Crime data explorer* https://crime-data-explorer.fr.cloud.gov/

Gardner, A., Aagaard, B., Cramer, J., & Pierce, E. (2021, September). *Using NIBRS data to reduce crime*. National Crime Statistics Exchange (NCS-X) Initiative Technical Assistance. www.theiacp.org/sites/default/files/NCSX_Using_NIBRS_Data_to_Reduce_Crime.pdf

Haberman, C. P., Clutter, J. E., & Lee, H. (forthcoming). A robbery is a robbery is a robbery? Exploring crime specificity in official police incident data. *Police Practice and Research*. https://doi.org/10.1080/15614263.2021.2009345

Hayes, R., & Downs, D. M. (2011). Controlling retail theft with CCTV domes, CCTV public view monitors, and protective containers: A randomized controlled trial. *Security Journal*, *24*(3), 237–250. https://doi.org/10.1057/sj.2011.12

Hinkle, J. C., Weisburd, D., Telep, C. W., & Petersen, K. (2020). Problem-oriented policing for reducing crime and disorder: An updated systematic review and meta-analysis. *Campbell Systematic Reviews*, *16*(2), e1089. https://doi.org/10.1002/cl2.1089

Kaplan, J. (2021). *Uniform Crime Reporting (UCR) program data: A practitioner's guide*. https://ucrbook.com/

Lantz, B. (forthcoming). Why more agencies and researchers should embrace the upcoming NIBRS transition: Contributions and promise of the NIBRS data. *American Journal of Criminal Justice* https://doi.org/10.1007/s12103-020-09606-5

National Academies of Sciences, Engineering, and Medicine. (2018). *Proactive policing: Effects on crime and communities*. The National Academies Press.

Nix, J., Richards, T. N., Pinchevsky, G. M., & Wright, E. M. (2021). Are domestic incidents really more dangerous to police? Findings from the 2016 National Incident Based Reporting System. *Justice Quarterly*, *38*(7), 1405–1427. https://doi.org/10.1080/07418825.2019.1675748

Pattavina, A., Socia, K. M., & Zuber, M. J. (2015). Economic stress and domestic violence: Examining the impact of mortgage foreclosures on incidents reported to the police. *Justice Research and Policy*, *16*(2), 147–164. https://doi.org/10.1177/1525107115623938

Rennison, C. M., & Addington, L. A. (2015). Rape against adolescent and emerging adult females: Using NIBRS to compare contexts and inform policy. *Justice Research and Policy*, *16*(2), 165–184. https://doi.org/10.1177/1525107115623940

Roberts, A. (2009). Contributions of the National Incident-Based Reporting System to substantive knowledge in criminology: A review of research. *Sociology Compass*, *3*(3), 433–458. https://doi.org/10.1111/j.1751-9020.2009.00209.x

Scott, T. L., Strom, K. J., & Planty, M. (forthcoming). Using national incident-based reporting system data to assess agency differences in clearance rates: A recommendation for law enforcement. *Police Practice and Research*.

Spelman, W., & Eck, J. E. (1987, January). *Problem-oriented policing*. U.S. Department of Justice, National Institute of Justice.

Strom, K. J., & Smith, E. L. (2017). The future of crime data: The case for the National Incident-Based Reporting System (NIBRS) as a primary data source for policy evaluation and crime analysis. *Criminology & Public Policy*, *16*(4), 1027–1048. https://doi.org/10.1111/1745-9133.12336

Uniform Crime Reporting Program (UCR). (2004). *Uniform crime reporting handbook.* U.S. Department of Justice, Federal Bureau of Investigation. https://ucr.fbi.gov/additional-ucr-publications/ucr_handbook.pdf

Weisburd, D., Telep, C. W., Hinkle, J. C., & Eck, J. E. (2010). Is problem-oriented policing effective in reducing crime and disorder? Findings from a Campbell systematic review. *Criminology & Public Policy*, *9*(1), 139–172. https://doi.org/10.1111/j.1745-9133.2010.00617.x

Reading 5.2 An Exploratory Analysis Examining the Relationship between Protective and Risk Factors of Bullying and Hate Crime Victimization within Schools

The National Crime Victimization Survey (NCVS) collects data about personal and household victimization. Since household members become eligible for participation at age 12, the NCVS data collection periods serve as an excellent opportunity for researchers to learn about victimization inside schools. The School Crime Supplement (SCS) is administered to NCVS respondents who are 12 to 18 years old and have attended a primary or secondary school within the past six months. The SCS collects information about both victimization and the students' perceptions of the schools they attend. Historical context is always important in social science research, so we must remember that the data were collected before the COVID-19 pandemic.

An Exploratory Analysis Examining the Relationship between Protective and Risk Factors of Bullying and Hate Crime Victimization within Schools

Hunter M. Boehme, John D. Burrow, and Sohee Jung

Introduction

The surge of bullying and hate crimes committed by K-12 students has brought increased attention from the scholarly and educational communities. To bring more awareness to discrimination committed by students in Vermont schools, the U.S. Attorney's Office launched an initiative for awareness and sensitivity of the harms of hate crimes (Department of Justice, 2023). While acts of hate broadly, and more specifically within schools, may attract significant law enforcement and national media attention (GAO K-12 Education, 2023), empirical research on the context, incidence, and predictors of school-based hate crimes and bullying in the U.S. is limited.

From 2019 to 2020, the FBI reported a 32% increase in race/ethnicity-related hate crimes from the previous year (Federal Bureau of Investigation, 2021). The FBI also reported that 9.6% and 4.2% of bias-motivated offenses occurred at schools/colleges in 2019 and 2020, respectively. However, from 2011–2015 the National Crime Victimization Survey (NCVS) revealed that 13.6% of hate incidents and 7% of non-hate crime occurred in schools, indicating an elevated risk of hate crime victimization within schools (Masucci & Langton, 2017).

Evidence suggests that bullying, akin to some hate crimes, is more ubiquitous in schools than previously thought. The National Center for Education Statistics (2018) reports that twenty-one percent of students aged twelve to eighteen reported bullying during the school year. The Virginia Department of Health (2019) found that approximately twenty-seven percent of high school students were victims of bullying, with higher rates for white and LGBT students (19% and 29.3% respectively). Comparable levels of bullying have also been observed in Michigan where twenty-one percent of students reported some form of bullying on school property and eighteen percent reporting electronic or cyber-bullying (Michigan Department of Education, 2019). While it is unclear whether a direct link between bullying and hate crimes in schools is not clear, it is conceivable that such a link does exist.

Despite scholars noting and theorizing some similarities between bullying and hate crimes in school (Englander, 2007; Steinberg et al., 2003; Stotzer, 2015), no empirical studies have closely examined these commonalities. Identifying these factors allows educational institutions or government agencies to develop targeted and comprehensive measures to address bullying and hate-related victimization, fostering safer and more supportive environments for students. This study utilizes the 2019 NCVS school crime supplement to assess the simultaneous effects of both protective and risk factors associated with bullying and hate-related victimization within schools. We draw on various theoretical traditions, propositions, and empirical evidence to inform our analysis and implications. Before presenting the data and methods, we review the theoretical traditions and literature guiding our analysis.

Theoretical Traditions

Previous school crime studies have drawn on the social disorganization (or school disorder) literature to assess protective (e.g., positive school climate) and risk factors (e.g., percentage of student body on free lunch vouchers) of crime and victimization within schools (Bradshaw et al., 2009; Lindstrom Johnson et al., 2017). The school disorder literature specifically explores how different dimensions of risk factors influence various types of students' self-reported victimization (Welsh, 2001). Others have drawn on the social control perspective since schools are a key source of control, including caring teachers/staff and rule enforcement (Cook et al., 2010; Lehman, 2019). Concepts derived from these perspectives also align with the routine activity perspective, particularly regarding protective and risk factors of victimization within schools. We largely apply the routine activity perspective, which we believe best addresses both the physical and psychological elements of bullying and hate-related victimization within schools. We detail these propositions below.

Routine activity theory suggests that when a potential victim, motivated offender, and lack of a capable guardian converge in space and time, crime is more likely to occur (Cohen & Felson, 1979). This theory has been applied across various social contexts including inner cities, college campuses, and cyberspace. Peguero (2009) argues that schools offer fertile environments for plenty of crime opportunities and victimizations. Among other reasons, schools provide a platform for large numbers of students interacting, with low visibility by capable guardians (e.g., teacher-to-student ratio) (Schreck et al., 2003). Further, students feeling alienated at school may be less likely to report victimization to school authorities and participate in school supervised activities (Wilcox et al., 2009).

Finkelhor and Asdigian (1996) extended routine activity theory to better explain youth victimization. The authors proffered the concepts of target vulnerability, target gratifiability, and target antagonism. Target vulnerability proposes that some youth may more likely be exposed to victimization due to their physical size, perceived weakness, and emotional/psychological problems. Target gratifiability, which most closely aligns with the original routine activity theory to target attractiveness, is defined as a target having a quality, skill, or attribute that an offender seeks to obtain. Finally, target antagonism involves a potential target having a characteristic(s) that insights anger or jealousy (e.g., minority youth). The authors conclude that these concepts better extrapolate to the context of youth offending, especially in school environments.

Empirical Knowledge of Bias in Schools

Some scholars argue that there is considerable overlap, yet clear differences between hate crime and bullying (Englander, 2007; Steinberg et al., 2003; Stotzer, 2015). Steinberg et al. (2003) suggest that youths who commit hate crimes also engage in bullying behavior, while Stotzer (2015) calls for clarity between the two incidences because bullying does not always develop into a level of crime that is covered under hate crime laws. What may complicate or obfuscate the link between bullying behavior and hate crime is that there is no universal definition of bullying (see Espelage et al., 2013). Olweus and Olweus (1993), for example, defines bullying as unprovoked and unpremeditated "goal-directed" behavior. In a later elaboration of the term, Olweus (2013) observed that three criteria must be observed to distinguish bullying from "ordinary" aggression: intentionality, repetitiveness, and an imbalance of power. Over the last quarter-century, several typologies have been offered to explain different types of bullying behaviors in schools (Khiat, 2012; Runions et al., 2018). Among these, Salmivalli (1999) argues that bullying encompasses both active and non-active participants inclusive of bullies, assistants, reinforcers, and defenders. Important, Salmivalli observes that bullies, victims, and peers are enmeshed within networks that define their needs and expectations.

Insights into the link between bullying and hate crime may be gleaned from Englander's (2007) proposed "junior hate crimes" thesis. First, a victim of bullying might be targeted due to their affiliation with a group or their physical characteristics like hate crime victims. Second, bullying behavior may parallel hate crimes concerning victim targeting, as bullies often choose children who differ from the mainstream group and are identified with a socially controversial group. More specifically, she argues that youth bullying and hate crimes are similar because both focus on those who are "different" and "unwelcome." Some evidence supports this view, given the findings from other scholars who have observed similar patterns among victims who identify as LGBTQ or other "perceived" outgroups (Swearer et al., 2008). Research testing the concepts of target vulnerability and antagonism support this claim that some characteristics about certain youth may result in intentional selection and victimization within schools (Cho & Park, 2023; Choi et al., 2022). Third, and finally, Englander (2007) argues that both bullying and hate crimes share a common trait in their use of debasing, humiliating, and offensive language to marginalize, diminish, or erase the personhood of the victim. While the targets of hate crimes are chosen due to the "real" or perceived membership in a particular group, the targets of bullying may be chosen because they have perceived "difference," rather than their membership. Notwithstanding the arguments of Englander (2007) and others, there is an overall dearth of empirical research that examines similarities between bullying and hate crimes (although see Hall & Hayden, 2007).

As we will argue, Finkelhor and Asdigian's (1996) reconceptualization of routine activity theory may be well suited to explain these similarities. First, target vulnerability is a key feature of bullying and hate-related victimization particularly as it relates to the "outsider status" of victims (Coleclough, 2022; Malecki et al., 2020). Because "outsider status" can assume myriad forms outside of the racial/ethnic context, acute differences in physical stature and even economic status may increase students' vulnerability to both types of victimization. Second, target gratifiability may increase students' susceptibility to bullying and hate-related victimization where school "resources" or commodities are not evenly distributed (e.g., exceptional grades, attention from teachers). Their scarcity means that they are highly desirable and likely coveted by students which may ultimately precipitate bullying and hate-related victimization (Laith & Vaillancourt, 2022). Third, target antagonism presumes that anger, jealousy, or other negative emotions emerge when particular presumably "neutral" traits or characteristics are displayed by students. In particular, "femininity" in boys or identification with racial/ethnic/cultural groups may precipitate an adverse response from other students (Rosen & Nofziger, 2019). Drawing on this perspective aids in addressing both the physical and psychological aspects of bullying and hate-related victimization.

Further, scholars still know very little about protective and risk factors associated with hate-related victimization within schools. Therefore, the present study utilizes the 2019 NCVS School Crime Supplement to test the claims of the junior hate crime hypothesis and unpack other relationships between bullying and hate-related victimization within America's schools. To our knowledge, no known study has assessed the relationship between school bullying and hate-related victimization. This study makes a unique contribution to the literature by testing this relationship as well as uncovering the protective and risk factors associated with both victimization types. Uncovering these relationships offer important implications for school safety, school policy, and potentially identifying stigmatized youth who are intentionally victimized and/or are at greater risk of school-based victimization. This research is an attempt to fill in some of the gaps in our knowledge about bullying and hate-related victims within schools. We seek to answer the following research questions:

> **RQ1:** Is there a relationship between bullying and hate-related victimization within schools?
> **RQ2:** What are the similarities and differences in protective and risk factors associated with bullying and hate-related victimization?

Data and Methods

Data and Sample

We used the 2019 NCVS School Crime Supplement (SCS) to examine predictors of victimization in schools. The NCVS employs a stratified multistage cluster sampling design to select representative households, and at each stage, the selection was proportionate to the population size, ensuring a self-weighting sample. In all households selected for the NCVS, the SCS selects the eligible respondents, aged 12–18, in primary or secondary education programs, and attending schools within the last six months before the survey (Bureau of Justice Statistics, 2019). The SCS asks various questions related to the school environment, risk/protective factors, crime victimization, and bullying and hate-related victimization. This data allows us to examine experiences with bullying and hate-related victimization at schools and other factors that may theoretically be associated with victimization.

We only included respondents who answered both the bullying and hate-related victimization questions (our dependent variables). We excluded those who were ever home-schooled and those who attended private schools. This approach has been used in previous research and is theoretically supported since there may be differential victimization opportunity structures between public, private, and home-schooled students (Burrow & Apel, 2008; Mayer & Leone, 1999; Robers et al., 2012). After removing cases that did not meet the inclusion criteria, our final sample consisted of 4,189 cases. There was no more than 1% missing information on key variables in the final sample, indicating no bias in estimates due to missingness (Parent, 2013).

Dependent Variables

All variable survey items can be found in Table A1 within the Appendix. The two dependent variables are 1) *hate-related victim* and 2) *bullying victim*, which are both dichotomous variables (1 = yes). The bullying variable serves as an independent variable in the hate-related victim model, while hate-related victim serves as an independent variable in the bullying victim model.

Risk Factors

We include risk factors largely derived from the opportunity theory perspective discussed above. For example, since a core tenet of the paradigm proposes that those may be more at risk of criminal victimization when they are in closer proximity to crime-prone areas or motivated offenders (Cohen & Felson, 1979), we include five risk factors:

(1) *Living neighborhood* – 1 to 4, where 1 indicates the respondent strongly disagrees there is elevated crime. (4 is strongly agree)
(2) S*chool neighborhood crime* – 1 to 4, where 1 indicates the respondent strongly disagrees there is elevated crime (4 is strongly agree)
(3) *School location* (1 = city/suburb, 0 = town/rural)
(4) *Misbehaving classmates* (1 = respondent was distracted by classmate(s) behavior.
(5) *Transiency* (1 = student attended two or more schools in the past year.

Protective Factors

We included ten potential protective factors that may be associated with bullying and hate crime victimization within schools (Crawford & Burns, 2015). Formal school security measures included dichotomous variables of whether there are

(1) *Police officer(s)*
(2) *Staff supervision in hallways*
(3) *Security cameras*
(4) Written *Code of conduct* in the school (1 = yes).
(5) *Enforcement of school rules*
(6) *Fairness of school rules*
(7) *Aware of school punishment*
(8) *Fairness of school punishment* (1 = yes) (Cook et al., 2010)
(9) *Respected teachers*
(10) *Adult cares* (1 = yes) (James et al., 2015)

Socio-demographic Factors

Finally, we considered several socio-demographic variables to assess the relationship of these factors with bullying and hate-related victimization. *Free lunch* serves as a proxy measure for socio-economic status, which is measured as the percentage of students (within the respondent school) eligible for free or reduced-price lunch. It was an ordinal variable including three levels (1 = less than 20%, 2 = 20 to 50%, and 3 = 50% or more). *Age* (12 to 18), *sex* (1 = male), and race variables (*Asian*, *Black*, *Hispanic*, *Other*, and *White* (reference category).

Results

We considered binary logistic regression models due to the dichotomous nature of the dependent variables. Since bullying and hate-related victimization are rare and skewed (23.80% and 7.60%, respectively), we estimated skewed logistic (scobit) regression models (Tay, 2016). We present average marginal effects coefficients which are more interpretable than odds ratios and log odds, particularly when estimating nonlinear models (Cameron & Trivedi, 2013). Variance inflation factors indicated that there were no concerns with multi-collinearity. Table A2 in the Appendix presents summary statistics of the variables used in the model. Based on summary statistics, we see that the average age of respondents was 14.8, with 52% of respondents being male. Hispanic respondents consisted of 23% of our sample, 5% were Asian, 11% were Black, 4% were other races, and 57% were White. More than two-thirds of respondents attended schools within a city/suburb area (64%), most students did not think that there is a lot of crime in the neighborhood where they live or go to school.

Table 1 presents findings from a scobit regression model on the hate-related victim outcome. Results show that respondents who were *bullying victims* were at a 13.7% increased chance of being a hate-related victim ($p < .05$) compared to those who were not bullied. Students whose schools had *security cameras* were at a 5.8% greater risk of experiencing a hate crime. However, students who attended schools with a written *code of student conduct* (-4.1%), respondents who perceived the *school rules to be fair* (-2.7%), were *aware of school punishments* (-2.4%), perceived

Table 1 Results from a skewed logistic regression model examining predictors of hate-related victimization

Variables	*dy/dx*	*P*	*S.E.*	*95% CIs*	
Risk factors					
Bullying victim	0.137	0.000	0.010	0.116	0.157
School location	0.002	0.777	0.008	-0.013	0.018
Neighborhood crime near home	0.004	0.437	0.006	-0.007	0.015
Neighborhood crime near school	0.001	0.797	0.006	-0.010	0.013
Misbehaving classmates	0.001	0.959	0.012	-0.024	0.025
Transiency	0.016	0.347	0.017	-0.017	0.048
Protective factors					
Security/police officers at school	0.012	0.232	0.010	-0.008	0.031
Staff supervision in hallways	-0.012	0.354	0.013	-0.038	0.014
Security cameras	0.058	0.025	0.026	0.007	0.109
School code of conduct	-0.041	0.023	0.018	-0.076	-0.006
Enforcement of school rules	-0.005	0.644	0.010	-0.024	0.015
Fairness of school rules	-0.027	0.023	0.012	-0.051	-0.004
Awareness of punishment	-0.024	0.022	0.010	-0.044	-0.003
Fairness of punishment	-0.021	0.027	0.010	-0.040	-0.002
Respect of teachers	-0.040	0.000	0.011	-0.063	-0.018
Adult cares	-0.021	0.210	0.017	-0.053	0.012
Socio-demographic factors					
Free lunch	0.012	0.027	0.006	0.001	0.023
Age	-0.004	0.060	0.002	-0.008	0.000
Sex	-0.005	0.528	0.007	-0.019	0.010
Asian	0.061	0.000	0.017	0.029	0.093
Black	0.021	0.070	0.012	-0.002	0.044
Hispanic	0.013	0.152	0.009	-0.005	0.032
Other race	0.045	0.002	0.015	0.016	0.074

Notes: dy/dx = average marginal effects, S.E. = standard errors, CIs = confidence intervals, Log likelihood = -802.90. White is the reference category for the race variables. Incorporating the SCS weight variable did not change our findings

school punishments to be fair (-2.1%) and had *respect for teachers* (-4.0%) were less likely to experience hate-related victimization ($p <$ .05). Students who attended schools with a greater percentage of students who receive *free lunch* were significantly more likely to experience hate-related victimization (1.2%, $p <$ .05). Finally, in comparison to *White* students, *Asian* students (6.1%) and students of *Other* races (4.5%) were significantly ($p <$ .05) more likely to experience hate-related victimization.

Table 2 shows the results predicting bullying victimization with the hate-related victim variable serving as an independent variable. Findings confirm the hate-related-bullying relationship. Students who were *hate-related victims* were 44% more likely to be bullying victims. Students who attended schools where the surrounding *neighborhood* had *elevated crime* rates (3.7%), students who were distracted from *misbehaving*

Table 2 Results from a skewed logistic regression model examining predictors of bullying victimization

Variables	*dy/dx*	*P*	*S.E.*	*95% CIs*	
Risk factors					
Hate-related victim	0.442	0.000	0.053	0.328	0.546
School location	0.015	0.234	0.013	-0.010	0.040
Neighborhood crime near home	0.001	0.933	0.010	-0.018	0.020
Neighborhood crime near school	0.037	0.000	0.010	0.017	0.057
Misbehaving classmates	0.160	0.000	0.021	0.118	0.201
Transiency	0.068	0.026	0.031	0.008	0.128
Protective factors					
Security/police officers at school	-0.025	0.106	0.015	-0.055	0.005
Staff supervision in hallways	-0.010	0.648	0.023	-0.055	0.034
Security cameras	-0.003	0.933	0.031	-0.063	0.058
School code of conduct	0.037	0.314	0.037	-0.035	0.109
Enforcement of school rules	-0.065	0.000	0.018	-0.099	-0.030
Fairness of school rules	-0.040	0.105	0.025	-0.089	0.008
Awareness of punishment	-0.041	0.032	0.019	-0.079	-0.004
Fairness of punishment	-0.099	0.000	0.018	-0.134	-0.063
Respectful teachers	-0.061	0.015	0.025	-0.111	-0.012
Adult cares	0.062	0.053	0.032	-0.001	0.124
Socio-demographic factors					
Free lunch	0.002	0.828	0.009	-0.015	0.019
Age	-0.020	0.000	0.003	-0.026	-0.014
Sex	-0.025	0.031	0.012	-0.048	-0.002
Asian	-0.126	0.000	0.034	-0.192	-0.059
Black	-0.055	0.006	0.020	-0.095	-0.016
Hispanic	-0.074	0.000	0.016	-0.105	-0.044
Other race	0.011	0.696	0.028	-0.044	0.065

Notes: dy/dx = average marginal effects, S.E. = standard errors, CIs = confidence intervals, Log likelihood = -1856.13. White is the reference category for the race variables. Incorporating the SCS weight variable did not change our findings

students (16.0%), and *transient students* (6.8%) were significantly more likely to be a victim of bullying ($p < .05$). Students who felt school *rules were enforced* (-6.5%), were *aware of punishments* (-4.1%), felt *punishments* were *fair* (-9.9%), and held *respect for teachers* (-6.1%) were significantly ($p < .05$) less likely to be bullying victims. Older respondents (-2.0%), *male* students (-2.5%), *Asian* students (-12.6%), *Black* students (-5.5%), and *Hispanic* students (-7.4%) were significantly ($p < .05$) less likely to experience bullying victimization.

Discussion

This research sought to assess Englander's (2007) theoretical claims regarding the relationship between bullying and hate-related victimization. While there was partial support for the "junior hate crime" hypothesis, indicating both victimizations were related to each other as well as some alignment in certain protective factors associated with both types of victimization, we also observed distinct differences in certain risk and socio-demographic factors. Subsequent discussion will highlight and expand upon these findings and offer important policy and research implications.

The Relationship between Bullying and Hate-Related Victimization, Protective, and Risk Factors

Regarding research question one, we found in both models that bullying and hate-related victimization were significantly associated with each other. Englander's (2007) "junior hate crime" hypothesis argues that bullying and hate crime victims may both be targeted due to perceived "difference." While caution is encouraged when comparing these results across different statistical models (Mood, 2010), we found noteworthy similarities among protective factors associated with both bullying and hate-related victimization. In both models, awareness of school punishment, perceived fairness of school punishment, and respect for teachers were significantly associated with lower chances of experiencing both bullying and hate-related victimization. These findings support the deterrence perspective and demonstrate the importance of fair and clearly presented school punishment policies within schools. Fair and clear punishments can serve as a form of deterrence (Mayworm & Sharkey, 2014), suggesting it is possible that student experiences are diffused to others within schools and serve as a cautionary tale that violations and violators will be swiftly, and sometimes severely, punished (Cook et al., 2010). Additionally, student respect for teachers may serve as an important social guardianship element to combat bullying and hate-related victimization. Not only may teachers be guardians but may be additional "eyes" in the hallways, classrooms, and around campus. Further, students' respect for teachers can foster a willingness to listen to authority figures across campus, which may also serve as a form of informal social control. Last, schools must redouble efforts to reduce discrepancies in students' perceptions of fair punishment in light of the research which shows that gaps in perceptions of fair punishment may result in lower social control and higher levels of delinquent activity (O'Neill & Vogel, 2020; Way, 2011).

Risk factors that were significantly associated with bullying were elevated crime rates of the neighborhood of the school, misbehaving classmates, and transient students. Misbehaving students may be indicative of an environment that exposes students to greater chance of bullying (Kupchik & Farina, 2016). Students who move schools frequently are more at-risk for bullying, a finding that has been replicated in other research (MacArthur & Higgins, 2007). Transient students (students who attend a school for a short period) may be vulnerable to bullying victimization because they have not yet had sufficient time to become embedded within peer and other social networks within the school (Bradshaw et al., 2009; Swearer et al., 2008). Transiency, it seems, may intensify students' isolation, and call even greater attention to their "outsider" status which unknowingly increases their bullying victimization risk. The research also finds that transient status is linked to poor school performance, especially among those who have changed schools three or more times (Scherrer & Preckel, 2021). Though this research did not test for interactions between transiency, academic performance, and bullying, a potential weakness, such students may be doubly disadvantaged to the extent that they can neither penetrate friendship nor scholastic networks. As such, social distance, distrust, and enmity may find outlets through bullying or criminal victimization (Burdick-Will et al., 2021).

As noted in our findings, students attending schools with codes of conduct experience 4% less hate-related victimization. We believe that the codes of conduct (school rules) implemented within school's outline or specify the bounds of discourse between students. This finding does seem to align with other empirical findings, though scarce, that have shown reduced hate crime-related incidents in schools that have "transparent" conduct codes (see Lehman, 2019). While this research cannot say with certainty which groups or behaviors are included within the various school conduct codes, the fact remains that clear rules which are designed to foster inclusiveness, reduce vulnerability, and regularly enforced are effective tools for reducing hate or bias-motivated behaviors among students.

Socio-demographic Factors Related to Bullying and Hate-Related Victimization

Aligning with this argument, the present study showed that physical differences such as race/ethnicity matter in both bullying and hate-related victimization, but for different reasons. While it is commonly accepted that racial or ethnic bias is linked to hate-related victimization (e.g., Asian, other races), no such relationship was observed concerning bullying victimization. That is, being Asian, Black, and/or Hispanic was associated with a significant decreased likelihood of bullying victimization. Although several studies have found that Asian students experience a heightened risk for bullying and other forms of victimization (see Hong et al., 2014), other studies have found that minority students may be more likely to underreport bullying victimization (Lai & Kao, 2018), which may be a plausible explanation for our findings. Note also that the structure of school rules, strict enforcement, and disciplinary systems may deter the more visible and overt forms of bullying.

However, being Asian or Other was associated with an increased chance of experiencing hate-related victimization at school (compared to White students). In this regard, Finkelhor and Asdigian's (1996) concept of target antagonism may have some merit. Asian students may be susceptible to what is termed "Orientalism" or "otherization" (Said, 1978). This term posits a dichotomous world or "East versus West," "Us versus Them," "Superiority versus Inferiority" discrimination. Presenting the world in such a binary form encourages hostility and negative stereotypes to flourish. As such, hate-related actions may be perpetrated against Asian students because they represent a collective threat whether it be in the form of academic excellence or other pernicious, but no less harmful, tropes and stereotypes such as vectors for disease (Liang et al., 2007; Niwa et al., 2011).

In addition to the apparent "physical" differences (Asian students) associated with hate-related victimization, there may also be an economic or socioeconomic dimension that requires further elaboration. In this research, students attending schools with a high percentage of students receiving free lunch were almost 3% more likely to experience hate-related victimization. Drawing on Blalock's (1967) "flexibility principle," we speculate that in schools where free lunch programs are offered, there may be an increased "threat" from disadvantaged groups to the socio-economic status of some students. While we do not believe that students are driven by the singular pursuit of status or power, the free lunch program may be a proxy measure for economic disadvantage thereby branding some students as undeserving. As such, an economic interpretation of Finkelhor and Asdigian's (1996) concept of target vulnerability may provide some needed insights into hate-relate victimization. At the same time, we should heed Blalock's (1967) observations who posited that we

> "overestimate the degree to which individuals are primarily motivated by considerations of status and power … [W]e may have minimized the importance of other types of goals, with the inherent danger of assuming that status and economic interests constitute a single 'master motive' in terms of which all other behavior can be explained." (p.39)

Such a reductionist label may make the scapegoating of these students more socially palatable while also normalizing verbal and physical attacks against them (Rahman, 2018). As applied to hate-related victimization, and with minor modification, Blalock's (1967) thesis would assume that there is a connection between minority group status (racial/ethnic, economic, etc.) and the means to an important goal. Because the free lunch program is need-based, and unavailable to most students in the school, some students may use the program to reinforce differences along racial and class lines.

Concerning bullying victimization, several significant relationships were observed among students' demographic characteristics including age, race/ethnicity, and gender, providing an important contrast to hate-related victimization. That is, as respondent age increased, there was a decreased chance of reported bullying victimization, indicating that younger students may be more susceptible to being bullied. It is possible that susceptibility to bullying victimization peaks by a certain age because students' social skills have evolved along with their levels of self-control (Cho & Park, 2022). Equally intriguing, some scholars have argued that there may be an age-graded decrease in bullying victimization because physical differences between students begin to equalize (Blaker & van Vugt, 2014; Craig et al., 2009). Additionally, female students were found to be at greater risk of bullying victimization, which has been discovered in previous research (see Kim et al., 2005).

Implications, Limitations, and Conclusion

Consistent with the findings, we propose several policy recommendations. First, schools at all levels should craft clearly written codes of student conduct that are sufficiently broad enough to cover both bullying and hate-related behaviors. Among other things, these codes of conduct should include definitions of bullying and hate crime that are theoretically driven and consistent with federal and state guidelines to promote uniformity and consistency of enforcement (Younan, 2018). Second, the enforcement of school violations should promote two goals: fairness/equity and prevention. Transparency of the rules and their enforcement will likely foster respect and tolerance of differences. We further emphasize the importance of student accessibility to teachers, or other adults, in whom they can informally confide in. As the scholarship suggests, teachers play an important role in establishing the tone of classrooms and establishing important normative boundaries for students. As such, schools may want to create or expand programs for students and teachers that will equip them with the skills needed to identify bullying and how to access support systems within the schools themselves (Wachs et al., 2018; Wang et al., 2015). Moreover, providing these resources to at-risk students such as transient and poorer students may be a proactive strategy to reduce various types of victimization.

There are a few limitations worth discussing. First, we analyzed cross-sectional data which only allowed us to make correlational conclusions such as if bullying victimization precedes hate-related victimization (or vice versa). Second, like in all non-experimental designs, there is the possibility of omitted variable bias in predicting bullying and hate crime victimization. Third, since we analyzed data from the 2019 SCS, caution should be taken in extrapolating findings to the current context which has experienced a global pandemic, elevated hate crimes, and new political leadership. Fourth, the SCS measure of hate-related victimization involved offensive words due to a student's identity; therefore, future studies should assess factors associated with hate crimes that go beyond words and into actions (e.g., violence). Future research should mitigate these limitations while continuing to explore the similarities and differences between bullying and hate crimes within schools.

This exploratory study sought to assess the relationship between bullying and hate-related victimization within America's schools. In doing so, we argued that there may be important similarities between Englander's "junior hate crime" hypothesis and school bullying/victimization. Protective factors such as clearly written school punishment(s), perceived fairness of punishment(s), and respect for teachers were associated with lower occurrence of bullying and hate-related victimization. While we can't say for certain why the enforcement of rules was not associated with lower risk of hate-related victimization, there may be a marginal deterrence gap due to the invariability of punishments for bullying and hate-related occurrences (Haber, 2015). In other words, if they are all equally punished, then there is no incentive not to commit hate-related acts or engage in bullying. This insight will be beneficial to schools as they consider how to structure or restructure specific rules regarding bullying and hate-related behaviors.

Finally, although the present study suggests that bullying and hate-related victimization are related to each other, schools should be cautious about punishing these offenses the same. Clearly, these types of victimization are not the same and schools should endeavor to decouple them to the greatest extent possible. School-based sensitivity and awareness programs alone may not achieve this goal. As such, school administrators and teachers should implement holistic interventions that focus on the multiple and intersecting pathways of bullying and hate-related victimization. Future research should continue to parse out these victimizations to make schools safer places for American youth.

Disclosure Statement

No potential conflict of interest was reported by the authors.

Discussion Questions

1. What is the junior hate crime hypothesis, and did the study authors find any support for it?
2. How are historical context and the fact that data were collected in 2019 relevant here in terms of understanding the results? How might the choice of a different research design have helped the authors study this?
3. What were the risk and protective factors measured in this study, and how were they related to bullying and hate crimes?

References

Blaker, N., & van Vugt, M. (2014). The status-size hypothesis: How cues of physical size and social status influence each other. In J. Cheng, J. Tracy, & C. Anderson (Eds.), *The psychology of social status*. Springer. https://doi.org/10.1007/978-1-4939-0867-7_6

Blalock, H. M. (1967). *Toward a theory of minority-group relations*. Wiley.

Bradshaw, C. P., Sawyer, A. L., & O'Brennan, L. M. (2009). A social disorganization perspective on bullying-related attitudes and behaviors: The influence of school context. *American Journal of Community Psychology*, *43*(3–4), 204–220. https://doi.org/10.1007/s10464-009-9240-1

Brantingham, P., & Brantingham, P. (1995). Criminality of place. *European Journal on Criminal Policy and Research*, *3*(3), 5–26. https://doi.org/10.1007/BF02242925

Burdick-Will, J., Nerenberg, K. M., Grigg, J. A., & Connolly, F. (2021). Student mobility and violent crime exposure at Baltimore city public elementary schools. *American Educational Research Journal*, *58*(3), 602–634. https://doi.org/10.3102/0002831220963908

Bureau of Justice Statistics. (2019). *School crime supplement, 2019*. Office of Justice Programs.

Burrow, J. D., & Apel, R. (2008). Youth behavior, school structure, and student risk of victimization. *Justice Quarterly*, *25*(2), 349–380. https://doi.org/10.1080/07418820802025181

Cameron, A. C., & Trivedi, P. K. (2013). *Regression analysis of count data* (Vol. 53). Cambridge University Press.

Cho, S., & Park, I. (2022). Explaining the patterns of bullying victimization trajectories: Assessing the generality of low self-control and crime opportunity models to bullying victims. *International Journal of Offender Therapy and Comparative Criminology*, 0306624X221102793. https://doi.org/10.1177/0306624X221102793

Cho, S., & Park, I. (2023). Understanding subtypes of bullying victims using target congruence and lifestyle-routine activities theories: A latent class analysis. *The Journal of Early Adolescence*, *43*(4), 418–454. https://doi.org/10.1177/02724316221105566

Choi, J., Kruis, N., & Lee, J. (2022). Target congruence as a means of understanding the risk of bullying victimization among multicultural family youth in South Korea. *Crime & Delinquency*, *68*(13–14), 2395–2421. https://doi.org/10.1177/00111287211022632

Cohen, L. E., & Felson, M. (1979). Social change and crime rate trends: A routine activity approach. *American Sociological Review*, *44*(4), 588–608. https://doi.org/10.2307/2094589

Coleclough, S. (2022). So many ways to be an outsider: 'Nerdism'and ethnicity as signifiers of otherness. *Exchanges: The Interdisciplinary Research Journal*, *9*(3), 62–83. https://doi.org/10.31273/eirj.v9i3.859

Cook, P. J., Gottfredson, D. C., & Na, C. (2010). School crime control and prevention. *Crime and Justice*, *39*(1), 313–440. https://doi.org/10.1086/652387

Craig, W., Harel-Fisch, Y., Fogel-Grinvald, H., Dostaler, S., Hetland, J., Simons-Morton, B., Molcho, M., de Mato, M. G., Overpeck, M., Due, P., & Pickett, W. (2009). A cross-national profile of bullying and victimization among adolescents in 40 countries. *International Journal of Public Health*, *54*(S2), 216–224. https://doi.org/10.1007/s00038-009-5413-9

Crawford, C., & Burns, R. (2015). Preventing school violence: Assessing armed guardians, school policy, and context. *Policing: An International Journal of Police Strategies & Management*, *38*(4), 631–647. https://doi.org/10.1108/PIJPSM-01-2015-0002

Department of Justice. (2023). U.S. Attorney's office hosts series of high school hate crime education presentations as part of DOJ's united against hate initiative. www.justice.gov/usao-vt/pr/us-attorneys-office-hosts-series-high-school-hate-crime-education-presentations-part#:~:text=Burlington%2C%20Vermont%20%E2%80%93%20U.S.%20Attorney%20Nikolas,and%20other%20civil%20rights%20violations

Englander, E. (2007). Is bullying a junior hate crime? Implications for interventions. *American Behavioral Scientist*, *51*(2), 205–212. https://doi.org/10.1177/0002764207306052

Espelage, D. L., Rao, M. A., & De La Rue, L. (2013). Current research on school-based bullying: A social-ecological perspective. *Journal of Social Distress and the Homeless*, *22*(1), 21–27. https://doi.org/10.1179/1053078913Z.0000000002

Federal Bureau of Investigation. (2021). *2020 FBI hate crimes statistics*. Department of Justice.

Finkelhor, D., & Asdigian, N. L. (1996). Risk factors for youth victimization: Beyond a lifestyles/routine activities theory approach. *Violence and Victims*, *11*(1), 3. https://doi.org/10.1891/0886-6708.11.1.3

GAO K-12 Education. (2023). U.S. Government Accountability Office. www.gao.gov/k-12-education

Haber, E. (2015). The meaning of life in criminal law. *Rutgers Law Review*, *68*, 763–808.

Hall, N., & Hayden, C. (2007). Is 'hate crime'a relevant and useful way of conceptualising some forms of school bullying. *International Journal on Violence and Schools*, *3*, 3–24.

Hong, J. S., Peguero, A. A., Choi, S., Lanesskog, D., Espelage, D. L., & Lee, N. Y. (2014). Social ecology of bullying and peer victimization of latino and Asian youth in the United States: A review of the literature. *Journal of School Violence*, *13*(3), 315–338. https://doi.org/10.1080/15388220.2013.856013

James, K., Bunch, J., & Clay-Warner, J. (2015). Perceived injustice and school violence: An application of general strain theory. *Youth Violence and Juvenile Justice*, *13*(2), 169–189. https://doi.org/10.1177/1541204014521251

Khiat, H. (2012). Unveiling the intricacies of bullying: Students' perspectives in a polytechnic in Singapore. *Asian Journal of Criminology*, *7*(1), 1–22. https://doi.org/10.1007/s11417-010-9085-4

Kim, Y. S., Koh, Y.-J., & Leventhal, B. (2005). School bullying and suicidal risk in Korean middle school students. *Pediatrics*, *115*(2), 357–363. https://doi.org/10.1542/peds.2004-0902

Kupchik, A., & Farina, K. A. (2016). Imitating authority: Students' perceptions of school punishment and security, and bullying victimization. *Youth Violence and Juvenile Justice*, *14*(2), 147–163. https://doi.org/10.1177/1541204014557648

Lai, T., & Kao, G. (2018). Hit, robbed, and put down (but not bullied): Underreporting of bullying by minority and male students. *Journal of Youth and Adolescence*, *47*(3), 619–635. https://doi.org/10.1007/s10964-017-0748-7

Laith, R., & Vaillancourt, T. (2022). The temporal sequence of bullying victimization, academic achievement, and school attendance: A review of the literature. *Aggression and Violent Behavior*, *64*, 101722. https://doi.org/10.1016/j.avb.2022.101722

Lehman, B. (2019). Stopping the hate: Applying insights on bullying victimization to understand and reduce the emergence of hate in schools. *Sociological Inquiry*, *89*(3), 532–555. https://doi.org/10.1111/soin.12296

Liang, B., Grossman, J. M., & Deguchi, M. (2007). Chinese American middle school youths' experiences of discrimination and stereotyping. *Qualitative Research in Psychology*, *4*(1–2), 187–205. https://doi.org/10.1080/14780880701473599

Lindstrom Johnson, S., Waasdorp, T. E., Cash, A. H., Debnam, K. J., Milam, A. J., & Bradshaw, C. P. (2017). Assessing the association between observed school disorganization and school violence: Implications for school climate interventions. *Psychology of Violence*, *7*(2), 181. https://doi.org/10.1037/vio0000045

MacArthur, J., & Higgins, N. (2007). *Addressing the needs of transient students: A collaborative approach to enhance teaching and learning in an area school*. Teaching & Learning Research Initiative.

Malecki, C. K., Demaray, M. K., Smith, T. J., & Emmons, J. (2020). Disability, poverty, and other risk factors associated with involvement in bullying behaviors. *Journal of School Psychology*, *78*, 115–132. https://doi.org/10.1016/j.jsp.2020.01.002

Masucci, M., & Langton, L. (2017). Hate crime victimization, 2004–2015. *NCJ, 250653*.

Mayer, M. J., & Leone, P. E. (1999). A structural analysis of school violence and disruption: Implications for creating safer schools. *Education and Treatment of Children*, *22*(3), 333–356. www.jstor.org/stable/42899578

Mayworm, A. M., & Sharkey, J. D. (2014). Ethical considerations in a three-tiered approach to school discipline policy and practice. *Psychology in the Schools*, *51*(7), 693–704. https://doi.org/10.1002/pits.21782

Michigan Department of Education. (2019). *Michigan high school youth risk behavior survey, 2019*. www.michigan.gov/mde/services/health-safety/curriculum/health/yrbs

Mood, C. (2010). Logistic regression: Why we cannot do what we think we can do, and what we can do about it. *European Sociological Review*, *26*(1), 67–82. https://doi.org/10.1093/esr/jcp006

National Center for Education Statistics. (2018). *Digest of education statistics, 2018*. https://nces.ed.gov/pubs2020/2020009.pdf

Niwa, E., Way, N., & Okazaki, S. (2011). Hostole hallways: Asian American adolescents' experiences of peer discriminationin school. In T. Leong, L. Juang, D. Qin, & H. Fitzgerald (Eds.), *Asian American and Pacific Islander children and mental health* (Vol. 1, pp. 193–217). ABC-CLIO.

Olweus, D. (2013). School bullying: Development and some important challenges. *Annual Review of Clinical Psychology*, *9*, 751–780. https://doi.org/10.1146/annurev-clinpsy-050212-185516

Olweus, D., & Olweus, D. (1993). What we know and what we can do. *Scandinavian Journal of Psychology*, *34*(1), 47–63. https://doi.org/10.1111/j.1467-9450.1993.tb01100.x

O'Neill, J., & Vogel, M. (2020). School cohesion perception discrepancy and student delinquency. *Journal of Youth and Adolescence*, *49*(7), 1492–1502. https://doi.org/10.1007/s10964-019-01170-4

Parent, M. C. (2013). Handling item-level missing data: Simpler is just as good. *The Counseling Psychologist*, *41*(4), 568–600. https://doi.org/10.1177/0011000012445176

Peguero, A. A. (2009). Opportunity, involvement, and student exposure to school violence. *Youth Violence and Juvenile Justice*, *7*(4), 299–312. https://doi.org/10.1177/1541204008330634

Rahman, K. S. (2018). Constructing citizenship: Exclusion and inclusion through the governance of basic necessities. *Columbia Law Review*, *118*, 2447.

Robers, S., Zhang, J., & Truman, J. (2012). Indicators of school crime and safety: 2011. NCES 2012-002/NCJ 236021. National Center for Education Statistics.

Rosen, N. L., & Nofziger, S. (2019). Boys, bullying, and gender roles: How hegemonic masculinity shapes bullying behavior. *Gender Issues*, *36*(3), 295–318. https://doi.org/10.1007/s12147-018-9226-0

Runions, K. C., Salmivalli, C., Shaw, T., Burns, S., & Cross, D. (2018). Beyond the reactive-proactive dichotomy: Rage, revenge, reward, and recreational aggression predict early high school bully and bully/victim status. *Aggressive Behavior*, *44*(5), 501–511. https://doi.org/10.1002/ab.21770

Said, E. (1978). *Orientalism: Western concepts of the orient*. Pantheon.

Salmivalli, C. (1999). Participant role approach to school bullying: Implications for interventions. *Journal of Adolescence*, *22*(4), 453–459. https://doi.org/10.1006/jado.1999.0239

Scherrer, V., & Preckel, F. (2021). Circadian preference and academic achievement in school-aged students: A systematic review and a longitudinal investigation of reciprocal relations. *Chronobiology International*, *38*(8), 1195–1214. https://doi.org/10.1080/07420528.2021.1921788

Schreck, C. J., Miller, J. M., & Gibson, C. L. (2003). Trouble in the school yard: A study of the risk factors of victimization at school. *Crime & Delinquency*, *49*(3), 460–484. https://doi.org/10.1177/0011128703049003006

Steinberg, A., Brooks, J., & Remtulla, T. (2003). Youth hate crimes: Identification, prevention, and intervention. *American Journal of Psychiatry*, *160*(5), 979–989. https://doi.org/10.1176/appi.ajp.160.5.979

Stotzer, R. L. (2015). Youth involvement in anti-gay and anti-lesbian bias crimes. *Violence and Victims*, *30*(2), 308–321. https://doi.org/10.1891/0886-6708.VV-D-13-00021

Swearer, S. M., Turner, R. K., Givens, J. E., & Pollack, W. S. (2008). You're so gay!: Do different forms of bullying matter for adolescent males? *School Psychology Review*, *37*(2), 160–173. https://doi.org/10.1080/02796015.2008.12087891

Tay, R. (2016). Comparison of the binary logistic and skewed logistic (scobit) models of injury severity in motor vehicle collisions. *Accident Analysis & Prevention*, *88*, 52–55. https://doi.org/10.1016/j.aap.2015.12.009

Virginia Department of Health. (2019). *Virginia youth survey, 2018*. www.vdh.virginia.gov/content/uploads/sites/69/2021/03/VYS-2019-High-School-Bullying-and-Teasing.pdf

Wachs, S., Bilz, L., Fischer, S. M., Schubarth, W., & Wright, M. F. (2018). Students' willingness to intervene in bullying: Direct and indirect associations with classroom cohesion and self-efficacy. *International Journal of Environmental Research and Public Health, 15*(11), 2577. https://doi.org/10.3390/ijerph15112577

Wang, C., Swearer, S. M., Lembeck, P., Collins, A., & Berry, B. (2015). Teachers matter: An examination of student-teacher relationships, attitudes toward bullying, and bullying behavior. *Journal of Applied School Psychology, 31*(3), 219–238. https://doi.org/10.1080/15377903.2015.1056923

Way, S. M. (2011). School discipline and disruptive classroom behavior: The moderating effects of student perceptions. *The Sociological Quarterly, 52*(3), 346–375. https://doi.org/10.1111/j.1533-8525.2011.01210.x

Welsh, W. N. (2001). Effects of student and school factors on five measures of school disorder. *Justice Quarterly, 18*, 911.

Wilcox, P., Tillyer, M. S., & Fisher, B. S. (2009). Gendered opportunity? school-based adolescent victimization. *Journal of Research in Crime and Delinquency, 46*(2), 245–269. https://doi.org/10.1177/0022427808330875

Younan, B. (2018). A systematic review of bullying definitions: How definition and format affect study outcome. *Journal of Aggression, Conflict and Peace Research, 11*(2), 109–115. https://doi.org/10.1108/JACPR-02-2018-0347

Appendix

Table A1 presents the survey items from the 2019 NCVS SCS used to create our measures for analyses. Table A2 shows the summary statistics of the measures used within the study.

Table A1 Survey item definitions

Hate-related victimization	"Has anyone called you a bad name having to do with your race/religion/ethnic background/national origin/disability/gender/sexual orientation?"
Bullying victimization	"During this school year, has another student (1) made fun of you, called you names, or insulted you, in a hurtful way; (2) spread rumors about you or tried to make others dislike you; (3) threatened you with harm; (4) pushed you, shoved you, tripped you, or spit on you; (5) tried to make you do things you did not want to do; excluded you from activities on purpose; destroyed your property on purpose?"
School location	1 = city/suburb, 0 = town/rural
Living neighborhood crime	"There is a lot of crime in the neighborhood where you live" (1 strongly disagree to 4 strongly agree)
School neighborhood crime	"There is a lot of crime in the neighborhood where you go to school" (1 strongly disagree to 4 strongly agree).
Misbehaving of classmates	"In your classes, how often are you distracted from doing your schoolwork because other students are misbehaving, for example, talking or fighting?" 1 = ever distracted.
Transiency	"How many different schools have you attended this school year?" 1 = student has attended 2+ schools in past year.
Security staff/police	"Does your school have security guards or assigned police officers?"
Supervision in hallways	"Does your school have other adults supervising the hallway, such as teachers, administrators, or parent volunteers?"
Security cameras in school	"Does your school have one or more security cameras to monitor the school?"
Code of conduct	"Does your school have a code of student conduct, that is, a set of written rules or guidelines that the school provides you?"

Table A1 (Continued)

Enforcement of school rules	"Are school rules strictly enforced"
Fairness of school rules	"Are rules fairly enforced"
Awareness of school punishment	"Are you aware of what punishment will follow if a rule is broken"
Fairness of school punishment	"The punishment for breaking school rules is the same no matter who you are"
Respected teachers	"There is a teacher or other adult at school who really cares about you
Adult cares	"An adult at the school really cares about me"
Free lunch	The percentage of students eligible for free or reduced-price lunch in the respondent's school. 1 = less than 20%, 2 = 20 to 50%, and 3 = 50% or more.
Age	12 through 18 years old
Sex	1 = male
Asian	1 = Asian race/ethnicity
Black	1 = Black race/ethnicity
Hispanic	1 = Hispanic race/ethnicity
Other	1 = American Indian, Alaska Native, Hawaiian, Pacific Islander, Biracial (e.g., Black and White), American Indian White, Asian White, and White Hawaiian/Pacific Islander
White	1 = White race/ethnicity

Table A2 Summary statistics of variables in the analyses

	Mean	*S.D.*	*Min*	*Max*
Dependent variables				
Hate-related victimization	0.08	0.27	0	1
Bullying victimization	0.24	0.43	0	1
Risk factors				
School location	0.64	0.48	0	1
Neighborhood crime near home	1.64	0.73	0	4
Neighborhood crime near school	1.72	0.71	0	4
Misbehaving classmates	0.83	0.37	0	1
Transiency	0.04	0.18	0	1
Protective factors				
Security/police officers at school	0.82	0.38	0	1
Staff supervision in hallways	0.93	0.25	0	1
Security cameras	0.96	0.19	0	1
School code of conduct	0.97	0.17	0	1
Enforcement of school rules	0.87	0.34	0	1
Fairness of school rules	0.93	0.25	0	1

(Continued)

Table A2 (Continued)

	Mean	*S.D.*	*Min*	*Max*
Awareness of punishment	0.89	0.31	0	1
Fairness of punishment	0.87	0.34	0	1
Respectful teachers	0.93	0.25	0	1
Adult cares	0.96	0.19	0	1
Socio-demographic factors				
Free lunch	2.20	0.73	1	3
Age	14.83	1.89	12	18
Sex	0.52	0.50	0	1
Asian	0.05	0.22	0	1
Black	0.11	0.31	0	1
Hispanic	0.23	0.42	0	1
Other	0.04	0.21	0	1
White	0.57	0.50	0	1

Notes: S.D. = standard deviation, min = minimum, max = maximum. N = 4,189.

6 Causation, Experimental, and Quasi-experimental Designs

So far, we have learned the difference between research we do to buy a new car and research adhering to the scientific method. We know about ethics and research, something that we must consider at all stages of planning and implementation of our studies. We have also tackled the issue of taking our concepts and figuring out ways that we can measure them. At this point, we are ready to dive into an exploration of different research designs. One thing that will become abundantly clear very quickly is that not all research is equal when it comes to quality. Research designs each have their own strengths and weaknesses. The selection of a design impacts the types of conclusions that we will be able to draw from the findings. Then why don't we always just select the best design and do that? That is not always possible for reasons that you will appreciate by the end of this book. The important thing for you to learn is that each design has its own pros and cons. Learning this will not only make you so much better prepared to recognize what works and what does not in criminal justice, but you will also be able to evaluate the quality of research in other fields too.

As I think of the late 2010s and the early 2020s, I can think of two good examples when evaluating sources of information and comprehending research were essential. The first was the COVID-19 pandemic. So many different groups shared claims about how it spread, the accuracy of testing, and possible treatments. What were we supposed to believe? More related to criminal justice, what about all the anti-immigration rhetoric, especially as it relates to the impact on the crime rate? A good starting point would be to use what you learned about the quality of sources in Chapter 2 to begin screening items by source and author. The next step is to apply what you are going to learn in the rest of this book, but particularly the next two chapters, to understand the quality of research. Between the two aforementioned steps, you should be able to distinguish good research from poorly designed work and flat-out pseudoscience. This will go a very long way toward helping you figure out what is real.

Correlation versus Causation

Did you know that, as the US government's spending on science, space, and technology increases, so do suicides by hanging, strangulation, and suffocation (Figure 6.1)? It is a strong correlation too. How about another cause of death—dying due to becoming tangled in bedsheets? There is a very strong correlation between that and per capita cheese consumption (Figure 6.2) (Vigen, n.d.). What should we make of this? Many of you are entering the field of criminal justice because you want to keep people safe. Same here, but I also really like cheese. These are really strong correlations, and people are dying, so should we confiscate all the cheese to keep people safe from their bedsheets? What about a return trip to the moon or a trip to Mars? Will that increase suicides in the United States? Of course not! You should not knock grilled cheese sandwiches out of strangers' hands in the name of saving lives. Additionally, I very much want us to explore space, and I am not afraid that increased exploration of space will result in a suicide epidemic here on Earth.

How can I be so confident of that, especially when lives are at stake? One possibility is that I'm just one of those people who buys into Mark Twain's famous "There's lies, damned lies, and

DOI: 10.4324/9781003661511-6

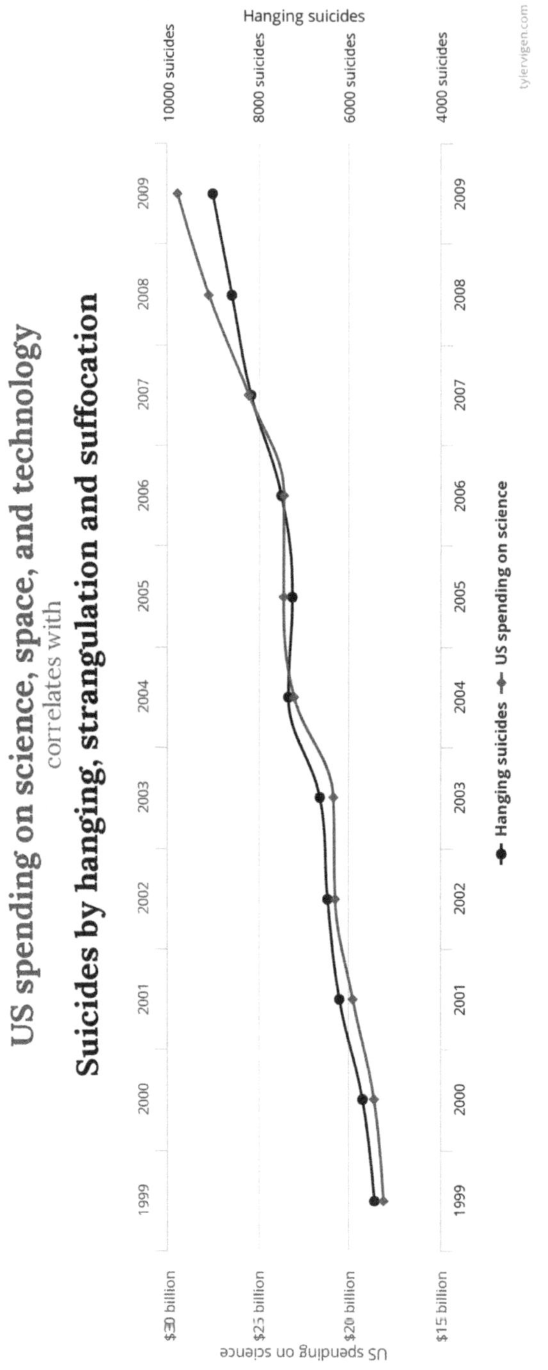

Figure 6.1 US spending on science, space, technology correlates with suicides by hanging, strangulation, and suffocation.
Source: Vigen (2024)

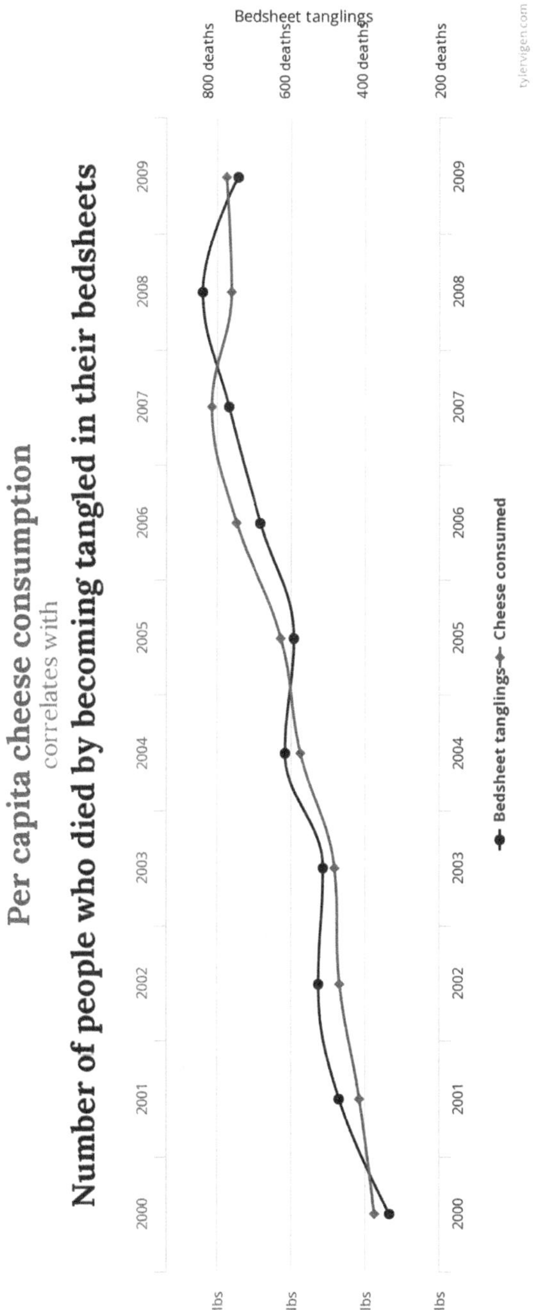

Figure 6.2 Per capita cheese consumption correlates with number of people who died by becoming tangled in their bedsheets.
Source: Vigen (2024)

statistics" statement, and believes that these findings are made up by some researcher with an axe to grind against space exploration and cheese. That certainly is not the case, as I also teach statistics classes and understand that the math behind the above statistical findings is solid. I am confident that we will not see a rise in suicides and deaths by bedsheet because I understand that correlation does *not* equal causation. Failure to distinguish the difference between correlation and causation is one of the biggest mistakes that people make when interpreting research results. If you want to see a great example of this, pick any news show that gives updates on recent health research. One day, coffee will be linked to increased chances of getting certain types of cancer. The next day, coffee will be linked to reduced chances of getting certain types of cancer. What gives? What they aren't telling you in that 60-second clip is that these are likely merely correlations. It doesn't mean that your morning cup of coffee is the one thing that will lead to cancer. The fact that correlation doesn't always mean that one thing causes the other is certainly good news for the ice cream industry, since there is a positive correlation between ice cream consumption and crime (Salkind, 2014). Why? Before you give up your favorite pint of ice cream in the name of public safety, let's learn a little about hypothesis testing.

Hypothesis Testing and the First Element of Causation—Relationships between Two Variables

As discussed in Chapter 1, hypotheses are predictions of relationships between variables. They are the researchers' educated guesses about what they will find when they collect and analyze data. Researchers construct hypotheses after they have considered theories and what we already know about topics in criminal justice. For example, therapeutic communities (TCs) were originally created to help veterans returning from World War II who were having difficulty adapting to civilian life (Lipton, 1998). TCs use therapeutic techniques and role playing to help individuals modify problematic behavior so that they can live successfully in the community. After finding evidence that these programs were associated with positive outcomes in the military community, researchers considered what they know about learning theory and, using deductive reasoning, hypothesized that the application of the TC model to drug-addicted and criminal offending populations would be associated with reduced drug use and offending.

Hypotheses predict relationships between independent and dependent variables. As noted in Chapter 4, independent variables are known as the predictor, treatment, intervention, or cause of something and often go by the abbreviations X or IV, while dependent variables are thought to be the outcome or effect and go by Y or DV. **Research hypotheses** predict that there will be a relationship between the independent and dependent variables. For the TC example, our research hypothesis would be that those who complete the TC program will be less likely to recidivate, or reoffend, within one year following program completion compared to those who did not complete the program. In this example, the independent variable is treatment participation, while the dependent variable is recidivism. In contrast to our research hypothesis, the **null hypothesis** predicts that there is no relationship between X and Y. In other words, completion of the TC program will *not* be associated with reduced odds of recidivism. In quantitative research, we conduct statistical analysis on data to test the *null* hypothesis. If we find enough evidence to confidently reject the null hypothesis, we are, by default, stating that we found support for the research hypothesis. If we do *not* find evidence to reject the null hypothesis, however, we fail to reject (but not accept!) the null hypothesis. Think of it like jury deliberations. The jury never declares the defendant innocent. Rather, they either find the person guilty or not guilty. We handle hypotheses the same way by rejecting or failing to reject the null hypothesis.

If we do decide to reject the null hypothesis and conclude that there is support for our research hypothesis, can we state that our X causes Y? Absolutely not! All we have accomplished thus far is establishing that X and Y are related. Completion of the TC program is associated with reduced recidivism. The problem is that a relationship between the independent and dependent variables is just one element of **causation**. What we accomplished by finding a relationship between X and Y is we found an association or **correlation** between the two. That is a good first step, but we are nowhere near establishing causation. Before I get to the other two requirements of causation, I want to discuss a little more about what we are accomplishing with hypothesis testing using statistics.

As I noted in Chapter 1, in quantitative research, we obtain large samples and conduct statistical analysis with the goal of seeking patterns, or what Maxfield and Babbie (2012) call regularities. Patterns or regularities reflect trends across the cases being studied and show us what is happening in most, but certainly not all, cases. Revisiting the TC example from earlier in this chapter, we will search for a pattern indicating that TC participation is associated with reduced recidivism, but even if the program is found to be helpful, there will often be exceptions and outliers. Exceptions and outliers are common in the social sciences, since we are dealing with human behavior.

Here is an example that should illustrate why predicting human behavior is so much more difficult than making predictions in other fields. Pawson and Tilley (1997) highlight differences between social science research and the natural sciences and mathematics by noting that natural scientists and mathematicians can prove things. For example, we can prove that flipping a switch will always lead to the light bulb turning on, provided that all conditions (circuitry, etc.) are correctly arranged. That is because, in the natural sciences, we know what conditions need to be present to make a light bulb work. Mathematicians conduct **proofs** that demonstrate that there are logically guaranteed conclusions in their field. Two plus two will always equal four, and that is an absolute certainty each time someone attempts addition. Phenomena studied by social scientists are less predictable. Humans do not behave the same way as light switches and circuitry. If a dozen people are exposed to the same stressor—walking into a bedroom and finding one's spouse in bed with one's best friend—we are likely to see different reactions from each person. We can set up a rehabilitation program that is evidence-based, staff it with credentialed professionals who implement that program exactly as planned, and fill it with clients who meet the admission criteria, and yet the program will rehabilitate some people but not others. The aforementioned conditions *should* lead to reduced recidivism, and likely will for a substantial number of people, but it is not nearly as certain as when we flip a light switch.

Given the complexity of human behavior, our research on the outcomes of a successful rehabilitation program will provide evidence that the program improved participants' chances of succeeding but does not present us with a 100% guarantee that it will address the problem we are seeking to solve. Why? Unlike circuitry, every person is different, meaning each person is in a different stage of readiness to change, has different home and family dynamics, has different attitudes and personality traits, and so forth. All these factors external to the TC program have the potential to impact the likelihood of success. So, the best we can do is find evidence of regularities among a large number of cases, or **aggregates**, rather than focus on individual exceptions.

The decision whether to reject or fail to reject the null hypothesis is made based on probability. After collecting data, we use statistics to test our hypotheses. The tricky aspect of statistics is that we can never be 100% confident in our results, as there is always the possibility that any difference we are seeing between our groups is a product of sampling error rather than an actual relationship between X and Y. Of course, researchers are always looking to minimize error, and we work to do so by careful sample selection. The possibility of error in statistics is why social scientists use less committal terms when describing their study results. Social scientists never claim that their results "prove" anything, nor do we declare that we have determined "X causes Y." If anyone is making such claims, be very suspicious.

Time Order—the Second Requirement for Causation

We did our hypothesis testing, ran our statistical analysis, and now feel comfortable that we have found a relationship between TC participation (our independent variable, or X) and reduced recidivism (our dependent variable, or Y). Despite all this work, we are now only one-third of the way toward being able to conclude that that X causes Y. The second requirement is determining the time order between X and Y. If we are to claim that our independent variable causes a change in the dependent variable, X must come before Y in time. For our TC example, that is easy, as we are looking at recidivism after people completed the program, so time order is built into the study. Unfortunately, it is not always so simple in criminal justice. Two examples that illustrate the importance of establishing the time order of X and Y are drug use and crime, and home security system ownership and burglary.

There are several theories that seek to explain the relationship between drug use and crime. Bennett, Holloway, and Farrington (2008) identified three categories of drug-crime theories, including those that (1) suggest a direct causal connection between drug use and crime, (2) posit an indirect causal connection, meaning that other variables cause both, or (3) suggest there is no causal connection. The first group of theories suggest that either drug use causes criminal behavior or criminal behavior causes drug use. Bennett et al. (2008) reviewed and analyzed the results of 30 empirical studies of drug use and crime and found that there is a strong association between the two. The odds of offending tended to be 2.8 to 3.8 times higher for drug users than nonusers, and these results varied by drug type. That is rather strong evidence of a relationship between drug use and crime, but which comes first, the drug use or the criminal behavior? Research results have been mixed, and there is currently no clear answer to this question.

Research on burglary and crime presents us with a similar dilemma. Contrary to what you might think, research suggests that burglar alarm ownership is associated with *greater* odds of victimization (Roth et al., 2018; Tseloni et al., 2014). What does this mean? Do burglar alarms make us *less* safe? We know that there is a positive relationship between alarm ownership and burglary, but we do not know the time order. It could be that the presence of a burglar alarm signals to potential burglars that there are valuables worth protecting in a house, but only if the alarms were installed before the burglaries. A possible explanation is that these houses installed burglar alarms after they were victimized, which is why it appears that houses with burglar alarms have more burglaries. Without knowing whether the burglaries or the alarm installations occurred first, our understanding of the relationship between the two is very limited.

Accounting for All Other Possible Explanations—the Third Requirement for Causation

The third element of causation is accounting for any other possible variable that could explain the relationship between X and Y. Remember that our consumption of ice cream is related to increases in crime. Eating ice cream does not cause crime, of course. It just looks that way, because there is a spurious relationship. **Spurious relationships** are those that are not genuine. What is happening here is that both X (ice cream) and Y (crime) are related to a third variable (Z)—the weather. Warmer weather prompts us to crave ice cream, but it also encourages us to change our behavior patterns and get out more. As we become more active, we leave our belongings at home, unattended, creating a greater opportunity for burglary. We also interact more with other people, presenting the possibilities of assault and robbery. According to the routine activities perspective, when we have the convergence in time and space of a motivated individual, a suitable target, and the absence of a capable guardian, crime is more likely to occur (Cohen & Felson, 1979). So, as the weather gets warmer and we change our routines, there is more opportunity for crime.

Statisticians who observe that increased ice cream consumption is associated with increased crime nationwide and that increased margarine consumption is correlated with higher divorce rates in Maine (Vigen, n.d.) must also think about other possible explanations for their findings. In other words, put the brakes on asserting that the correlation is equivalent to causation until all other possibilities are considered. These other possibilities are called **rival causal factors** (Z), defined as any variable other than X that may be responsible for the changes in Y. Remember when I mentioned that the success rates of people completing TC programs might vary because of their personality characteristics, home lives, employment readiness, and other aspects of their lives? Those are all rival causal factors. The presence of these other variables is known as **threats to internal validity** (TIVs) (Hagan, 2007). What this means is that people in Maine can put some margarine on a piece of toast without fearing that they are ruining someone's marriage.

Threats to Internal Validity

Threats to internal validity are any factors, besides the independent variable, that exert influence on our dependent variable. We cannot conclude that X causes Y while there are other variables that are producing variation in Y. According to Cook and Campbell (1979), there are several threats to internal validity. Following is a short summary of them:

History

History refers to events external to research that can influence the results. Imagine that you are studying a school district as it overhauls its school security procedures with the hope that it will increase both actual safety and students' perceptions of safety. You conduct a pretest of students' opinions about their safety before the administration starts to implement the changes to get a baseline. After the overhaul, you conduct the posttest and find that students are more fearful now. Did the security measures backfire? Maybe. Another possible explanation might be that a historical event impacted opinions. If the pretest was administered around a time when there were no publicized school shootings, but the posttest took place within a week of a shooting that received extensive media coverage, the publicity could be what impacted students' assessment of their own safety, not the new safety measures.

White and Weisburd (2018) were studying the use of a police-social work co-responder model to address calls for service for people suffering from mental illness in Baltimore, Maryland, when history intervened. Freddie Gray died while in police custody under very controversial circumstances, leading to civil unrest in Baltimore. Since extra police were needed to respond to protests and property damage, the co-response program was suspended for a few weeks. This impacted residents' perceptions of the program, as they were frustrated by the team's absence. Such circumstances, which had nothing to do with the efficacy of the co-responders, impacted residents' impressions of the program.

Testing Effects

Testing may become more of a problem the more often respondents are asked to take the test. If people are asked to take both a pretest and a posttest, the pretest content might sensitize participants to the purpose of the study. This might increase respondents' motivation either to provide desirable answers on the posttest or to change behavior that they realize is being observed. The consequence is that the posttest results will not be an accurate reflection of participants' true performance or opinions. In this case, changes in performance or opinions are not related to the impact of the independent variable on the dependent variable but instead reflect the influence of the pretest on the outcome.

Instrumentation

Instrumentation refers to a change in a data collection tool, resulting in difficulty comparing information across time. As was noted in Chapter 5, the National Crime Victimization Survey (NCVS) is the largest source of victimization data in the United States, with researchers conducting 240,000 interviews on criminal victimization each year. The NVCS has been in existence since 1973, but over the years, the Bureau of Justice Statistics (BJS) has found it necessary to conduct multiple redesigns of their survey instrument. One major redesign that had a substantial impact on victimization estimates took place in 1992. BJS adjusted questions to allow for better stimulation of respondents' memories and asked additional questions to elicit more responses about sexual victimization and domestic violence. These changes resulted in increased reporting of victimization. Someone who was unaware of this change might look at NCVS statistics over time and incorrectly assume that there was a substantial crime wave in the early 1990s. Fortunately, the NCVS makes it very clear in their data tables that year-to-year changes during this time period likely reflect an instrumentation issue rather than a surge in victimization (Kinderman, Lynch, & Cantor, 1997).

Statistical Regression

Inclusion of people with extremely high or low pretest scores in research will likely result in some movement of their scores toward the group mean by the second testing, regardless of the planned intervention. This is known as **statistical regression** or regression to the mean. The same goes for neighborhoods or prisons that are selected for study due to their high rates of crimes and disciplinary infractions. Farrington and Welsh (2006) found that, when selecting a high-crime area for a crime prevention initiative and using a control area with a moderate crime rate, statistical regression accounted for about 4% of the crime reduction in the high-crime area from the pretest time to posttest. Grambsch (2008) studied homicide rates in states throughout the United States from 1976 through 2001. Between 1981 and 1996, 25 states passed shall-issue laws that require states to issue permits for carrying concealed weapons to all residents meeting certain criteria. Previous research touted these laws as producing a reduction in homicide rates. Grambsch found declines in homicides not only in states that passed shall-issue laws, but also in states that did not. In fact, those that had not passed such laws experienced greater reductions in homicide rates over the 25-year period. Grambsch concluded that the apparent relationship between shall-issue laws and declines in homicides is more of a product of regression to the mean rather than substantial policy changes.

Selection (Sample) Bias

The manner in which we seek and accept participants for studies is a threat to internal validity when it produces a sample that is unlike the population from which it was drawn or when we wind up comparing groups that are nonequivalent. Comparing recidivism rates of people who were sentenced to prison to those who were sentenced to probation is problematic, because there is likely a reason why judges deemed some people appropriate for incarceration while others were considered safe enough to be placed on community supervision. If we find that those returning from prison recidivated more often, it will be difficult to determine whether it was due to the harm caused by incarceration or whether they were already higher-risk individuals.

Mortality/Attrition

Studies that involve multiple periods of data collection or tracking people over time are likely to lose participants. This is known as **mortality**, and it can arise for numerous reasons. A better fitting term might be **attrition bias**, as mortality tends to make people assume that we are losing research participants due to death. While that could certainly be a reason why someone leaves a study, a much more common reason is that people lose interest in the study and drop out. Other possibilities are they move out of the area, complete their correctional supervision term, or otherwise become ineligible for continued study participation. Not only does such attrition make data analysis more difficult due to its impact on the sample size, but it can also be especially problematic if certain types of individuals are more likely than others to withdraw or disappear. Imagine you want to study drug use and delinquency among high school students. You decide to do a panel study, which means you are going to collect data from the same group of people multiple times, in this instance at the start of every school year. Data collection is taking place in the school, so students must be enrolled and present on the data collection days to participate. Over four years, you will lose students for a variety of reasons, but you are likely to lose more adolescents with higher involvement in drug use and delinquency, as they are more likely to be suspended, expelled, sent to another school, or to skip school. The result is that you will likely have higher attrition levels for individuals who are more involved in delinquency, resulting in a likely underestimation of drug use and criminal involvement of juveniles. This attrition bias is very likely to impact your findings.

Maturation

Maturation can threaten the validity of findings when biological or psychological changes result in different performance or responses from pretest to posttest. Children become physically stronger as they enter adolescence. Teenagers become impulsive risk-takers, but that behavior changes as they transition to adulthood. Changes to impulsiveness levels are natural as people transition from adolescence to adulthood, so we need to be careful in attributing any such observed differences to an independent variable, such as a behavioral intervention, that we are studying at the time.

Selection-Maturation Interaction

The two threats of selection bias and maturation can combine to be problematic when groups are selected unevenly, resulting in maturation impacting groups at different times. Fletcher and Tims (1992) caution that **selection-maturation** can be a problem in drug treatment evaluations, as people with greater maturity and fewer psychological challenges might be more predisposed to enter and remain in treatment. Even if we take it upon ourselves to assign half our participant group to treatment, there can still be problems. Imagine if we take a large sample of people on probation who are currently struggling with drug use, and we assign them to two groups. One group is going to be mandated to the experimental stimulus, in this case TC treatment, as part of their probation, while the other group is going to just get probation. We should do some testing to find out characteristics of our participants first, to make sure that the two groups are similar before the treatment intervention. If we have a situation where we accidentally select the people who are more ready to change, are older, and have fewer psychological challenges into one of the groups, that group might fare better regardless of the intervention. They might be motivated to change on their own or seek assistance outside of probation to address their needs. Similarly, if we try to split our population into two groups and compare offending patterns, the groups might differ in criminal activities because the sampling process resulted in one group having older, more mature participants than the other group.

Diffusion of Treatment

If we have one group being exposed to a treatment stimulus (X) and another, similar group not exposed for comparison purposes, we must make sure that the comparison group remains unexposed to X. I once worked with a social service group that was interested in helping justice-involved individuals with mental illness. These groups tended to be stigmatized quite a bit. The social service agency aimed to reduce their isolation and build up their social capital so that they could live happier, more productive lives. We randomized the agency's client group so that one half would get the new treatment from the social workers, while the other half would receive the regular case management work that the agency traditionally did with their clients. To maintain this second group of clients not receiving the new services, we had to be very careful to limit training of the new techniques and discussion of that work to just the staff engaging with the clients getting the new services. We worried that too much discussion of the new program among the whole staff would result in all clients getting the new services. In other words, there would be **diffusion of treatment** into the comparison group. That could be a problem, because when we went to evaluate the effectiveness of the program, we would likely see that the two groups fared the same over that time period. That would lead us to believe, perhaps erroneously, that the treatment failed when, in fact, the two groups were equal because they all received the same treatment. Diffusion of the treatment is also known as contamination of the comparison group.

Compensatory Equalization of Treatment

There may be legitimate ethical concerns about withholding treatment from a group of people and, to combat this, it might be tempting for practitioners to deviate from the research plan and provide extra services or perks to that group. I mentioned the Kansas City Preventive Patrol Experiment in Chapter 4. Researchers and the police department arranged for some parts of Kansas City to get extra police patrols (proactive beats), others were going to get normal routine patrols (control beats), and a third area would only get police attention when someone called for assistance (reactive beats). The researchers found no differences in crime rates in the three areas, nor did residents in the three beats notice differences in police behavior (Kelling et al., 1974). One drawback to the study, however, was that police officers had the discretion to engage in "patrol-initiated activity" in the different beats. The officers seemed to do so very frequently in the beats that were intended to receive less police attention, to the point where there was little difference in the observed levels of police presence in the different areas (Larson, 1975). What some police did here was provide **compensatory equalization of treatment** by finding excuses to make themselves visible in the reactive beats neighborhoods, because they were convinced that their presence was essential to public safety.

Compensatory Rivalry and Demoralization/Resentment

Compensatory rivalry can arise when the group getting the treatment, or X, and the comparison group not receiving it are aware of each other's presence, and the latter group attempts to outperform the former or otherwise portray itself in a better light. **Demoralization** is the opposite, where members of the comparison group become discouraged and experience reduced productivity and morale in the face of their deprivation relative to the experimental group.

Statistical Conclusion Validity

Maxfield and Babbie (2012) define **statistical conclusion validity** as "whether we are able to determine if two variables are related" (p. 114). Statistical procedures only provide valid information if we implement them properly. One drawback to statistical tests is they require a sufficient sample size in order to have enough "power." **Power** refers to the probability of correctly rejecting a null hypothesis. For a detailed discussion of power analysis and of determining appropriate sample sizes, you should consult an introductory statistics textbook. What you should understand for now is that we can make errors when drawing conclusions based on our statistical findings, and a small sample size can increase the chance of error.

Generalizability and Threats to External Validity

If, after doing careful analysis, we are comfortable stating that we have found evidence of an actual (not spurious) relationship between X and Y, our next step is to think about whether it is appropriate to assume those results would apply to other samples or to the population from which we selected our original sample. If we find support for our research hypothesis and are comfortable that our sample is representative of the population we are studying, we can generalize our findings, meaning we can assume that the pattern we witnessed in our sample also exists in the larger population. **Generalizability** is an important goal of research, as we study samples to learn about populations that are too expensive or time-consuming for us to study.

A type of generalizability is **external validity**, or the likelihood of being able to replicate our findings if we did the same study at another time or place (Maxfield & Babbie, 2012). There are several characteristics of our research designs that can impact external validity. Following is a list:

Selection (Sample) Bias

This threat to internal validity could also influence external validity. If you wanted to study whether students at a specific university thought classes were rigorous enough, but your sample consisted only of students in the honor's program, it would be unlikely that you would get similar findings if you repeated the study with another sample of students from the same school.

Reactivity

Reactivity is individuals' awareness that they are being observed and their corresponding changes of behavior. Most people would not attempt to break into a car or a house if they knew that someone was observing them. I should know, as one of my many research jobs in graduate school was to make myself as inconspicuous as possible while hanging out in high-crime areas and observing what people do. In criminal justice research, we must be aware of the impact of our involvement in the study. In this instance, the person's decision not to commit a crime might have been a product of a researcher's visible presence, and if we replicated this situation without a researcher in sight, results would likely have been different.

While the presence of researchers can inhibit the behavior of people thinking about breaking the law, it can motivate employees who feel the need to be at peak performance while being observed. The **Hawthorne Effect** refers to people behaving atypically due to their knowledge of being watched. It got its name from a study of workers at the Hawthorne Plant, where staff were suddenly much more efficient once they learned that they were being observed (Landsberger, 1958).

Findings based on such changes to behavior are not generalizable to the population of factory workers, nor would they be replicated in another study where the researchers remained out of sight.

Testing Effects

This is another threat to internal validity that can also impact external validity. Participants might gain knowledge or increase their sensitivity to the topic being studied simply by being exposed to the pretest instrument. If that is the case, posttest results might be partially or completely a product of testing effects rather than a reaction to the treatment stimulus. That means that we would not find the same results elsewhere unless we also administered a pretest. That is problematic if we are testing a new curriculum, such as a law enforcement ethics training course, that we are pilot testing with pre- and posttests now. If the plan is to implement the new curriculum statewide without a corresponding research evaluation, it is imperative that the curriculum itself, and not the pretest, is what is producing the desired change.

History

History could have a far-reaching impact on the study results and the extent to which we could expect to replicate the study and find similar outcomes. If a historical event produced some or all the observed changes in the dependent variable, we are unlikely to find the same results at another place or time absent that historical event.

Multiple Treatment Interference

In criminal justice, agencies frequently attempt multiple interventions at the same time. Incarcerated people might be simultaneously enrolled in anger management, drug counseling, and job readiness programs and then, upon release, be placed on parole with the requirement of participation in additional programs. Police departments might consider engaging in community policing citywide, hotspots policing in certain areas, and then perhaps a very specific problem-oriented policing initiative in one neighborhood. If we see that people participating in more than one correctional program were less likely to recidivate or that crime went down in the city, **multiple treatment interference** would make it difficult to determine which, exactly, contributed to our positive outcomes (Hagan, 2007).

The Importance of Replication in Research

I have used the word "replicate" a few times over the last few pages because **replication** is an important part of research, albeit time-consuming and expensive. When searching for programs that work in criminal justice, it is essential that we exercise caution and refrain from rushing to change policies or adopt new programs based on just one study, even if it was quality work. The reason is that there could be something unique about that one place or time that contributed to a program's success. A recent example of the need for replication before drawing conclusions about programs is the story of Project HOPE, which originally stood for the Hawaii Opportunity Probation with Enforcement program. As the program moved from Hawaii to the US mainland, the "H" was changed from "Hawaii" to "Honest." Project HOPE is a program that de-emphasizes rehabilitation and, instead, promotes swift, certain, and fair graduated sanctions for people on probation with the goal of deterring negative behavior. The program was run by a very charismatic judge and evaluated by well-regarded researchers. After the researchers conducted two evaluations and reported reductions in recidivism, the researchers and the judge worked to publicize the program. Project HOPE was quickly adopted all over the United States, with 160 programs popping up in a little over a decade. Subsequent evaluations, however, did not support the Hawaii findings. On the contrary, replications of this program indicated that Project HOPE did not produce reductions in recidivism. There were 160 programs funded and staffed using this seemingly ineffective model. What happened? We did not slowly introduce this program elsewhere, replicate the research, and wait for the findings before concluding that it worked. Instead, we assumed the findings of the Hawaii evaluations would be generalizable to everywhere else. But why weren't they? One possible reason is that the probation officers in Hawaii received cognitive-behavioral programming treatment, making them uniquely prepared to help their clients. This is something that most other probation jurisdictions do not do. Another possibility is the performance or involvement of the judge. Then, there is the flaw in the entire theory underpinning this program. Just about all the existing research on deterrence-based programs indicates that they are not effective in reducing recidivism, and that alone should have given everyone pause and encouraged replication studies before mass adoption of the program (Cullen et al., 2018). Replication may seem like a waste of time if a program appeals to "common sense" and there is some early evidence that it is effective. This is just one example of an ineffective, criminal justice program being prematurely adopted by jurisdictions before adequate replication work is completed.

Classical Experiments

Now that we have reviewed the pitfalls of research, we are going to spend the next 1.5 chapters discussing different types of designs and learn how each fares in avoiding threats to validity. Something that you must keep in mind is that there is no perfect research design. We just do our best within the confines of what ethical rules, our budgets, the availability of data, and our schedules allow. Our goal is to design a study in a way that will get us closest to being able to find a causal pattern between our independent and dependent variables. To get there, we must remember the three elements of causation: (1) a relationship between X and Y, (2) X precedes Y in time, and (3) all rival causal factors (Z) are explained away. Out of all the designs we will review in this chapter and the next, the **classical experiment** gets us closest to our goal.

There are three characteristics that distinguish the classical experiment from other research designs (Figure 6.3). First, the participants, groups, or geographic areas being studied are divided into at least two groups—experimental and control. The **experimental group** will be exposed to whatever stimulus represents the independent variable, while the **control group** will serve as a comparison that, hopefully, differs only in that they will not be exposed to X. Second, assignment to either the experimental or the control group must be handled in a way that maximizes the chances that the two groups will be equivalent. In a classical experiment, this is achieved through random selection of participants to either the experimental or control group. While randomization does not guarantee that the groups will be equivalent, the chances of it producing similar groups grow with a randomized design as we increase the sample size. Third, the study must include at least one measurement of the groups before introduction of the experimental stimulus and at least one measurement after exposure. In other words, there needs to be at least one pretest to measure the dependent variable before the appearance of X and at least a posttest after X is introduced.

The goal of a classical experiment is to acquire experimental and control groups that are similar in every way that is relevant to what is being studied. Revisiting the TC example, we would seek to obtain a large sample of potential participants who are somewhat similar. We would set specific inclusion and exclusion criteria with the goal of acquiring participants with

Classical Experiment				Quasi-Experiment		
R	O	X	O	O	X	O
R	O		O	O		O

R = Random assignment
X = Independent variable
O = observation

Figure 6.3 Classical and quasi-experimental designs
Source: Author

similar offending histories and criminogenic needs (personality traits, attitudes, association with delinquent peers, education levels, etc.). We could accomplish this by restricting participation to only individuals with certain criminal charges and those who scored within a specific range on a reliable and valid risk assessment test. Once we have identified a pool of eligible participants, they would be randomly assigned to either the TC program or to treatment-as-usual that is offered through probation services. Researchers can then look at a number of outcomes, or dependent variables, to see whether there are differences between the two groups before and after treatment. Some ideas for dependent variables could be whether participants in the two groups are rearrested during a certain time period, how long they remain in the community before being rearrested, or the percent of people in both groups who are able to obtain legal jobs within a time period.

The classical experiment would allow us to (1) study whether there is a relationship between X (type of treatment received while on probation) and Y (an outcome such as recidivism or employment) and (2) establish time order by measuring both groups before and after the experimental group is exposed to the independent variable. The third requirement for causation, controlling for all possible rival explanations, is more difficult to address.

The primary advantage to classical experiments is the degree of control the research team can have. Researchers in the natural sciences, and even psychology, can run classical experiments inside laboratories where they are able to control just about everything, including the lighting, temperature, exposure to outside information and influences, and other environmental factors. This level of control allows them to be confident that the introduction of X is truly the only difference between groups. This is an important feature because it addresses the third requirement for causality—eliminating other possible explanations for the relationship between X and Y. Of course, laboratory experiments are generally not feasible in criminal justice, as we seek to observe and measure behaviors of humans in real-world settings.

The classical experiment is a very strong research design and can help to reduce or eliminate some, but not all, threats to internal validity. Maxfield and Babbie (2012) observed that attrition/mortality could continue to be a problem, despite the safeguards built into classical experimental designs, because dropout rates could be higher in the experimental or control group for a variety of reasons, including the desirability of exposure to the independent variable. Cook and Campbell (1979) note that demoralization of the control group could generate a spurious relationship between X and Y, because the control group's dampened mood or diminished performance can create the appearance of a difference between the two groups that would incorrectly be attributed to the independent variable. For other threats, such as compensatory rivalry, compensatory equalization, and diffusion of treatment, these problems can obscure a relationship between X and Y that actually exists.

External validity is a potential problem with classical experiments, particularly those implemented in a tightly controlled environment. While those controls help to enhance internal validity, they introduce a degree of artificiality into the study. That artificiality will weaken external validity, since implementation of the same study in a real-world setting will likely produce different results (Maxfield & Babbie, 2012).

Variations on the Classical Experimental Designs

Solomon Four-Group Design and Factorial Design

A few designs incorporate the elements of the classical experiment—two groups, equivalence, and pre- and posttests, but take additional steps to address potential threats to validity. One of these is the **Solomon four-group design** (Figure 6.4). This design can be rather cumbersome, but it serves as a check for testing bias. As the name implies, researchers randomly divide participants into four groups. The first two groups are the same as they are in the classical experiment, with both taking a pretest, followed by only one group's exposure to the independent variable, and then both groups taking the posttest. The Solomon design adds two more groups, neither of which get the pretest. Instead, one group gets exposed to the independent variable and takes the posttest, while the last group just takes the posttest. We are hypothesizing here that the two groups exposed to the experimental stimulus will have been impacted by that experience and will, therefore, have different posttest scores than the two groups that were not exposed to X. We can check to see whether the pretest had any impact on the results by comparing the pretest-no stimulus-posttest group to the posttest-only group. If the pretest had no impact, those two groups should be the same that was not exposed to X. Additionally, posttest scores for the pretest-X-posttest and the X-posttest-only groups should also be the same if there were no testing effects.

The **factorial design** is a classical experiment with an additional group added to test a second type of treatment (Figure 6.4). We could use a factorial design if we have two types of drug treatment options that we want to add as enhancements to regular probation and then test their effectiveness against that of standard probation. We could randomly assign one group of people on probation to cognitive-behavioral treatment plus probation, one to medication-assisted treatment plus probation, and then the third group to standard probation conditions.

Equivalent Groups Posttest-Only Design

Pretests are not always possible, and in those instances, an **equivalent-groups posttest-only** design might be the only option. Gates, Ariel, and Assaraf (2025) wanted to test the efficacy of using virtual police visits to handle calls for service for low-level offenses in Great Britain. They worked with two police departments to randomly assign these cases to virtual visits (treatment condition) or the traditional in-person visits (control condition). After the police interaction, respondents assigned to the virtual visits reported higher levels of satisfaction with the police and faster response from law enforcement. The obvious drawback here is that we have no baseline or pretest data to gauge how the two groups perceived the police prior to this most recent contact. Skeptics of virtual visits could argue that the control group might have consisted of a pool of individuals who had more negative views of police before they called for service. Of course, the use

Solomon four-group design		
R O	X	O
R O		O
R	X	O
R		O

Factorial design		
R O	X_1	O
R O	X_2	O
R O		O

Equivalent groups posttest-only design		
R	X	O
R		O

Crossover design		
R	X	O
R		O X

R = Random assignment
X = Independent variable
O = Observation

Figure 6.4 Variations of experimental designs
Source: Author

of randomization goes a long way toward increasing the chance that the two groups were similar at baseline.

Crossover Design

When working with criminal justice and social service programs, researchers often have to work around what the implementing agencies have decided to do. A common challenge is that the agency wants or needs to expose everyone to the new treatment, leaving no control group for comparison purposes. This is understandable and might be guided by ethical practice or even law. If we have a potentially helpful rehabilitation program, we would not want to deny anyone admission. Similarly, if the law dictates that police need to receive training, all must receive it. If everyone needs to be exposed to X, then how do we learn about how people who didn't get it performed in terms of Y? One way to do that is through a **crossover design**. Rehabilitation programs only have so many seats, and training programs usually need to be phased in over time. So, the waiting list can become the control group. Engel et al. (2022) were faced with this dilemma when they partnered with the Louisville (Kentucky) Metro Police Department. The entire department had to receive de-escalation training (X). Training the whole department would take time, so it had to be done in phases. The researchers took the nine divisions of the department, randomly selected clusters of those officers to either the intervention or the control group, and set a calendar for all the control group members to eventually permanently cross over into the treatment group. While the waiting list officers comprised the control group, researchers collected data on use-of-force incidents, officer injuries, and resident injuries (all Ys) and then compared this to the performance of officers who already completed the training. One potential drawback here is that this plan will only work if people are scheduled to be in the control group long enough for researchers to collect sufficient data on the dependent variable.

Quasi-experiments

A **quasi-experiment** differs from the classical experimental design in that it is missing one of the three elements that characterize the classical experiment (Cook & Campbell, 1979). Random assignment of participants into treatment or control groups is not always possible, especially when researchers are dependent on an external agency to provide access to research participants. When groups are selected nonrandomly, we will still have an experimental group, but the control group will be referred to as a **comparison group** instead. The inability to randomly assign participants to the treatment and comparison groups has the potential to introduce threats to internal validity here, including selection bias and selection-maturation interaction.

While less than ideal, quasi-experiments can be very valuable, especially when researchers take steps to match the treatment and comparison groups or use statistical controls to account for the differences between groups. **Matching** involves either manually, or with statistical procedures, pairing experimental participants with comparison group members based on theoretically relevant variables. Returning to the TC example, the criminal justice, mental health, or drug treatment agency associated with the intervention may not be in a position to allow the researchers to randomly assign people to either probation or treatment-as-usual. Strah et al. (2018) faced this exact challenge when studying an in-prison cognitive-behavioral treatment (CBT) program. The corrections department's policy was that joining CBT had to be voluntary, so random assignment to treatment modality was prohibited. The researchers responded by matching program volunteers to individuals who either started the program and later dropped out or those who did not volunteer. Individuals in both groups were matched on several demographic and institutional misconduct variables to produce similar treatment and comparison groups.

An alternative to matching is to use statistical techniques to account for potential differences between the treatment and comparison groups with the goal of isolating the effects of the treatment. A mental health agency near my university was partnering with the county jail and some police departments to offer diversion and reentry services to individuals with mental illness who were committing low-level crimes. The agency felt an ethical obligation to provide services to all who were eligible and willing to participate, so it was impossible to randomize half of those eligible into a control group. Instead, I constructed a comparison group by identifying people who were eligible for services but did not receive them because they either lived outside of the agency's treatment area or staff were unable to contact them. I then used multivariate statistical models to learn whether program participation remained a predictor of recidivism after controlling for demographic and legal characteristics of the two groups (Tartaro, 2015).

The other type of quasi-experiment is a **time series** (Jennings & Reingle Gonzalez, 2019; Lu et al., 2019; Maxfield & Babbie, 2012) (Figure 6.5). Time-series designs involve multiple data collection points. This would not be appropriate for use with the TC or CBT program example, as there would not be enough data collection points to make a time series possible. For evaluations of those programs, you would likely compare outcomes at two, possibly three different data points, such as number of incarcerations in the three years before the treatment program (time 1) versus number of incarcerations in the first-year post-completion (time 2), and then maybe the number of incarcerations three years after completion (time 3). That is not enough for a time series. Time series is very useful when you want to look at changes in crime patterns, such as

Interrupted time series

O O O O O O O O O O O O X O O O O O O O O O O O O O

Interrupted time series with nonequivalent comparison group

O O O O O O O O O O O O X O O O O O O O O O O O O O
O O O O O O O O O O O O O O O O O O O O O O O O O

Interrupted time series with treatment removal

O O O O O O X O O O O O O O O O O O -X O O O O O O O

X = independent variable
O = observation

Figure 6.5 Time-series designs
Source: Author

monthly crime statistics over a period of a few years or yearly statistics over several decades. For example, Mayhew, Clarke, and Elliott (1989) studied yearly rates of motorcycle theft in Germany in the 1970s and 1980s, during which the German government passed a law requiring people on motorcycles to wear helmets. The researchers looked at yearly rates throughout the two decades. The new law was phased in gradually. Theft rates remained stable during the phase-in period but fell sharply once police began writing tickets. Mayhew and colleagues concluded that the reduction in thefts was due to fear of being caught stealing. Most motorcycle thefts are crimes of opportunity, with someone looking for transportation committing the theft at a time and place when he or she is unlikely to be caught. Once police started to pull over and ticket motorists without helmets, stealing a bike became very risky unless one happened to be carrying around a helmet in anticipation of stealing a bike. Mayhew and associates did an **interrupted time series**. The interruption is the introduction of the independent variable, which in this case was the helmet law with enforcement.

There are multiple variations of time-series designs, including the **interrupted non-equivalent comparison group time series** (Figure 6.5). This would allow researchers to assess the impact of a new policing tactic on calls for service data over several months while also collecting the same type of police data from a neighboring city that is not introducing any new police initiatives (Braga, et al., 2001). Is legalization of marijuana associated with increases in crime? That argument was used for decades to maintain prohibition of the drug. When some states started to legalize it, Lu et al. (2019) obtained crime data from Washington and Colorado, two of the earliest states to legalize, and states where marijuana remained prohibited at the time of their data collection. They found no long-term impact of legalization of marijuana on violent or property crime, with the exception of a *decline* in burglary rates in Washington following legalization.

Another possibility is **interrupted time series with treatment removal**, including several observation periods, introduction of a stimulus, more observation periods, removal of the stimulus, and then additional observation points. This design is appropriate for observing the impact of placement and then removal of crime prevention initiatives, such as road barriers to deter drug dealing and sex work.

Quasi-experimental designs are desirable in that they do provide safeguards against some threats to validity. If nonequivalent comparison groups are included, testing and instrumentation would likely impact both groups equally, as would history and maturation. Selection bias and selection-maturation remain possibilities, given the lack of equivalence between the experimental and comparison groups. As was noted earlier, it is possible to minimize the differences between the groups with matching techniques or statistical controls to isolate the impact of the independent variable on the dependent variable. As with classical experiments, diffusion of treatment, compensatory equalization, demoralization, and compensatory rivalry remain potential threats to validity.

Summary

This chapter covered some very important topics in research methods. I always tell my students that, if they are to walk away from my class having learned one thing, I would like it to be the elements of causality. We can only conclude that X causes Y when we find evidence that there is a relationship between X and Y, X precedes Y in time, and we can control for, or explain away, the influence of all other possible explanations. We seek evidence of associations between X and Y through hypothesis testing and accompanying statistical procedures. The results of our statistical analysis tell us whether we can reject the null hypothesis (prediction of no relationship between X and Y) or whether we lack sufficient evidence to take that step. If we reject the null hypothesis, we can be confident that there *is* an association between the independent and dependent variables, and depending on our sampling procedures, we might feel comfortable generalizing those results to the population from which we obtained our sample. Our results will reflect patterns among our sample, but they will not necessarily explain every case that was studied.

No research is perfect, and even among strong designs, there are threats to internal and external validity. Threats to internal validity are factors other than our independent variable that might impact the values of our dependent variable. Threats to external validity reduce the possibility of our finding similar results if we replicate the same study at another place or time. A goal of quantitative research is to generalize our results, meaning we feel confident that our findings with the sample we studied would also apply to the population from which the sample was selected.

The gold standard for research designs is the classical experiment, which includes participants randomly divided into experimental and control groups. Participants are pretested prior to the introduction of the treatment stimulus, and then both groups are posttested. The goal is to generate two groups that are as similar as possible so that the only difference is that the experimental group was exposed to treatment stimulus (X) while the control group was not. If the values for the dependent variable for the experimental group change from pretest to posttest, but the values for the control group remain steady or move in the opposite direction from the experimental group, we can conclude that the independent variable is associated with the dependent variable.

When conducting research, it is often difficult to find circumstances that allow for random assignment of participants into groups. It can be particularly challenging when there are clear ethical problems related to denying one group of participants access to treatment, or if a criminal justice agency involved in the study has strict rules about how people are assigned to treatments or punishments. For that reason, quasi-experiments with nonrandom assignments to experimental and comparison groups are a common and useful alternative to the classical experiment.

Key Terms

Research hypothesis	Null hypothesis	Causation
Correlation	Proofs	Aggregates
Spurious relationship	Rival causal factors	Threats to internal validity
History	Testing effects	Instrumentation
Statistical regression	Selection (sample) bias	Mortality
Attrition bias	Maturation	Selection-maturation interaction
Diffusion of treatment	Compensatory equalization of treatment	Compensatory rivalry
Demoralization	Statistical conclusion validity	Power
Generalizability	External validity	Reactivity

Hawthorne effect	Multiple treatment interference	Replication
Classical experiment	Experimental group	Control group
Solomon four-group design	Factorial design	Equivalent groups posttest-only design
Crossover design	Quasi-experiment	Comparison group
Matching	Time series	Interrupted time series
Interrupted time-series with non-equivalent comparison group	Interrupted time-series with treatment removal	

Discussion Questions

1. What is a spurious relationship? Besides what was mentioned in this chapter, can you think of any other relationships in the world that might be spurious?
2. Besides a relationship between X and Y, what other factors are required to determine a causal relationship between two variables?
4. If a researcher cannot put together a classical experiment due to the inability to randomize selection into the experimental and control groups, what options does the researcher have to limit the impact of non-randomization on the study's results?
5. How might changes in instrumentation impact our ability to interpret data over a period of years?
6. What are some of the drawbacks to the classical experimental design?

References

Bennett, T., Holloway, K., & Farrington, D. (2008). The statistical association between drug misuse and crime. *Aggression and Violent Behavior, 13*, 107–118. https://doi.org/10.1016/j.avb.2008.02.001

Braga, A. A., Kennedy, D. M., Waring, E. J., & Piehl, A. M. (2001). Problem-oriented policing, deterrence, and youth violence: An evaluation of Boston's youth violence. *Journal of Research in Crime and Delinquency, 38*, 195–225.

Cohen, L. E., & Felson, M. (1979). Social change and crime rate trends: A routine activity approach. *American Sociological Review, 44*(4), 588–608. https://doi.org/ 10.2307/2094589

Cook, T. D., & Campbell, D. T. (1979). *Quasi-experimentation: Design and analysis issues for field settings.* Rand-McNally.

Cullen, F. T., Pratt, T. C., Turanovic, J. J., & Butler, L. (2018). When bad news arrives: Project HOPE in a post-factual world. *Journal of Contemporary Criminal Justice, 34*(1), 13–34.

Engel, R. S., Cosaro, N., Isaza, G. T., & McManus, H. D. (2022). Assessing the impact of de-escalation training on police behavior: Reducing police use of force in the Louisville, KY Metro Police Department. *Criminology & Public Policy, 21*(2), 199–234.

Farrington, D., & Welsh, B. C. (2006). How important is "regression to the mean" in area-based crime prevention research? *Crime Prevention & Community Safety, 8*, 50–60. https://doi.org/10.1057/palgrave.cpcs.8150017

Fletcher, B. W., & Tims, F. M. (1992). Methodological issues: Drug abuse treatment research in prisons and jails. In C. G. Leukfeld & F. M. Tims (Eds.), *Drug abuse treatment in prisons and jails* (pp. 246–260). National Institute on Drug Abuse.

Gates, S., Ariel, B., & Assaraf, N. (2025). Responding to nonemergency calls for service via video: A randomized controlled trial. *Criminology & Public Policy, 24*, 309–331. https://doi.org/10.1111/1745-9133.12690.

Grambsch, P. (2008). Regression to the mean, murder rates, and shall-issue laws. *The American Statistician, 62*(4), 289–295. https://doi.org/10.1198/000313008X362446

Hagan, F. (2007). *Essentials of research methods in criminal justice and criminology* (2nd ed.). Pearson.

Jennings, W. G., & Reingle Gonzalez, J. M. (2019). *Criminological and criminal justice research methods.* Wolters Kluwer.

Kelling, G. L., Pate, T., Diekman, D., & Brown, C. E. (1974). *The Kansas City preventive patrol experiment.* The Police Foundation.

Kinderman, C., Lynch, J., & Cantor, D. (1997). *Effects of the redesign on victimization estimates.* United States Department of Justice, Bureau of Justice Statistics.
Landsberger, H. A. (1958). *Hawthorne revisited.* The New York State School of Industrial and Labor Relations.
Larson, R. C. (1975). What happened to patrol operations in Kansas City? A review of the Kansas City preventive patrol experiment. *Journal of Criminal Justice, 3*, 267–297.
Lipton, D. S. (1998). Therapeutic community treatment programming in corrections. *Psychology, Crime, and Law, 4*, 213–263. https://doi.org/10.1080/10683169808520010
Lu, R., Willits, D., Stohr, M. K., Makin, D., Snyder, J., Lovrich, N., ... Hemmens, C. (2019). The cannabis effect on crime: Time-series analysis of crime in Colorado and Washington State. *Justice Quarterly, 38*(4), 565–595. https://doi.org/10.1080/07418825.2019.1666903
Maxfield, M. G., & Babbie, E. (2012). *Basics of research methods for criminal justice and criminology* (3rd ed.). Thomson Wadsworth.
Mayhew, P., Clarke, R. V., & Elliott, D. (1989). Motorcycle theft, helmet legislation, and displacement. *Howard Journal of Criminal Justice, 28*, 1–8. https://doi.org/10.1111/j.1468-2311.1989.tb00631.x
Pawson, R., & Tilley, N. (1997). *Realistic evaluation.* Sage Publications.
Roth, J., Lee, S., & Joo, J. (2018). The effectiveness of community-level alarm ownership on burglary rates. *Journal of Applied Security Research, 13*(2), 160–171. https://doi.org/10.1080/19361610.2018.1422360
Strah, B. M., Frost, N. A., Stowell, J. I., & Taheri, S. A. (2018). Cognitive-behavioral programming and the value of failed interventions: A propensity score evaluation. *Journal of Offender Rehabilitation, 57*(1), 22–46, https://doi.org/10.1080/10509674.2017.1416437
Tartaro, C. (2015). An evaluation of the effects of jail diversion and reentry for mentally ill offenders. *Journal of Offender Rehabilitation, 54*(2), 85–102. https://doi.org/10.1080/10509674.2015.1009966
Tseloni, A., Thompson, R., Grove, L., Tilley, N., & Farrell, G. (2014). The effectiveness of burglary security devices. *Security Journal, 30*, 646–664. https://doi.org/10.1057/sj.2014.30
White, C., & Weisburd, D. (2018). A co-responder model for policing mental health problems at crime hot spots: Findings from a pilot project. *Policing, 12*(2), 194–209. https://doi.org/10.1093/police/pax059
Vigen, T. (2024). *Spurious correlations.* https://tylervigen.com/

Reading 6.1 An Examination of Prison-Based Programming and Recommitment to Prison

As we discussed in Chapter 6, there might be ethical issues associated with randomly assigning people to a control group and preventing them from possibly benefiting from the study's experimental condition. In the corrections setting, it is clear why we would want to see people eager and willing to engage in rehabilitation programs. That is why evaluations of many prison-based rehabilitation programs must resort to quasi-experiments rather than classical experiments. Given the lack of randomization, there is a greater chance that the experimental group will somehow differ from those placed in the comparison group(s), so it is important to proactively address this potential sample bias. Rodriguez and Usman (2023) did that by utilizing propensity score matching, a statistical technique that allowed them to match rehabilitation program participants with individuals in two other groups—those who did not participate and program non-completers—on characteristics that might be associated with the probability of recidivating. While this did not eliminate the possibility that the three groups differed, it did serve to make them much more comparable, thereby enhancing the validity of the findings.

An Examination of Prison-Based Programming and Recommitment to Prison

Nancy Rodriguez and Hina Usman

Introduction

Since the 1970s, the U.S. has experienced an unprecedented increase in its prison population (Raphael, 2011; Travis, Western, & Redburn, 2014; Wagner & Walsh, 2016; Western, 2006). The drivers of the prison boom include sentencing policies, determinate sentencing schemes, and select legal measures for enhanced sentences (e.g., criminal histories, gang affiliation, and drug offenses). As individuals enter and leave prisons, efforts focused on recidivism reduction also note the importance of improving individual key indicators. The Programme for the International Assessment of Adult Competencies (PIAAC) is a recent survey of the literacy and numeracy skills of individuals incarcerated in U.S. state and federal prisons. The most recent estimate from PIACC reports that almost 30% of the incarcerated individuals have not completed their high school (Rampey & Keiper, 2014). Two-thirds of incarcerated individuals have a substance abuse disorder (Karberg & James, 2005; Lindquist et al., 2015) and almost half of incarcerated persons in state prisons exhibit symptoms of psychotic, manic or depressive disorders (James & Glaze, 2006). Women in prison have higher rates of substance abuse, victimization, and mental health challenges than men (Miller, 2021). Individuals released from prison often have unstable access to housing before their imprisonment (Morenoff & Harding, 2014; Western, 2019; Western & Sirois, 2019) and their housing challenges are only exacerbated upon release (Lutze, Rosky, & Hamilton, 2014).

Prison-based programming plays an important role in addressing the needs of incarcerated persons, in skill development, and improving post-release outcomes, including reducing recidivism. Although often described under one umbrella, correctional programs vary in type and purpose. The most common types of treatment programs focus on educational and work/vocational training, cognitive behavioral treatment, and substance abuse treatment. Each type of program has its own established evidence base with varying degrees of depth and known impact on institutional (e.g., misconduct) and post-release outcomes (e.g., employment and recidivism) (Duwe, 2017; Pompoco et al., 2017; Weisburd, Farrington, & Gill, 2017). To be clear, correctional programs have the capacity to improve outcomes of participants but only to the degree that individuals have access and can successfully complete designated correctional programming. Unfortunately, programs have limited capacity, often serving a fraction of those who need treatment.

Experts have outlined the key dimension of correctional programming research (Doleac, 2018; Weisburd et al., 2017). Among these include the importance of program implementation and fidelity (La Vigne & Willison, 2020; Taxman, 2020), the alignment between level of risk, programs, and responsivity to programming (Andrews & Bonta, 2010; James, 2015, 2018; Latessa, 2020; Lipsey & Cullen, 2007; Silver et al., 2020; Solomon et al., 2008; Warwick, Dodd, & Neusteter, 2012), and national clearinghouses dedicated to sharing evidence on what works (Crime Solutions, 2017). As scholars stress the value of implementation science and the relationship between risk and recidivism, correctional facilities continue to administer prison-based programs to serve the needs of incarcerated persons in order to achieve one of the most important goals of public safety: reduce recidivism of formerly incarcerated persons.

Unfortunately, the landscape of research on in-prison program effectiveness relies on different and broad measures of recidivism. For example, some studies rely on any new arrest, while others measure technical violations for community supervision alongside arrests, and others rely on returns to prison (Cho & Tyler, 2010; Kim & Clark, 2013; Pompoco et al., 2017; Rhodes et al., 2016). These differences exist in research across program types, as well as among studies of the same type of program (Duwe, 2017). Researchers have documented the limitations associated with relying on an overall measure of recidivism to ascertain the impact of rehabilitation programs (Lattimore, 2020) and propose the value of capturing more refined measures of recidivism, such as type of crime (Lattimore, 2020; Soloman & Scherer, 2021).

In this study, we take stock of the evidence on prison-based programming to examine the impact of five programs delivered by the Arizona Department of Corrections, Rehabilitation and Reentry (ADCRR) on recommitment to prison. Specifically, we examine the population of incarcerated persons in ADCRR from July 1, 2013 through June 30, 2018 and use propensity score matching models and survival analyses to examine the impact of educational and work/vocational training programs, cognitive behavioral treatment, and substance abuse treatment on return to prison within three years. We examine the landscape of prison-based programming in the state, providing a broader view of state supported programming and its impact on the population of individuals, which allows leaders to make decisions about what programs need to be scaled and/or reassessed. In light of the various calls for additional research on the impact of programs on incarcerated persons (Duwe, 2017; Taxman, 2020; Weisburd et al., 2017) and more detailed measures of recidivism (Lattimore, 2020; Soloman & Scherer, 2021), we seek to assist in filing this important gap for correctional leaders and policy makers alike.

Literature Review

Contemporary Research on What Works in Institutional Programming and Reentry

As with most criminal justice activity, state and local jurisdictions play a critical role in the implementation and processing of justice involved populations. According to research, state level correctional programs can reduce recidivism by 5-10 percentage points (Byrne, 2020). Prison-based programming covers a broad array of programs and intervention areas, including educational/vocational training, cognitive behavioral therapy, substance abuse programs, as well as specialized treatment for sex offenders. While evidence indicates that successful interventions often invest heavily on individual level treatment and changes, such as attainment of educational credentials, cognitive change, and substance abuse treatment (Andrews & Bonta, 2006; MacKenzie, 2006), the research on in-prison based programs is varied in depth and rigor.

Educational programs (e.g., high school and GED certification) exist in most correctional settings, offering basic and secondary education courses for individuals looking to improve educational outcomes (Bozick et al., 2018). Importantly, research has found that educational programming is associated with lower rates of imprisonment. A meta-analysis revealed that individuals who participated in correctional education programs had lower rates of recidivism than the control group (Davis et al., 2014). However, researchers have also found that correctional education does not lead to post-release employment relative to individuals who did not receive correctional education (Bozick et al., 2018). Other studies have found participation in prison education programs (GED, vocational training, and college classes) significantly reduces the chances of reincarceration but do not impact misconduct (Pompoco et al., 2017). Despite their effectiveness in reducing recidivism, access to educational opportunities within institutions remains scarce (Austin, 2017).

Vocational training programs are often classified and grouped alongside educational programs given the focus on education *and* technical skill development. Vocational training or correctional technical training programs focus on developing specific occupational skills that will facilitate employment opportunities and reduce recidivism (Bozick et al., 2018). Studies have produced mixed findings on the impact of vocational training interventions on job market outcomes and recidivism. Some studies have found that work training programs (i.e., occupational training, job placement programs, and basic skills training) and employment services do not reduce rates of recidivism (Visher et al., 2017; Visher & Farrell, 2005), while others have found lower levels of recidivism and improved employment outcomes (Bauldry & McClanahan, 2008; Duwe, 2017; James, 2015).

Cognitive-behavioral treatment (CBT) has proven to be an effective tool in correctional and community settings (Duwe, 2017; Landenberger & Lipsey, 2005). CBT relies on strategies to increase participants' awareness of themselves and their behavior with regards to others. This approach trains individuals in skills such as cognitive restructuring, strategies to cope with difficult situations, and problem solving. Cognitive-behavioral programs have proven effective for improving problem-solving skills and social control, developing moral reasoning and boosting self-efficacy (Milkman & Wanberg, 2007). Cognitive-behavioral therapy has also been linked to reduced recidivism (Chadwick, DeWolf, & Serin, 2015; Landenberger & Lipsey, 2005). Behavioral and cognitive therapies have shown positive results for those who suffer from mental health challenges during reentry, especially programs which facilitate the prison to community transition (James, 2015; Lattimore & Visher, 2009).

Studies evaluating substance abuse treatment in facilities indicate that the most effective treatment provides services to individuals consistently and for sufficiently long periods of time during imprisonment and post-release. Substance abuse treatment programs (e.g., therapeutic communities, group counseling programs and residential treatment programs) have shown to reduce relapse and are associated with lower levels of recidivism (CASA 2010; Mitchell, Wilson, & MacKenzie, 2007). For example, researchers examining data from the Iowa Department of Corrections found that completing alcohol and drug treatment plays an important role in post-release success (Peters et al., 2015). Despite the need for substance abuse treatment in correctional settings, it is estimated that only 15% of individuals in state prisons receive drug-related treatment (Visher, Yahner, & La Vigne, 2010).

Examining Prison Returns within the Context of Prison-Based Programs

The access to treatment and the ability to successfully complete correctional programming are pragmatic realities of rehabilitation programs in prison. Put simply, the vast majority of incarcerated individuals will be unable to participate in correctional programming because resources are limited (e.g., programs can only serve a small number of clients, limited staff availability, and programs are only offered in certain facilities) (Kaiser et al., 2021) or because individuals do not meet program criteria (e.g., literacy requirements, risk level, or length of stay) (Austin, 2017). And still, there are individuals who will be given access to programs but will drop-out and be unable to complete the program. An important dimension of addressing the "revolving door" of imprisonment and providing the treatment that incarcerated individuals need includes identifying correctional programming that can be most effective for those individuals who have access *and* can complete the programs.

Recidivism remains the primary measure when establishing what works and doesn't work in prison-based programming. According to the Bureau of Justice Statistics' (BJS) recidivism study with a 10-year follow-up period, 82 percent of formerly incarcerated individuals released in 2008 were rearrested within 10 years and 61 percent returned to prison for a parole or probation violation or a new offense (Durose & Antenangeli, 2021). Researchers have noted the value in moving beyond general measures of recidivism to more specific measures, such as type of crime involved in the rearrests or reincarceration (La Vigne & Willison, 2020; Soloman & Scherer, 2021). More specificity on the type of crime an individual commits post release can inform assessment of participants, classification, and delivery of services. Research on the relationship between in-prison programming and recidivism is vital for policy makers and correctional leaders who must allocate limited resources to programs that will improve the outcomes of individuals.

Current Study

In the current study, we pursue an examination of prison-based programs and reincarceration among individuals released from the Arizona Department of Corrections, Rehabilitation, and reentry (ADCRR). Specifically, we examine the impact of cognitive behavioral, substance abuse treatment, educational and work/vocational training programs on reincarceration among program participants and non-participants. Further, we examine the impact of prison-based programs among program completers and program non-completers on reincarceration.

Methods

ADCRR Prison-Based Programs

We offer a brief description of the five programs in our review and analyses. The *cognitive thinking program* is a cognitive restructuring program, which aims to teach prosocial life skills that improve individuals' behavior inside prisons and upon release. The components of the cognitive thinking program are similar to those of other CBT programs offered in prisons (Clark, 2010; Crime Solutions, 2016). The *substance abuse treatment program*, which is a six-month program addresses individuals' substance-use related issues and encourages addiction-free behavior. The program mirrors national models for residential substance abuse treatment in correctional settings (Bureau of Justice Assistance, 2005). The goal of *functional literacy* classes is for individuals to pass the minimum eighth-grade literacy standard. The program is designed to provide reading, writing, mathematical, and other basic skills necessary for an individual to adjust in a working environment. The *GED program* targets those individuals who do not have a high-school diploma or GED. Program participants study for and take the GED test, and upon completion of the program, receive a diploma from the Arizona Department of Education. *Vocational skills training programs* aim to teach individuals employability skills to help them obtain employment in prison and upon release. Programs range from six months to two years in duration. The work-based programs aim to teach practical skills such as construction technology, automotive technology, building maintenance, welding, upholstery, horticulture, carpentry, and business technology.

Data and Sample

This study uses a quasi-experimental design to test whether programming improved reincarceration outcomes for individuals who participated and completed programming. The data set used in this study contains information on 27,548 individuals released from all facility units of ADCRR between July 1st, 2013 and June 20th, 2015. The individual panel data set provides detailed information on individuals' demographic characteristics, programming status, release and admission dates, prior offense history, sentencing offense, and reincarceration. Dependent variables, independent variables, and control variables used in the study are discussed below.

Reincarceration Binary Variables

There are seven dependent variables that are the post-release outcomes of the incarcerated individual measured from a three-year time point, i.e., measured within three years of release. *Reincarceration* is a binary variable indicating whether an individual returned to prison within three years of release or not. *New felony offense* is a binary variable indicating whether an individual returned to prison due to a new felony. *New felony—violent offense* is a binary variable indicating whether an individual returned to prison due to a new felony—violent offense. *New felony—assault offense* is a binary variable indicating whether an individual returned to prison due to a new felony—assault offense. *New felony—drug offense* is a binary variable indicating whether an individual returned to prison due to a new felony—drug offense. *New felony—burglary* offense is a binary variable indicating whether an individual returned to prison due to a new felony—burglary offense. Finally, *new felony—theft offense* is a binary variable indicating whether an individual returned to prison due to a new felony—theft offense. As shown in Table 1 Panel B, *Reincarceration* mean in the overall sample is 40%, while 16% of the individuals were reincarcerated due to a *new felony.* The mean of *new felony—violent offense* is 4%, while the sample mean for *new felony—assault offense* is 3%. Similarly, sample means for *new felony—drug offense* and *new felony—theft offense* is 12% and 3% respectively. Finally, 3% of the individuals were reincarcerated due to a *new felony—burglary offense.*

Table 1 Treatment and dependent variable mean

Panel A – Treatment Variables	
Treatment Variable	*Mean*
Cognitive Thinking – Program Participation	29.10%
Cognitive Thinking – Program Completion	84.76%
Substance Abuse – Program Participation	5.98%
Substance Abuse – Program Completion	70.75%
Functional Literacy – Program Participation	35.17%
Functional Literacy – Program Completion	87.06%
GED – Program Participation	22.13%
GED – Program Completion	38.74%
Vocational Skills – Program Participation	20.91%
Vocational Skills – Program Completion	56.16%
Panel B – Dependent Variables	
Dependent Variable	*Mean*
Reincarceration	40.02%
New Felony – All	16.73%
New Felony – Violent Offense	3.61%
New Felony – Assault offense	2.82%
New Felony – Drug offense	12.35%
New Felony – Theft offense	2.56%
New Felony – Burglary offense	2.89%

Variables for Survival Curves

In addition to binary outcomes, we compare the conditional reincarceration risk of individuals by treatment status using survival curves. The two key variables for the survival curves are *event* and *time to event.* In the context of our study, the *event* is reincarceration. Released individuals were considered at risk for reincarceration (recorded in event variable as "survive") until the month they were reincarcerated (recorded in the event variable as "fail"). *Time to reincarceration* is measured in months, and it captures the month in which the individual is reincarcerated.

Independent Variables

Based on the program participation and completion status, we construct two different types of treatment and comparison groups. The first is *program participation,* which is a binary variable of whether the individual participated in the program or not. The second is *program completion,* which represent a binary variable of whether the individual completed the program or not. According to Table 1 Panel A, 29% of the individuals participated in cognitive thinking program, and 85% completed the program. For the substance abuse treatment program, 6% of the individuals were program participants, and 71% were program completers. Compared to other programs, functional literacy has the highest percentage of participants and completers; 35% of the individuals were program participants, and 87% were program completers. In contrast, 22% of the individuals participated in the GED program, and 39% completed the program. Finally, 21% participated in the vocational skills program, and 56% completed the program.

Control Variables

Several covariates are included in the propensity score models. *Race* is measured with six binary variables that indicate whether the individual is White, Black, Native American, Latino, Asian, or belongs to another race. *Sex* is dichotomized as male (1) and female (0). *Age* is measured in years at time of release. Current *incarceration offense type* is measured with nine binary variables that indicate whether the individual was incarcerated for a sex offense, assault, kidnapping, arson, robbery, larceny, theft, auto theft, or other offenses. *Risk score* is a measure of an individual's risk of recidivism. It ranges from one to five, where five represents the highest risk of recidivism and one represents the lowest risk of recidivism. *Time served* in prison is measured in days spent in prison for the sentencing offense. *Release year* is measured with binary variables for each release year to account for unobserved time trends in the release year that could bias our estimates. *Prior felony record* is a binary variable indicating whether an individual has at least one prior felony record. Finally, *prior juvenile adjudication record* is a binary variable representing whether an individual has at least one prior juvenile adjudication record.

Propensity Score Matching

Propensity score matching (PSM) is a popular quasi-experimental research design that is used in program evaluations to make treatment and comparison groups comparable. More specifically, matching involves comparing individuals across treatment and comparison groups who are identical on covariates that we observe. In practice, such covariates are *pre-determined* and are observed before treatment assignment. PSM is a two-step process in which the first step provides estimates of the conditional probability of selection to a treatment group based on the observed covariates (Rosenbaum & Rubin, 1985). We generate the conditional probability of treatment, known as propensity scores, using a logistic regression model that takes treatment status as the dependent variable and characteristics of individuals as independent variables. In the second step, we match individuals in the treatment group to similar individuals in the control group based on the propensity scores estimated in the first step.

After obtaining propensity scores for individuals in the treatment and comparison groups for each program, we match individuals across these groups using the nearest 1:1 neighbor matching procedure with replacement (Abadie & Imbens, 2002). Matching with replacement allows individual observations to be used as a match more than once. Moreover, compared to matching without replacement, this method lowers the bias and also retains a higher number of observations while matching individual observations (Abadie & Imbens, 2002). Next, we evaluate the degree to which PSM effectively reduced observable selection bias. To do so, we compare the standardized mean differences in covariates of the treatment and comparison groups. Figure 1 presents the standardized mean difference between each treatment and comparison group for each of the programs. The figure shows that balance between the treatment and comparison group is achieved after matching as standardized bias for most of the covariates is well below 20% (or 0.2).

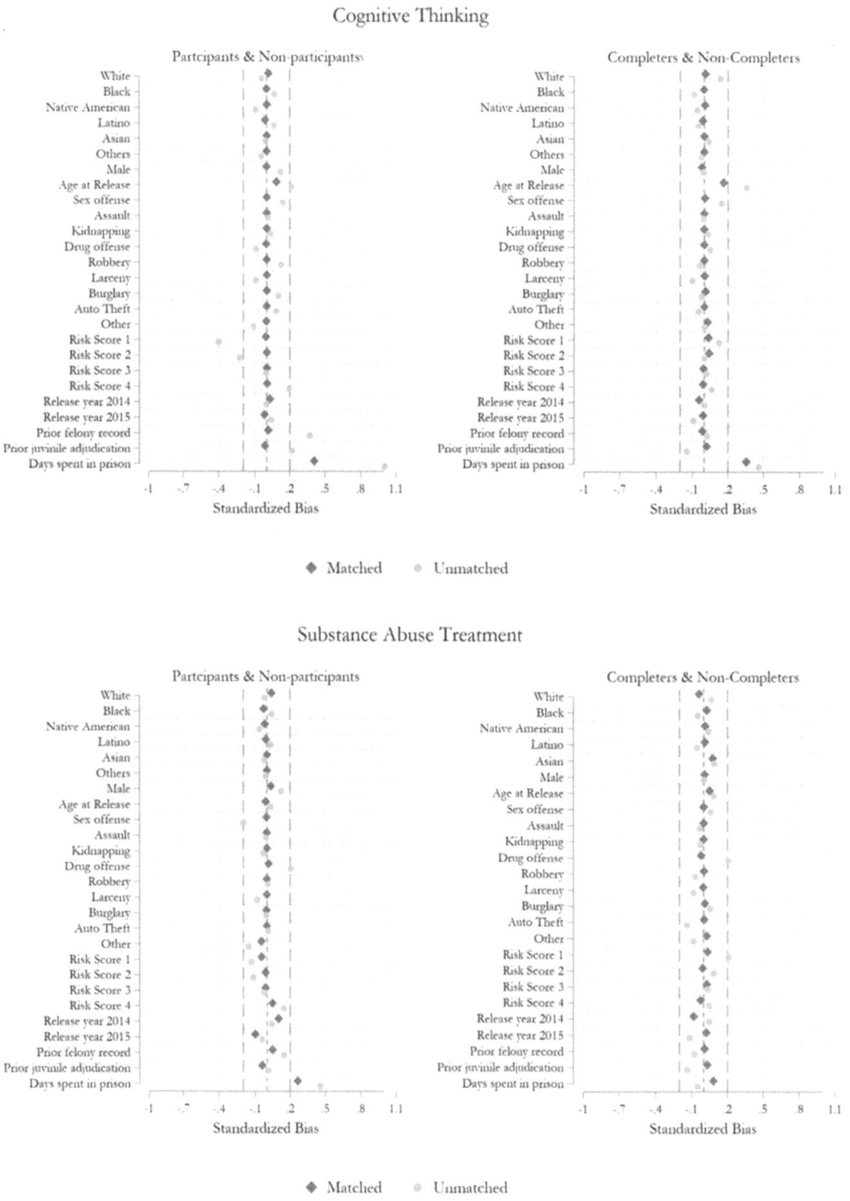

Figure 1 Propensity score matching and covariate balance using standardize bias

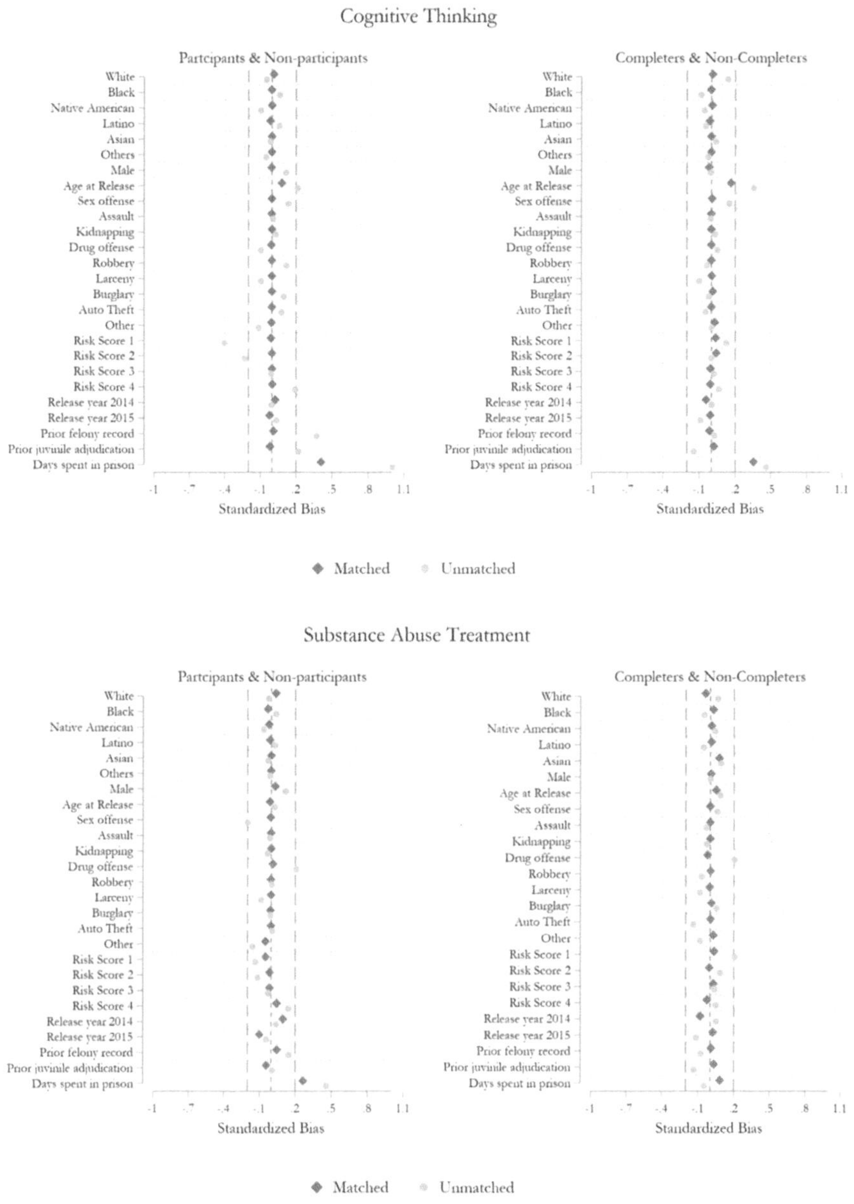

Figure 1 (Continued)

Statistical Analysis

Reincarceration binary variables

We evaluate the treatment effect for each program using the matched sample constructed using PSM. We first estimate the treatment effect on binary outcomes, which include: *reincarceration, reincarceration due to a new felony, reincarceration due to a new felony—violent offense, a new felony—assault offense, a new felony—drug offense, a new felony—theft, and new felony—burglary offense.* As indicated earlier, the binary outcomes are measured from a three-year standpoint, i.e.,

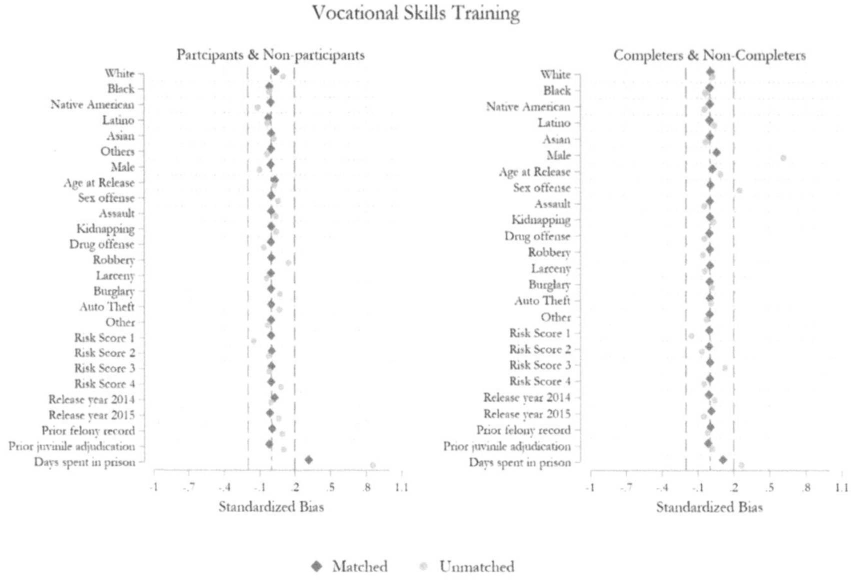

Figure 1 (Continued)

whether an individual is reincarcerated within three years of release. We estimate the bias-corrected matching estimator for the average treatment effect (ATE) introduced by Abadie and Imbens (2002) instead of a simple matching estimator. To test the statistical significance of the computed ATEs, we calculate robust standard errors (Abadie & Imbens, 2006).

Analysis with Survival Curves

We use survival curves to estimate the reincarceration survival rates of individuals across the treatment and comparison groups. For survival curves, time to reincarceration is measured as the difference between the month of release and the month the individual is reincarcerated. In our study, the "cut off" time frame for survival analysis is 36 months. With time to reincarceration as an outcome (or event) of interest, survival curves tell us the proportion of individuals who are not reincarcerated by an arbitrary month *t*. To conduct informative comparisons of survival rates for treatment and comparison groups, we use matched treatment and comparison groups constructed using 1:1 nearest neighbor matching (Abadie & Imbens, 2002) with replacement as discussed in the earlier section. Finally, we use the Kaplan-Meier method to estimate survival function for matched treatment and comparison groups (Austin, Thomas, & Rubin, 2020).

Results

Reincarceration Binary Variables

The analysis of binary outcomes presents two main findings. First, individuals who participated in any program have lower reincarceration predicted probabilities than the program non-participants. Second, conditional on participation, program completion led to higher reductions in predicted reincarnation probability compared to program non-completion.

For cognitive thinking program, we find that program participants have significantly lower probabilities of *reincarceration, new felony offense, new felony—violent offense, new felony—assault offense, and new felony—theft offense* compared to program non-participants. The predicted probability of reincarceration among program participants is 37.38%, while the predicted probability of reincarceration among program non-participants is 41.08%. Conditional on participation, program completers have significantly lower predicted probabilities of *reincarceration, new felony—violent offense, and new felony—assault offense.* Conditional on participation, the predicted probability of reincarceration among program completers is 40.41%, while the predicted probability of reincarceration among program non-completers is 49.58%.

Program participants of the substance abuse program have significantly lower probabilities of *reincarceration, new felony offense, new felony—violent offense, and new felony—assault offense* compared to program non-participants. Our findings show that the predicted probability of reincarceration among program participants is 34.68%, while the predicted probability of reincarceration among program non-participants is 40.49%. Program completers have significantly lower predicted probabilities of *reincarceration, new felony offense, new felony—drug offense, new felony—burglary offense, and new felony—theft offense.* Conditional on participation, the predicted probability of reincarceration among program completers is 32.42%, while the predicted probability of reincarceration among program non-completers is 48.05%.

For functional literacy program, we find that program participants have significantly lower probabilities of *reincarceration, new felony offense, and new felony—drug offense* compared to program non-participants. Predicted probability of reincarceration among program participants is 38.71%, while the predicted probability of reincarceration among program non-participants is 41.34%. Conditional on participation, program completers have significantly lower predicted probabilities of *reincarceration, new felony offense, new felony—violent offense, new felony—assault offense, and new felony—drug offense.* Conditional on participation, the predicted probability of reincarceration among program completers is 36.24%, while the predicted probability of reincarceration among program non-completers is 47.22%.

Analysis for the GED program show that program participants have significantly lower probabilities of *reincarceration*, and *new felony offense*. Predicted probability of reincarceration among program participants is 38.16%, while the predicted probability of reincarceration among program non-participants is 40.17%. Additional analysis show that the program completers have significantly lower predicted probabilities of *reincarceration, new felony offense, new felony—theft offense,* and *new felony—burglary offense*. The predicted probability of reincarceration among program completers is 36.90%, while the predicted probability of reincarceration among program non-completers is 44.98%.

Finally, our findings show that program participants of the vocational skills training program have significantly lower probabilities of *reincarceration, new felony offense, new felony—drug offense, new felony—theft offense,* and *new felony—burglary offense* than program non-participants. Predicted probability of reincarceration among program participants is 35.88%, while the predicted probability of reincarceration among program non-participants is 41.31%. The analysis also reveals that program completers have lower predicted probability of *new felony—theft offense.* Conditional on participation, the predicted probability of *new felony—theft offense* among program completers is 2.03%, while the predicted probability of reincarceration among program non-completers is 3.35%.

Survival Curves

Figure 2 displays a series of survival curves differentiated by treatment and comparison groups for all programs. Each sub-figure plots months since release on the x-axis and reincarceration survival rates on the y-axis. The following main findings emerge from the survival analysis. First, program completers have lowest predicted reincarceration risk compared to participants, non-participants, and non-completers as indicated by their survival curves for all programs. Second, for most of the

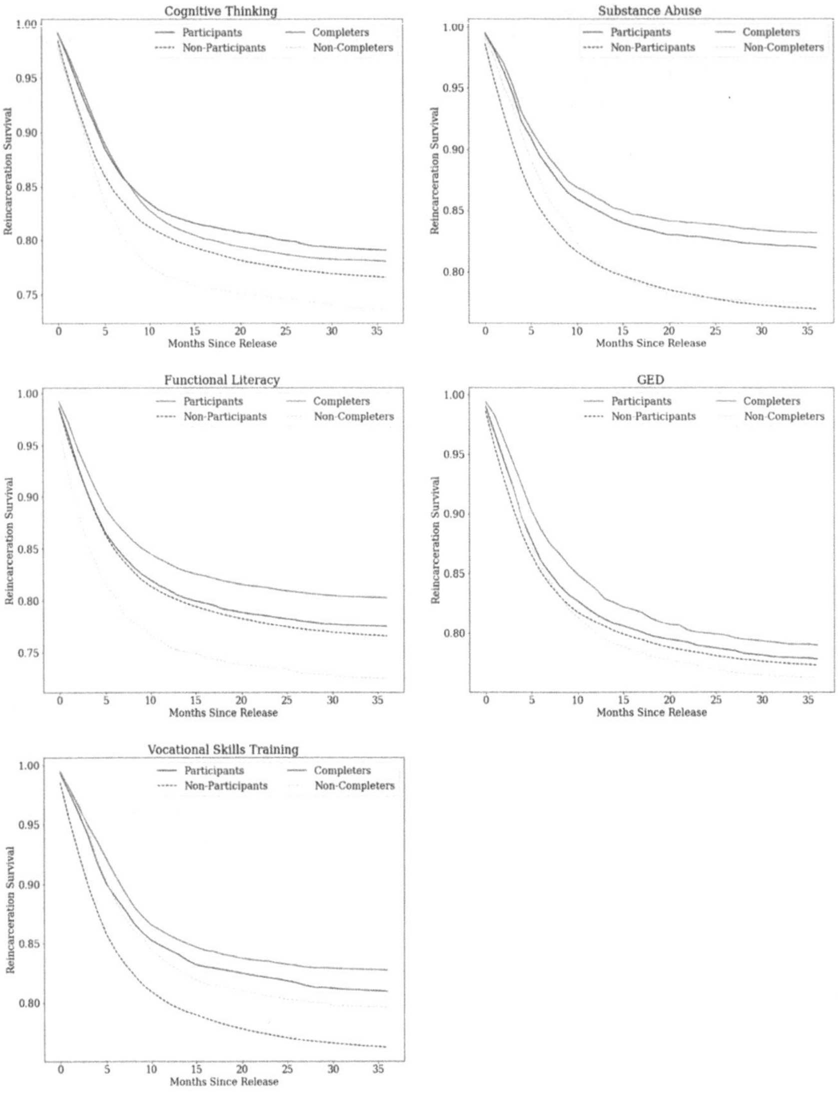

Figure 2 Survival curves by treatment status for all programs

programs, the decline in survival rate is sharpest among program non-completers and program non-participants which implies that they exhibit higher reincarceration risk compared to participants and completers.

The survival curves for the treatment and comparison groups of cognitive thinking program show that program non-completers pose the highest reincarceration risk as indicated by the sharpest decline in survival rate compared to other groups. For program participants and program completers, there is some intersection in reincarceration trajectories in the earlier months; however, the gap in the reincarceration trajectories widens after eight months. These findings imply that the reincarceration risk of program participants and completers are similar after eight months. Unlike cognitive thinking program, non-participants of substance abuse program pose the highest reincarceration risk as indicated by the sharpest decline in survival rate compared to others. The gap in reincarceration trajectories exist for program non-completers and non-participants; however, their reincarceration trajectories overlap after one year. The survival curve for program completers of substance abuse program is situated above program non-completers, participants, and non-participants which indicates that program completers maintain lowest reincarceration risk compared to others.

The analysis of survival curves for treatment and comparison group of the functional literacy program exhibits the following main findings. First, like cognitive thinking program, non-completers pose highest reincarceration risk as indicated by the sharp decline of survival curve. Second, reincarceration trajectories of program participants and non-participants overlap in the first few months; however, the gap in their reincarceration trajectories widens after six months. Third, like cognitive thinking and substance abuse programs, completers of functional literacy program exhibit lowest reincarceration risk compared to others.

The reincarceration trajectories of program participants, non-completers, and non-participants of GED program initially overlap in the first few months; however, the gap in reincarceration trajectories widens after ten months. Initially, program non-participants exhibit highest reincarceration risk, however, after one year, program non-completers exhibit highest reincarceration risk. The survival curve for program completers of GED program lies above the survival curves of program participants, non-participants, and non-completers which shows that completers have lowest reincarceration risk compared to others. Lastly, the survival curve of program non-participants of vocational skills program exhibits sharpest decline which shows that non-participants are at the highest reincarceration risk compared to others. Like GED program, there exists overlap in the reincarceration trajectories of program participants and non-completers of vocational skills training program; however, the gap in their reincarceration trajectories widens after six months. Similar to the findings of other programs, completers of vocational skills program pose lowest reincarceration risk compared to other groups.

Discussion

This study examined the effects of in-prison programming on reincarceration using a panel data set of incarcerated persons from the Arizona Department of Corrections Rehabilitation and Reentry. Analyses reveal several key findings. First, we find that program participants of all programs have lower predicted reincarceration rates than program non-participants. Second, conditional on participation, program completers of cognitive thinking, substance abuse, functional literacy, and GED programs exhibit lower predicted recidivism rates than program non-completers. Finally, the analysis of survival curves show that program completers have higher reincarceration survival rates than program non-completers for all programs.

The present study advances correctional program research in important ways. The study offers breadth and depth to the understanding of prison-based programming, as most existing studies focus on binary outcomes of prison returns. In contrast, we examine crime-specific prison returns and survival curves, which offers a more comprehensive understanding of the impact of prison-based programs. In addition, analyses of multiple correctional programs present a more comprehensive understanding of these programs' impact on public safety outcomes. Overall, our research answers the policy question of what works in correctional programming, as well as *which* correctional programs have the most impact.

Findings from the study have implications for correctional programs and practices throughout the U.S. First, our results have implications for the investment strategy of in-prison programs. All program participants have lower *reincarceration* and *new felony* rates compared to program non-participants. Findings from survival curves show that reincarceration survival rates decline at a higher rate for program non-participants compared to program participants. Therefore, the general pattern of our findings points toward the importance of program participation. This implies resource allocation toward prison-based programming expansion can result in greater public safety. Second, and related, our work informs which programs yield more impact than others. While the exact mechanisms of our findings are unclear, functional literacy and GED programs are worth investing in for the following possible reasons. First, education-based programs can increase the knowledge or skills of individuals, which ultimately increase the probability of being employed post-release. Second, a GED may hold a signaling value for employers, which can help individuals to acquire employment opportunities post-release. We would also encourage correctional leaders to consider the benefits of cognitive thinking and substance abuse programs beyond reincarceration, such as improved behavioral health outcomes. In comparison to other programs, vocational skills program resulted in insignificant difference in the probability of reincarceration of completers and non-completers. Based on these findings, we recommend further assessment of these types of program.

Study findings point towards the importance of program retention. The findings imply that prisons can adopt and implement various strategies that enhance program completion. For instance, prisons may offer incentives to individuals to complete programs or prioritize program completion over logistical barriers, including the movement of individuals across facilities before program completion. In addition, existing theories and evidence suggest that lack of motivation leads to high program incompletion rates among incarcerated individuals. Therefore, strategies like inclusion of post-release success stories of former program completers in the teaching curriculum may boost motivation among program participants.

Our study points to several noticeable differences between program participants and completers of various programs and type of felony for reincarceration. For example, cognitive thinking program participation and completion decreases the probability of reincarceration due to a *new felony—violent offense* and *new felony—assault offense.* In contrast, no such differences exist for GED and vocational skills training program. An important implication of these findings is that cognitive thinking program might teach individuals pro-social life skills thereby improving their mental health, ensuring smooth transition in communities, and ultimately enhancing public safety. Second, our results demonstrate that GED program completion decreases the probability of reincarceration due to a *new felony—theft offense* and a *new felony—burglary offense.* This implies knowledge-enhancing programs like GED may help with the immediate monetary needs of the individuals by opening new employment opportunities, ultimately increasing the opportunity cost of committing crimes like burglary and theft. Third, compared to other programs, substance abuse program completion leads to a sizeable decrease in the probability of reincarceration due to a *new felony—drug offense.* In light of the intersection of substance abuse and crime (i.e., commit crime to obtain money for drugs), assisting individuals with need-based substance abuse treatment can reduce crime.

Lastly, our findings have implications for reentry and the timing of services. The general pattern of survival curves initially shows a steep slope implying sharp declines in the reincarceration survival rates in the first few months of release for all groups. Program non-completers and non-participants exhibit sharpest declines in reincarceration survival rates compared to participants and completers. This implies that post-release programs that ensure smooth transition of individuals in their communities can be helpful, particularly, in the first few months of release. The results also imply that prison-based programming coupled with post-release programs can further reduce crime. For instance, post-release work placement programs for functional literacy participants can help individuals find legal employment thereby increasing the opportunity cost of committing crimes.

Despite these important policy and practice implications, several study limitations are worth noting. First, due to data limitations, our study does not highlight specific mechanisms through which in-prison programs reduce recidivism. Identifying mechanisms is important as it guides which policy levers to pull to reduce recidivism. For instance, our findings show that program completers of GED program have lower predicted probabilities of reincarceration due to a new felony theft offense or new felony burglary offense. The question arises whether GED program completion leads to better and faster employment opportunities or whether the program completion increases the skillset of individuals permanently. Data related to employment and the specific time period it took for individuals to find employment after release can highlight mechanisms through which GED program affects prison returns. Second, programs such as vocational skills training and functional literacy programs have multiple components that contribute to the overall structure of the course. Due to data limitations, we cannot test which specific component of the courses resulted in a reduction in recidivism. For instance, individuals who participated in different types of vocational skills training programs (carpentry, construction, etc.) are pooled in a single measure. With the current analysis, it is unclear which specific component led to a reduction in reincarceration rates. Finally, while our study attempts to generate unbiased estimates using PSM, future work in this area can improve the research design by exploiting natural variation in program participation or experimental setting.

In sum, understanding the impact of in-prison programming is a critical dimension of reducing recidivism and improving public safety. In this study, we expand the evidence base by showing how multiple types of programs in prison impact individuals' post-release success. As such, we shed light on the benefits associated with program participation and program completion, as it relates to reincarceration. While we recognize that across (and even within) states there exist unique challenges that makes a one-size-fits-all approach to recidivism unfeasible, the common link between all states is that prison crowding and budget constraints create the need for implementing promising practices and strategies for successful reentry. Our research findings inform these efforts. We conclude with a reminder that supporting and scaling in-prison correctional programs for individuals can improve their outcomes in important ways. In order for correctional systems to effectively serve individuals, it will require targeting individuals for correctional programs and supporting their retention and program completion. Doing so will yield short and long terms benefits.

Discussion Questions

1. Why did the authors believe that one measure of recidivism would be inadequate? Discuss the multiple ways that they approached the concept of recidivism.
2. What variables did the authors choose when working to match the three different groups? Were there any additional variables that would have been helpful to use here?
3. How did having so many different measures of recidivism help us better understand how these different programs are assisting people upon release from prison?

References

Abadie, A., & Imbens, G. (2002). *Simple and bias corrected matching estimators for average treatment effects.* NBER.

Abadie, A., & Imbens, G. W. (2006). Large sample properties of matching estimators for average treatment effects. *Econometerica, 74*(1), 235–267. https://doi.org/10.1111/j.1468-0262.2006.00655.x

Andrews, D. A., & Bonta, J. (2006). *The psychology of criminal conduct* (4th ed.). LexisNexis.

Andrews, D. A., & Bonta, J. (2010). Rehabilitating criminal justice policy and practice. *Psychology, Public Policy, and Law, 16*(1), 39–55.

Austin, J. (2017). Limits of prison education. *Criminology & Public Policy, 16*(2), 563–570. https://doi.org/10.1111/1745-9133.12301

Austin, P. C., Thomas, N., & Rubin, D. B. (2020). Covariate-adjusted survival analyses in propesnity-score method samples: Imputed

potential time-to-event outcomes. *Statistical Methods in Medical Research, 29*(3), 728–751. https://doi.org/10.1177/0962280218817926
Bauldry, S., & McClanahan, W. (2008). *Ready4Work. Final research report,* pp. 1–46. U.S. Department of Labor.
Becker, S. O., & Caliendo, M. (2007). mhbounds-sensitivity analysis for average treatment effects. *IZA*, Paper No. 2542.
Bozick, R., Steele, J., Davis, L., & Turner, S. (2018). Does providing inmattes with education improve post release outcomes? A meta-analysis of correctional education programs in the US. *Journal of Experimental Criminology, 14*(3), 389–428. https://doi.org/10.1007/s11292-018-9334-6
Bucklen, K. B., Sheets, M., Bohm, C., Bell, N., Campbell, J., Flaherty, R., & Wiede, K. V. (2022). *Recidivism 2022 Report.* Technical. The Bureau of Planning, Research, and Statistics.
Bureau of Justice Assistance. (2005). *Residential Susbstance Abuse Treatment for State Prisoners (RSAT)*. Online. Office of Justice Programs.
Byrne, J. M. (2020). The effectiveness of prison programming: A review of the research literature examing the impact of federal, state, and local inmate programming on post-release recidivism. *Federal Probation, 84*(1), 3–20.
Center on Addiction and Substance Abuse. (2010). *Behind Bars II: Substance Abuse and America's prison population.* Online. Center on Addiction and Substance Abuse.
Chadwick, N., DeWolf, A., & Serin, R. (2015). Effectively training community supervision officers: A meta-analytic review of the impact on offender outcome. *Criminal Justice and Behavior*, *42*(10), 977–989.
Cho, R. M., & Tyler, H. J. (2010). Does prison-based adult basic education improve postrelease outcomes for male prisoners in Florida? *Crime and Delinquency, 50*(7), 975–1005. https://doi.org/10.1177/0011128710389588
Clark, P. (2010). Preventing future crime with cognitive behavioral therapy. *NIJ Journal (NIJ Journal), 265*, 22–25.
Crime Solutions. (2016). *Crime solutions.* National Institute of Justice. 2 9. https://crimesolutions.ojp.gov/ratedpractices/57#pd.
Crime Solutions. (2017). *Crime solutions*. National Institute of Justice. 9 5. https://crimesolutions.ojp.gov/ratedprograms/558.
D'Amico, R., Geckeler, C., & Kim, H. (2016). *An evaluation of seven second chance act adult demonstration programs: Impact findings at 18 months.* Online. SPR: Social Policy Research Associates.
Davis, L. M., Steele, J. L., Bozick, R., Williams, M. V., Turner, S., Miles, J. N., ... Steinberg, P. S. (2014). *How effective is correctional education, and where do we go from here? The results of a comprehensive evaluation.* Rand Corporation.
Doleac, J. L. (2018). Strategies to productively reincorporate the formerly-incarcerated into communities: A review of literature. *IZA Institute of Labor Economics: Discussion Paper Series*, June: IZA DP No. 11646.
Drake, E. K., & Fumia, D. (2017). Evolution of correctional education evaluations and directions for future research. *Criminology and Public Policy, 16*(2), 549–562. https://doi.org/10.1111/1745-9133.12291
Durose, R. M., & Antenangeli, L. (2021). *Recidivism of prisoners released in 34 states in 2012: A 5-year follow-up period (2012–2017).* Technical. Beauru of Justice Statistics.
Duwe, G. (2017). *The use and impact of correctional programming for inmates on pre- and post-release outcomes.* Technical. National Institute of Justice.
Fagan, A. A., & Buchanan, M. (2016). What works in crime prevention? *Criminology and Public Policy, 15*(3), 617–649. https://doi.org/10.1111/1745-9133.12228
Groger, A., Harding, D. J., & Henderson, H. (2021). *Prisoner reentry*. Technical. Brookings Institute.
James, D. J., & Glaze, L. E. (2006). *Mental health problems of prison and jail inmates*. U.S. Department of Justice, Office of Justice Programs, Bureau of Justice Statistics.
James, N. (2015). *Offender reentry: Correctional statistics, reintegration into the community and recidivism*. Online. Congressional Research Service.
James, N. (2018). *Risk and needs assessment in federal prison system*. Technical. Congressional Research Service.
Kaiser, K., Keena, L., Piquero, A., & Howley, C. (2021). Barriers to inmate program participation in a private southern prison. *Journal of Crime and Justice*, *44*(2), 165–179.
Karberg, J. C., & James, D. J. (2005). *Substance dependence, abuse, and treatment of jail inmates. U.S.* Department of Justice, Office of Justice Programs, Bureau of Justice Statistics.
Kim, R. H., & Clark, D. (2013). The effect of prison-based college education programs on recidivism: Propensity score matching approach. *Journal of Criminal Justice*, *41*(3), 196–204. https://doi.org/10.1016/j.jcrimjus.2013.03.001
La Vigne, N., & Willison, J. B. (2020). Integerating lived experience into reentry evaluation design. In B. Orrell (Ed.), *Rethinking reentry* (pp. 72–87). American Enterprise Institute.
Landenberger, N. A., & Lipsey, M. W. (2005). The positive effects of cognitive-behavioral programs for offenders: A meta-analysis of factors associated with effective treatment. *Journal of Experimental Criminology*, *1*(4), 451–476.

Latessa, E. (2020). Triaging of services for individuals returning from prison. In B. Orrell (Ed.), *Rethinking reentry* (pp. 39–72). American Enterprise Institute.

Lattimore, P. K. (2020). Considering reentry program evaluation: Thouts from SVORI. In B. Orrell (Ed.), *Rethinking reentry* (pp. 7–380). American Enterprise Institute.

Lattimore, P. K., Steffey, D. M., & Visher, C. A. (2010). Prisoner reentry in the first decade of the twenty-first century. *Victims and Offenders, 5*(3), 253–267.

Lattimore, P. K., & Visher, C. A. (2009). *The multisite evaluation of SVORI: Summary and synthesis*. Urban Institute.

Leverentz, A. (2020). Interviewing the "rabble class": Recruitment and retention in studies of prisoner reentry. In A. Leverentz, E. Y. Chen, & J. Christian (Eds.), *Beyond recidivism: New approaches to research on prisoner reentry and reintegration* (pp. 100–135). New York University.

Lindquist, C., Lattimore, P., Willison, J. B., Steffey, D., Loveman, W., & Eisenstat, J. (2018). *Cross-site evaluation of the Bureau of Justice Assistance FY 2011 Second Chance Act adult offender reentry demonstration projects*. National Criminal Justice Reference Service.

Lindquist, C., McKay, T., Bir, A., & Steffey, D. (2015). *The experiences of families during a father's incarceration: Descriptive findings from the baseline data collection for the multi-site study on incarceration, parenting and partnering*. Research. RTI International.

Lipsey, M. W., & Cullen, F. T. (2007). The effectiveness of correctional rehabilitation: A review of systematic reviews. *Annual Review of Law and Social Science, 3*, 297–320.

Lutze, F. E., Rosky, J. W., & Hamilton, Z. K. (2014). Homelessness and reentry: A multisite outcome evaluation of Washington State's reentry housing program for high risk offenders. *Criminal Justice and Behavior, 41*(4), 471–491.

MacKenzie, D. L. (2006). *What works in corrections: Reducing the criminal activities of offenders and delinquents*. Cambridge University Press.

Milkman, H. B., & Wanberg, K. W. (2007). *Cognitive-behavioral treatment: A review and discussion for corrections professionals*. U.S. Department of Justice, National Institute of Corrections.

Miller, H. V. (2021). *Female reentry and gender-responsive programming: Recommendations for policy and practice*. Technical. National Institute of Justice.

Mitchell, O., Wilson, D. B., & MacKenzie, D. L. (2007). Does incarceration-based drug treatment reduce recidivism? A meta-analytic synthesis of the research. *Journal of Experimental Criminology, 3*(4), 353–375.

Morenoff, J. D., & Harding, D. J. (2014). Incarceration, prisoner reentry, and communities. *Annual Review of Sociology, 40*, 411–429.

Papp, J., Wooldedge, J., & Pompoco, A. (2019). Timing of prison programs and the odds of returning to prison. *Corrections: Policy, Practice and Research, 6*(2), 124–149.

Peters, D. J., Hochstetler, A., DeLisi, M. et al. (2015). Parolee recidivism and successful treatment completion: Comparing hazard models across propensity methods. *Journal of Quantitative Criminology, 31*, 149–181. https://doi.org/10.1007/s10940-014-9229-2

Petersilia, J. (2005). Hard time: Ex-offenders returning home after prison. *Corrections Today, 67*(2), 66–71.

Pompoco, A., Wooldredge, J., Lugo, M., Sullivan, C., & Latessa, E. J. (2017). Reducing inmate misconduct and prison returens with facility education programs. *Criminology and Public Policy, 16*(2), 515–547.

Przybylski, R. (2008). *What works: Effective recidivism reduction and risk-focused prevention programs*. RKC Group.

Rampey, B. D., & Keiper, S. (2014). *Highlights from the U.S. PIAAC survey of incarcerated adults: Their skills, work, experience, education, and training*. Technical. U.S. Department of Education.

Raphael, S. (2011). Incarceration and prisoner reentry in the United States. *The Annals of the American Academy of Political and Social Science, 635*(1), 192–215.

Rhodes, W., Gaes, G., Luallen, J., Kling, R., Rich, T., & Shively, M. (2016). Following incarceration, most released offenders never return to prison. *Crime & Delinquency, 62*(8), 1003–1025.

Rosenbaum, P. R., & Rubin, D. B. (1985). Constructing a control group using multivariate matched sampling methods that incorporate the propensity score. *The American Statistician, 39*(1), 33–38. https://doi.org/ 10.2307/2683903

Silver, I. A., Cochran, J. C., Motz, R. T., & Nedelec, J. L. (2020). Academic achievement and the implications for prison program effectiveness and reentry. *Criminal Justice and Behavior, 47*(7), 848–866. https://doi.org/10.1177/0093854820919790

Solomon, A. L., Osborne, J. W., Winterfield, L., Elderbroom, B., Burke, P., Stroker, R. P., & Burrell, W. D. (2008). *Putting public safety first: 13 parole supervision strategies to enhance reentry outcomes*. Urban Institute.

Soloman, A. L., & Scherer, J. (2021). *Desistance from crime*. National Institute of Justice.

Taxman, F. S. (2020). Implementation and intervention sciences: New frontiers to improve research on reentry. In B. Orrell (Ed.), *Rethinking reentry* (pp. 88–118). American Enterprise Institute.

Travis, J., Western, B., & Redburn, F. S. (2014). *The growth of incarceration in the United States: Exploring causes and consequences.* The National Academies Press.

Visher, C., Debus, S., & Yahner, J. (2008). *Employment after prison: A longitudinal study of releasees in three states.* Urban Institute, Justice Policy Center.

Visher, C., & Farrell, J. (2005). *Chicago communities and prisoner reentry.* Urban Institute.

Visher, C., Yahner, J., & La Vigne, N. (2010). *Life after prison: Tracking the experiences of male prisoners returning to Chicago.* Urban Insitute.

Visher, C. A., Lattimore, P. K., Barrick, K., & Tueller, S. (2017). Evaluating the long-term effects of prisoner reentry services on recidivism: What types of services matter? *Justice Quarterly, 34*(1), 136–165.

Wagner, P., & Walsh, A. (2016). *States of incarceration: The global context.* Prison Policy Initiative.

Warwick, K., Dodd, H., & Neusteter, S. R. (2012). *Case management strategies for successful jail reentry.* Urban Institute.

Weisburd, D., Farrington, D. P., & Gill, C. (2017). What works in crime prevention and rehabilitation. *Criminology and Public Policy, 16*(2), 415–449. https://doi.org/ 10.1111/1745-9133.12298

Western, B. (2006). *Punishment and inequality in America.* Russell Sage Foundation.

Western, B. (2019). Race, poverty, and justice reform. *Du Bois Review, 16*(1), 177–180. https:// doi.org/ 10.1017/S1742058X19000225

Western, B., & Sirois, C. (2019). Racialized reentry: Labor market inequality after incarceration. *Social Forces, 97*(4), 1517–1542.

Reading 6.2 Does Depth of Information Matter?

Students are not randomly assigned to college classes, and that fact created a dilemma for Harmon et al. (2024). They wanted to test the late Supreme Court Justice Thurgood Marshall's statement about death penalty opinions. In his written dissent for the landmark *Furman v. Georgia* (1972), Justice Marshall asserted that if people were fully informed about the death penalty, they would oppose it. A number of researchers have attempted to test Marshall's hypothesis, but Harmon et al. took this one step further by studying whether depth of information matters. They decided to collect data by exposing students to one of three conditions—a full semester-long course on the death penalty, a course that covered the death penalty for just once week, and a sociology course with no death penalty instruction. Since it was impossible for the professors to randomly assign students to any of the three classes, they had to resort to a quasi-experimental design. Students' race and gender could impact their opinions on the death penalty. Rather than attempting to match the students in the three classes on race and gender, the researchers decided to statistically control for these variables to see whether either was associated with changes in students' opinions about the death penalty during the study period.

Does Depth of Information Matter? An Empirical Test of the Marshall Hypothesis

Talia Harmon, David Taylor, Todd Schoepflin, Chelsea Henning, and Diana Falco

Introduction

The recent execution of Eugene Smith on 25 January 2024, in Alabama sparked renewed media attention on the death penalty as he was the first person to be executed in the United States using nitrogen gas (Chandler, 2024). While support for the death penalty has been on the decline, more than one-half of the US population continues to support the death penalty for first degree murder (Gallup, Inc, 2023). On the other hand, in October 2023, for the first time, it was found that a majority of Americans felt the death penalty was applied unfairly (Brenan, 2023). While death sentences and executions have also been on a decline in the past few decades, 2020 saw a resurgence in the use of the death penalty in an unprecedented number of federal cases with 13 individuals being executed over a 7-month period (Harmon et al., 2021a). There are also various states (e.g. Oklahoma and Florida) that have announced a desire to increase the frequency of executions within their state. In 2022, Oklahoma initiated plans to execute approximately one inmate per month over the following 2 years (Segura, 2023). However, only a couple weeks after Oklahoma conducted its first execution in 2023, the recently appointed State Attorney General, Gentner Drummond, took action to slow the state's rapid pace of executions, while also opening an independent investigation into the case of Richard Glossip, a controversial death row inmate who has consistently maintained his innocence (Segura, 2023). Drummond claimed, 'Reassessment of the current execution schedule is necessary to maintain confidence in the system … the current pace of executions is unsustainable in the long run, as it is unduly burdening the (Department of Corrections) DOC and its personnel' (Segura, 2023, p. 1). The new schedule allows for only four executions in 2023, placing 60 days between each execution (Segura, 2023). As the pace has slowed, Oklahoma's State House

Judiciary Criminal Committee has also begun to consider placing a moratorium on the death penalty, with State Representative Kevin McDugle citing concerns over innocence as well as the appropriate identification of offenders 'who deserve the death penalty' (Murphy, 2023).

In contrast, Florida has been altering its laws in a way that increases the availability of the death penalty as a punishment. First, the state no longer requires a unanimous jury to sentence inmates to death; it has reverted back to requiring only 8 of 12 of the jury votes to impose the punishment (Ebert, 2023). The state pushed for this shift last year after a split 9–3 jury prevented the Parkland school shooter, Nikolas Cruz, from receiving the death penalty (Associated Press, 2023). In 2023, Florida also enacted a law permitting capital punishment for the rape of a child under 12 years of age (Harding, 2023). Governor Ron DeSantis of Florida stated after he signed it into law: 'These are really the worst of the worst. The perpetrators of these crimes are often serial offenders' (Harding, 2023). This is a controversial law that will likely be challenged, as the Supreme Court has previously ruled in (Louisiana, 2008), that child rape is not a death-eligible crime as it does not result in the death of another human being (*Kennedy v. Louisiana*, 2008), making the law unconstitutional. However, given the current composition of the United States Supreme Court, it will be interesting to see if the *Kennedy* decision is revisited and possibly overruled (Berg & Shokoor, 2023; Wheeler, Robinson, & Sadek, 2023, p. 1). Although these state developments may be anomalies, given the current makeup of the Supreme Court with the more recent appointments of conservative justices appointed by former President Trump, it is difficult to predict what the future holds for capital punishment in the United States. It is safe to say, though, that the Court will likely not accept a global challenge to the constitutionality of capital punishment anytime soon (Death Penalty Information Center, 2023a; Steiker & Steiker, 2019). We have just passed the 50th anniversary of *Furman v. Georgia* in which the Supreme Court examined the constitutionality of the death penalty and ruled that the death penalty as then administered violated the Eighth Amendment and constituted cruel and unusual punishment (Furman, 1972). For a brief period, this ruling halted executions in the United States, until multiple states rewrote their death penalty statutes to comply with the provisions in *Furman* (Lain, 2007). At present, 27 states continue to allow for capital punishment, and as of January 2023, just over 2,300 inmates remain sitting on death row (Death Penalty Information Center, 2023b).

It is appropriate to conduct a new empirical test of the hypotheses established by Justice Thurgood Marshall in his concurring decision in *Furman*. His second assertion, which is most pertinent to our study, suggested that 'people who were fully informed as to the purposes of the penalty and its liabilities would find the penalty, shocking, unjust and unacceptable' (p. 361). While numerous empirical studies have been conducted to test this hypothesis and will be reviewed below, the purpose of this study is to add to the existing literature by investigating whether the amount or *depth of information* about capital punishment is more likely to be associated with increased opposition to capital punishment.

This study introduces a new methodology to extend the previous work conducted by Harmon et al. (2021a, 2021b). We compare change in death penalty opinion when information is gained by both undergraduate and graduate students over the course of a full semester as opposed to a single lecture on the death penalty. Consequently, this analysis will explore the following untested research question: does the amount or depth of information on capital punishment have an impact on death penalty opinion? To test this hypothesis, data were collected by an instructor who taught a full semester-long death penalty class, an instructor who only taught one lecture on the topic, and a comparison group of students enrolled in a class that did not cover death penalty or criminal justice topics. The authors predict the results will suggest that a full semester-long course will have more of a significant effect on change in student opinion than the single lecture or control group, thereby lending support to Justice Marshall's second hypothesis.

Literature Review

Prior Research: Tests of the Marshall Hypothesis

The thrust of this proposed research focuses on the second of Justice Marshall's three hypotheses: It is this hypothesis that has received the most attention over the past five decades and that has, much like the concept of 'fully informed' itself, proven most elusive to be able to test and confirm. On its face, the contention is simple enough: if the American public better understood (i.e. they were 'fully informed') the application and impact of the death penalty, a majority would not support it. The hypothesis has been subjected to numerous tests over 50 years with primarily supportive results.

Methodologically, much of the research examining Justice Marshall's hypotheses has faced significant limitations. For example, Sarat and Vidmar (1976) acknowledge that, given the short time frame and brevity of the readings they used, there was a lack of opportunity and 'time to reflect on or discuss in any depth the issues raised in the essays' (p.195). Studies looking at the impact of specific information on change in opinion also utilized single topical essays, mainly focused on innocence and deterrence (Clarke, Lambert, & Whitt, 2001; Lambert & Clarke, 2001). The methodology employed in many of the early studies rarely allowed students the time and space necessary to think deeply about and to wrestle with their opinions (Bohm, 2014; Kennedy-Kollar & Mandery, 2010). Several studies employed short lectures to impart knowledge to subjects, and two others used a single questionnaire to assess pre- and post-test opinions at the same time while providing a short fact sheet of death penalty information as the information vehicle in between the tests (Kennedy-Kollar & Mandery, 2010; LaChappelle, 2014).

The first researchers to improve the methodology and employ a semester-long college classroom as a means of imparting information to produce 'fully informed people' were Bohm (1989) and his colleagues (1990). With a longer course, subjects can acquire a significantly larger amount of knowledge while also being provided more time and intellectual space to process it. Bohm was also the first to introduce and require a textbook as the knowledge to be obtained on capital punishment issues. Bohm utilized Bedau's Death Penalty in America textbook (Bedau, 1982) (see also Bohm, 1989, 1990; Bohm & Vogel, 1991, 1994, 2004; Bohm, Clark, & Aveni, 1990, 1991; Bohm, Vogel, & Maisto, 1993). Others continued to use textbooks for their classroom experiments (Sandys, 1995; Wright, Bohm, & Jamieson, 1995). Some of these semester-long studies also included follow-up studies (Bohm & Vogel, 2004; Bohm, Vogel, & Maisto, 1993; Cochran & Chamlin, 2005; Michel & Cochran, 2011), the use of journals to record change in opinion as knowledge was gained (Bohm & Vogel, 1991; Sandys, 1995), and the utilization of control groups (Bohm, 1990; Bohm & Vogel, 1994; Bohm, Clark, & Aveni, 1991; Lee, Bohm, & Pazzani, 2014).

Harmon, Falco, and Taylor (2021a), conducted two tests of the *Marshall* hypothesis. The first study was a general test of Marshall's second hypothesis and found qualified support for Marshall's second hypothesis that knowledge is significantly related to an increase in death penalty opposition. Additionally, cost, victim's race, and evolving societies were significant predictors of overall change in subjects' opinions. Surprisingly, the innocence survey items did not appear to have a statistically significant effect on changing opinions. The second study explored the effect of different modes of delivery of information to students and found that the method of course delivery was significantly related to change in opposition toward capital punishment. More specifically, hybrid/online offerings were more likely to result in increased opposition toward the death penalty after taking the class. In the current study, we seek to expand on these two previous studies to compare the use of a semester-long course requiring text readings (including a myriad of issues), with a single lecture utilizing a single article/essay, and a control group with no required readings at all. This is the first study to compare these different methodologies across students enrolled at a single university at the same time in answering a very important untapped research question: does amount of information matter in altering death penalty opinion? Thus, we are filling a significant gap in the literature on this historic and integral hypothesis. In other words, this study extends knowledge on the topic from previous studies by being the first study of its kind to determine if depth of information is a key component that fosters change in opinion.

Methodology

The methodology used to test this hypothesis involved the following data collection of surveys on capital punishment opinion and death penalty knowledge (see survey adapted from Lee, Bohm, & Pazzani, 2014). Researchers received IRB approval prior to conducting the research. Utilizing a quasi-experimental pre-test/post-test design, treatment and control groups were created using the following format: (1) Treatment Group A: a full-semester capital punishment course at the undergraduate and graduate level (n = 30 students), (2) Treatment Group B: a 1-week capital punishment lecture in an Introductory Criminal Justice course (n = 64 students), and (3) Comparison Group: a full semester course that did not cover anything regarding capital punishment in an Introductory Sociology course (n = 74 students). The final N consisted of 168 students.

The full semester-long class (Treatment Group A) consisted of lectures, debates, and films. Students were given a pre-test on the first day of class, which included questions on their opinions and knowledge relating to the death penalty. The same post-test survey was issued at the end of the semester to assess if students' opinions had changed over the course of the semester. The same information was presented in all of the semester-long classes, and consistent with previous research, all of the classes required the same readings (see, for example, Acker, Bohm, & Lanier, 2014; Latzer & McCord, 2011). In addition, all the classes were assigned comparable course requirements such as papers and discussion forums. The classes covered the following topics in depth: racial bias, innocence, deterrence, cost, legal developments regarding landmark Supreme Court decisions, current statistics, methods of execution, and the overall central arguments in the debate.

Treatment Group B included an instructor who delivered a single lecture on capital punishment and taught sections of the course that met three times per week. Students were surveyed during the first class of the week, then provided with an article to read prior to the next class period. During the second class, the instructor reviewed and discussed the article and shared the latest data on capital punishment from the most recent fact sheet produced by the Death Penalty Information Center. The reading used was Radelet and Borg (2000) which provides an overview of the six primary arguments that continue to frame the national debate around the death penalty: retribution, deterrence, incapacitation, cost, innocence, and caprice and bias. The article is ideal in cases where only one reading would be assigned, as the authors provide comprehensive coverage of the topics, yet they adopt no position on the death penalty. Finally, for those in the comparison group, the instructor who taught Introduction to Sociology administered the survey on two occasions to students in two sections of the course, in the span of 1 month's time.

Variables

Students' knowledge and opinions about the death penalty were surveyed (pre- and post-tests) after a full semester-long course, a 1-week session embedded in an Introduction to Criminal Justice course, and an Introduction to Sociology course where the death penalty was not discussed at all. The survey items used to measure both death penalty knowledge and support for the death penalty were adopted from Lee, Bohm, and Pazzani (2014).

For the purpose of this study, the researchers focused on five knowledge items covering the areas of cost, deterrence, innocence, evolving societies, and racial disparities. Respondents were asked to state whether each statement is true or false. The knowledge items (for both pre- and post-tests) were combined to construct a latent variable that was measured on a scale of 0–5. Each correct response added 1 point to the scale. A score of '0' represented no correct responses. A score of '5' represented 100% correct responses.

The death penalty opinion items included 11 questions that made up the two sub-scales (both pre- and post-tests. Respondents were asked to provide their level of agreement with each statement using 5-point Likert response categories (ranging from 1 = strongly agree to 5 = strongly disagree). An additive scale was created with scores ranging from 11 (strongest possible score for a proponent who strongly agreed with each item) to a 55 (strongest possible score for an opponent who strongly disagreed with each of the 11 items). Thus, higher scale scores indicate greater opposition to the death penalty.

Data Analysis

Data were collected in the academic years of 2021 and 2022. As a first step, basic descriptive statistics and frequencies were conducted for all survey items. Our sample consisted of primarily white (76%), females (67%), who were Catholic or Christian (72%) (see Table 1). Next, classes were selected out separately. Paired samples t-tests were conducted to determine significant differences for each type of class separately on both the pre- and post-test for the knowledge and opinion scales. At the outset, it is important to mention that the groups were not significantly different on either knowledge or opinion at pre-test.

The paired samples t-tests found that students enrolled in the full-semester class had significantly higher knowledge scores at post-test at the .01 level. Students in the 1-week class had higher knowledge scores at post-test that were approaching significance at the .10 level, and students in the control group saw no significant differences from pre-test to post-test. More specifically for the 1-week topic class, although average knowledge increased from pre-test to post-test, the increase was only nearing significance (p = .06). Then, ANOVA (Analysis of Variance) was conducted for each group on the knowledge and opinion scales. At the outset, the groups were not significantly different on either knowledge scale (F = 2.113, p = .124) or opinion scale (F = .124, p = .883) at pre-test. This sheds light on whether there are any significant differences in knowledge and opinion based upon the type of class the students were enrolled in (from pre to post-test). A comparison of these items based on class type was evaluated, and any significant changes in students' opinions were identified (see Tables 2 and 3).

To further examine factors impacting death penalty opposition at post-test, we conducted bi-variate regression analyses on each of the independent variables in the study (class type, race, gender, and knowledge). All theoretically significant variables were subsequently

Table 1 Sample descriptives: theoretically important independent variables

Variables	*Categories N (valid percentage)*				
Gender	Males	55 (33%)	Females	113 (67%)	
Race	White	128 (76%)	Non-White	40 (24%)	
Religion	Catholic	71 (42%)	Christian	50 (30%)	Other 47 (28%)

Total N=168.

Table 2 Mean comparison: post-knowledge scale means by type of class

Type of Class	*Average (Mean)*	*Standard Deviation*	N
Full-semester Class	4.2	.925	30
One-Week Topic Class	2.65	1.415	64
Comparison Class	2.58	1.443	74
T-tests for Paired Samples Pre- and Post-Knowledge Scores:			
Full-Semester Class	t = -5.637	p <.001	
One-Week Topic Class	t = −1.918	p = .06	
Comparison Class	t = −.545	p = .587 (NS)	
Type of Class	*Post-Average (Mean)*	*SD*	*N*
Means Comparison: Post-Opinion Scale Means by Type of Class			
Full-semester Class	35.80	13.568	30
One-Week Topic Class	33.23	10.850	64
Comparison Class	32.44	9.805	74
T-tests for Paired Samples Pre- and Post-Opinion Scores:			
Full-Semester Class	t = −1.871	p = .07	
One-Week Topic Class	t = .747	p = .458 (NS)	
Comparison Class	t = .991	p = .325 (NS)	

Total $N = 166$

Table 3 Analysis of variance model: type of class and post-knowledge means

Type of Class	*Average (Mean)*	*Standard Deviation*	N
Full-semester Class	4.2	.925	30
One-Week Topic Class	2.65	1.415	64
Comparison Class	2.58	1.443	74

F Stat = 16.968, $p < .001$ Statistically significant difference between groups/classes, $n = 166$

included in a multiple regression model. None of the bivariate regressions were statistically significant except for knowledge at post-test (see Table 4). The multiple OLS regression model was specifically chosen given the presence of normally distributed dependent variables and to allow the researchers to control for the influence of more than one independent variable on the dependent variable. Although multiple regression models call for the use of all interval level data, it is not uncommon in criminal justice research for lower levels of measurement to be used, particularly with dichotomous independent variables (see Harmon et al., 2021a). We ran a multiple regression with all of the same theoretically important independent variables: knowledge scores at post-test, dichotomized gender, dichotomized race, and dummy variables for Type of Class (the control group was removed from the analysis as the comparison category). This model showed that the only predictor that was significant in the model was knowledge at post-test, which significantly predicted death penalty opposition at post-test ($t = 2.118, p < .05$).

Table 4 Bivariate regression for each theoretically important independent variable on post-opinion scores

Independent Variable	*Unstandardized Slopes (Std. Error)*	*Standardized Coefficients/Beta*	*T*
Post-Knowledge	1.489 (.577)	.201	2.581*
Race	1.020 (2.056)	.039	.496
Gender	-2.668 (2.974)	−.071	−.897
Full-Semester	3.363 (2.38)	.119	1.408
One-Week	.789 (1.907)	.035	.414

*Significance at the .01 level, $N = 160$.

Discussion of Findings

Based upon the results of the ANOVA, the Type of Class (Depth of Information) was related to Knowledge at post-test thus suggesting an indirect effect may exist through the main effect of Type of Class impact on knowledge. Knowledge level at post-test was related to an increase in death penalty opposition, thus offering support for Justice Marshall's second hypothesis. Type of Class appears to have an indirect effect on opinion through knowledge at post-test. This finding ultimately supports the main research question that we tested in this paper: namely, that depth of information *does* appear to influence public opinion through knowledge level at post-test. Thus, this finding also provides support for Justice Marshall's second hypothesis. Moreover, none of the controls were significant in the models, thus providing powerful support for our conjecture that depth of information seems to matter most in classroom instruction and is influential in this context of change in public opinion/support. Finally, the type and amount of information imparted to students on the topic of capital punishment had a significant impact on the level of knowledge of the students at post-test. Thus, this evidence may provide tentative support for the conjecture that the use of in-depth textbooks, varied supplemental readings, casebooks, in-class debates, and documentary films is a superior method of instruction. The full-semester long course also provides ample opportunity for reflection and processing of information through discussion forums/posts. It would also seem that it is more advantageous to impart knowledge to students during the lengthier full semester long course. Based on the high degree of complexity and controversy surrounding the overall topic, this teaching approach is more likely to provide deeper learning, active learning strategies such as discussion boards, group debates, and reflection papers that facilitate increased knowledge and sustained critical engagement and learning to students by the end of the semester (Robinson, 2000). As such, in general, courses that tend to involve more controversial, debatable topics should be considered in Criminal Justice departments as stand-alone courses that last a full semester as opposed to including them or highlighting them in a more superficial, swift fashion where they are embedded within more general or introductory level courses.

Limitations

Several limitations in this study must be addressed. First, we had a modest sample size. In addition, the data were collected at one private Catholic university in the Northeast, in a non-death penalty state; thus, there is limited generalizability of the findings reported herein. There were some limitations based on the survey items that were collected which could be considered 'subjective to a certain extent' (Harmon et al., 2021a, p. 19). There is also the potential for instructor influence that could not be accounted for in the analysis. There also exists the possibility for a rebound effect to occur in follow-up studies years later (see Bohm & Vogel, 2004; Bohm, Vogel, & Maisto, 1993). The rebound effect suggests that the change in opinion after the course is only temporary and subjects may return back to their original pre-test opinion after several years have elapsed.

Future Research

Future research should continue to explore these issues with larger, more diverse samples from various universities in different locations including active death penalty states. Moreover, the cumulative effect of knowledge through multiple course offerings in a department curriculum would provide an extension of these findings in this important area of scholarly research. Another area for future research could involve qualitative interviews of students to get a sense of the information related to the death penalty that they may be consuming outside of class. In-depth answers about what content in the death penalty course they found impactful and related reasons why could be obtained. Relatedly, it would be interesting to determine which arguments in opposition to the death penalty were presented in the course and found to be especially persuasive among students. It would also be helpful to differentiate the precise point when the amount and type of information begins to alter opinions or whether at some point the extra amount of information ceases to have an impact. It could also be the case that when students are simply given the extra amount of time to process the information, that becomes the pivotal distinction for the full semester-long course. This type of examination of depth of information would also lend itself well to courses outside of criminal justice that examine law-related issues that are nuanced, complex, and sensitive topics such as reproductive rights, affirmative action, and the Second Amendment.

Conclusion

In sum, the depth of information taught on capital punishment significantly has an impact on the level of knowledge for college-level participants on the topic. Results also suggest that increased knowledge gained over the course of a full semester of instruction reduced the level of students' support for the death penalty. Public opinion remains critical to examine, even though the Supreme Court will probably not address it at present (see Steiker & Steiker, 2019); notwithstanding this reality, the analysis may still be used in the future in their continued legal analysis or state's analyses of capital punishment under the Eighth Amendment. In fact, while the spotlight rightfully remains on what the highest court in the land might do, equally important are what governors, state representatives, county prosecutors, and state attorney generals might do. Equally relevant is the potential for Eighth Amendment legal analysis under state constitutions. Issues of racial bias, innocence, cost, and methods of execution still continue to be prominent in public discourse and debate on this controversial punishment.

Finally, additional confirmation of depth of information may have even more wide-ranging implications beyond the academic setting. Bloomberg estimates that the 2024 political campaign season will shatter the $10 billion advertisement ceiling, and many of these advertisements attempt to persuade viewers to adopt their positions on particular campaign issues like crime or immigration (Allison & Korte, 2023). They rely heavily on sound bites, particularly with highly charged and emotive issues. However, if such snapshot efforts are ineffective at swaying public opinion, it raises questions about whether those funds might be used more effectively elsewhere.

Disclosure Statement

No potential conflict of interest was reported by the author(s).

Discussion Questions

1. What were the independent, dependent, and control variables for this study?
2. How did including pretests in this study strengthen the authors' findings?

3. How did the three classes of student differ, and how might those differences have impacted students' knowledge and opinions?

References

Acker, J. R., Bohm, R. M., & Lanier, C. S. (2014). *America's experiment with capital punishment* (3rd ed.). Carolina Academic Press.

Allison, B., & Korte, G. (2023, September 12). Election 2024 advertising spending to hit record $10.2 billion. *Bloomberg.com*. Retrieved December 1, 2023, from www.bloomberg.com/news/articles/2023-09-12/election-2024-advertising-spending-to-hit-record-10-2-billion

Associated Press. (2023, April 20). Unanimous juries are no longer required for Florida death penalty sentences. *WUSF*. Retrieved December 1, 2023, from www.wusf.org/politics-issues/2023-04-20/unanimous-juries-are-no-longer-required-for-florida-death-penalty-sentences

Bedau, H. A. (1982). *The death penalty in America*. Oxford University Press.

Berg, N., & Shokoor, J. (2023, May 4). *Florida's multifaceted expansion of the death penalty raises constitutional concerns*. American Bar Association. Retrieved December 1, 2023, from www.americanbar.org/groups/committees/death_penalty_representation/publications/project_blog/florida-expands-the-death-penalty/

Bohm, R. M. (1989). The effects of classroom instruction and discussion on death penalty opinions: A teaching note. *Journal of Criminal Justice*, *17*(2), 123–131. https://doi.org/10.1016/0047-2352(89)90005-6

Bohm, R. M. (1990). Death penalty opinions: A classroom experience and public commitment. *Sociological Inquiry*, *60*(3), 285–297. https://doi.org/10.1111/j.1475-682X.1990.tb00146.x

Bohm, R. M. (2014). American death penalty opinion: Past, present and future. In J. R. Acker, R. M. Bohm, & C. S. Lanier (Eds.), *America's experiment with capital punishment* (3rd ed., pp. 39–75). Carolina Academic Press.

Bohm, R. M., Clark, L. J., & Aveni, A. F. (1990). The influence of knowledge on reasons for death penalty opinions: An experimental test. *Justice Quarterly*, *7*(1), 175–188. https://doi.org/10.1080/07418829000090521

Bohm, R. M., Clark, L. J., & Aveni, A. F. (1991). Knowledge and death penalty opinion: A test of the Marshall hypotheses. *The Journal of Research in Crime and Delinquency*, *28*(3), 360–387. https://doi.org/10.1177/0022427891028003006

Bohm, R. M., & Vogel, B. L. (2004). More than ten years after: The long-term stability of informed death penalty opinions. *Journal of Criminal Justice*, *32*(4), 307–327. https://doi.org/10.1016/j.jcrimjus.2004.04.003

Bohm, R. M., & Vogel, R. E. (1991). Educational experiences and death penalty opinions: Stimuli that produce changes. *Journal of Criminal Justice Education*, *2*(1), 69–80. https://doi.org/10.1080/10511259100082291

Bohm, R. M., & Vogel, R. E. (1994). A comparison of factors associated with uninformed and informed death penalty opinions. *Journal of Criminal Justice*, *22*(2), 125–143. https://doi.org/10.1016/0047-2352(94)90108-2

Bohm, R. M., Vogel, R. E., & Maisto, A. A. (1993). Knowledge and death penalty opinion: A panel study. *Journal of Criminal Justice*, *21*(1), 29–45. https://doi.org/10.1016/0047-2352(93)90004-7

Brenan, M. (2023, November 6). New 47% low say death penalty is fairly applied in U.S. *Gallup*. Retrieved November 28, 2023, from https://news.gallup.com/poll/513806/new-low-say-death-penalty-fairly-applied.aspx

Chandler, K. (2024, January 26). Alabama executes a man with nitrogen gas, the first time the new method has been used. *AP news*. https://apnews.com/article/nitrogen-execution-death-penalty-alabama-6998968154 86f019f804a8afb7032900

Clarke, A. W., Lambert, E., & Whitt, L. A. (2001). Executing the innocent: The next step in the Marshall hypotheses. *New York University Review of Law & Social Change*, *26*(3), 309–346.

Cochran, J. K., & Chamlin, M. B. (2005). Can information change public opinion? Another test of the Marshall hypotheses. *Journal of Criminal Justice*, *33*(6), 573–584. https://doi.org/10.1016/j.jcrimjus.2005.08.006

Cox, A. K. (2013). Student death penalty attitudes: Does new information matter? *Journal of Criminal Justice Education*, *24*(4), 443–460. https://doi.org/10.1080/10511253.2013.787638

Death Penalty Information Center. (2023a, October 3). Analysis shows supreme court's changing view of death penalty cases. Retrieved December 1, 2023, from https://deathpenaltyinfo.org/news/analysis-shows-supreme-courts-changing-view-of-death-penalty-cases

Death Penalty Information Center. (2023b, November). *DPIC fact sheet*. https://dpic-cdn.org/production/documents/pdf/FactSheet.pdf

Ebert, A. (2023, June 20). *DeSantis death penalty law leads to pause in ongoing cases*. Bloomberg Law. https://news.bloomberglaw.com/product/blaw/bloomberglawnews/exp/eyJpZCI6IjAwMDAwMTg4LWRhMDQtZDlmZC1hYmZiLWRiMzRlNTc3MDAwMSIsImN0eHQiOiJMV05XIiwidXVpZCI6IjJFdnZ3MUZWWjJ1U0NhR2FtTDl0WWc9PXBXQW9hZU9RWE03Q2R1U0x1WE RWeHc9PSIsInRpbWUiOiIxNjg3MzQ1MzYwNzA0Iiwic2lnIjoiWXg1ZE9ha25XdW02blpDQXdqajcxZlhjZHRZPSIsInYiOiIxIn0=

Fattah, E. (1983). Canada's successful experience with the abolition of the death penalty. *Canadian Journal of Criminology*, *25*(4), 421–431. https://doi.org/10.3138/cjcrim.25.4.421

Furman v. Georgia, 408 US 238. (1972).

Gallup, Inc. (2023, May). *Death penalty: Gallup historical trends*. Gallup.com. https://news.gallup.com/poll/1606/death-penalty.aspx

Harding, A. (2023, October 1). Death penalty for child rape goes into effect in Florida. *WJXT*. Retrieved December 1, 2023, from www.news4jax.com/news/local/2023/10/01/death-penalty-for-child-rape-goes-into-effect-in-florida/#:~:text=Child%20rapists%20can%20now%20face,violation%20of%20the%208th%20Amendment

Harmon, T., Falco, D., & Taylor, D. (2021a). The impact of specific knowledge on death penalty opposition: An empirical test of the Marshall hypothesis. *Crime & Delinquency*, *68*(9), 1516–1537. https://doi.org/10.1177/00111287211052441

Harmon, T., Falco, D., & Taylor, D. (2021b). The impact of teacher method of delivery and the Marshall hypothesis: JCJE. *Journal of Criminal Justice Education*, *33*(3), 442–459. https://doi.org/10.1080/10511253.2021.1986086

Kennedy-Kollar, D., & Mandery, E. J. (2010). Testing the Marshall hypothesis and its antithesis: The effect of biased information on death-penalty opinion. *Criminal Justice Studies*, *23*(1), 65–83. https://doi.org/10.1080/14786011003634480

LaChappelle, L. (2014). Capital punishment in the era of globalization: A partial test of the Marshall hypothesis among college students. *American Journal of Criminal Justice*, *39*(4), 839–854. https://doi.org/10.1007/s12103-014-9263-5

Lain, C. (2007). Furman fundamentals. *Washington Law Review*, *82*(1), 1–74.

Lambert, E., & Clarke, A. (2001). The impact of information on an individual's support of the death penalty: A partial test of the Marshall hypothesis among college students. *Criminal Justice Policy Review*, *12*, 215–234. https://doi.org/10.1177/0887403401012003003

Latzer, B., & McCord, D. (2011). *Death penalty cases* (3rd ed.). Butterworth-Heinemann.

Lee, G. M., Bohm, R. M., & Pazzani, L. M. (2014). Knowledge and death penalty opinion: The Marshall hypotheses revisited. *American Journal of Criminal Justice*, *39*(3), 642–659. https://doi.org/10.1007/s12103-013-9229-z

Lord, C. G., Ross, L., & Lepper, M. R. (1979). Biased assimilation and attitude polarization: The effects of prior theories on subsequently considered evidence. *Journal of Personality & Social Psychology*, *37*(11), 2098–2109. https://doi.org/10.1037/0022-3514.37.11.2098

Louisiana, K. V., 554 U.S. 407. (2008).

Merrill, M. (2022). Resistance, rage, paralysis, and paralysis by proxy: Reflecting on reactions to contentious content in the classroom. *Teaching Sociology*, *50*(2), 146–154. https://doi.org/10.1177/0092055X211063495

Michel, C., & Cochran, J. K. (2011). The effects of information on change in death penalty support: Race- and gender-specific extensions of the Marshall hypotheses. *Journal of Ethnicity in Criminal Justice*, *9*(4), 291–313. https://doi.org/10.1080/15377938.2011.609430

Murphy, S. (2023, October 5). Republican-led Oklahoma committee considers pause on executions amid death case scrutiny | AP news. *AP News*. https://apnews.com/article/death-penalty-oklahoma-moratorium-wrongful-convictions-1ee3bf8d9e730cbf59bc4fdc46658b19#lnn77lgthod62zah8o5

Payne, B. K., & Gainey, R. R. (2000). Developing and dealing with controversial issues in criminal justice courses. *Journal of Criminal Justice Education*, *11*(2), 313–325. https://doi.org/10.1080/10511250000084941

Radelet, M. L., & Borg, M. J. (2000). The changing nature of death penalty debates. *Annual Review of Sociology*, *26*(1), 43–61. https://doi.org/10.1146/annurev.soc.26.1.43

Robinson, M. (2000). Using active learning in criminal justice: Twenty-five examples. *Journal of Criminal Justice Education*, *11*(1), 65–78. https://doi.org/10.1080/10511250000084761

Salkind, N. J. (2014). *Statistics for People who (Think They) Hate Statistics.* (5th ed.) Sage Publications.

Sandys, M. (1995). Attitudinal change among students in a capital punishment class: It May Be possible. *American Journal of Criminal Justice*, *20*(1), 37–55. https://doi.org/10.1007/BF02886117

Sarat, A., & Vidmar, N. (1976). Public opinion, the death penalty, and the eighth amendment: Testing the Marshall Hypothesis. *Wisconsin Law Review*, *17*, 171–206.

Segura, L. (2023, January 28). Oklahoma slows down frenzied execution spree and launches probe into Richard Glossip case. *The Intercept*. https://theintercept.com/2023/01/28/oklahoma-execution-spree-richard-glossip/

Steiker, C. S., & Steiker, J. M. (2019). *Comparative capital punishment*. Edward Elgar Publishing.

Thompson, D. (2022, January 31). California moves to dismantle nation's largest death row. *AP News*. Retrieved 26, 2024, from https://apnews.com/article/california-death-row-closed-prisons-gavin-newsom-d59ae606239abadb2dfa03be71e54649

Tollini, C. (2009). The behaviors that college students classify as political bias: Preliminary findings and implications. *Teaching Sociology*, *37*(4), 379–389. https://doi.org/10.1177/0092055X0903700406

Vidmar, N., & Dittenhoffer, T. (1981). Informed public opinion and death penalty attitudes. *Canadian Journal of Criminology*, *23*(1), 43–56. https://doi.org/10.3138/cjcrim.23.1.43

Wheeler, L., Robinson, K. S., & Sadek, N. (2023, September 26). Death row inmates find fewer paths to supreme court reprieves (1). *Bloomberg Law*. https://news.bloomberglaw.com/pharma-and-life-sciences/death-row-inmates-find-fewer-paths-to-supreme-court-reprieves

Wright, H. O., Jr., Bohm, R. M., & Jamieson, K. M. (1995). A comparison of uninformed and informed death penalty opinions: A replication and expansion. *American Journal of Criminal* Justice, *20*(1), 57–87. https://doi.org/10.1007/BF02886118

7 Pre-experimental, Longitudinal, and Cross-Sectional Designs

Classical and quasi-experiments are ideal when evaluating the effectiveness of a program. Those designs allow us to safeguard the study against several threats to internal validity. There are, however, circumstances in which classical and experimental designs are not possible or are not appropriate for what we are looking to research. That is why there are a variety of other designs available for consideration. In this chapter, I will describe three different types of studies: pre-experimental, longitudinal, and cross-sectional designs.

Pre-experimental Designs

Ideally, we would like to utilize the most rigorous methodology every time we engage in research. However, the reality is because criminal justice research takes place in the real world, we are often forced to modify our plans to fit the situation at hand. Sometimes, that means that the only available option for a program evaluation might be a **pre-experimental design**. Whereas quasi-experiments lack one of the three requirements of a classical experiment, pre-experimental designs lack two of the three elements. So, here we get designs that not only lack randomization of participants into experimental and control groups, but we might not even have a comparison group or pretest data.

One-Group Before-After Design

In Chapter 4, I discussed how Stauss et al. (2018) evaluated a letter writing program to help incarcerated mothers improve their communication skills while they worked to bond with their children. Their work was an example of a **one-group before-after design**. While the researchers were able to measure differences in the participants before versus after their involvement in the program, they did not have access to a sample of incarcerated people outside of the program who were available to take surveys for comparison purposes. Stauss and colleagues reported posttest scores that indicated reduced parental stress compared to the pretest results. Participants also reported in the interviews that the program helped them work on becoming more empathetic mothers, increased their confidence, and allowed them to have a more positive view of themselves as parents. This type of evaluation holds value in that it helps us establish a relationship between X (the classes) and Y (parenting stress), and it provides evidence that the introduction of X preceded the observed changes in Y. The design does not, however, address multiple potential threats to internal validity, including maturation. Without a comparison group, we cannot tell whether the changes observed in the participants would have occurred absent the intervention.

One- and Two-Group Posttest-Only Designs

The **two-group posttest-only design** addresses the problem of lacking a comparison group, but a significant problem is the lack of a pretest to tell us whether the two groups were similar

DOI: 10.4324/9781003661511-7

or different before introduction of the independent variable. The **one-group posttest-only design** has the most limitations of any of the plans we have discussed thus far, with no comparison group and no data to indicate where the treatment group was at baseline before being exposed to the independent variable. There are occasions when that is the only feasible option. Early in my career, I received a frantic phone call from a criminal justice agency. They had been implementing a three-year grant-funded program for the past two years and nine months. The problem was that one of the grant stipulations was they had to have an outside researcher evaluate the program. While they attempted to contract with another researcher at the outset of the project, that deal fell through, and the agency was now desperate to find someone who would step in at the last minute to do an evaluation. I agreed to help with the understanding that I was coming in too late to monitor the data collection process and could not promise the quality of what I would be able to produce. The practitioner who called me was confident that all would be well, because the person responsible for implementing the program had been distributing pre- and posttests all along. Unfortunately, that was only partially correct. There were no pretests. The program consisted of a series of 12-week sessions with a different group of juveniles each time. When I came on board, I asked for what I expected to be piles of pre- and posttests, but I only received the latter. Consequently, I had no choice but to explain to the grant agency that a one-group posttest-only design was the only possible option. I submitted a report but made it clear I could not make any statements regarding the efficacy of the program, because I had no idea whether the participants changed from the beginning of the program to the end. Even if I did have the pretests and would have been able to do a one-group before-after design, I would have had to note that any changes seen in the juveniles might have been a case of maturation rather than program effectiveness, since I also lacked a comparison group of similarly aged juveniles in the same setting.

Potential Drawbacks of Pre-experimental Designs

Studies utilizing pre-experimental designs can be very useful and help to advance our field, but we must use caution when considering the results. Researchers have compared results of program evaluations based on pre-experimental, quasi-experimental, and experimental designs. Chin et al. (2023) noted that researchers are more likely to find support for more desirable findings when using methodologically weaker designs. Because there is evidence that selection of research design can impact results, researchers should make every effort to choose the most rigorous design possible.

Longitudinal Designs

You have already learned about some **longitudinal designs**. Classical and quasi-experiments and one-group before-after methods involve data collection at multiple points in time. Time-series studies include several data collection points over a period of weeks, months, or years. In this section, I am going to describe a few additional types of designs that require multiple waves of data collection but not necessarily a comparison group.

Trend Studies

Trend studies are exactly how they sound in that they examine trends in populations over time. A review of the FBI's Uniform Crime Reports (UCR) homicide statistics over a 30-year period would give us a good overview of homicide trends in the United States. More and more states are enacting criminal justice reform, with one of the targets of reform being reduction of pretrial incarceration. States are working to limit the use of pretrial incarceration based on fairness, as being released on bail is often more of a matter of a person's wealth than an assessment of their threat to the community. As states enact bail reform, residents are concerned with whether the decision to grant pretrial release will produce increases in crime in the community. Criminal justice practitioners share the community's concern about crime, but they also keep a close eye on the jail population sizes, as bail reform efforts aim to substantially reduce incarceration. Trend studies can help us monitor both the community crime rates and the jail population statistics over time.

Panel Studies

Panel studies are a type of longitudinal design that involves repeatedly collecting data on the same individuals over time. Examples of large-scale panel designs are the National Youth Survey (NYS) and the National Crime Victimization Survey. As discussed in Chapter 5, the NCVS collects victimization data at the household level from all persons 12 and older residing in each selected home. Once a house is selected, it remains part of the study for three years. The first interview is conducted in person, and then the majority of the subsequent six interviews (at six-month intervals) are completed via telephone (United States Bureau of Justice Statistics, n.d.). The **Communities that Care Youth Survey** is another example of a panel study. The surveys were part of a program aimed at reducing health and behavioral problems among children and adolescents. For data collection, researchers tracked 4,407 students, half of whom were part of the Communities that Care Program and half of whom were in the control group, and surveyed the same students each year, starting when they were in the fifth grade (Communities that Care Plus, n.d.).

Cohort Studies

Cohort studies involve following people who are grouped together. While cohorts are often age groups, they can be categorized in other ways, such as by grade in school or police academy class. Perhaps the most famous cohort study in our discipline was the **Philadelphia Birth Cohort Study** conducted by Marvin Wolfgang, Robert Figlio, and Thorsten Sellin (1972) and published in *Delinquency in a Birth Cohort.* Wolfgang and colleagues identified 9,945 males born in Philadelphia in 1945 and used police records to trace their delinquent activity from their 10th through 18th birthdays. Their work was groundbreaking in that they discovered that a very small proportion (6 percent of the entire cohort) was responsible for over half of the entire cohort's criminal offending and nearly three-quarters of serious offending. Several years later, Wolfgang, Figlio, and Sellin (1987) followed up this work by continuing to track 10 percent of the original Philadelphia sample through the age of 30. This research taught us that a small percentage of the population is responsible for a disproportionate amount of crime and, contrary to what was conventional wisdom at the time, individuals generally do *not* specialize in a particular type of criminal behavior.

Accelerated or Intensive Longitudinal Designs

The **Monitoring the Future** (MTF) Survey, which surveys 8th, 10th, and 12th graders, college students, and young adults, is another example of a cohort design. By looking at all these different age groups at once, MTF provides us with indicators of age effects, cohort effects, environmental effects (high school, college, employment), and change in years across all included age groups (Monitoring the Future, n.d.). This use of multiple cohorts at the same time is known as a cohort-sequential longitudinal design or as an **accelerated or intensive longitudinal design**. Unlike traditional cohort designs, which take years to generate results, these accelerated designs provide information in a much shorter time (Galbraith, Bowden, & Mander, 2017). Intensive longitudinal designs can include frequent measurements of the same participants or repeated use of cross-sectional data for the same population or crime type (Jennings & Reingle Gonzalez, 2019).

Counterbalanced Design

What if the research involves questions about what order is best for the delivery of a new curriculum or participation in various rehabilitation programs in a correctional facility? To put this in terms very relatable to you, faculty must grapple with figuring out the best sequence of college courses for students. Should it be Intro, Theories, Methods, then Statistics? What about Intro, Methods, Statistics, then Theories, or Intro, Statistics, Theories, then Methods? A good way to find out would be to do a **counterbalanced design**. Take a large group of students and randomly assign them to a different sequence (Figure 7.1). Once students complete all four courses, we can study their grades, survey them to ask them their thoughts about the sequence they experienced, and survey the faculty about their perceptions of students' readiness and performance in the classes.

Potential Drawbacks of Longitudinal Designs

Longitudinal studies have numerous strengths, with the most prominent one being establishing time order between the independent and dependent variables, a requirement for causation. An important disadvantage is that any research that involves multiple data collection periods over time is also going to be susceptible to some threats to validity. For example, instrumentation, or a change in the way the data are being collected and recorded, must be closely monitored throughout the study. Data collection practices change for various reasons, including adjustments to the way we are asking questions and how data are being input into databases. Attrition, also known in research as mortality, is likely in any study that takes place over time. Researchers may need to consider selecting a larger sample size than what will ultimately

One-group before-after design			
	O	X	O
Two-group posttest-only design			
		X	O
		X	O
One-group posttest-only design			
		X	O

X = Independent variable
O = Observation

Figure 7.1 Pre-experimental designs
Source: Author

be needed for analysis to account for attrition. Of course, if participant attrition occurs in nonrandom fashion, what will be left is a sample that no longer resembles the study population. Incentives to maintain participation, such as a small renumeration at each wave of data collection, might help to reduce attrition.

Cross-Sectional Design

Cross-sectional designs involve just one wave of data collection. The FBI's Uniform Crime Reports (UCR) and the National Incident-Based Reporting System (NIBRS) are both examples of cross-sectional studies. The NCVS is a panel design, but just one wave of data collection for that project is considered cross-sectional. Cross-sectional studies are good options whenever we need to learn about something quickly, and they can provide very good descriptive data. As the country deals with the opioid epidemic, some cities are looking to open supervised injection facilities as a harm-reduction measure. One question that policymakers have is whether drug users would be willing to use them. Leon et al. (2018) used a cross-sectional design to survey a sample of people who use drugs in the Boston area to learn how likely they would be to use such facilities and, if not, why. This descriptive data can help city officials and rehabilitation agency coordinators design injection sites that are most likely to be used by city residents struggling with drug addiction.

Cross-sectional designs are not hampered by attrition problems, nor are changes in instrumentation over time a concern. What we do lose here is the ability to learn about time order. We might be able to find that there is a relationship between an independent and a dependent variable, but we will not know whether the change in Y preceded or followed the introduction of X. As I noted in previous chapters, research on home security systems has been hampered by this problem. Do burglar alarms prevent burglaries? It is difficult to tell with cross-sectional research. Cross-sectional research only helps us establish that there is some sort of relationship between alarm ownership and burglaries but not whether the alarm installation came before or after the break-in.

Approximating Longitudinal Designs with Cross-Sectional Data

Since longitudinal studies are time-consuming and expensive, researchers may attempt to use cross-sectional designs in a way that can allow us to get a picture of what interests us over time.

Retrospective Studies

A common way of approaching crime and victimization research is to ask participants to recall past events. Individuals might be asked to keep diaries to record their recent alcohol or drug consumption. Women who have been in abusive relationships are interviewed about their experiences and reasons why they chose informal or formal avenues of assistance. Adults can be asked to recall their juvenile offending patterns and the age at which they became involved in delinquency. Researchers can also search official records to learn about recidivism of a sample of people who completed a rehabilitation program one year ago.

Researchers refer to cross-sectional designs that involve use of data sources to examine past behavior as **retrospective designs**. Carr, Baker, and Cassidy (2016) conducted a retrospective quasi-experiment of justice-involved individuals with mental illness who went to a specialized day reporting center over a five-year period and compared them to a similar group of people on probation. The outcome of interest here was recidivism, measured as new convictions. The researchers constructed a comparison group based on their knowledge of the characteristics of the experimental group, and then they searched non-public agency records for conviction data. The researchers were able to use databases to get a picture of participants' criminal offending over time, even though they were collecting the data at one time period. Such retrospective work is sometimes used in program evaluation when researchers are not brought in to study the effectiveness of a program until well after the program started. Keep in mind, though, that this type of research is susceptible to instrumentation problems. While the researcher is collecting the data at one time, the agency records were collected over a period of years, and the data collection procedures could have changed during that time.

Retrospective designs are much quicker to implement than prospective designs. For retrospective designs, we ask people to recall past events, sometimes years preceding the survey, or we go into databases to measure things that have already happened. **Prospective designs** involve starting with a sample and then observing participants or asking them to self-report as time progresses. An example of a retrospective study would be to ask 25-year-old men to tell us the age at which they first drank alcohol. For a prospective study, we might identify a sample of 10-year old boys and then interview them every two to three years until they turn 25. During those interviews, we will ask them if they have had alcohol since the last study period. The latter study is clearly going to be more expensive and take 15 years, so the retrospective design is advantageous in terms of time and money.

The downside is that, when we rely on individuals to recall events, there is always the possibility that they will not be forthcoming, will forget about an incident, or their memory will not be an accurate representation of what really occurred. When we ask people to recall events, even if they do remember something happening, there is the possibility of telescoping. Telescoping involves placing events into an improper time frame. In other words, something happened 14 months ago (outside of the time frame of the survey question), but I mistakenly report that it occurred nine months ago (within the survey time frame). More trivial events are also less likely to remain in our memories. Emiko et al. (2004) analyzed data from the **Lehigh Longitudinal Study**, a research project that involved data collection of prospective parental reports of child maltreatment as well as retrospective reports from those parents' children. When comparing the prospective and retrospective measures, the authors found that two-thirds of adolescents whose parents prospectively reported child abuse retrospectively reported that same abuse. In other words, the retrospective accounts were associated with substantial underreporting of abuse.

The **Cambridge Study in Delinquent Development** is a prospective longitudinal survey of 411 males from London who were first contacted when they were eight to nine years old in the early 1960s. Researchers then interviewed the boys again at ages 10, 14, 16, 18, 21, 25, and 32. Since this was a prospective design, researchers were able to ask questions about the onset of criminal behavior. As the respondents aged, they were also asked to retrospectively report on their juvenile offending patterns. Findings revealed that retrospective studies are not necessarily an adequate substitution for prospective designs. Nearly 90 percent of the males interviewed at age 32 failed to report at least one offense that they had reported when they were juveniles. The lack of reporting differed by offense type, with respondents much more likely to forget or otherwise neglect to mention less serious offenses. Retrospective reporting was especially problematic for people with serious substance use problems, which should not be surprising given the impact that substance use has on memory. Retrospective interviews were also less useful for identifying the age at which people began offending as juveniles or young adults (Kazemian & Farrington, 2005). When should we use retrospective designs to collect self-report data? Kaemian and Farrington concluded that data collected retrospectively tends to be more valid and reliable when used to measure more serious offending and more memorable events, as more trivial incidents are likely to be lost with time.

Summary

Pre-experimental designs lack two of the three elements of classical experiments. Not only are these designs missing random assignment of individuals into treatment and control groups, but some lack a comparison group. Pre-experimental designs may also fail to utilize pretest measurements. These studies are limited in what they can tell us about what is being studied, because they fail to address numerous threats to internal validity. They might be the only options available for researchers due to data or program access constraints.

The primary strengths of longitudinal designs are their ability to establish time order between X and Y and to study phenomena over time. Some vitally important data have come from longitudinal studies, including data collected as part of the Cambridge Study in Delinquent Development and the Philadelphia Birth Cohort Study. Of course, significant barriers to longitudinal research are the time and money that they take to complete. It is difficult to secure funding and to wait years, or even decades, to collect all the desired data. That is why cross-sectional retrospective research is an attractive alternative to prospective panel or cohort designs. Of course, anything that is an easier and cheaper alternative comes with limitations, and retrospective designs have been found to produce underestimations of offending and victimization incidents compared to prospective work designed to measure the same variables.

Discussion Questions

1. How do trend studies, panel studies, and cohort designs differ from each other?
2. What are the advantages and disadvantages of using a prospective instead of a retrospective design?
3. What threats to internal validity might be present with a two-group posttest only design?

References

Carr, W. A., Baker, A. B., & Cassidy, J. J. (2016). Reducing criminal recidivism with an enhanced day reporting center for probationers with mental illness. *Journal of Offender Rehabilitation, 55,* 95–112. https://doi.org/10.1080/10509674.2015.1124958

Chin, J. M., Pickett, J. T., Vazire, S., & Holcombe, A. O. (2023). Questionable research practices and open science in quantitative criminology. *Journal of Quantitative Criminology, 39*(1), 21–51. https://doi.org/10.1007/s10940-021-09525-6

Communities that Care Plus. (n.d.). *Research and results.* University of Washington. www.communitiesthatcare.net/research-results/

Emiko, T., Herrenkohl, T. I., Huang, B., & Whitney, S. D. (2004). Measuring child maltreatment: A comparison of prospective parent reports and retrospective adolescent reports. *American Journal of Orthopsychiatry, 74*(4), 424–435. https://doi.org/10.1037/0002-9432.74.4.424

Galbraith, S., Bowden, J., & Mander, A. (2017). Accelerated longitudinal designs: An overview of modeling, power, costs, and handling of missing data. *Statistical Methods in Medical Research, 26*(1), 374–398. https://doi.org/10.1177/0962280214547150.

Jennings, W. G., & Reingle Gonzalez, J. M. (2019). *Criminological and criminal justice research methods.* Wolters Kluwer.

Kazemian, L., & Farrington, D. P. (2005). Comparing the validity of prospective, retrospective, and official onset for different offending categories. *Journal of Quantitative Criminology, 21*(2), 127–147.

Leon, C., Cardoso, L., Mackin, S., Bock, B., & Gaeta, J. (2018). The willingness of people who inject drugs in Boston to use a supervised injection facility. *Substance Abuse, 39*(1), 95–101. https://doi.org/10.1080/08897077.2017.1365804

Monitoring the Future. (n.d.). *About Monitoring the Future.* https://monitoringthefuture.org/about/

Stauss, K., Sparks, L., Thomas, J., & Grant, K. (2018). Letters to children: Findings of a program to enhance communication of incarcerated mothers and their children. *Corrections, 3*(4), 225–247, https://doi.org/10.1080/23774657.2017.1381054

United States Bureau of Justice Statistics. (n.d.). *National Crime Victimization Survey methodology.* United States Department of Justice, Bureau of Justice Statistics. www.bjs.gov/developer/ncvs/methodology.cfm

Wolfgang, M. E., Figlio, R. M., & Sellin, T. (1972). *Delinquency in a birth cohort.* University of Chicago Press.

Wolfgang, M. E., Figlio, R. M., & Sellin, T. (1987). *From boy to man, from delinquency to crime.* University of Chicago Press.

Reading 7.1 Do Cannabis and Amphetamine Use in Adolescence Predict Adult Life Success

Prospective research designs can be incredibly time-consuming. The researchers involved in the Mater-University of Queensland Study of Pregnancy (MUSP) in Australia collected their data over a period of 30 years. The benefit, of course, is that they produced data reflecting the pregnancy, birth, and growth of individuals into their 30s. This is the best way to study the impact of early childhood development and adolescence on drug use in early adulthood and their relationship with life success. Research centers engage in these long-running data collection projects and then make the data available, sometimes to the public and other times through membership-based organizations, to maximize what we can learn from their efforts. Najman et al. (2022) filled a gap in the existing drugs and life-course research by examining simultaneous use of marijuana and amphetamines during early adulthood and its association with success in later adulthood.

Do Cannabis and Amphetamine Use in Adolescence Predict Adult Life Success: A Longitudinal Study

Jake M. Najman, David P. Farrington, William Bor, Alexandra M. Clavarino, Tara R. McGee, James G. Scott, Gail M. Williams, and Rebecca McKetin

Introduction

Despite an extensive literature documenting the adverse consequences of the use of cannabis (Volkow et al., 2014; Airagnes et al., 2019; Campeny et al., 2020) and amphetamines (Degenhardt et al., 2017; Farrell et al., 2019; McKetin et al., 2019) there remain important gaps in what is known. These gaps include that: (i) there is a need to distinguish the harms associated with the use of cannabis and amphetamines as well as determine whether there are specific harms associated with their co-use. (ii) adolescence is a period of the life course which involves substantial biological, psychological and social changes. There is a possibility that drug use during this period may be transient or may have longer-term consequences. It is presently not known which of these two possibilities is supported by the evidence. (iii) previous (often cross-sectional) studies determine harms associated with cannabis and/or amphetamines using samples derived from clinical or treatment services. Patterns of drug use in community samples are likely to involve lower levels of use than in clinical samples and be a better indicator of harms experienced by the majority of those who use cannabis and/or amphetamines. (iv) drug use in community samples is associated with a variety of life circumstances, for example, family poverty and parental marital breakdown and child aggressive/delinquent behavior. These same life circumstances also predict a range of adverse life outcomes. Analyses need to distinguish the effects of drug use from their correlated early life predictors of adverse outcomes. (v) adolescent drug use is associated with drug use in adulthood. In determining whether adolescent drug use leads to adult age adverse outcomes it is important that patterns of drug use in both the adolescent and adult stages of the life course be identified and distinguished in analyses. (vi) there are few long-term prospective studies of adolescent drug use. Such studies are needed to estimate the duration of adverse consequences associated with adolescent drug use. (vii) the majority of studies documenting the harms associated with drug use focus on specific mental and physical health, delinquency, crime and sometimes family life outcomes. There is a need to extend our understanding of the possible consequences of adolescent drug use to include more global measures of overall social and economic outcomes. Life success is one such outcome.

The present paper takes data from a long-running longitudinal study and uses self-reported cannabis and amphetamine use as well as cannabis and amphetamine use meeting the clinical criteria for a substance use disorder, retrospectively recalled at the 21 years of age data collection, to predict life success at the 30 years of age data collection, with adjustment for cannabis and amphetamine use at 30 years of age. Covariates are taken from the 14 years of age data collection and are used as controls.

Cannabis

There is ample evidence that some levels of cannabis use are associated with a wide range of adverse life course outcomes (Lynskey & Hall, 2000; Fergusson & Boden, 2008; Horwood et al., 2010; Danielsson et al., 2014; Hasin, 2018; Airagnes et al., 2019; Boden et al., 2020). Early age of onset and many years of continuing cannabis use has been found to predict psychosis-related outcomes. (McGrath et al., 2010). Outcomes associated with higher levels of cannabis use span the range of factors that are arguably indicators of life success including later life course depression (Schoeler et al., 2018), aggressive and violent behavior (Schoeler et al., 2016), as well as reduced educational achievement and socioeconomic status (Lynskey & Hall, 2000; Fergusson & Boden, 2008; Horwood et al., 2010), poor mental health, reduced wellbeing and less satisfactory intimate relationships (Hall et al., 2016; Hasin, 2018). The adverse impact of cannabis use on education in adolescence may also have a downstream effect on occupational outcomes, while adolescent cannabis use has been reported to result in poorer relationships and reduced life satisfaction in adulthood (Fergusson & Boden, 2008).

Amphetamines

The use of amphetamines is similarly associated with poor health and social outcomes, including an elevated risk of cardiovascular complications, stroke, injury, risk of HIV and hepatitis infection, sexually transmitted infections and poor mental health as well as antisocial behavior (McKetin et al., 2019; Foulds et al., 2020; McKetin et al., 2020). Relatively little is known about the level of harm associated with specific levels of amphetamine use. Further, many of the health harms attributed to the use of amphetamines may dissipate with abstinence from substance use, though some impacts may be longer-lasting. For example, although psychosis risk associated with the use of drugs is largely transient, a minority of people are at elevated risk of developing schizophrenia (Kendler et al., 2019), with consequent long-term impacts on social and occupational outcomes (Chong et al., 2016). While these examples demonstrate the plausibility of cannabis and amphetamine use having a long-lasting effect on functioning, with the exception of Fergusson and Boden (2008) and Boden et al. (2020), most studies focus on specific health behaviors and harm experienced proximate in time to the use of cannabis and amphetamines and do not capture the duration or level of drug use involved nor consider the broader extent of the likely impact of drug use on later adult functioning.

In particular, there has been a dearth of studies addressing the co-use of cannabis and amphetamines. Cannabis and amphetamines are associated with the highest number of drug arrests and both are responsible for substantial numbers of hospital admissions (AIHW, 2021). Their use and couse are of policy importance.

Life Success

One measure that has the potential to capture the global impact of substance use on functioning is life success. The case for the development of the concept of life success reflects (i) the need for a multifaceted measure of life course outcomes, (ii) extent societal changes which render more traditional measures of life course outcomes such as social class and family poverty less relevant, (iii) the need for a measure of life course outcomes that may be relevant to a wide variety of study designs and research questions. Life success, as a concept, will have advantages and limitations much as do the related concepts of social class and the quality of life (see Moons et al., 2006).

Life success has been measured using objective (Craig et al., 2020) and subjective (Layard et al., 2014) indicators. Many studies of life success have focused on objective indicators such as social or occupational status and wealth (Parker & Chusmir, 1992; Ullrich et al., 2008). Objective measures of life success have included employment in the highest levels of the professions or business (Holahan, 2021). Subjective rankings of what is perceived to contribute to life success commonly include satisfaction with family life (Sears, 1977). In the Cambridge Study of Delinquent Development, involving a selected sample of economically disadvantaged children, life success was measured using a composite of indicators taken from multiple life domains (Farrington et al., 2006).

Parker and Chusmir (1992) have moved some way toward the validation of the concept of life success using a large pool of items mentioned in the literature, with factor analysis to select a set of 42 items (and six subscales) that met the criteria for construct validity including good internal consistency, test-retest reliability, and very good convergent validity. While life success can and is measured in multiple ways, many of those measures are correlated and the selection of specific indicators is likely to be less informative than the use of a composite indicator (Farrington et al., 2006).

We examine the relationship between the use of cannabis and amphetamines in adolescence and life success at 30 years of age. To measure life success we have developed a 9-item scale which includes objective as well as subjective measures of life success along the lines suggested by Farrington et al. (2006) and Parker and Chusmir (1992). We adopt the suggestion that the adolescent period now extends to the early 20s (Sawyer et al., 2018). We use data from a long-running birth cohort study (the Mater-University of Queensland Study of Pregnancy – MUSP) which has had six waves of data collection from the period during pregnancy to the 30-year follow-up (Najman et al., 2015). Data on cannabis and amphetamine use were available at the 21- and 30-year follow-ups. Covariates were measured at birth and the 14-year follow-up. Life success was measured at the 30-year follow-up. We examine here the extent to which cannabis and amphetamine use up to 21 years of age, predicts life success at the 30-year follow-up, adjusting for a wide range of prior life experiences and behaviors. We also adjust for concurrent cannabis and amphetamine use at the 30-year follow-up to distinguish the consequences of adolescent use of cannabis and amphetamines from those associated with concurrent use.

Research Questions

1. Do cannabis and/or amphetamine use or use disorder by 21 years of age predict life success in adulthood independently of the early life adversities that predict both illicit drug use and life success?
2. Does adolescent cannabis and/or amphetamine use or use disorder by 21 years of age predict life success independently of cannabis and/or amphetamine use in adulthood?

Materials and Methods

Beginning in early 1981 all consecutive pregnant women attending their first visit at an obstetrical service at a major (public) hospital were invited to participate in the study. This obstetrical service accounted for almost half the births in the city of Brisbane, Australia. Of the 8556 women invited to participate in the study, 8448 agreed, of whom 7223 women gave birth to a live singleton baby, defined as the MUSP study cohort. Data were obtained on the offspring immediately after the birth and at 6 months, 5, 14, 21 and 30 years. Some 2900 children provided some data at the 30-year follow-up.

While 2900 offspring provided some data at the 30-year follow-up (excluding deaths this comprises 41% of the original sample), only about 2350 offspring (numbers vary slightly due to missing data) provided useable data at the 30-year follow-up and this group comprises the study sample for the current paper.

We have previously published more extensive details of the sampling, recruitment, study design and response rates for each phase of the study (Najman et al., 2005, 2015). We have noted that loss to follow-up is selective with low income, single-parent families, families reporting high levels of adversity and mothers experiencing anxiety and depression more frequently lost to follow-up. We have addressed the issue of possible attrition bias in a number of papers using methods such as multiple imputations and inverse probability weighting as well as specific testing the likely effects of attrition comparing data on those retained and lost to follow-up (Saiepour et al., 2019). This issue is discussed in the study limitations.

At all phases of data collection ethical approval was obtained from the Human Research Ethics Committee of the University of Queensland and the Ethics Committee of the Mater Hospital. Up to the 14-years, follow-up mothers provided consent for their own participation and the participation of their child. From 14 years onwards the offspring also provided consent.

Measurement of Cannabis and Amphetamine Use

We administered the Composite International Diagnostic Interview (CIDI) including the module detailing past use of cannabis and amphetamines at the 21-year follow-up. The CIDI is a structured clinical interview based upon DSM-IV clinical criteria for substance abuse and dependence. The CIDI includes questions providing details of the age of onset of a disorder meeting the relevant clinical criteria. The CIDI has good validity in identifying cases that meet DSM-IV criteria for diagnosed mental health disorders (Reed et al., 1998). Of 2550 respondents who completed the CIDI, 21.9% (N = 558) had ever had a cannabis use disorder and 4.1% (N = 105) had an amphetamine use disorder. The mean age of the first onset for a cannabis use disorder was 16.4 years (SD = 2.14yrs) and for an amphetamine use disorder was 17.4 years (SD = 2.19yrs). Combining these cannabis and amphetamine use disorder variables, 77.4% (N = 1972) of the sample have never had a cannabis or amphetamine use disorder, 18.5% (N = 472) report only cannabis use disorder, 0.7% (N = 19) only an amphetamine use disorder and 3.4% (N = 86) both a cannabis and amphetamine use disorder by 21 years of age.

At the 21-year follow-up, respondents were asked how often they had ever used cannabis. Some 49.8% of respondents reported ever using cannabis. Respondents were also asked if they had ever used amphetamines like speed, uppers or pep pills. Response options included using but not in the last year. Some 21.4% of respondents reported ever using amphetamines. We then created a variable combining lifetime ever cannabis and amphetamine use. Of 3748 respondents from whom data were available 48.4% (N = 1815) were categorized as never using cannabis or amphetamines, 30.2% (N = 1131) only ever using cannabis, 1.7% (N = 64) only ever using amphetamines while 19.7% (N = 738) were categorized as ever using both cannabis and amphetamines.

At the 30-year follow-up, the now young adults were asked questions about whether they had used cannabis or amphetamines in the last 12 months. Respondents were also asked if cannabis (or amphetamines) were used, for how many days and the quantity they used on those days. They were also asked the age at which they first regularly used cannabis or amphetamines. From answers to these questions, we created a composite variable of no use or lower 50% and higher 50% levels of use (the modest numbers of users at the 30-year follow-up precludes more narrowly defined subgroups of use).

Measuring Life Success

We selected 9 indicators of life success all taken from the 30-year follow-up. These are in 3 categories of a variable, socioeconomic level (3 variables), subjective perceptions of quality of life (3 variables) and stability and perceived quality of intimate relationships (3 variables).

To measure the socioeconomic status of respondents we have used family income, level of education and ownership of own accommodation. To measure stability and perceived quality of intimate relationships we asked questions about the past number of intimate relationships and whether the respondent currently was in an intimate relationship as well as perceived satisfaction with that relationship (three questions). To measure subjective perceptions of quality of life we have three questions concerning satisfaction and happiness with life. The 9 life success items were added together and divided by the number of life success items for which there was available data. Those in the lowest quintile of life success scores were categorized as having low life success outcomes. Using the 9 items we find a Cronbach alpha reliability coefficient of 0.76 suggesting the 9 items are measuring a consistent underlying construct (see Supplementary Table 1 for more details of items in the life success scale).

Measurement of Covariates

Covariates were selected on the basis that they precede the onset of illicit drug use and are all (based upon previous research) likely early-life predictors of the use of illicit drugs. Two predictors were from the time the mother was recruited to the study, namely mothers' age and her education. For analytic purposes, these do not change over the early life course. We have extracted 8 other covariates from the data set. These are all from the 14-year follow-up. Family income, mothers' number of changes of partner between 7 and 14 years, child ever contacts with police as well as contacts with juvenile aid or suspension from school, are all reported by the mother. At the 14-year follow-up, the adolescent was administered a short form of Raven's Progressive Matrices and the Wide Range Achievement Test (WRAT) (to measure IQ) and the Achenbach youth self-report (YSR) to measure anxiety and depression (subscales were combined) and aggression and delinquency (subscales were combined).

Analytic Strategy

First, we examine the association between the sociodemographic variables and life success (Table 1) and drug use recalled at 21 years (Table 2). Table 3 presents the association between sociodemographic covariates and drug use at the 30-year follow-up. Table 4 has details of the association between cannabis and amphetamine use and use disorder up to 21 years of age and life success at 30 years with successive adjustments for covariates and drug use at 30 years. Table 5 provides the cross-sectional data for drug use and life success at 30 years of age. We use either binomial or multinomial logistic regression to assess all associations between early life exposures and cannabis and/or amphetamines use or use disorders at the 21-year follow-up, and cannabis and amphetamine use at 21 years and life success at the 30-year follow-up.

Results

The association between early life course exposures and life success is presented in Table 1. Consistent with expectations mothers' education and family income are predictors of offspring success at 30 years of age. A number of other early life (adolescent) characteristics of the child are strong and consistent predictors of life success including YSR externalizing behavior (at age 14), child contact with police, child suspension from school and child school performance. There is a very strong pattern of associations between the child's aggressive

Table 1 Sociodemographic characteristics of the mother and/or child predicting life success at 30 years of age (Odds ratio, 95% CI)

Variable	*Values*	*High success (80%)*	*Low success (20%)*
Maternal age	19 yrs or less	1	1.30 (0.98, 1.74)
	35 yrs or more	1	1.25 (0.80, 1.96)
	20–34 yrs	1	1
Maternal education	Incomplete high	1	1.49 (1.07, 2.08)
	Complete high	1	1.03 (0.80, 1.33)
	Post high	1	1
Family income (14)	Lowest	1	1.27 (1.02, 1.58)
	Higher	1	1
Raven's 14yr IQ (14)	Bottom 10%	1	2.27 (1.48, 3.49)
	Higher	1	1
WRAT 14yr IQ (14)	Bottom 10%	1	1.67 (1.12, 2.49)
	Higher	1	1
YSR-Internalizing (14)	Highest 10%	1	1.63 (1.23, 2.15)
	Normal	1	1
YSR-Externalizing (14)	Highest 10%	1	2.24 (1.64, 3.07)
	Normal	1	1
Child contact with Police/ Juvenile aid (14)	Yes	1	3.04 (2.13, 4.33)
	No	1	1
Child suspended from school (14)	Yes	1	2.25 (1.47, 3.44)
	No	1	1
Child School Performance (14)	Below average	1	3.25 (2.44, 4.31)
	Normal	1	1.22 (0.96, 1.54)
	Above average	1	1
Maternal partner changes (7–14 yrs)	Three+	1	1.39 (0.85, 2.27)
	One-two	1	1.02 (0.79, 1.33)
	Nil	1	1

All 95% CI are highlighted in bold.

and/or delinquent behavior in the early adolescent period and the child's life success when an adult.

Table 2 provides details of the association between early life course covariates and cannabis and amphetamine use by the 21-year follow-up. These include measures of adolescent behavior including YSR externalizing behavior, contact with the police, suspension from school, and poor school performance. Mothers who report more frequent partner changes over the period up to the 14-year follow-up have children who more often use cannabis and amphetamines by 21 years of age, as do children who have higher levels of externalizing behavior, contact with police/juvenile aid and problems at school. For these latter children, rates of co-use of cannabis and amphetamines appear to be very high.

Early adolescent behaviors (age 14 years) also strongly predict the use of cannabis and amphetamines at the 30-year data collection. Adolescent externalizing behavior, contact

Table 2 Sociodemographic characteristics of mother and/or child by 14 years and drug use by 21 years of age (Odds ratio, 95% CI)

Variable	*Values*	*Nil drugs (N = 1815)*	*Cannabis only (N = 1131)*	*Amphetamine only (N = 64)*	*Cannabis & amphetamine (N = 738)*
Maternal age	19 yrs or less	1	1.05 (0.84, 1.32)	1.19 (0.58, 2.45)	1.27 (0.77, 1.62)
	35 yrs or more	1	0.80 (0.56, 1.15)	1.28 (0.45, 3.62)	0.88 (0.58, 1.33)
	20–34 yrs	1	1	1	1
Maternal education	Incomplete high	1	1.16 (0.91, 1.49)	0.85 (0.33, 2.23)	1.11 (0.83, 1.49)
	Complete High	1	1.10 (0.91, 1.33)	1.33 (0.68, 2.60)	1.17 (0.94, 1.46)
	Post High	1	1	1	1
Family Income	Lowest	1	1.07 (0.90, 1.26)	1.49 (0.87, 2.56)	1.15 (0.95, 1.39)
	Higher	1	1	1	1
Raven's 14yr IQ	Bottom 10%	1	0.82 (0.59, 1.15)	0.81 (0.25, 2.67)	0.87 (0.59, 1.29)
	Higher	1	1	1	1
WRAT 14yr IQ	Bottom 10%	1	0.76 (0.55, 1.05)		0.77 (0.53, 1.13)
	Higher	1	1	1	1
YSR-Internalizing	Highest 10%	1	1.03 (0.80, 1.31)	0.21 (0.07, 1.16)	1.35 (1.04, 1.75)
	Normal	1	1	1	1
YSR-Externalizing	Highest 10%	1	2.89 (2.11, 3.94)		6.03 (4.43, 8.19)
	Normal	1	1	1	1
Child contact with	Yes	1	2.39 (1.75, 3.28)	1.18 (0.36, 3.87)	3.67 (2.66, 5.08)
Police/Juvenile aid	No	1	1	1	1
Child suspended from School	Yes	1	2.51 (1.72, 3.66)		4.65 (3.19, 6.73)
	No	1	1	1	1
Child school performance	Below average	1	1.57 (1.26, 1.97)	0.83 (0.36, 1.90)	2.05 (1.58, 2.65)
	Normal	1	1.36 (1.15, 1.61)	0.87 (0.49, 1.55)	1.99 (1.63, 2.42)
	Above average	1	1	1	1
Maternal partner changes (7–14yrs)	Three+	1	2.56 (1.71, 3.84)	1.50 (0.35, 6.38)	2.33 (1.47, 3.70)
	One-Two	1	1.41 (1.41, 2.06)	1.69 (0.93, 3.09)	1.81 (1.46, 2.25)
	Nil	1	1	1	1

All 95% CI are highlighted in bold.

with police/juvenile aid and suspension from school predict the use of both cannabis and amphetamines at 30 years of age. In general, these associations are strong and consistent (Table 3)

The unadjusted and adjusted associations between self-reported cannabis and amphetamine use and use disorder by the 21-year follow-up and life success some nine years later are presented in Table 4. Lower life

Table 3 Sociodemographic characteristics of mother and/or child by 14 years and drug use at 30 years of age (Odds Ratio, 95% CI) (Reference Category is No Drug Use)

	Cannabis use 30yr			*Amphetamine use 30yr*		
	No use	*Lowest 50%*	*Highest 50%*	*No use*	*Lowest 50%*	*Highest 50%*
Maternal age						
19 yrs or less	1	0.87 (0.54, 1.41)	1.36 (0.89, 2.09)	1	1.61 (0.85, 3.05)	1.02 (0.52, 2.01)
35 yrs or more	1	0.64 (0.28, 1.48)	0.84 (0.38, 1.84)	1	2.09 (0.88, 4.97)	0.79 (0.25.2.57)
20–34yrs	1	1	1	1	1	1
Maternal education						
Incomp. high	1	0.84 (0.50, 1.39)	0.82 (0.48, 1.40)	1	1.29 (0.57, 2.91)	0.61 (0.27, 1.40)
Complete high	1	0.77 (0.53, 1.11)	0.82 (0.57, 1.19)	1	1.08 (0.57, 2.02)	0.85 (0.50, 1.43)
Post high	1	1	1	1	1	1
Family income						
Lowest	1	1.03 (0.74, 1.45)	1.2 (0.87, 1.71)	1	0.97 (0.57, 1.67)	0.62 (0.36, 1.09)
Highest	1	1	1	1	1	1
Raven's 14 yr IQ						
Bottom 10%	1	0.65 (0.26, 1.63)	0.93 (0.42, 2.06)	1	0.90 (0.28, 2.93)	0.83 (0.26, 2.68)
Higher	1	1	1	1	1	1
WRAT 14yr IQ						
Bottom 10%	1	0.58 (0.25, 1.35)	0.69 (0.32, 1.52)	1	1.48 (0.62, 3.51)	0.42 (0.10, 1.74)
Higher	1	1	1	1	1	1
YSR internalizing						
Highest 10%	1	1.35 (0.89, 2.05)	1.09 (0.69, 1.73)	1	0.87 (0.41, 1.83)	0.98 (0.50, 1.93)
Normal	1	1	1	1	1	1
YSR externalizing						
Highest 10%	1	1.60 (0.98, 2.63)	2.40 (1.54, 3.75)	1	1.49 (0.70, 3.17)	2.53 (1.39, 4.61)
Normal	1	1	1	1	1	1
Child contact police/juvenile						
Yes	1	1.09 (0.56, 2.14)	3.34 (2.10, 5.32)	1	3.31 (1.69, 6.50)	2.43 (1.22, 4.84)
No	1	1	1	1	1	1
Child suspended from school						
Yes	1	1.95 (1.01, 3.77)	4.00 (2.36, 6.80)	1	2.47 (1.04, 5.87)	3.81 (1.89, 7.67)
No	1	1	1	1	1	1
Child school performance						
Below average	1	1.09 (0.67, 1.77)	2.06 (1.32, 3.21)	1	1.93 (1.02, 3.66)	1.07 (0.49, 2.34)
Average	1	0.92 (0.66, 1.29)	1.36 (0.96, 1.93)	1	1.02 (0.59, 1.78)	1.65 (1.02, 2.67)
Above average	1	1	1	1	1	1
Maternal partner changes						
Three+	1	1.61 (0.85, 3.05)	1.02 (0.52, 2.01)	1	0.92 (0.39, 2.15)	1.42 (0.67, 3.01)
One-two	1	2.09 (0.88, 4.97)	0.79 (0.25, 2.57)	1	1.19 (0.82, 1.74)	1.67 (1.16, 2.39)

(Continued)

Table 3 (Continued)

	Cannabis use 30yr			*Amphetamine use 30yr*		
	No use	*Lowest 50%*	*Highest 50%*	*No use*	*Lowest 50%*	*Highest 50%*
Nil	1	1	1	1	1	1

All 95% CI are highlighted in bold.

Table 4 Cannabis and amphetamine use and use disorder by 21 + years predicting life success at 30 years

	High life success	*Drug use by 21 yrs Low life success*	*Drug use disorder by 21 yrs Low life success*
Cannabis use/use disorder			
Unadjusted	1	1.18 (0.92, 1.53)	2.29 (1.68, 3.14)
Adjusted [1]	1	1.34 (0.97, 1.83)	2.16 (1.48, 3.14)
Adjusted[2]	1	1.04 (0.74, 1.45)	1.52 (0.99, 2.31)
Amphetamine use/use disorder			
Unadjusted	1	1.37 (0.61, 3.04)	1.39 (0.38, 5.08)
Adjusted[1]	1	1.11 (0.37, 3.38)	1.27 (0.23, 6.94)
Adjusted[2]	1	1.11 (0.37, 3.38)	1.00 (0.17, 5.98)
Cannabis and amphetamine use/use disorder			
Unadjusted	1	1.92 (1.45, 2.52)	2.23 (1.16, 4.29)
Adjusted[1]	1	1.83 (1.28, 2.61)	2.40 (1.11, 5.17)
Adjusted[2]	1	1.17 (0.78, 1.76)	1.35 (0.56, 3.23)

(Reference categories are no use or no use disorder). Odds ratio, 95% CI.

+ Numbers in cells vary somewhat depending upon missing values.

Adjusted[1] Adjusted for maternal education, family income, child IQ, child internalizing and externalizing, contact with police/juvenile aid, suspended from school, school performance and maternal partner changes.

Adjusted[2] Adjusted for above plus cannabis and amphetamine use at 30-year follow-up.

All 95% CI are highlighted in bold.

success appears to be predicted by cannabis and amphetamine use but not by the use of only cannabis or amphetamines. Cannabis use disorder by the 21-year data collection also predicts low life success. These associations are largely unaffected after adjustment for early life covariates. However, adjustment for cannabis and amphetamine use at the 30-year follow-up indicates that cannabis and amphetamine use and use disorder by 21 years no longer predicts life success at 30 years of age.

The association between cannabis use and amphetamine use at 30 years and life success at 30 years, shown in Table 5, is adjusted for earlier life course covariates as well as concurrent use of amphetamines (for cannabis) and cannabis (adjusted for amphetamine use). Most associations in Table 5 are very strong and consistent.

Table 5 Association between cannabis or amphetamine use and life success at 30-year follow-up (Reference category is no cannabis or amphetamine use)

Cannabis use	*Life success*	
	High	*Low*
Lowest 50%		
Unadjusted	1	1.92 (1.36, 2.72)
Adjusted[1]	1	2.72 (1.80, 4.10)
Adjusted[2]	1	2.76 (1.81, 4.21)
Highest 50%		
Unadjusted	1	3.75 (2.72, 5.18)
Adjusted[1]	1	4.40 (2.96, 6.55)
Adjusted[2]	1	3.83 (2.47, 5.94)
Amphetamine use		
Lowest 50%		
Unadjusted	1	3.28 (2.00, 5.36)
Adjusted[1]	1	3.66 (2.04, 6.57)
Adjusted[2]	1	2.53 (1.35, 4.74)
Highest 50%		
Unadjusted	1	1.89 (1.16, 3.08)
Adjusted[1]	1	2.34 (1.35, 4.07)
Adjusted[2]	1	1.22 (0.66, 2.25)

+ Number in cells vary depending upon missing values.

Adjusted[1] Adjusted for maternal education, family income, child IQ, child internalizing and externalizing, contact with police/juvenile aid, suspended from school, school performance and maternal partner changes

Adjusted[2] Is for above plus amphetamines for cannabis use and adjusted for cannabis for amphetamine use.

All 95% CI are highlighted in bold.

Persons using cannabis or amphetamines at 30 years of age consistently report low life success. For cannabis use, there appears to be a dose-related relationship, with high cannabis use being associated with the highest rates of low life success. This is not apparent with the users of amphetamines with both low and high use generally having similar rates of low life success. Adjustment for concurrent cannabis use renders the association between amphetamine use at 30 years and life success no longer statistically significant.

Discussion

Figure 1 presents a visual summary of the analyses and main findings. The most salient features are the extent to which age 14 evidence of adolescent behavior problems predicts cannabis and amphetamine use at age 21 years and at age 30 years, as well as predicting life success at 30 years. It is the consistency and strength of some of these associations that is notable.

In the context of an existing body of literature which suggests that early age of onset of drug use is a strong predictor of adult health and well-being (Hasin, 2018; Airagnes et al., 2019; Farrell et al., 2019; Campeny et al., 2020) our findings could be seen to provide some contrary evidence. From a policy perspective our findings that adolescent-onset of aggressive and delinquent behavior and school problems predicting a wide range of drug use and life success outcomes represents an opportunity to alter the young person's subsequent life trajectory. From a research perspective these findings emphasize the potential for early life experiences and behaviors that may lead to misleading interpretations of any associations observed between drug use and later life outcomes.

The early age of use of cannabis and/or amphetamines, or prior cannabis and/or amphetamine use disorder does not appear to independently predict life success at the 30-year follow-up. There is a need to test this finding and consider its validity and generalizability. Three issues need to be considered in the above context. First, is it likely that early age of onset of drug use may not lead to adverse life course outcomes; second, does the type/level or pattern of drug use suggest some drugs or patterns of use are of greater concern; and third, is life success a valid or generalizable measure of the outcome?

At the 21-year follow-up, we have two measures of cannabis and amphetamine use. Those whose pattern or cannabis and amphetamine use meet the criteria for DSM-IV use disorder (dependence or abuse) identify a subgroup of users with high levels of use at a young age.

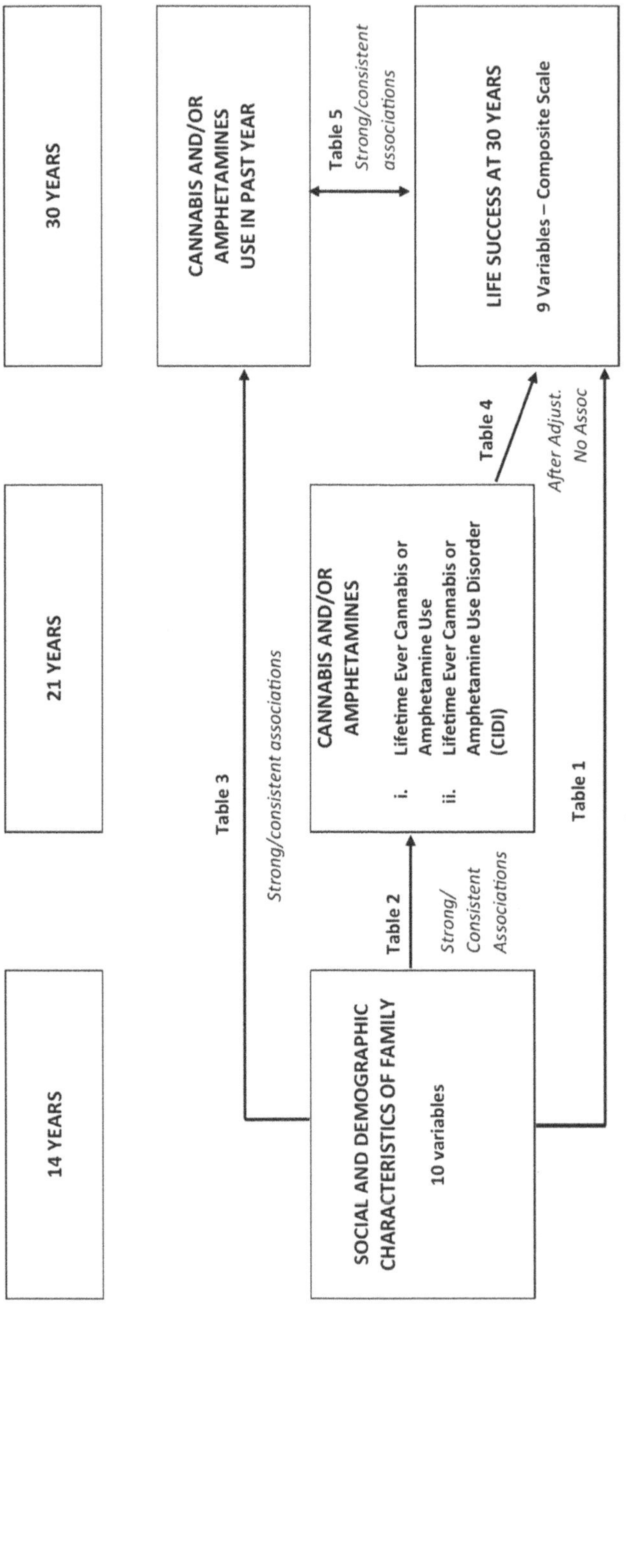

Figure 1 Research model—possible causal pathways. (Respondent age at time data were obtained)

We also reported last year's use of cannabis and/or amphetamines at the 30-year follow-up. In this community-based sample of users, the level of cannabis use was modest (of those who had ever used cannabis only about 25% had used at the level of multiple times in the last month), while the level of amphetamine use was even lower (13% of ever users had used multiple times a month). The numbers using cannabis or amphetamines every day are low in our sample and suggest that the longer terms harm we report for users may largely reflect what are low levels of drug use in a community sample. The lack of an association between amphetamine use and life success may simply reflect low levels of amphetamine use in a community sample.

When we consider those who have had a history of clinically diagnosed cannabis and amphetamine use disorder, we note that some 75% of those who had a cannabis use disorder had their first episode in the 15-to-18-year age range while of those who have ever had an amphetamine use disorder, over 80% were in the 17-to-19-year age range. These respondents exhibit both early ages of onset and high levels of use. Our data on cannabis and amphetamine use suggests that a large majority of those who had ever met the criteria for a drug use disorder were no longer using at clinically significant levels by 21 years of age.

We find little evidence that the early age of onset of cannabis and/or amphetamine use or use disorder predicts adult life success. This may be attributable (i) the low rate of clinically significant drug use in a community-based sample (ii) the ability to distinguish users whose use continues into adulthood (iii) a sample that has a modest proportion who exhibit continuing and persistent use of cannabis and amphetamines.

Perhaps most surprising is the finding that cannabis and amphetamine co-use does not predict adverse outcomes independently of those who are using drugs at the 30-year follow-up. Co-use or polydrug use is frequently associated with a range of adverse outcomes (Darke et al., 2014) but it is difficult to find previous studies documenting co-use of cannabis and amphetamines in a community sample.

It is also notable that there are few in this sample who only report using amphetamines with most amphetamine users also reporting they use cannabis. This is consistent with our CIDI derived data with more respondents reporting a past cannabis and amphetamine use disorder than only reporting an amphetamine use disorder. The co-use of cannabis and amphetamines is relatively common in this population-based sample suggesting the co-use of these drugs warrants greater attention.

In any event, the frequency of a past cannabis and amphetamine co-use disorder in this sample appears to be low and it is not possible to determine whether co-use involved concurrent or serial co-use. Our measure of co-use is limited in detail but does confirm the more general finding that early age of cannabis and amphetamine use, either separately or over a similar time period appears to predict few consequences for life success at 30 years of age.

Of those who had a cannabis use disorder by 21 years of age, 36% report using cannabis at the 30-year follow-up. Of those who had had a cannabis and amphetamine use disorder by 21 years, 60% report using cannabis at 30 years. Comparable comparisons for amphetamine use at 30 years are lower with about 20% of those with a drug use disorder at 21 years using amphetamines at 30 years. At 30 years, when respondents were asked the age at which they first used cannabis and amphetamines "regularly", some 92% of cannabis users and 77% of amphetamine users reported their first regular use was at 21 years of age or less. The data seems to suggest that those using cannabis and/or amphetamines at 30 years comprise substantial numbers of those who experienced a young age of first use. It appears to be the persistence of cannabis and amphetamine use that best predicts low life success outcomes. In any event, it is not possible to determine, at the 30-year follow-up, whether drug use has contributed to low life success or whether low life success may have contributed to drug use, or indeed whether both causal sequences may occur.

Limitations

In interpreting these findings, the limitations of the current study are noted. This study involves a 30-year follow-up of a sample of children recruited in 1981-4. The loss to follow-up is substantial and has been a focus of a number of our research papers (Najman et al., 2015; Saiepour et al., 2019). In many of our papers, we have used multiple imputations, inverse probability weighting or propensity analysis to adjust for selective attrition. In no instances has this adjustment altered the substance of our findings. More recently we have engaged in a series of modeling exercises testing the impact of substantial bias in attrition as well as very high rates of attrition on our findings (Saiepour et al., 2019). The modeling suggests that the observed associations are similar within the group lost to follow-up as well as the group remaining in the study. While loss to follow-up does affect population estimates, for example, we likely lose a higher proportion of respondents who are heavier users of drugs, the association between drug use and life course outcomes is likely unaffected.

The data on cannabis and amphetamine use were obtained over a decade ago and changes in both the prevalence of the use of cannabis and amphetamines as well as changes in the concentration of active ingredients need to be considered in the current context (Volkow et al., 2014; Degenhardt et al., 2017; Stuyt, 2019). Population rates of cannabis and amphetamine use have not changed greatly in Australia in recent years. However, it does appear that more concentrated forms of both cannabis and amphetamine are being used and that the impact of higher concentrations of cannabis and amphetamine has implications both for the extent to which use patterns may increase but also the possibility that there may be a greater impact of newer forms of substances on life success.

The high rates of low life success for those concurrently using cannabis and amphetamines also need to be considered in a broader context. We do not have adequate data on other illicit drugs that may be being used, for example, ecstasy, opiates and even synthetic drugs. A subset of those using cannabis as well as amphetamines may also be using a range of other drugs and it may be that our findings reflect polydrug use generally rather than the specific use of cannabis and amphetamines.

Conclusion

Our findings suggest that the young age of onset of cannabis and amphetamine use has minimal impact on later life success for people who do not continue to use these drugs into their adulthood. However, those who do continue to use amphetamines and/or cannabis, even at moderate levels of use, into their later adulthood have significantly lower levels of life success. The major impacts of concurrent drug use on life success are substantial and involve most domains of life success. While the use of cannabis and amphetamines in a community sample of adolescents does confirm lower levels of educational achievement, most harms are concentrated in the small number of users whose use continues into their 30s. Policies that respond to the findings of this study would firstly act to address the factors predicting the onset of drug use (early adolescent aggressive/delinquent/school-related behavior problems), secondly to discourage cannabis and amphetamine use in the late adolescent and young adult period and, thirdly, focus on support and treatment for those whose pattern of drug use continues into their 30s.

Disclosure Statement

No potential conflict of interest was reported by the author(s).

Funding

This work was supported by the Australian Research Council; National Health and Medical Research Council.

Discussion Questions

1. Najman et al. used several variables collected during four different waves of data collection. What variables did they use, and when was data on each collected?

2. What were the pros and cons associated with this being a prospective study?
3. The relationship between drug use and life success found here was rather nuanced. Explain what the researchers found and what kind of implications this has for policy.

References

AIHW. (2021). Alcohol, tobacco & other drugs in Australia. Retrieved from Canberra: www.aihw.gov.au/reports/alcohol/alcohol-tobacco-other-drugs-australia

Airagnes, G., Lemogne, C., Meneton, P., Plessz, M., Goldberg, M., Hoertel, N., Roquelaure, Y., Limosin, F., & Zins, M. (2019). Alcohol, tobacco and cannabis use are associated with job loss at follow-up: Findings from the CONSTANCES cohort. *PLOS One*, *14*(9), e0222361–e0222361.

Boden, J. M., Dhakal, B., Foulds, J. A., & Horwood, L. J. (2020). Life-course trajectories of cannabis use: A latent class analysis of a New Zealand birth cohort. *Addiction*, *115*(2), 279–290.

Campeny, E., López-Pelayo, H., Nutt, D., Blithikioti, C., Oliveras, C., Nuñno, L., Maldonado, R., Florez, G., Arias, F., Fernáandez-Artamendi, S., et al. (2020). The blind men and the elephant: Systematic review of systematicreviews ofcannabisuse related healthharms. *European Neuropsychopharmacology*, *33*, 1–35.

Chong, H. Y., Teoh, S. L., Wu, D. BC., Kotirum, S., Chiou, CF., & Chaiyakunapruk, N. (2016). Global economic burden of schizophrenia: A systematic review. *Neuropsychiatric Disease and Treatment*, *12*, 357–373.

Craig, J. M., Piquero, A. R., & Farrington, D. P. (2020). Not all at-risk boys have bad outcomes: Predictors of later life success. *Crime and Delinquency*, *66*(3), 392–419.

Danielsson, A. K., Agardh, E., Hemmingsson, T., Allebeck, P., & Falkstedt, D. (2014). Cannabis use in adolescence and risk of future disability pension: A 39-year longitudinal cohort study. *Drug and Alcohol Dependence*, *143*(1), 239–243.

Darke, S., Marel, C., Mills, K. L., Ross, J., Slade, T., Burns, L., & Teesson, M. (2014). Patterns and correlates of non-fatal heroin overdose at 11-year follow-up: Findings from the Australian treatment outcome study. *Drug and Alcohol Dependence*, *144*, 148–152.

Degenhardt, L., Sara, G., McKetin, R., Roxburgh, A., Dobbins, T., Farrell, M., Burns, L., & Hall, W. D. (2017). Crystalline methamphetamine use and methamphetamine-related harms in Australia. *Drug and Alcohol Review*, *36*(2), 160–170.

Farrell, M., Martin, N. K., Stockings, E., Bórquez, A., Cepeda, J. A., Degenhardt, L., Ali, R., Tran, L. T., Rehm, J., & Torrens, M. (2019). Responding to global stimulant use: Challenges and opportunities. *The Lancet*, *394*(10209), 1652–1667.

Farrington, D. P., Coid, J. W., Harnett, L. M., Jolliffe, D., Soteriou, N., Turner, R. E., & West, D. J. (2006). Criminal careers up to age 50 and life success up to age 48: New findings from the Cambridge study in delinquent development.

Fergusson, D. M., & Boden, J. M. (2008). Cannabis use and later life outcomes. *Addiction, 103*(6), 969–976.

Foulds, J. A., Boden, J. M., McKetin, R., & Newton-Howes, G. (2020). Methamphetamine use and violence: Findings from a longitudinal birth cohort. *Drug and Alcohol Dependence*, *207*, 107826–107826.

Hall, W. D., Patton, G., Stockings, E., Weier, M., Lynskey, M., Morley, K. I., & Degenhardt, L. (2016). Why young people's substance use matters for global health. *The Lancet Psychiatry*, *3*(3), 265–279.

Hasin, D. S. (2018). US epidemiology of cannabis use and associated problems. *Neuropsychopharmacology*, *43*(1), 195–212.

Holahan, C. K. (2021). Achievement across the life span: Perspectives from the Terman Study of the Gifted. *The Gifted Child Quarterly*, *65*(2), 185–195.

Horwood, L. J., Fergusson, D. M., Hayatbakhsh, M. R., Najman, J. M., Coffey, C., Patton, G. C., Silins, E., & Hutchinson, D. M. (2010). Cannabis use and educational achievement: Findings from three Australasian cohort studies. *Drug and Alcohol Dependence*, *110*(3), 247–253.

Kendler, K. S., Ohlsson, H., Sundquist, J., & Sundquist, K. (2019). Prediction of onset of substance-induced psychotic disorder and its progression to schizophrenia in a Swedish national sample. *AJP*, *176*(9), 711–719.

Layard, R., Clark, A. E., Cornaglia, F., Powdthavee, N., & Vernoit, J. (2014). What predicts a successful life? A life-course model of well-being. *The Economic Journal*, *124*(580), F720–F738.

Lynskey, M., & Hall, W. (2000). The effects of adolescent cannabis use on educational attainment: A review. *Addiction*, *95*(11), 1621–1630.

McGrath, J., Welham, J., Scott, J., Varghese, D., Degenhardt, L., Hayatbakhsh, M. R., Alati, R., Williams, G. M., Bor, W., & Najman, J. M. (2010). Association between cannabis use and psychosis-related outcomes using sibling pair analysis in a cohort of young adults. *Archives of General Psychiatry*, *67*(5), 440–447.

McKetin, R., Boden, J. M., Foulds, J. A., Najman, J. M., Ali, R., Degenhardt, L., Baker, A. L.,

Ross, J., Farrell, M., & Weatherburn, D. (2020). The contribution of methamphetamine use to crime: Evidence from Australian longitudinal data. *Drug and Alcohol Dependence*, *216*, 108262–108262.

McKetin, R., Leung, J., Stockings, E., Huo, Y., Foulds, J., Lappin, J. M., Cumming, C., Arunogiri, S., Young, J. T., & Sara, G. (2019). Mental health outcomes associated with of the use of amphetamines: A systematic review and meta-analysis. *EClinicalMedicine*, *16*, 81–97.

Moons, P., Budts, W., & De Geest, S. (2006). Critique on the conceptualisation of quality of life: A review and evaluation of different conceptual approaches. *International Journal of Nursing Studies*, *43*(7), 891–901.

Najman, J. M., Alati, R., Bor, W., Clavarino, A., Mamun, A., McGrath, J. J., McIntyre, D., O'Callaghan, M., Scott, J., & Shuttlewood, G. (2015). Cohort profile update: The Mater-University of Queensland Study of Pregnancy (MUSP). *International Journal of Epidemiology*, *44*(1), 78–78.

Najman, J. M., Bor, W., O'Callaghan, M., Williams, G. M., Aird, R., & Shuttlewood, G. (2005). Cohort profile: The Mater-University of Queensland Study of Pregnancy (MUSP). *International Journal of Epidemiology*, *34*(5), 992–997.

Najman, J. M., Farrington, D. P., Bor, W., Clavarino, A. M., McGee, T. R., Scott, J. G., Williams, G. M., & McKetin, R. (2022). Do cannabis and amphetamine use in adolescence predict adult life success: A longitudinal study. *Addiction Research & Theory*. www.tandfonline.com/doi/abs/10.1080/16066359.2022.2032679

Parker, B., & Chusmir, L. H. (1992). Development and validation of a life-success measures scale. *Psychological Reports*, *70*(2), 627–637.

Reed, V., Gander, F., Pfister, H., Steiger, A., Sonntag, H., Trenkwalder, C., Sonntag, A., Hundt, W., & Wittchen, H. U. (1998). To what degree does the Composite International Diagnostic Interview (CIDI) correctly identify DSM-IV disorders? Testing validity issues in a clinical sample. *International Journal of Methods in Psychiatric Research*, *7*(3), 142–155.

Saiepour, N., Najman, J. M., Ware, R., Baker, P., Clavarino, A. M., & Williams, G. M. (2019). Does attrition affect estimates of association: A longitudinal study. *Journal of Psychiatric Research*, *110*, 127–142.

Sawyer, S. M., Azzopardi, P. S., Wickremarathne, D., & Patton, G. C. (2018). The age of adolescence. *The Lancet Child & Adolescent Health*, *2*, 223–228.

Schoeler, T., Monk, A., Sami, M. B., Klamerus, E., Foglia, E., Brown, R., Camuri, G., Altamura, A. C., Murray, R., & Bhattacharyya, S. (2016). Continued versus discontinued cannabis use in patients with psychosis: A systematic review and meta-analysis. *The Lancet Psychiatry*, *3*, 215–225.

Schoeler, T., Theobald, D., Pingault, J., Farrington, D., Coid, J., & Bhattacharyya, S. (2018). Developmental sensitivity to cannabis use patterns and risk for major depressive disorder in mid-life: Findings from 40 years follow-up. *Psychological Medicine*, *48*, 2169–2176.

Sears, R. R. (1977). Sources of life satisfactions of the Terman gifted men. *American Psychologist*, *32*(2), 119–128.

Stuyt, E. (2019). The problem with the current high potency THC marijuana from the perspective of an addiction psychiatrist. *Missouri Medicine*, 482–486.

Ullrich, S., Farrington, D. P., & Coid, J. W. (2008). Psychopathic personality traits and life-success. *Personality and Individual Differences*, *44*(5), 1162–1171.

Volkow, N. D., Baler, R. D., Compton, W. M., & Weiss, S. R. (2014). Adverse health effects of marijuana use. *New England Journal of Medicine*, *370*(23), 2219–2227.

Reading 7.2 A Comparison between Two Retrospective Alcohol Consumption Measures and the Daily Drinking Diary Method with University Students

Repeated alcohol consumption among specific individuals is nearly impossible to observe, as drinking can occur in multiple locations at any time of the day. The most practical way to capture such data is to rely on people to self-report their drinking. As Patterson, Hogan, and Cox (2019) discovered, not every self-report method is equally valid and reliable. Researchers continue to search for measures that are easy for respondents to use but still provide accurate estimates of daily drinking habits. Patterson and colleagues compared three different ways to measure drinking habits retrospectively. Each measure required respondents to catalog their drinking habits differently. This article is an excellent example of how the decisions we make when collecting data have an impact on the results that we find.

A Comparison between Two Retrospective Alcohol Consumption Measures and the Daily Drinking Diary Method with University Students

Chris Patterson, Lee Hogan, and Miles Cox

Recent epidemiological evidence has identified that as little as one heavy-drinking episode per week increases a person's chances of dying from a long-term illness (1). Considering the significant risks and consequences posed by excessive alcohol consumption, accurate alcohol consumption measurement is essential (2).

The most widely used method of assessing and evaluating alcohol consumption is self-report. This is because it: (a) is less intrusive, and easier and cheaper to administer and interpret than alternative methods (i.e., biochemical); (b) provides detailed information that can be used to identify alcohol misuse and dependency; and (c) has consistently been shown to be a reliable and valid method of measuring alcohol consumption (3). There are three main categories of self-report measures: (1) retrospective, summary measures; (2) retrospective, daily drinking measures; and (3) concurrent, daily drinking measures. Retrospective summary measures (e.g., Quantity-Frequency measures) require respondents to report their average quantity of alcohol consumed on a drinking occasion and average frequency of drinking occasions for a specified period in the past. These quantity and frequency estimates are then multiplied together to calculate total alcohol consumption (4).

The earlier, more simplistic QF measures were criticized for being unable to identify the variability of a person's drinking (5). For instance, they were unable to distinguish between different drinking patterns when the total number of units consumed was the same: (1) drinking two units of alcohol on each day of the week; (2) drinking seven units twice a week; and (3) drinking 14 units once a week. Information about drinking pattern variability is essential, especially considering the unique risks associated with particular drinking patterns, such as heavy drinking (6). In response to this criticism, researchers (7) designed more sophisticated QF measures that could classify respondents' drinking (e.g., abstainer, light, moderate, and heavy).

Quantity-Frequency measures have been consistently shown to produce reduced estimates of alcohol consumption and to be poor at distinguishing different drinking patterns, compared to daily drinking measures (8–10). For example, in Flegal's study (10), 31% of heavy drinkers—identified by a daily drinking measure—were classified as moderate drinkers by the QF method. Similarly, in Redman et al.'s study (9), the QF method failed to detect 78% of heavy drinkers identified by a daily drinking measure.

CONTACT Chris Patterson psuc1a@bangor.ac.uk School of Psychology, Brigantia Building, Bangor University, Bangor, Gwynedd, North Wales, UK LL57 2DG

Fitzgerald and Mulford (8) managed to quantify the QF method's insensitivity for capturing atypical drinking. Participants in Fitzgerald and Mulford's study (8) were asked to complete a standard QF measure (i.e., reporting their typical drinking pattern) and then separately asked to report any atypical drinking. The addition of atypical drinking questions resulted in 35% of participants reporting more drinking, thus increasing the total alcohol consumption estimate by 14%. Adapted QF measures (that also ask respondents to report atypical and heavy drinking) have been found to produce estimates of alcohol consumed that are similar to those obtained from concurrent drinking records (11).

The Timeline Followback (TLFB) (i.e., retrospective, daily drinking) is widely accepted as the gold standard alcohol consumption measure. This is because it can capture detailed information about people's drinking behavior, including drinking pattern and variability (12). Moreover, the reliability and validity of drinking data captured by the TLFB have been shown to be high (13).

Clinicians favor the TLFB because its data can be reviewed to help identify individuals' triggers to use, high-risk situations and relapse periods, increase individuals' motivation and commitment to change (14). As a product of the precision with which the TLFB captures alcohol consumption, however, the TLFB's administration is more time consuming and more demanding than other measures (i.e., QF measures). The TLFB may, therefore, be unsuitable in time-limited situations where precise information is not required, for example, some survey studies. Survey studies that have used the TLFB have reported high rates of attrition (15).

Concurrent daily drinking measures require respondents to make concurrent, detailed, records of their daily alcohol consumption (e.g., recording amount, frequency, mood, and urges). This approach has been used extensively to monitor different behaviors in clinical settings (16). Many researchers believe that the Daily Drinking Diary (DDD) method produces the most accurate reports of alcohol consumption, as respondents are less likely to misreport their consumption as a consequence of forgetting (17). As a result of its increased accuracy, the DDD method often produces higher estimates of drinking frequency in studies.

This concurrent daily drinking method is recommended to researchers and clinicians who require precise information about the frequency of alcohol consumption (12). Additionally, researchers and clinicians may ask their clients to keep a daily record of their drinking during treatment. Clients might also be asked to record other variables such as their mood at the time of drinking. This information can be used to identify the antecedents to their drinking; for example, a person might consume alcohol as a means of avoiding unwanted emotional experiences, such as anxiety. DDD data can also be used to track a client's progress during treatment.

It is important to consider that the DDD method has a number of limitations. First, individuals might not adhere to self-monitoring instructions (18). Second, the DDD method cannot be used to gather information about pre-treatment alcohol consumption. In cases where pretreatment drinking information is required, researchers and clinicians would have to use a retrospective measure (12). Third, respondents tend to reduce their drinking as a product of recording their alcohol consumption concurrently (i.e., recording one's own drinking is reactive). For instance, when DDDs have been used as control or waiting conditions in clinical trials, significant reductions in alcohol consumption have been reported (19). Reactivity, however, can be beneficial in clinical settings, where the aim of treatment is to reduce alcohol consumption and change harmful drinking patterns.

This study aimed to compare the accuracy of two retrospective alcohol consumption measures, the Timeline Follow Back (TLFB) and the Typical and Atypical Drinking Diary (TADD) to an assessment of alcohol consumption captured concurrently in Daily Drinking Diaries (DDD) during a 28-day period. The administration of the retrospective drinking questionnaires was to be delayed for a further 28 days after the completion of the diaries in order to prevent the easier recall of estimates following the daily diary procedure. Comparisons of drinking estimates would focus on three aspects of drinking behavior: (1) the total amount of alcohol consumed, (2) the total number of drinking days, and (3) the total number of heavy drinking episodes. There is a strong body of evidence indicating that the DDD method provides the most accurate record of alcohol consumption. It was hypothesized that the gold standard TLFB would provide the most accurate retrospective estimates of alcohol consumption. If the TADD was found to produce estimates that were as accurate, or more accurate, than those provided by the TLFB, this would offer certain advantages to professionals within the field. There would then be evidence that the self-administered and easy to administer TADD can produce reliable and valid estimates of total alcohol consumption, drinking patterns, and drinking variability.

Method

Participants

Out of the 75 psychology undergraduates who initially volunteered to participate in this study, 43 managed to complete the study and provide valid data: 34 females (79.1%) and nine males (21.9%), whose ages ranged from 18 to 46 years (M = 20.8, SD = 5.1). Twenty participants were first-year students (46.5%), 21 were second-year students (48.8%), and two were third-year students (4.7%). The majority of participants identified themselves as White (76.7%), while the remainder identified themselves as Asian (23.3%). There were 33 British students (76.7%), five from other European countries (11.2%) and five from Asia (11.2%). Participation in this study was rewarded with course credit, as well as tickets for a prize draw where monetary prizes could be won: participants who provided all the necessary data gained the maximum number of tickets. The School of Psychology's Ethics Committee approved this study prior to its commencement.

Procedure

Participants met with the investigator in a quiet experimental room in groups of five or less (*M* =2.41, *SD* = 1.40), between 25 and 33 days (*M* = 28.20, *SD* = 3.34) after the start of the second semester. Participants were required to read the participant information sheet and provide their informed consent before commencing this study. Participants were then provided with their first drinking diary and instructed on how to complete the diary correctly (see DDD section).

As agreed, participants met with the investigator for 10 min once a week for 4 weeks. During these meetings, participants handed over their completed diaries and received new diaries. If participants completed their diaries correctly, they were praised. If they completed their diaries incorrectly, they were given extra instruction.

Between 28 and 41 days after completing the DDD (*M* = 34.02, *SD* = 3.96), participants met with the investigator, in groups of six or less (*M* = 2.38, *SD* = 1.52), for approximately 30 min. Participants filled in a demographics form and then estimated their alcohol consumption for the period of time that they recorded their drinking using the DDD (i.e., a time period that was approximately 56 days to 28 days previously) using two retrospective measures: the

TADD and TLFB (in that order). Subsequently, participants were debriefed, thanked, and dismissed. A prize draw was conducted when data collection was complete.

Instruments

DDD

The DDD is a method of concurrently recording alcohol consumption information. The DDD method has been used widely in research validating retrospective alcohol consumption measures. In this study, participants recorded their daily alcohol consumption for 28 consecutive days, detailing the alcohol percentages, volumes, and quantities of beverages consumed: this information enabled the calculation of units. Participants recorded their alcohol consumption the day after it had occurred on a 7-day diary created specifically for this study. They submitted each of their four weekly diaries directly to one of the researchers. Due to not being a standardized alcohol consumption measure, the DDD does not have any psychometric properties to report.

TADD

The six-item TADD was developed by Hogan (20), as a method of retrospectively estimating alcohol consumption and drinking patterns for a specified time period. It can also calculate peak blood–alcohol concentration (BAC) for each drinking session if required (21). The TADD comprises two weekly diaries: one for *typical* weeks and the other for *atypical* weeks (21) (i.e., heavier or lighter drinking weeks). In the typical drinking diary section, respondents stated the types of drinks, alcohol percentages, volumes, and quantities of the beverages that they consumed for each day of a 7-day week (i.e., Monday through to Sunday) and then they estimated how many weeks they drank this *typical* amount during a specified time (in this instance 4 weeks). In the atypical drinking diary section, respondents provide all of the same information, but for a pattern of drinking that might be an atypical week for the respondent (i.e., either greater or lesser than *typical* weekly pattern). Again, they estimated how many weeks they drank this *atypical* amount during the 4 weeks of the drinking diary period. Typical beverage sizes and their alcohol content were shown in an accompanying table, to aid recall. Hogan (20) reported a Cronbach's alpha, a measure of internal consistency (reliability), of .78 (n = 170) for the TADD. In terms of (concurrent) validity, when compared with the TFLB, the TADD's ICC = .872 (95% CI = .677–.935) for an 84-day period.

TLFB

The TLFB (22) is a retrospective daily drinking alcohol consumption measure, which can be used to gain a detailed picture of a person's daily drinking over a specified time period. There is a robust body of evidence attesting the TLFB's ability to produce reliable and valid estimates of alcohol consumption with a wide range of clinical and nonclinical populations (12,22,23). For example, the TLFB has been reported to have a Cronbach's alpha of .84 (24), and test-retest reliability ranging between r = .80–1.00 for a number of drinking variables over a 90-day interval (25).

In an interview with the investigator, who was trained to administer the TLFB, respondents used the calendar-based TLFB form to retrospectively estimate their daily drinking over a specified period of time: the 28-day period where they concurrently recorded their daily alcohol consumption using the DDD method. To aid recall, participants were provided with a sheet outlining the volume and alcohol content of the most commonly consumed beverages.

Design

This study used a within-subjects design to compare participants' reports of alcohol consumption on three instruments.

Statistical Analysis

Summary statistics (i.e., means and standard deviations) were obtained for the three alcohol consumption measures on three drinking variables: total alcohol consumption, number of drinking days, and number of heavy drinking episodes.

Intra-class correlations (ICC) were employed to establish how similar the estimates provided by the TLFB and the TADD in comparison to those produced by the DDD. ICC used the two-way mixed subjects and absolute agreement methods. Moreover, Koo and Li's (26) guideline for reporting ICC was used. This guideline states that values less than 0.5 are 'poor', between 0.5 and 0.75 are 'moderate', between 0.75 and 0.9 are 'good', and greater than 0.9 are 'excellent'.

Paired-sample *t*-tests were applied to ascertain whether the TLFB and the TADD's estimates were significantly different to those yielded from the DDD.

Drinking Definitions

In this study, alcohol consumption was calculated using the UK's unitary system. According to this system, one unit is equal to 8 g or 10 mL of pure alcohol. One UK unit is equivalent to 0.56 standard drinks in the USA. Heavy drinking is referred to in the following results section. This term refers to instances where male participants consumed 8 or more UK units (4.51 or more standard drinks in the USA) and female participants consumed 6 or more UK units in a single drinking session (3.38 or more standard drinks in the USA).

Results

Using data obtained from the concurrent DDD method, the mean weekly consumption of alcohol in UK units was 15.33 (SD = 11.10). On average, students drank alcohol on 8.83 days over the 28-day period they recorded their drinking (*SD* = 4.06), and drank heavily on 4.02 days (*SD* = 3.48). Overall, 86% of students drank heavily on at least one occasion during the 28-day period, and 46.5% drank heavily at least once per week. In Table 1, summary statistics are shown for each of the three methods for assessing alcohol consumption.

Comparison of the DDD and TLFB for overall alcohol consumption had an ICC = .735 (95% CI .229–.886), which is 'moderate'. When compared, the DDD and TADD's overall alcohol consumption estimates had an ICC = .908 (95% CI .832–.950), which is 'excellent'. With regard to estimated number of drinking days, the DDD and TLFB had an ICC = .498 (95% CI –.087 to .758), which is 'poor'. Comparison of the DDD and TADD for number of days drinking had an ICC = .886 (95% CI .789–.938), which is 'good'. The ICC between the DDD and TLFB's estimated number of heavy drinking episodes was = .799 (95% CI .493–.907), which is 'good'. Similarly, the ICC between the DDD and TADD's estimated number of heavy drinking episodes was = .757 (95% CI .555–.868), which is 'good'.

Table 1 Summary statistics of drinking measures for the concurrent Daily Drinking Diary (DDD) and the retrospective measures of the Typical and Atypical Drinking Diary (TADD) and the Timeline Follow Back (TLFB)

	Total alcohol consumption	*Number of drinking days*	*Number of heavy drinking episodes*
	M (*SD*)	M (*SD*)	M (*SD*)
DDD	61.34 (44.39)	8.83 (4.06)	4.02 (3.48)
TADD	65.80 (43.34)	9.0 (4.05)	4.86 (4.29)
TLFB	36.39 (33.13)	5.49 (2.91)	2.51 (2.93)

Note. Total alcohol consumption is reported in terms of the number of UK alcohol units consumed.

Paired-samples *t*-tests revealed no significant difference between the TADD and the DDD in terms of total alcohol consumption, t $(42) = -1.16$, $p = .254$, number of drinking days, t $(42) = -0.41$, $p = .686$, and number of heavy drinking episodes, t $(42) = -1.61$, $p = .115$. Further paired-samples *t*-tests demonstrated that the TLFB, in comparison to the DDD, produced significantly lower estimates of alcohol consumption, t $(42) = 5.35$, p t $(38) = 6.07$, p t $(42) = 4.23, p < 001$.

Discussion

This study established that it is possible to accurately estimate alcohol consumption using a retrospective alcohol consumption measure. The TADD provided highly accurate estimates of three important drinking variables: total alcohol consumption, number of drinking days, and number of heavy drinking episodes. In contrast, the TLFB significantly underestimated total alcohol consumption, number of drinking days, and number of heavy drinking episodes.

Why did the TLFB under-report actual consumption? In line with Fishburne and Brown's (27) social desirability hypothesis, students in this study might have feared that the interviewer was going to judge them negatively as the TLFB was administered in a one-to-one interview. In contrast, the TADD was completed independently without an interviewer scrutinizing the drinking estimates. It is hypothesized that this level of independence enabled respondents to describe their alcohol consumption patterns without fear of judgment.

The results from this study provide further evidence that QF measures can provide accurate retrospective estimates of alcohol consumption and drinking variability, as long as they ask questions about both typical and atypical drinking (8,11,28). Giving respondents a full weekly pattern of assessment for their alcohol consumption for a typical week and for an atypical week in the TADD provided sufficient range/variability to capture a reasonable estimate of actual drinking. The independent administration of the TADD gives it a greater advantage over the TLFB in terms of ease of administration and reduced burden on respondents.

A number of limitations exist in this study. For example, it is possible that the estimate of alcohol consumption using the DDD might not have accurately estimated actual consumption: the DDD was also an estimate of consumption rather than objective independent report. The procedure of administering the TADD prior to the TLFB might have influenced the completion of the TLFB; however, it was felt that the completion of the TLFB first was highly likely to improve recall on the TADD.

The generalizability of this study's results is also limited by the study's sample size, as well as the under-representation of male students. While a sufficient number of individuals initially volunteered to participate in this study, a large number failed to complete it. This high rate of attrition is likely to have been associated with this study's demanding data collection procedure. If this study was to be replicated, researchers should consider replacing face-to-face contact with communication via email. The ratio of male-to-female students in this study was characteristic of the anecdotal underrepresentation of male psychology undergraduates. In retrospect, it would have been beneficial if students studying other subjects were recruited to balance this ratio.

Conclusion

These results can be taken as preliminary evidence that the TADD can be a quick and easy to administer instrument that provides accurate estimates of total alcohol consumption, number of drinking episodes, and number of heavy drinking episodes. In the future, therefore, clinicians and researchers should consider using the TADD if they require accurate retrospective information about a client's total alcohol consumption and drinking variability, especially if they are time-limited.

Financial Disclosures

The authors report no financial conflicts.

Funding

This study was initially conducted as part of an MSc thesis (Foundations of Clinical Psychology) at Bangor University, North Wales. As such, the university provided the author with £200 to cover any costs. This money was spent on the prize draw. No other funding was sourced.

Discussion Questions

1. If the TADD and the TLFB were both retrospective consumption measures, what is the likely explanation for why they produced such different results?
2. From a research participant's standpoint, what were the pros and cons to having to fill out each of the three data collection instruments?
3. How did the fact that participants had to complete one of the forms in front of a research staff member impact those results?

References

1. Holmes, J., Angus, C., Buykx, P., Ally, A., Stone, T., Meier, P., & Brennan, A. (2016). *Mortality and morbidity risks from alcohol consumption in the UK: Analyses using the Sheffield Alcohol Policy Model (v. 2.7) to inform the UK Chief Medical Officers' review of the UK lower risk drinking guidelines*. ScHARR, University of Sheffield.
2. Gmel, G., & Rehm, J. (2004). Measuring alcohol consumption. *Contemporary Drug Problems, 31*, 467. https://doi.org/10.1177/009145090403100304
3. Del Boca, F. K., & Noll, J. A. (2000). Truth or consequences: The validity of self-report data in health services research on addictions. *Addiction, 95*(11s3), 347–360. https://doi.org/10.1046/j.1360-0443.95.11s3.5.x
4. Midanik, L. T. (1994). Comparing usual quantity/frequency and graduated frequency scales to assess yearly alcohol consumption: Results from the 1990 US National Alcohol Survey. *Addiction, 89*(4), 407–412.
5. Alanko, T. (1984). An overview of techniques and problems in the measurement of alcohol consumption. In R. G. Smart, H. D. Cappell, F. B. Glaser, et al. (Eds.), *Research advances in alcohol and drug problems* (pp. 209–226). Springer. https://doi.org/10.1007/978-1-4613-2719-6_7
6. Connor, J. (2017). Alcohol consumption as a cause of cancer. *Addiction, 112*(2), 222–228. https://doi.org/10.1111/add.13477
7. Polich, J. M., & Orvis, B. R. (1979). *Alcohol problems: Patterns and prevalence in the US air force*. RAND CORP.
8. Fitzgerald, J. L., & Mulford, H. A. (1987). Self-report validity issues. *Journal of Studies on Alcohol, 48*(3), 207–211. https://doi.org/10.15288/jsa.1987.48.207
9. Redman, S., Sanson-Fisher, R. W., Wilkinson, C., Fahey, P. P., & Gibberd, R. W. (1987). Agreement between two measures of alcohol consumption. *Journal of Studies on Alcohol, 48*(2), 104–108. https://doi.org/10.15288/jsa.1987.48.104
10. Flegal, K. M. (1990). Agreement between two dietary methods in the measurement of alcohol consumption. *Journal of Studies on Alcohol, 51*(5), 408–414. https://doi.org/10.15288/jsa.1990.51.408
11. Wyllie, A., Zhang, J. F., & Casswell, S. (1994). Comparison of six alcohol consumption measures from survey data. *Addiction, 89*(4), 425–430. https://doi.org/10.1111/j.1360-0443.1994.tb00917.x
12. Sobell, L. C., & Sobell, M. B. (1995). Alcohol consumption measures. *Assessing Alcohol Problems, 2*, 75–99.
13. Sobell, L. C., Maisto, S. A., Sobell, M. B., & Cooper, A. M. (1979). Reliability of alcohol abusers' self-reports of drinking behavior. *Behaviour Research and Therapy, 17*(2), 157–160. https://doi.org/10.1016/0005-7967(79)90025-1
14. Sobell, L. C., Cunningham, J. A., Sobell, M. B., Agrawal, S., Gavin, D. R., Leo, G. I., & Singh, K. N. (1996). Fostering self-change among problem drinkers: A proactive community intervention. *Addictive Behaviors, 21*(6), 817–833. https://doi.org/10.1016/0306-4603(96)00039-1
15. Cunningham, J. A., Ansara, D., Wild, T. C., Toneatto, T., & Koski-Jännes, A. (1999). What is the price of perfection? The hidden costs of using detailed assessment instruments to measure alcohol consumption. *Journal of Studies on Alcohol, 60*(6), 756–758. https://doi.org/10.15288/jsa.1999.60.756
16. Korotitsch, W. J., & Nelson-Gray, R. O. (1999). An overview of self-monitoring research in assessment and treatment. *Psychological Assessment, 11*(4), 415. https://doi.org/10.1037/1040-3590.11.4.415
17. Sobell, M. B., Bogardis, J., Schuller, R., Leo, G. I., & Sobell, L. C. (1989). Is self-monitoring of alcohol consumption reactive. *Behavioral Assessment, 11*(4), 447–458.

18. Sanchez-Craig, M., & Annis, H. M. (1982). 'Self-monitoring' and 'recall' measures of alcohol consumption: Convergent validity with biochemical indices of liver function. *Alcohol and Alcoholism, 17*(3), 117–121.
19. Kavanagh, D. J., Sitharthan, T., Spilsbury, G., & Vignaendra, S. (1999). An evaluation of brief correspondence programs for problem drinkers. *Behavior Therapy, 30*(4), 641–656. https://doi.org/10.1016/S0005-7894(99)80030-6
20. Hogan, L. M. (2005). *Developing and evaluating brief, computerised interventions for excessive drinkers* [Doctoral dissertation]. University of Wales.
21. Hogan, L. M. (2008). *Relationships among alcohol use, emotion, motivation, and goals* [Doctoral dissertation]. University of Wales.
22. Sobell, L. C., & Sobell, M. B. (1992). Timeline follow-back. In *Measuring alcohol consumption* (pp. 41–72). Humana Press.
23. Sobell, L. C., & Sobell, M. B. (2000). Alcohol Timeline Followback (TLFB). In *Handbook of psychiatric measures B2* (pp. 477–479). American Psychiatric Association.
24. Wennberg, P., & Bohman, M. (1998). The timeline follow back technique: Psychometric properties of a 28-day timeline for measuring alcohol consumption. *German Journal of Psychiatry, 2*, 62–68.
25. Sobell, L. C., Sobell, M. B., Leo, G. I., & Cancilla, A. (1988). Reliability of a timeline method: Assessing normal drinkers' reports of recent drinking and a comparative evaluation across several populations. *British Journal of Addiction, 83*(4), 393–402.
26. Koo, T. K., & Li, M. Y. (2016). A guideline of selecting and reporting intraclass correlation coefficients for reliability research. *Journal of Chiropractic Medicine, 15*(2), 155–163. https://doi.org/10.1016/j.jcm.2016.02.012
27. Fishburne, J. W., & Brown, J. M. (2006). How do college students estimate their drinking? Comparing consumption patterns among quantity-frequency, graduated frequency, and timeline follow-back methods. *Journal of Alcohol and Drug Education, 50*(1), 15.
28. Rehm, J., Dawson, D., Frick, U., Gmel, G., Roerecke, M., Shield, K. D., & Grant, B. (2014). Burden of disease associated with alcohol use disorders in the United States. *Alcoholism, 38*(4), 1068–1077. https://doi.org/10.1111/acer.12331

8 Sampling

Polling agencies constantly survey the general public to find out what we think of the latest presidential, senate, and gubernatorial candidates or how favorably we perceive proposed legislation. We will watch a presidential debate one night and have polling results identifying the general public's "winner" that same week. That is pretty impressive, given that there are over 200 million people in the United States who are of voting age. How do the polling groups do it? By taking samples that are, hopefully, representative of the voting population.

It is often too expensive and too time-consuming to reach the entire population of interest when we do research. In fact, it is so challenging that we only attempt it every 10 years when we do the national census. Otherwise, we rely on **samples**. Sampling involves selecting a subunit of the population of interest, with the hopes of then generalizing the results of the research to the entire population.

One of the first steps that we must take when planning research is to determine our unit of analysis. The unit of analysis is who or what the researcher chooses to study. Maxfield and Babbie (2012) identified four different types of units of analysis, including (1) individuals, such as people who are incarcerated, (2) groups, including prison gangs, (3) organizations, such as prisons or jails, or (4) social artifacts, including media content, prison disciplinary records, or police data. The **unit of observation** is frequently, but not always, the same as the unit of analysis. The unit of observation is exactly who is providing us with information about the unit of analysis. Let's go over a few examples to make this clear. When Klein, Bailey, and Sample (2018) were interested in learning about the lives of people on the sex offender registry list, they reached out to the individuals themselves. In this case, both the unit of analysis and the unit of observation here were the same—individuals. I was once interested in the design and management characteristics of jails that were identified in the National Institute of Corrections directory as podular direct supervision facilities. To learn more about these jails, I sent a mail survey to each facility, and I asked for someone in administration to complete it. All the questions on the survey were aimed at getting information about the jail itself, so my unit of analysis was the organization. Since I needed a representative of that organization to complete it, the unit of observation was the responding jail administrator. We must identify our units of analysis and observation at a very early stage in the research plan. Knowing this will guide not only our sampling plan but our entire data collection strategy.

We need to identify the units of analysis and observation for two reasons. First, as I already noted, we need to know who or what we are studying before we actually do the study. If you plan to survey households, then you must decide who in the household is going to serve as the representative for the inhabitants. The National Crime Victimization Survey (NCVS) surveys every member of the selected household who is at least 12 years old for personal victimization interviews. For those surveys, NCVS had to determine what constitutes a household member. The researchers decided that people who are using the sampled home's address as their usual place of residence at the time of the interview *and* currently lack any other usual places of residence would count as household members. For the section of the NCVS interview that just concerns crimes against the household, such as vandalism and burglary, the interviewers need to identify a reference person

DOI: 10.4324/9781003661511-8

who will represent the entire house. That person is usually the owner or renter, but that does not necessarily have to be the case. They generally seek the person who is most knowledgeable about the house, and that individual becomes the unit of observation for the household, which is the unit of analysis (Morgan & Oudekerk, 2019).

The second reason why the unit of analysis matters is that it impacts the conclusions we can safely draw from the results. We want to avoid making mistakes of ecological fallacy and exception fallacy. **Ecological fallacy** means that we come to conclusions about individuals based on research conducted on groups or organizations. This is problematic because researchers have found examples where there was a relationship between two variables when comparing groups, but when that same variable was tested with individuals, the relationship disappeared (Schwartz, 1994). Findings from medical marijuana research provides a good illustration of this problem. Each year, more states allow for the use of medical marijuana. Naturally, there is concern that more widespread availability of medical marijuana will result in greater misuse of the drug. Findings that there is an association between state-level medical marijuana laws and increases in drug treatment admissions in those same states has only served to reinforce those worries. Caputi (2020) cautions, however, that we cannot take those state-level findings and draw conclusions about individuals. A state-level association between the legality of medical marijuana and the number of individuals checking into drug treatment does not tell us whether the people checking into rehab are the same who used medical marijuana. There are a number of possibilities why this state-level association would exist, including a concurrent legalization of medical marijuana and expansion of drug treatment slots in the state. The increase in the number of people entering treatment might be a reflection of the number of beds that are now available. In this example, we should not take a state-level analysis and draw conclusions about the behaviors of individuals. To find out whether the increased availability of marijuana is responsible for the uptick in people seeking treatment, we would need to research *individuals* entering rehab to find out what drugs they used and, if they used marijuana, whether they obtained it using the medical marijuana program.

Exception or individualistic fallacy is another potential problem but in the opposite way from ecological fallacy. Here, we attempt to draw conclusions about large groups after learning about an exceptional circumstance with one or a few individuals. Earlier in this book, I discussed the problem of using anecdotal evidence to dismiss clear trends found in research. We should not conclude that stop-and-frisk is an effective policy based on one big arrest while ignoring the outcomes of hundreds of thousands of such stops. For another example, think about when we hear of a particularly upsetting crime, and based on that one case, we call for policy changes that will affect large groups of people. In 2007, two people on parole in Connecticut committed a heinous crime, murdering three members of a family in their home. That same year, one other person on parole from Connecticut stole a car at knifepoint. In the wake of those two incidents, the governor suspended parole for everyone convicted of a violent offense in the entire state and ordered all other people on parole to be returned to prison for the remainder of their terms for even the smallest of violations (Berman & Fox, 2016). The vast majority of those people were not going to commit a violent crime but had their parole revoked due to the behavior of three individuals. These are just two of many examples in criminal justice of us taking stories of one or two unique events and generalizing them to entire populations.

Sample Bias

As I mentioned earlier, the goal of sampling is to select a subset of the population that closely resembles the population. Failure to handle sampling well may result in sample bias, which is a threat to both the internal and external validity of research. Sample bias can impact the results and, in turn, threaten our ability to generalize the results to the population from which we selected the sample. Sample bias can occur due to purposeful actions by those who are involved in research, or it can be completely unintentional and just a matter of chance. One potential motivation for intentional sample bias is a desire to see a program succeed. People whose jobs rely on the existence of a program, or even people who are just passionate about it succeeding might, consciously or not, select only participants they believe are most likely to succeed. This is known as **creaming**, since they are selecting only the "cream of the crop" to be in the program. This is why there have been instances of correctional interventions and school programs being populated with lower-risk, higher-achieving individuals. The goal of such selection bias is to include people thought to be most likely to succeed. Even in instances where people with a stake in the program's success lack control over who is admitted to the program, they may attempt to introduce sample bias into the program evaluation to skew the results. Years ago, I was tasked with evaluating a parenting program in a medium-security juvenile facility. While I was conducting observations, the instructor, whose employment was contingent on the continued funding of the program, repeatedly requested that I conduct interviews with three of her former students. The research plan that I agreed to with the facility administration did not involve any interviews, but the instructor kept pushing it, as she felt it was crucial to the program evaluation. I later learned that she had developed a very close relationship with these three students, had used her own money to purchase them lots of clothing and other items, and they had remained in the community for some time without recidivating. The instructor was only expressing a desire to contact and arrange meetings for me to interview those three individuals, and not the other 42 program participants. So, while this practitioner had been unable to cream the participant list, she was attempting to facilitate the researcher's access to only the most successful participants who would undoubtably have nothing but good things to say about her.

Sample bias can appear for other reasons, including how the poll or survey is made available to potential participants. With the proliferation of websites and media outlets, people now have the ability to choose to get only news (or even conspiracy theories being peddled as news) from sources that ascribe to particular political leanings. When a site chooses to conduct a poll by posting a survey link on their web page, those who are most likely to see and respond to it are people who share the political views espoused by that show, publication, or network. It is unlikely that a poll shared in that manner will reach people with diverse opinions. When a conservative radio show or website asks its fans to provide approval ratings of a liberal politician, the results are likely to be very negative. The same goes for opinions about conservative politicians being judged by fans of a liberal talk show. This type of sample bias can impact criminal justice opinion polls and surveys. National Public Radio (NPR) conducted a randomized telephone survey in 2018, asking respondents about their preferred television news network and their opinion regarding the question "are immigrants an important part of our American identity?" Seventy-eight percent of respondents who preferred CNN responded affirmatively, compared to just 52% of those who prefer Fox News. So, if a poll appears on a CNN or Fox News website and invites people to click to vote, there is likely to be a good deal of sample bias built into the design (Rose, 2018). But if studies like this are biased, why should we even trust the results of the NPR survey? We can feel comfortable with it, because they conducted a telephone survey of a random sample of households instead of posting a link in a location where only certain people would see it.

Over the next few pages, I will discuss sampling techniques and how they might impact our chances of selecting a representative sample. After that, I will revisit the sample bias issue and review ways to detect bias.

Probability Sampling

The preferred approach to sampling is a design that incorporates the **Equal Probability Selection Method** (EPSM), which includes probability sampling. Probability sampling ensures that every possible participant has an equal chance of being selected, and the hope is that this will prevent sample bias. To do this, researchers randomly select participants, cases, locations, or groups to be involved in the study. Since everyone has an equal chance of being selected by randomization, this also maximizes our chances of selecting a sample that will most closely represent the population. Randomization is also considered the fairest way to separate participants into experimental and control groups. One step typically involved in EPSM sampling is to get access to a **sampling frame**, or a comprehensive list of everyone or everything in the population from which we are about to select our sample. If I wanted to survey students at my university regarding their opinions of the state of parking on campus, I would need to get a list of all students who are registered for at least one class or were on maintenance of matriculation status for that particular semester. Then, once I have that, I would be able to engage in any of the EPSM sampling methods listed here. As you read about the different types of proportional sampling methods, please remember that these do not guarantee a bias-free representative sample of the population you are seeking to study. These methods just reduce the chances of sample bias.

Simple Random Sampling

At some point, you have probably participated in **simple random sampling**. In its most basic form, it involves picking a name out of a hat. All that is required for the process to be fair is for all the possible names to be placed in the hat and for the hat to undergo a good shaking. Of course, this is impractical if you are taking a sample from a population of 1,000, as that would require a giant hat. Fortunately, there are random number generators available online that allow us to input our sample size. It will then generate a number (97 for this example). We would select the 97th person, case, or location on the sampling frame and then select again and again until we have the desired sample size.

Polling agencies often use random digit dialing when conducting telephone surveys. If the target population lives in a certain area, the researchers will program phones to dial certain area codes followed by randomized phone numbers. If the researchers are seeking a very specific area, they can use specific area codes and prefixes (the first three digits of a phone number) and then randomize the last four digits. Of course, use of random digit dialing for specific locations is complicated by geographically mobile people keeping their cell phone numbers when they move to a new area.

Systematic Random Sampling

Systematic random sampling techniques are easy for those who have access to a sampling frame. Once the researchers have a list of the population, they will choose every nth (5th, 10th, etc.) participant to obtain the desired sample size. When I was conducting an evaluation at my local county jail, I needed a sample of 500 recently released individuals to serve as a comparison group for a reentry program evaluation. The jail staff identified 5,000 potential comparison group members, so I asked them to select every 10th person on the list. A potential drawback and threat to randomization is if the sampling frame is listed in some sort of order that could generate sample bias if every certain number of cases or people are selected. It is recommended that researchers select a random start point on the sampling frame and then proceed with picking every nth case.

Stratified Random Sampling

Stratified random sampling requires that researchers be a bit more knowledgeable about the characteristics of the sampling frame from which the sample is being selected. That is because stratified random sampling involves dividing the population into different strata, often based on demographics such as sex, race, age, or socioeconomic status, depending on how important adequate representation of these groups is for the study (Hagan, 2007). From there, researchers select random samples of participants from each stratum. This sampling plan is appropriate anytime it is particularly important for certain segments of the population to be adequately represented. Randomization maximizes, but does not guarantee, a representative sample. Stratification safeguards researchers against accidentally randomly selecting mostly Whites for a study when it is essential to hear from various racial groups.

Stratified sampling techniques can be proportionate or disproportionate. **Proportionate stratified samples** include selection of enough cases or individuals to ensure that each stratified group has the same ratio of representation in the sample as they have in the population. It might be desirable to select a sample that has proportions of representation that do not match the population, and that is when it is appropriate to conduct **disproportionate stratified sampling**. For disproportionate stratified sampling, we would oversample some groups and undersample others. Researchers who are looking to study the impact of racial discrimination on the lives of residents of a particular county or state would likely want to oversample racial minorities.

Multistage Cluster Sampling

As I noted, stratified sampling requires some knowledge about the individuals or cases who are being stratified, as their membership in certain groups needs to be apparent to the researchers in the early stages of sampling. **Multistage cluster sampling** involves division of census tracts, blocks, other areas, or even population units and then taking a probability sample from each cluster (Hagan, 2007; Maxfield & Babbie, 2012). This can be particularly useful when a sampling frame is not available. When studying the impact of police intervention on possible crime displacement, Weisburd et al. (2006) identified both intervention areas and nearby catchment areas that might be impacted by spatial displacement. Data collection involved random selection of street segments within those clusters for social observations and random selection of households in the same clusters for victimization surveys.

The NCVS utilizes a stratified, multistage cluster sample to select households for their panel study of victimization. The first step of their sampling plan is to stratify by primary sampling units (PSUs), including counties, groups of counties, and large metropolitan areas. All the large PSUs are automatically included in the sample, but the smaller ones are grouped by geographic and demographic characteristics derived from the US Census. After randomly selecting some of the smaller PSUs, the researchers divide all the PSU areas into types of housing (such as group quarters, individual houses, etc.) and select clusters of units from those housing types (United States Bureau of Justice Statistics, n.d.).

Nonprobability Sampling

It is not always possible to conduct random sampling for a variety of reasons. For one, placement into the criminal justice system does not occur at random. Judges do not randomly assign people to either probation or incarceration. Even within those specific populations, such as incarcerated individuals, it might not be possible to obtain a random sample for research purposes. Administrators of only some of the prisons might have granted researchers access, and the correctional administration might only be providing the new treatment program being evaluated on certain units. Incarcerated people are not placed in prisons or particular units at random, as their security/custody level and treatment needs dictate where they will live. When studying therapeutic interventions, there may be ethical issues that will prevent the use of random assignment. There are a number of scenarios in criminal justice where it is not going to be possible to conduct any of the previously reviewed sampling procedures. Instead, you will likely have to do **nonprobability sampling**, which encompasses any sampling plan that does not abide by the Equal Probability Selection Method. Nonprobability, or nonrandom selection plans, vary in their ease of implementation and their quality.

Convenience and Accidental Sampling

Convenience or accidental sampling is simply a sampling plan designed to be convenient for the researcher. Examples include research that professors conduct by handing out surveys to their own students (Hartley, 2011), or "man on the street" interviews where local news reporters and a camera crew step outside their studios and ask two or three people walking down the street what they think of an issue (Hagan, 2007). A more modern example of convenience sampling is placing a survey on your social media page and asking people to complete it. If you wanted to get students' opinions about your university's newest academic policies and you set up a table outside of one of the school dining halls on a Tuesday, that would be a convenience sample. You might have chosen a Tuesday afternoon because that is the only day you are free during lunch. While you will get responses, you are going to miss everyone who does not have class on Tuesday, does not eat in that dining hall, or only comes to school at night. Earlier, I discussed posting surveys on websites for news organizations. Special interest groups and even sports teams might post links to surveys this same way. These are all very easy and convenient ways for the researchers to collect responses, but these techniques are very unlikely to produce samples that are representative of the population.

A drawback to convenience sampling is that the sample that you generate might not be the most appropriate to address the research question (Chenane & Hammond, 2022). Going back to the idea of setting up a table outside a university cafeteria, if the research question pertains to commuter parking and the participant recruitment table is located at a cafeteria that primarily serves residential students, you are likely to miss the people who have actual experience with commuter parking. Along those same lines, if a website specializing in covering a specific sports team posts a poll on their site asking people who they think will win this week's matchup, only those who visit that website will see it and be eligible to participate. Just posting the poll in one location was convenient for the web designers, but it is sure to generate a nonrepresentative sample. Gathering a sample of research participants by just posting a link to the survey on your social media page is unlikely to provide you with a very diverse pool of respondents, as we all tend to gravitate to like-minded individuals. Additionally, if only younger people tend to utilize that site, then you will not receive responses from many older individuals. That could be a problem if you are looking for a sample that resembles most communities.

Purposive Sampling

Purposive sampling plans are based on the researchers' needs but also involve the researchers' judgment about how to obtain an appropriate sample. A colleague and I became curious about students' motivations for selecting criminal justice as a major. For sampling, we perceived two challenges. First, we knew that we needed to reach a variety of criminal justice students, ideally from different colleges in multiple states, for generalizability purposes. Second, we realized that, even within majors, some students would be attracted to certain classes while avoiding others based on their academic and career interests. Unfortunately, we were not in possession of the names and email addresses of every criminal justice college student in the nation, nor did we have extensive connections at every school in the United States, so we had to get creative. We addressed our first concern by contacting colleagues at universities in multiple states and requested their assistance with survey dissemination. Next, we decided to target specific classes. We wanted to avoid electives, as students are likely to self-select into different electives based on their career goals,

We decided to target two mandatory core courses—Introduction to Law Enforcement and Research Methods—to ensure that we reached a good cross-section of majors at each university (Krimmel & Tartaro, 1999; Tartaro & Krimmel, 2003). While we could not arrange for a random sample of college criminal justice students across the nation, our purposive sampling plan likely produced a more representative group of students than if we had just surveyed students in our own classes at the two colleges where we worked, or surveyed students in elective courses.

A common use for purposive sampling is the construction of **focus groups**, or small groups of people (usually 8 to 15) brought together at one time for moderated group interviews. Ideally, the participants should be unfamiliar with each other, and they are typically selected because they all have certain common characteristics (e.g., they are all shoppers at a particular type of store, all registered voters in a state, all employees of a university, etc.) (Marczak & Sewell, n.d.). Focus groups are common in marketing research and political polling. In the social sciences, focus groups can be particularly helpful in the early stages of research when the research team is working on constructing surveys. Focus group members can help the researchers consider aspects of the topic that they had not thought of previously. For practitioners, these interviews allow service providers to hear directly from consumers about their needs.

It is common for people to confuse convenience and purposive sampling methods. Chenane and Hammond (2022) noted that the key difference is, where convenience sampling allows participation for anyone willing and able to participate, purposive sampling is more focused based on the researchers' knowledge of the sample. While there is no guarantee that purposive sampling will result in a representative sample, this technique does allow researchers to focus on a population of interest for the research. The drawback here is that, since researchers are human, their bias, conscious or not, may prompt selection of a sample that would support the researchers' hypothesis.

Quota Sampling

Quota sampling is similar to stratified random sampling, but it does not involve randomization. As with stratified sampling, the goal of quota sampling is to guarantee that certain groups are represented in the sample. Eaton, Ramjee, and Saunders (2023) wanted to study sextortion and its relationship with intimate partner violence and needed a diverse sample. Since they were circulating an online survey and were unable to set up probability sampling, they utilized proportional quota sampling. This allowed them to ensure that their sample included adequate representation of different genders, races, ages, sexual identities, and geographic regions. The decisions that the researchers made during the sampling process had important implications for what they were able to discover in their analysis, as groups that make up a small proportion of the population, such as Native Americans and sexual identity minorities, were more likely to have reported experiencing sextortion. Failure to include these groups in their quota categories and to disproportionately sample them would have prevented them from discovering this information.

Snowball Sampling

Snowball sampling is a nonprobability technique that can help researchers access very hard-to-reach populations. The goal here is to find at least one member of the population of interest and then have that person refer others. Those referrals will, hopefully, introduce the researchers to more potential participants, and so on until the small sample increases in size, just like a snowball being rolled through the snow. Perhaps the most well-known example of snowball sampling in criminal justice research is Wright et al.'s (1992) research on active residential burglars. People actively involved in criminal activity are an especially tough-to-find group. Researchers cannot exactly put an ad in the newspaper or post something online asking for active criminals to please call a number or click on a link to be part of a study. This is a very suspicious group, and for good reason. Admitting to illegal behavior carries with it the possibility of arrest and prosecution. The most common way that researchers get access is through police, courts, and corrections departments. The drawback, of course, is that everyone known to the criminal justice system has been caught and, to a certain extent, can be seen as someone who failed at being adept at committing crimes. For that reason, Wright and associates wanted to obtain a sample of active burglars in a way other than going through criminal justice system records. Instead, they hired a well-regarded individual in the neighborhood who used to be involved in crime but was paralyzed in a shooting. This individual acted as a **gatekeeper** who helped to vouch for the credibility of the researchers and made the potential research participants comfortable about discussing their criminal activity. Through these introductions, Wright and colleagues did some initial interviews and then encouraged the new participants to introduce them to their associates. The researchers found that their sample of people actively involved in crime did, indeed, differ from the sample they would have obtained by going through the corrections system. Forty-two percent of Wright and colleagues' sample had never been arrested for burglary, while 33% had been arrested for, but never convicted of, burglary. Those who had never been arrested reported breaking into nearly twice as many homes as the respondents who had been arrested for burglary.

Snowball sampling is an important tool for researchers, as it allows us to reach groups that would otherwise be impossible to locate, but it does come with a substantial drawback, and that is the very strong possibility of sample bias. I am sure you have heard the saying "birds of a feather flock together." There is truth to that. If you are doing gang research and start a snowball sample with one or two members of one gang, you are likely to finish your study with a sample consisting of members of that gang and maybe some people in allied gangs. It is very unlikely that the people you meet and interview will introduce you to members of rival gangs. One way to mitigate, but not eliminate, the sample bias inherent in snowball sampling is to use **respondent-driven sampling**. This is a type of snowball sample that seeks to reduce the influence of the initial informant or informants by (1) using as many initial informants as possible, and (2) limiting the number of referrals from each initial informant. The goal here is reduce the influence of the small number of initial informants and then to draw a more diverse sample (Weisheit, 2015).

Revisiting Sample Bias

Checking Your Data—Confidence Intervals and Confidence Levels

When we take a sample, how do we know whether it is representative of the population? There are ways that we can check this. I do want to caution you that even the best researchers will always find at least a little difference between the sample and the population, as it is inevitable. That difference is called **sampling error**, and it is simply part of research life. As I have discussed throughout this chapter, there are ways to increase one's chances of selecting a representative sample, thereby reducing sampling error. One way includes use of random selection. The other is selecting a large enough sample size. I will get to appropriate sample size in a little bit. Before I do that, however, I want to discuss how to compare your sample to the population from which it was selected.

The first way to compare your sample to the population is the easiest, and that is to just look at the **sample statistics** and **population parameters** (Maxfield & Babbie, 2012). A sample statistic provides a summary description of a variable in the sample, whereas the population parameter gives the same information about a variable in the population. Whenever population parameters are known, we can get an idea of how representative our sample is by comparing the numbers to our sample statistics. If I took a random sample of residents in a particular state, I could then look at my sample statistics for resident demographics, such as race and sex, and compare those numbers to the state's published census results.

When we do not have the population statistics available, we can use some very basic statistical techniques to determine confidence intervals and confidence levels. **Confidence intervals** are a range of values in which the true population parameter is likely to be. For example, let's take a sample of jails across the country and ask administrators to indicate the percent capacity at which they were operating on June 30 that year. We get a range of responses and calculate the mean facility capacity of our sample to be at 84%. We can figure out the size of the confidence interval, where the population capacity mean lies, by determining our **confidence level**, or the probability that our population value falls within a particular confidence interval. So, we have our sample mean of 84% capacity for the jails. We now need a few other statistics, including the standard deviation, which is a measure of the average deviation from the mean for each of our sample statistics. We also need to know the size of the sample we selected. Once we have those figures, we could calculate a confidence interval. We could then adjust the size of the confidence interval depending on how confident we wanted to be that we captured the population parameter. The drawback here is that the higher our confidence *level*, the less precise our confidence *interval* will be.

Let me share an example I often use with my students to illustrate the trade-off between our confidence level and the size of the confidence interval. I'll ask someone what time of day they were born. Let's say the student answers 2:15pm. Then, I ask if they are really sure, and the student responds, "well, sometime between 1:30 and 2:45." Next, I tell the student that they will get an automatic F in the class if I find out that they are wrong, and they respond, "sometime between 1pm and 3pm." I have done this in statistics classes several times, and the higher I make the stakes for being wrong, the less precise the student gets, because they want to be as sure as possible that their time interval captures the actual time that they are born. So, as the student's level of confidence in the correctness of their response increases, their confidence interval (in this case range of time in which they were born) gets larger.

To assess how much sampling error we have, we could use our available sample mean, standard deviation, and sample size to calculate it. The smaller the calculated sampling error, the better our sample matches the population. Returning to my hypothetical jails example, my mean occupancy rate was 84%. I could then use this information and the other statistics that I already mentioned and calculate a confidence interval. If I wanted to be just 50% sure that I knew what the actual jail capacity average was, I might calculate a confidence interval that is 84% + or – 3%, meaning that I am 50% sure that the nationwide jail occupancy rate is somewhere between 81% and 87%. People rarely only want to be 50% sure, though. We are much more likely to want to be 95% or 99% confident in our results. If I were to calculate the confidence interval with a 95% confidence level, that would produce a larger confidence interval, perhaps 84% + or – 7%, or anywhere from 77% to 91% occupancy rate.

I began this chapter discussing political polls. Have you ever noticed that poll results are always accompanied by a margin of error, usually 1 to 5 percent? That is because the poll is based on a sample, not the whole voting population, and the margin of error is the confidence interval. If there is an upcoming election and Politician A has 50% support, while Politician B has 48%, why is it that the reporters say that they are in a "statistical dead heat" when one is 2% ahead in the polls? That is because there is likely at least a 3% margin of error associated with this sample, so the true population level of support for Politician A is actually anywhere from 47% to 53%, and for Politician B the confidence interval is 45% to 51%. Therefore, based on this sample, we cannot completely rule out the possibility that the two are tied or even that Politician B is ahead in the polls.

Attempting to Minimize Sample Bias

Ways to Compensate for Lack of Random Assignment in an Evaluation

As was noted in Chapter 6, the ideal situation for any type of evaluation is for us to get a pool of research participants who are similar in every theoretically important respect and then to randomly assign them to either the experimental group that gets the treatment stimulus (X) or the control group that does not. We then observe how both groups fare in terms of the dependent variable (Y). What if we want to test the impact of body-worn cameras (X) on incidence of police use of force (Y), but the large department can only afford a small batch of cameras this year? While you might suggest that they randomly assign officers either to get a camera or go without, criminal justice agencies often have their own ideas about how to prioritize usage of equipment. We can still go forward with the evaluation, but as we learned in Chapter 6, this is going to be a quasi-experimental design, since officers will not be randomly selected to receive the cameras. This could result in a problem with sample bias, as our groups might differ on some key characteristics. What if one unit is selected to get the cameras first because they have more of a history of controversial interactions with civilians? We could limit sample bias introduced by the lack of randomization through matching. This can be done manually, but another approach is to engage in **propensity score matching** (PSM). PSM allows researchers to match individuals or cases from different groups to each other based on theoretically relevant variables. Jennings et al. (2017) utilized propensity score matching when they were unable to randomly assign police officers either to wear body cameras or to serve as control group members without cameras. Instead, they had 60 officers with cameras and used propensity score matching to find 60 officers without cameras in the same jurisdiction who also matched the experimental group officers on sex, race/ethnicity, age, years of law enforcement experience, and number of physical-response-to-resistance incidents in the previous 12 months. The PSM procedure made the two groups much more comparable, and while there is still the possibility of sample bias due to other variables that were not considered, this matching technique substantially enhanced the validity and generalizability of the results.

Another sophisticated type of matching involves researchers using their statistical skills to create synthetic comparison groups to match with the experimental group in certain circumstances. Ashby (2020) encountered one of those circumstances when studying the impact of COVID-19 on police calls for mental health assistance in the early weeks of the pandemic. It was not possible for the researcher to find a genuine control or comparison group, because the entire country was taking precautions to mitigate the spread of COVID. Instead, the author used statistical skills to forecast what the weekly frequency of mental health calls for service would likely have been in the study cities based on calls for service data years prior to COVID-19. Wu and McDowall (2023) did something similar when studying the impact of bail reform on crime in New York. The authors created a "synthetic New York" by taking crime data from other states that most closely matched New York in the years leading up to bail reform. They then compared differences in crime between New York after the start of bail reform to the synthetic New York.

Finding the right sample size—statistical power

As I noted in Chapter 6, statistical conclusion validity may be a problem when we test our hypotheses, as it could affect our ability to correctly discern whether the independent and dependent variables are related. During the sampling phase of research, we might be able to be proactive and take steps to prevent this from being a problem for data analysis. To review, smaller sample sizes might leave our statistical tests lacking sufficient power. **Power** impacts the probability of us correctly rejecting a null hypothesis when it is appropriate to reject it. As we set up our data collection protocol, it might be possible to increase our sample size. I say "might" because, as someone who frequently engages in small program evaluations for individual criminal justice agencies, there are times when I have no say in the number of program participants.

If researchers have the freedom to determine the sample size, it would be wise to conduct a power analysis, which is a quick mathematical test that will inform you how large your sample size must be for you to be confident that you have enough statistical power. There are free and easy-to-use power calculators available on the internet. Generally, increasing the sample size increases our chances of preventing "flukes" such as accidentally picking a small sample that tends to be unlike the rest of the population. Think of coin flips. If you flip a coin 10 times, you might wind up getting tails eight out of 10 times. If you were betting on getting tails, this probably made you happy and led you to believe you were on a hot streak. Before you become convinced that you are onto something and head to the nearest casino, keep flipping. If you flip1,000 times, the heads/tails ratio will likely be even or extremely close to it. That is because, as you increased your sample size, you would have encountered a few streaks where you continually got heads too, canceling out the influence of your tails streak. Large sample sizes are much less susceptible to these flukes, which is why they are more likely to represent the population.

Is Randomization Perfect?

Random assignment is important, as it can increase our chances of selecting samples that are representative of the population. Randomization, however, is not a guarantee against sample bias if the pool of potential participants you recruit is somehow different from the general population. In Chapter 3, I discussed the Zimbardo Stanford Prison Experiment that had to be discontinued after just six days due to the aggressive behavior of the young men who were randomly selected to act as corrections officers. As I noted in Chapter 3, one reason to be concerned about the validity and generalizability of these results is that there is evidence that Zimbardo encouraged the same aggressive behavior that he later found so noteworthy. Another problem with the study was his sample selection.

To find participants, Zimardo put an ad in a local newspaper calling for "volunteers for a study of the psychological effects of prison life." Once he gathered a pool of volunteers, the research team conducted "diagnostic interviews and personality tests to eliminate candidates with psychological problems, medical disabilities, or a history of crime or drug abuse," giving Zimbardo a sample of "an average group of healthy, intelligent, middle-class males" (Zimbardo, 2020). After that, he randomly selected participants to become either a "prisoner" or a "guard" and assumed that his study would be generalizable. What Zimbardo either did not consider or failed to discuss in his research findings was the strong possibility of sample bias generated by his recruitment approach. Remember, Zimbardo only utilized random selection after people made the decision to volunteer for a study about prison life. Carnahan and McFarland (2007) replicated Zimbardo's recruitment plan while simultaneously advertising for paid volunteers for a more generic psychological test. They advertised for two fictitious studies. The first had the same wording as Zimbardo's solicitation, just with a higher offer of pay to account for inflation. The second ad also called for paid participants for a "psychological study" but left out any further details. The researchers administered personality tests to the volunteers for both advertised studies, and they found that the people who expressed interest in the prison study had higher scores on measures of aggressiveness, authoritarianism, narcissism, social dominance, and Machiavellianism. It appears that people who are attracted to research where they could role-play being part of the prison system have some personality characteristics that make them not necessarily representative of the typical college-age male population. While Zimbardo did randomly assign students to the "prisoner" condition and the "guard" condition, the manner in which he acquired the volunteers prior to that randomization introduced sample bias. I note this, because I noticed that my students tend to see the word "randomization" and immediately conclude that there cannot be any problems with the sample, and that is not always the case. We must consider how the participant pool being randomized was selected.

Summary

We do not always have the time or money to observe or survey an entire population, so sampling is a common component of most research designs. The goal of sampling is to select one that is representative of the population from which it was selected. The only exception to this rule is when it is necessary to oversample a group to ensure adequate representation of certain individuals in the sample. The fairest, least biased way of selecting a sample is through random selection, where every potential participant has an equal chance of being selected. There are several different approaches to random sampling.

Random sampling is not always possible for a number of reasons, so researchers may have to resort to using a nonprobability sampling method. These techniques vary in quality, and researchers must be mindful of how the selected sample might differ from the population. Sample bias is a threat to both the internal and external validity of a study, so researchers must be mindful of how representative their sample appears to be before generalizing the results to the population. There are ways to check for similarities and differences between samples and populations, and if the research involves splitting the sample into treatment and non-equivalent comparison groups, matching techniques can help to reduce the group differences. It is important to remember that even random sampling does not guarantee a representative sample. The larger a sample size gets, the more likely it is to be representative of the population.

Key Terms

Sample	Unit of observation	Ecological fallacy
Exception or individualistic fallacy	Creaming	Probability sampling
Equal Probability Selection Method (EPSM)	Sampling frame	Simple random sampling
Systematic random sampling	Stratified random sampling	Proportionate stratified sampling
Disproportionate stratified sampling	Multistage cluster sampling	Nonprobability sampling
Convenience/accidental sampling	Purposive sampling	Focus groups
Quota sampling	Snowball sampling	Gatekeeper
Respondent-driven sampling	Sampling error	Sample statistic
Population parameter	Confidence interval	Confidence level
Propensity score matching (PSM)	Power	

Discussion Questions

1. Discuss steps that we can take to try to avoid sample bias.
2. Why is using the EPSM method no guarantee that you will produce a representative sample? Discuss steps that you can take to check to see if your sample appears to be representative of the population.
3. Identify the pros and cons of snowball sampling.

References

Ashby, M. P. J. (2020). Changes in police calls for service during the early months of the 2020 coronavirus pandemic. *Policing: A Journal of Policy and Practice*, *14*(4), 1054–1072. https://doi.org/10.1093/police/paaa037

Berman, G., & Fox, A. (2016). *Trial and error in criminal justice reform: Learning from failure (revised edition).* The Urban Institute Press.

Caputi, T. L. (2020). Medical marijuana laws, substance use, treatment admissions, and the ecological fallacy. *Addiction, 115*(1), 188.
Carnahan, T., & McFarland, S. (2007). Revisiting the Stanford Prison Experiment: Could participant self-selection have led to the cruelty? *Personality and Social Psychology Bulletin, 33*(5), 603–614. https://doi.org/10.1177/0146167206292689
Chenane, J. L., & Hammond, Q. (2022). Using social media to recruit participants for scholarly research: Lessons from African female immigrants in the United States. *Journal of Criminal Justice Education, 33*(4), 509–525. https://doi.org/10.1080/10511253.2021.1991411
Eaton, A. A., Ramjee, D., & Saunders, J. F. (2023). The relationship between sextortion during COVID-19 and pre-pandemic intimate partner violence: A large study of victimization among diverse U.S. men and women. *Victims & Offenders, 18*(2), 338–355. https://doi.org/10.1080/15564886.2021.2022057
Hagan, F. (2007). *Essentials of research methods in criminal justice and criminology* (2nd ed.). Pearson.
Hartley, R. D. (Ed.). (2011). *Snapshots of research.* Sage Publications.
Jennings, W. G., Fridell, L. A., Lynch, M., Jetelina, K. K., & Reingle Gonzalez, J. M. (2017). Aquasi-experimental evaluation of the effects of police body-worn cameras (BWCs) on response-to-resistance in a large metropolitan police department. *Deviant Behavior, 38*(11), 1332–1339. https://doi.org/10.1108/PIJPSM-03-2017-0032
Klein, J. L., Bailey, D. J. S., & Sample, L. L. (2018). Researching the registered: Challenges and suggestions for researchers studying sex offender populations. *Criminal Justice Studies, 31*(2), 192–211. https://doi.org/10.1080/1478601X.2018.1430033
Krimmel, J. T., & Tartaro, C. (1999). Career choices and characteristics of criminal justice undergraduate students. *Journal of Criminal Justice Education, 10*(2), 277–290. https://doi.org/10.1080/10511259900084591
Marczak, M., & Sewell, M. (n.d.). Using focus groups for evaluation. *CYFERnet – Evaluation.* University of Arizona. https://cals.arizona.edu/sfcs/cyfernet/cyfar/focus.htm
Maxfield, M. G., & Babbie, E. (2012). *Basics of research methods for criminal justice and criminology* (3rd ed.). Thomson Wadsworth.
Morgan, R. E., & Oudekerk, B. A. (2019). *Criminal Victimization, 2018.* United States Department of Justice, Bureau of Justice Statistics.
Rose, J. (2018). Poll: Where you watch TV news predicts your feelings on immigration. *National Public Radio.* www.npr.org/2018/07/16/629320653/poll-where-you-watch-tv-news-predicts-your-feelings-on-immigration
Schwartz, S. (1994). The fallacy of ecological fallacy: The potential misuse of a concept and the consequences. *American Journal of Public Health, 84*(5), 819–824.
Tartaro, C., & Krimmel, J. T. (2003). The effect of race on criminal justice students' career choices. *American Journal of Criminal Justice, 28*(1), 109–124.
United States Bureau of Justice Statistics (n.d.). *National Crime Victimization Survey methodology.* United States Department of Justice, Bureau of Justice Statistics.
Weisburd, D., Wyckoff, L. A., Ready, J., Eck, J. J., Hinkle, J. C., & Gajewski, F. (2006). Does crime just move around the corner? A controlled study of spatial displacement and diffusion of crime control benefits. *Criminology, 44*(3), 549–592. https://doi.org/10.1111/j.1745-9125.2006.00057.x
Weisheit, R. A. (2015). Researching drug crime using qualitative methods. In H. J. Copes & M. Miller (Eds.), *The Routledge handbook of qualitative criminology* (pp. 191–203). Routledge.
Wright, R., Decker, S. H., Redfern, A. K., & Smith, D. L. (1992). A snowball's chance in hell: Doing fieldwork with active residential burglars. *Journal of Research in Crime and Delinquency, 29,* 148–161. https://doi.org/10.1177/0022427892029002003
Wu, S., & McDowall, D. (2023). Does bail reform increase crime in New York State: Evidence from interrupted time-series analyses and synthetic control methods. *Justice Quarterly, 41*(3), 1–29. https://doi.org/10.1080/07418825.2023.2209145
Zimbardo, P. G. (2020). *The Stanford prison experiment.* www.prisonexp.org/setting-up

Reading 8.1 Attitudes about Rehabilitation among Jail Correctional Officers

In Chapter 8, we discussed the unit of analysis, meaning who or what we are studying. Most studies include one unit of analysis, as researchers make a decision to examine something from one perspective, such as the organization or the individual employees themselves. Occasionally, we decide to include multiple types of units of analysis within one study. The work of Jossie, Lane, and Cook (2023) provides an example of that. They were interested in characteristics of individual officers working in various jails throughout Florida and how those individual-level characteristics are associated with opinions about rehabilitation in jails. At the same time, they were also wondering whether there was variation in aggregate officer opinion across the jails themselves. For the latter analysis, the jails were the units of analysis, with responding officers serving as the units of observation. This second analysis was important to add to the study, given previous research that has shown support for rehabilitation to vary across institutions.

Attitudes about Rehabilitation among Jail Correctional Officers

McKenzie L. Jossie, Jodi Lane, and Carrie L. Cook

Jail Officer Attitudes toward Those They House

Despite the large number of people who pass through jails every year in the United States – about 10.3 million admissions in 2019 – there is little research on jail officer attitudes about how institutions should treat those they house (Zeng & Minton, 2021). There is more research on job satisfaction and job stress among jail officers (Ellison & Caudill, 2020; Lambert et al., 2016; Lambert & Paoline, 2008). Those studies that have examined their attitudes toward jailed people have more often centered on sexual victimization (e.g., Cook & Lane, 2012, 2015, 2017), willingness to use force (Griffin, 1999, 2002; M. L. Griffin, 1999), or safety risk (Ellison & Gainey, 2020; Lambert et al., 2018), but few examine predictors of their attitudes toward rehabilitation (e.g., Farkas, 1999). Although, there are more studies of rehabilitative attitudes among prison officers (e.g., Antonio & Young, 2011; Lambert et al., 2009; Lerman & Page, 2016).

One reason that research on jail officer attitudes toward rehabilitation may be scarcer is due to the nature of jails, including short average stays and high population turnover, which makes custody more important than rehabilitation efforts there (Kifer et al., 2003). Jail population turnover is high, with an average jail stay in 2019 of just 26 days (Zeng & Minton, 2021). Stays are shorter in part because people may be there pre-trial, on hold for a probation or parole violation hearing, or awaiting a transfer (Castle, 2008; Farkas, 1999; Zeng & Minton, 2021). Yet, some people may be there for up to a year, providing plenty of time to participate in and benefit from rehabilitative services. Consequently, there are practical benefits to learning more about jail officer attitudes toward rehabilitation. Jail administrators may be better able to provide at least some rehabilitative services (e.g., counseling, workshops, or classes) if their staff support these efforts and are willing to be trained and help implement the programming.

Moreover, like prison officers, jail officers work close to those they manage and control the institutional environment, meaning their opinions and attitudes may affect incarcerated individuals' willingness to participate in and perceptions of rehabilitative programming (Antonio et al., 2009; Antonio & Young, 2011; Patrick & Marsh, 2001). Research shows that training correctional officers to support and extend rehabilitation has the potential to be both successful and cost-effective (Burton et al., 2018; Lerman & Harney, 2019; Young et al., 2009); yet, it would be helpful to know more about jail officers' attitudes before implementing training efforts. A primary goal of this manuscript is to increase understanding of how officer personal characteristics and job attitudes impact attitudes toward rehabilitation among a large sample of jail officers in Florida. We also consider whether rehabilitative attitudes differ between jails.

Jail Specific Studies

Unfortunately, there are not many studies of jail correctional officer attitudes toward the people housed there. Some studies do compare attitudes of correctional officers in jails and prisons, and findings differ. While employees tend to agree on the goals of corrections, prison staff place more value on both incapacitation and rehabilitation (Kifer et al., 2003). Also, one study found that because county jails tend to offer limited programming and primarily focus on custody, staff tend to be less supportive of rehabilitation (Kifer et al., 2003). One qualitative study in multiple U.S. jails that focused specifically on incarcerated women found that most officers understood the hardships people there faced but felt helpless to assist because of insufficient funding and inadequate training (Belknap et al., 2016). Still, jail officers are more likely to focus on the importance of incapacitation when compared to incarcerated people, who believe rehabilitation is more important (Collins et al., 2013).

Similar to studies in prisons, jail studies show that officer characteristics matter. Many results echo those found in research on prison officers. Specifically, studies sometimes show that female officers tend to be more interested in rehabilitation and more likely to prefer counseling roles (Farkas, 1999; Griffin, 2002; Kifer et al., 2003), while others show no gender differences (Cook & Lane, 2014; Stohr et al., 1996). Jail officers who are older and with longer tenure, tend to be less punitive, less custodial, and more likely to prefer counseling roles and rehabilitation (Farkas, 1999; Griffin, 2002); while those with less authoritative power and who fear victimization tend to be more punitive (Griffin, 2002). Interestingly, one study suggests that while the majority of jail correctional officers support rehabilitative programming generally, they did not support correctional officers taking on counseling roles themselves (Farkas, 1999). Yet, some correctional officers think their coworkers are much less progressive about rehabilitation than they are (Cook & Lane, 2014).

While many prior studies of jail officers focus on correlates of job satisfaction (Castle, 2008; Griffin, 2001), job stress (Castle & Martin, 2006; Ellison & Caudill, 2020), or both (Lambert et al., 2016; Lambert & Paoline, 2005, 2008), this study examines how job satisfaction and job stress influence their attitudes about rehabilitation and treatment. We found only one other study examining this question, and it was conducted outside the United States (in South Korea). There, officers with high levels of job satisfaction were more likely to support rehabilitation, while job stress had no impact (Moon & Maxwell, 2004a). However, those with more job stress were more likely to support punitive orientations (Moon & Maxwell, 2004a).

Using the same dataset as this study, (Cook & Lane, 2015) assessed the impact of social distance. They found that jail officers who preferred more social distance were more likely to blame incarcerated victims of sexual assault, while those who did not were more willing to talk about the risk of sexual assault and to respond to incidents when they occurred (Cook & Lane, 2015; Cook & Lane, 2017). In jails, it may be easier to maintain social distance, because stays are shorter, and staff are less likely to be expected to deliver rehabilitation services than in prisons (Cook & Lane, 2014).

Location also matters. Studies find that urban jails are more likely than rural ones to have treatment and work programs and educational opportunities (Applegate & Sitren, 2008; Mays & Thompson, 1988; Ruddell & Mays, 2007). Providing mental health care is more difficult in rural jails, but overall need for these services may be more pronounced in urban facilities (Mays & Thompson, 1988; Powell et al., 1997; Ruddell & Mays, 2007). Small jail administrators are more likely than those in larger jails to report a lack of resources (Ruddell & Mays, 2007) and concern about insufficient training (Kerle, 1982; Miller, 1982). The varying challenges and difficulties posed by facility location (rural versus urban) may impact officer attitudes toward rehabilitation due to resource (un)availability and (un)familiarity with rehabilitative efforts within jails.

In summary, there are few studies that examine attitudes about rehabilitation among correctional officers, and even fewer focus specifically on jail officers. These prior studies show that personal characteristics matter, although sometimes differ on how. While research has examined job experiences, such as satisfaction and stress, these are primarily the dependent variable. Very little information exists about how these experiences impact attitudes toward rehabilitation. We also do not know enough about how facility differences and preference for social distance affect rehabilitation attitudes among jail officers. The goal here is to help close this research gap.

Methodology

Data Collection and Sample

Researchers contacted jail administrators via e-mail and telephone in Florida's 67 county jails to request they allow their staff to participate in the survey. Administrators at 13 jails agreed to participate (19.4% of jail agencies), including at least one jail in each administrative region in the state. The participating facilities varied from small jails in rural counties with fewer than 15,000 people to large urban jails in counties with more than one million people. We used a non-probability purposive sampling method. Researchers distributed surveys and consent forms to all correctional officers at participating jails during shift briefings or pre-shift meetings during one 24-hour period to encourage participant representation for all shifts. To limit disruption within the facilities, respondents were to return the survey via mail using the provided addressed, stamped envelope. There was no compensation for completing the survey. Researchers distributed 1,161 surveys to the 41% of correctional officers employed (n = 2,822) at the participating jails who attended either a shift briefing or pre-shift meeting during the one 24-hour period in which the team visited each jail. Respondents returned 376 surveys (32.4% response rate), with response rates ranging from 11% to 63% per facility. Using the selected survey methodology, we should expect response rates between 30% to 50% (Dillman et al., 1995).

Table 1 presents descriptive statistics of the independent variables. Respondents included 260 males (69.3%) and 115 females (30.7%). The proportion of male to female correctional officers was consistent with the proportion of males and females working in these facilities. The majority of respondents were White (80.9%) and married (64.8%). The average highest level of school completed was more than one year of college, but less than an associate degree. The average respondent was 36 to 40 years old, described his/her political orientation as "middle of the road," and reported moderate religiosity. Ten years was the average length of employment as a jail officer. On a scale of 1 (not at all satisfied) to 10 (extremely satisfied), the average correctional officer response about job satisfaction was a 6.9. The average level of stress reported on a scale from 1 (no stress) to 10 (extreme stress) was moderate (6.0).

We asked respondents to report the estimated number of correctional officers employed (measured continuously) at their jail facility. On average, the facilities employed an estimated 432 correctional officers (minimum: 5, maximum: 3,000). We also asked respondents to report the estimated number of inmates currently housed (measured continuously) at their jail facility. The facilities housed an average of 2,051 individuals (minimum: 2, maximum: 5,000) at the time of the survey. Respondents indicated whether their work facility was in a rural (in the open country or in a town of less than 2,500 people), urban (area with a total population of 50,000 or more),

Table 1 Sample characteristics

	Coding	*Sample (N = 376)*	%	*M*	*SD*
Personal Characteristics					
Female	1	115	30.7		
Nonwhite	1	69	19.1		
Not married	1	131	35.2		
Education				3.2	1.3
HS or GED	1	38	10.1		
Some college < 1 year	2	79	21.1		
> 1 year college	3	102	27.2		
Associate	4	78	20.8		
Bachelor's	5	71	18.9		
Master's	6	6	1.6		
Professional/Doctorate	7	1	0.3		
Missing		1	0.3		
Age				4.4	1.9
18–25	1	26	7.0		
26–30	2	40	10.7		
31–35	3	58	15.6		
36–40	4	79	21.2		
41–45	5	71	19.0		
46–50	6	44	11.8		
51–55	7	29	7.8		
56–60	8	18	4.8		
Over 60	9	8	2.1		
Missing		3	0.8		
Conservatism				4.4	1.0
Extremely liberal	1	4	1.1		
Very liberal	2	7	2.0		
Liberal	3	26	7.3		
Middle of the road	4	163	45.5		
Conservative	5	119	33.2		
Very conservative	6	28	7.8		
Extremely conservative	7	11	3.1		
Missing		18	4.8		
Religiosity	1 (Not at all religious)- 10 (Extremely religious)			5.8	2.4
Missing		4	1.1		
Experience (to nearest year)				10.2	7.0
Missing		10	2.7		
Officer Attitudes					
Job satisfaction	1 (Not at all satisfied)- 10 (Extremely satisfied)			6.9	2.1
Missing		1	0.3		

(*Continued*)

Table 1 (Continued)

	Coding	*Sample (N = 376)*	%	*M*	*SD*
Job stress	1 (No stress)- 10 (Extreme stress)			6.0	2.2
Missing		8	2.1		

Note: HS = high school; GED = general educational development

or suburban area (somewhere between rural and urban; United States Census Bureau, 1995, 2000; United States Department of Agriculture, 2004). The majority of the facilities (69.7%) were located in urban areas. Jails varied in terms of types of housing utilized, including podular, dormitory, and linear. The majority of the facilities (85%) utilized a podular jail design either exclusively or in combination with other housing types. Jails also varied in terms of whether they had remote surveillance, direct surveillance, or both. Approximately 38% of the facilities utilized remote surveillance, about 38% utilized direct surveillance, and the remaining facilities utilized both direct and remote supervision.

Measures

Dependent Variable

Support for Rehabilitation

The survey asked respondents to reflect on their beliefs about rehabilitation. The dependent variable is an index of nine attitudinal items. Three items directly measured support for rehabilitation: "rehabilitating a criminal is just as important as making a criminal pay for his or her crime," "the only effective and humane cure to the crime problem in America is to make a strong effort to rehabilitate offenders," and "I would support expanding the rehabilitation programs with criminals that are now being undertaken in our prisons" (*strongly disagree = 1 to strongly agree = 6*). We reverse coded six items so that higher values represented more support for rehabilitation (so that *strongly agree* (1), *agree* (2), *not sure but probably agree* (3), *not sure but probably disagree* (4), *disagree* (5), or *strongly disagree* (6)). These were: "the only way to reduce crime in our society is to punish criminals, not try to rehabilitate them," "we should stop viewing criminals as victims of society who deserve to be rehabilitated and start paying more attention to the victims of these criminals," "the rehabilitation of prisoners has proven to be a failure," "the rehabilitation of adult criminals just does not work," "all rehabilitation programs have done is allow criminals who deserve to be punished to get off easily," and "rehabilitation programs are a waste of time and money" (Cullen et al., 1985; Whitehead et al., 1987). The factor loadings and reliability analysis suggest that correctional officers view these items as conceptually similar, and the index is reliable (Cronbach's $\alpha = 0{:}90$) (see, Table 2). Table 2 presents descriptive statistics for the index variables, along with factor loading and reliability analyses. The index variable added all response values across all variables in the index and divided by the number of variables in the index for an average response. Higher values in the index reflect more support for rehabilitation.

Independent Variables

Personal Characteristics

We included several demographic variables in the current analyses based on the findings from prior research. These are sex (*female* = 1 and *male* = 0), race (*nonwhite*–including Black, Asian/Pacific Islander, biracial, and other = 1 and *White* = 0), marital status (*not married* = 1 and *married* = 0), highest degree or level of school completed (higher values represent higher levels of completed education, 1 = *high school/ GED* and 7 = *professional or doctorate degree*), age (higher values represent older age groups, 1 = *18–25* and 9 = *Over 60*), and length of employment as a correctional officer (experience to the nearest year)[1]. We also measured self-reported conservatism (*extremely liberal = 1* to *extremely conservative* = 7) and religiosity (*not at all religious = 1 to extremely religious = 10*) (Cook & Lane 2012, 2014, 2015, 2017; Davis et al., 1998).

Officer Attitudes

We include several variables measuring officer attitudes, which include job satisfaction (*not at all satisfied = 1 to extremely satisfied = 10*), job stress (*no stress = 1 to extreme stress = 10*), and preference for social distance from those incarcerated (Cook & Lane, 2012, 2014, 2015, 2017). Consistent with prior literature, we assessed preferences about maintaining social distance with the following five items: "a correctional officer should work hard to earn trust from inmates," "it's important for a correctional officer to have compassion," "you get to like the inmates you supervise," "sometimes a correctional officer should be an advocate for an inmate," and "the way to get respect from inmates is to take an interest in them" (Cook & Lane, 2012, 2014, 2015, 2017; Klofas & Toch, 1982; Toch & Klofas, 1982; Whitehead et al., 1987). The questions utilized a 6-point Likert scale with the options of *strongly agree* (1), *agree* (2), *not sure but probably agree* (3), *not sure but probably disagree* (4), *disagree* (5), or *strongly disagree* (6). The index variable added all response values across all variables in the index and divided by the number of variables in the index for an average response. We coded the social distance index so that higher values reflect more preference for social distance from incarcerated individuals. The factor loadings and reliability analysis suggest that correctional officers view these items as conceptually similar, and the index is reliable (Cronbach's $\alpha = 0{:}67$) (see, Table 2).

Analytic Strategy

We first conducted bivariate correlations to determine which independent variables were significantly correlated with support for rehabilitation. Second, we estimated a set of ordinary least squares (OLS) regression models predicting support for rehabilitation. Hierarchical linear modeling is not appropriate given the guidelines for an acceptable number of level 1 and level 2 units.[2] Model 1 examines the impact of personal characteristics. Models 2 and 3 add job satisfaction and then job stress. Finally, model 4 adds preference for social distance from those serving time. This approach to the analysis allows us to assess the change in R^2 between models and examine the differential impact of these factors on support for rehabilitation (Moon & Maxwell, 2004a). Lastly, we conducted a one-way ANOVA and Tukey HSD to determine if there were significant differences in the mean scores for support for rehabilitation across jails.

Results

Table 3 presents the Pearson product-moment and Spearman rank-order correlation coefficients. Female, nonwhite, conservatism, religiosity, job satisfaction, and social distance are significantly correlated with support for rehabilitation. At the bivariate level, female and nonwhite correctional officers reported more support for rehabilitation. Moreover, as religiosity and job satisfaction increase, support for rehabilitation increases. Conservatism is negatively correlated with support for rehabilitation, so those who were more conservative reported less support for rehabilitation. Social distance is also negatively correlated with support for rehabilitation, so those who preferred more social distance from the people they manage were less supportive of rehabilitation.

All correlations for the independent variables are below 0.8, the highest Variation Inflation Factor (VIF) value in the full model is 1.47 (age), and the lowest tolerance statistic in the full model is 0.68 (age), indicating that multicollinearity is not a problem. Generally,

Table 2 Descriptives for index variables, factor loadings, and reliability analyses

	N = 376	*Minimum, Maximum, Skew*	*M (SD)*	*Cronbach's Alpha*	*Factor Loading*
Dependent variable:	357	1, 5.89, 0.02	3.15 (1.08)	0.90	
Rehabilitation: 9-item index					
Rehabilitating a criminal is just as important as making a criminal pay for his or her crime	371	1, 6	3.96 (1.57)		0.73
The only effective and humane cure to the crime problem in America is to make a strong effort to rehabilitate offenders	372	1, 6	3.17 (1.55)		0.74
The only way to reduce crime in our society is to punish criminals, not try to rehabilitate them	371	1, 6	3.39 (1.60)		0.81
We should stop viewing criminals as victims of society who deserve to be rehabilitated and start paying more attention to the victims of these criminals	374	1, 6	2.01 (1.19)		0.66
The rehabilitation of prisoners has proven to be a failure	373	1, 6	2.79 (1.33)		0.77
The rehabilitation of adult criminals just does not work	372	1, 6	3.04 (1.39)		0.80
I would support expanding the rehabilitation programs with criminals that are now being undertaken in our prisons	368	1, 6	3.27 (1.40)		0.76
All rehabilitation programs have done is allows criminals who deserve to be punished to get off easily	372	1, 6	3.19 (1.35)		0.73
Rehabilitation programs are a waste of time and money	372	1, 6	3.58 (1.44)		0.81
Independent variable:					
Social distance: 5-item index	358	1.4, 6, -0.09	3.73 (0.88)	0.67	
A correctional officer should work hard to earn trust from inmates	371	1, 6	3.39 (1.54)		0.55
It's important for a correctional officer to have compassion	371	1, 6	3.03 (1.33)		0.68
You get to like the inmates you supervise	372	1, 6	4.09 (1.28)		0.66
Sometimes a correctional officer should be an advocate for an inmate	368	1, 6	3.97 (1.33)		0.64
The way to get respect from inmates is to take an interest in them	371	1, 6	4.21 (1.24)		0.77

Table 3 Pearson product-moment and Spearman rank-order correlation coefficients between independent variables and support for rehabilitation (N = 376)

Independent Variable	*Correlation Coefficient*
Female	0.15**
Nonwhite	0.32***
Not married	0.01
Education+	0.03
Age+	-0.01
Conservatism+	-0.22***
Religiosity	0.21***
Experience	-0.10
Job satisfaction	0.15**
Job stress	-0.03
Social distance	-0.34***

Note.

* p < .05. ** p < .01 *** p < .001

+ = Spearman Rank-Order Correlation Coefficient.

multicollinearity is a problem if VIF values are greater than five and tolerance values are less than 0.20 (Tabachnick & Fidell, 1989).

Table 4 reports the results of the regression models predicting support for rehabilitation among jail correctional officers. In model 1, we regress the dependent variable on personal characteristics (including female, nonwhite, not married, highest degree/level of school completed, age, conservatism, religiosity, and length of employment as CO). This allows us to observe how personal characteristics affect correctional officers' attitudes toward rehabilitation before other correlates are added in the model. Race, conservatism, and religiosity are significant predictors, accounting for 19% of variance in attitudes about rehabilitation. Consistent with the bivariate relationships, nonwhite correctional officers and those who are more religious are significantly more likely to support rehabilitation. Those who are more conservative are significantly less likely to support rehabilitation.

In model 2 we add job satisfaction, and the same personal factors are significant. Job satisfaction is a significant predictor, although the R^2 value only changes by 1%. This is consistent with the bivariate results, which shows a relationship between job satisfaction and rehabilitation attitudes. The model fit is significant, accounting for 20% of the variance in rehabilitation attitudes, although this model does not explain much more variance than Model 1, including only personal characteristics (R^2 value changed 1%). In model 3, we add job stress, which is not a significant predictor. This is consistent with the bivariate results, which shows no relationship between job stress and rehabilitation attitudes. Job satisfaction is still significant with those who are more satisfied being more likely to support rehabilitation. The same personal characteristics are significant. The R^2 value changed by 1%.

In the final model (4), we add preference for social distance, and the model remains significant. Preference for social distance is significant, and this model explains much more variance than the previous ones (29%). As in the prior models, nonwhites and those who are more religious are more likely to support

Table 4 OLS regression models predicting support for rehabilitation

Independent Variables	*Model 1*	*Model 2*	*Model 3*	*Model 4*
	B (RSE)	*B (RSE)*	*B (RSE)*	*B (RSE)*
Personal Characteristics				
Female	0.20 (0.13)	0.19 (0.13)	0.21 (0.13)	0.25 (0.12)*
Nonwhite	0.74 (0.15)***	0.75 (0.15)***	0.74 (0.15)***	0.73 (0.15)***
Not married	-0.11 (0.12)	-0.09 (0.12)	-0.06 (0.12)	-0.15 (0.12)
Highest Degree/Level of School Completed	0.03 (0.04)	0.03 (0.04)	0.03 (0.04)	0.03 (0.04)
Age	0.02 (0.04)	0.02 (0.04)	0.03 (0.04)	0.00 (0.04)
Conservatism	-0.22 (0.06)***	-0.21 (0.06)***	-0.21 (0.06)***	-0.17 (0.06)**
Religiosity	0.09 (0.02)***	0.08 (0.02)**	0.08 (0.03)**	0.06 (0.02)*
Length of Employment as CO	-0.01 (0.01)	-0.01 (0.01)	-0.01 (0.01)	-0.01 (0.01)
Officer Attitudes				
Job Satisfaction		0.06 (0.02)*	0.06 (0.03)*	0.05 (0.02)*
Job Stress			-0.00 (0.03)	0.00 (0.03)
Social Distance				-0.37 (0.07)***
Constant	3.39***	3.00***	2.94***	4.39***
Model fit				
F	9.69***	9.56***	8.46***	11.94***
R^2	0.19	0.20	0.21	0.29
df	8	9	10	11
N	317	317	314	306

Note.

CO = Correctional officer; B = unstandardized coefficients; RSE = robust standard error; df = degrees of freedom; * p < .05 ** p < .01 *** p < .001

rehabilitation, while those who are more conservative are less likely to. Those who are more satisfied are still more likely to support rehabilitation. Respondents who preferred more social distance from those housed in the jail are significantly less likely to support rehabilitation. Female is now significant, with female jail officers more supportive of rehabilitation than males, meaning that once we controlled for preference for social distance, sex mattered.

Table 5 presents the results of the one-way ANOVA. There is a statistically significant difference in mean support for rehabilitation scores across the thirteen jails. Tukey's HSD post-hoc test, used to determine which pairwise comparisons in the sample differ, reveal that support for rehabilitation was significantly higher among jail officers in County 12 (M = 4.33, SD = 0.47) compared to those in County 3 (M = 2.43, SD = 1.08). There were no statistically significant differences for any other jails.

Discussion and Conclusions

Summary of Findings & Research Implications

The purpose of our study was two-fold. First, we examined the connection between personal characteristics, officer attitudes, and support for rehabilitation among jail correctional officers,

Table 5 *Jail descriptives and one-way ANOVA results*

Independent Variable: Jail County (N = 376)	*Jail Descriptives*					*One-Way ANOVA Results*			
	Estimated # of COs employed (Mean)	*Estimated # of inmates housed*	*Location*	*Housing type*	*Supervision type*	*Mean*	*SD*	*F*	*df (Between- groups, Within-groups)*
1	364	2,653	Urban	Podular	Remote	2.69	0.85	1.83*	(12, 344)
2	14	65	Rural	Podular	Remote	3.50	1.18		
3	29	107	Urban	_+	_+	2.43	1.08		
4	146	591	Suburban	Dormitory, Podular	Direct	2.93	1.07		
5	178	1,073	Urban	Podular	Direct	3.41	1.32		
6	106	465	Suburban	Dormitory, Linear, Podular	Remote	3.22	1.15		
7	227	1,006	Rural	Podular	Direct	3.08	1.09		
8	42	242	Rural	Dormitory, Podular	Remote	3.44	0.71		
9	321	1,892	Urban	Dormitory, Linear, Podular	Direct	3.49	0.98		
10	724	2,984	Urban	Dormitory, Podular	Direct, Remote	3.23	1.08		
11	215	1,261	Urban	Dormitory, Linear	Direct, Remote	2.86	1.26		
12	31	135	Rural	Podular	Remote	4.33	0.47		
13	193	971	Urban	Podular	Direct	2.75	1.05		
						Significant contrasts			
						Tukey HSD			Jail 12 > Jail 3

Note.

* $p < .05$ ** $p < .01$ *** $p < .001$; CO = Correctional Officer; + = County 3 did not provide this information.

a group that has received little attention in prior studies of correctional staff. Second, we compared the mean differences in support for rehabilitation across the thirteen jails. In the final regression model, we found that females were more likely than males to support rehabilitation, which is partially consistent with some previous research showing that women have a humanizing influence on correctional attitudes toward rehabilitation (Applegate et al., 2002). Across all models, we found that nonwhite respondents were more likely than White respondents to support rehabilitation, which is consistent with previous prison research (Cullen et al., 1989; Lerman & Harney, 2019; Maahs & Pratt, 2001). Those that were more religious were more likely to support rehabilitation, which was consistent across all models and in alignment with the empirical literature (Teske & Williamson, 1979). Jail officers that were more satisfied with their jobs also showed greater support for rehabilitation, consistent with prior research (Arthur, 1994; Kerce et al., 1994; Moon & Maxwell, 2004a). In contrast, those who indicated they were more conservative were less likely to support rehabilitation. While the impact of conservatism on officer support for rehabilitation can vary by state and institution, these findings are in line with prior research (Lerman & Harney, 2019; Lerman & Page, 2016).

Those who preferred more social distance from individuals housed in the jail were less likely to support rehabilitation in the final model. Prior research on this data set indicates that jail officers who prefer more social distance are also less interested in discussing sexual assault risk, more likely to blame incarcerated victims of sexual assault, and less willing to respond to sexual assault incidents (Cook & Lane, 2015, 2017). These results imply that correctional officers who are more comfortable with social proximity to individuals housed in jails may be more apt to provide assistance and support rehabilitative efforts. They may also be the ones best suited to deliver any programming related to those efforts in jails, because attitudes of correctional staff involved can affect the attitudes of those they serve (see, Beijersbergen et al., 2015; Molleman & Leeuw, 2012). Moreover, when hiring new officers, especially in jails where being helpful is valued, management might consider screening for preferences related to social distance.

The results of the one-way ANOVA shed light on the impact of facility on jail officer attitudes toward rehabilitation. This is consistent with some prior research indicating that officer orientation is affected by jail location (rural versus urban) and jail size (Applegate & Sitren, 2008; Mays & Thompson, 1988; Ruddell & Mays, 2007; Toch & Klofas, 1982). Although, of the thirteen facilities, only one of the pairwise comparisons indicated statistically significant differences in mean support for rehabilitation.

One limitation of the current study is that the data is comprised of jail officers from only one state (Florida), and it is possible that attitudes toward rehabilitation could be a function of the location; southern residents generally have more negative and punitive attitudes toward individuals who are criminal justice involved (Chiricos et al., 2004; Hirschfield & Piquero, 2010). Because we utilized a convenience sample, the data may not be representative of those who did not complete the survey, all jail officers in Florida or jail officers generally. It may be that those who returned the survey were interested in the topic and had attitudes that were not reflective of the population from which they were sampled. There may also be self-selection bias among jail administrators who disallowed their staff to participate, potentially limiting the respondents in the study. Despite these limitations, these findings add to the very limited jail officer literature by showing factors related to their opinions about rehabilitation.

Future research should continue to explore predictors of attitudes toward rehabilitation among both jail officers and incarcerated individuals. The factors we examined accounted for about 29% of observed variance in support for rehabilitation among jail officers, which is comparable to prior studies (Cullen et al., 1989; Lambert et al., 2009, 2011; Van Voorhis et al., 1991). Yet, in our final models a number of variables were not significant, including many personal characteristics (e.g., marital status, level of education, age, length of employment) and officer attitudes (job stress). These findings are consistent with some prior research, as the impact of personal characteristics (Antonio & Young, 2011; Lerman & Harney, 2019; Maahs & Pratt, 2001) and officer attitudes (Lambert & Hogan, 2009; Moon & Maxwell, 2004a) on attitudes about rehabilitation are mixed. Future research in different locations may find different results and may be able to explain how or why these factors impact attitudes (or do not). Qualitative research with jail officers may be useful in helping gain a more in-depth understanding of the multitude of factors that may affect these attitudes, including personal and facility variables (Wooldredge & Steiner, 2016). Future studies could examine other possibly relevant issues such as noise level, indicators of physical disorder, ratio of officers to population, and jail design. Future research may also further examine sex differences between jail officer attitudes toward rehabilitation. Our study suggests that sex may matter in some circumstances but does not provide much information on when and to what extent.

Policy and Practice Implications

As policymakers look to reduce spending within the criminal justice system and reduce staff while also hoping to reduce recidivism, utilizing correctional officers as an asset in rehabilitation can be essential. As one qualitative study of multiple jail facilities suggested, jail officers may feel undertrained to play an active role in rehabilitation (Belknap et al., 2016). Jail officers may also be less familiar with rehabilitation because treatment programs in jails are not that common (Applegate & Sitren, 2008; Ruddell & Mays, 2007). Prison officers trained in correctional rehabilitation have reported greater support for it, suggesting that training jail officers on this topic may help (Antonio et al., 2009; Lerman & Harney, 2019; Lerman & Page, 2016; Young et al., 2009).

More specifically, the results of the current study suggest that jail officers that are comfortable with social proximity to housed individuals are more likely to support rehabilitative efforts and may be more apt to provide assistance. Previous research shows that law enforcement officers that receive Crisis Intervention Team (CIT) training, a collaborative mental health treatment model, express reduced stigma and a decreased preference for social distance from those with psychiatric conditions (Bahora et al., 2008; Compton et al., 2006; Hanafi et al., 2008). Researchers examined the CIT model in local jails to determine if the benefits expressed by police officers also apply to jail officers. Following implementation, jail officers reported feeling better prepared and reported an increased use of deescalation tactics (Public Health Research Institute, 2005; University of New England Center of Health Policy, Planning and Research, 2007). Increased jail officer training such as this may lower officer preference for social distance and in turn increase support for rehabilitative efforts.

Training may also improve relations between officers and those they manage. According to prison research, incarcerated people tend to have more positive views about correctional officers and their circumstances when officers have more positive views about treatment (Beijersbergen et al., 2015; Molleman & Leeuw, 2012), and residents are more likely to perceive rehabilitation to be a main goal of the facility when officers value treatment (Patrick & Marsh, 2001). If staff relations with those incarcerated are good, rehabilitation efforts in jails could be more successful. Given that some people stay in these facilities for up to a year and may lose many of their community supports during that time (Mowen & Visher, 2016), including friends and jobs, it is worth the effort to try rehabilitation because it can improve the lives of those incarcerated and reduce the chances of recidivism upon release (Miller et al., 2016, 2019).

Disclosure Statement

No potential conflict of interest was reported by the author(s).

Discussion Questions

1. The authors stated that their data collection method was paper and pencil survey, but what kind of research design do they appear to have used here? Review Chapters 6 and 7 if you need a refresher.
2. What were the two units of analysis for this study, and what did the results for the tests on those units of analysis find?
3. How might the authors' reliance on a convenience sample have influenced their findings?

Note

1 The current study has a small sample size of Black (N=61), Asian/Pacific Islander (N=1), biracial (N=5), and Other (N=2) respondents, therefore we examine race as a dichotomous variable (nonwhite and White). While we realize that this prohibits an understanding of the differences among nonwhite groups, we do not have enough statistical power to examine each group individually.

References

Angrist, J. D., & Pischke, J. S. (2009). *Mostly harmless econometrics: An empiricist's companion*. Princeton University Press.

Antonio, M. E., & Young, J. L. (2011). The effects of tenure on staff apathy and treatment orientation: A comparison of respondent characteristics and environmental factors. *American Journal of Criminal Justice*, *36*(1), 1–16. https://doi.org/10.1007/s12103-010-9103-1

Antonio, M. E., Young, J. L., & Wingeard, L. M. (2009). When actions and attitude count most: Assessing perceived level of responsibility and support for inmate treatment and rehabilitation programs among correctional employees. *The Prison Journal*, *89*(4), 363–382. https://doi.org/10.1177/0032885509349554

Applegate, B. K., Cullen, F. T., & Fisher, B. S. (2002). Public views toward crime and correctional policies: Is there a gender gap? *Journal of Criminal Justice*, *30*(2), 89–100. https://doi.org/10.1016/S0047-2352(01)00127-1

Applegate, B. K., & Sitren, A. H. (2008). The jail and the community: Comparing jails in rural and urban contexts. *The Prison Journal*, *88*(2), 252–269. https://doi.org/10.1177/0032885508319207

Arthur, J. A. (1994). Correctional ideology of black correctional officers. *Federal Probation*, *58*(1), 57–66.

Bahora, M., Hanafi, S., Chien, V. H., & Compton, M. T. (2008). Preliminary evidence of effects of crisis intervention team training on self-efficacy and social distance. *Administration and Policy in Mental Health and Mental Health Services Research*, *35*(3), 159–167. https://doi.org/10.1007/s10488-007-0153-8

Baldursson, E. (2000). Prisoners, prisons and punishment in small societies. *Journal of Scandinavian Studies in Criminology and Crime Prevention*, *1*(1), 6–15. https://doi.org/10.1080/14043850050116228

Beijersbergen, K. A., Dirkzwager, A. J. E., Molleman, T., van der Laan, P. H., & Nieuwbeerta, P. (2015). Procedural justice in prison: The importance of staff characteristics. *International Journal of Offender Therapy and Comparative Criminology*, *59*(4), 337–358. https://doi.org/10.1177/0306624X13512767

Belknap, J., Lynch, S., & DeHart, D. (2016). Jail staff members' views on jailed women's mental health, trauma, offending, rehabilitation, and reentry. *The Prison Journal*, *96*(1), 79–101. https://doi.org/10.1177/0032885515605485

Blevins, K. R., Cullen, F. T., & Sundt, J. L. (2007). The correctional orientation of "child savers": Support for rehabilitation and custody among juvenile correctional workers. *Journal of Offender Rehabilitation*, *45*(3–4), 47–83. https://doi.org/10.1300/J076v45n03_03

Burton, A. L., Lux, J. L., Cullen, F. T., Miller, W. T., & Burton, V. S. (2018). Creating a model correctional officer training academy: Implications from a national survey. *Federal Probation*, *81*(1), 26–36.

Butler, H. D., Tasca, M., Zhang, Y., & Carpenter, C. (2019). A systematic and meta-analytic review of the literature on correctional officers: Identifying new avenues for research. *Journal of Criminal Justice*, *60*(2), 84–92. https://doi.org/10.1016/j.jcrimjus.2018.12.002

Castle, T. L. (2008). Satisfied in the jail?: Exploring the predictors of job satisfaction among jail officers. *Criminal Justice Review*, *33*(1), 48–63. https://doi.org/10.1177/0734016808315586

Castle, T. L., & Martin, J. S. (2006). Occupational hazard: Predictors of stress among jail correctional officers. *American Journal of Criminal*

Justice, *31*(1), 65–80. https://doi.org/10.1007/BF02885685

Center of Health Policy, Planning, and Research. (2007). *Crisis Intervention Team (CIT) training for correctional officers: An evaluation of NAMI Maine's 2005–2007 expansion program*. University of New England.

Chen, G., & Einat, T. (2015). The relationship between criminology studies and punitive attitudes. *European Journal of Criminology*, *12*(2), 169–187. https://doi.org/10.1177/1477370814551211

Chiricos, T., Welch, K., & Gertz, M. (2004). Racial typification of crime and support for punitive measures. *Criminology*, *42*(2), 359–389. https://doi.org/10.1111/j.1745-9125.2004.tb00523.x

Collins, P. A., Iannacchione, B., Hudson, M., Stohr, M. K., & Hemmens, C. (2013). A comparison of jail inmate and staff correctional goal orientations: Results from across the line. *Journal of Crime and Justice*, *36*(1), 100–115. https://doi.org/10.1080/0735648X.2012.692892

Compton, M. T., Esterberg, M. L., McGee, R., Kotwicki, R. J., & Oliva, J. R. (2006). Brief reports: Crisis intervention team training: Changes in knowledge, attitudes, and stigma related to schizophrenia. *Psychiatric Services*, *57*(8), 1199–1202. https://doi.org/10.1176/ps.2006.57.8.1199

Cook, C. L., & Lane, J. (2012). Examining differences in attitudes about sexual victimization among a sample of jail officers: The importance of officer gender and perceived inmate characteristics. *Criminal Justice Review*, *37*(2), 191–213. https://doi.org/10.1177/0734016812436548

Cook, C. L., & Lane, J. (2014). Professional orientation and pluralistic ignorance among jail correctional officers. *International Journal of Offender Therapy and Comparative Criminology*, *58*(6), 735–757. https://doi.org/10.1177/0306624X13476285

Cook, C. L., & Lane, J. (2015). Blaming the victim: Perceptions about incarcerated sexual assault victim culpability among a sample of jail correctional officers. *Victims & Offenders*, *12*(3), 347–380. https://doi.org/10.1080/15564886.2015.1065531

Cook, C. L., & Lane, J. (2017). Responding to incidents of sexual victimization in correctional institutions: Correctional officer perspectives. *International Journal of Offender Therapy and Comparative Criminology*, *61*(15), 1651–1681. https://doi.org/10.1177/0306624X16631347

Cullen, F. T., Clark, G. A., Cullen, J. B., & Mathers, R. A. (1985). Attribution, Salience, and Attitudes toward Criminal Sanctioning. *Criminal Justice and Behavior*, *12*(3), 305–331. https://doi.org/10.1177/0093854885012003003

Cullen, F. T., Latessa, E. J., Burton, V. S., & Lombardo, L. X. (1993). The correctional orientation of prison wardens: Is the rehabilitative ideal supported? *Criminology*, *31*(1), 69–92. https://doi.org/10.1111/j.1745-9125.1993.tb01122.x

Cullen, F. T., Lutze, F. E., Link, B. G., & Wolfe, N. T. (1989). The correctional orientation of prison guards: Do officers support rehabilitation? *Federal Probation*, *53*(1), 33–42.

Davis, J. A., Smith, T. W., & Marsden, P. V. (1998). *General social surveys, 1972–1998: Cumulative codebook*. National Opinion Research Center.

Dillman, D. A., Dolsen, D. E., & Machlis, G. E. (1995). Increasing response to personally-delivered mail-back questionnaires. *Journal of Official Statistics*, *11*(2), 129–139.

Dowden, C., & Tellier, C. (2004). Predicting work-related stress in correctional officers: A meta-analysis. *Journal of Criminal Justice*, *32*(1), 31–47. https://doi.org/10.1016/j.jcrimjus.2003.10.003

Ellison, J. M., & Caudill, J. W. (2020). Working on local time: Testing the job-demand-control-support model of stress with jail officers. *Journal of Criminal Justice*, *70*(1), 1–11. https://doi.org/10.1016/j.jcrimjus.2020.101717

Ellison, J. M., & Gainey, R. (2020). An opportunity model of safety risks among jail officers. *Journal of Criminal Justice*, *66*, 1–12. https://doi.org/10.1016/j.jcrimjus.2019.101632

Farkas, M. A. (1999). Correctional officer attitudes toward inmates and working with inmates in a "get tough" era. *Journal of Criminal Justice*, *27*(6), 495–506. https://doi.org/10.1016/S0047-2352(99)00020-3

Griffin, M. L. (1999). The influence of organizational climate on detention officers' readiness to use force in a county jail. *Criminal Justice Review*, *24*(1), 1–26. https://doi.org/10.1177/073401689902400102

Griffin, M. L. (2001). Job satisfaction among detention officers: Assessing the relative contribution of organizational climate variables. *Journal of Criminal Justice*, *29*(3), 219–232. https://doi.org/10.1016/S0047-2352(01)00086-1

Griffin, M. L. (2002). The influence of professional orientation on detention officers' attitudes toward the use of force. *Criminal Justice and Behavior*, *29*(3), 250–277. https://doi.org/10.1177/0093854802029003002

Hanafi, S., Bahora, M., Demir, B. N., & Compton, M. T. (2008). Incorporating Crisis Intervention Team (CIT) knowledge and skills into the daily work of police officers: A focus group study. *Community Mental Health Journal*, *44*(6), 427–432. https://doi.org/10.1007/s10597-008-9145-8

Helfgott, J. B., & Gunnison, E. (2008). The influence of social distance on community corrections officer perceptions of offender reentry needs. *Federal Probation, 72*(1), 2–12.

Hemmens, C., & Stohr, M. K. (2000). The two faces of the correctional role: An exploration of the value of the correctional role instrument. *International Journal of Offender Therapy and Comparative Criminology, 44*(3), 326–349. https://doi.org/10.1177/0306624X00443006

Hepburn, J. R. (1984). The erosion of authority and the perceived legitimacy of inmate social protest: A study of prison guards. *Journal of Criminal Justice, 12*(6), 579–590. https://doi.org/10.1016/0047-2352(84)90115-6

Hirschfield, P. J., & Piquero, A. R. (2010). Normalization and legitimation: Modeling stigmatizing attitudes toward ex-offenders. *Criminology, 48*(1), 27–55. https://doi.org/10.1111/j.1745-9125.2010.00179.x

Hox, J. J. (1998). Multilevel modeling: When and why. In I. Balderjahn, R. Mathar, & M. Schader (Eds.), *Classification, data analysis, and data highways* (pp. 147–154). Springer.

Hussemann, J. M., & Page, J. (2011). Gender diversity and the prospects for progressive prison reform. *Women & Criminal Justice, 21*(4), 267–289. https://doi.org/10.1080/08974454.2011.609397

Jiang, S., Jin, X., Xiang, D., Goodlin-Fahncke, W., Yang, S., Xu, N., & Zhang, D. (2016). Punitive and rehabilitative orientations toward offenders among community correctional officers in China. *The Prison Journal, 96*(6), 771–792. https://doi.org/10.1177/0032885516671867

Johnsen, B., Granheim, P. K., & Helgesen, J. (2011). Exceptional prison conditions and the quality of prison life: Prison size and prison culture in Norwegian closed prisons. *European Journal of Criminology, 8*(6), 515–529. https://doi.org/10.1177/1477370811413819

Jurik, N. C. (1985). Individual and organizational determinants of correctional officer attitudes toward inmates. *Criminology, 23*(3), 523–540. https://doi.org/10.1111/j.1745-9125.1985.tb00352.x

Kerce, E. W., Magnusson, P., & Rudolph, A. (1994). *The attitudes of Navy corrections staff members: What they think about confinees and their jobs*. Navy Personnel Research and Development Center.

Kerle, K. (1982). The rural jail: Its people, problems, and solutions. In S. D. Cronk, J. Jankovic, & R. K. Green (Eds.), *Criminal justice in rural America* (pp. 189–204). National Institute of Justice, Office of Development, Testing, and Dissemination.

Kifer, M., Hemmens, C., & Stohr, M. K. (2003). The goals of corrections: Perspectives from the line. *Criminal Justice Review, 28*(1), 47–69. https://doi.org/10.1177/073401680302800104

Kim, A., DeValve, M., DeValve, E. Q., & Johnson, W. W. (2003). Female wardens: Results from a national survey of state correctional executives. *The Prison Journal, 83*(4), 406–425. https://doi.org/10.1177/0032885503260176

Kjelsberg, E., Skoglund, T. H., & Rustad, A. (2007). Attitudes towards prisoners, as reported by prison inmates, prison employees and college students. *BMC Public Health, 7*(71), 1–9. https://doi.org/10.1186/1471-2458-7-71

Klofas, J., & Toch, H. (1982). The guard subculture myth. *Journal of Research in Crime and Delinquency, 19*(2), 238–254. https://doi.org/10.1177/002242788201900207

Lambert, E. G., Gordon, J., Paoline, E. A., III, & Hogan, N. L. (2018). Workplace demands and resources as antecedents of jail officer perceived danger at work. *Journal of Crime and Justice, 41*(1), 98–118. https://doi.org/10.1080/0735648X.2016.1218355

Lambert, E. G., Griffin, M. L., Hogan, N. L., & Kelley, T. (2015). The ties that bind: Organizational commitment and its effect on correctional orientation, absenteeism, and turnover intent. *The Prison Journal, 95*(1), 135–156. https://doi.org/10.1177/0032885514563293

Lambert, E. G., & Hogan, N. L. (2009). Exploring the predictors of treatment views of private correctional staff: A test of an integrated work model. *Journal of Offender Rehabilitation, 48*(6), 504–528. https://doi.org/10.1080/10509670903081334

Lambert, E. G., Hogan, N. L., Altheimer, I., Jiang, S., & Stevenson, M. T. (2010). The relationship between burnout and support for punishment and treatment: A preliminary examination. *International Journal of Offender Therapy and Comparative Criminology, 54*(6), 1004–1022. https://doi.org/10.1177/0306624X09348585

Lambert, E. G., Hogan, N. L., & Barton, S. M. (2002). Satisfied correctional staff: A review of the literature on the correlates of correctional staff job satisfaction. *Criminal Justice and Behavior, 29*(2), 115–143. https://doi.org/10.1177/0093854802029002001

Lambert, E. G., Hogan, N. L., Barton, S. M., & Elechi, O. O. (2009). The impact of job stress, job involvement, job satisfaction, and organizational commitment on correctional staff support for rehabilitation and punishment. *Criminal Justice Studies, 22*(2), 109–122. https://doi.org/10.1080/14786010902975374

Lambert, E. G., Hogan, N. L., & Barton-Bellessa, S. M. (2011). The association between perceptions of distributive justice and procedural justice with support of treatment and support of punishment among correctional staff. *Journal of Offender Rehabilitation, 50*(4), 202–220. https://doi.org/10.1080/10509674.2011.552586

Lambert, E. G., Hogan, N. L., & Paoline, E. A., III. (2016). Differences in the predictors of job stress and job satisfaction for Black and White jail staff. *Corrections*, *1*(1), 1–19. https://doi.org/10.1080/23774657.2016.1105654

Lambert, E. G., Morrow, W., Vickovic, S. G., Leone, M. C., Keena, L. D., Haynes, S. H., & May, D. (2021). Work–family conflict's association with the work attitudes of job involvement, job satisfaction, and organizational commitment among southern prison staff. *Criminal Justice Policy Review*, *32*(8), 865–889.

Lambert, E. G., & Paoline, E. A., III. (2005). The impact of medical issues on the job stress and job satisfaction of jail staff. *Punishment & Society*, *7*(3), 259–275. https://doi.org/10.1177/1462474505053829

Lambert, E. G., & Paoline, E. A., III. (2008). The influence of individual, job, and organizational characteristics on correctional staff job stress, job satisfaction, and organizational commitment. *Criminal Justice Review*, *33*(4), 541–564. https://doi.org/10.1177/0734016808320694

Lerman, A. E., & Harney, J. (2019). Feedback effects and the criminal justice bureaucracy: Officer attitudes and the future of correctional reform. *The ANNALS of the American Academy of Political and Social Science*, *685*(1), 227–249. https://doi.org/10.1177/0002716219869907

Lerman, A. E., & Page, J. (2016). Does the front line reflect the party line? The politicization of punishment and prison officers' perspectives towards incarceration. *The British Journal of Criminology*, *56*(3), 578–601. https://doi.org/10.1093/bjc/azv061

Maahs, J., & Pratt, T. (2001). Uncovering the predictors of correctional officers' attitudes and behaviors: A meta-analysis. *Corrections Management Quarterly*, *5*(2), 13–19.

Mays, G. L., & Thompson, J. A. (1988). Mayberry revisited: The characteristics and operations of America's small jails. *Justice Quarterly*, *5*(3), 421–440. https://doi.org/10.1080/07418828800089801

Miller, J. M., Miller, H. V., & Barnes, J. C. (2016). Outcome evaluation of a family-based jail reentry program for substance abusing offenders. *The Prison Journal*, *96*(1), 53–78. https://doi.org/10.1177/0032885515605482

Miller, J. M., Miller, H. V., & Barnes, J. C. (2019). Treating co-occurring disorders in jails: Outcome findings from a second chance act offender reentry program. *Crime & Delinquency*, *65*(5), 583–605. https://doi.org/10.1177/0011128718789860

Miller, R. (1982). A needs assessment for small jails in the United States. In S. D. Cronk, J. Jankovic, & R. K. Green (Eds.), *Criminal justice in rural America* (pp. 205–229). National Institute of Justice, Office of Development, Testing, and Dissemination.

Molleman, T., & Leeuw, F. L. (2012). The influence of prison staff on inmate conditions: A multilevel approach to staff and inmate surveys. *European Journal on Criminal Policy and Research*, *18*(2), 217–233. https://doi.org/10.1007/s10610-011-9158-7

Moon, B., & Maxwell, S. R. (2004a). Assessing the correctional orientation of corrections officers in South Korea. *International Journal of Offender Therapy and Comparative Criminology*, *48*(6), 729–743. https://doi.org/10.1177/0306624X04266681

Moon, B., & Maxwell, S. R. (2004b). The sources and consequences of corrections officers' stress: A South Korean example. *Journal of Criminal Justice*, *32*(4), 359–370. https://doi.org/10.1016/j.jcrimjus.2004.04.006

Mowen, T. J., & Visher, C. A. (2016). Changing the ties that bind: How incarceration impacts family relationships. *Criminology & Public Policy*, *15*(2), 503–528. https://doi.org/10.1111/1745-9133.12207

Patrick, S., & Marsh, R. (2001). Perceptions of punishment and rehabilitation among inmates in a medium security prison: "A consumers' report." *Journal of Offender Rehabilitation*, *33*(3), 47–63. https://doi.org/10.1300/J076v33n03_03

Powell, T. A., Holt, J. C., & Fondacaro, K. M. (1997). The prevalence of mental illness among inmates in a rural state. *Law and Human Behavior*, *21*(4), 427–438. https://doi.org/10.1023/A:1024811303834

Public Health Research Institute. (2005). *Evaluation report of NAMI CIT implementation at the Androscoggin County jail*. Public Health Research Institute.

Rhineberger-Dunn, G., Mack, K. Y., & Baker, K. M. (2017). Comparing demographic factors, background characteristics, and workplace perceptions as predictors of burnout among community corrections officers. *Criminal Justice and Behavior*, *44*(2), 205–225. https://doi.org/10.1177/0093854816666583

Richter, T. (2006). What is wrong with ANOVA and multiple regression? Analyzing sentence reading times with hierarchical linear models. *Discourse Processes*, *41*(3), 221–250. https://doi.org/10.1207/s15326950dp4103_1

Robinson, D., Porporino, F. J., & Simourd, L. (1997). The influence of educational attainment on the attitudes and job performance of correctional officers. *Crime & Delinquency*, *43*(1), 60–77. https://doi.org/10.1177/0011128797043001004

Ruddell, R., & Mays, G. L. (2007). Rural jails: Problematic inmates, overcrowded cells, and cash-strapped counties. *Journal of Criminal Justice*, *35*(3), 251–260. https://doi.org/10.1016/j.jcrimjus.2007.03.002

Shannon, S. K. S., & Page, J. (2014). Bureaucrats on the cell block: Prison officers' perceptions of work environment and attitudes toward prisoners. *Social Service Review*, *88*(4), 630–657. https://doi.org/10.1086/678448

Stohr, M. K., Lovrich, N. P., & Wood, M. J. (1996). Service versus security concerns in contemporary jails: Testing general differences in training topic assessments. *Journal of Criminal Justice*, *24*(5), 437–448. https://doi.org/10.1016/0047-2352(96)00030-X

Tabachnick, B. G., & Fidell, L. S. (1989). *Using Multivariate Statistics*. Harper & Row.

Teske, R. H. C., & Williamson, H. E. (1979). Correctional officers' attitudes toward selected treatment programs. *Criminal Justice and Behavior*, *6*(1), 59–66. https://doi.org/10.1177/009385487900600109

Tewksbury, R., & Mustaine, E. E. (2008). Correctional orientations of prison staff. *The Prison Journal*, *88*(2), 207–233. https://doi.org/10.1177/0032885508319163

Toch, H., & Klofas, J. (1982). Alienation and desire for job enrichment among correction officers. *Federal Probation*, *46*(1), 35–44.

United States Census Bureau. (1995). *Urban and rural definitions*. Geography Division.

United States Census Bureau. (2000). *Census 2000 geography glossary*. Geography Division.

United States Department of Agriculture. (2004). *Measuring rurality: Rural-urban continuum codes*. Economic Research Service.

Van Voorhis, P., Cullen, F. T., Link, B. G., & Wolfe, N. T. (1991). The impact of race and gender on correctional officers' orientation to the integrated environment. *Journal of Research in Crime and Delinquency*, *28*(4), 472–500. https://doi.org/10.1177/0022427891028004007

Ward, G., & Kupchik, A. (2010). What drives juvenile probation officers?: Relating organizational contexts, status characteristics, and personal convictions to treatment and punishment orientations. *Crime & Delinquency*, *56*(1), 35–69. https://doi.org/10.1177/0011128707307960

Whitehead, J. T., & Lindquist, C. A. (1989). Determinants of correctional officers' professional orientation. *Justice Quarterly*, *6*(1), 69–88. https://doi.org/10.1080/07418828900090051

Whitehead, J. T., Lindquist, C. A., & Klofas, J. (1987). Correctional officer professional orientation: A replication of the Klofas-Toch measure. *Criminal Justice and Behavior*, *14*(4), 468–486. https://doi.org/10.1177/0093854887014004004

Wooldredge, J., & Steiner, B. (2016). Further inspection into the effects of correctional officers' sex, race, and perceptions of safety on job-related attitudes. *The Prison Journal*, *96*(4), 576–599. https://doi.org/10.1177/0032885516650882

Young, J. L., Antonio, M. E., & Wingeard, L. M. (2009). How staff attitude and support for inmate treatment and rehabilitation differs by job category: An evaluation of findings from Pennsylvania's department of corrections' employee training curriculum 'reinforcing positive behavior.' *Journal of Criminal Justice*, *37*(5), 435–441. https://doi.org/10.1016/j.jcrimjus.2009.07.003

Zeng, Z., & Minton, T. D. (2021). *Jail inmates in 2019* (NCJ 255608). Bureau of Justice Statistics.

Reading 8.2 Police-Related Social Media Exposure and Adolescents' Interest in Becoming a Police Officer

For years, policing jobs were in very high demand, but that has changed over the past decade. Now, police departments and other law enforcement agencies across the United States are struggling to recruit good candidates. A possible reason for that is residents' change in views regarding police legitimacy. Given the pervasive nature of social media in our lives, we should not be surprised to find that it can influence our views on a number of issues, including our impressions of police. While the impact of social media on police perceptions had previously been tested on college students, Cross and Fine (2022) wanted to reach potential police recruits at an earlier stage in their lives, specifically during their teenage years. That is a much more difficult group to access, since the researchers could not simply rely on students from their universities to serve as their respondent pool. Cross and Fine sought the assistance of a research firm that recruits and compensates people for their survey participation to find a nationally representative sample of adults who had teenage children willing to participate in the survey.

Police-Related Social Media Exposure and Adolescents' Interest in Becoming a Police Officer

Allison R. Cross and Adam D. Fine

Introduction

Research on people's perceptions of police is surging largely because studies routinely find that the public's perceptions of the police are vitally important for law-abiding behavior (Sunshine & Tyler, 2003; Walters & Bolger, 2019). For instance, personally or vicariously experiencing respectful and fair treatment, or procedural justice, often promotes law-abiding behavior, more willingness to report witnessed crimes, and a shared moral obligation to obey the law (Cohn et al., 2010; Harris & Jones, 2020; Tyler & Jackson, 2014). Yet beyond these behaviors, it is likely that perceptions of police impact a host of other critical outcomes, such as desire to enter policing careers. The harsh reality is that few people today are pursuing careers in law enforcement (Police Executive Research Forum, 2019). In this increasingly digital age, exposure to unjust policing is becoming even more ubiquitous, which may impact people's perceptions of law enforcement and their interest in joining police departments (Nix & Pickett, 2017). However, this association has not been systematically examined among adolescents – the population that will become the next generation of law enforcement.

Adolescents' perceptions of police are essential to study for several reasons. First, adolescents are the future pool of police applicants. Second, youths' perceptions of law enforcement and felt obligation to obey the law appear to be more malleable than during any other developmental period (Cohn et al., 2010; Fine et al., 2020; Jackson et al., 2012; Tyler & Trinkner, 2018). Third, despite the ubiquity of social media in the lives of modern adolescents (Anderson & Jiang, 2018) and the fact that many users may encounter videos, posts, and news stories about police on social media before they themselves experience direct interactions with officers, only a handful of studies have actually examined the impact of media exposure on individuals (e.g. Maguire et al., 2017) and virtually none have focused on adolescents. The current study leveraged the procedural justice framework to examine how exposure to police officer content on social media affects adolescents' perceptions of police and, in turn, their willingness to become a police officer.

Police Officer Workforce Crisis

Policies have been put into place to encourage police departments to diversify their departments and recruit officers who can better handle modern-day social issues (Police Executive Research Forum, 2019; President's Task Force on 21st Century Policing, 2015). Yet even with these new policies implemented, police departments are struggling to recruit suitable police officers who have desirable characteristics because the pool of applicants is shrinking. The reality is that sixty-three percent of police departments in the United States reported a decrease in police officer applicants within the past five years (Police Executive Research Forum, 2019), and law enforcement agencies across the nation are facing similar challenges in recruiting the next generation of officers.

Procedural Justice Framework

Studies are beginning to leverage the procedural justice framework to explain why fewer people may be less willing to become police officers (Morrow et al., 2020; Todak, 2017). On a broad level, procedural justice theorists argue that if people believe that the police treat them fairly, they will have more positive perceptions of the legitimacy of the law and legal system (Fagan & Tyler, 2005; Sunshine & Tyler, 2003). Consequently, the more positively they view law enforcement, the more interested they would be in joining law enforcement.

More specifically the procedural justice framework consists of three components: (1) procedural justice, (2) legitimacy, and (3) behavioral outcomes. Police procedural justice refers to the perception of fair treatment by police officers (Fagan & Tyler, 2005; Sunshine & Tyler, 2003). People base their perceptions of procedural justice on four key factors: ability to participate in the legal process, respectful treatment by the officer, neutrality in the decision-making process, and trust in the motives of the decision-maker (Tyler, 1990). These assessments of procedural justice may be grounded in how individuals are directly treated by the police or in how the police treat others (Fine et al., 2020; Harris & Jones, 2020). Direct exposure to the police is characterized by immediate contact with a police officer, such as being pulled over in a traffic stop, whereas vicarious exposure to the police is characterized by observing, witnessing, or hearing how others are treated (Harris & Jones, 2020). Both direct and vicarious assessments of procedural justice have been found to affect perceptions of police legitimacy (Fine et al., 2020; Harris & Jones, 2020).

Police legitimacy constitutes the second component of the procedural justice framework (Fagan & Tyler, 2005; Sunshine & Tyler, 2003; Walters & Bolger, 2019; Wolfe et al., 2016). Briefly, legitimacy is the perception that the authority of the police is right and just and that police can use their authority to dictate proper behavior (Fagan & Tyler, 2005; McLean et al., 2019; Sunshine & Tyler, 2003). A prevailing view is that legitimacy consists of three core features: right to power, authority to govern, and motivation (Jackson, 2018). Right to power refers to the individual's belief in the entity's rightful authority, which is often based on the normative appropriateness of the institution. Authority to govern refers to the normative duty that citizens feel to obey the authorities that they believe are appropriate. The third is the motivation of people who deem an institution to be legitimate to either strengthen or diminish the authority of the said institution by abiding by the laws and rules of that institution (Jackson, 2018). The procedural justice model posits that positive experiences with how police officers treat people during interactions, or procedural justice, are related to more positive perceptions of police legitimacy, while negative experiences with police officers, or procedural *in*justice, are related to more negative perceptions of police legitimacy (Fagan & Tyler, 2005; Johnson et al., 2017; Maguire et al., 2017; McLean et al., 2019; Sunshine & Tyler, 2003).

Even though procedurally just and procedurally unjust treatment has been found to impact legitimacy perceptions, more recent procedural justice theorists have found that positive and negative experiences may not impact legitimacy perceptions to the same extent (Skogan, 2006; Slocum & Wiley, 2018). The asymmetry hypothesis indicates that negative experiences with police may have a greater impact on legitimacy perceptions than positive experiences do (Skogan, 2006; Slocum & Wiley, 2018). That is, numerous procedurally just encounters with police may not greatly enhance positive legitimacy perceptions, but one procedurally unjust encounter with police has the potential to drastically reduce legitimacy perceptions of police.

Legitimacy perceptions are important because they have behavioral implications. The final component of the procedural justice framework focuses on the behavioral outcomes of procedural justice and police legitimacy. When people view police as more legitimate, they are more likely to cooperate with the police and are more apt to comply with laws (Cohn et al., 2010; Jackson et al., 2012; Tyler & Jackson, 2014). Further, people who have positive legitimacy views of police report that they feel a moral obligation to obey the law and are more willing to cooperate with police (Cohn et al., 2010; Jackson et al., 2012; Tyler & Jackson, 2014). Conversely, when people view the police as more illegitimate, they are more likely to commit crimes, are less willing to cooperate with police, and feel less morally obligated to obey the law. The behavioral outcomes associated with positive legitimacy perceptions are essential to maintaining an orderly society (Tyler, 2006).

Social Media

Researchers suggest that the police are currently facing a post-Ferguson era legitimacy crisis (Morrow et al., 2020; Nix & Pickett, 2017; Nix & Wolfe, 2017). In other words, many people have lost their trust in the police and do not believe that they have a right to exert legal authority. Researchers have speculated that the legitimacy crisis is the main cause for the decrease in police officer applicants (Morrow et al., 2020; Police Executive Research Forum, 2019). A qualitative study sampling criminology and criminal justice students interested in policing careers asked the students about their expectations of becoming police officers during the current legitimacy crisis (Todak, 2017). Many of the students voiced that they were afraid of making mistakes as police officers and acknowledged that they may face increased difficulty and criticism by choosing that profession (Todak, 2017). The results from that study indicated that prospective police applicants consider the public mistrust and scrutiny of police in their decisions of whether they want to become police officers.

Recent advancements in technology over the past several years has allowed for much more rapid dissemination of information (Morrow et al., 2020; Nix & Pickett, 2017; Parry et al., 2019). The increased availability and use of technology provide a growing and understudied platform for people to be exposed to the way in which people are treated by the police. In particular, recorded police encounters that demonstrate inappropriate police use of force against Black, indigenous, and people of color saturate social media outlets such as Facebook, Twitter, and Instagram, which simultaneously provide people with the additional opportunity to broadcast and share their reactions to the content and police-related opinions more generally (Parry et al., 2019). Adolescents, in particular, may be disproportionately exposed to police-related content considering the most recent Pew Research Center report on teenage social media usage found that 95% of adolescents aged 13 to 17 reported having access to a Smartphone and 89% reported being online 'almost constantly' or 'several times a day' (Anderson & Jiang, 2018). This increased significantly from 2014, where only 56% of adolescents reported being online more than once a day. Altogether, only 3% of adolescents reported that they do not use social media (Anderson & Jiang, 2018).

Media's impact on legitimacy has been examined in a handful of studies, yet typically with undergraduate students. For instance, in a study of undergraduate college students, researchers found that students who reported that they read news online had more negative perceptions of police legitimacy (Intravia et al., 2018). In addition, other studies have exposed participants to videos of police actions. For instance, Maguire et al. (2017) manipulated participants' exposure to different types of police videos. In this study, participants viewed police body camera footage of a procedurally just or unjust police interaction. The participants who viewed the procedurally just police interaction video reported more trust and confidence in the police compared to those who viewed the procedurally unjust police interaction video (Maguire et al., 2017). While these few studies capitalize on how exposure to media influences perceptions of legitimacy in young adults, impacts on adolescents have been understudied.

The Current Study

Although adolescents spend an exorbitant amount of time on social media and are by definition situated to become the next generation of police officers, research has yet to examine how social media shapes teenagers' perceptions of police legitimacy and their willingness to become a police officer. This is surprising in light of the current crisis in police recruitment and the widespread conversations surrounding the future of policing in the United States (Fine et al., 2019; Intravia et al., 2018; Maguire et al., 2017). The current study leveraged the procedural justice model to examine the relation that police-related valence of social media exposure to police content has to youths' willingness to become a police officer, particularly through its relation to youths' perceptions of police legitimacy. The procedural justice model suggests that exposure to procedural justice leads to more positive perceptions of police legitimacy and promotes more positive law-related outcomes (Tyler, 1990). Therefore, we hypothesized that more positive exposure to content related to police on social media would be correlated with more positive legitimacy perceptions and more willingness to become a police officer. Additionally, we hypothesized that more positive legitimacy perceptions would be correlated with more willingness to become a police officer. Lastly, grounded in the procedural justice model, we hypothesized that legitimacy would mediate the relation between more positive exposure to content related to police officers on social media and more willingness to become a police officer (see Figure 1). That is, we speculate that seeing on social media how police treat others may be associated with more positive legitimacy perceptions which would, in turn, be associated with an increased desire to become a police officer as posited by the procedural justice model.

The models accounted for whether the participant had ever been arrested, had been a victim of a crime in the past two years, or if they personally knew a police officer. Whether participants had been arrested before was controlled for because researchers have found that adolescents who have more contact with law enforcement have lower perceptions of police legitimacy compared to those who have less contact with law enforcement (Vidal

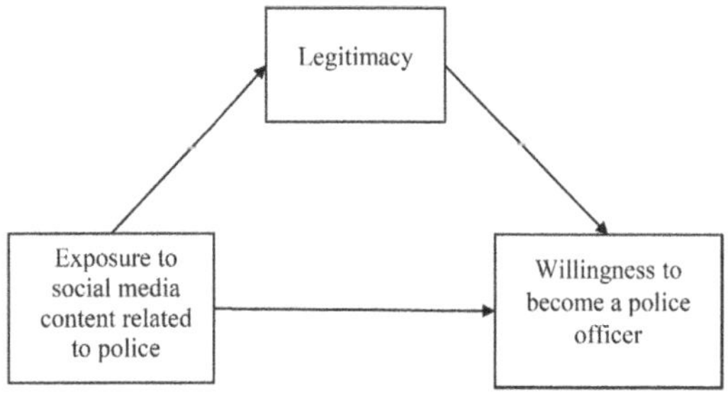

Figure 1 Hypothesized mediation model

et al., 2017). Whether or not the participant had been a victim of a crime was controlled for because researchers have indicated that police treatment after crime victimization may impact perceptions of police (Koster et al., 2016). Whether participants personally know a police officer was controlled for because people who know a police officer may have more positive perceptions of police officers compared to those who do not know a police officer.

The demographic variables of age, sex, and race/ethnicity were also controlled for in the models. Age was controlled for because research has demonstrated that older adolescents have more negative perceptions of police officers compared to younger adolescents (Fine et al., 2021; McLean et al., 2019). Sex was controlled for because more males than females become police officers (Police Executive Research Forum, 2019). Race/ethnicity was controlled for because adolescents who are Black tend to report lower perceptions of police officers compared to Latinx individuals, who in turn tend to report worse perceptions than White adolescents (Fine et al., 2017; Peck, 2015).

Method

Participants

CloudResearch, formerly known as TurkPrime, collects data from nationally representative panels of adults who are pre-screened for eligibility and who are recruited into sampling quotas for demographic categories proportional to the U.S. Census (e.g. age, sex, ethnicity, Hispanic/Latinx), similar to Qualtrics or Survey Monkey (Litman et al., 2017; McDonald et al., 2018). We contracted CloudResearch to create a nationally representative sample of adult parents using census-matched quotas. CloudResearch first creates a pool of adults who are parents. Then, using demographic categories that are proportional to the U.S. Census on age, gender, and race/ethnicity, it then recruits from this pool adults that fit into the sampling strata. Adults complete the consent process for their adolescent children to participate in the survey, and then the youth themselves are surveyed. As such, the sample consisted of 951 adolescent children of a nationally representative sample of adults from the U.S. using CloudResearch. One hundred twenty-nine (13.6%) responses were eliminated from analyses for failed attention checks (e.g. *Please select 'always' for this question*) or inappropriately short response times (less than four minutes). The final sample consisted of 822 adolescents ranging in age from 13 to 17 (M = 15.41, SD = 1.40). About half were female (50.31%) and half were male (49.69%). Sixty-three percent of the participants were White, 17% were Black, 11% were Latinx/Hispanic, and 9% were another race/ethnicity.

Measures

Covariates

Participants selected their age and sex. To assess race/ethnicity, participants were asked if they identify with one or more of the following categories: Latinx/Hispanic, White, African American/Black, Asian, and Native American. Participants also had the option to write in a different race/ethnicity in an 'Other' category. Participants were grouped into one of four categories: White (only selected 'White'), Black (any part Black), Latinx/Hispanic (not Black and any part Latinx/Hispanic), and Other (all other participants). Mixed racial participants were grouped into the "other" category due to the small sample size. Dummy-coded variables were created comparing White to Black, Latinx/Hispanic, and Other.

To measure if participants personally knew a police officer, they were asked, '*Do you know anyone (like friends, family, or neighbors) who is a police officer?*' Three hundred sixty-six participants knew a police officer (44.63%; coded as 1). To measure if participants had been a victim of a crime in the past two years, they were asked, '*In the past 2 years, have you personally been a victim of a crime?*' Seventy-six participants had been a victim of a crime in the past two years (9.27%; coded as 1). To measure if participants had ever been arrested, they were asked, '*Have you ever been arrested before?*' Few participants had been arrested (4.03%; coded as 1).

Exposure to Social Media (SM) Content Related to Police

To explore the association between being exposed to positive or negative social media content related to police officers, analyses needed to focus on adolescents who had been exposed to social media content related to police officers. First, participants were asked, '*Considering all that you are exposed to on social media, how often do you see content about police officers?*' Participants answered on a 5-point Likert scale from *never* to *very often*. To focus on those who had been exposed to content related to police officers, those who selected *never* (N = 28) were excluded from analyses. Those who indicated that they had seen social media content about police officers were asked the follow-up question, '*Has the social media content that you have seen about police officers been positive or negative*?' (Nix & Pickett, 2017). Participants responded on a 4-point scale where *1 = very negative, 2 = negative, 3 = positive*, and *4 = very positive*. Higher scores indicated more exposure to positive social media content about police officers, $M = 2.11$, $SD = .81$.

Legitimacy

Participants were presented with six items and rated each item on a 5-point Likert scale of *strongly disagree* to *strongly agree*. Four of the items originated from Tyler's (1990) legitimacy scale (e.g. *I have a great deal of respect for the police*) that is used in both longitudinal (McLean et al., 2019) and cross-sectional studies of youth (Fine et al., 2020). Two additional items assessed the normative alignment aspect of legitimacy, the extent to which people believe that police officers have the same moral values as they do (Jackson et al., 2012; e.g. *The police usually act in ways that are consistent with my own ideas about what is right and wrong*). The items were mean scored to create one measure based on the results of a factor analysis (Tom et al., 2021). Scores ranged from 1 to 5 with higher scores indicating higher perceptions of police legitimacy, $M = 3.53$, $SD = .99$, $\alpha = .93$.

Willingness to Become a Police Officer (PO)

Participants were asked to rate how much they agree or disagree with the statement, '*When I grow up, I might want to be a police officer*,' using a 5-point Likert scale that ranged from *strongly disagree* to *strongly agree*. Scores ranged from 1 to 5 with higher scores indicating more willingness to become a police officer and lower scores indicating less willingness to become a police officer, $M = 2.25$, $SD = 1.36$.

Procedure

The study was approved by the Arizona State University Institutional Review Board. Adolescents whose parents consented to their participation were informed of the purpose of the study and were ensured of the anonymity of their responses. The data used in the current study were from the survey portion of an experiment that aimed to assess the impact of viewing procedurally just and unjust videos of a traffic stop on cooperation with police officers. As a result, participants in the study were randomly assigned to one of three video conditions: a procedurally just video of a traffic stop, a procedurally unjust (but nonviolent) video of a traffic stop, or a control condition where they did not view any video (Maguire et al., 2017). Afterwards, participants answered a series of questions about their perceptions of police officers. Initially, the plan was to exclude participants in the two treatment conditions (i.e. just and unjust videos) and to focus the analyses on the control group who did not watch a video. However, youths' perceptions of police legitimacy did not differ depending on condition (Tom et al., 2021). Therefore, all participants were included in this analysis and the conditions were dummy coded in the model. It is important to note that the results are consistent regardless of if the models only included participants in the control group or if the models included all participants in the sample.

Results

Bivariate Correlations

Bivariate correlations are presented in Table 1. Older youth reported more exposure to negative social media content about police officers. More exposure to positive social media content about police officers was positively correlated with perceptions of police legitimacy and willingness to become a police officer. As expected, legitimacy was positively related to adolescents' willingness to become a PO. These associations were in the hypothesized direction to support testing the mediation model.

Mediation Path Analysis Model

We hypothesized that more exposure to positive SM content about police officers would be associated with more positive legitimacy perceptions of police, and, in turn, would be associated with more willingness to become a PO. To examine the hypothesized model, a mediation path model with asymmetric bootstrapping set to 10,000 was examined. The unstandardized coefficients for the model are presented in Table 2.

Willingness to Become a PO on Covariates

Within the mediation model, four covariates were significantly related to willingness to become a PO. First, males were more willing to become police officers than females (b = .39, SE = .08, *95% CI* [-.48, -.01]). Second, adolescents who personally knew a police officer were more willing to become a police officer compared to adolescents who did not personally know a police officer (b = .22, SE = .08, *95% CI* [.07, .38]). Third, adolescents who had been a victim of a crime were more willing to become a police officer compared to adolescents who had not been a victim of a crime (b = .45, SE = .15, *95% CI* [.15, .75]). Lastly, Black adolescents were less willing to become a police officer compared to White adolescents (b = -.22, SE = .12, *95% CI* [-.48, -.01]). The covariates of age, Latinx/Hispanic (vs. White), other race/ethnicity (vs. White), ever been arrested, and video condition were not significantly related to willingness to become a police officer.

Legitimacy on Covariates

Additionally, six covariates were related to the mediator of police legitimacy. Black adolescents (b = -.59, SE = .09, *95% CI* [-.79, -.42]) and Latinx/Hispanic adolescents (b = -.36, SE = .11, *95% CI* [-.57, -.16]) had more negative police legitimacy perceptions than White adolescents. Males had more positive legitimacy perceptions compared to

Table 1 Descriptives and correlations

Variable	*Descriptive Statistics*				*Correlations*		
	M	*SD*	*Min*	*Max*	*1. Exposure to SM*	*2. Legitimacy*	*3. Willingness to be a PO*
1. Exposure to SM	2.11	0.81	1	4	1.00		
2. Legitimacy	3.53	0.99	1	5	0.35***	1.00	
3. Willingness to be a PO	2.25	1.36	1	5	0.40***	0.42***	1.00

Note. Pearson's correlation was used for the correlation between legitimacy and age. Spearman's rho was used for correlations using the variables exposure to social media (SM) and willingness to be a police officer (PO).

* $p < .05$. ** $p < .01$. *** $p < .001$

Table 2 Hypothesized mediation model unstandardized coefficients

Path	*b*	*SE*	*95% CI*	*p-value*
			Lower	*Upper*
On Legitimacy (mediator)				
Age	<0.01	0.02	-0.04	0.05 0.002
Race/ethnicity (vs. White)				
Black	-0.59	0.094	-0.79	-0.42<.001
Latinx/Hispanic	-0.36	0.11	-0.57	-0.160.001
Other	-0.21	0.10	-0.42	0.00 0.04
Male (vs. Female)	0.19	0.06	0.07	0.32 0.002
Know a police officer	0.17	0.06	0.05	0.30 0.005
Victim of a crime	-0.31	0.11	-0.52	-0.090.006
Ever been arrested	-0.35	0.18	-0.68	-0.01 0.051
Video condition (vs. control)				
Unjust	0.04	0.07	-0.10	0.19 0.59
Just	0.13	0.08	-0.01	0.29 0.09
Exposure to SM	0.40	0.04	0.31	0.48 <.001
On willingness to be a PO (dependent variable)				
Age	-0.03	0.03	-0.09	0.03 0.27
Race/ethnicity (vs. White)				
Black	-0.22	0.12	-0.48	-0.01 0.07
Latinx/Hispanic	0.11	0.13	-0.18	0.33 0.41
Other	0.03	0.15	-0.27	0.32 0.8
Male (vs. Female)	0.39	0.08	0.24	0.55 <.001
Know a police officer	0.22	0.08	0.07	0.38 0.005
Victim of a crime	0.45	0.15	0.15	0.75 0.003
Ever been arrested	0.17	0.19	-0.22	0.55 0.89
Video condition (vs. control)				
Unjust	0.04	0.09	-0.15	0.22 0.66
Just	<0.01	0.10	-0.19	0.19 0.96
Legitimacy	0.41	0.05	0.32	0.50 <.001
Exposure to SM	0.46	0.06	0.35	0.60 <.001

Note. Coefficient *b* is unstandardized. Standard errors and confidence intervals are bootstrapped to 10,000. SM refers to social media. PO refers to police officer.

females (*b* = .19, *SE* = .06, *95% CI* [.07, .32]). Adolescents who personally knew a police officer had more positive perceptions of police legitimacy than adolescents who did not personally know a police officer (*b* = .17, *SE* = .06, *95% CI* [.05, .30]). Lastly, adolescents who had been arrested compared to those who had not been arrested (*b* = -.35, *SE* = .18, *95% CI* [-.68, -.01]) and been a victim of a crime compared to those who had not been a victim of a crime (*b* = -.31, *SE* = .11, *95% CI* [-.52, -.09]) had more negative legitimacy perceptions. When accounting for the other variables in the model, age, other race/ethnicity (vs. White), and video condition were not significantly related to legitimacy perceptions.

Hypothesized Mediation Model

Exposure to SM had a direct effect on willingness to become a PO (b = .46, SE = .06, *95% CI* [.35, .60]); as expected, more positively valenced exposure to police content on social media was associated with more willingness to become a police officer. Exposure to SM was also indirectly associated with willingness to become a PO through police legitimacy; more positively valenced social media exposure to police content was associated with more positive perceptions of police legitimacy (b = .40, SE = .04, *95% CI* [.31, .48]) which, in turn, were associated with more willingness to become a police officer (b = .41, SE = .05, *95% CI* [.32, .50]). Support was found for a partial mediation; legitimacy accounted for 35.65% of the effect that exposure to SM had on willingness to become a PO.

Supplemental Analysis

Due to high profile policing incidents against Black, indigenous, and people of color (BIPOC) in the U.S., we conducted supplemental and post-hoc analyses to determine if our mediation path models differed depending on racial/ethnic identification. As such, we conducted three additional mediation path models in Mplus 8 with asymmetric bootstrapping set to 10,000 to determine if the associations within the mediation path model were different for White adolescents, Black adolescents, and Latinx/Hispanic adolescents. All three of these mediation models were significant. Exposure to SM was directly related to increased willingness to become a PO for White (b = .40, SE = .08, *95% CI* [.24, .56]), Black (b = .53, SE = .18, *95% CI* [.19, .88]), and Latinx/Hispanic adolescents (b = .35, SE = .14, *95% CI* [.06, .61]). For all three racial/ethnic groups, more positive exposure to police related content on social media was associated with more willingness to enter a policing career. Exposure to SM was also indirectly associated with willingness to become a PO through police legitimacy for White adolescents (b = .24, SE = .04, *95% CI* [.16, .33]), Black adolescents (b = .14, SE = .08, *95% CI* [.01, .31]), and Latinx/Hispanic adolescents (b = .14, SE = .05, *95% CI* [.04, .23]). For all three racial/ethnic groups, more positive social media exposure to police content was related to more positive legitimacy perceptions and, in turn, more willingness to enter a policing career.

However, despite similar overall findings, differences between these three racial/ethnic groups were apparent when examining the percent of the mediation effect. That is, we uncovered tentative evidence that legitimacy mediated the relation between exposure to SM and willingness to become a PO more and less strongly depending on the youth's racial/ethnic identity. For the entire sample, legitimacy accounted for 35.65% of the effect that exposure to SM had on willingness to become a PO. For White adolescents, legitimacy accounted for 60.59% of the effect that exposure to SM had on willingness to become a PO. For Black adolescents, legitimacy accounted for only 25.35% of the effect that exposure to SM had on willingness to become a PO. Lastly, for Latinx/Hispanic adolescents, legitimacy accounted for 47.64% of the effect that exposure to SM had on willingness to become a PO.

Discussion

While many police departments have enacted policies in an attempt to diversify their departments to better represent the population, better handle social problems, and recruit officers with desirable characteristics, this has become increasingly difficult because the applicant pool in recent years has been both small and shrinking (Police Executive Research Forum, 2019). The reality is that police departments are becoming increasingly homogenous (Leatherby & Oppel, 2020). Even though adolescents spend a copious amount of time on the Internet (Anderson & Jiang, 2018) and are the future of the police force, extant literature has not assessed how adolescents' social media exposure affects their perceptions of police and their desire to become a police officer.

While many researchers have speculated that the decrease in police applicants may be due to the legitimacy crisis in the United States, no research to date has quantitatively assessed the relation between legitimacy perceptions and willingness to become a police officer. Qualitative data has demonstrated that criminology and criminal justice students express fear around becoming a police officer and expect harsh criticism for deciding to become a police officer due to negative perceptions of police in the United States (Todak, 2017). Morrow et al. (2020) found that criminology students who believe that police are impacted by the legitimacy crisis express more apprehension towards becoming a police officer, but these researchers did not examine participants' own perceptions of legitimacy. The current study expanded on this research by examining this desire in adolescents and testing the empirical relations between legitimacy perceptions and willingness to become a police officer. The results clearly indicated that youths' perceptions of police legitimacy were related to their willingness to become a police officer. Based on the findings from this current study and the research of Todak (2017) and Morrow et al. (2020), it appears that decreased perceptions of police legitimacy may play a role in the decrease in police applicants in the United States. The implications are quite clear; if police officers continue to treat citizens unjustly and if police brutality continues to occur in the United States, police departments will continue to struggle in their recruitment of applicants.

The current study also assessed a gap in the extant literature by assessing how social media exposure is related to adolescents' desire to become a police officer. A previous nationally representative study determined that 97% of adolescents report that they use social media (Anderson & Jiang, 2018). In this current study, 97% of adolescents reported that they are exposed to police-related content on social media. It is possible that most, if not all, adolescents who use social media are exposed to at least some police-related content. Perhaps more importantly, there was a direct relation between youths' valence of social media exposure to police content and their willingness to become a police officer. On the other hand, more social media exposure to negative policing content was related to less desirability to become a police officer. These findings demonstrate how important the content about police officers is on social media. This should inform individual officers about the impact that their actions can have if they are recorded and posted on social media.

Further, we found that social media content about police was related to legitimacy perceptions, where more negative social media content about policing was associated with more negative perceptions of police legitimacy. Researchers have speculated that the decrease in police legitimacy perceptions may stem from increased media exposure to police-related content (Nix & Pickett, 2017). Previous research has demonstrated that media exposure is related to perceptions of police legitimacy in samples of young adults, but studies have not considered social media content specifically related to police or these associations in adolescent samples. For instance, Maguire et al. (2017) found that exposure to procedurally just virtual police encounters predicted more positive legitimacy while exposure to procedurally unjust virtual police encounters predicted more negative legitimacy. The results from this current study highlight the importance that social media exposure may have on the legitimacy crisis and, in turn, adolescent desire to become a police officer. Given that there are so few studies in this area, more research is clearly necessary.

Lastly, we found that perceptions of legitimacy partially mediated the relation between valence of social media exposure to police content and willingness to become a police officer. About 1/3 of the effect that social media exposure to police-related content had on adolescents' willingness to become a police officer was explained through legitimacy perceptions. That means that while legitimacy perceptions were important in explaining the relation, social media exposure appears to have more of a direct influence on the desirability of policing careers. The partially mediated results may be understood through the procedural justice model, which indicates that personal and vicarious experiences with police predict perceptions of trust in the police and, in turn, behavioral outcomes (Sunshine & Tyler, 2003). Social media clearly constitutes a mechanism through which adolescents are vicariously exposed to police-related content; in this study, almost all the adolescents indicated being exposed to police-related content.

Social media has been described as an *information limiting environment*, a term coined by Kitchens et al. (2020) meaning that the platform's 'homophily and algorithmic filtering constrains the information sources that individuals choose to consume.' This concept includes both echo chambers, wherein people are exposed more to conforming opinions than contradicting opinions (Sunstein, 2002), and filter bubbles, wherein social media algorithms personalize content based on opinions and amplify exposure to conforming opinions (Pariser, 2011). Researchers have highlighted that when individuals use social media and search engines to find news articles, they are both more likely to have polarized political ideations and are more likely to be exposed to differing views (Flaxman et al., 2016; Kitchens et al., 2020). Altogether, social affiliation and algorithmic filtering may heavily influence the type of police-related content that youth are exposed to on social media. Youth may seek information and online 'friends' that confirm their beliefs about police, which may also be amplified by social media algorithms meant to expose users to supporting information. If adolescents do not regularly encounter police through direct exposure, it is plausible that their legitimacy perceptions come mostly from their vicarious exposure, especially on social media. Through the procedural justice model, we can see how this vicarious experience might influence legitimacy perceptions and, in turn, adolescents' desire to become a police officer, further demonstrating the impact police-related content can have on adolescents.

The current study has implications for police departments who are attempting to improve themselves through the three goals identified by the Police Executive Research Forum (2019): diversifying, better handling social problems, and possessing desirable characteristics. While exposure to negative police-related content was associated with less willingness to become a police officer, exposure to positive police-related content was still associated with more willingness to become a police officer. Because adolescents spend so much time on social media, as demonstrated by this study and the 2018 Pew Research Report, police departments that are committed to diversifying officers should consider leveraging social media to showcase to youth the changes that departments are trying to make and the types of people they are attempting to recruit. On one hand, a prior study of adults' perceptions of police found that perceptions became more positive in communities whose police departments actively used Twitter to keep the community informed of what their officers are doing day-to-day (Grimmelikhuijsen & Meijer, 2015). Creating police department social media accounts for community members to stay connected to news related to police may be a route for police departments to expose community members to positive content related to police in hopes of diversifying the future faces of law enforcement.

On the other hand, the current research also demonstrates the importance of individual officers' actions. Many of the 'negative' social media posts to which youth are exposed likely reference incidents of police use of force, typically inappropriate use of force. These issues are currently front and center, and legitimately lead to many people having a negative view of police and policing. In the past, if an individual police officer treated an individual unjustly, perceptions of legitimacy would have theoretically decreased for the individual who was treated unjustly (direct exposure) and the friends and family who were told about the unjust encounter (immediate vicarious exposure). Currently, social media vastly expands the number of people who have the potential to be affected by unjust police behavior. When police behave unjustly in the age of social media, the scope and scale of the vicarious impact is dramatically larger. Individual officers must be aware that their actions can have wide-ranging effects. The unjust treatment of a single person could impact the entire population of people who directly use social media or whose communities use social media. It is important to note that this is not to say that procedurally unjust content should be banned from social media. Indeed, sunshine and transparency are clearly needed for enacting change. Rather, these findings indicate that police officers must be aware of the mass impact their actions can have on adolescents who use social media and who enters the entire future workforce in policing.

This study also has implications for research on adolescents' exposure to police. Studies to date focus primarily on the behavioral outcomes of youth that stem from direct and vicarious exposure to police. For instance, a recent study found that 26.8% of youth are directly exposed to police, 50.2% are vicariously exposed through their neighborhood, 47.9% are vicariously exposed through school, and 55.6% are exposed through someone they know (Harris & Jones, 2020). Exposure to police through social media, however, appears much more extensive than direct and vicarious exposure. The current study found that almost all of adolescents are vicariously exposed to police contact through social media. The exposure of adolescents to police contact through social media is astronomical and nearly ubiquitous in our sample. Vicarious exposure through social media was associated with how youth perceived police legitimacy, as would be expected by the procedural justice model. These findings suggest that social media exposure to police should be incorporated in future studies that attempt to understand youths' perceptions of police. Considering nearly two-thirds of the association between social media exposure and interest in becoming a police officer was direct, it also indicates that we are just beginning to scratch the surface of understanding the implications of adolescents' social media exposure to police.

Limitations and Future Directions

One limitation of this study was the use of single-item measures to assess social media exposure to police-related content and willingness to become a police officer. However, this was necessary in order to access this sample of adolescents. Future studies should assess these constructs using multi-item scales, though the face validity of the items we included was strong. Further, this study was cross-sectional and correlational. It cannot be determined if social media exposure had a causal effect on police legitimacy and youths' willingness to become a police officer. We attempted to mitigate endogeneity issues, wherein youth who are more likely to perceive police negatively may be more likely to be exposed to and choose to view negative social media posts about police and vice versa, through accounting for key variables including whether youth personally know a police officer, whether they've been arrested, and whether they've ever been the victim of a crime. However, while that approach partially mitigates the issue, the issue remains nonetheless; the study suggests a key relation that should be parsed further by future work to identify what constellations of factors cause the outcome. Relatedly, no conclusions can be drawn about longitudinal effects. Future studies should attempt to manipulate social media exposure and assess the effect that this exposure has on later willingness to become a police officer. Additionally, we were unable to control for all negative direct encounters with police to isolate the effect of vicarious social media exposure to police. We attempted to control for this by asking if the adolescent had ever been arrested. However, many adolescents may not be arrested but may have frequent negative interactions with police. Relatedly, they may not know at what point they have been arrested (e.g. placed in handcuffs or in the back of a police car). Future study should more robustly control for direct negative encounters with police. Further, future research should more comprehensively assess personal and vicarious effects, including the role of adolescents' family and friends' perceptions of police. That may better isolate and measure the strength of these associations. It may also be the case that family and friends hold certain beliefs and post on behalf of those beliefs on social media. Therefore, the beliefs of family and friends may be more indicative of the relation between youths' social media exposure and their perceptions of police legitimacy, such as the 'echo chamber' theory that people tend to gravitate towards websites and news outlets that support their already held beliefs (Flaxman et al., 2016; Graziano & Gauthier, 2017). On a related note, political orientation should also be assessed in the future to determine how this variable affects perceptions of legitimacy and willingness to become a police officer.

Lastly, due to the racially charged nature of police brutality, future analyses should assess whether the association between the mediation models in this paper change depending on race. We conducted supplemental analyses to assess if the mediation model differed depending on racial/ethnic identification. While we found that the mediation model was significant across races/ethnicities, there were notable differences in the percent in which legitimacy mediated the relation between exposure to social media content about police and willingness to become a police officer. Legitimacy mediated more of the relation for White adolescents than Latinx/Hispanic adolescents and Black adolescents. Additionally, legitimacy mediated more of the relation for Latinx/Hispanic adolescents than Black adolescents. It is possible that social media posts about police may influence non-BIPOC adolescents more, but due to some of the high-profile police brutality instances against BIPOC, Black adolescents in particular may not have as strong of a mediation effect because their perceptions of police may not change as readily when exposed to social media content about police. For them, exposure to unjust police behavior may be a more prevalent feature of their everyday lived experience. Because this was a post-hoc analysis, these results should be used with caution. Future research on these associations is necessary.

Conclusion

Adolescents' exposure to social media content about police was related to their perceptions of police legitimacy and their desire to become a police officer. While many police departments have enacted policies in an attempt to more efficiently handle social problems by diversifying and recruiting officers with desirable characteristics (Police Executive Research Forum, 2019), the recent decreases in applicants makes it very difficult for police departments to recruit officers who have the qualities needed to improve and diversify the police force. Although this study found that higher amounts of exposure to negative police-related content on social media was related to less of a desire to become a police officer, social media itself is not the problem. As long as police officers continue to behave unjustly, there will be negative content about police on social media, which may continue to erode adolescents' perceptions of police and lessen their interest in becoming police officers. Police officers should be aware of the negative implications that their actions can have on adolescents.

Disclosure Statement

No potential conflict of interest was reported by the author(s).

Discussion Questions

1. How did Cross and Fine derive their sample of adolescents? What were reasons for some surveys being discarded?
2. How is police legitimacy associated with perceptions of police? What did Cross and Fine find with regard to how social media influences perceptions of legitimacy and police?
3. Based on your reading of Chapters 6 and 7 of this book, how would you label this research design?

References

Anderson, M., & Jiang, J. (2018). *Teens, Social Media & Technology 2018*. Pew Research Center. http://assets.pewresearch.org/wpcont

ent/uploads/sites/14/2018/05/31102617/PI_2018.05.31_TeensTech_FINAL.pdf

Cohn, E., Bucolo, D., Rebellon, C., & Van Gundy, K. (2010). An integrated model of legal and moral reasoning and rule-violating behavior: The role of legal attitudes. *Law and Human Behavior*, *34*(4), 295–309. https://doi.org/10.1007/s10979-009-9185-9

Fagan, J., & Tyler, T. R. (2005). Legal socialization of children and adolescents. *Social Justice Research*, *18*(3), 217–241. https://doi.org/10.1007/s11211-005-6823-3

Fine, A., Amemiya, J., Frick, P., Steinberg, L., & Cauffman, E. (2021). Perceptions of police legitimacy and Bias from ages 13 to 22 among black, latino, and white justice-involved males. *Law and Human Behavior*, *45*(3), 243–255. https://doi.org/10.1037/lhb0000445

Fine, A., Cavanagh, C., Donley, S., Frick, P. J., Steinberg, L., & Cauffman, E. (2017). Is the effect of justice system attitudes on recidivism stable after youths' first arrest? Race and legal socialization among first-time youth offenders. *Law and Human Behavior*, *41*(2), 146–158. https://doi.org/10.1037/lhb0000229

Fine, A., Simmons, C., & Rowan, Z. (2019). Do politics trump race in determining America's youths' perceptions of law enforcement? *Journal of Criminal Justice*, *61*, 48–57. https://doi.org/10.1016/j.jcrimjus.2019.01.003

Fine, A., Thomas, A., van Rooij, B., & Cauffman, E. (2020). Age-graded differences and parental influences on adolescents' obligation to obey the law. *Journal of Developmental and Life-Course Criminology*, *6*(1), 25–42. https://doi.org/10.1007/s40865-020-00134-8

Flaxman, S., Goel, S., & Rao, J. M. (2016). Filter bubbles, echo chambers, and online news consumption. *Public Opinion Quarterly*, *80*(S1), 298–320. https://doi.org/10.1093/poq/nfw006

Graziano, L. M., & Gauthier, J. F. (2017). Media consumption and perceptions of police legitimacy. *Policing: An International Journal of Police Strategies & Management*, *41*(5), 593–607. https://doi.org/10.1108/PIJPSM-12-2016-0177

Grimmelikhuijsen, S. G., & Meijer, A. J. (2015). Does twitter increase perceived police legitimacy? *Public Administration Review*, *75*(4), 598–607. https://doi.org/10.1111/puar.12378

Harris, J. W., & Jones, M. S. (2020). Shaping youths' perceptions and attitudes toward the police: Differences in direct and vicarious encounters with police. *Journal of Criminal Justice*, *67*, 101674. https://doi.org/10.1016/j.jcrimjus.2020.101674

Hyland, S. S., & Davis, E. (2019 October). *Local police departments 2016: Personnel*. Bureau of Justice Statistics. https://bjs.ojp.gov/content/pub/pdf/lpd16p.pdf

Icenogle, G., Steinberg, L., Duell, N., Chein, J., Chang, L., Chaudhary, N., Di Giunta, L., Dodge, K. A., Fanti, K. A., Lansford, J. E., Oburu, P., Pastorelli, C., Skinner, A. T., Sorbring, E., Tapanya, S., Uribe Tirado, L. M., Alampay, L. P., Al-Hassan, S. M., Takash, H. M. S., & Bacchini, D. (2019). Adolescents' cognitive capacity reaches adult levels prior to their psychosocial maturity: Evidence for a "maturity gap" in a multinational, cross-sectional sample. *Law and Human Behavior*, *43*(1), 69–85. https://doi.org/10.1037/lhb0000315

Intravia, J., Wolff, K. T., & Piquero, A. R. (2018). Investigating the effects of media consumption on attitudes toward police legitimacy. *Deviant Behavior*, *39*(8), 963–980. https://doi.org/10.1080/01639625.2017.1343038

Jackson, J. (2018). Norms, normativity, and the legitimacy of justice institutions: International perspectives. *Annual Review of Law and Social Science*, *14*(1), 145–165. https://doi.org/10.1146/annurev-lawsocsci-110316-113734

Jackson, J., Bradford, B., Hough, M., Myhill, A., Quinton, P., & Tyler, T. R. (2012). Why do people comply with the law? *British Journal of Criminology*, *52*(6), 1051–1071. https://doi.org/10.1093/bjc/azs032

Johnson, D., Wilson, D. B., Maguire, E. R., & Lowrey-Kinberg, B. V. (2017). Race and perceptions of police: Experimental results on the impact of procedural (in)justice. *Justice Quarterly*, *34*(7), 1184–1212. https://doi.org/10.1080/07418825.2017.1343862

Kitchens, B., Johnson, S. L., & Gray, P. (2020). Understanding echo chambers and filter bubbles: The impact of social media on diversification and partisan shifts in news consumption. *MIS Quarterly*, *44*(4), 1619–1649. https://doi.org/10.25300/MISQ/2020/16371

Koster, N. S. N., Kuijpers, K. F., Kunst, M. J. J., & Van der Leun, J. P. (2016). Crime victims' perceptions of police behavior, legitimacy, and cooperation: A review of the literature. *Victims & Offenders*, *11*(3), 392–435. https://doi.org/10.1080/15564886.2015.1065532

Leatherby, L., & Oppel, R. A., Jr. (2020, September 23). Which police departments are as diverse as their communities? *The New York Times*. www.nytimes.com/interactive/2020/09/23/us/bureau-justice-statistics-race.html

Litman, L., Robinson, J., & Abberbock, T. (2017). TurkPrime.com: A versatile crowdsourcing data acquisition platform for the behavioral sciences. *Behavior Research Methods*, *49*(2), 433–442. https://doi.org/10.3758/s13428-016-0727-z

Maguire, E. R., Lowrey, B. V., & Johnson, D. (2017). Evaluating the relative impact of positive and negative encounters with police: A randomized experiment. *Journal of Experimental*

Criminology, *13*(3), 367–391. https://doi.org/10.1007/s11292-016-9276-9

McDonald, C. C., Kennedy, E., Fleisher, L., & Zonfrillo, M. R. (2018). Factors associated with cell phone use while driving: A survey of parents and caregivers of children ages 4-10 years. *The Journal of Pediatrics*, *201*, 208–214. https://doi.org/10.1016/j.jpeds.2018.06.003

McLean, K., Wolfe, S. E., & Pratt, T. C. (2019). Legitimacy and the life course: An age-graded examination of changes in legitimacy attitudes over time. *Journal of Research in Crime and Delinquency*, *56*(1), 42–83. https://doi.org/10.1177/0022427818793934

Morrow, W. J., Vickovic, S. G., & Shjarback, J. A. (2020). Motivation to enter the police profession in the post-Ferguson era: An exploratory analysis of procedural justice. *Criminal Justice Studies*, *34*(2), 1–21. https://doi.org/10.1080/1478601X.2020.1802591

Muthén, B. O., Muthén, L. K., & Asparouhov, T. (2017). *Regression and mediation analysis using Mplus*. Muthén & Muthén.

Muthén, L. K., & Muthén, B. O. (1998–2011). *Mplus user's guide* (6th ed.). Muthén & Muthén.

Nix, J., & Pickett, J. T. (2017). Third-person perceptions, hostile media effects, and policing: Developing a theoretical framework for assessing the Ferguson effect. *Journal of Criminal Justice*, *51*, 24–33. https://doi.org/10.1016/j.jcrimjus.2017.05.016

Nix, J., & Wolfe, S. E. (2017). The impact of negative publicity on police self-legitimacy. *Justice Quarterly*, *34*(1), 84–108. https://doi.org/10.1080/07418825.2015.1102954

Pariser, E. (2011). *The Filter Bubble: What the Internet is hiding from you*. Penguin Press.

Parry, M. M., Moule, R. K., & Dario, L. M. (2019). Technology-mediated exposure to police–citizen encounters: A quasi-experimental assessment of consequences for citizen perceptions. *Justice Quarterly*, *36*(3), 412–436. https://doi.org/10.1080/07418825.2017.1374435

Peck, J. H. (2015). Minority perceptions of the police: A state-of-the-art review. *Policing: An International Journal of Police Strategies & Management*, *38*(1), 173–203. https://doi.org/10.1108/PIJPSM-01-2015-0001

Police Executive Research Forum. (2019). *The workforce crisis, and what police agencies are doing about it*. www.policeforum.org/assets/WorkforceCrisis.pdf

President's Task Force on 21st Century Policing. (2015). *Final report of the President's task force on 21st century policing*. Office of Community Oriented Policing Services.

Skogan, W. G. (2006). Asymmetry in the impact of encounters with police. *Policing & Society*, *16*(2), 99–126. https://doi.org/10.1080/10439460600662098

Slocum, L. A., & Wiley, S. A. (2018). "Experience of the expected?" Race and ethnicity differences in the effects of police contact on youth. *Criminology (Beverly Hills)*, *56*(2), 402–432. https://doi.org/10.1111/1745-9125.12174

Sunshine, J., & Tyler, T. R. (2003). The role of procedural justice and legitimacy in shaping public support for policing. *Law & Society Review*, *37*(3), 513–548. https://doi.org/10.1111/1540-5893.3703002

Sunstein, C. R. (2002). The law of group polarization. *Journal of Political Philosophy*, *10*(2), 175–195. https://doi.org/10.1111/1467-9760.00148

Todak, N. (2017). The decision to become a police officer in a legitimacy crisis. *Women & Criminal Justice*, *27*(4), 250–270. https://doi.org/10.1080/08974454.2016.1256804

Tom, K. E., Fine, A. D., & Pickrel, E. (2021). *Do police videos impact youths' willingness to cooperate with the police?: Results from a national experiment*. Unpublished.

Tyler, T. R. (1990). *Why people obey the law*. Yale University Press.

Tyler, T. R. (2006). Psychological perspectives on legitimacy and legitimation. *Annual Review of Psychology*, *57*(1), 375–400. https://doi.org/10.1146/annurev.psych.57.102904.190038

Tyler, T. R., & Jackson, J. (2014). Popular legitimacy and the exercise of legal authority: Motivating compliance, cooperation, and engagement. *Psychology, Public Policy, and Law*, *20*(1), 78–95. https://doi.org/10.1037/a0034514

Tyler, T. R., & Trinkner, R. (2018). *Why children follow rules: Legal socialization and the development of legitimacy*. Oxford University Press.

Vidal, S., Cleary, H., Woolard, J., & Michel, J. (2017). Adolescents' legal socialization: Effects of interrogation and Miranda knowledge on legitimacy, cynicism, and procedural justice. *Youth Violence and Juvenile Justice*, *15*(4), 419–440. https://doi.org/10.1177/1541204016651479

Walters, G. D., & Bolger, P. C. (2019). Procedural justice perceptions, legitimacy beliefs, and compliance with the law: A meta-analysis. *Journal of Experimental Criminology*, *15*(3), 341–372. https://doi.org/10.1007/s11292-018-9338-2

Wolfe, S. E., Nix, J., Kaminski, R., & Rojek, J. (2016). Is the effect of procedural justice on police legitimacy invariant? Testing the generality of procedural justice and competing antecedents of legitimacy. *Journal of Quantitative Criminology*, *32*(2), 253–282. https://doi.org/10.1007/s10940-015-9263-8

Reading 8.3 Impaired Driving and Other Risky Drug Use and Sex Behaviors

Rural individuals and areas tend to be overlooked in research, likely because they are hard to reach with their wide geographic areas and small sample sizes. As Webster et al. (2024) make clear, it is important to do research on rural populations and locations, as these areas and the people living in them might be facing unique issues. A perfect example of this is Webster et al.'s observation that those involved in car accidents in rural areas will likely have to wait longer for help to arrive and face long trips to the hospital, increasing the chances that injuries will become fatal. The authors of this study were fortunate that they did not have to make multiple trips to the three participating rural jails for years to collect the data, since they were able to use an available dataset for the analysis. The fact remains that some researchers, not just Webster et al., did have to do the sampling and data collection work, and this involved a two-stage sampling plan. The researchers responsible for data collection relied on a purposive sample of women incarcerated in one of three rural jails with a specific release time frame to establish a sampling frame. The second step was to take a random sample of women from that list.

Impaired Driving and Other Risky Drug Use and Sex Behaviors: A Cross-Sectional Examination of High-Risk Rural Women Incarcerated in Jail

J. Matthew Webster, Megan F. Dickson, Martha Tillson, and Michele Staton

Introduction

Impaired driving, or driving under the influence (DUI) of alcohol or drugs, remains a significant public health problem.[1] In 2018, an estimated 20.5 million Americans drove under the influence of alcohol, and an estimated 12.6 million drove while impaired by an illicit drug.[2] Given the significant implications for public safety, impaired driving remains an important area of inquiry with researchers continuing to examine characteristics of emerging groups of impaired drivers and their associated behavior. Two areas of impaired driving research that have grown in recent years include a focus on women and impaired driving in rural communities, though both remain largely understudied.

Women and Impaired Driving

Recent research has highlighted that an increasing proportion of individuals arrested for impaired driving are women,[3,4] and a growing number of women are involved in impaired driving crashes,[5] including those that result in a fatality.[6] Several explanations for women's increasing role in impaired driving offenses and crashes have been offered, including: (1) increasing rates of women who drive and longer distances traveled, (2) women's changing substance use patterns, (3) the lowering of the legal blood alcohol concentration (BAC) limits from .10 g/dL to .08 g/dL, and (4) more consistent law enforcement practices in arresting men and women for impaired driving (i.e., no longer being more lenient with women).[7] Other research suggests that risky driving behaviors, in general, have become more common among women, particularly younger women, which may also help explain their increase in impaired driving.[6,8]

Thus, more research attention has been placed on understanding the characteristics of women who drive impaired. For example, compared to male impaired drivers, female impaired drivers have been found to be younger, more likely to be white, less likely to be married, and have more severe mental health, trauma histories, and substance use problems.[9,10] While most studies of female impaired drivers have focused on women arrested for DUI and their behavioral health treatment needs and recidivism risk,[10,11] few studies have examined impaired driving in the context of other health risk behaviors, particularly among women living in rural communities where substance use and related problems may be more prevalent and health services more limited.[12,13]

Rural Impaired Drivers

Overall, rural impaired drivers have been identified as a group warranting more attention.[1,14] National data indicate higher impaired driving arrest rates in less populated, nonmetropolitan areas compared to metropolitan areas of the United States.[15] Similarly, the majority of U.S. studies included in a recent scoping review of alcohol-related harm found higher prevalence of alcohol impaired driving in rural areas compared to urban areas.[16] This finding is consistent with Fatality Analysis Reporting System data, which indicate that fatal traffic accidents involving an alcohol-impaired driver occur at a disproportionately higher rate in rural areas of the U.S.[17]

Prior research has identified several differences between rural and urban impaired drivers. One early study directly compared clinical assessment records for rural and urban impaired drivers and found greater drug use severity and higher rates of substance use disorders, as well as lower compliance with clinical referrals, among rural impaired drivers.[18] Other research has shown greater risk of heavy alcohol use among rural impaired drivers with fewer drug differences between groups.[19] More recently, high rates of drugged driving among rural impaired drivers have been noted. In a purposive sample of rural impaired drivers, 77% reported driving after illicit drug use during their lifetime and 60% indicated they had driven drug-impaired in the past year.[20] Another study examining individuals with multiple impaired driving convictions found higher rates of substance use and mental health problems among rural impaired drivers compared to several earlier studies which utilized urban samples.[21]

Only a few impaired driving studies, however, have focused specifically on rural women. This is a noteworthy gap given the increasing number of female impaired drivers,[3,4] the higher rates of impaired driving and road fatalities in rural areas,[14,22] and the significant health disparities experienced by rural women related to mental health, substance use, and access to care.[23–25] A recent study examined correlates of past year impaired driving histories as well as the types of substances involved in impaired driving episodes in a sample of high-risk rural women incarcerated in jails.[26] Despite all participants having a recent history of substance use, women who reported driving impaired were significantly more likely to use eight of 11 different substances, but no differences in the number of mental health problems or criminal history were found. Although this study added new information on the types of substances involved in impaired driving as well as the substance use, mental health, and criminal histories among high-risk rural women, it only examined whether women used a particular substance in the year prior to incarceration, ignoring the substance use severity and level of risk associated with their substance use. Furthermore, with the exception of impaired driving and criminal history, no other risk behaviors associated with substance use were examined or how they may be associated with a history of impaired driving. This is an important knowledge gap given that rural women who use substances, especially those who are also justice-involved, have been shown to increasingly engage in other health risk behaviors.[27]

Current Study

The objective of the present study was to reexamine the sample of high-risk rural women incarcerated in jails described by Webster et al.[26] to assess the extent impaired driving history is related to engaging in risky substance use and related health risk behaviors. Specifically, it was hypothesized that impaired drivers would report more severe and riskier patterns of substance use than women who did not drive impaired in the past year. Furthermore, it was expected that a higher proportion of impaired drivers would report engaging in other health risk behaviors (e.g., trading sex) often associated with substance use.

Materials and Methods

Participants

Four hundred women from three rural jails in rural Kentucky were randomly selected, screened, and consented to participate in a larger intervention study on drug use and health risk behavior among rural, justice-involved women. Similar to previous impaired driving research,[18] rurality was defined as a county having a Rural-Urban Continuum Code of five or greater.[28] Eligibility criteria included: (1) moderate risk of substance abuse based on the NIDA-modified Alcohol, Smoking and Substance Involvement Screening Test (NM-ASSIST) score of 4+ for any drug;[29] (2) self-reported sex risk behaviors in the three months before arrest, based on five questions from the risk behavioral assessment;[30] (3) residing in a designated rural Appalachian county before incarceration; (4) an anticipated release date between two weeks and three months from screening (to accommodate the intervention); (5) and a willingness to participate.

Procedure

Recruitment and Screening

Recruitment dates were randomized monthly for each of the three jails between December 2012 and August 2015. On each date, research staff worked with jail administrators to review jail rosters and identify women who had at least two weeks but no more than three months remaining on their sentence according to jail records. This timeframe was critical for the delivery of the intervention as part of the larger study on drug use and health risk behavior. All women with a release date meeting this criterion were included in the sampling frame and had equal opportunity to be selected for the study screening session.

Research staff then randomly selected 10 to 20 women from this sampling frame for study screening on each recruitment day. A total of 900 women were randomly selected from the three rural jails and invited to participate in one of several group screening sessions to determine study eligibility. Screening sessions were conducted by research staff in a confidential room in the jail. No jail staff were present. Research staff provided study details and answered questions. Women interested in participating provided written informed consent and completed measures to determine eligibility. Additional details about the screening procedures have been described previously.[27]

A total of 688 women (76.44% of those randomly selected) completed the eligibility screening. Those who did not participate in the screening either refused (n = 101) or were released from jail between screening recruitment and their scheduled screening session (n = 111). Of those participating in a screening session, 440 (63.95%) met all study eligibility criteria for the intervention study. The majority of women who were ineligible for the study could not participate because they reported release dates falling outside the two-week to three-month window despite initial screening from jail rosters (n = 203). Significantly fewer women were ineligible based on the NM-ASSIST (n = 9), risky sex behavior (n = 15), or residence (n = 21) criteria. Forty of the 440 women who met all study eligibility criteria were released from jail prior to being scheduled for a baseline interview. Thus, the final sample consisted of 400 high-risk women incarcerated in jail with histories of substance use and risky sex.

Baseline Interview

Individuals who provided consent and met screening criteria were scheduled for a baseline interview. Structured interviews were conducted face-to-face by a trained female interviewer from the study team in a private room at the jail; no jail staff were present for baseline interviews. Participants responded to questions about their drug use and other health risk behaviors prior to entering jail. Responses were recorded using computer-assisted personal interview software by the research interviewer. Participants were paid $25 for their time. All study screening and data collection procedures were approved after full review by the University of Kentucky Medical Institutional Review Board #6 (protocol #12-0372-F6A approved on 5/16/2012; Lexington, KY) and performed in accordance with the principles stated in the Declaration of Helsinki. Participant responses were protected under a federal Certificate of Confidentiality.

Measures

Demographics

Demographic information collected from participants included their age, race, marital status, years of education, and employment status in the six months prior to incarceration. Given that the sample was recruited from jails, the length of their current incarceration was collected. Participants also reported if they had ever served time in prison as a proxy measure for more serious criminal involvement.

Because mental health has been shown to be an important contributor to risk behavior, particularly among substance-using populations,[31] a measure of mental health symptoms was included. Participants completed the mental health section of the Global Appraisal of Individual Needs (GAIN).[32] The GAIN is a screening instrument used to assess symptoms associated with major depressive disorder, generalized anxiety disorder, and posttraumatic stress disorder. For purposes of the present study, participants were coded as either having or not having symptoms consistent with diagnostic criteria for any of the three disorders.

Risk Behaviors

Because the present study involved secondary analysis of an existing data set, authors reviewed the data codebook to identify all health risk behavior variables. These included measures of substance use, injection drug practices, sex risk behaviors, and impaired driving.

Substance use. The NIDA-Modified Alcohol, Smoking, and Substance Involvement Screening Test (NM-ASSIST);[29] was used to measure participants' drug use problem severity and level of risk. At screening, participants were asked six questions related to intensity and frequency of use of cannabis, cocaine, prescription stimulants, methamphetamine, inhalants, hallucinogens, sedatives, street opioids, and prescription opioids in the three months prior to incarceration. A Substance Involvement (SI) score was computed using standard scoring procedures for each drug, which ranged from 0 to 39 with higher scores indicating more risky use. Items comprising each SI score had acceptable internal consistency (Cronbach's alpha: cannabis [α=.82], cocaine [α=.90], prescription stimulants [α=.90], methamphetamine [α=.92], inhalants [α=.92], hallucinogens [α= .90], sedatives [α=.89], street opioids [α=.92], and prescription opioids [α=.88]).

Participants also completed the Substance Problem Scale (SPS) of the GAIN. This 16-item measure of problematic alcohol and drug use is based on DSM-IV-TR criteria (α=.94). The SPS was included as a second measure of drug use because it corresponds to the same timeframe (i.e., one year prior to incarceration) used for other measures of risk behaviors used in the study. However, unlike the NM-ASSIST, the SPS provides a single (0 to 16) score of substance use severity, rather than scores for individual drugs. Higher SPS scores indicate more severe substance use problems.

Injection drug use practices. Participants were also asked about their injection drug use practices in the year prior to incarceration: whether they injected drugs, used shared needles/injection equipment, and the number of people with whom they shared needles/injection equipment.

Sex risk behaviors. Participants provided information on their sex risk behaviors in the year prior to incarceration. Specifically, participants reported their number of sex partners and casual sex partners as well as whether they engaged in transactional sex (i.e., traded sex for money/drugs/food). The casual sex partner variable was dichotomized to stay consistent with the measurement of other risk behaviors (i.e., injection drug use, transactional sex, and riding with an impaired driver), whereas the number of sex partners was left continuous since having multiple sex partners, not simply having a sex partner, is typically viewed as riskier behavior.

Impaired driving. Finally, participants were asked whether they had driven under the influence of drugs or alcohol in the year prior to incarceration. They also reported whether they were the passenger of an impaired driver during this time period.

Analytic Plan

Nine participants from the full sample were removed due to missing data. Two of these were missing the impaired driving variable used to define groups for analysis. The remaining removed participants had missing data on measures of other risk behavior (NM-ASSIST scores [n = 4], injection drug use [n = 2], or trading sex [n = 1]), leaving 391 participants for analyses. Then, the data were stratified based on whether participants indicated they had driven under the influence of drugs or alcohol in the year prior to incarceration (n = 260 yes; n = 131 no). These two groups were compared on demographic characteristics, including mental health, using a series of t-tests for continuous variables and chi-square analyses for dichotomous variables. The purpose of these analyses was to identify any preexisting group differences that should serve as covariates in subsequent analyses examining group differences in risk behaviors.

Next, the two groups were compared on their risky drug- and sex-related risk behaviors controlling for demographic differences. Multivariate analysis of covariance (MANCOVA) was used as an omnibus test for continuous measures of risk behavior (SPS and SI scores, number of people with whom they shared needles/injection equipment, and number of sex partners). Box's M Test of Equality of Covariance Matrices and Pillai's Trace were used to test for homogeneity of variance-covariance and homogeneity of regression slopes. Post-hoc analysis of covariance analyses were then conducted to determine group differences on individual, continuously measured variables. With a sample size of 391, analyses were powered at 99% to detect a medium effect size (η^2 =.06) between group differences with a two-tailed alpha = .05.

Logistic regression analyses were used for risk behaviors measured dichotomously (past year injection drug use, sharing needles/injection equipment, having a casual sex partner, traded sex, and passenger of an impaired driver). Variance Inflation Factor (VIF) and Tolerance were used to test for multicollinearity in logistic models. Results indicated that no variable had a tolerance level below the cutoff value of 0.1, and no variable had a VIF value higher than 10. A Box-Tidwell test was used to test for linearity in the logit. The logistic regression models were powered at 89% to detect an odds ratio of 2.0 with a two-tailed alpha=.05.

All group differences were considered statistically significant at $p < .05$. Analyses were conducted using SPSS 28.[33]

Results

The average age of study participants was 32.74 (SD = 8.23) years old. Most of the sample was white (98.98%) and had less than a high school education (11.09 years of education, SD = 2.28). Approximately one-fourth (23.02%) of participants were employed at least part-time prior to incarceration, and 37.34% of participants were married or living as married. As shown in Table 1, age was the only demographic variable that significantly

Table 1 Demographic information by past year impaired driving

	Past year Impaired driving		*Total (N = 391)*
	Yes (n = 260)	*No (n = 131)*	
Age (years)**	31.90	34.42	32.74
% White	98.85	99.24	98.98
% Married/living as married	36.92	38.17	37.34
Education (years completed)	11.24	10.79	11.09
% Employed at least part-time 6 months prior to incarceration	25.00	19.08	23.02
Days currently incarcerated	74.69	62.27	70.53
% Ever served time in prison	17.69	12.98	16.11
% Having symptoms consistent with a mental health disorder	83.07	78.62	81.59

Note. *$p \leq .05$, **$p \leq .01$, and ***$p \leq .001$ indicates significant differences between women who drove impaired in the past year and those who did not.

differed between impaired drivers and the comparison group of other high-risk rural women incarcerated in jail with impaired drivers being significantly younger (M = 31.90, SD = 7.67 vs. M = 34.42, SD = 9.04; t[226.62] = 2.73, p = .007, d = .309, 95% CI [0.098, 0.520]). Thus, age was the only demographic variable included as a covariate in subsequent analyses.

The MANCOVA examining the linear combination of all continuously measured risk behaviors yielded a significant main effect of past year impaired driving history, F(12, 377) = 6.14, $p < .001$, Wilks' λ = 0.84, partial η^2 = 0.16. As shown in Figure 1, post-hoc ANCOVA analyses found that impaired drivers reported significantly higher SPS scores (M = 13.97, SD = 3.12) than the comparison group (M = 10.21, SD = 6.03; F[16, 363] = 4.90, $p < .001$, partial η^2 = .0.17, 95% CI [-0.87, -0.48]). Additionally, impaired drivers had higher substance involvement scores on the NM-ASSIST for cannabis (M = 12.79, SD = 11.62 vs. M = 10.60, SD = 12.00; F[36, 353] = 1.64, p=.014, partial η^2 = 0.14, 95% CI [-0.69, -0.07]), prescription opioids (M = 30.48, SD = 12.26 vs. M = 22.20, SD = 14.89; F[36,353] = 1.88, p = .002, partial η^2 = 0.16, 95% CI [-0.51, -0.17]), and sedatives (M = 21.92, SD = 14.34 vs. M = 16.16, SD = 14.82; F[38, 351] = 1.85, p = .002, partial η^2 = 0.17, 95% CI [-0.42, -0.11]). Impaired drivers also reported sharing needles and/or injection equipment with significantly more people (M = 3.26, SD = 8.53 vs. M = 1.61, SD = 5.74; F[16, 373] = 1.82, p = .027, partial η^2 = 0.07, 95% CI [-3.28, -0.03]). The number of sex partners did not significantly differ between groups.

Logistic regression analyses controlling for age also detected multiple group differences (see Figure 2). Specifically, impaired drivers were significantly more likely to report injecting drugs (69.2% vs. 41.98%; B = 1.07, SE = 0.23, $p < .001$; AOR = 2.90, 95% CI [1.86, 4.55]); using shared needles and/or shared injection equipment (69.23% vs. 40.46%; B = 1.11, SE = 0.23, $p < .001$; AOR = 3.05, p=.000, 95% CI [1.95, 4.77]); having a casual sex partner (47.31% vs. 25.95%; B = 0.88, SE = 0.24, p = < .001; AOR = 2.41, 95% CI [1.51,3.84]); having traded sex for drugs and/or money (31.15% vs. 15.27%; B = 0.86, SE = 0.28, p = .002; AOR = 2.36, 95% CI [1.37,4.09]); and being the passenger of an impaired driver (78.08% vs. 53.44%; B = 1.05, SE = 0.24, $p < .001$; AOR = 2.85, 95% CI [1.80, 4.52]) in the past year.

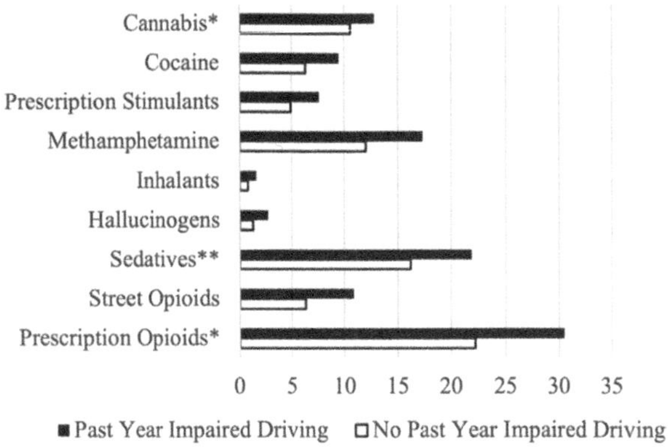

Figure 1 Average NM-ASSIST substance involvement scores by past year impaired driving history

Note. Group comparisons were performed with ANCOVA controlling for participant age. Statistically significant group differences are indicated by *p ≤ .05, **p ≤ .01, ***p ≤ .001.

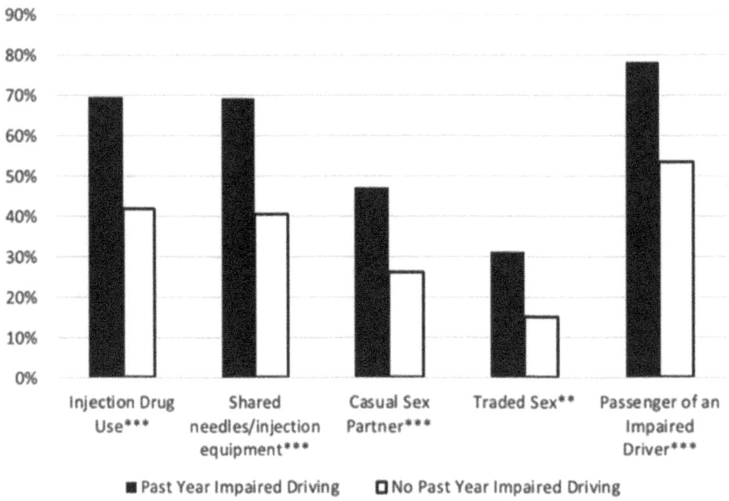

Figure 2 Other past year health risk behaviors by past year impaired driving history

Note. Group comparisons were performed with logistic regression controlling for participant age. Statistically significant group differences are indicated by *p ≤ .05, **p ≤ .01, ***p ≤ .001.

Discussion

The present study compared the health risk behaviors of women who self-reported impaired driving in the past year to women who did not in a sample of high-risk rural women incarcerated in jail with histories of substance use and risky sex. Overall, impaired drivers reported engaging in more drug use prior to incarceration and other health risk behaviors than women in the comparison group. These findings add to the impaired driving literature in two important ways.

First, to our knowledge, this is the only study to use an evidence-based screening tool to examine drug use problem severity for specific drugs and level of risk among rural female impaired drivers. The use of the NM-ASSIST allowed for the examination of SI scores for nine separate drug types, providing both drug use breadth and severity information. Although the sample consisted entirely of drug-involved women, impaired drivers had a consistent pattern of higher NM-ASSIST SI scores for all nine drugs with differences for cannabis, sedatives, and prescription opioids reaching statistical significance. These SI scores are consistent with other studies showing that cannabis is the drug most frequently involved in impaired driving[34] with prescription medications among the next most prevalent.[35] Furthermore, the drug use profiles of the impaired drivers are consistent with another examination of rural (convicted) impaired drivers, which reported cannabis, sedatives, and prescription opioids as the drugs most frequently involved in self-reported drugged driving episodes.[20]

Differences in SPS scores among impaired drivers provide further support for higher levels of problematic substance use among rural female impaired drivers in this sample. Taken together, the SI and SPS scores suggest that, even among a rural sample of high-risk women incarcerated in jail, those with an impaired driving history may be at a heightened need for substance use treatment not only to address their own needs but to reduce the threat to public safety they present.[1] Untreated substance use may lead to further impaired driving, which is particularly risky in rural areas where delays in crash detection and farther distances to medical care contribute to higher rates of traffic fatalities.[14]

Second, the current study adds to our understanding of other health risk behaviors among rural female impaired drivers, which included higher rates of drug injection use and risky injection practices, having casual sex, engaging in transactional sex, and riding with an impaired driver. Although existing research has highlighted substance use problem severity as a correlate of each of these health risk behaviors,[27,36,37] to our knowledge the associations found between impaired driving and both injection drug use and risky sex behavior is a new finding. The literature on the clustering of risk behaviors has shown consistent associations between substance use and risky sex, particularly among adolescent and young adult samples.[36,38] Fewer studies, however, have examined impaired driving in the context of other co-occurring risk behaviors,[39,40] and none to our knowledge have examined impaired driving and other risk behavior among rural women. Future research should more carefully explore these relationships to determine if they are replicated in other samples of impaired drivers.

Although the present study found no association between self-reported impaired driving and mental health symptoms, it is notable that more than 80% of participants had symptoms consistent with a mental health disorder. Multiple studies have shown that individuals with mental health issues are more likely to engage in risk behaviors,[36,41] and so a closer examination of the role of mental health and other risk behavior among impaired drivers is warranted.

Study findings also point to the importance of comprehensive assessment of women who drive impaired to identify and appropriately target intervention and treatment efforts. While substance use is typically the primary intervention focus for women convicted of an impaired driving offense, the present study with self-reported impaired drivers suggests that other health risk behaviors, such as transactional sex, may be more prevalent among this group and therefore could benefit from additional services. Because higher levels of injection drug use and risky sex behavior put individuals at risk for infections such as HIV and HCV,[42–44] early intervention could prevent the spread of infection and may be particularly important in rural communities, which experience a disproportionate risk for burden of disease[45] in part due to limited or inadequate resources and services.[46]

In addition to highlighting the need for comprehensive assessment of rural women incarcerated in jail, results suggest that knowledge of recent impaired driving behavior (regardless of arrest) could help identify women in jail who are at higher risk for engaging in significant health risk behavior once released. Previous research indicates community reentry as a vulnerable time for individuals with a history of drug use. Without appropriate resources and supports, many individuals who used drugs prior to incarceration will return to drug use once released from jail, putting them at risk for multiple negative health consequences including overdose.[47] If future research were to establish that impaired driving prospectively predicts engaging in other health risk behavior, screening for impaired driving history during incarceration might function as a useful tool for identifying individuals in most need of prevention services.

Limitations

Study limitations should be considered when interpreting results. First, sample characteristics may limit the generalizability of study findings to other rural female impaired drivers or groups of justice-involved women. Future researchers should attempt to examine impaired driving and other health risk behaviors in more heterogeneous samples. Second, impaired driving and other health risk behaviors were examined only in the year prior to incarceration; as a result, the relationship between long-term patterns of health risk behavior and impaired driving among rural females is unknown. Third, the present study examined impaired driving and most other health risk behaviors as dichotomous variables. A closer examination between impaired driving frequency and the frequency of other health risk behaviors may provide more detailed information on the associations between these health risk behaviors. Finally, all data were self-reported. While self-report is common in social and behavioral research and has been shown to be valid for self-reported substance use,[48,49] the accuracy of these data could not be assessed.

Despite these limitations, the current study has several strengths. First, this is among the first studies to examine co-occurring risk behaviors in a sample of high-risk women with a history of impaired driving, and to our knowledge, perhaps the only to examine these behaviors among rural female impaired drivers. In addition, the current study examined multiple risk behaviors, all using a uniform one-year timeframe. Although other studies have shown a clustering of risk behaviors, the present research found new associated risk behaviors (e.g., impaired driving and injection drug use) in this sample. Furthermore, an evidence-based substance use screening instrument was used, providing a substance use risk score which future impaired driving research could incorporate. Finally, the high rates of health risk behavior found in the present study point to clear opportunities to intervene with rural women in jail with histories of impaired driving. Taken together, these strengths mitigate study limitations and provide a foundation for future research in this area.

Conclusion

This study found a consistent association between past year impaired driving and a range of drug use- and sex-related risk behaviors in a sample of high-risk rural women incarcerated in jail. These findings add to the literature on rural women impaired drivers, which is particularly important given the increasing number of women who drive impaired and the limited information on rural impaired drivers despite disproportionately higher rates of fatal accidents caused by impaired drivers in rural areas. Research should continue to develop a better understanding of these groups of impaired drivers with the goal of reducing their participation in this dangerous behavior.

Disclosure Statement

No potential conflict of interest was reported by the authors.

Funding

This was work supported by the National Institute on Drug Abuse under Grant R01DA033866 (Staton, PI). Opinions expressed are those of the authors and do not represent the position of the National Institute on Drug Abuse.

Discussion Questions

1. The researchers who collected the data for the Webster et al. study had two different stages of sampling to find their group of incarcerated women to participate in their interviews. Describe both.
2. Webster et al. relied on secondary data for their study, meaning that they did not collect the data themselves. Instead, they relied on a dataset that other researchers made in the process of doing their own research. In what ways did relying on others' data impact their study, and what could Webster et al. have done differently had they been in charge of the data collection plan?
3. How were high-risk behaviors in the Webster et al. study operationalized?

References

1. Wyatt, B., & Novotna, G. (2021). Driving under the influence of alcohol and drugs: A scoping review. *Journal of Social Work Practice in the Addictions*, *21*(2), 119–138. http://doi.org/10.1080/1533256X.2021.1893952
2. Center for Behavioral Health Statistics and Quality. (2019). *Results from the 2018 national survey on drug use and health: Detailed tables*. www.samhsa.gov/data/report/2018-nsduh-detailed-tables
3. Oh, S., Vaughn, M. G., Salas-Wright, C. P., AbiNader, M. A., & Sanchez, M. (2020). Driving under the influence of alcohol: Findings from the NSDUH, 2002–2017. *Addictive Behaviors*, *108*, 106439. http://doi.org/10.1016/j.addbeh.2020.106439
4. Schwartz, J., & Beltz, L. (2018). Trends in female and male drunken driving prevalence over thirty years: triangulating diverse sources of evidence (1985–2015). *Addictive Behaviors*, *84*, 7–12. http://doi.org/10.1016/j.addbeh.2018.03.024
5. Vaca, F. E., Romano, E., & Fell, J. C. (2014). Female drivers increasingly involved in impaired driving crashes: Actions to ameliorate the risk. *Academic Emergency Medicine*, *21*(12), 1485–1492. http://doi.org/10.1111/acem.12542
6. Romano, E., Kelley-Baker, T., & Voas, R. B. (2008). Female involvement in fatal crashes: Increasingly riskier or increasingly exposed? *Accident Analysis & Prevention*, *40*(5), 1781–1788. http://doi.org/10.1016/j.aap.2008.06.016
7. Robertson, A. A., Liew, H., & Gardner, S. (2011). An evaluation of the narrowing gender gap in DUI arrests. *Accident Analysis & Prevention*, *43*(4), 1414–1420. http://doi.org/10.1016/j.aap.2011.02.017
8. Beck, K. H., Daughters, S. B., & Ali, B. (2013). Hurried driving: Relationship to distress tolerance, driver anger, aggressive and risky driving in college students. *Accident Analysis & Prevention*, *51*, 51–55. http://doi.org/10.1016/j.aap.2012.10.012
9. Hohman, M., Barker, M., & Woodruff, S. (2017). What lies beneath: Trauma events, PTSD, and alcohol misuse in driving under the influence program clients. *Journal of Social Work Practice in the Addictions*, *17*(1–2), 95–113. http://doi.org/10.1080/1533256X.2017.1302885
10. Reilly, K., Woodruff, S. I., Hohman, M., & Barker, M. (2019). Gender differences in driving under the influence (DUI) program client characteristics: Implications for treatment delivery. *Women & Health*, *59*(2), 132–144. http://doi.org/10.1080/03630242.2018.1434589
11. Robertson, A. A., Zhou, Q. M., Tatch, A., Walsh, M. (2019). Gender-specific predictors of recidivism among DUI offenders. *Journal of Studies on Alcohol and Drugs*, *80*(6), 641–650. http://doi.org/10.15288/jsad.2019.80.641
12. Jones, C. M., Compton, W. M., & Mustaquim, D. (2020). Patterns and characteristics of methamphetamine use among adults—United States, 2015–2018. *MMWR Morbidity and Mortality Weekly Report*, *69*(12), 317–323. http://doi.org/10.15585/mmwr.mm6912a1
13. Moody, L. N., Satterwhite, E., & Bickel, W. K. (2017). Substance use in rural central Appalachia: Current status and treatment considerations. *Journal of Rural Mental Health*, *41*(2), 123–135. http://doi.org/10.1037/rmh0000064
14. Robertson, R. D., Wicklund, C., Holmes, E., & Biderman, P. (2016). *Impaired driving in rural jurisdictions: Problems and solutions*. www.deslibris.ca/ID/10050905
15. Federal Bureau of Investigation (FBI). (2018). *Crime in the United States, 2017*. https://ucr.fbi.gov/crime-in-the-u.s/2017/crime-in-the-u.s.-2017/tables/table-31
16. Friesen, E. L., Bailey, J., Hyett, S., Sedighi, S., de Snoo, M. L., Williams, K., Barry, R., Erickson, A., Foroutan, F., Selby, P., et al. (2022). Hazardous alcohol use and alcohol-related harm in rural and remote communities: A scoping review. *The Lancet Public Health*, *7*(2), e177–e187. http://doi.org/10.1016/S2468-2667(21)00159-6

17. National Center for Statistics and Analysis. (2020). *Rural/urban comparison of traffic fatalities: 2018 data.* (DOT HS 812 957; Traffic Safety Facts). National Highway Traffic Safety Administration.
18. Webster, J. M., Dickson, M. F., Duvall, J. L., & Clark, D. B. (2010). Rural and urban differences in Kentucky DUI offenders. *Journal of Addiction Medicine*, *4*(3), 186–190. http://doi.org/10.1097/ADM.0b013e3181c6cb24
19. Malek-Ahmadi, M., & Degiorgio, L. (2015). Risk of alcohol abuse in urban versus rural DUI offenders. *The American Journal of Drug and Alcohol Abuse*, *41*(4), 353–357. http://doi.org/10.3109/00952990.2015.1043436
20. Webster, J. M., Dickson, M. F., & Staton, M. (2018). A descriptive analysis of drugged driving among rural DUI offenders. *Traffic Injury Prevention*, *19*(5), 462–467. http://doi.org/10.1080/15389588.2018.1450980
21. Dickson, M. F., Wasarhaley, N. E., & Webster, J. M. (2013). A comparison of first-time and repeat rural DUI offenders. *Journal of Offender Rehabilitation*, *52*(6), 421–437. http://doi.org/10.1080/10509674.2013.813616
22. Duren, M., Ehsani, J., Grant, B., & Fowler, D. (2019). Geographic variation and trends in opioid-involved crash deaths in Maryland: 2006–2017. *Accident Analysis & Prevention*, *125*, 1–6. http://doi.org/10.1016/j.aap.2019.01.012
23. American College of Obstetricians and Gynecologists. (2014). Health disparities in rural women. *Obstetrics & Gynecology*, *123*(2 Pt 1), 384–388.
24. Bolin, J. N., Bellamy, G., Ferdinand, A. O., Kash, B. A., & Helduser, J. W. (Eds.). (2015). *Rural healthy people 2020*. Vol. 1. Texas A&M Health Science Center School of Public Health, Southwest Rural Health Research Center.
25. Bushy, A. (2012). Health issues of women in rural United States: An overview. In B. D. Leipert, B. Leach, & W. E. Thurson (Eds.), *Rural women's health* (pp. 80–97). University of Toronto Press.
26. Webster, J. M., Tillson, M., Dickson, M. F., & Staton, M. (2020). Impaired driving among rural female drug-involved offenders. *Traffic Injury Prevention*, *21*(8), 513–520. http://doi.org/10.1080/15389588.2020.1810244
27. Staton, M., Ciciurkaite, G., Havens, J., Tillson, M., Leukefeld, C., Webster, M., Oser, C., & Peteet, B. (2018). Correlates of injection drug use among rural Appalachian women. *The Journal of Rural Health*, *34*(1), 31–41. http://doi.org/10.1111/jrh.12256
28. United States Department of Agriculture Economic Research Service. (2020). 2013 Rural-Urban continuum codes. www.ers.usda.gov/data-products/rural-urban-continuum-codes.aspx
29. National Institute on Drug Abuse (NIDA). (2009). *NIDA modified-ASSIST*. http://www.drugabuse.gov/nidamed/screening/
30. Wechsberg, W. M. (1998). *The revised risk behavior assessment*. Research Triangle Institute.
31. Morley, K. I., Lynskey, M. T., Moran, P., Borschmann, R., & Winstock, A. R. (2015). Polysubstance use, mental health and high-risk behaviours: Results from the 2012 Global Drug Survey. *Drug and Alcohol Review*, *34*(4), 427–437. http://doi.org/10.1111/dar.12263
32. Dennis, M. L. (1998). *Global Appraisal of Individual Needs (GAIN)*. Chestnut Health Systems.
33. *IBM SPSS Statistics for Macintosh (28.0)*. (2021). [Computer software]. IBM.
34. Pearlson, G. D., Stevens, M. C., & D'Souza, D. C. (2021). Cannabis and driving. *Frontiers in Psychiatry*, *12*, 689444. http://doi.org/10.3389/fp-syt.2021.689444
35. National Institute on Drug Abuse (NIDA). (2021). *Drugged driving drug facts*. www.drugabuse.gov/publications/drugfacts/drugged-driving#ref
36. Luk, J. W., Worley, M. J., Winiger, E., Trim, R. S., Hopfer, C. J., Hewitt, J. K., Brown, S. A., & Wall, T. L. (2016). Risky driving and sexual behaviors as developmental outcomes of co-occurring substance use and antisocial behavior. *Drug and Alcohol Dependence*, *169*, 19–25. http://doi.org/10.1016/j.drugalcdep.2016.10.006
37. Roberts, W., Moore, K. E., Pittman, B. P., Fillmore, M. T., & McKee, S. A. (2019). High risk of alcohol-impaired driving in adults with comorbid alcohol and substance use disorders in the U.S. population. *Journal of Studies on Alcohol and Drugs*, *80*(1), 114–119. http://doi.org/10.15288/jsad.2019.80.114
38. Meader, N., King, K., Moe-Byrne, T., Wright, K., Graham, H., Petticrew, M., Power, C., White, M., & Sowden, A. J. (2016). A systematic review on the clustering and co-occurrence of multiple risk behaviours. *BMC Public Health*, *16*(1), 1–9. http://doi.org/10.1186/s12889-016-3373-6
39. Cook, S., Shank, D., Bruno, T., Turner, N. E., & Mann, R. E. (2017). Self-reported driving under the influence of alcohol and cannabis among Ontario students: associations with graduated licensing, risk taking, and substance abuse. *Traffic Injury Prevention*, *18*(5), 449–455. http://doi.org/10.1080/15389588.2016.1149169
40. McDonald, C. C, Sommers, M. S., & Fargo, J. D. (2014). Risky driving, mental health, and health-compromising behaviours: Risk clustering in late adolescents and adults. *Injury Prevention*, *20*(6), 365–372. http://doi.org/10.1136/injuryprev-2014-041150

41. Kwan, M. Y., Arbour-Nicitopoulos, K. P., Duku, E., & Faulkner, G. (2016). Patterns of multiple health risk–behaviours in university students and their association with mental health: Application of latent class analysis. *Health Promotion and Chronic Disease Prevention in Canada, 36*(8), 163–170. http://doi.org/10.24095/hpcdp.36.8.03
42. Centers for Disease Control and Prevention. (2019). *Injection drug use and HIV risk*. www.cdc.gov/hiv/pdf/risk/cdc-hiv-idu-fact-sheet.pdf
43. Jenness, S. M., Kobrak, P., Wendel, T., Neaigus, A., Murrill, C. S., & Hagan, H. (2011). Patterns of exchange sex and HIV infection in high-risk heterosexual men and women. *Journal of Urban Health, 88*(2), 329–341. http://doi.org/10.1007/s11524-010-9534-5
44. Liang, T. J., & Ward, J. W. (2018). Hepatitis C in injection-drug users—A hidden danger of the opioid epidemic. *New England Journal of Medicine, 378*(13), 1169–1171. http://doi.org/10.1056/NEJMp1716871
45. Van Handel, M. M., Rose, C. E., Hallisey, E. J., Kolling, J. L., Zibbell, J. E., Lewis, B., Bohm, M. K., Jones, C. M., Flanagan, B. E., Siddiqi, A. E. A., et al. (2016). County-level vulnerability assessment for rapid dissemination of HIV or HCV infections among persons who inject drugs, United States. *JAIDS Journal of Acquired Immune Deficiency Syndromes, 73*(3), 323–331. http://doi.org/10.1097/QAI.0000000000001098
46. Browne, T., Priester, M. A., Clone, S., Iachini, A., DeHart, D., & Hock, R. (2016). Barriers and facilitators to substance use treatment in the Rural South: A qualitative study: Substance use treatment barriers and facilitators. *The Journal of Rural Health, 32*(1), 92–101. http://doi.org/10.1111/jrh.12129
47. Binswanger, I. A., Nowels, C., Corsi, K. F., Glanz, J., Long, J., Booth, R. E., & Steiner, J. F. (2012). Return to drug use and overdose after release from prison: A qualitative study of risk and protective factors. *Addiction Science & Clinical Practice, 7*(1), 3. http://doi.org/10.1186/1940-0640-7-3
48. Del Boca, F. K., & Noll, J. A. (2000). Truth or consequences: the validity of self-report data in health services research on addictions. *Addiction, 95*(11), 347–360. http://doi.org/10.1046/j.1360-0443.95.11s3.5.x
49. Rutherford, M. J., Cacciola, J. S., Alterman, A. I., McKay, J. R., & Cook, T. G. (2000). Contrasts between admitters and deniers of drug use. *Journal of Substance Abuse Treatment, 18*(4), 343–348. http://doi.org/10.1016/S0740-5472(99)00079-3

Reading 8.4 Legal Barriers and Re-Victimization for Survivors of Intimate Partner Violence Navigating Courts in Utah, United States

Having to navigate the criminal justice system as a victim can be traumatizing and lead to secondary victimization. Gezinski and Gonzales-Pons (2022) wanted to reach people who have had to face the criminal justice system, either as victims or as victim advocates, and hear directly from them about the challenges that they faced. One difficult aspect of this research is finding such individuals. The victim advocates themselves were not particularly difficult to find, as the researchers simply had to contact their place of business and request participation. The interpersonal violence victims were more difficult to access. The authors had to rely on the cooperation of victim advocates, who helped to spread the word and even assist with setting up the interviews. Of course, deriving most or all the sample from people who are connected with victim advocates and support groups does lead to the potential for sample bias.

Legal Barriers and Re-Victimization for Survivors of Intimate Partner Violence Navigating Courts in Utah, United States

Lindsay B. Gezinski and Kwynn M. Gonzalez-Pons

Introduction

Partner violence remains a pressing concern in the United States (U.S.). More than one in three women (36.4%) reported contact sexual violence, physical violence, and/or stalking by an intimate partner in their lifetime (Smith et al., 2018). As a result, survivors find themselves navigating the legal system, whether for a protection order, divorce, or child custody agreement. These proceedings may be initiated by either the survivor or perpetrator and result in numerous hearings across various court systems for an extended period of time. This convoluted process, which includes abusive litigation and forced contact with the perpetrator, results in secondary victimization that negatively impacts survivors' physical and mental health (Laing, 2017). In fact, survivors have reported that the court process prolongs their trauma, resulting in great emotional and financial strain (Ragusa, 2013). The following literature review describes these challenges in more detail, including those related to survivors' limited legal representation and poor treatment in court settings.

Literature Review

Manipulation through Courts

While survivors may self-initiate court proceedings, many become embroiled due to a manipulative ex-partner who uses the family law system to maintain contact with them (Coy et al., 2015; Laing, 2017). Utilization of the court system to exert control over the survivor has been termed "paper abuse" (Miller & Smolter, 2011, p. 637). This paper abuse may include the perpetrator's repeat filing of petty lawsuits, false accusations of child abuse, and cross-petition for civil protection orders. As a result, the court becomes a tool of manipulation for the perpetrator, especially when he possesses class privilege relative to the survivor. These extensive court contacts have implications for survivors who must negotiate work, childcare, and transportation arrangements leaving them at the mercy of their ex-partner (Bell et al., 2011; Miller & Smolter, 2011; Ragusa, 2013).

Legal Representation

Obtaining legal counsel is difficult for those with limited financial resources and results in survivors representing themselves in court proceedings. Over half of survivors represented themselves in private law contact court proceedings in recent studies conducted in the United Kingdom (U.K.) and rural Australia (Coy et al., 2015; Ragusa, 2013). Because survivors lack knowledge of court processes, such as how to present evidence to meet the legal definition of abuse or crossexamine witnesses, their court rulings are negatively impacted (Coy et al., 2015; Durfee, 2009). In fact, those without legal representation are less likely to be granted an order of protection (Durfee, 2009). Still, even those who *did* obtain legal counsel reported mixed experiences with attorneys (Ragusa, 2013). For instance, survivor dissatisfaction was linked to attorney skepticism and the survivor not feeling believed (Coy et al., 2015). Criminal prosecutors were more likely to proceed with high severity cases that involved white women and children, as well as perpetrators with a history of IPV and substance use (Cerulli et al., 2014).

The Role of Judges

The survivor court experience is also influenced by the presiding judge who may make a determination about what constitutes abuse. Research suggests that judges recognize physical violence more so than other forms, such as emotional and psychological violence (Coy et al., 2015). Child custody court judges demonstrated knowledge of IPV, but they tended to minimize physical violence and not recognize patterns of coercive control (Coy et al., 2015). Moreover, judges perceived legitimate IPV as consisting of severe physical violence and threats of future violence (Kafka et al., 2019). Judges utilized heuristics in their decision-making and dichotomized cases as either genuine IPV or frivolous cases used to manipulate the abusive partner (Agnew-Brune et al., 2017; Kafka et al., 2019). Those presiding over domestic violence protection order (DVPO) cases indicated that judges first probe for physical signs of violence and that a certain threshold of abuse must be reached for a DVPO to be granted (Agnew-Brune et al., 2017). Factors that influenced judges' DVPO decisions included the severity of the violent incident, whether or not the survivor appeared afraid, courtroom dress and demeanor, the amount of time that had passed since the abusive episode(s), and the presence of children at violent incidents (Agnew-Brune et al., 2017; Person et al., 2018). Judges themselves indicated that they are often forced to make decisions based on minimal case file information, including that which pertains to details of the abuse or to the presence of firearms (Person et al., 2018).

Treatment of Survivors in Court Settings

Survivors expressed mixed reactions to their experiences with judges, attorneys, and other court personnel (Bell et al., 2011). Racialized minority women in Canada reported encountering indifferent court personnel who often lacked cultural sensitivity (Tam et al., 2016). This apathy was felt by survivors in Australian family courts, too, who described a lack of understanding about the dynamics of abuse by court personnel (Roberts et al., 2015). Survivors also reported invalidation, victim blaming, fearing for their safety, and inadequate consequences for perpetrators (Laing, 2017; Roberts et al., 2015; Tam et al., 2016). Moreover, Indigenous courts in the U.S. reportedly lacked consistency in sentencing and were described as giving perpetrators a "slap on the wrist" (Burnette, 2015, p. 1539). Survivors reported being pressured to agree to parenting arrangements they deemed to be unsafe for their children (Laing, 2017). Finally, survivors described how they were revictimized in court settings. Namely, this was attributed to cross-examination and the reliving of abuse in hearings and affidavits, which exacerbated and prolonged trauma (Laing, 2017; Roberts et al., 2015).

Purpose of the Present Study

As described above, research has been conducted with survivors and judges in Australia, Canada, the U.K., and the U.S. However, survivor court experiences have been mixed. While DVPOs have been examined from the perspective of judges, more qualitative research is needed from the perspective of survivors themselves. The purpose of this research study was to explore survivors' experiences with their IPV-related court appearances in Utah, U.S. as they attempt to ensure safety for themselves and their children. Utah has a policy of mandatory arrest, meaning that the perpetrator, survivor, or both are likely to come into contact with the criminal justice system if the abuse is reported to police (Robinson & Williams, 2018). DVPOs represent one mechanism that survivors invoke in an attempt to protect themselves and their children from the abuser. In Utah, an individual may approach the district court to file for a protection order in the county where the survivor lives, where the perpetrator lives, or where the abuse took place (WomensLaw.org, 2019). The petitioner completes the associated forms with information pertaining to the most recent violent incident and the resultant physical harm. If a full protection order is requested, the court date is required to occur within 20 days of filing. An ex parte order may be granted prior to this court date if the judge determines that the survivor is in immediate danger.

One question guided this research study: (1) What are the lived experiences of survivors of IPV as they attempt to navigate the legal system? Informed by Feminist Standpoint Theory, which centers marginalized voices in knowledge production (Harding, 2004), this research study was conducted with survivors and service providers across the state of Utah. The inclusion of survivors and service providers was based on the assumption that both occupy less status in the court setting, especially in relation to judges who have been appreciably studied regarding their decision-making in IPV-related cases. Based on this lower status, survivors and service providers share certain epistemic advantages as knowledge producers (see Harding, 2004) in the documentation of their interactions with courts. As well, both survivors and service providers were included as a method to triangulate the data, assuming that each group would have a slightly different, but equally valuable, perspective concerning legal proceedings. The next section outlines the methodology associated with this research study.

Methods

This research study was approved by the Institutional Review Board at University of Utah. This article is based on data collected during a larger research study that examined the structural challenges survivors experience upon leaving an abusive relationship. Though a multitude of themes emerged from this research study, the focus of this article is survivors' involvement with the legal system specifically. Grounded theory guided this research study due to its emphasis on inductive meaning making and theory development (Glaser & Strauss, 1967). Meaning, concepts and theory emerge from the research process rather than a priori (Corbin, 2017). Thus, grounded theory guided both data collection and data analysis. The study sample consisted of 102 participants, including 43 survivors and 59 service providers. All participants completed either a semi-structured focus group or interview. The methods section describes the study sampling and recruitment strategy, participant demographics, data collection, measures and processes, and data analysis.

Sampling and Recruitment

Purposive sampling was utilized to reach survivors and service providers to ensure that both urban and rural areas were represented. As well, targeted sampling was utilized to ensure participation of hard-to-reach populations, such as plural families, immigrants, $LGBTQ_+$ persons, and Tribal communities. For the purposes of recruitment, "service provider" was defined as a person who devotes a significant amount of time responding to IPV as a function of their employment. However, the majority of service providers worked in a DV service organization at the time of study. The research team collaborated with the state DV coalition to identify organizations serving survivors of IPV. An associated victim's advocate made initial contacts with agencies to assess their interest in participating in the research study. Then, the victim's advocate and a member of the research team worked together to schedule and arrange the locations for the focus groups. Service providers who expressed interest in participating were emailed a flyer with the date, time, and location of the focus group in their area. Service providers were encouraged to forward this flyer to other service providers who may be interested in participating. This means that focus groups were typically cross-pollinated, with several different agencies represented in a single focus group. English-speaking ability was a requirement for study participation.

Focus groups with survivors were conducted separately to ensure that they felt comfortable sharing their concerns without fear of reprisal. The majority of survivor participants were recruited through DV service organizations. The research team created separate flyers for survivor focus groups. These were emailed to various organizations serving survivors of IPV, and staff at these organizations posted the flyer and verbally publicized the research study. Survivor focus groups were typically held in agency settings, meaning that residents of the agency were able to attend with relative ease and were permitted to drop-in to the focus group. Some survivors advertised the research study to their peers resulting in snowball sampling.

Participants

On average, survivors were 39.9 years of age, while service providers were 43.3. All survivors and almost 90% of service providers self-identified as women. Of those who completed the sexual orientation item, the majority of survivors and service providers identified as straight or heterosexual, 88.9% and 96% respectively. Of those who indicated their race, participants identified pre-dominantly as white (68.3% of survivors, 89.7% of service providers) or Indigenous/Native American (22% of survivors, 8.6% of service providers). Over 90% of both survivors and service providers were born in the U.S., and approximately 10% of both survivors and service providers reported Latinx or Hispanic identity. Service providers had, on average, higher levels of education (27.1% some college, 62.7% college degree) compared to survivors who answered the question (38.1% high school diploma or GED, 21.4% some college, 23.8% college degree). Two-thirds of participants identified as religious (67.4% for survivors and 64.4% for service providers), which was ascertained with a dichotomous (yes/no) survey item. Survivors reported accessing IPV-specific services in nine Utah counties with 25.6% specifying that they accessed services in Salt Lake County, the most populous county in the state. Service providers represented both urban and rural regions of the state, and the majority (66.1%) of service providers reported current employment in a DV service organization. Please see Table 1.

Data Collection

From March 2016 to February 2017, in-depth and semi-structured focus groups and interviews were conducted with IPV survivors and service providers throughout the state of Utah. Eight focus groups were conducted with survivors, and nine separate focus groups were held with service providers. While ranging in size, there were an average of six participants in each focus group. All focus groups were facilitated by two cisgender female research team members, while a victim's advocate observed nonverbal behavior and was available to provide support to participants if needed.

Table 1 Demographics of study participants

	Survivors (n = 43) Mean (SD)	*Service Providers (n = 59) Mean (SD)*
Age	*39.86 (12.75)*	*43.26 (12.65)*
	Count (%)	*Count (%)*
Gender Identity		
Female	43 (100%)	53 (89.8%)
Male	0 (0%)	5 (8.5%)
Transgender	0 (0%)	1 (1.7%)
Sexual Orientation		
LGBQ+	4 (9.3%)	2 (3.4%)
Straight/ Heterosexual	32 (74.4%)	48 (81.4%)
No Answer	7 (16.3%)	9 (15.3%)
Race		
African American/ Black	3 (7%)	0 (0%)
Asian	1 (2.3%)	1 (1.7%)
Indigenous/Native American	9 (20.9%)	5 (8.5%)
White	28 (65.1%)	52 (88.1%)
No Answer	2 (4.6%)	1 (1.7%)
Latinx/Hispanic	4 (9.3%)	6 (10.2%)
Born Outside U.S.	4 (9.3%)	4 (6.8%)
Education Level		
Did Not Graduate HS	7 (16.3%)	1 (1.7%)
HS Diploma/GED	16 (37.2%)	5 (8.5%)
Some College	9 (20.9%)	16 (27.1%)
College Degree	10 (23.3%)	37 (62.7%)
No Answer	1 (2.3%)	0 (0%)
Religious	29 (67.4%)	38 (64.4%)

However, some participants preferred to be interviewed individually with four survivors and two service providers selecting this option. The majority of focus groups and interviews were conducted in agency settings; however, some interviews were conducted in the first author's office or at a local cafe with the location chosen by the participant.

Measures and Processes

Prior to the start of each focus group and interview, informed consent and confidentiality were discussed. Participants were informed that participation was completely voluntary and that they may end participation at any point without penalty. Each participant completed a demographic form immediately after the informed consent discussion. Open-ended, semi-structured interview guides were utilized for all focus groups and interviews. While interview guides were used, participants guided the focus groups and interviews allowing space for participants to speak to issues of most importance to them. Service providers were asked open-ended questions like, "In your opinion, what are the largest barriers to victims of DV accessing services at your agency?" and "Are there any issues facing victims that the public/law enforcement/clergy/etc. are not aware of, and should be?" Similarly, survivors were asked questions such as, "What are some of the biggest obstacles you have faced when looking for help?" and "How did you learn about services available, and how long did it take you to try to access them?" All focus groups and interviews were conducted in English and lasted between 1 and 2 hours. Survivors received a $20 grocery gift card for their participation, while service providers received no incentive for participation in this research study.

Data Analysis

All focus groups and interviews were audio-recorded with the participants' consent and transcribed verbatim. Data collection and data analysis occurred simultaneously, meaning that transcription and data analysis occurred soon after each focus group and interview to assess emergent themes (see Noaks & Wincup, 2004). Again, grounded theory guided the interpretive analysis and consisted of the development of concepts, categories, and themes (see Corbin, 2017). First, each transcript was read multiple times by each author. Then, data were entered in

NVivo 10 to conduct initial open coding through line-by-line analysis (Strauss, 1987). This was followed by axial coding wherein data were coded based on emerging categories. Finally, selective coding assisted with the identification of themes and development of matrices to uncover relationships between themes and categories. Thematic codes were analyzed separately for survivors and service providers with the expectation that themes would differ for each group; however, themes were largely consistent across sub-group. Meaning, analyzed data showed great similarity for survivor and service provider focus groups. Therefore, data from all focus groups and interviews were analyzed together. Two research team members coded all transcripts separately and compared themes and categories to ensure inter-rater reliability. Any discrepancies were discussed between these researchers and resolved prior to the selection of final categories. Confidentiality was of utmost concern; therefore, no names have been included here.

Results

Several themes emerged pertaining to survivors' engagement with the legal system, including: (1) insufficient legal representation, (2) protection order access and enforcement, (3) revictimization in court settings, and (4) disparities in accountability. Participants reported that the number of public assistance and pro bono attorneys is insufficient to meet the demand, and survivors' own criminal charges affect their access to legal aid. This results in survivors representing themselves in court. Service providers assisted survivors with the completion of DVPO forms, but they emphasized their limited ability to provide legal advice. Furthermore, survivors pointed to a lack of enforcement of DVPOs, mandated child visitation with the perpetrator, and lenient sentencing as evidence that the legal system favors perpetrators. Survivors described being bullied and re-victimized by judges and attorneys who they expressed lack a solid understanding of IPV.

Insufficient Legal Representation

This theme was related to a lack of pro bono attorneys and affordable legal representation. Participants described survivors' difficulty navigating the legal system, often requiring traversing multiple courts, including criminal and civil courts. Although survivors often require legal representation, service providers reported that DV service organizations do not have the capacity to provide attorneys or legal advice on-site, nor are staff trained on the complexities of the legal system. Lack of public assistance and pro bono attorneys was cited as a barrier for survivors. As illustrated by a service provider:

> We have [nonprofit law office] but... it's only like one person. They come down for two hours every third Wednesday of the month for a two-hour window period, and if people can't make it, then they can't make it. Or the lines are too long. [Survivors] go, and they don't even have a chance to be seen or heard or get assistance.

Even when a survivor does qualify for free or low-cost legal assistance, she may be excluded from services due to her own criminal record. For survivors who have criminal charges, including DV charges related to self-defense, their ability to access legal assistance is impacted. For example, an advocate employed at the prosecutor's office stated: "If [a survivor] has charges, pending charges, it becomes a conflict for us to help them," and it "shuts off all help for them." The high costs associated with obtaining legal representation were illustrated by a houseless survivor who indicated that attorneys "automatically want cash or something before they even seen [sic] you... It's like, I'm on the street. I'm down at the river. I don't have any money. There's usually nowhere you can turn, so you just give up." As a result, many survivors described taking out loans to cover legal costs resulting in a precarious financial situation.

Survivors, especially those without legal representation, reported dismay as their perpetrators were bestowed legal counsel and offered court-sponsored counseling. One participant who was both a survivor and a service provider stated:

> Whether [the offender is] in jail or he's outside, [the court has] ordered [the offender] to do this, and it's all paid for. And he's getting the help he needs, you know, going to rehab or getting a mental health evaluation... And since the court ordered it, the state is paying for it... Where's the victim? And that's when [legal professionals] say, 'oh, well try and get restitution,' and then it never works out [for the survivor]. So, it's almost like we're re-victimizing [survivors] again in the current system we have. I felt revictimized that way.

Thus, not only are many survivors unable to access legal representation, they are also not afforded other resources, such as mental health counseling, that are essential to their own recovery.

Still, countless survivors are left to navigate the legal system alone and report unfamiliarity with court processes. Survivors who represent themselves "lose in protective order hearings or custody battles," as one service provider noted. A lack of awareness of available resources was apparent, as many survivors were uninformed that they may be entitled to advocate support during their court proceedings. Moreover, the legal process was described as especially difficult for survivors who have an intellectual disability, as a service provider stated:

> Have you ever talked in court in front of a judge? It's like terrifying whether you [have an intellectual disability or not]. I get terrified and I know the judge... The whole situation is terrifying, and so you add [an intellectual disability] on top of it and not completely functioning as soon as [survivors] get up there, they just lose their whole thought process.

Protection Order Access and Enforcement

Fearing for their safety, survivors approached courts in an effort to secure a DVPO. Applying for a DVPO took a toll on already traumatized survivors who were required to recount their victimization experiences in order to justify their request. The protection order theme centered around barriers to access, lack of enforcement, and associated safety risks. For instance, access issues were linked to filing timelines and the length of time it took some survivors to get a DVPO approved. As stated above, the court date for a full DVPO is required to occur within 20 days of filing. However, survivors described difficulty attending prompt court dates because of their work schedules. These work schedules were often released several weeks in advance. Further, survivors reported waiting months for orders to be granted, which implied a lack of urgency on the part of the courts. Service providers described how their ability to assist survivors in obtaining a DVPO was hampered by requirements around the last abusive incident. For instance, various service providers claimed that survivors were required to have experienced physical and/or sexual assault within the last 30 days to qualify for a DVPO in Utah. As one service provider stated:

> We do protective orders at our agency. We use the utcourts.gov website... and it specifically asks if there has been physical or sexual abuse or a threat in the last thirty days, and there are a lot of people that come in and they know something's going to happen. But it hasn't been in the last thirty days, and so there is nothing you can do at this point and you basically have to send them out the door and say, "When it happens, come back."

According to legal statute, though, the assumption that violence must have occured within the last 30 days in order to acquire a DVPO is incorrect (personal communication, January 2018). This is concerning, because survivors supplied with this faulty information may not even apply.

Safety risks still remained for survivors who were granted DVPOs, due in part to a lack of enforcement and measures that jeopardize their privacy. One survivor described: "I had protective orders that he would constantly violate... I have some records, like I have an entire file, like I'd go get phone records of harassment." This lack of enforcement led survivors to perceive that their victimization experiences were not taken seriously. Here, a service provider highlights the need to validate survivors: "I just think the accountability, perpetrator accountability [is needed]... Like, victims could be validated a little bit more in their experience." Privacy and safety concerns persisted for survivors regarding listing their address on the DVPO form. For example, a survivor described the impact of this when the perpetrator was served:

> That is actually how he found me the first time, and he broke in. And so the next house I moved to now, I opted to not put my physical address... And so legally right now my home is not protected under it, but he doesn't know where I live.

Survivors reported feelings of revictimization when their DVPO was not enforced. In fact, engaging with the legal system was a precursor to more violence for some. Rather than feeling protected by the legal system, one survivor illustrated how the DVPO put her safety at risk, because it further infuriated the perpetrator. She explained: "The courts, the justice system, it sucks. It's made to piss [perpetrators] off more and then just have us sitting there like sitting ducks."

Revictimization in Court Settings

Both survivors and service providers illustrated how the legal process resulted in trauma and revictimization. This trauma was attributed to perpetrator, judge, and attorney statements and behaviors. Perpetrators were described as "working the system" to exert control and manipulate survivors as well as to deplete survivors both financially and emotionally. These included using custody issues, protection order continuances, or divorce proceedings as a facade to string along survivors, costing them time, adding to their stress, and draining them of any financial resources they had left. As described by one service provider: "... abusers use the legal system against [survivors]. [Perpetrators] may have a lot of money, and just keep [survivors] in court. [The survivor ends up] taking out loans and wasting money and getting nowhere." Keeping the survivor embroiled in the legal process represents a mode of manipulation for perpetrators. This is combined with survivors missing work, which also contributes to financial instability. One service provider noted how involvement in the court system was "draining the woman of economic and mental and emotional resources that could be better used elsewhere that she's caught up in going to court. She's caught up in having to deal with all this stuff."

Survivors, especially those who represented themselves, feared the overall court process. Survivors expressed being re-traumatized when they are forced to face their abusers in court and recount their victimizations. One survivor explained: "Do you know how scary and terrifying that was for me to even just walk from here to go to the courthouse and sit in that courtroom anticipating... your husband, that's your attacker?! You're sitting there by yourself scared." One service provider illustrated how "a lot of cases are dropped, because [survivors] just can't stand that pressure." Despite survivors being encouraged to seek help for their IPV victimization, legal system engagement did not equate to safety for some survivors.

Survivors perceived a lack of awareness among judges and attorneys regarding the extent and the seriousness of their abuse as well as feeling "bullied" and not knowing "how to work the court system." They reported instances where their abusive experiences were minimized and their pleas for protection ignored. Survivors watched, despite their pleas, as judges granted child visitation rights to their perpetrator. One survivor explained: "I repeatedly said, 'I'm scared for my children. I'm scared for my life.' And they would just push child support and visitation." Survivors expressed concern for the impact of mandated visitation on their children and feeling like the perpetrator was more supported. For example, a survivor said, "the court process with victims isn't very friendly. And I know that the focus is more on the offender than it ever is the victim."

Disparities in Accountability

Finally, survivors described lacking perpetrator accountability connected to minimal jail time and sentencing disparities. For instance, some survivors saw their perpetrators receive less jail time and more court-appointed assistance options than they did. One survivor related how, even though she was physically assaulted by her partner, he served no jail time: "When he hit me and nearly killed the baby, all he gets is 50 hours of community services. He gets away with that so easy." Another survivor described how her partner gave her a concussion and fled from the police, only to serve six days in jail. And yet another survivor described how her perpetrator was charged with "cruelty to a child, willful cruelty to a spouse and destruction of property. He spent 14 days in jail, considered time served, let go on probation and the judge ordered a [criminal protective order]." In contrast, participants highlighted harsh consequences for survivors who "fought back in self-defense" or who remained in the household with their children despite the violence. For example, a service provider described the process of Division of Child and Families Services (DCFS) becoming involved in the court system:

> There's a really crazy case that I'm dealing with, and [the survivor is] involved with DCFS and the court system… I'm just appalled at the way they're treating her as a victim of very serious abuse and long-standing abuse. For the court to look at her as a perpetrator of abuse for her child, because she stayed for a few months because he was threatening her.

Discussion

The results presented here suggest that survivors of IPV face difficulty navigating courts in the U.S., as documented in the Australian and Canadian contexts (see Laing, 2017; Roberts et al., 2015; Tam et al., 2016). In fact, themes were consistent for both survivors and service providers. Akin to past research conducted in Australia and the U.K. (Coy et al., 2015; Ragusa, 2013), this study found that survivors are often unable to access affordable legal representation, nor is the availability of legal aid and pro bono attorney services sufficient to meet the demand. Past research has found that English and Welsh survivors accumulated significant debt when they were not afforded free or low-cost legal counsel (Coy et al., 2015). These findings were replicated in this study, with survivors taking out loans to pay for legal counsel. Other survivors were forced to represent themselves in court settings. This further served to support survivors' belief that perpetrators, who are afforded legal representation and sometimes mandated to attend counseling, are favored by the criminal justice system. While alleged perpetrators have a Constitutional right to a public defender, survivors are not automatically afforded legal representation. This led survivors to perceive that their abusers were more supported, or even protected, by the legal system. Survivors expressed disappointment and a loss of faith in a system they felt favored perpetrators.

Of particular importance, we found that survivors' own criminal charges affected their access to legal counsel. Even when these charges were connected to self-defense, survivors were precluded from accessing legal aid. Participants described how survivors themselves were charged with abuse to a child as a result of staying with the perpetrator, which in turn affected child custody. While survivors' own charges affected their access to legal assistance, they also influenced their status as a "victim." Research has documented characteristics that influence the approval of DVPOs (Agnew-Brune et al., 2017; Person et al., 2018). The existing study showed that even when granted, DVPOs are often unenforced, especially when severe physical violence is absent. Several challenges were associated with DVPOs, namely filing timelines and listing of addresses, and they sometimes resulted in escalated violence.

Contrary to past research that found mixed experiences (Ragusa, 2013), survivors in this study reported consistent poor treatment in court settings. They spoke of victim-blaming that prolonged their trauma, which provides further support for the concept of secondary victimization (see Laing, 2017) in the legal system. This secondary victimization is likely to occur when judges and attorneys are uneducated about abuse dynamics, how abuse presents, and trauma-informed practices. Granting or mandating the abuser visitation rights sent a clear message to the survivor, namely that maintaining the father in the child's life is more important than the survivor's safety. Granting visitation rights may present risks to survivor and child safety, as well as allow the perpetrator to continue to manipulate the survivor through their children. Similar to Burnette's (2015) finding in Tribal courts, this study found sentencing disparities as well. Survivors reported a range of criminal sentences for their perpetrators and were bewildered by the short length of sentences. Overall, participants discussed intimidation associated with the legal system, especially if the survivor was attempting to navigate it alone.

Implications

The present research study has implications for both practice and future research. First, findings indicate the need for the education of judges and attorneys regarding the dynamics of IPV broadly as well as those specifically related to the legal system, such as how perpetrators manipulate court systems to further exert control. Stereotypes related to the manifestation of violence should be addressed to ensure the recognition of a variety of abuse types, rather than severe physical violence only. While mandatory training exists for judges, prosecutors, and public defenders in some locations, others have limited access to training (Hyman & Aldrich, 2012; Tsai, 2000). Therefore, consistent training is needed across court systems, regardless if the court is general or DV-specific. This may be paired with an Integrated DV Court (IDVC).

While specialized DV courts have existed for decades (Newmark et al., 2001; Tsai, 2000), survivors' experiences are mixed (Coulter et al., 2005; Gover et al., 2007). More recently, IDVCs have emerged, primarily in New York, and involve a single judge hearing both criminal charges and civil cases in one court (Hyman & Aldrich, 2012; Koshan, 2018). This has the potential to reduce the number of court dates the survivor must attend and allow judges to have more complete case information. However, more research is needed on survivors' experiences in IDVCs. In addition, there is a great need for increased availability of affordable legal representation, particularly public assistance and pro bono legal services, and greater on-site presence of attorneys to provide legal advice at DV service organizations. This is especially true for survivors with criminal charges who are often unable to access legal representation.

More research is needed on several aspects of the legal system as it pertains to partner violence. First, as secondary victimization continues to be a problem (Laing, 2017; Ragusa, 2013), research should examine whether this victimization deters survivors from subsequently engaging with the legal system. Second, research is needed that follows survivors longitudinally through the court process and that quantitatively measures their well-being and safety proceeding court involvement. Finally, research should compare survivors with and without legal representation on the timeliness of court processes, enforcement of DVPOs, and sentencing decisions. An examination of court experiences at the intersections of identity, especially related to intellectual disability, would be particularly beneficial.

Strengths and Limitations

The study presented here has a wealth of strengths. First, the study had a large sample size by qualitative research standards, which allowed for the representation of survivor and service provider voices across the state, regardless of geographic location or proximity to the research institution. Further, by including perspectives of both survivors and service providers, the study was able to present findings that were reinforced by more than one party with different stakes in the process, adding weight to the findings. Finally, the study presented several unique findings that further support survivors' needs in legal settings as well as opening discussions for new areas of practice and research.

Still, despite these novel research findings, several limitations should be noted. While qualitative research methods allow for great depth, they have limited generalizability. This research study was limited to survivors and service providers in the state of Utah. Thus, these research findings cannot be generalized to these overall populations. However, these findings are likely applicable to the rest of the U.S. as well as other countries, such as Australia and Canada, and comparison research is needed in the future. Moreover, the majority of the survivors had accessed DV service organizations, namely shelter services. As such, perspectives from survivors who do not interact with these services are not present here. Further, many survivors experienced a lower socioeconomic status, which has potential implications for access to attorneys as well as judges' reception of them. The majority of survivor participants are white and likely afforded better treatment than survivors of color. Finally, all survivors identified as women, and future research should include male and gender nonconforming survivors.

Conclusion

Overall, survivors recounted being re-victimized by a legal system that handed down lenient sentences to their perpetrators, incarcerated victims for defending themselves, failed to address DVPO violations, and mandated child visitation schedules for perpetrators. The result was often a negative experience that deterred survivors from seeking legal help in the future.

Regardless of their criminal records, survivors need low-cost or free legal representation to advance procedural justice. Judges, attorneys, and other court personnel require IPV education that goes beyond physical violence to understand coercive control. The integration of trauma- informed practices in courts (see McKenna & Holtfreter, 2020) may reduce re-traumatization of survivors.

Disclosure Statement

No potential conflict of interest was reported by the author(s).

Discussion Questions

1. How did Gezinski and Gonzalez-Pons gain access to survivors of interpersonal violence for their research?
2. What are the advantages and disadvantages to the sampling plan that Gezinski and Gonzalez-Pons used to recruit both service providers and survivors of IPV?
3. What steps did Gezinski and Gonzalez-Pons take to improve the validity and reliability of their research? How can future research build upon their findings?

References

Agnew-Brune, C., Moracco, K. E., Person, C. J., & Bowling, J. M. (2017). Domestic violence protective orders: A qualitative examination of judges' decision-making processes. *Journal of Interpersonal Violence, 32*(13), 1921–1942. https://doi.org/10.1177/0886260515590126

Bell, M. E., Perez, S., Goodman, L. A., & Dutton, M. A. (2011). Battered women's perceptions of civil and criminal court helpfulness: The role of court outcome and process. *Violence against Women, 17*(1), 71–88. https://doi.org/10.1177/1077801210393924

Burnette, C. E. (2015). From the ground up: Indigenous women's after violence experiences with the formal service system in the United States. *British Journal of Social Work, 45*(5), 1526–1545. https://doi.org/10.1093/bjsw/bcu013

Cerulli, C., Kothari, C. L., Dichter, M., Marcus, S., Wiley, J., & Rhodes, K. V. (2014). Victim participation in intimate partner violence prosecution: Implications for safety. *Violence against Women, 20*(5), 539–560. https://doi.org/10.1177/1077801214535105

Corbin, J. (2017). Grounded theory. *The Journal of Positive Psychology, 12*(3), 301–302. https://doi.org/10.1080/17439760.2016.1262614

Coulter, M. L., Alexander, A., & Harrison, V. (2005). Specialized domestic violence courts. *Women & Criminal Justice, 16*(3), 91–106. https://doi.org/10.1300/J012v16n03_05

Coy, M., Scott, E., Tweedale, R., & Perks, K. (2015). 'It's like going through the abuse again': Domestic violence and women and children's (un)safety in private law contact proceedings. *Journal of Social Welfare and Family Law, 37*(1), 53–69. https://doi.org/10.1080/09649069.2015.1004863

Durfee, A. (2009). Victim narratives, legal representation, and domestic violence civil protection orders. *Feminist Criminology, 4*(1), 7–31. https://doi.org/10.1177/1557085108324961

Glaser, B. G., & Strauss, A. L. (1967). *The discovery of grounded theory: Strategies for qualitative research.* AldineTransaction.

Gover, A., Brank, E., & Macdonald, J. (2007). A specialized domestic violence court in South Carolina: An example of procedural justice for victims and defendants. *Violence against Women, 13*(6), 603–626. https://doi.org/10.1177/1077801207301553

Harding, S. (2004). *The feminist standpoint theory reader: Intellectual and political controversies.*

Hyman, E. M., & Aldrich, L. (2012). Rethinking access to justice: The need for a holistic response to victims of domestic violence. *Women's Rights Law Reporter, 33*(4), 449–462.

Kafka, J. M., Moracco, K. E., Barrington, C., & Mortazavi, A. L. (2019). Judging domestic violence from the bench: A narrative analysis of judicial anecdotes about domestic violence protective order cases. *Qualitative Health Research, 29*(8), 1132–1144. https://doi.org/10.1177/1049732318821691

Koshan, J. (2018). Specialised domestic violence courts in Canada and the United States: Key factors in prioritising safety for women and children. *Journal of Social Welfare and Family Law, 40*(4), 515–532. https://doi.org/10.1080/09649069.2018.1519656

Laing, L. (2017). Secondary victimization: Domestic violence survivors navigating the family law system. *Violence against Women, 23*(11), 1314–1335. https://doi.org/10.1177/1077801216659942

McKenna, N. C., & Holtfreter, K. (2020). Trauma-informed courts: A review and integration of justice perspectives and gender responsiveness. *Journal of Aggression, Maltreatment & Trauma, 2020,* 1–21.https://doi.org/10.1080/10926771.2020.1747128

Miller, S. L., & Smolter, N. L. (2011). "Paper abuse": When all else fails, batterers use procedural stalking. *Violence Against Women, 17*(5), 637–650. https://doi.org/10.1177/1077801211407290

Newmark, L., Rempel, M., Diffily, K., & Kane, K. M. (2001). *Specialized felony domestic violence courts: Lessons on implementation and impacts from the Kings County experience.* Urban Institute.

Noaks, L., & Wincup, E. (2004). *Criminological research: Understanding qualitative methods.* Sage.

Person, C. J., Moracco, K. E., Agnew-Brune, C., & Bowling, J. M. (2018). "I don't know that I've ever felt like I got the full story": A qualitative study of courtroom interactions between judges and litigants in domestic violence protective order cases. *Violence Against Women, 24*(12), 1474–1496. https://doi.org/10.1177/1077801217738582

Ragusa, A. T. (2013). Rural Australian women's legal help seeking for intimate partner violence: Women intimate partner violence victim survivors' perceptions of criminal justice support services. *Journal of Interpersonal Violence, 28*(4), 685–717. https://doi.org/10.1177/0886260512455864

Roberts, D., Chamberlain, P., & Delfabbro, P. (2015). Women's experiences of the processes associated with the family court of Australia in the context of domestic violence: A thematic analysis. *Psychiatry, Psychology and Law, 22*(4), 599–615. https://doi.org/10.1080/13218719.2014.960132

Robinson, P. H., & Williams, T. S. (2018). *Mapping American criminal law: Variations across the 50 states.* ABCCLIO.

Smith, S. G., Zhang, X., Basile, K. C., Merrick, M. T., Wang, J., Kresnow, M., & Chen, J. (2018). *The National Intimate Partner and Sexual Violence Survey (NISVS): 2015 data brief – Updated release.* National Center for Injury Prevention and Control, Centers for Disease Control and Prevention.

Strauss, A. L. (1987). *Qualitative analysis for social scientists.* Cambridge University Press.

Tam, D. M., Tutty, L. M., Zhuang, Z., & Paz, E. (2016). Racial minority women and criminal justice responses to domestic violence. *Journal of Family Violence, 31*(4), 527–538. https://doi.org/10.1007/s10896-015-9794-7

Tsai, B. (2000). The trend toward specialized domestic violence courts: Improvements on an effective innovation. *Fordham Law Review, 68*(4), 1285–1328. https://ir.lawnet.fordham.edu/flr/vol68/iss4/8

WomensLaw.org. (2019). *Utah restraining orders.* www.womenslaw.org/law/ut/restraining-orders/protective-orders-due-domestic-violenceabuse#node-36786

9 Surveys and Interviews

Surveys and interviews are essential to criminal justice research, because they allow us to learn about things that are difficult or impossible to observe. We can only learn about residents' fear of crime in their neighborhoods by asking them about it, as we obviously cannot observe feelings. We cannot follow large groups of people every day for years to record the number of times they are victimized or are perpetrators of illegal activity. The mere presence of the researcher on the street looking to witness a burglary or robbery is likely to deter any would-be offender at that place and time. Researchers have been very innovative in finding ways to observe crime, but even when they are able to conceal themselves enough, they run into another problem: crime is (thankfully) a rare occurrence. What we can do is survey people about their thoughts and behaviors. It is much easier to sample a large number of individuals, households, or businesses and ask about victimization experiences or to survey people to ask about offending patterns than it is to try to observe crimes. Collecting data this way allows us to obtain a large enough sample size for quantitative data analysis.

In this chapter, I will review the elements of survey construction. Just as I warned readers in Chapter 4 that writing survey questions might initially seem like an easy task, I want to remind you that it is not. There is so much more to this process than most people realize, and I think that will be very clear by the end of this chapter. When we consider how to collect data, we need to decide whether to conduct interviews, either in person, via video chat, or over the phone, or to distribute surveys for respondents to complete on their own. Each method has advantages and disadvantages in terms of its impact on response rates, participant privacy, and the impact of social desirability on answers. Finally, we will consider specific types of surveys, such as focus groups and self-report questionnaires.

Survey Construction

The process of turning vague concepts into measurable variables is difficult, but it is important to get this right. You will only have one shot at getting someone to respond to your survey. While this project might mean a lot to you and your future, it is often seen as a burden to the respondent. Believe me, you will not get away with having people complete a survey and then asking them to complete it again because you just realized that some of your wording was vague or the way you ordered the questions was problematic.

As you prepare to make a survey, the first step is to create a list of all the variables that you need to remember to include in the survey. If you are putting together a very short document, this probably isn't necessary, but if it is going to be a long survey with lots of variables, you could check your list against the final draft of the survey to make sure you have everything that you need in there. Next, think about your goal, as this will help you determine the appropriate survey format. If you are interested in hypothesis testing, you might want to use close-ended survey items, where respondents choose from a set of available answer options. These are very helpful when it comes to doing quantitative data analysis because there is no additional coding. Surveys with just

DOI: 10.4324/9781003661511-9

close-ended questions are known as **structured surveys**. If you think that you might not be able to imagine every possible answer that respondents will give or you really want the respondents to describe things in their own words, then open-ended questions would be better. A questionnaire made entirely of open-ended questions is known as an **unstructured survey**. An advantage to unstructured surveys is they eliminate the problem of you forgetting to include an answer option, but a substantial drawback is that you will later have to code the answers into categories yourself if the responses are going to be included in quantitative analysis. Open-ended items and less structured surveys are particularly helpful in introducing the researchers to ideas that they had not previously considered. Decker and Rosenfeld (1995) assumed that they knew all the methods that people use to avoid HIV transmission, including using condoms, practicing monogamy, getting regular testing, and practicing celibacy. They used open-ended questions when surveying people who were recently arrested and were surprised at the answers they received when they asked for respondents' most frequently used method of avoiding HIV transmission. People responded that they would have their partners drink orange juice and ask them if it burned when they urinated, because they thought this served as an at-home HIV test (it does not). Others reported washing their genitals with gasoline to kill infection (it does not). These are ideas that the researchers never would have thought to include as answer options on a structured survey. Another possibility is to have a combination of close-ended and open-ended questions in a **semi-structured survey**. A final option is to not have an actual written survey and to just have a few key words available to guide interviewers as they conduct depth interviews. **Depth interviews** are long conversations, some of which take hours, where the respondents can fully explain their circumstances and the researcher is free to think of and ask additional questions as topics arise. Less structured surveys and depth interviews are advantageous when researchers are working on theory and hypothesis development or when they are looking to get ideas for what to include in a structured survey.

If you decide against depth interviews and need a survey, pause before diving into survey construction. There are currently hundreds, if not thousands, of surveys that have already been written, some of which have been tested for validity and reliability. Rather than trying to create your own measures, it might be better to use or even adapt an existing survey for use in your research. As you work on learning about your topic, you should do an extensive review of the existing literature. While doing so, pay attention to how others measured the variables that currently interest you. Are there instruments that have already been tested for their reliability and validity? Someone looking to research depression and suicidal ideation may want to choose from forms that have been validated several times. For example, the Beck Depression Inventory-II (BDI-II) (Beck, Steer, & Brown, 1996), the Beck Hopelessness Scale (Beck, 1988; Beck & Steer, 1988), and the Suicide Probability Scale (Cull & Gill, 1998) are good tools for measuring suicidal ideation. There are even suicide screening tools designed specifically for use with people housed in prisons and jails, such as the Brief Jail Mental Health Screen (Kohl et al., 2024; Steadman et al., 2005; Veysey et al., 1998), the Suicide Risk Assessment Scale (Wichmann et al., 2002), and the Suicide Concerns for Offenders in Prison Environment (Perry & Olason, 2009).

Before using an existing survey, you need to first consider whether it is permissible. Some surveys are free for others to use and reproduce, provided that adequate credit is given to the survey creators. Others may only be used for a fee. You should look into that and, when in doubt, reach out to the people who developed the survey to ask permission. Provided that you have permission, your second step is to see whether the existing survey captures all the variables that you need for your study. If it does not, you may have to add additional items. Third, think about whether the survey is appropriate for your study population. While it might have been found to be valid and reliable with one group of people, it may not also be valid and reliable if you use it with a different population. Going back to the suicide questionnaire example, the reason why there are tools specific to the justice-involved population is because some community-level depression and suicide screening surveys lack validity when used to evaluate individuals in custody. For example, the BDI-II is a valid measure of depression in the community, but it includes statements such as "I feel particularly guilty" and "I feel I am being punished." Those items are intended to measure feelings of depression, but when people in custody reflect on those items, they might answer while thinking about how guilty they feel about their crimes and whether they feel that being in jail for that is punishment (Perry et al., 2010). In other words, for some people, those statements might wind up measuring something other than depression, and that presents a validity problem. Another question to consider as you think about the appropriateness of an existing survey for your own research is whether it is composed at a suitable reading and comprehension level for your respondents. Fourth, if this is an assignment for a course or some other graded project, always check with your instructor to confirm that you are permitted to adopt a survey from another source. Your instructor may want you to create your own for the learning experience.

Survey Content

Assuming you do need to make your own survey, here are some issues to consider:

1. Think about who is supposed to complete the survey. If your unit of analysis is an organization, what is your unit of observation? Do you want it to be the chief or executive director of an organization, or can it be a lower-level employee? Ask yourself the same question if your unit of analysis is the household. Do you want the unit of observation to be anyone over the age of 18 living in the house, the oldest person in the home, the person who does most of the household shopping, or the person whose birthday is coming up next? You need to collect data in a consistent manner. Figuring out who is going to be completing the survey will help you with some of the next decisions.
2. Make sure the survey is written in a way that is geared toward the people who will be completing it. If I am surveying judges, I will write for a highly educated population and use legal terminology. If I am surveying people living in prison, I will make sure everything is written at a fourth-grade reading level.
3. If you are using close-ended questions, make sure your response options are mutually exclusive and exhaustive. To review, mutually exclusive means that respondents will only be able to select one, and only one, answer option. Exhaustive means that there will be an answer option available for every respondent taking the survey. See Chapter 4 if you need a refresher.
4. Do not ask leading questions. I once received a "survey" in the mail asking me how I felt about a certain political party's "partisan witch hunt" against a specific politician. Is it any wonder how the writers of that survey hoped I would respond? Has anyone ever thought, "I really do enjoy a good partisan witch hunt?" To be fair, a few weeks later, I received a survey from a group at the other end of the political spectrum asking me how concerned I was about "the government's harsh immigration policies that trample on the due process rights…" What decent person would be in favor of trampling on people's rights? If I respond that I am *not* concerned, what kind of person am I? Of course, most surveys are much more subtle than these two examples, but they can still wind up introducing bias into the questions. Choose your wording carefully, as some words can be leading. For example, anytime anyone wants an industry to look bad, they add the word "big" before its name. We have had "big tobacco," "big oil," and "big pharma" in media reports over the past few decades. Labeling these industries as "big" communicates that these companies are so overwhelmingly powerful that they can, and will, barrel over the public good for the sake of their own interests. Whether that is true is a debate for another time. The items on a survey are not supposed to lead people to

think any particular way about a topic, since we want to get respondents' opinions, not their opinions after we slip ideas into their heads. You have to be careful not only with the survey questions themselves but with the introductory statement. I recently received a survey that began with "we want to know what parts of the federal government are most harmful to the American people." Before asking any questions, the authors of this survey communicated to respondents an expectation that everyone has negative feelings toward aspects of the federal government.

5. Be clear and concise. The wordier questions are, the more likely people are to get confused, and the more likely tired respondents are to skip parts of the question.
6. Avoid vague wording. I distributed a survey to jail administrators years ago with the question "How many sworn staff members work at your facility?" It was a mail survey, and I included my phone number on the cover letter in case people had questions. Within a week of the mailing, I knew I had a problem. I received several phone calls about that one item. It seems that people were interpreting it one of three ways. Some respondents thought I meant "How many sworn staff members are working *this shift*"; others thought, "How many sworn staff members are working *today*"; and a third group of people thought, "How many sworn staff members work here *in total*?" About a dozen people called for clarification, but the other nearly 200 respondents did not and, instead, just interpreted it one of the three aforementioned ways and wrote down a number. I was too vague with my wording, and it ruined the question.
7. Make sure you ask only one question at a time. Do not ask double-barreled questions, such as "Did you bring your lunch or get something to eat at the cafeteria today?" If someone answers "yes," what did you learn about what they did for lunch?
8. Hagan (2007) suggests that researchers avoid "response set" patterns by using reversal questions. In other words, if there are a number of questions where, on a rating of 1 to 5, "5" means that the person is a good student, people who are good students might get bored and start circling "5." To keep people paying attention, switch things up a bit so an answer of "1" would mean good student for a few of the questions.
9. Consider using an attention check. This is an item to make sure that people are paying attention. The attention check could be something as simple as "This item is to confirm that you are paying attention. If so, circle '3'." Another option is to ask a question quizzing the respondents about something that was in an earlier part of the survey. Surveys that involve vignettes, or stories/scenarios, might involve an attention check where respondents are quizzed about a part of the story. Surveys with failed attention checks should not be used for data analysis.

Flow and Appearance of Survey

The order in which items appear on the questionnaire can impact both the probability of participants completing it and the types of answers they provide. For most surveys, the demographic questions are almost always placed at the very end. Demographic questions are boring and certainly do not capture respondents' interest. They can also be off-putting to some. It is wise to save them for the end after the respondents have made a bit of a time investment in the project. Surveys should begin with questions that are interesting but not too sensitive or controversial. It is prudent to build up to those more difficult questions after people have warmed up a bit to the survey. For face-to-face administration, researchers can take the time to build a rapport before getting to the delicate questions.

The order in which survey items appear could influence how people answer questions later in the questionnaire, introducing bias into the responses. Picture a survey including lots of items about the opioid epidemic and its impact on public health and neighborhood safety. Toward the end of the survey, the researcher asks people to write what they believe to be the top five greatest threats to our communities. In this case, the opioid epidemic will likely be one of the top five issues that respondents raise, even if it was not something that respondents considered a particularly serious problem before starting the survey. By focusing attention on a specific problem for several minutes before asking respondents to come up with a list of community challenges, the survey structure likely helped to plant that idea in the heads of at least some people. In this scenario, the question about the greatest threats to the community should have come first, before respondents were exposed to any questions that would give them ideas.

Surveys should be as short as possible to encourage people to complete them. Researchers are often tempted to cram as many questions into a small number of pages to give the appearance of brevity (And perhaps to save money on copies and postage as I did with my own dissertation mail-survey!). While you want to make it appear as short as possible, be very careful. Do not reduce the font to the point where it will be hard to read, as that will irritate people and make it more difficult to complete. Cramming items anywhere they fit on the page will increase the chances that people will accidentally skip items. The survey's appearance should serve to improve the chances that all items will be seen and answered. If there are unstructured questions, remember to leave room for people to write responses.

One way to facilitate the flow of the survey is to use matrices, meaning that there will be a set of questions or statements that all have the same answer options. The **matrix** in Figure 9.1 was adapted from Peterson, Speer, and McMillan (2007) and used by Tartaro et al. (2021) when surveying police officers in New Jersey. One drawback to matrices is that they could lull participants into response sets, meaning they fall into a pattern of circling one number. The example in Figure 9.1 contains just a few items, so it is unlikely that participants will grow tired and start answering them without reading. If the matrix were larger, it would be wise to reverse some items in the middle of the matrix to have a high score indicate that the police do *not* feel supported by their communities.

Using the following scale, please rate your agreement on the following statements. As you read the questions, keep in mind the communities you police, not other communities or American social trends as a whole.

	Strongly Disagree				*Strongly Agree*
As a police officer, I can get what I need from the community I currently police.	1	2	3	4	5
Members of the community I police help me fulfill my needs as a police officer.	1	2	3	4	5
As a police officer, I feel like a member of the community I police.	1	2	3	4	5
As a police officer, I belong in the community I police.	1	2	3	4	5
As a police officer, I have a say about what goes on in the community I police.	1	2	3	4	5
As a police officer, I feel connected to the community I police.	1	2	3	4	5
As a police officer, I have a good bond with others in the community I police.	1	2	3	4	5
People in the community I police are good at influencing each other.	1	2	3	4	5

Figure 9.1 Matrix example

Sources: Peterson, N.A., Speer, P.W., & McMillan, D.W. (2007). Validation of a brief sense of community scale: Confirmation of the principle theory of sense of community. *Journal of Community Psychology, 36*(1), 61–73. https://doi.org/10.1002/jcop.20217 Tartaro, C., Bonnan-White, J., Mastrangelo, M. A. & Mulvihill, R. (2021). Police officers' attitudes toward mental health and crisis intervention: Understanding preparedness to respond to community members in crisis. *Journal of Police and Criminal Psychology,* DOI: 10.1007/s11896-021-09459-6

Another tool to assist with survey organization is the inclusion of **contingency questions**. It might not be necessary for every participant to complete every question and section of the survey. For a victimization survey, respondents who have not been burglarized in the past year should be able to skip the questions about what was stolen, whether they were home when it happened, and whether they reported the incident to the police. So, when they answer "no" to "has your house or apartment been burglarized in the past 12 months," self-administered paper/pencil surveys should include directions for the respondent to skip ahead to the next section. Computer or internet-based surveys can be programmed with **skip logic** to move respondents to the next appropriate question contingent on how they respond to previous items. Perhaps you might have been asked to participate in an online survey, but then after answering one or two questions, you were thanked for your time and the survey closed. That means that you answered a contingency question in a way that excluded you from further participation. This type of survey organization allows researchers to gather the data they need without needlessly taking up respondents' time.

Pretesting

As I noted earlier, researchers have one chance to get the survey right. The contingency questions must work properly to direct people to the next part of the survey, all questions must be worded clearly and lack biased language, and the format must make every question clearly visible. Researchers should spend a lot of time constructing, reviewing, and then re-reviewing the instrument. Individuals can only look at things for so long, however, and we are likely to inadvertently overlook things after multiple reviews of the same document. To mitigate making mistakes, you should do two things. First, walk away from the survey, let it sit for a few days, and then take another look with a fresher set of eyes. You are much more likely to find errors after a break. Second, pretest it with respondents who have a lot in common with your target population. If you plan to survey a sample of police captains, seek out some retired high-level police personnel or some police captains who are not in your intended sample and ask them to take the survey with an eye for anything that might be confusing or inaccurate. My colleagues and I were reminded of the value of pretesting when we asked some police officers to give us their opinions about our survey. We included what we considered an unambiguous question about whether they discharged their firearm while on duty in the past 12 months. The officers suggested that we reword the question, because there was something we failed to consider. While we were attempting to measure their involvement in life-threatening situations, we did not realize that officers in rural jurisdictions regularly use their firearms to put down wildlife hit by cars or injured by hunters. Given their advice, we reworded the question to ask about discharge of firearms over the past year, excluding incidents involving putting down an injured animal. Had we proceeded with distributing the survey to our sample without the pretest, we would have likely wound up with some very confusing results that would make it appear that officers in low-crime areas had to routinely resort to deadly force.

Ways of Distributing Surveys

In-Person Surveys

Sharing the same space with research participants has numerous advantages. One benefit is that it presents numerous survey construction and distribution possibilities. When in person, we have flexibility in the types of questions we can ask, the length of time spent interacting with participants, and the extent of contact that we want to have with them. When we are in person, we can use any type of survey format, from depth interviews to completely structured surveys with close-ended questions. Face-to-face is really the best option when considering doing a depth interview or anything that is going to take at least 30 minutes. Two people are more likely to sit and talk for hours when they are together having coffee. They are less likely to make such a time commitment to talk on the phone, fill out a mail survey, or complete an online survey.

Face-to-face interviews and in-person surveys are also desirable because they tend to elicit a greater response rate. It is so easy to delete an email asking for survey participation, toss a paper survey in the recycle bin, ignore a pop-up survey link while online, or neglect to answer the phone when caller ID indicates it is a research firm or an "unknown number." It is much more difficult to say no to another human standing in front of you. Nix et al. (2019) reviewed hundreds of policing articles and found that surveys involving any type of in-person administration, whether through an interview or even just in-person distribution of forms, had a 24% higher response rate than surveys circulated via telephone, mail, or online. Also, whereas survey response rates overall have been diminishing over the years, response rates for in-person surveys have remained steady.

When in the presence of respondents, researchers can use multimedia presentations, use audio or video recording devices (provided consent is given), and can be available to answer any questions that may arise. If the data collection involves an interview, researchers can not only note the individuals' verbal responses but also observe their body language. If the interview is being conducted in a home setting, observation of the home itself might also add some important context. For example, if you are interviewing a parent about their parenting skills and sense of responsibility and that person is giving answers that would indicate that they are a model parent but then stops and screams at a child for no apparent reason, that action is more telling than their survey answers.

When the researchers are on-site, they can clear up any misunderstandings or answer questions having to do with the research, something that is not possible with mail or internet surveys. Researchers administering surveys can even probe for more information. Probing is a gentle, neutral prompt from the researchers to encourage the respondents to elaborate on their answers. Researchers can probe with a few different techniques. One is silence. If someone asks you a question, you answer it, and the person just stares at you in silence, the silence is likely to make you uncomfortable and prompt you to talk more. It is a nonverbal way of communicating that the first answer really was not enough. Another probe is to repeat the question. Other options are to say things such as "like what" or "how" to elicit more of a response. In the most recent revision of the National Crime Victimization Survey (NCVS), research teams added follow-up probes for interviewers as they asked about victimization. These additional probes resulted in higher proportions of incidents being properly classified as crimes and the recording of more detailed information about criminal events when compared to the previous version of the NCVS (Truman & Brostsos, 2022).

Finally, on-site researchers can provide assistance to those who are unable to complete a self-administered survey due to language or literacy barriers. If the survey is going to be administered in a language other than the one in which it was originally written, it should first be completely translated by qualified individuals. Failure to do so could impact the validity and reliability of the survey, as each translator may word questions differently if left on their own to interpret the surveys.

Interacting with the Respondents

The presence of a researcher has a multitude of advantages, but researcher/respondent interaction must be handled very carefully. Just as researchers can read the body language of respondents, the opposite is also true. Researchers can unknowingly introduce bias into the interview if they fail to carefully regulate their own behavior. Researchers' unscripted comments can be particularly problematic during an interview. If the goal is to do a depth interview, the researcher will lack a script and will have to use his/her own skills to generate conversation in a way that is non-judgmental and refrains from leading the conversation in a way that would produce biased results. For example, if I am interviewing someone about victimization in a neighborhood, and upon hearing a response I remark, "Oh how awful, that must have been terrifying," I am leading the conversation in a specific direction. Through my comments, I am expressing my opinion that I believe that there are frightening incidents taking place in the area, and this might prompt the respondent to elaborate on the dangers more than would have happened had I just said, "I am sorry to hear that" or "Oh really, can you tell me more about that?" For scripted, more structured surveys, interviewers should be trained to stay on the precise script that is provided, with the exception of acting human and making neutral remarks from time to time.

Verbal responses are not the only way for researchers to influence the respondents' answers. A sigh, gasp, or eye roll can be just as powerful as a comment. People generally dislike being judged, and if it takes place in a situation where they are completing a survey for which the results really don't matter to them, what's the use in putting up with the judgment when one can just provide more socially acceptable answers, feel less shame, and just finish the interview? If I am interviewing someone about drinking habits and my face gives away my anger when the person recalls driving while under the influence, the person is likely to be reluctant to continue to divulge sensitive, unflattering information. Criminal justice researchers hear a lot of bad things. It is imperative that researchers withhold their personal opinions and judgments while performing their jobs as researchers.

For in-person work, researchers must give consideration to what they wear to the meetings with respondents. If the research team will be entering office space and interviewing judges or administrators, professional attire is appropriate. Instances where the interviews will take place in booking areas of jails or inside jail visitation rooms are different, however, and I have always found it helpful to dress casually to avoid making it seem like I was someone in a position of authority who might be considered a threat to the respondents. The general rule for choosing attire is to dress in a way that is similar to the level of dress of respondents. Pashea and Kochel (2016) worked on a large crime hot spots project that involved numerous face-to-face interviews of residents. Their interviewers initially dressed in khaki pants and collared shirts because they thought that a show of professionalism would attract more survey respondents. They learned that neighborhood residents were more likely to be receptive to and comfortable with interviewers who dressed casually rather than in a uniform.

Drawbacks to In-Person Surveys

In addition to the risk of biasing the survey through researcher-participant interaction, three further potential drawbacks to in-person survey distribution in criminal justice are time, money, and safety. Researchers must often travel to the respondents for in-person research. In criminal justice, we often work with people who lack financial resources and/or transportation, and in some cases, people are not free to travel on account of incarceration or conditions of community supervision. Researchers can work to arrange or pay for participants to travel to interview locations, but there's concern in our field that this might introduce some artificiality to the work by interviewing people outside of their usual environments. That is why, in most cases, researchers travel to the participants. Logan et al. (2008) researched domestic violence among families in Appalachia, requiring approximately four hours of driving each day, plus any interview time. Researchers must find funding for the gas, tolls, and the time it takes to do this work, or face having to pay for it themselves. Since we are often interviewing offenders or people whose lives have been impacted by crime, we frequently visit neighborhoods, housing projects, and correctional facilities that pose safety risks. It is important to have safety protocols in place, such as requiring researchers to stay together, in some fieldwork settings. This will be discussed in more detail in Chapter 10.

Video as a Substitution for Physical Presence

In recent years, being present via technology has become an option for researchers. Having an online presence through the use of videos for interviews is a potentially inexpensive alternative for data collection, particularly if travel would otherwise need to be involved. It also reduces safety concerns for researchers. Being online over video with someone will never completely replicate the personal experience of being physically present in a room, so for depth interviews or situations where it would be very helpful to see someone's physical surroundings, the in-person approach is still ideal. The online option does contain multiple benefits similar to the in-person data collection approach, as the private chat function can be used to clear up any misunderstandings in a group setting, and researchers can still get a sense of the respondent's body language. Some video conferencing systems even come with built-in recording and/or transcription services that can free the researcher from having to take notes during interviews. We do need to consider that this type of data collection might be problematic for some types of criminal justice research. Older individuals are less likely to want or even be able to do this type of interview. We often work with individuals experiencing high levels of poverty who have low levels of education. That means they may lack technical know-how, the financial resources to access the technology, or access to a private setting suitable to maintain confidentiality while online. Additionally, we work with people who are concerned about their privacy and about being monitored, so such participants may not want to be on video for fear that it will be secretly recorded. Finally, corrections researchers looking to connect with incarcerated individuals could utilize the video visitation system for interviews, but that comes with the drawbacks of lack of confidentiality (the video visits are monitored), time limits to those sessions, and cost. The lack of confidentiality will likely make proposals to do online interviews with incarcerated people a violation of research ethics requirements.

Computer Assistance with Survey Administration

If there is a possibility that social desirability might impact participants' survey answers, it might be best to allow them to respond to the survey privately with **computer-assisted interviewing** (CAI) or **computer-assisted survey instruments** (CASIs). CASIs can be placed on laptops and tablets, have the benefit of being able to use skip-logic to seamlessly move people from one contingency question to the next appropriate section, and they allow for either the respondent to take the whole survey online or for the interviewer to read the question while the respondent keys in the answer. Regardless of whether the interviewer is reading the questions or the participant is reading and answering on the tablet, the interviewer will never see the respondents' answers. When taking an in-person survey, CASIs may afford people more privacy than a paper/pencil option. When people are taking long paper/pencil surveys, others in the room can see how long someone is taking on a particular page or section. They can also detect when someone answers a contingency question in a way that results in a skip to another section several pages later, as the paper flipping will be visible. An additional potential advantage to using the CAI or CASI technology includes time and cost saving due to not having to hire data entry staff to log responses from paper surveys. While researchers doing face-to-face surveys without CASI can only promise confidentiality, CASI provides the extra benefit of anonymity. This is an important distinction. With confidentiality, researchers promise participants that they will never divulge their specific responses to anyone, but the researchers still know how participants answered. With anonymity, even the research team is unable to match the respondents with the completed surveys. Anonymity provides the participants with greater privacy, and it frees them from having to worry about being judged by the researcher for giving socially undesirable responses to questions. It is also a much safer way for respondents to self-report illegal activities.

Spark and associates (2015) surveyed adults about their sexual behavior, which is clearly a sensitive topic. They administered nearly 4,500 surveys, half through paper/pencil and half using CASI. The participants who entered their data with CASI were less likely to skip questions pertaining to their sexual behavior and were more likely to report having a greater number of sexual partners in the past 12 months compared to those who took the paper/pencil survey. The researchers found that, for this study, administration using CASI was cheaper than paper/pencil administration after accounting for copies, postage, and having to pay staff for data entry.

Potential drawbacks to using CASI are front-end costs to purchase the equipment and set up the programs. Anytime technology is involved, there is the possibility that something will go wrong and data will be lost. Additionally, if one is reliant on internet access for survey administration, lack of access to Wifi and unstable connections can complicate data collection.

Telephone Surveys

Like in-person survey administration, telephone surveys do allow for a degree of interaction between the survey administrator and respondents. Researchers have the benefit of being able to provide clarification if anything is unclear, probe for longer answers when necessary, and be able to note any significant changes in the respondents' tone as the interview progresses. Of course, whenever we can hear the respondents, they can hear us, so it is imperative that the telephone interviewers are properly trained to avoid biasing the interview. As with in-person surveys, it is possible to use technology, with **computer-assisted telephone interviewing** (CATI). CATI lets the researcher read questions from a computer and then immediately input the answers into a database, cutting down on time and money needed for subsequent data entry. CATI does not, however, give participants the anonymity and privacy associated with CASI.

Telephone interviews are beneficial in that calls are very cheap, so the costs for this type of work are substantially lower than for in-person research. It can also be much faster, as the time between phone calls can be seconds, whereas travel between locations for on-site work could take minutes, hours, or days. The safety risks to research staff are also eliminated, as they will remain in a call center instead of being in potentially dangerous environments. Another advantage to phone work is the ease of supervision of workers. One supervisor can be in a room listening to several interviewers at once. This makes it much easier to check for interviewer bias. If the sample is ethnically heterogeneous, there might be a need for bilingual interviewers, and using telephone interviewers in call centers makes it possible to quickly engage staff members who speak the appropriate language. Such quick switching out of interviewers is less likely to be an option when researchers have to fan out through neighborhoods on foot while doing in-person work.

Drawbacks to Telephone Surveys

There are, of course, disadvantages to phone surveys. While it is possible to do long interviews, people are generally very hesitant to stay on the telephone with strangers for long. In graduate school, I was involved in a phone survey project, and if respondents had personally been victimized in a few different ways, the survey could take up to 35 minutes to complete. It was very difficult to convince people to stay on the phone that long, as they tended to lose interest around 20 minutes into the call. Another drawback to this modality is the proliferation of caller ID. Now that it is possible to see who is calling, some people avoid researchers' calls. Telephone survey response rates decreased from 36% in 1997 to just 9% in 2016 (Keeter et al., 2017).

Another more recent development is the decline in landlines in favor of cellphones. In 2003, over 95% of American homes had landlines, but that percentage began decreasing immediately thereafter (Kempf & Remington, 2007). The National Center for Health Statistics tracks the percentages of adults and children who live in homes with and without landlines. As of 2023, three-quarters of adults in the United States lived in a house without a landline phone. Additionally, the decision to go wireless-only is not random, with younger families, Latinos, families with incomes below the poverty level, and adults who rented homes being less likely to have a landline (Blumberg & Luke, 2024). These differences are relevant to criminal justice research, as demographics are associated with crime involvement and victimization.

The popularity of cell phones at the expense of landlines also presents difficulty with identifying the unit of analysis for the study. Landlines generally belong to the entire household, whereas an individual cellphone belongs to a person (Kempf & Remington, 2007). Landlines are easier to work with for survey purposes, as it is possible to identify which exchanges belong to businesses, but that is not the case with cell phones. The growth of the prepaid cell phone business has also generated phones that are regularly activated and then deactivated. Landlines also lack portability, so people who move from one area code to another with a landline have had to change their phone numbers. Cell phone owners keep their numbers regardless of where they move. This makes it difficult to sample a geographic region using random digit dialing of area codes and the first three digits of phone numbers (Kempf & Remington, 2007). A final concern about the involvement of cell phones in surveys is that, when we call landlines, we know that people are in their homes and not behind the wheel of a car. We also know that they are in at least a semi-private location rather than in a grocery store or office. There are concerns that people on cell phones will be more likely to be multitasking during interviews. In addition to this possibly being dangerous, it could impact their responses. People may give more socially desirable responses when they lack privacy or may be more rushed and give answers that they think will end the interview sooner (Kempf & Remington, 2007; Link et al., 2007). Even if multitasking cell phone users are trying to concentrate on the survey, they may still lack a degree of cognitive engagement (Link et al., 2007).

One final issue that I want to note about telephone surveys is that the quality largely rests on how well the staff are trained and supervised. Have you ever gotten a call from a researcher who you could hear reading the survey to you? I have and, as a researcher, it bothers me a great deal. The staff should have the greeting statement/paragraph memorized and practiced to the point where it can be recited as if the researcher is having a friendly conversation with another individual. As for the rest of the survey, it is not necessary for staff to memorize it, but they must be comfortable enough to be able to go through it while *not* sounding as if they are reading the questions. If the staff is using a paper/pencil survey, they must know where the contingency questions are and be prepared to move to the next section without delay. Researchers often inconvenience respondents by taking up their time, and it is our responsibility to show respondents respect by being well prepared for the job.

Self-Administered Surveys

Traditional Mail or Paper/Pencil

Utilizing the mail to distribute paper and pencil surveys is a very inexpensive option. Mail surveys have the benefit of allowing researchers to reach a wide geographic region, even globally, with very little cost. Mail surveys are also possible without a research team. My dissertation was based on a mail survey of approximately 1,700 jails, and I handled the mailing myself, with the assistance of a few relatives who were willing to stuff envelopes.

Surveys that participants can complete independently have less potential to be impacted by social desirability, as they don't have to worry about facing someone who might judge them. Patterson, Hogan, and Cox (2019) utilized different methods of collecting self-reported alcohol consumption data from college students. Respondents tended to provide more conservative estimates of their drinking when data were collected through face-to-face interaction with research staff versus completing a drinking diary at home.

Unlike in-person or telephone interviews, surveys that are mailed or otherwise distributed with return instructions can be completed at a time convenient for the respondent, and this could encourage the person to put more consideration into answers. It can also give participants the needed time to look up answers. This is particularly helpful when we are asking criminal justice practitioners information about the populations their agencies serve, as they are unlikely to have that information committed to memory. Finally, the lack of researcher presence eliminates the possibility of interviewer bias.

Online/Email

The fastest, cheapest, and most convenient way to distribute surveys is through websites and email. Online survey distribution is especially useful when you already have a sampling frame containing the email addresses, and you are targeting a population that regularly uses technology. Online surveys are particularly helpful if your instrument relies on contingency questions, as existing survey tools can use skip logic to automatically move people to the next appropriate section of the survey.

Drawbacks to Self-Administered Surveys

Of course, there are disadvantages to self-administered surveys that are sent through the mail or email or are available online. Just as the researchers' absence is an advantage in that it eliminates interviewer bias, it also removes all the benefits of having interviewers present. It will not be possible to collect data about respondent body language or make observations about the house or neighborhood where the respondent lives. The researcher will also not be present to clarify anything or probe for more information. Researchers' lack control over when, if ever, people will complete the surveys and return them, and this often leads to low response rates.

Researchers working on the NCVS redesign wanted to explore the possibility of conducting the initial interview of household members in person but then switching to online survey administration instead of their traditional follow-up telephone interviews. The potential benefits of the switch are lower costs due to reduced need for staff involvement in survey administration and additional respondent privacy as they work through providing details about victimizations. The researchers found that, while online survey administration is cheaper and more efficient, it is not always better for collecting data. Responses collected via follow-up telephone interviews revealed higher violent victimization rates than did the online survey responses. A likely explanation for this is that personal interaction with the researcher over the phone, combined with the researchers' skills at probing, encouraged respondents to pay greater attention and put more effort into recalling and disclosing events (Cantor et al., 2023).

Another concern with using self-administered surveys instead of interviews is that respondents may become less motivated and invested in the survey without the presence of a research staff member to encourage accountability. Krosnick (1991) observed that, by asking someone to participate in a survey, we are asking people to expend cognitive effort in exchange for little to no reward. Even if they are initially interested in the survey, that interest is likely to fade as the survey continues and fatigue and even frustration take hold. Krosnick cautioned that respondents may resort to **satisficing**, which involves respondents seeking to provide what they believe to be a satisfactory answer to a survey question without expending cognitive effort. Satisficing can take multiple forms, including choosing the first response option that appears to constitute a reasonable answer, endorsing the status quo, utilizing the "don't know" option, or randomly choosing among available answer options.

Part of satisficing is trying to complete the survey as quickly as possible while expending little effort to do so. One way to accomplish this is to skip over directions and even the wording of survey questions. With self-administered surveys, particularly those including close-ended questions or statements that involve circling or checking answers, a very valid concern is whether people get bored and start answering at random or fall into a pattern of providing a particular response set. Researchers can check for this using attention checks. Flippinn, Reisig, and Trinkner (2019) surveyed college students on their likely responses to hypothetical 911 calls where the dispatcher was either respectful and professional or rude and confrontational. One survey item was completely unrelated to their hypothesis testing, as it asked participants to indicate why the 911 call was being made (the correct answer was either a bicycle accident or a burglary). Less than 3% of respondents failed the attention check. Those surveys with the incorrect attention check answers were removed from analysis.

While attention checks are a good way of detecting lack of respondent attention, it is not possible to detect all forms of satisficing without administering the same survey in a different modality, such as telephone or in-person. The NCVS redesign research provided a rare opportunity for this when researchers compared the telephone interviews to the pilot-tested online surveys. In the Police Performance section of the surveys, telephone respondents reported a greater number of contacts with police. Additionally, for both Police Performance and Community Safety sections, it appears that the online respondents were more likely to frequently select the neutral or middle response categories on Likert scales. Online survey participants also tended to complete the surveys faster than those who responded over the phone (Cantor et al., 2023).

Perhaps the biggest drawback to mail and internet surveys is the response rate. In-person interviews have the best response rates, followed by telephone interviews (although those rates have been declining with the growth of caller ID and reliance on cell phones). With in-person and telephone interviews, there is some social desirability pressure to agree to participate so as not to disappoint the person on the phone or at the front door. Since people toss out junk mail every day, there is little guilt associated with throwing out a letter from a researcher or polling organization. Returning to our NCVS example, when the researchers attempted online surveys, those had lower response rates than the telephone interviews, particularly for minor children respondents (Cantor et al., 2023). A $20 financial incentive did help, with 61% of respondents offered the incentive completing the survey, compared with the 37% completion figure for those not offered money (Edwards et al., 2023).

Online surveys tend to have an even lower response rate than mail surveys. Sax, Gilmartin, and Bryant (2003) studied differences in survey completion when students were given four options: paper-only, paper with internet option, internet-only with response incentive, and internet-only without response incentive. The total response rate across all four types was 21.5%, with the online options having the lowest rates. The researchers speculated that this could be a product of students not checking their college email regularly as well as possible concerns about privacy. British Columbia Health Survey (BCHS) researchers distributed surveys through a combination of mail and online requests but were more likely to receive responses through traditional mail (Guo et al., 2016).

There are a few possible reasons for the lower response rates for online and email-generated surveys. First, the proliferation of spam has resulted in inboxes being flooded with unwanted email, and while we also get unwanted paper mail, there is a greater risk involved with opening an email or clicking on a link that might contain malware. Second, not everyone uses email and the internet, with the elderly and people living in poverty being less likely to be online. Third, of all the survey options to ignore, emails with survey links and online links to surveys are the easiest.

The timing for sending out the initial survey and subsequent reminders is very important. The holidays, particularly between Thanksgiving and New Year's Day, for example, are not good times to send surveys. It is helpful to think about your target population and their lives. If you are considering surveying accountants about people's tax evasion habits, do not send them during tax season when accountants are especially busy.

Since mail and internet surveys often have poor response rates, it is frequently necessary to conduct follow-ups. If the survey is distributed by mail, this will increase how much money it takes to complete the project. While postage is cheap, researchers must pay for postage and self-addressed stamped return envelopes to make it easy for respondents to return the surveys. Never make participants go through the trouble of finding their own envelope and paying for their own postage. Project costs multiply with each additional mailing, but it will likely be necessary. When is the right time to send out follow-ups? Track the number of responses you are getting each day. They will eventually peak, and as they start to diminish, that would be a good time to get the next batch ready.

Anyone who does a mail or internet survey is going to need to give serious consideration to how they can work to maximize response rates. Wu and colleagues (2022) screened over 8,000 studies utilizing online surveys and found that there were some promising tactics for increasing response rates. They reported that research protocols involving prenotifying potential participants, calling people to remind them about the surveys, and using other types of survey distribution in addition to the online option tended to have higher response rates. Prenotifications can also serve to test the physical or email addresses and confirm that they are still accurate and/or functional (Jennings & Reingle Gonzales, 2019).

One way to encourage people to fill out a survey is to get an endorsement or sponsorship from a well-regarded individual or organization. Approval from a professional association can lend legitimacy to a survey, especially when practitioners might not understand how the work could help the discipline. In Chapter 2, I noted how I asked for and received assistance from a high-ranking member of the American Jail Association when I was planning to send surveys to hundreds of jail administrators. After my initial mailing and two follow-ups, I had a 50% response rate, which is very good for a mail survey. The American Jail Association endorsement was important, as jail administrators who opened the envelope immediately saw a cover letter with the AJA logo.

Regardless of whether you can get someone or some influential group to write the cover letter for you, the letter or introductory email/message itself is very important, and you should take great care writing it. You will not personally be there to plead your case why your research is important and why it is worthy of anyone's time. The letter is your one chance to do it. At minimum, you should identify yourself and your affiliation (likely a college or university right now), and explain what you are studying and how the results of the study could be beneficial to individuals, groups, agencies, or society in general. Don't overstate this, though, or you will lose credibility. Give respondents the opportunity to let you know if they would like to see a copy of the results once you are finished with data collection and analysis. When you explain the purpose of the study, keep in mind that you might need to be a bit vague to prevent introducing bias into the results. If you find that you need to be vague and omit any information in the cover letter, you could include a debriefing statement at the end of the survey. The cover letter also usually has the contact information of the person who can answer any questions that the participants might have. For surveys, cover letters may also serve as informed consent documents, so please review Chapter 3 for a refresher on that.

Hagan (2007) provided additional suggestions for attempting to boost response rates, including renumeration, appeals to altruism, and using an attractive survey format, personalization, and a shortened format. Researchers with the BCHS tested types of data collection methods to see if they had an impact on response rates. Renumeration served as a good incentive for survey completion. Surveys sent with an instant lottery ticket were 35% more likely to be returned than those that were not. The researchers found that providing instant financial compensation was more persuasive than a promise of sending compensation upon completion of the survey. The BCHS researchers also found that people were more likely to complete and return a 10-minute version of the survey than they were the 30-minute version (Guo et al., 2016), but others have not found survey length to be associated with differences in response rates (Stolzmann et al., 2019).

There might be a time when some of the aforementioned options aren't possible. In the incarceration setting, incentives might be prohibited, and prenotifications and reminder phone calls aren't feasible. Pickett et al. (2014) came up with a unique way to encourage survey participation among incarcerated individuals by appealing to their desire for autonomy, something that people in prison lack. Instead of asking for their consent and then providing one survey, each incarcerated individual was given a consent form and then permitted to choose from two different surveys that contained the same questions but in a different order. This served to give participants a sense of control, which is rare inside prisons. The sample of individuals who were given a choice of survey had higher response rates and higher item-completion percentages when compared to a random sample of incarcerated individuals who were not permitted to select a preferred survey format.

What about increasing the sample size? Does that improve response rates? Nix et al. (2019) reviewed 380 articles in policing and criminal justice journals that involved a variety of survey methods and found that, for every additional 100 individuals invited to respond to a survey, the response rate declined by about 1 percent. When Wu et al. (2022) reviewed the performance of online surveys in educational research, they found that smaller sample sizes were associated with higher response rates. The researchers recommended that targeting a clearly defined and refined population for survey completion is likely to be more successful in improving response rates compared to increasing sample sizes.

Specific Types of Surveys

Focus Group

Focus groups are a type of in-person interview popular with market research firms, as they are a quick and easy way to get feedback about a product. They consist of small groups, usually eight to 15 people, who participate in a guided discussion with a facilitator. Focus groups are usually constructed through purposive sampling, with the goal of bringing together certain groups of individuals, such as household members responsible for weekly grocery shopping or registered voters from a specific community. Companies that are nearing the release of a product might gather a sample of shoppers to get their opinions about the taste, texture, and even the bottle shape of a new type of salad dressing. News networks frequently put together focus groups of potential voters to watch political candidates debate and then engage in guided discussions about each politician's performance.

Focus groups can be useful as researchers prepare to write structured surveys but have not yet decided what to ask and what answer options to use. Data obtained from focus groups can also be used to supplement survey data to better understand the nature of the problem at hand. Dyson (2005) distributed structured questionnaires to young men housed in Scottish correctional facilities but also hosted 11 small focus groups with an average of four to seven juveniles. The groups revealed factors impacting bullying that the researcher had not included in the survey, specifically how bullying might differ by officer shift. With regard to validity and reliability, juveniles' descriptions of bullying differed between what was said in the focus groups and what juveniles reported on the anonymous surveys. In the surveys, juveniles disclosed being bullied by both staff and other juveniles but would only discuss staff bullying in the group setting. It appears that the juveniles did not want to "rat" out their peers or admit to being victims of peer bullying when they were speaking in front of other juveniles.

It is generally desirable to select focus group members who do not already know each other, as familiarity might mean that already established social dynamics will influence who gets to speak the most during the sessions (Dyson, 2005; Rainbow, 2024). In the above bullying example, Dyson (2005) was unable to arrange for the focus groups to consist of strangers, as all the young men were incarcerated together. As a result, the facilitator noticed that sessions tended to be dominated by one or two people, while the rest usually quietly agreed with the points made by the vocal individuals. This is because social hierarchies had already been established among this group of people who knew each other.

Self-Report

Self-report surveys serve an important purpose in our discipline, as they give us the opportunity to ask people directly about their behavior. Researchers have employed self-report surveys in various ways, ranging from interviews with a single person to large, nationally representative data collection endeavors such as the **National Youth Survey** (NYS), Monitoring the Future (MTF), and the **Arrestee Drug Abuse Monitoring** (ADAM and ADAM II) Program. The NYS started in 1976 with a national sample of juveniles aged 11 to 17 years old living in the United States. The NYS is a longitudinal design including numerous waves of data collection with the goal of studying delinquent behavior (Brauer, 2009; Pogarsky et al., 2005). NYS results have been used in several publications and are considered valid and reliable data. The MTF survey began in 1975 and serves as a measure of adolescent attitudes and drug behavior. Each year, MTF staff survey over 25,000 students in the 8th, 10th, and 12th grades as well as approximately 20,000 adults between the ages of 19 and 65 (Monitoring the Future, 2024). MTF helps researchers and policymakers understand trends in drug use, including newer developments such as vaping. The ADAM Program, originally called the Drug Use Forecasting Program, was discontinued in 2003 due to budget cuts. It was reinstated as ADAM II in 2007 and was discontinued again in 2013. ADAM researchers interviewed newly arrested individuals and asked them to self-report drug use and provide a urine sample to enhance validity and reliability (National Institute of Justice, n.d.).

With self-reports, we are usually asking people to admit to behavior that might not make them look very good. The behavior in question, if it were to become publicly available, could bring embarrassment, impact one's employment or student status, and even lead to arrest. That means there are reasons why people would be tempted to be less than forthcoming. Fortunately, research indicates that self-reports generally have good validity and reliability. Connell and Farrington (1997) studied the reliability and validity of self-reported bullying and victimizations in correctional facilities, and Sekol and Farrington (2013) did a follow-up several years later. The results of both studies support the use of self-reports as reliable indicators of bullying in institutions. Sutton et al. (2011) surveyed incarcerated individuals and asked them to self-report criminal behavior. The researchers conducted a follow-up survey three months later to check for reliability, and their test-retest strategy provided evidence of good reliability.

There are steps that researchers can take to help to enhance the accuracy and stability of self-reports. As with any survey asking for information over time, telescoping, or placing an incident into an incorrect time period, could be a problem here. For example, if I am filling out a survey and am asked if I have gotten a traffic ticket anytime over the last year, I might accidentally write "yes" when my most recent ticket was actually 18 months ago. To combat this, researchers doing longitudinal self-report surveys could employ bounding, or do an initial interview as a panel study and then use that first interview as a time boundary (Hagan, 2007). After the initial interview, researchers might start an interview by saying, "since our last interview...", to hopefully help respondents place incidents in the correct time frame. If researchers are not implementing a panel design, another suggestion would be to try to use memorable moments as a reference point. For students, asking them about incidents that occurred during specific times in their lives, such as "since the start of the semester" or "during summer break" might help to prevent telescoping.

We can increase our confidence in self-report data by conducting reliability checks. As noted earlier, the ADAM data collection project involved the use of multiple data collection methods. Not only did participants answer questions about their drug use, but they also provided a urine sample. Researchers asking students about their delinquent activity might include some questions that can then be verified using other records. For example, schools have records of suspensions, so researchers can ask students to self-report the number of suspensions they received this year and check this against school records later. Reliability checks, including using test-retest and measures of internal consistency (see Chapter 4 for a review) are also valuable tools to monitor respondents' consistency.

An obviously difficult aspect of some self-report surveys is broaching sensitive subjects with people who are complete strangers. There are some things that we have not even admitted to our own friends and families, and yet we might find ourselves sitting across from a researcher or staring at a computer screen and being asked to disclose this information. There are a few ways for researchers to approach asking about sensitive information. One is the **randomized response technique** (RRT) designed by Warner (1965). A research participant would flip a coin or use some other randomization technique to select one of two available statements: "I cheated on my taxes at least once" or "I have never cheated on my taxes" and then answer that question. Only the respondent will know which question was actually asked, shielding them from the embarrassment of having to give a socially undesirable answer to the researcher. A drawback to RRT is that it is a rather complicated scheme to understand, and people will only shed their social desirability concerns if they both understand the process and trust that their anonymity is being protected (Jann et al., 2012). Yan and Cantor (2019) also suggest either using a "forgiving introduction" or asking questions presupposing the behavior. **Forgiving introductions** aim to lessen the impact of social desirability by prefacing the questions with a brief statement about how commonly some things occur, such as taking office supplies or being stopped by the police. Yan and Cantor describe questions that presuppose the behavior as types of "loaded" questions that assume that people committed a particular behavior at least once. Instead of asking whether a person ever took home office supplies, one might ask, "how many times in the past six months did you take home office supplies?"

Is a Survey the Right Tool for Your Study?

Surveys are obviously very powerful tools in our data collection arsenal. They allow us to get information about thoughts and feelings as well as incidents that are too difficult to observe. Without surveys, we would have little information on crimes not reported to the police. Maxfield and Babbie (2012) observed that surveys generally perform well on reliability but may lack validity. With surveys, we are not observing what people did, but instead we are asking what they did or what they *would* do in certain situations. Due to social desirability, recall error, dishonesty, or an unrealistic view of oneself, the answers might not reflect people's true behavior. Additionally, the way we construct the survey might inhibit our full understanding of an issue. Structured surveys are quick and can be very reliable, but if we forget to ask some questions or to include a full range of answer options, we could emerge from the project with a limited understanding of the topic.

When conducting surveys, we must remember that our sample may not be truly representative of the population. The US Census Bureau (2019) identified four categories of hard-to-count (HTC) populations—hard to locate, hard to contact, hard to persuade, and hard to interview. Among these groups are very marginalized segments of our society, including people who are homeless, transient, incarcerated, have language barriers, or have disabilities. This is especially concerning given that these groups' lives tend to be disproportionately impacted by crime, whether as offenders or as victims. Projects with large budgets and staff members can put resources into working to identify and locate HTC individuals, work with community organizations to gain trust, and attempt to have these groups represented in data collection. This is obviously much more difficult, if not impossible, for studies involving fewer resources. The result is sample bias. The NCVS, which surveys households, does work to collect data from residents living in dormitories, rooming houses and religious group dwellings, but they do not survey people who are in military barracks or institutions (including correctional facilities) (United States Bureau of Justice Statistics, n.d.). While a survey might ultimately be the best option for what you are looking to study, it is important to keep in mind that there are difficult-to-reach populations that you will likely miss, and their exclusion will result in sample bias.

Is a self-report appropriate for what you are looking to study? Self-reports can be very helpful when we are trying to collect data on criminal behavior and victimization, particularly when we are seeking to capture information on crimes not known to the police. If you are aiming to find out about the age of onset for individuals' criminal offending, Moffitt et al. (2001) found that self-report data will likely yield different information than official records. Specifically, self-reports tend to reveal offending commencing about three to five years before people start to develop arrest histories that would be found by searching official records. While that's a strength of self-reports relative to official records, self-reports have also been found to be less precise than official records on account of memory and honesty issues with respondents. Farrington et al. (2003) noted that, while self-reports might be less precise on dates, they can provide us with information that may not be available in official records, particularly the UCR/NIBRS, such as specifics regarding the offense, motives, and levels of planning involved.

Summary

Since we cannot always observe the activities that we wish to study, we frequently rely on surveys in criminal justice to understand thoughts and behaviors. How we choose to construct a survey will likely impact the quality of the data we collect. We must decide whether we want to provide answer options or have respondents answer using their own words. While the former will be easier to use during data analysis, it also comes with the risk that we might fail to consider and include every possible answer option that respondents would want to choose. As we work to construct surveys, we must think about our sample and their reading and verbal comprehension levels, because the survey language must be written in a way that they can understand. Questions and statements on surveys must be completely unambiguous to reduce problems with validity and reliability. The physical layout of the survey can impact the chances of participants seeing and responding to every item. Researchers must be very careful when they construct surveys, and they have to spend a tremendous amount of time writing, reviewing, editing, and re-reviewing the instruments. Pretesting with a few people who are similar to the target population is a valuable experience that can prevent distribution of a survey before it is ready.

The various methods of survey distribution—in-person, telephone, mail, email/web—each have strengths and weaknesses. In-person distribution tends to produce the highest response rates.

Face-to-face survey administration can provide us not only with survey data but information about the respondents' surroundings, their body language, and possibly their interactions with family and friends. While this is very helpful, we must be mindful of the potentially costly drawbacks to this type of data collection. Work that requires researchers to travel will cost more time and money, and in criminal justice, it might also require data collectors to risk their personal safety. Video conferencing might be a viable substitute for in-person interviewing provided that the interviews are not too long, the respondents are able to access and use technology, and they can find a private setting to do so. Telephone surveys present an opportunity for very fast data collection while still allowing for some researcher-respondent interaction. Any time the researchers speak to respondents, they need to be properly trained to administer the survey so that they avoid biasing the interview. Telephone surveys have become more of a challenge over the past few decades with the proliferation of caller-ID and the reduction of landlines in favor of cell phones. Mail and email/web surveys are also inexpensive alternatives that give respondents a good amount of privacy and plenty of time to complete the survey, but low response rates are common. Of the types of survey administration, mail and email/web surveys are the easiest for people to discard.

Self-report surveys give researchers the opportunity to learn about behaviors that we are probably unlikely to witness. In criminal justice, these surveys often address sensitive topics, including asking people to recall victimization experiences and their offending histories. Given the risks associated with disclosing such information, it is natural to wonder how forthcoming and truthful respondents will be. If possible, reliability checks should be conducted to inform researchers about how confident they should be in the results. Any time researchers ask individuals to share personal information, it is the research team's duty to follow ethical rules to safeguard the data and prevent respondents from being harmed by their willingness to participate in the study.

Key Terms

Structured survey	Unstructured survey	Semi-structured survey
Depth interview	Matrix	Contingency question
Skip logic	Computer-assisted interviewing (CAI)	Computer-assisted survey instruments (CASI)
Computer-assisted telephone interviewing (CATI)	Satisficing	Arrestee Drug Abuse Monitoring (ADAM)
	National Youth Survey (NYS)	
Randomized response technique (RRT)	Forgiving introduction	

Discussion Questions

1. Discuss each type of survey administration and how it fares with getting good response rates. What kind of steps can researchers take to improve their response rates?
2. What are the advantages and disadvantages to using structured or unstructured surveys?
3. What are the pros and cons to using computer-assisted survey instruments (CASI)?
4. Discuss the different ways that our wording on surveys could serve to confuse respondents or introduce bias.
5. How can the appearance of a survey instrument encourage or discourage full and accurate completion of the survey?

References

Beck, A. T. (1988). *BHS, Beck Hopelessness Scale*. Psychological Corporation.

Beck, A. T., & Steer, R. A. (1988). *Manual for the Beck Hopelessness Scale*. Psychological Corporation.

Beck, A. T., Steer, R. A., & Brown, G. K. (1996). *BDI-II, Beck Depression Inventory*. Psychological Corporation.

Blumberg S. J., & Luke J. V. (2024). *Wireless substitution: Early release of estimates from the National Health Interview Survey, July-December 2023*. National Center for Health Statistics. https://doi.org/10.15620/cdc/156660

Brauer, J. (2009). Testing social learning theory using reinforcement's residue: A multilevel analysis of self-reported theft and marijuana use in the National Youth Survey. *Criminology, 47*(3), 929–970. https://doi.org/10.1111/j.1745-9125.2009.00164.x

Cantor, D., Edwards, W. S., Giambo, P., Towsent, R., Yan, T., & DeMatteis, J. (2023). *NCVS redesign – comparison of interviewer and web survey modes*. Westat. www.ojp.gov/pdffiles1/bjs/grants/306998.pdf

Connell, A., & Farrington, D. P. (1997). The reliability and validity of resident, staff, and peer reports of bullying in young offender institutions. *Psychology, Crime, and Law, 3*(4), 287–300. https://doi.org/10.1080/10683169708410824

Cull, J. G., & Gill, W. S. (1998). *Suicide Probability Scale (SPS) manual*. Western Psychological Services.

Decker, S. H., & Rosenfeld, R. (1995). "My wife is married and so is my girlfriend": Adaptations to the threat of AIDS in an arrestee population. *Crime & Delinquency, 41*(1), 37–53.

Dyson, G. (2005). Examining bullying among institutionalized young offenders: Triangulation of questionnaires and focus groups. In J. L. Ireland (Ed.), *Bullying among prisoners* (pp. 84–108). Willan Publishing.

Edwards, W. S., Cantor, D., Yan, T., Sun, H., & Giambo, P. (2023). *National Crime Victimization Survey redesign letter and incentive experiment report*. Westat. www.ojp.gov/pdffiles1/bjs/grants/306158.pdf

Farrington. D. P., Jolliffe, D., Hawkins, J. D., Catalano, R. F., Hill, K. G., & Kosterman, R. (2003). Comparing delinquency careers in court records and self-reports. *Criminology, 41*(3), 933–958. https://doi.org/10.1111/j.1745-9125.2003.tb01009.x

Flippin, M., Reisig, M. D., & Trinkner, R. (2019). The effect of procedural injustice during emergency 911 calls: A factorial vignette-based study. *Journal of Experimental Criminology, 15*, 651–660. https://doi.org/10.1007/s11292-019-09369-y

Guo, Y., Kopec, J. A., Cibere, J., Li, L. C., & Goldsmith, C. H. (2016). Population survey features and response rates: A randomized experiment. *American Journal of Public Health Methods, 106*(8), 1422–1426. https://doi.org/10.2105/AJPH.2016.303198

Hagan, F. (2007). *Essentials of research methods in criminal justice and criminology* (2nd ed.). Pearson.

Jann, B., Jerke, J., & Krumpal, I. (2012). Asking sensitive questions using the crosswise model. *Public Opinion Quarterly, 76*(10), 32–49. https://doi.org/10.2307/41345966

Jennings, W. G., & Reingle Gonzalez, J. M. (2019). *Criminological and criminal justice research methods*. Wolters Kluwer.

Keeter, S., Hatley, N., Kenedy, C., & Lau, A. (2017). *What low response rates mean for telephone surveys*. Pew Research Center. https://assets.pewresearch.org/wp-content/uploads/sites/12/2017/05/12154630/RDD-Non-response-Full-Report.pdf

Kempf, A. M., & Remington, P. L. (2007). New challenges for telephone survey research in the twenty-first century. *Annual Review of Public Health, 28*(1), 113–126. http://doi.org/10.1146/annurev.publhealth.28.021406.144059

Kohl, S. A., & Tovar, E. G. (2024). Screening for serious mental illness in a correctional setting. *The Nurse Practitioner, 49*(5), 41–47. https://doi.org/10.1097/01.NPR.0000000000000178

Krosnick, J. (1991). Response strategies for coping with the cognitive demands of attitude measures in surveys. *Applied Cognitive Psychology, 5*(3), 213–223.

Link, M. W., Battaglia, M. P., Frankel, M. R., Osborn, L., & Mokdad, A. H. (2007). The U.S. cell phone generation: Comparison of cell phone survey results with an ongoing landline telephone survey. *Public Opinion Quarterly, 71*(5), 814–839. https://doi.org/10.1093/poq/nfm051

Logan, T. K., Walker, R., Shannon, L., & Cole, J. (2008). Combining ethical considerations with recruitment and follow-up strategies for partner violence victimization research. *Violence Against Women, 14*(11), 1226–1251. https://doi.org/10.1177/1077801208323976

Maxfield, M. G., & Babbie, E. (2012). *Basics of research methods for criminal justice and criminology* (3rd ed.). Thomson Wadsworth.

Moffitt, T., Caspi, A., Rutter, M., & Silva, P. A. (2001). *Sex differences in antisocial behavior.* Cambridge University Press.

Monitoring the Future. (2024). *Monitoring the future.* https://monitoringthefuture.org/

National Institute of Justice. (n.d.). *NIJ's drugs and crime research: Arrestee drug abuse monitoring programs.* https://nij.ojp.gov/topics/articles/nijs-drugs-and-crime-research-arrestee-drug-abuse-monitoring-programs#descriptions

Nix, J., Pickett, J., Baek, H., & Alpert, G. P. (2019). Police research, officer surveys, and response rates. *Policing and Society, 29*(5), 530–550. https://doi.org/10.1080/10439463.2017.1394300

Pashea, J. J., Jr., & Kochel, T. R. (2016). Face-to-face surveys in high crime areas: Balancing respondent cooperation and interviewer safety. *Journal of Criminal Justice Education, 27*(1), 95–120. https://doi.org/10.1080/10511253.2015.1091487

Patterson, C., Hogan, L., & Cox, M. (2019). A comparison between two retrospective alcohol consumption measures and the daily drinking diary method with university students. *The American Journal of Drug and Alcohol Abuse, 45*(3), 248–253. https://doi.org/10/1080/00952990.2018.1514617

Perry, A. E., Marandos, R., Coulton, S., & Johnson, M. (2010). Screening tools assessing risk of suicide and self-ham in adult offenders: A systematic review. *International Journal of Offender Therapy & Comparative Criminology, 54*(3), 803–828. https://doi.org/10.1177/0306624X09359757

Perry, A. E., & Olason, D. T. (2009). A new psychometric instrument assessing vulnerability to risk of suicide and self-harm behaviour in offenders. *International journal of Offender Therapy & Comparative Criminology, 53*(4), 385–400. https://doi.org/10.1177/0306624X08319418

Peterson, N. A., Speer, P. W., & McMillan, D. W. (2007). Validation of a brief sense of community scale: Confirmation of the principle theory of sense of community. *Journal of Community Psychology, 36*(1), 61–73. https://doi.org/10.1002/jcop.20217

Pickett, J. T., Metcalfe, C. F., Baker, T., Gertz, M., & Bedard, L. (2014). Superficial survey choice: An experimental test of potential method for increasing response rates and response quality in correctional surveys. *Journal of Quantitative Criminology, 30,* 265–284.

Pogarsky, G., Kim, K., & Paternoster, R. (2005). Perceptual change in the National Youth Survey: Lessons for deterrence theory and offender decision-making. *Justice Quarterly, 22*(1), 1–29. https://doi.org/10.1080/0741882042000333627

Rainbow, J. A. (2024). *Researching prisons.* Routledge.

Sax, L. J., Gilmartin, S. K., & Bryant, A. N. (2003). Assessing response rates and nonresponse bias in web and paper surveys. *Research in Higher Education, 44*(4), 409–432.

Sekol, I., & Farrington, D. P. (2013). The reliability and validity of self, peer and staff reports of bullying and victimization in correctional and care institutions. *Psychology, Crime & Law, 19*(4), 329–344. https://doi.org/10.1080/1068316X.2011.631541

Spark, S., Lewis, D., Vaisey, A., Smyth, E., Wood, A., Temple-Smith, M., Lorch, R., Guy, R., & Hocking, J. (2015). Using computer-assisted survey instruments instead of paper and pencil increased completeness of self-administered sexual behavior questionnaires. *Journal of Clinical Epidemiology, 68,* 94–101. https://doi.org/10.1080/1068316X.2011.631541

Steadman, H. J., Scott, J. E., Osher, F., Agnese, T., K., & Robbins, P. C. (2005). Validation of the brief jail mental health screen. *Psychiatric Services, 56*(7), 816–822. https://doi.org/10.1176/appi.ps.56.7.816

Stolzmann, K., Meterko, M., Mller, C. J., Belanger, L., Seibert, M. N., & Bauer, M. S. (2019). Survey response rate and quality in a mental health clinic population: Results from a randomized survey comparison. *Journal of Behavioral Health Services & Research, 46*(3), 521–532. https://doi.org/10.1007/s11414-018-9617-8

Sutton, J. E., Bellair, P. E., Kowalski, B. R., Light, R., & Hutcherson, D. T. (2011). Reliability and validity of prisoner self-reports gathered using the life event calendar method. *Journal of Quantitative Criminology, 27,* 151–171. https://doi.org/10.1007/s10940-010-9101-y

Tartaro, C., Bonnan-White, J., Mastrangelo, M. A., & Mulvihill, R. (2021). Police officers' attitudes toward mental health and crisis intervention: Understanding preparedness to respond to community members in crisis. *Journal of Police and Criminal Psychology*, 36, 579-591. https://doi.org/10.1007/s11896-021-09459-6

Truman, J. L., & Brotsos, H. (2022). *Update on the NCVS instrument redesign.* United States Department of Justice, Bureau of Justice Statistics.

United States Bureau of Justice Statistics. (n.d.). *National Crime Victimization Survey methodology.* United States Department of Justice, Bureau of Justice Statistics. www.bjs.gov/developer/ncvs/methodology.cfm

United States Census Bureau. (2019). *Counting the hard to count in a census.* U.S. Census Bureau. www.census.gov/content/dam/Census/library/working-papers/2019/demo/Hard-to-Count-Populations-Brief.pdf

Veysey, B. M., Steadman, H. J., Morrissey, J. P., Johnsen, M., & Beckstead, J. W. (1998). Using the referral decision scale to screen mentally ill jail detainees: Validity and implementation issues. *Law & Human Behavior, 22*(2), 205–215. https://doi.org/10.1023/a:1025794104048

Warner, S. L. (1965). Randomized response: A survey technique for eliminating evasive answer bias. *Journal of the American Statistical Association, 60*, 63–69. https://doi.org/10.1080/01621459.1965.10480775

Wichmann, C., Serin, R., & Abracen, J. (2002). *Women offenders who engage in self-harm: A comparative investigation.* Correctional Service of Canada.

Wu, M.J., Zhao, K., & Fils-Aime, F. (2022). Response rates of online surveys in published research: A meta-analysis. *Computers in Human Behavior Reports*, *7*, 100206. https://doi.org/10.1016/j.chbr.2022.100206

Yan, T., & Cantor, D. (2019). Asking survey questions about criminal justice involvement. *Public Health Reports, 134*(1), 46s–56s. https://doi.org/10.1177/0033354919826566

Reading 9.1 The Relationship between Sextortion during COVID-19 and Pre-pandemic Intimate Partner Violence

While technology has become an essential part of our everyday lives, it took on even greater importance during the COVID-19 pandemic. We used technology to work from home, connect with extended family, and have online social events with friends. It also presented the opportunity for criminal victimization, including sextortion. Eaton, Ramjee, and Saunders (2023) sought to test whether sextortion has some of the same victimization patterns as other types of interpersonal violence. The use of online samples can produce sample bias in some studies, because researchers utilizing them are likely to miss those who spend little time online or lack the technological skills to use computers or the internet. In this case, an online sample was a very appropriate choice because the authors were studying victimization that involves the use of the internet.

The Relationship between Sextortion during COVID-19 and Pre-pandemic Intimate Partner Violence: A Large Study of Victimization among Diverse U.S Men and Women

Asia A. Eaton, Divya Ramjee, and Jessica F. Saunders

Introduction

While the widespread use of information and communication technology has brought about many societal benefits, such changes have also enabled online violence in various forms (Clevenger et al., 2018; Henry, McGlynn et al., 2020; Jane, 2020). For example, growing proportions of people in the United States are reporting experiencing online harassment, including stalking, sexual harassment, and threats (Vogels, 2021). The COVID-19 pandemic may have exacerbated this public health problem, as it necessitated a massive shift to web-based information and communication technologies (ICTs), enabling millions of Americans to work, attend classes, perform errands, and sustain social and civic connections while maintaining physical distance from others.

Indeed, since the start of the pandemic, nonprofit organizations, government institutions, and legal professionals in the U.S. have reported a substantial increase in technology-facilitated sexual violence (Boniello, 2020; CCRI, personal communication, June 2, 2020; FBI, 2020, 2021). Technology-facilitated sexual violence (TSFV) is defined as sexual abuse via electronic or digital means, and can include nonconsensual pornography (also known as “revenge porn”), deepfakes, cyber harassment, cyber stalking, cyber dating violence, and sexual extortion or “sextortion” (Henry & Powell, 2018). In all these forms of abuse, technology is used to violate a survivor’s sexual autonomy, whether by producing, procuring, and/or distributing their intimate images without consent, and/or using intimate images to threaten and extort.

Technology-Facilitated Sexual Violence

Empirical research on TFSV is sparse, though growing, and more work is needed regarding the manner in which technology is used to facilitate TFSV and who is most at risk of victimization and perpetration (Fisico & Harkins, 2021). According to Henry and Powell’s (2018) review of existing empirical research, there are five types of TFSV studies on adults: 1) online sexual harassment, 2) gender- and sexuality-based harassment, 3) cyber-obsessive pursuit (cyberstalking), 4) image-based sexual exploitation, and 5) the use of a service to perpetrate an assault or coerce an unwanted sexual experience. While these are distinct dimensions, they can overlap and interact with each other depending on the type of offense being investigated.

Certain forms of TFSV have received increased scholarly attention over the last decade. For example, by 2020, sufficient work on the psychology of nonconsensual porn had been conducted to allow for a review of 32 empirical articles (Eaton & McGlynn, 2020). Nonconsensual porn (NCP) refers to the distribution of intimate images of individuals without their consent, including threats to share without consent (Citron & Franks, 2014). In this review, the authors found that NCP has been studied using a variety of psychological frameworks, including the Power and Control Wheel (Eaton et al., 2020), gender roles and sexual scripts (Hall & Hearn, 2019; Henry & Flynn, 2019; Van Oosten et al., 2020), social norms theory (Ehman & Gross, 2019), and individual difference theories (Pina et al., 2017).

However, other forms of technology-facilitated sexual violence are less researched, such as sextortion. Sextortion also appears to have increased during the pandemic according to complaints to the FBI Internet Crime Complaint Center (FBI, 2020, 2021). In this paper, we test the relationship between sextortion during the COVID-19 pandemic and pre-pandemic intimate partner violence (IPV) among diverse men and women in the U.S.

Sextortion

Sextortion, a combination of "sexual" and "extortion," is the act of threatening to expose or distribute sexually explicit materials unless a victim complies with certain demands (Acar, 2016; Clevenger et al., 2018; Powell et al., 2019; Wolak & Finkelhor, 2016). In this regard, it falls within the umbrella of NCP, but does not necessarily include the actual distribution of material (Citron & Franks, 2014; O'Malley & Holt, 2022). Sextortion is an evolving term, and may also be referred to as "threatening with NCP" or "online sexual coercion and extortion" (e.g., Equality Now, 2021).

As the majority of sextortion victims in the U.S. are under the age of 18 (Brookings, 2016; O'Malley & Holt, 2022), most academic research on sextortion has been done on minors (e.g., Gámez-Guadix & Incera, 2021; Patchin & Hinduja, 2020; Wolak et al., 2018). However, sextortion has been increasing among adults (Wittes et al., 2016), especially in the last few years (FBI, 2020, 2021). Based on the little work that exists on adult victims of sextortion, we know that sextortion can occur when perpetrators hack into victim's electronic devices, accessing stored images and webcams (for a review including young adults, see, Paat & Markham, 2020). Sextortion may also be perpetrated as the result of sexual acts (consensual or forced) that are nonconsensually-recorded. Consensually-shared sexual images may also be used for sextortion by former and current intimate partners. Finally, perpetrators may target victims in scams, such as online dating scams where they are lured to a dating profile, groomed by a perpetrator, and then sexually extorted (Whitty, 2015).

Sextortion and Intimate Partner Violence

Here, we examine the relationship between in-person IPV victimization and later experiences with sextortion during COVID-19. There are a number of reasons in-person IPV victimization before the pandemic should positively predict sextortion victimization during the pandemic. First, in-person IPV and sextortion may be related tactics committed by the same abusive partner. Indeed, research with college undergraduates by Ross et al. (2019) found overlap between sexual coercion and sexting coercion victimization in intimate relationships. Research also finds that abusive partners sometimes use intimate images to control their victims (Bates, 2017; Eaton et al., 2020). Based on a content analysis of 366 U.S. news articles, Eaton et al. (2020) established NCP as a form of IPV that can be perpetrated using intimidation, economic control, or coercion and threats (i.e., sextortion).

Next, even among those who changed intimate partners from before-to-during the pandemic, there is reason to expect a positive correlation between in-person IPV from a pre-pandemic partner and sextortion from a new partner during the pandemic. Specifically, research suggests that individuals in abusive relationships tend to leave those relationships for other relationships that also contain violence and aggression (Carbone-Lopez et al., 2012). For example, young women who experience dating violence in adolescence are more likely to experience dating violence in college (Smith et al., 2003). Thus, those experiencing abuse from one partner in the form of in-person IPV should be more likely to experience abuse from a later partner in the form of sextortion.

Finally, those who were victims of sextortion from someone other than an intimate partner may also share the risk factor of previous in-person IPV. Adults who have been victims of one form of violence have also been found to be victims of other types of violence- a phenomenon called polyvictimization (Hamby & Grych, 2013). For example, nationally-representative data from the National Intimate Partner and Sexual Violence Survey (NISVS) pilot study found that that women who had experienced violence by intimate partners were typically more likely to also experience violence by non-intimate partners (Krebs et al., 2011). Experiences of polyvictimization in the form of both online and offline violence is also common (DeKeseredy et al., 2019). DeKeseredy et al. (2019) found that women who received sexts and other unwanted digital sexual messages and images were 3.4 times more likely to also be sexually assaulted offline than college students who never received such digital sexual messages. Indeed, polyvictimization may be especially likely when both forms of violence are sexual in nature (Gidycz et al., 1995; Sabina & Straus, 2008).

Therefore, our first hypothesis is that in-person IPV victimization before the pandemic should positively predict sextortion victimization during the pandemic for both women and men adults (H1). While some recent research has found links between cyber victimization and in-person experiences of psychological, physical, and sexual IPV among adults, that research has come from convenience samples, samples of college students, or samples of females only (e.g., DeKeseredy et al., 2019, 2018; Marganski & Melander, 2018; Reed et al., 2016) prohibiting generalization as well as limiting understandings of victimization risk across dimensions of social identity.

Sextortion and Identity

Based on a person's social location, they may be more or less at-risk for TFSV such as sextortion. First, research finds that women are victimized more often by sexual crimes (e.g., rape and assault) than men in the U.S. (Statista, 2021), including TFSV (for a review, see, Henry, Flynn et al., 2020; for exceptions, see, Patel & Roesch, 2020; Powell & Henry, 2019). Sociological and feminist thinking on technology and gender has proposed that TFSV lies on a continuum of violence (McGlynn et al., 2017), as a result of old and new gender roles and scripts (Henry & Powell, 2015; Ruvalcaba & Eaton, 2020). Though there have been limited studies on the role of gender in sextortion victimization (Hinduja & Patchin, 2018; Powell & Henry, 2019), sextortion may also be used disproportionately against women because of the gendered nature of sexual violence and TFSV, driven by gender roles and sexual double standards. Thus, our second hypothesis is that women will more often report being victims of sextortion during the pandemic than men (H2).

Given the higher prevalence of TFSV among young adults (Paat & Markham, 2020; Ruvalcaba & Eaton, 2020), they may also be at greater risk for sextortion than adults of other ages. For example, work by Ruvalcaba and Eaton (2020) found that emerging adults in the U.S. (age 18–29; Arnett, 2014) had more often been victimized by NCP than adults in other developmental periods. This may be the product of their greater sexual and relationship experimentation compared to older adults (Maheux & Choukas-Bradley, 2021), as well as the high rate at which they use technology (Pew Research Center, 2021). Therefore, we also hypothesized that age would be negatively associated with TSFA victimization among adults, with emerging adults experiencing the highest levels of sextortion during the pandemic (H3).

Due to the social, economic, and health consequences of structural racism in the U.S., adults' risk for TFSV may also vary across racial/ethnic groups. First, Black and Native people in the U.S. have been found to be more at-risk for sexual violence, generally, than their White, LatinX, and Asian counterparts (Black et al., 2011). For example, African American college women are more likely to report experiencing sexual assault than their White counterparts (Abbey et al., 1996), and Native Americans are twice as likely to experience a rape or sexual assault compared to those from other racial groups (Perry, 2004).

Black and Native individuals are also typically more likely than other groups to experience sexual and reproductive coercion in relationships (Grace & Anderson, 2018). In nationally-representative research by Basile et al. (2021), Black women and men had significantly higher lifetime prevalence of reproductive coercion in intimate relationships than other groups (Basile et al., 2021). Native women and men, meanwhile, have been found to have higher rates of lifetime sexual coercion than their non-Hispanic White counterparts (Caponera, 2018). Rates of adult sextortion across racial/ethnic groups, however, have not been directly examined to the authors' knowledge, perhaps as a result of racial/ethnic homogeneity in samples of sextortion victims (e.g., Wolak et al., 2018). In the current study, we hypothesize that Black and Native individuals will be more likely to report sextortion during the pandemic than other racial/ethnic groups (H4).

Finally, we expect that members of LGBTQ community will more often report having been victims of sextortion during the pandemic than heterosexuals (H5). LGBTQ individuals have been found to more often be victims of sexual violence and more likely to experience polyvictimization than heterosexuals (Daigle & Hawk, 2021; Schwab-Reese et al., 2021). Bisexual individuals have been shown to be especially at risk for rape and sexual violence committed by any perpetrator, and also of rape, physical violence, and/or stalking by intimate partner (Schwab-Reese et al., 2021; Walters et al., 2013). Research on adolescents has found that bisexual, homosexual, pansexual, asexual, and queer adolescents have more often been victims of online sextortion than heterosexual adolescents (Gámez-Guadix & Incera, 2021). However, this study will be the first to the authors' knowledge examining sextortion rates among LGBTQ adults in the U.S.

Methods

Qualtrics panels were used to apply proportional quota sampling (Trochim et al., 2015) to collect online survey data from diverse men and women adults across the United States. Quotas were established for age group (18–24, 25–34, 35–44, 45–54, 55–64, and 65+), region of the U.S. (South East, North East, Mid-West, West, and South West), gender (woman/transwoman, man/transman), race (White or European Non-Hispanic, Black/Afro-Caribbean/African, Latino/a or Hispanic, Asian, and Native American or Alaskan Native (Lavrakas, 2008), and sexual identity (LGBTQ, heterosexual). Additionally, we oversampled for racial and ethnic minorities, to give adequate power to statistical analyses comparing racial/ethnic groups. The sampling approach was not intended to produce a perfectly representative sample for the purpose of prevalence estimates, but to allow for adequately-powered examinations of associations between variables of interest, with robust comparative analyses across relevant population subgroups.

Data were collected in January–March 2021, marking approximately one year since the start of the pandemic in March 2020. Data collection included 3,150 adult U.S. participants. This larger sample was restricted to individuals who reported having a partner prior to COVID, resulting in a final data set of 2,006

Table 1 Sample demographics

Variable	*Grouping*	%	*n*
Age			
	18–29	17.6	354
	30–40	25.1	503
	41–65	44.2	886
	65+	13.1	263
Education			
	Some High School	2.2	44
	High School/ GED	30	599
	Associate's Degree	16.8	335
	Bachelor's Degree	29.3	586
	Master's Degree	16.5	329
	Doctorate	2.4	48
	Professional Degree	2.9	58
Employment			
	Not Employed	36.2	725
	Employed Part-time	15.2	304
	Employed Full-time	48.7	975

participants (52.4% female). Fifty-four and a half percent of participants identified as "White or European (Non-Hispanic)," 10% as "Black, Afro-Caribbean, or African," 14.9% as "Latino/a or Hispanic," 8.9% as "Asian," 9.4% as "Native American or Alaska Native," and 2.3% as "Other." Eighty eight percent identified as Heterosexual, 2.4% identified as gay, 1.4% identified as lesbian, 6.1% identified as bisexual, and 1.6% identified as "other." Twenty seven percent of participants indicated living in the South East U.S., 22% in the North East, 22% in the Mid-West, 17% in the West, and 12% in the South West. See Table 1 for additional demographic data.

Measures

Participants were asked to complete an online survey including measures assessing intimate partner violence victimization before the pandemic, sextortion victimization during the pandemic, and a number of demographic items. The survey also included additional measures not relevant to the current study, such as experience with other forms of cyber abuse, technology use, gender role attitudes, well-being, social support, and alcohol use.

In-person IPV victimization pre-COVID was examined using the psychological aggression, physical assault, and sexual coercion victimization subscales from the Revised Conflict Tactics Scale (CTS-2), which is considered reliable and valid (Archer, 1999; Straus et al., 1996). To assess these forms of IPV pre-COVID, participants were first asked "did you have a romantic partner before COVID-19 (e.g., boyfriend/girlfriend, spouse)?" Participants who answered "yes" to this question were then asked to complete the CTS-2 subscales by indicating "how many times your most recent partner did these before COVID-19." Across the three subscales, participants indicated the frequency with which each form of IPV victimization occurred, from *this has never happened* (0) to *more than 20 times before the pandemic* (6). An example of the 8-item psychological aggression subscale is "my partner insulted or swore at me" This subscale had a Cronbach's $\alpha = .90$ (Straus et al., 1996). The physical assault subscale is a 12-item subscale (e.g., "my partner punched or hit me with something that could hurt") with a Cronbach's $\alpha = .97$ (Straus et al., 1996). The sexual coercion subscale is a seven-item subscale with a Cronbach's $\alpha = .89$ (Straus et al., 1996). An example item is "my partner used threats to make me have sex." Sextortion victimization was examined by asking participants if they had ever been the victim of sextortion. Sextortion was defined for participants as "the act of threatening to expose a nude or sexually explicit image in order to get a person to do something such as send more nude or sexually explicit images, pay someone money, or perform sexual acts." Response options included "yes, before the pandemic," "yes, after the pandemic," and "no, never." Responses were coded to reflect whether the participant had been a victim of sextortion during the pandemic (1) or not (0).

Results

Multi-group Logistic Path Analysis

The relationship between physical IPV, psychological IPV, and sexual IPV victimization before the pandemic and sextortion victimization after the pandemic began were next examined for both men and women. Neither prior victimization by physical IPV (Male OR = 1.03, 95% CI [.99, 1.06], p = .16; Female OR = .96, 95% CI [.90, 1.02], p = .26) or psychological IPV (Male OR = .99, 95% CI [.96, 1.04], p = .98; Female OR = .96, 95% CI [.91, 1.01], p = .20) prior to the pandemic were significant predictors of sextortion once the pandemic began (see, Figure 1 for all multi-group logistic path analysis results). However, sexual IPV levels pre-pandemic were significant predictors of sextortion during the pandemic (Male OR = 1.05, 95% CI [1.02, 1.09], p = .01; Female OR = 1.17, 95% CI [1.06, 1.30], p = .009), partially supporting H1.

Higher levels of sexual IPV pre-pandemic resulted in 1.05 times greater risk of sextortion for men and 1.17 times greater risk of sextortion for women. A Wald test on this significant pathway indicated that the strength of this relation did not differ for men and women, χ (1) = 2.79, p = .09. Of the covariates also included in the model, IPV that was previously perpetrated by a partner was also a significant predictor of sextortion for both men and women (Male OR = 3.23, 95% CI [1.29, 8.10], p = .04; Female OR = 9.76, 95% CI [3.09, 30.86], p < .001). The strength of the effect of IPV that was previously perpetrated by a partner on sextortion during the pandemic was not significantly different by gender, χ (1) = 1.53, p = .22.

Group Level Differences

Differences in the frequency with which sextortion since the pandemic was reported were identified by gender, age, sexuality, race, and race and gender combined. Four and a half percent of men and 2.3% of women reported experiencing sextortion since the pandemic began. In contrast to H2, a significantly higher percentage of men reported sextortion than women, $\chi2(1)$ = 7.82, p = .005. Age at victimization did not differ between men and women, $t(65)$ = .22, p = .83. However, participants who were victims of sextortion were significantly younger (M = 38.64, SD = 14.46) than participants who were not victims of sextortion during the pandemic (M = 45.32, SD = 15.37). Using logistic regression with age as a continuous variable, age was a significant,

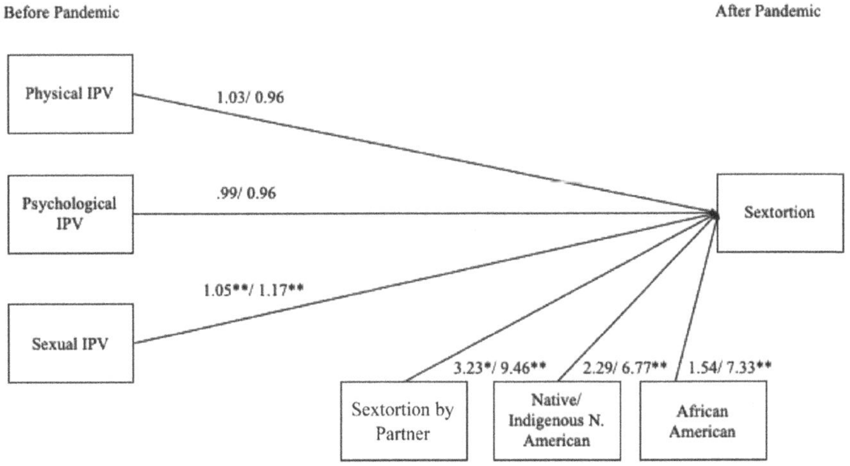

Figure 1 Multi-group logistic regression examining predictors of sextortion during the pandemic. *Note: Coefficients before the "/" represent estimates for males, coefficients after the "/" represent estimates for females. Only significant covariates are pictured ** p < .01 ***p < .001

negative predictor of sextortion during the pandemic, OR = .97, 95% CI [.95, .99], b = -.03 ($\chi^2(1) = 11.83, p < .001$), supporting H3. When examining individuals based on their developmental periods (see, Table 1 for sample distribution across developmental groups) those between the ages of 18–29 were most likely to report sextortion victimization during the pandemic, with 5.4% (n = 19) of this sub-sample reporting an experience of sextortion, followed by 4.3% (n = 21) of individuals between the ages of 30–40, 2.7% (n = 24) of individuals between the ages of 41–64, and 1.1% (n = 3) of participants over age 65, ($\chi^2(3) = 10.63, p = .01$), further supporting H3.

Racial differences in the frequency with which sextortion was reported were also identified, $\chi^2(5)$ = 14.35, p = .014. Supporting Hypothesis 4, 7% of Black, Afro-Caribbean, or African and 5.3% of Native American or Alaskan Native participants reported sextortion, compared to 3.4% of Latinx, 2.8% of Asian, and 2.6% of White participants. These racial differences were significant for women ($\chi2(5)$ = 21.32, p < .001) but not for men ($\chi^2(5) = 2.64, p = .76$). Seven percent of Black, Afro-Caribbean, or African women and 5% of Native American or Alaskan Native women reported sextortion, while 2.4% of Latinas, 2% of Asian women, and 0.8% of White women reported sextortion. Identifying as Native Alaskan or Indigenous North American compared to White (OR = 6.77, 95% CI [2.11, 21.78], p < .001), or as an African American compared to White (OR = 7.33, 95% CI [2.34, 22.98], p < .001), were significant predictors of sextortion during the pandemic for women but not men. Native Alaskan and Indigenous North American women were 6.77 times more likely than White women to experience sextortion, while African American women were 7.33 times more likely than White women to experience sextortion during the pandemic.

The distribution of sextortion during the pandemic also significantly differed by sexual orientation, $\chi2(4)$ = 15.50, p = .004, in support of Hypothesis 5. Two-point-nine percent of heterosexual, 2.0% of gay, 7.1% of lesbian, 8.9% of bisexual, and 6.3% of participants who self-identified as "other" sexual orientation reported experiences of sextortion during the pandemic. The most commonly reported perpetrator of sextortion against victims was "a stranger" (29%), followed by "a current romantic partner" (20%), a "former romantic partner" (18%), a "friend outside of work or school" (9%), "someone I met online" (9%), "someone from work" (7%), "someone from school" (4%), and "someone I met outside of work or school" (4%). The frequency of perpetrator identity did not differ by gender, ($\chi^2(7) = 11.09$, $p = .14$) or by race, ($\chi^2(35) = 46.16, p = .10$).

Discussion

The COVID-19 pandemic has brought increased scientific, legal, and public attention to digital crimes that can be perpetrated from a distance, including technology-facilitated sexual violence (Boman & Gallupe, 2020). One of the forms of TFSV that has gained increased attention during the pandemic is sextortion (FBI, 2020, 2021), or the threat to distribute intimate materials unless a victim complies with a perpetrator's demands (O'Malley & Holt, 2022). A unique aspect of sextortion is that, unlike other forms of TFSV, the victim and perpetrator may never interact offline; perpetrators may gain possession of a victim's images through a variety of means, including coercion and hacking (Liggett, 2019).

In the present study, we surveyed a large diverse sample of U.S. adults to better understand the relationship between in-person IPV and TFSV victimization. We found that experience with sexual IPV pre-pandemic (but not physical or psychological IPV) was a significant predictor of sextortion during the pandemic for both men and women. In addition, we examined the occurrence of sextortion victimization during the pandemic across gender, race/ethnicity, and sexual orientation in the U.S. We found that men, Native American and Black women, and sexual identity minorities (specifically lesbians, bisexuals, and "others") more often reported sextortion victimization during the pandemic than their counterparts. Finally, we found that victims of sextortion during the pandemic tended to be younger than non-victims, with emerging adults (age 18–29) reporting the highest levels of victimization. This is consistent with research on TFSV in Australia finding that younger individuals were generally at greater risk for TFSV than other age groups (Douglass et al., 2018; Powell & Henry, 2019).

Sextortion and Gender

Our finding that men were more often victims of sextortion during the pandemic than women was contrary to our initial predictions. However, not all work on TFSV finds that women are disproportionately victimized (e.g., Patel & Roesch, 2020; Powell & Henry, 2019). The primary forms of TFSV that appear to more often affect women include the distribution of NCP and online sexual harassment (for a review, see, Henry & Powell, 2018). Gender differences in the frequency of threats to distribute intimate images, however, has not been systematically examined among U.S. adults until now. Our research is consistent with findings from the office of Australia's eSafety commissioner in 2020, which found that seven out of 10 victims of sextortion in Australia were men (Yi, 2020).

There are several reasons U.S. men may have more often reported being victims of sextortion during the pandemic than women. First, recent research has highlighted gender disparities in unpaid care work and household-related work since the beginning of the pandemic (Xue & McMunn, 2021; Zamarro & Prados, 2021); it is possible that men had more time to spend online than women during the pandemic. Although the finding that men were more likely than women to be victimized was contrary to our hypothesis, a recent study with a representative sample of U.S. middle and high school students found that boys reported sextortion victimization more frequently than girls (Patchin & Hinduja, 2020). According to the authors of that study, there is a strong correlation between male offenders and male victims such that individuals with experience in one role are likely to also experience the other (Patchin & Hinduja, 2020). Male online dating patterns, such as being less selective than women (Whyte & Torgler, 2017), may have also contributed to the current finding. Finally, research indicates that men and highly educated individuals are more likely to be victims of cyberscams, including consumer, charity, and romance scams (Whitty, 2015); this victimization may extend beyond cyberscams to sextortion.

Sextortion and Sexual IPV

The finding that sexual IPV pre-pandemic (and not physical or psychological) was positively associated with sextortion during the pandemic only partially supported our initial prediction. However, it is consistent with research finding that different types of sexual victimization (e.g., rape and verbal sexual coercion) are highly correlated (e.g., Abbey et al., 2004; Mellins et al., 2017). However, the limited work on the relationship between IPV and cyber abuse among adults rarely separately analyzes different types of IPV (e.g., sexual and non-sexual) and their individual relationships to different types of cyber abuse (e.g., sexual and non-sexual; Wolford-Clevenger et al., 2016). For example, work by Sargent et al. (2016) found that cyber victimization was related to psychological IPV among first-year college students. However, the type of cyber victimization participants reported could have included sexual and non-sexual types. Our work suggests that teasing apart the subtypes of victimization experienced by polyvictims may be key to understanding the nature of polyvictimization, generally, and predictors of sextortion victimization, specifically.

Limitations

This work represents the first study on sextortion using a large and diverse sample of U.S. adults during the COVID-19 pandemic. However, it comes with a number of limitations. First, the data were collected cross-sectionally. This inhibits our ability to establish temporal precedence for the different forms of sexual violence examined, and it increases the risk of within-survey order effects (Laursen et al., 2012; Shadish et al.,

2002). Future research should examine the relationship between IPV types and TFSV using a longitudinal design.

Second, our data consisted only of self-reports, making it possible that differences obtained between groups, for example, were a function of group-level differences in sexual violence perceptions or norms, rather than actual rates of victimization. Next, our data were collected during the first year of the COVID-19 pandemic, and may not represent rates or relationships during non-pandemic periods, or during the subsequent part of the pandemic. Next, we did not assess how many times sextortion victimization occurred during the pandemic- only whether or not it had occurred. This measure prohibits us from examining the relationship between in-person IPV and TFSV frequency or severity.

Finally, the current paper did not test mediators of group-level differences in IPV. Future research should examine potential explanations for differences by race, age, gender, and so on. For example, age-related differences may be the result of emerging adults using technology more frequently than older people (Powell & Henry, 2017), or engaging in more relationship and sexual experimentation than older adults (Maheux & Choukas-Bradley, 2021).

Conclusion

Given the rise in TFSV over time, and sextortion during the pandemic specifically, it has become increasingly urgent to better understand the nature of cyber sexual abuse. This large, study of U.S. adults suggests that sextortion victimization can be predicted by gender, race, age, sexual orientation, and sexual IPV, with men, Native and Black women, LGBTQ people, and sexual IPV victims all being at greater risk for sextortion.

Disclosure Statement

No potential conflict of interest was reported by the author(s).

Funding

This work was funded by the National Science Foundation under Grant #2035686.

Discussion Questions

1. How did the decision to utilize a cross-sectional design impact the findings? How might the use of a longitudinal analysis have impacted this study?
2. What were the independent and dependent variables? How did the researchers measure them?
3. The findings about respondent gender and victimization were surprising. What are possible explanations for that finding?

References

Abbey, A., BeShears, R., Clinton-Sherrod, A. M., & McAuslan, P. (2004). Similarities and differences in women's sexual assault experiences based on tactics used by the perpetrator. *Psychology of Women Quarterly*, *28*(4), 323–332. https://doi.org/10.1111/j.1471-6402.2004.00149.x

Abbey, A., Ross, L. T., McDuffie, D., & McAuslan, P. (1996). Alcohol and dating risk factors for sexual assault among college women. *Psychology of Women Quarterly*, *20*(1), 147–169. https://doi.org/10.1111/j.1471-6402.1996.tb00669.x

Acar, K. V. (2016). Sexual extortion of children in cyberspace. *International Journal of Cyber Criminology*, *10*(2), 110–126. https://doi.org/10.5281/zenodo.163398

Andersen, J. P., Zou, C., & Blosnich, J. (2015). Multiple early victimization experiences as a pathway to explain physical health disparities among sexual minority and heterosexual individuals. *Social Science & Medicine*, *133*, 111–119. https://doi.org/10.1016/j.socscimed.2015.03.043

Archer, J. (1999). Assessment of the reliability of the conflict tactics scales: A meta-analytic review. *Journal of Interpersonal Violence*, *14*(12), 1263–1289. https://doi.org/10.1177/088626099014012003

Arnett, J. J. (2014). *Emerging adulthood: The winding road from the late teens twenties* (2nd ed.). Oxford University Press. http://dx.doi.org/10.1093/oxfordhb/9780199795574.013.9

Basile, K. C., Smith, S. G., Liu, Y., Miller, E., & Kresnow, M. J. (2021). Prevalence of intimate partner reproductive coercion in the United States: Racial and ethnic differences. *Journal of Interpersonal Violence*, *36*(21–22),

NP12324–NP12341. https://doi.org/10.1177/0886260519888205

Bates, S. (2017). Revenge porn and mental health: A qualitative analysis of the mental health effects of revenge porn on female survivors. *Feminist Criminology*, *12*(1), 22–42. https://doi.org/10.1177/1557085116654565

Black, M. C., Basile, K. C., Breiding, M. J., Smith, S. G., Walters, M. L., Merrick, M. T., … Stevens, M. R. (2011). *The National Intimate Partner and Sexual Violence Survey (NISVS): 2010 summary report*. National Center for Injury Prevention and Control, Centers for Disease Control and Prevention. www.cdc.gov/violenceprevention/pdf/nisvs_report2010-a.pdf

Boman, J. H., & Gallupe, O. (2020). Has COVID-19 changed crime? Crime rates in the United States during the pandemic. *American Journal of Criminal Justice*, *45*(4), 537–545. https://doi.org/10.1007/s12103-020-09551-3

Boniello, K. (2020). Virtual sextortion surging as more men stay home during coronavirus lockdowns. *New York Post*. https://nypost.com/2020/05/02/virtual-sextortion-scams-rising-during -coronavirus-lockdowns/

Brookings. (2016). *Sextortion: Cybersecurity, teenagers, and remote sexual assault*. www.brookings.edu/research/sextortion-cybersecurity-teenagers-and-remote-sexual-assault/

Caponera, B. (2018). *Sexual violence among Native Americans (American Indians and Alaskan Natives) in the United States and New Mexico*. New Mexico Coalition of Sexual Assault Programs, Inc. https://nmcsap.org/wp-content/uploads/NativeAmericanData_Feb2018.pdf

Carbone-Lopez, K., Rennison, C. M., & Macmillan, R. (2012). The transcendence of violence across relationships: New methods for understanding men's and women's experiences of intimate partner violence across the life course. *Journal of Quantitative Criminology*, *28*(2), 319–346. https://doi.org/ 10.1007/s10940-011-9143-9

Cho, H. (2012). Racial differences in the prevalence of intimate partner violence against women and associated factors. *Journal of Interpersonal Violence*, *27*(2), 344–363. https://doi.org/10.1177/0886260511416469

Citron, D. K., & Franks, M. A. (2014). Criminalizing revenge porn. *Wake Forest Law Review*, *49*, 345. https://scholarship.law.bu.edu/faculty_scholarship/643

Clevenger, S., & Navarro, J. (2021). The "third-victimization": The cybervictimization of sexual assault survivors and their families. *Journal of Contemporary Criminal Justice*, *37*(3), 356–378. https://doi.org/10.1177/10439862211001616

Clevenger, S. L., Navarro, J. N., & Gilliam, M. (2018). Technology and the endless "cat and mouse" game: A review of the interpersonal cybervictimization literature. *Sociology Compass*, *12*(12), e12639. https://doi.org/10.1111/soc4.12639

Daigle, L. E., & Hawk, S. R. (2021). Sexual orientation, revictimization, and polyvictimization. *Sexuality Research and Social Policy*. https://doi.org/10.1007/s13178-021-00543-4

DeKeseredy, W. S., Schwartz, M. D., Harris, B., Woodlock, D., Nolan, J., & Hall-Sanchez, A. (2019). Technology-facilitated stalking and unwanted sexual messages/images in a college campus community: The role of negative peer support. *SAGE Open*, *9*(1), 215824401982823. https://doi.org/10.1177/2158244019828231

DeKeseredy, W. S., Schwartz, M. D., Nolan, J., Mastron, N., & Hall-Sanchez, A. (2018). Polyvictimization and the continuum of sexual abuse at a college campus: Does negative peer support increase the likelihood of multiple victimizations? *The British Journal of Criminology*, *58*(5), 1107–1126. https://doi.org/10.1093/bjc/azy036

Douglass, C. H., Wright, C. J. C., Davis, A. C., & Lim, M. S. C. (2018). Correlates of in-person and technology-facilitated sexual harassment from an online survey among young Australians. *Sexual Health*, *15*(4), 361. https://doi.org/10.1071/SH17208

Eaton, A. A., Jacobs, H., & Ruvalcaba, Y. (2017). *2017 Nationwide online study of nonconsensual porn victimization and perpetration: A summary report*. Cyber Civil Rights Initiative. www.cybercivilrights.org/wp-content/uploads/2017/06/CCRI-2017-ResearchReport.pdf

Eaton, A. A., & McGlynn, C. (2020). The psychology of nonconsensual porn: Understanding and addressing a growing form of sexual violence. *Policy Insights from the Behavioral and Brain Sciences*, *7*(2), 190–197. https://doi.org/10.1177/2372732220941534

Eaton, A. A., Noori, S., Bonomi, A., Stephens, D. P., & Gillum, T. L. (2020). Nonconsensual porn as a form of intimate partner violence: Using the power and control wheel to understand nonconsensual porn perpetration in intimate relationships. *Trauma, Violence, & Abuse*, *22*(5), 1140–1154. https://doi.org/10.1177/1524838020906533

Ehman, A. C., & Gross, A. M. (2019). Sexual cyberbullying: Review, critique, & future directions. *Aggression and Violent Behavior*, *44*, 80–87. http://dx.doi.org/10.1016/j.avb.2018.11.001

Equality Now. (2021). *Ending online sexual exploitation and abuse of women and girls: A call for International standards*. https://live-equal

ity-now.pantheonsite.io/wp-content/uploads/2021/11/Ending-OSEA-Report.pdf
FBI. (2020). *Online extortion scams increasing during the Covid-19 crisis*. www.ic3.gov/media/2020/200420.aspx
FBI. (2021). *FBI warns about an increase in sextortion complaints*. www.ic3.gov/Media/Y2021/PSA210902
Fernet, M., Hébert, M., Brodeur, G., & Théorêt, V. (2021). "When you're in a relationship, you say no, but your partner insists": Sexual dating violence and ambiguity among girls and young women. *Journal of Interpersonal Violencei*, *36*(19–20), 9436–9459. https://doi.org/10.1177/0886260519867149
Fisico, R., & Harkins, L. (2021). Technology and sexual offending. *Current Psychiatry Reports*, *23*(59), 1–8. https://doi.org/10.1007/s11920-021-01269-1
Gámez-Guadix, M., & Incera, D. (2021). Homophobia is online: Sexual victimization and risks on the internet and mental health among bisexual, homosexual, pansexual, asexual, and queer adolescents. *Computers in Human Behavior*, *119*, 106728. https://doi.org/10.1016/j.chb.2021.106728
Gidycz, C. A., Hanson, K., & Layman, M. J. (1995). A prospective analysis of the relationships among sexual assault experiences: An extension of previous findings. *Psychology of Women Quarterly*, *19*(1), 5–29. https://doi.org/10.1111/j.1471-6402.1995.tb00276.x
Gilbar, O., & Ford, J. (2020). Indirect effects of PTSD and complex PTSD in the relationship of polyvictimization with intimate partner violence victimization and perpetration among men in mandated treatment. *European Journal of Psychotraumatology*, *11*(1), 1794653. https://doi.org/10.1080/20008198.2020.1794653
Grace, K. T., & Anderson, J. C. (2018). Reproductive coercion: A systematic review. *Trauma, Violence, & Abuse*, *19*(4), 371–390. https://doi.org/10.1177/1524838016663935
Hall, M., & Hearn, J. (2019). Revenge pornography and manhood acts: A discourse analysis of perpetrators' accounts. *Journal of Gender Studies*, *28*(2), 158–170. https://doi.org/10.1080/09589236.2017.1417117
Hamby, S., & Grych, J. (2013). Tracing the threads of the web: The epidemiology of interconnections among forms of violence and victimization. In *The web of violence* (pp. 9–27). SpringerBriefs in Sociology. Springer. https://doi.org/10.1007/978-94-007-5596-3_2
Harwell, D. (2020). Thousands of Zoom video calls left exposed on open web. *The Washington Post*. www.washingtonpost.com/technology/2020/04/03/thousands-zoom-video-calls-left-exposed-open-web/?fbclid=IwAR3cGg-5v4YZRvis0baGTncTy6zv9g74WFrPelMIMANg-QHFzplqlPuxFd8&utm_campaign=wp_main&utm_medium=social&utm_source=facebook
Henry, N., & Flynn, A. (2019). Image-based sexual abuse: Online distribution channels and illicit communities of support. *Violence Against Women*, *25*(16), 1932–1955. https://doi.org/10.1177/1077801219863881
Henry, N., Flynn, A., & Powell, A. (2020). Technology-facilitated domestic and sexual violence: A review. *Violence Against Women*, *26*(15–16), 1828–1854. https://doi.org/10.1177/1077801219875821
Henry, N., McGlynn, C., Flynn, A., Johnson, K., Powell, A., & Scott, A. (2020). *Image-based sexual abuse: A study on the causes and consequences of non-consensual nude or sexual imagery*. Routledge.
Henry, N., & Powell, A. (2015). Embodied harms: Gender, shame and technology–facilitated sexual violence in cyberspace. *Violence Against Women*, *21*(6), 758–779. https://doi.org/10.1177/1077801215576581
Henry, N., & Powell, A. (2018). Technology-facilitated sexual violence: A literature review of empirical research. *Trauma, Violence, & Abuse*, *19*(2), 195–208. https://doi.org/10.1177/1524838016650189
Hinduja, S., & Patchin, J. W. (2018). *Cyberbullying identification, prevention, and response*. Cyberbullying Research Center (cyberbullying.org).
Jane, E. A. (2020). Online abuse and harassment. In K. Ross, I. Bachmann, V. Cardo, S. Moorti, & M. Scarcelli (Eds.), *The international encyclopedia of gender, media, and communication*. https://doi.org/10.1002/9781119429128.iegmc080
Krebs, C., Breiding, M. J., Browne, A., & Warner, T. (2011). The association between different types of intimate partner violence experienced by women. *Journal of Family Violence*, *26*(6), 487–500. https://doi.org/10.1007/s10896-011-9383-3
Lagdon, S., Armour, C., & Stringer, M. (2014). Adult experience of mental health outcomes as a result of intimate partner violence victimisation: A systematic review. *European Journal of Psychotraumatology*, *5*(1), 24794. https://doi.org/10.3402/ejpt.v5.24794
Laursen, B., Little, T. D., & Card, N. A. (2012). *The handbook of developmental research methods*. Guilford Press.
Liggett, R. (2019). Exploring online sextortion offenses: Ruses, demands, and motivations. *Sexual Assault Report*, *22*(4), 58–62.
Maheux, A. J., & Choukas-Bradley, S. (2021). Sexuality and mental health in emerging adulthood. In E. M. Morgan & M. H. M. van

Dulmen (Eds.), *Sexuality in emerging adulthood* (pp. 452–470). Oxford University Press.
Marganski, A., & Melander, L. (2018). Intimate partner violence victimization in the cyber and real world: Examining the extent of cyber aggression experiences and its association with in-person dating violence. *Journal of Interpersonal Violence*, *33*(7), 1071–1095. https://doi.org/10.1177/0886260515614283
McGlynn, C., Rackley, E., & Houghton, R. (2017). Beyond "revenge porn": The continuum of image-based sexual abuse. *Feminist Legal Studies*, *25*(1), 25–46. https://doi.org/10.1007/s10691-017-9343-2
Mellins, C. A., Walsh, K., Sarvet, A. L., Wall, M., Gilbert, L., Santelli, J. S., Thompson, M., Wilson, P. A., Khan, S., Benson, S., Bah, K., Kaufman, K. A., Reardon, L., & Hirsch, J. S. (2017). Sexual assault incidents among college undergraduates: Prevalence and factors associated with risk. *PLoS One*, *12*(11), e0186471. https://doi.org/10.1371/journal.pone.0186471
Muthén, B., & Asparouhov, T. (2002). *Latent variable analysis with categorical outcomes: Multiple-group and growth modeling in Mplus*. Mplus Web Notes: No. 4. www.statmodel.com
Muthén, L. K., & Muthén, B. O. (2007). *Mplus user's guide* (6th ed.). Muthén & Muthén.
O'Malley, R. L., & Holt, K. M. (2022). Cyber sextortion: An exploratory analysis of different perpetrators engaging in a similar crime. *Journal of Interpersonal Violence*, *37*(1–2), 258–283. https://doi.org/10.1177/0886260520909186
Paat, Y. F., & Markham, C. (2020). Digital crime, trauma, and abuse: Internet safety and cyber risks for adolescents and emerging adults in the 21st century. *Social Work in Mental Health*, 1–23. https://doi.org/10.1080/15332985.2020.1845281
Patchin, J. W., & Hinduja, S. (2020). Sextortion among adolescents: Results from a national survey of U.S. youth. *Sexual Abuse*, *32*(1), 30–54. https://doi.org/10.1177/1079063218800469
Patel, U., & Roesch, R. (2020). The prevalence of technology-facilitated sexual violence: A meta-analysis and systematic review. *Trauma, Violence, & Abuse*. https://doi.org/10.1177/1524838020958057
Perry, S. W. (2004). *American Indians and crime-A BJS statistical profile 1992-2002*. Bureau of Justice Statistics, US Department of Justice, Office of Justice Programs. https://bjs.ojp.gov/content/pub/pdf/aic02.pdf
Pew Research Center. (2021). *About three-in-ten U.S. adults say they are 'almost constantly' online*. www.pewresearch.org/fact-tank/2021/03/26/about-three-in-ten-u-s-adults-say-they-are-almost-constantly-online/
Pina, A., Holland, J., & James, M. (2017). The malevolent side of revenge porn proclivity: Dark personality traits and sexist ideology. *International Journal of Technoethics*, *8*(1), 30–43. https://doi.org/10.4018/IJT.2017010103
Powell, A., & Henry, N. (2017). *Introduction. Sexual violence in a digital age*. Palgrave MacMillian.
Powell, A., & Henry, N. (2019). Technology-facilitated sexual violence victimization: Results from an online survey of Australian adults. *Journal of Interpersonal Violence*, *34*(17), 3637–3665. https://doi.org/10.1177/0886260516672055
Powell, A., Henry, N., Flynn, A., & Scott, A. J. (2019). Image-based sexual abuse: The extent, nature, and predictors of perpetration in a community sample of Australian adults. *Computers in Human Behavior*, *92*, 393–402. https://doi.org/10.1016/j.chb.2018.11.009
Reed, L. A., Tolman, R. M., & Ward, L. M. (2016). Snooping and sexting: Digital media as a context for dating aggression and abuse among college students. *Violence Against Women*, *22*(13), 1556–1576. https://doi.org/10.1177/1077801216630143
Ross, J. M., Drouin, M., & Coupe, A. (2019). Sexting coercion as a component of intimate partner polyvictimization. *Journal of Interpersonal Violence*, *34*(11), 2269–2291. https://doi.org/10.1177/0886260516660300
Ruvalcaba, Y., & Eaton, A. A. (2020). Nonconsensual pornography among U.S. adults: A sexual scripts framework on victimization, perpetration, and health correlates for women and men. *Psychology of Violence*, *10*(1), 68–78. https://doi.org/10.1037/vio0000233
Sabina, C., & Straus, M. A. (2008). Polyvictimization by dating partners and mental health among U.S. college students. *Violence & Victims*, *23*(6), 667–682. https://doi.org/10.1891/0886-6708.23.6.667
Sargent, K. S., Krauss, A., Jouriles, E. N., & McDonald, R. (2016). Cyber victimization, psychological intimate partner violence, and problematic mental health outcomes among first-year college students. *Cyberpsychology, Behavior and Social Networking*, *19*(9), 545–550. https://doi.org/10.1089/cyber.2016.0115
Schwab-Reese, L. M., Currie, D., Mishra, A. A., & Peek-Asa, C. (2021). A comparison of violence victimization and polyvictimization experiences among sexual minority and heterosexual adolescents and young adults. *Journal of Interpersonal Violence*, *36*(11–12), NP5874–NP5891. https://doi.org/10.1177/0886260518808853
Shadish, W. R., Cook, T. D., & Campbell, D. T. (2002). *Experimental and quasi-experimental*

designs for generalized causal inference (2nd ed.). Houghton-Mifflin.

Smith, P. H., White, J. W., & Holland, L. J. (2003). A longitudinal perspective on dating violence among adolescent and college-age women. *American Journal of Public Health, 93*(7), 1104–1109. https://doi.org/10.2105/AJPH.93.7.1104

Snyder, J. A., Scherer, H. L., & Fisher, B. S. (2021). Poly-victimization among female college students: Are the risk factors the same as those who experience one type of victimization? *Violence Against Women, 27*(10), 1716–1735. https://doi.org/10.1177/1077801220952176

Statista. (2021). *Number of rape or sexual assault victims in the United States per year from 2000 to 2019, by gender*. www.statista.com/statistics/642458/rape-and-sexual-assault-victims-in-the-us-by-gender/

Straus, M. A., Hamby, S. L., Boney-mccoy, S., & Sugarman, D. B. (1996). The revised conflict tactics scales (CTS2): Development and preliminary psychometric data. *Journal of Family Issues, 17*(3), 283–316. https://doi.org/10.1177/019251396017003001

Tjaden, P., & Thoennes, N. (2000). Prevalence and consequences of male-to-female and female-to-male intimate partner violence as measured by the national violence against women survey. *Violence Against Women, 6*(2), 142–161. https://doi.org/10.1177/10778010022181769

Trochim, W., Donnelly, J. P., & Arora, K. (2015). *Research methods: The essential knowledge base*. Nelson Education.

van Oosten, J. F. M., & Vandenbosch, L. (2020). Predicting the willingness to engage in non-consensual forwarding of sexts: The role of pornography and instrumental notions of sex. *Archives of Sexual Behavior, 49*(4), 1121–1132. https://doi.org/10.1007/s10508-019-01580-2

Vogels, E. A. (2021). *The state of online harassment*. Pew Research Center. www.pewresearch.org/internet/2021/01/13/the-state-of-online-harassment/

Walters, M. L., Chen, J., & Breiding, M. J. (2013). *The national intimate partner and sexual violence survey (NISVS): 2010 Findings on victimization by sexual orientation*. National Center for Injury Prevention and Control, Centers for Disease Control and Prevention. www.cdc.gov/violenceprevention/pdf/nisvs_sofindings.pdf

Whitty, M. T. (2015). Anatomy of the online dating romance scam. *Security Journal, 28*(4), 443–455. https://doi.org/10.1057/sj.2012.57

Whyte, S., & Torgler, B. (2017). Preference versus choice in online dating. *Cyberpsychology, Behavior, and Social Networking, 20*(3), 150–156. https://doi.org/10.1089/cyber.2016.0528

Wittes, B., Poplin, C., Jurecic, Q., & Spera, C. (2016). *Sextortion: Cybersecurity, teenagers, and remote sexual assault*. Brookings Institution. www.brookings.edu/research/sextortion-cybersecurity-teenagers-and-remote-sexual-assault/

Wolak, J., & Finkelhor, D. (2016). *Sextortion: Findings from a survey of 1,631 victims*. Crimes Against Children Research Center, University of New Hampshire. www.humantraffickingsearch.org/wp-content/uploads/2018/09/Sextortion_Report.pdf

Wolak, J., Finkelhor, D., Walsh, W., & Treitman, L. (2018). Sextortion of minors: Characteristics and dynamics. *Journal of Adolescent Health, 62*(1), 72–79. https://doi.org/10.1016/j.jadohealth.2017.08.014

Wolfe, D. A. (2018). Why polyvictimization matters. *Journal of Interpersonal Violence, 33*(5), 832–837. https://doi.org/10.1177/0886260517752215

Wolford-Clevenger, C., Zapor, H., Brasfield, H., Febres, J., Elmquist, J., Brem, M., Shorey, R. C., & Stuart, G. L. (2016). An examination of the partner cyber abuse questionnaire in a college student sample. *Psychology of Violence, 6*(1), 156–162. https://doi.org/10.1037/a0039442

Xue, B., & McMunn, A. (2021). Gender differences in unpaid care work and psychological distress in the UK Covid-19 lockdown. *PLoS One, 16*(3), e0247959. https://doi.org/10.1371/journal.pone.0247959

Yi, B. L. (2020). Growing number of young men in Australia targeted for 'sextortion.' *Reuters*. www.reuters.com/article/us-australia-technology-crime/growing-number-of-young-men-in-australia-targeted-for-sextortion-idUSKBN20Z1MQ

Zamarro, G., & Prados, M. J. (2021). Gender differences in couples' division of childcare, work and mental health during COVID-19. *Review of Economics of the Household, 19*(1), 11–40. https://doi.org/10.1007/s11150-020-09534-7

Zhong, L. R., Kebbell, M. R., & Webster, J. L. (2020). An exploratory study of technology-facilitated sexual violence in online romantic interactions: Can the Internet's toxic disinhibition exacerbate sexual aggression? *Computers in Human Behavior, 108*, 106314. https://doi.org/10.1016/j.chb.2020.106314

Reading 9.2 Pivoting from In-Person to Phone Survey Assessment of Alcohol and Substance Use

The COVID-19 pandemic forced most people to make changes to how they did their jobs, and researchers were no exception. At the time of the outbreak, researchers worldwide were conducting longitudinal studies with in-person interviews. Proceeding with business as usual was not an option. Research teams had to choose between suspending data collection or pivoting to other modalities. Suspending data collection would result in the loss of valuable data, but there are also risks associated with changing modalities. Tierney et al. (2024) decided to continue their data collection, which started in 1949, by utilizing telephone surveys instead of in-person interviews in 2020.

Pivoting from In-Person to Phone Survey Assessment of Alcohol and Substance Use: Effects on Representativeness in a United States Prospective Cohort of Women Living with and without HIV

Hannah R. Tierney, Yifei Ma, Peter Bacchetti, Adaora A. Adimora, Aruna Chandran, Mirjam-Colette Kempf, Lauren F. Collins, Jack DeHovitz, Ralph J. DiClemente, Audrey L. French, Deborah L. Jones, Anjali Sharma, Amanda B. Spence, Judith A. Hahn, Jennifer C. Price, and Phyllis C. Tien

Introduction

The COVID-19 pandemic led to unprecedented changes in the way clinical care and research are conducted in the United States (US). Early in the pandemic, many clinical research and population studies pivoted from in-person survey administration to phone-based survey methods (1). The shift in survey methods offers an opportunity to examine the effect of rapidly adapting research study methods in the context of a widespread crisis as well as specific patterns in participant study engagement based on survey method.

Phone survey methods are convenient for collecting real-time data but have higher nonresponse rates than in-person visits, introducing a nonresponse selection bias if certain subgroups who are more or less likely to have the outcome do not respond (1,2). Survey nonresponse for alcohol and substance use has been described in studies prior to the COVID-19 pandemic and has variably resulted in biased prevalence estimates of alcohol and substance use related outcomes (3–10). Furthermore, self-reported alcohol consumption may vary by survey method. The National Alcohol Survey of 1990 found similar response rates between in-person and phone surveys. However, there was an underrepresentation of low-income participants and lower reported alcohol consumption quantities with phone surveys compared to in-person surveys (10). The 1985 National Household Survey on Drug Abuse also found lower reports of substance use by phone surveys compared to in-person surveys, especially among racial minorities (3). Since then, similar results have been replicated in other large epidemiology studies such as the National Survey on Drug Use and Health and the Canadian Addiction Survey (7,9).

Phone communication norms have shifted over the years with the decreasing use of landlines, and widespread use of cell phones, caller identification and text messages, creating an ongoing need to reevaluate phone survey modalities. Furthermore, widespread shifts in participant priorities due to economic insecurity, role strain, and health considerations early in the COVID-19 pandemic made data collection during this time period unique compared to pre-pandemic surveys. At the same time, substance use-related deaths and alcohol consumption have been increasing in the US, underscoring the importance of accurately estimating alcohol and substance use among at-risk subpopulations (11–14). This is particularly relevant for women, who may have been disproportionately impacted by the COVID-19 pandemic and had greater increases in alcohol consumption compared to men (12,13,15– 18). However, the impact of changes from in-person assessments to phone survey methods on the response rate to alcohol and substance use questionnaires among women during the COVID-19 pandemic remains unexplored.

Leveraging data collected from the Women's Interagency HIV Study (WIHS), a multicenter US prospective cohort of adult women living with and without HIV, we aimed to 1) determine the response rate to an alcohol and substance use phone survey administered early in the COVID-19 pandemic among women recently engaged in in-person assessments; 2) identify sociodemographic and clinical factors associated with response to an alcohol and substance use phone survey; and 3) assess the impact of phone survey nonresponse on COVID-19 pandemic prevalence estimates of alcohol and substance use.

Materials and Methods

Data Source

Established in 1994, WIHS is the longest prospective cohort study of women living with and without HIV enrolled from 10 US sites (19). In 2019, WIHS merged with the MACS (Multicenter AIDS Cohort Study), a long-standing cohort study of men living with and without HIV, to become the MACS/WIHS Combined Cohort Study (MWCCS) (20). At the time of the merger, 86% of participants from both cohorts had completed a visit within the previous year. There were 2,115 WIHS participants and the majority of participants had been enrolled for at least 5 years, as the last enrollment wave for WIHS was from 2011 to 2015. The WIHS is representative of women living with HIV in the US and also includes demographically similar women living without HIV for comparison. Recruitment, retention, and other study procedures are described in detail elsewhere (19–22). Briefly, women were recruited from a wide variety of venues including community-based organizations, support groups, substance use treatment programs, medical settings such as HIV and STI clinics, and other research studies. This was done primarily through flyers and word-of-mouth. Visits and phone surveys were conducted in English and Spanish, and participants were compensated. Study staff made multiple attempts to contact a participant. Contact methods (e.g., phone, text, e-mail) were site dependent and based upon preexisting modes of reaching participants for study visits. Data collection forms are available publicly (https://statepi.jhsph.edu/mwccs/). Clinical assessments and self-report surveys on medical, psychiatric, and social measures in WIHS were collected at inperson semiannual visits through February 2020. From April through September 2020, participants were invited to complete surveys by phone regarding COVID-19 symptoms, testing, and hospitalization, as well as mental health, alcohol, and substance use.

Ethics Statement

The WIHS and now MWCCS are approved by the Institutional Review Board at each study site. Written consent was obtained from all participants. Participants were also verbally consented before proceeding with the phone survey.

Study Sample

Women living with and without HIV who had a pre-pandemic visit from April 2019 through September 2019 and who remained enrolled in the study during 2020 were included. This pre-pandemic visit was considered the index visit for the current analysis. If index data were missing, data from the preceding visit (October 2018 to March 2019) were carried forward and only observations that ultimately had complete index data were retained in the analysis.

Alcohol and Substance Use Measures

A survey on alcohol and substance use was conducted in-person at the index pre-pandemic visit and by phone during the pandemic from August to September 2020. In both instances, participants were asked questions adapted from the Alcohol Use Disorders Identification Test – Consumption (AUDIT-C), and responses were used to calculate the average number of drinks per week either since their last visit (during the pre-pandemic index visit) or since pandemic start (in the 2020 phone survey), respectively (23). Responses were used to assess risky drinking (>7 drinks/week or >3 drinks/day). Participants were also asked a single question about substance use since their last visit or the pandemic start for each substance (i.e., heroin, crack, cocaine, methamphetamine, sedatives, other non-prescribed drugs). Responses were dichotomized into any substance use versus none. Pandemic phone survey response was the primary study outcome. Participants were considered "responders" or "nonresponders" based on whether they had available alcohol and substance use data for this survey.

Sociodemographic Measures

Age, study site region, race/ethnicity, education, employment, health insurance, annual household income, housing status, HIV serostatus, depressive symptoms (20-item Center for Epidemiologic Studies Depression Scale [CES-D], range 0–60, score >16 indicative of depression) (24,25), tobacco use, and cannabis use were captured from the index visit. These variables were selected based on previously published and hypothesized associations with phone survey nonresponse and retention in clinical research studies among women living with HIV (5,7,9,21,22,26–29). Study site region (categorized as Midwest, Southeast, Northeast, West) was included due to potential differences in demographic and clinical characteristics as well as the varying impact of the COVID-19 pandemic and related policies in different regions across the US. Homelessness and unstable housing was broadly defined as staying outdoors, in a transitional setting, or staying with someone else.

Statistical Analysis

Descriptive statistics were used to assess index demographics, clinical characteristics, and alcohol and substance use measures. Univariable and multivariable logistic regression models were used to identify factors associated with phone survey response. Inverse response probability weights (IRPW) generated from the multivariable logistic regression model were used to obtain nonresponse-adjusted estimates of risky drinking and substance use prevalence in the COVID-19 pandemic. These were compared to the estimates from the unweighted sample to assess for the presence of selection bias due to participant nonresponse. For example, if the weighted estimates were higher than the unweighted estimates it would indicate that the sample was biased due to lower response rates among those with greater alcohol or substance use. There were no extreme weights on visual assessment, so all observations were retained. RStudio version 1.4.1717 was used for the analysis (30).

Results

There were 1,968 women with an index pre-pandemic visit. Missing data included educational attainment (2.8%), employment (2.9%), health insurance (3.2%), annual household income (6.8%), housing status (2.8%), drinks per week (3.1%), tobacco use (3.1%), cannabis use (3.1%), substance use (3.1%), depression (3.4%). These data were imputed by carrying forward data from the visit prior. After excluding participants who still did not have complete index visit data, or who were no longer followed in the study, 1,847 women qualified for this analysis, of whom 1,433 (77.6%) responded to the pandemic alcohol and substance use phone survey (Figure 1).

The majority of participants were Black/African American (61.9%), had stable housing (88.2%), and were living with HIV (71.2%); nearly, half (46.0%) had an annual income <$12K (Table 1). The median age was 53 (IQR 46–59) years. Tobacco and cannabis use were relatively common (39.5% and 23.5% respectively), while risky drinking and substance use were less common (12.7% and 7.4% respectively).

In univariable analysis, nearly all sociodemographic and clinical measures – except racial and ethnic groups, HIV serostatus, risky drinking, and cannabis use – had statistically significant associations with response to the pandemic alcohol and substance use phone survey (Table 2). In the adjusted model, the odds of responding were lower among women residing in the Western (aOR 0.35 95% CI: 0.21–0.57) and Southern (aOR 0.29 95% CI: 0.19–0.44) regions compared with Midwestern US regions; among women of Hispanic ethnicity (aOR 0.47 95% CI: 0.33–0.66, ref=Black/African American); and among those who reported pre-pandemic substance use (aOR 0.63 95% CI: 0.41–0.98) (Table 2). By contrast, the odds were higher for White women (aOR 1.64 95% CI: 1.02–2.70, ref=

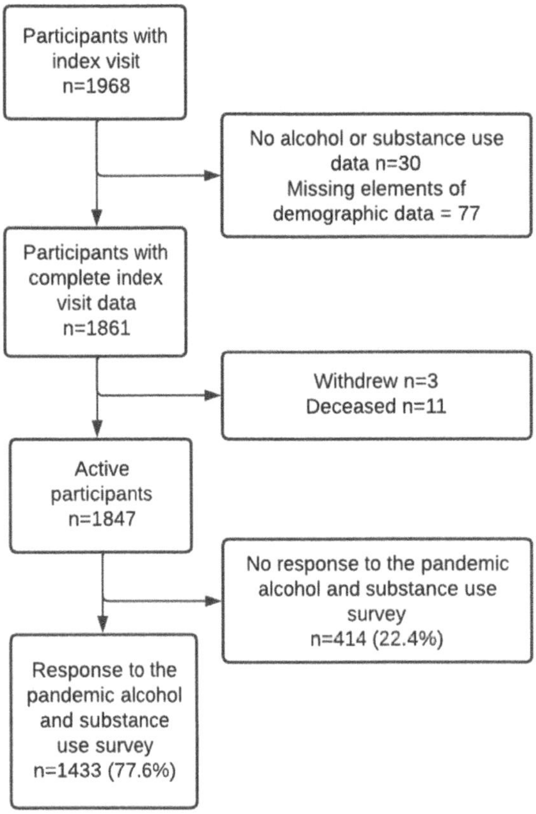

Figure 1 Participant flow diagram

Table 1 Index visit sociodemographic and clinical factors for participants who did and did not respond to the alcohol and substance use phone survey early in the COVID-19 pandemic (August–September 2020)

	Total n = 1847	*Responders n = 1433 (77.6%)*	*Nonresponders n = 414 (22.4%)*
N (%)			
Age, years, median (IQR)	53 (46–59)	53 (47–60)	52 (44–57)
Region			
Northeast	772 (41.8)	678 (47.3)	94 (22.7)
South	612 (33.1)	398 (27.8)	214 (51.7)
Midwest	223 (12.1)	192 (13.4)	31 (7.5)
West	240 (13.0)	165 (11.5)	75 (18.1)
Race and Ethnicity			
Black/African American	1144 (61.9)	884 (61.7)	260 (62.8)
Hispanic	263 (14.2)	191 (13.3)	72 (17.4)
White	151 (8.2)	126 (8.8)	25 (6.0)
Multiracial	257 (13.9)	212 (14.8)	45 (10.9)
Other/Unknown	32 (1.7)	20 (1.4)	12 (2.9)
Educational attainment			
High school incomplete	606 (32.8)	451 (31.5)	155 (37.4)
High school complete	565 (30.6)	446 (31.1)	119 (28.7)
Some college or above	676 (36.6)	536 (37.4)	140 (33.8)
Employed	716 (38.8)	577 (40.3)	139 (33.6)
Health Insurance*	1777 (96.2)	1392 (97.1)	385 (93.0)
Annual household income			
<$12,000/year	850 (46.0)	633 (44.2)	217 (52.4)
$12,000–30,000/year	560 (30.3)	441 (30.8)	119 (28.7)
>$30,000/year	437 (23.7)	359 (25.1)	78 (18.8)
Stable Housing	1629 (88.2)	1296 (90.4)	333 (80.4)
HIV Positive	1315 (71.2)	1014 (70.8)	301 (72.7)
Number of drinks per week, mean (sd)	2.6 (7.5)	2.4 (7.2)	3.1 (8.7)
Risky drinking	234 (12.7)	175 (12.2)	59 (14.3)
Tobacco use	730 (39.5)	535 (37.3)	195 (47.1)
Cannabis use	434 (23.5)	326 (22.7)	108 (26.1)
Substance use**	137 (7.4)	85 (5.9)	52 (12.6)
Depression (CESD ≥16***)	545 (29.5)	398 (27.8)	147 (35.5)

*Includes the Ryan White HIV/AIDS Program.

**Includes heroin, crack, cocaine, methamphetamine, sedatives, other non-prescribed drugs.

***Center for Epidemiologic Studies Depression Scale (CESD), range 0–60, score > 16 suggestive of depression.

Black/African American) and those with stable housing (aOR 1.74 95% CI: 1.24–2.43). Unweighted versus IRPW prevalence estimates were 11.03% vs. 11.55% (standard error 0.89%) for risky drinking and 6.07% vs. 6.86% (standard error 0.73%) for substance use. While the difference between the weighted and unweighted estimates of risky drinking

Table 2 Logistic regression for response (vs. no response) to the alcohol and substance use phone survey early in the COVID-19 pandemic (August–September 2020)

	Unadjusted OR (95% CI)	*p-value*	*Adjusted OR (95% CI)*	*p-value*
Age, years	**1.02 (1.01–1.03)**	<.001	1.01 (1.00–1.03)	.066
Region				
Midwest	REF		REF	
Northeast	1.17 (0.74–1.78)	.494	1.20 (0.75–1.86)	.440
South	**0.30 (0.20–0.45)**	<.001	**0.29 (0.19–0.44)**	<.001
West	**0.36 (0.22–0.56)**	<.001	**0.35 (0.21–0.57)**	<.001
Race and Ethnicity				
Black/African American	REF		REF	
Hispanic	0.78 (0.58–1.06)	.110	**0.47 (0.33–0.66)**	<.001
White	1.48 (0.96–2.38)	.087	**1.64 (1.02–2.70)**	.046
Multiracial	1.39 (0.99–1.99)	.068	1.33 (0.92–1.94)	.138
Other/Unknown	0.49 (0.24–1.05)	.055	**0.41 (0.18–0.93)**	.028
Educational Attainment				
High school incomplete	REF		REF	
High school complete	1.29 (0.98–1.69)	.069	1.23 (0.92–1.66)	.164
Some college or above	**1.32 (1.01–1.71)**	.039	1.17 (0.86–1.58)	.321
Employed	**1.33 (1.06–1.68)**	.014	1.25 (0.93–1.67)	.140
Health Insurance*	**2.56 (1.56–4.15)**	<.001	1.66 (0.96–2.87)	.069
Annual household income				
<$12,000/year	REF		REF	
$12,000–30,000/year	1.27 (0.99–1.64)	.065	1.13 (0.85–1.50)	.416
>$30,000/year	**1.58 (1.19–2.12)**	.002	0.97 (0.67–1.39)	.852
Stable Housing	**2.30 (1.70–3.10)**	<.001	**1.74 (1.24–2.43)**	.001
HIV Positive	0.91 (0.71–1.16)	.442	0.79 (0.59–1.04)	.095
Number of drinks per week	0.99 (0.98–1.00)	.124	1.01 (0.99–1.02)	.309
Tobacco use	**0.67 (0.54–0.84)**	<.001	0.84 (0.65–1.09)	.186
Cannabis use	0.83 (0.65–1.08)	.159	1.09 (0.82–1.46)	.577
Substance use**	**0.44 (0.31–0.64)**	<.001	**0.63 (0.41–0.98)**	.037
Depressive symptoms (CESD ≥16)***	**0.70 (0.55–0.88)**	.002	0.90 (0.70–1.17)	.425

Statistically significant values are bolded.

*Includes the Ryan White HIV/AIDS Program.

**Includes heroin, crack, cocaine, methamphetamine, sedatives, other non-prescribed drugs.

***Center for Epidemiologic Studies Depression Scale (CESD), range 0–60, score > 16 suggestive of depression.

represents a 4.77% increase, the unweighted estimate falls within the standard error of the weighted estimate. The difference between the weighted and unweighted estimates of substance use represents a 13.00% increase, with the unweighted estimate falling just outside of the standard error for the weighted estimate.

Discussion

The transition from in-person to remote survey methods in population and clinical research studies during the COVID-19 pandemic is an important opportunity for understanding the impact of rapid adaptations of remote research methods and to inform future best practices for study retention. Examining this question in a longitudinal cohort of socioeconomically disadvantaged US women living with and without HIV is critically important, because these women are underrepresented in research studies and may be more difficult to retain using traditional methods (32,33).

When we examined women from our cohort who were previously engaged in in-person assessments, over one-fifth did not respond to a phone-based alcohol and substance use survey. After adjusting for sociodemographic factors, HIV serostatus, and evidence of depression, we found that Black/African American and Hispanic women, those who were unstably housed or homeless, and women who reported pre-pandemic substance use had lower odds of responding to the phone survey. These findings raise concern that the transition to phone survey methods led to the underrepresentation of subgroups of women. Furthermore, these same subgroups were disproportionally burdened by COVID-19 illness and early pandemic policies, making data collection for these participants all the more important (34–36). Despite differences in survey response by sociodemographic and clinical subgroups, we found only small increases in prevalence estimates of risky drinking and substance use early in the COVID-19 pandemic after applying survey IRPW to the sample.

Our findings of differential survey response by sociodemographic factors and substance use are consistent with previous studies of survey nonresponse and study retention in both alcohol and substance use research as well as more broadly in cohort studies of men and women (3,5,21,22,27,28,37). A WIHS analysis among participants observed from 1994 through 2006 found that in-person study visit nonattendance was associated with temporary housing, substance use, and study site (22). Our findings in the context of these earlier WIHS data raise additional concern that a switch to phone survey methods could exacerbate low engagement rates in vulnerable subgroups given that we only included participants who were already engaged in the cohort. General population surveys including the U.S. Census Bureau Current Population Survey Annual Social and Economic Supplement (29,38) and National Health Interview Survey (26) also found similar results to our study when they switched to phone survey methods in the pandemic.

Underlying factors that mediate the lower response rates in these subgroups remain understudied. Members of racial and ethnic minority groups are more likely to be essential workers, experienced disproportionate job loss in the pandemic, had higher COVID-19 related hospitalization rates, and often have a higher number of medical comorbidities, making the navigation of early COVID-19 pandemic changes even more challenging (36). These factors may have contributed to lower response rates among these subgroups. While some of these circumstances were unique to the COVID-19 pandemic, persistent factors that underpin these disparities such as multilevel racism and the social marginalization of people who use drugs and people experiencing homelessness could continue to influence survey response moving forward. In the MACS/WIHS, in-person visits were resumed later in 2020, so it is unknown if lower response rates among these subgroups have persisted beyond the early phase of the COVID-19 pandemic with the use of phone surveys.

The use of phone surveys in research will continue to grow, underscoring the need for best practices and additional or alternative retention methods for phone surveys that are tailored toward specific participant populations, especially those who have been underrepresented in research historically and often face worse social and health outcomes (33). Current best practices for retention in longitudinal cohort studies focus on in-person study assessments (39). Future research should expand on the role of phone retention interventions such as calling at different times of day, providing participants with cell phones, and ensuring participants save study phone numbers at enrollment so that an unrecognized number is not ignored (2,40–42). Furthermore, having contingencies for contacting participants is important for future periods of social disruption and crisis.

Tradeoffs in the use of phone surveys in clinical research should be considered in the context of study populations and participant preferences. In addition to avoiding disease transmission, phone surveys can facilitate real-time data collection and reach of subgroups who have difficulty attending in-person study visits, such as people in rural locations, those with full-time work schedules, or those without access to transportation or childcare (43). However, these methods may exclude participants who do not have access to a personal phone or a private space to participate in a phone call, which is especially important in the context of discussing sensitive matters such as substance use (44). In a survey of participants enrolled in clinical research studies at one medical center early in the COVID-19 pandemic, about one-fifth to two-fifths preferred participating in study visits over the phone or internet, while others were neutral or preferred inperson visits, highlighting diverse participant preferences (31). In a discrete choice experiment of preferences for engaging in medical care early in the COVID- 19 pandemic among PLWH who were experiencing homelessness/unstable housing, telehealth was not preferred to in-person visits even if patient navigation was available to help with technology barriers (45). Given that phone survey methods will continue to become more common, investigators should consider these tradeoffs, account for participant preferences, and try to mitigate the risk of selection bias.

After applying IRPW, we found small increases in the prevalence estimates of risky drinking and substance use that may be partially attributable to statistical imprecision and are therefore unlikely to have public health implications. However, true increases in alcohol and substance use among women living with HIV and their demographically similar peers could translate to important health and social consequences given that this population is already at greater risk for poor health outcomes. In the National Epidemiologic Survey on Alcohol and Related Conditions, where there were also no meaningful differences in prevalence estimates of alcohol use after adjusting for survey nonresponse (27). These findings contrast with previous studies such as the Canadian Addiction Survey, where there was a doubling of prevalence estimates for substance use after adjusting for nonresponse (9) and the Mental Health Surveillance Study, where there were differences in 53% of alcohol and substance use measures after applying response weights (7). The variability in these findings highlights the importance of testing missing data assumptions and assessing for bias in each data source.

Limitations

This study focuses on adult women in the US who are socioeconomically disadvantaged and have a high burden of medical comorbidities, limiting the generalizability of these findings. It is also limited to a single, early COVID-19 pandemic time point. The longitudinal nature of the WIHS introduces a selection bias toward response due to the participants' demonstrated history of ongoing engagement in research. Furthermore, we excluded those with missing data at the index visit, including alcohol and substance use data, which could result in an overestimation of response rates, but an under-representation of subgroups in the overall sample for this study. Due to the sensitive nature of alcohol and substance use, these measures are also subject to social desirability bias, which can lead to underestimated alcohol and substance use prevalence. There may be factors associated with phone survey response and our outcome measures that were not included in our adjusted analysis, leading to inaccurate weighted prevalence estimates of risky drinking and substance use. Furthermore, the factors in the analysis were derived from a pre-pandemic index visit and may have changed in relation to the pandemic (e.g., employment, income, and housing changes).

Conclusion

Among a sample of women living with and without HIV who previously attended in-person study visits, participants of Hispanic ethnicity (compared to Black/African American race) and those who reported pre-pandemic substance use had lower odds of responding to an alcohol and substance use phone survey administered early in the COVID-19 pandemic, while those of White race (compared to Black/African American race) and those with stable housing had increased odds of responding, suggesting an underrepresentation of those most impacted by the COVID-19 pandemic. As remote survey methods become more common, best practices for using remote study methods are needed to ensure that data remain representative of the target population and investigators should assess for selection bias.

Disclosure Statement

RJD has received consulting fees from the Department of Defense, Morehouse School of Medicine, Benten Technologies, and Northwell Health. AAA has received consulting fees from Merck and Gilead; Merck and Gilead have provided her institution with funding for her research. AS has received consulting fees from Gilead; Gilead has provided her institution with funding for her research. Gilead, Merck, and Abbvie have provided JCP's institution with funding for her research. Merck and Gilead have provided PCT's institution with funding for her research. JAH has received consulting fees from Pear Therapeutics. The other authors have no conflicts of interest.

Discussion Questions

1. How might switching from in-person interviews to telephone surveys be beneficial?
2. What groups tended to be under-represented in the telephone surveys compared to the in-person interviews?
3. Do you think the researchers made the right decision by going forward with the study rather than suspending it? Why or why not? Could they have done anything to improve their data collection during the pandemic?

References

1. De Man, J., Campbell, L., Tabana, H., & Wouters, E. (2021). The pandemic of online research in times of COVID-19. *BMJ Open*, *11*, e043866. http://doi.org/10.1136/bmjopen-2020-043866
2. Menon, S., Sonderegger, P., & Totapally, S. (2021). Five questions to consider when conducting COVID-19 phone research. *BMJ Global Health*, *6*, e004917. http://doi.org/10.1136/bmjgh-2020-004917
3. Aquilino, W. S. (1991). Telephone versus face-to-face interviewing for household drug use surveys. *International Journal of Addictions*, *27*, 71–91. http://doi.org/10.3109/10826089109063463
4. Boniface, S., Scholes, S., Shelton, N., Connor, J., & Schooling, C. M. (2017). Assessment of non-response bias in estimates of alcohol consumption: Applying the continuum of resistance model in a general population survey in England. *PLoS One*, *12*, e0170892. http://doi.org/10. 1371/journal.pone.0170892
5. McCabe, S. E., & West, B. T. (2016). Selective nonresponse bias in population-based survey estimates of drug use behaviors in the United States. *Social Psychiatry and Psychiatric Epidemiology*, *51*, 141–153. http://doi.org/10.1007/s00127-015-1122-2
6. Nwaru, C. A., Lövestad, S., Gunnarsdóttir, H., Sundh, V., & Hensing, G. (2021). Determinants of non-response in a longitudinal study of participants in the women and alcohol in Gothenburg project. *Women & Health*, *61*, 452–60. http://doi.org/10.1080/03630242.2021.1917482
7. Peytcheva, E., Wang, K., Bose, J., Hedden, S., Hunter, D., & Tice, P. (2017). *Nonresponse bias in demographic and survey estimates from the mental health surveillance study of the national survey on drug use and health.* Substance Abuse and Mental Health Services Administration.
8. Rehm, J., Kilian, C., Rovira, P., Shield, K. D., & Manthey, J. (2021). The elusiveness of representativeness in general population surveys for alcohol. *Drug and Alcohol Review*, *40*, 161–165. http://doi.org/10.1111/dar.13148
9. Zhao, J., Stockwell, T., & Macdonald, S. (2009). Non-response bias in alcohol and drug population surveys. *Drug and Alcohol Review*, *28*, 648–657. http://doi.org/10.1111/j.1465-3362.2009.00077.x

10. Greenfield, T. K., Midanik, L. T., & Rogers, J. D. (2000). Effects of telephone versus face-to-face interview modes on reports of alcohol consumption. *Addiction, 95*, 277–84. http://doi.org/10.1046/j.1360-0443.2000.95227714.x
11. Ahmad, F., Rossen, L., & Sutton, P. (2021). *Provisional drug overdose death counts*. National Center for Health Statistics.
12. Barbosa, C., Cowell, A. J., & Dowd, W. N. (2020). Alcohol consumption in response to the COVID-19 pandemic in the United States. *Journal of Addiction Medicine, 15*, 341–344. http://doi.org/10.1097/ADM.0000000000000767
13. Pollard, M. S., Tucker, J. S., & Green, H. D., Jr. (2020). Changes in adult alcohol use and consequences during the COVID-19 pandemic in the US. *JAMA Network Open, 3*, e2022942. http://doi.org/10.1001/jamanetworkopen.2020.22942
14. Rodriguez, L. M., Litt, D. M., & Stewart, S. H. (2020). Drinking to cope with the pandemic: The unique associations of COVID-19-related perceived threat and psychological distress to drinking behaviors in American men and women. *Addictive Behaviors, 110*, 106532. http://doi.org/10.1016/j.addbeh.2020.106532
15. Connor, J., Madhavan, S., Mokashi, M., Amanuel, H., Johnson, N. R., Pace, L. E., & Bartz, D. (2020). Health risks and outcomes that disproportionately affect women during the covid-19 pandemic: A review. *Social Science & Medicine, 266*, 113364. http://doi.org/10.1016/j.socscimed.2020.113364
16. Jones, D. L., Rodriguez, V. J., Salazar, A. S., Montgomerie, E., Raccamarich, P. D., Uribe Starita, C., Barreto Ojeda, I. T., Beauchamps, L., Vazquez, A., & Martinez, T., et al. (2021). Sex differences in the association between stress, loneliness, and COVID-19 burden among people with HIV in the US. *AIDS Research and Human Retroviruses, 37*, 314–21. http://doi.org/10.1089/aid.2020.0289
17. Philpot, L. M., Ramar, P., Roellinger, D. L., Barry, B. A., Sharma, P., & Ebbert, J. O. (2021). Changes in social relationships during an initial "stay-at-home" phase of the COVID-19 pandemic: A longitudinal survey study in the U.S. *Social Science & Medicine, 274*, 113779. http://doi.org/10.1016/j.socs cimed.2021.113779
18. Rodriguez, L. M., Litt, D. M., & Stewart, S. H. (2020). Drinking to cope with the pandemic: The unique associations of COVID-19-related perceived threat and psychological distress to drinking behaviors in American men and women. *Addictive Behaviors, 110*, 106532. http://doi.org/10.1016/j.addbeh.2020.106532
19. Adimora, A. A., Ramirez, C., Benning, L., Greenblatt, R. M., Kempf, M. C., Tien, P. C., Kassaye, S. G., Anastos, K., Cohen, M., & Minkoff, H., et al. (2018). Cohort profile: The women's interagency HIV study (WIHS). *International Journal of Epidemiology, 47*, 393–4i.
20. D'Souza, G., Bhondoekhan, F., Benning, L., Margolick, J. B., Adedimeji, A. A., Adimora, A. A., Alcaide, M. L., Cohen, M. H., Detels, R., & Friedman, M. R., et al. (2021). Characteristics of the MACS/WIHS combined cohort study: Opportunities for research on aging with HIV in the longest US observational study of HIV. *American Journal of Epidemiology, 190*, 1457–1475.
21. Hessol, N. A., Schneider, M., Greenblatt, R. M., Bacon, M., Barranday, Y., Holman, S., Robison, E., Williams, C., Cohen, M., & Weber, K. (2001). Retention of women enrolled in a prospective study of human immunodeficiency virus infection, impact of race, unstable housing, and use of human immunodeficiency virus therapy. *American Journal of Epidemiology, 154*, 563–573. http://doi.org/10.1093/aje/154.6.563
22. Hessol, N. A., Weber, K. M., Holman, S., Robison, E., Goparaju, L., & Alden, C. B., et al. (2009). Retention and attendance of women enrolled in a large prospective study of HIV-1 in the United States. *Journal of Women's Health, 18*, 1627–1637. http//doi.org/10.1089/jwh.2008.1337
23. Higgins-Biddle, J. C., & Babor, T. F. (2018). A review of the alcohol use Disorders identification test (AUDIT), AUDIT-C, and USAUDIT for screening in the United States: Past issues and future directions. *The American Journal of Drug and Alcohol Abuse, 44*, 578–586. http://doi.org/10.1080/00952990.2018.1456545
24. Devins, G. M., Orme, C. M., Costello, C. G., Binik, Y. M., Frizzell, B., Stam, H. J., & Pullin, W. M. (1988). Measuring depressive symptoms in illness populations: Psychometric properties of the center for epidemiologic studies depression (CES-D) scale. *Psychology and Health, 2*(2), 139–156. http://doi.org/10.1080/08870448808400349
25. Thomas, J. L., Jones, G. N., Scarinci, I. C., Mehan, D. J., & Brantley, P. J. (2001). The utility of the CES-D as a depression screening measure among low-income women attending primary care clinics. *The International Journal of Psychiatry in Medicine, 31*, 25–40. http://doi.org/10.2190/FUFR-PK9F-6U10-JXRK
26. Dahlhamer, J. M., Bramlett, M. D., Maitland, A., & Blumberg, S. J. (2021). *Preliminary evaluation of the nonresponse due to the COVID-19 pandemic on national health interview survey estimates, April-June 2020*. Centers for Disease Control and Prevention.
27. Dawson, D. A., Goldstein, R. B., Pickering, R. P., & Grant, B. F. (2014). Nonresponse bias in

survey estimates of alcohol consumption and its association with harm. *Journal of Studies on Alcohol and Drugs*, *75*, 695–703. http://doi.org/10.15288/jsad.2014.75.695
28. Haley, D. F., Lucas, J., Golin, C. E., Wang, J., Hughes, J. P., Emel, L., El-Sadr, W., Frew, P. M., Justman, J., & Adimora, A. A., et al. (2014). Retention strategies and factors associated with missed visits among low income women at increased risk of HIV acquisition in the US (HPTN 064). *AIDS Patient Care and STDs*, *28*, 206–217.
29. Ward, J. M., & Anne Edwards, K. (2021). Assessing the link between survey interview method and survey outcomes: Evidence from the CPS and the COVID-19 pandemic. *Labour Economics*, *72*, 102060. http://doi.org/10.1016/j.labeco.2021.102060
30. Team, R. (2020). RStudio: Integrated development for R. In R. Team (Ed.), RStudio, PBC.
31. Hsia, D. S., Williams, K. M., & Beyl, R. A. (2022). Participant perspectives concerning resuming clinical research in the era of COVID-19. *Journal of Clinical Medicine Research*, *14*, 165–169. http://doi.org/10.14740/jocmr4670
32. Falcon, R., Bridge, D. A., Currier, J., Squires, K., Hagins, D., & Schaible, D., et al. (2011). Recruitment and retention of diverse populations in antiretroviral clinical Trials: Practical applications from the gender, race and clinical experience study. *Jounal of Women's Health*, *20*, 1043–1050. http://doi.org/10.1089/jwh.2010.2504
33. Kelty, M., Bates, A., & Pinn, V. W. (2012). Chapter 13 – National institutes of health policy on the inclusion of women and minorities as subjects in clinical research. In J. Gallin & F. Ognibene (Eds.), *Principles and practice of clinical research* (3rd ed., pp. 147–59). Academic Press.
34. Melamed, O. C., Hauck, T. S., Buckley, L., Selby, P., & Mulsant, B. H. (2020). Article commentary: Covid-19 and persons with substance use Disorders: Inequities and mitigation strategies. *Substance Abuse*, *41*, 286–291. http://doi.org/10.1080/08897077.2020.1784363
35. Perri, M., Dosani, N., & Hwang, S. W. (2020). COVID-19 and people experiencing homelessness: Challenges and mitigation strategies. *Canadian Medical Association Journal*, *192*, E716–E719. http://doi.org/10.1503/cmaj.200834
36. Tai, D. B. G., Shah, A., Doubeni, C. A., Sia, I. G., & Wieland, M. L. (2021). The disproportionate impact of COVID-19 on racial and ethnic minorities in the United States. *Clinical Infectious Diseases*, *72*, 703–706. http://doi.org/10.1093/cid/ciaa815
37. Link, M. W., Mokdad, A. H., Stackhouse, H. F., & Flowers, N. T. (2006). Race, ethnicity, and linguistic isolation as determinants of participation in public health surveillance surveys. *Preventing Chronic Disease*, *3*, A09–A.
38. Rothbaum, J., & Bee, A. (2021). *Coronavirus infects surveys, too: Survey nonresponse bias and the coronavirus pandemic*. U.S. Census Bureau.
39. Abshire, M., Dinglas, V. D., Cajita, M. I. A., Eakin, M. N., Needham, D. M., & Himmelfarb, C. D. (2017). Participant retention practices in longitudinal clinical research studies with high retention rates. *BMC Medical Research Methodology*, *17*. http://doi.org/10.1186/s12874-017-0310-z
40. Stewart, C., Kopinski, H., Liebschutz, J., Holmdahl, I., Keosaian, J., Herman, D., Anderson, B., & Stein, M. (2018). The provision of cell phones as a recruitment and retention strategy for people who inject drugs enrolling in a randomized trial. *Drug and Alcohol Dependence*, *184*, 20–25.
41. Teague, S., Youssef, G. J., Macdonald, J. A., Sciberras, E., Shatte, A., Fuller-Tyszkiewicz, M., Greenwood, C., McIntosh, J., Olsson, C. A., & Hutchinson, D., et al. (2018). Retention strategies in longitudinal cohort studies: A systematic review and meta-analysis. *BMC Medical Research Methodology*, *18*. http://doi.org/10.1186/s12874-018-0586-7
42. Pertl, K., Petluri, R., Wiest, K., Hoffman, K., McCarty, D., Levander, X. A., Chan, B., Martin, S. A., & Korthuis, P. T. (2023). Recruitment challenges for a prospective telehealth cohort study. *Contemporary Clinical Trials Communications*, *31*, 101043. http://doi.org/10.1016/j.conctc.2022.101043
43. Tipre, M., Scarinci, I. C., Pandya, V. N., Kim, Y. I., Bae, S., Peral, S., Hardy, C., & Baskin, M. L. (2022). Attitudes toward telemedicine among urban and rural residents. *Journal of Telemedicine and Telecare*, 1357633X2210942. http://doi.org/10.1177/1357633X221094215
44. Nguyen, M. L., Garcia, F., Juarez, J., Zeng, B., Khoong, E. C., Nijagal, M. A., Sarkar, U., Su, G., & Lyles, C. R. (2022). Satisfaction can co-exist with hesitation: Qualitative analysis of acceptability of telemedicine among multilingual patients in a safety-net healthcare system during the COVID-19 pandemic. *BMC Health ServicesResearch*, *22*. http://doi.org/10.1186/s12913-022-07547-9
45. Imbert, E., Hickey, M. D., Del Rosario, J. B., Conte, M., Kerkhoff, A. D., Clemenzi-Allen, A., Riley, E. D., Havlir, D. V., & Gandhi, M. (2022). Heterogeneous preferences for care engagement among people with HIV experiencing homelessness or unstable housing during the COVID-19 pandemic. *Journal of Acquired Immune Deficiency Syndromes*, *90*, 140–145. http://doi.org/10.1097/QAI.0000000000002929

Reading 9.3 Community Policing during the Pandemic

Police departments face multiple challenges when attempting to adopt community-oriented policing (COP) programs. As with most other jobs, the COVID-19 pandemic only made the work more difficult. Given COP's emphasis on interactions with members of the community, how do police carry out this work at times when lockdowns and social distancing are mandatory? Since Smylie, Duxbuty, and Bennell (2024) wanted to learn about police experiences with COP during the pandemic, they chose to run focus groups with patrol officers responsible for community policing.

Community Policing during the Pandemic

Christina Smylie, Linda Duxbury, and Craig Bennell

Introduction

Gill et al. (2017) define community-oriented policing (COP) as a law enforcement philosophy that 'emphasizes the "co-production" of public safety by police and citizens' (p. 5). COP programs require police and community members to work collaboratively to 'define, prioritize, and address crime problems by drawing on a range of resources…instead of relying on the use of traditional law enforcement powers such as arrest' (Gill et al., 2017, p. 5). Community police officers (CPOs) are expected to seek out face-to-face interactions with the public by adopting alternative patrol strategies (e.g., foot, bike) and are, ideally, assigned to the same beat for an extended period of time. These strategies are expected to help officers familiarize themselves with community concerns and develop positive relationships with residents. In theory, COP should reorient policing's 'core functions' away from a crime control perspective towards a model that emphasizes relationship building, problem-solving, crime prevention, reassurance, and order maintenance. COP is commonly mentioned by both practitioners and academics as a feasible way to reform policing, address concerns relating to police-community relations, and reduce public dissatisfaction with reactive models of policing (Gill et al., 2014, 2017; Neyroud, 2021).

Despite widespread interest in this model of policing, efforts to implement COP programs and practices in a way that delivers on expectations can be challenging given the vast number of contextual variables that can influence how such programs are delivered and perceived (e.g., human capital and structural resources available to support COP programs, the socio-economic status of communities, the level of trust and the type of relationship that exists between the police and the public within communities; Dias Felix & Hilgers, 2020; Lum et al., 2020; Lum et al., 2017; Neyroud, 2021). A greater understanding of the contexts in which COP programs are delivered, and how those contexts impact perceptions of these programs is, therefore, required to help interested police services implement effective COP programs.

Evaluations of COP have not paid sufficient attention to context (Mastrofski, 2006). We took the opportunity provided by the COVID-19 pandemic to examine the implementation of a COP program in an extreme context where government regulations and public health requirements (e.g., lockdowns, social distancing, masking) made it difficult, if not impossible, for CPOs to deliver on the central tenants of COP (e.g., engage in face-to-face relationship building activities with the public). In doing so we were able to test the theoretical assumptions on which COP is based; namely that relationship building and the establishment of trust in police are key to the success of this form of policing. Our study illustrates how disruptions to these key processes influence the ability of police services to deliver on the expected benefits of COP.

Literature Review

The COP model was developed in response to concerns regarding poor relationships between the community and the police that could be linked to the reactive model of policing practiced in the 1960's (Eve et al., 2003). Early discussions around police legitimacy pushed police services to try proactive strategies, such as assigning officers to designated beats where they could engage with the community (Neyroud, 2017). As Sherman (1986) notes, however, these early attempts to apply proactive policing strategies often failed because services did not have a clear model or structure of how to implement such programs.

In the following decades, rising crime rates and high-profile research studies revealed a disconnect between what citizens want the police to do and what police actually do. Researchers reported that while policing, in general, was not particularly effective at impacting crime rates, proactive strategies (i.e., foot patrol) made police more visible and citizens less fearful of crime (Kelling et al., 1974; Pate et al., 1981). These early studies demonstrated the breadth of the policing role and encouraged the development of the COP philosophy, which reoriented strategies from a narrow focus on law enforcement and crime fighting to a broader view centered around community concerns (Cordner, 1997). As discussed in more detail below, Cordner's (1997, 1998) work provided the necessary structure to support the use of COP teams by strategically linking broad ideas and beliefs to specific programs and practices, and identifying the structural changes needed to support them.

The COP Philosophy

Cordner (1997, 1998) developed a structure that frames discussions of COP around four pillars: philosophical, strategic, tactical, and organizational. As a *philosophy*, COP assumes that the community is central to the identification of, and response to, crime and safety concerns. *Strategically*, COP links the broad ideas and beliefs of community policing to the specific programs and practices that are implemented. The *tactical* pillar focuses on the concrete programs and practices that are implemented as part of a COP program while the *organizational* pillar identifies structural changes that need to occur within police services for COP to succeed.

COP requires police to change how they operate (Reisig, 2010), expanding the roles and duties of police officers to enable them to provide personalized service delivery and engage in both proactive and follow-up policing activities (Segrave & Ratcliffe, 2004). CPOs are expected to spend less time in cars and on patrol and more time on local problem solving, crime prevention education, and developing positive relationships with community members. They are expected to seek out face-to- face interactions with the public and are assigned to the same beat for an extended period. These strategies are expected to help officers develop positive relationships with residents and to familiarize themselves with community concerns. Researchers believe that such changes should result in increased levels of public trust in the police and support from the community (Reisig, 2010).

Segrave and Ratcliffe (2004) observe that from an operational perspective COP programs can include any or all the following approaches: establishing community partnerships, focusing on public relations/media campaigns, developing mini-police stations, setting up Neighbourhood Watch programs, and hosting community meetings. Reisig (2010) points out that tactically, CPOs are encouraged to engage in local problem solving to help them understand the issues that are important to the communities they serve and tailor community-specific solutions to address those problems.

COP is expected to have impacts that differ from those associated with traditional policing (Greene, 2000). In a systematic review of the academic literature relating to COP, Gill et al. (2014) provide empirical evidence to support positive outcomes associated with COP, including increased community capacity to resist and prevent crime and social disorder, a reduction in citizen's fear of crime and enhanced perceptions of safety, improved relationships between community members and police, and community perceptions that police are legitimate and trustworthy. Due to these positive findings, the COP model has received considerable attention over the years from police administrators, practitioners, and academics leading to global COP implementation (for a review, see Mazerolle et al., 2013).

However, even though there is a considerable amount of research supporting the effectiveness of certain COP initiatives, especially those that involve very targeted interventions by police (e.g., Braga et al., 2014), there is less research that focuses specifically on the underlying mechanisms that make these initiatives effective. The COVID-19 pandemic provides a unique opportunity for researchers to consider COP implementation in a context where it is difficult, if not impossible, for officers to deliver on the central tenants of COP, such as community engagement and relationship building. As such, our research adds to the body of scholarly work that already exists on this topic, which has relied on methodologies that are very different from the extreme case study that we report on here (e.g., Hawdon & Ryan, 2003; Peyton et al., 2019).

The COVID-19 Pandemic: An Extreme Context

An extreme context can be defined as one in which events occur that rupture the normal functioning, and/or routines, of organizations and require an organized response that has significant consequences for individuals and groups who are members of, or related to, the organization (Hällgren et al., 2018). COVID-related events required an organized response from all levels of government (see Table 1) that resulted in unprecedented changes for most Canadians, including police officers. While there is limited research available that explores the impact of the pandemic on CPOs, several recent studies do speak to how the pandemic has impacted police more generally. For example, a survey study of 1000+ front-line Canadian police officers undertaken by Compeau and Duxbury (2021) during the third wave of the pandemic (February to June 2021) determined that police officers faced several unique challenges during the pandemic. They reported that following COVID-19 protocols, managing calls related to COVID-19 issues (on average, officers spent 6.5 hours per week dealing with COVID-19 related activities), and the need to work extra hours to replace colleagues who were absent from work because they had been exposed to or contracted the virus) had increased their work-role demands.

Other research links the initiatives taken by the government to limit the spread of the virus to changes in expectations regarding the responsibilities of police officers, and the number and type of calls for service that were being received (e.g., increase in domestic violence calls, decrease in traffic violations; Maskály et al., 2021). Of relevance to the current study are data showing that the pandemic changed how often officers engage in reactive (e.g., arrests) versus proactive (e.g., COP activities) policing strategies. More specifically, the available literature provides support for the idea that during the pandemic police agencies reduced arrests for less serious crimes as well as other enforcement actions, while also limiting proactive police activities (Alexander & Ekici, 2020; Lum et al., 2020; Maskály et al., 2021).

Drew and Martin (2021) reported that the expectation that police officers would enforce COVID-19 related restrictions was a significant source of stress for officers who worried about enforcing restrictions on non-compliant individuals. This worry seems justified given that research has linked publicized accounts of

Table 1 COVID-19 events in CANCITY

Date	*COVID-19 events in CANCITY1*
2020	
March 11	First identified COVID-19 case is recorded.
March 25	First COVID-19 death is confirmed and city enters a state of emergency.
May 2	Anti-lockdown protesters gather downtown despite emergency orders.
May 16	City begins a phased reopening.
July 7	Mask mandate and non-compliance fines are implemented.
September 16	Record daily increases in cases and 66% of cases are from racialized communities.
September 18	Second wave begins.
December 14	COVID vaccines arrive in CANCITY.
December 26	City goes into lockdown.
2021	
January 6	First vaccines are delivered.
February 14	Front line police officers receive vaccines.
February 17	Third wave begins.
February 20	108 fines are given for illegal gatherings and businesses operating during lockdown.
March 31	CANCITY food banks cite crisis level food insecurity
April 1	Vulnerable populations are hit hard by outbreaks and require additional protection.
April 3	COVID cases rise by 25% and city goes into lockdown.
April 8	Hospital and ICE admissions rise and officials declare a state of emergency.
April 16	Mayor gives police authority to enforce restrictions.
May 20	Re-opening plan is announced as cases drop and vaccine rates increase.
August 1	Large social gatherings identified as super spreaders and cases spike among youth.
August 12	Fourth wave begins.
September 21	Proof of vaccination is federally mandated for some locations and services.

officers applying COVID-related enforcement to negative perceptions of the police (Meško, 2021). Other research provides support for the idea that government enforced lockdown measures imposed during the pandemic and the concomitant decrease in foot traffic reduced the number of opportunities that CPOs had to interact and communicate with members of the community (Ashby, 2020; Lum et al., 2020). These actions meant that CPOs were less visible, which is unfortunate given research showing that officer visibility is positively associated with the likelihood that people within the community will perceive that the police are effective (Ghaemmaghami et al., 2021). Finally, existing research provides support for the idea that the COVID-19 pandemic made it more challenging for CPOs to engage with community members and build the relationships necessary to support this form of policing (Ashby, 2020; Lum et al., 2020; Meško, 2021) and to access resources from community agencies to address crime (Laufs & Waseem, 2020).

The Current Study

The literature presented above supports our claim that the COVID-19 pandemic created an extreme context that has the potential to rupture the normal functioning of COP officers. Our study capitalized on the opportunity offered by the pandemic to conduct a case study examining how this extreme context impacted the ability of six separate COP teams operating in

Table 2 CANCITY police service evolution events

Year	*Changes to CANCITY police service* [2]
1995	CANCITY police services amalgamate into largest municipal service in the country.
1997	60 full-time CPOs and 8 staff sergeants deployed in each of the three CANCITY districts.
2012	Mental health facilities closed and police demand increases.
2015	Budget cuts led to the restructuring of police services.
2017	CPOs are redeployed to front-line duties and COP program is abolished due to limited capacity resulting in public backlash.
2018	Community problems surge, 93% of calls for service go unanswered, and public expresses dissatisfaction with police.
2019	Police service admits flaws and re-introduces 60 CPOs in priority communities.

a mid-sized Canadian city (CANCITY) to execute a COP program.

To contextualize our findings, it is important to describe the police service implementing the model, the history of COP in CANCITY, and the CANCITY communities where the model is being implemented (see Table 2). The CANCITY police service is a reasonably large municipal police service in Canada. The service is under-resourced in terms of human capital, and it struggles to meet the demands of the community. CANCITY includes several socio-economically challenged communities. Within these communities most police calls can be linked to homelessness, social disorder, and mental health issues. COP initiatives were introduced in 2017 to address the needs of residents in these high priority socioeconomically challenged communities. These initiatives were not, however, evaluated and were discontinued in 2017 due to funding pressures. Due in part to community backlash over this decision, COP teams were re-introduced in CANCITY in 2019 in various priority neighbourhoods. It is these teams that are the focus of the current study.

The six CANCITY communities where the COP teams have been assigned have diverse racialized populations, experience a variety of socio-economic challenges, report high levels of crime and social disorder, and account for the largest proportion of CANCITY police calls for service (information provided by CANCITY police). The media in CANCITY is replete with stories that demonstrate the challenges the CPOs face trying to build positive relationships with disenfranchised members of these communities. However, these stories are offset by others expressing community support for the COP initiative, suggesting that some in the community see it as a way to improve their quality of life.

Methods

The Sample

During the fourth wave of the pandemic (August to November 2021) we conducted focus groups with the CPOs deployed in six CANCITY neighbourhoods. Information about the focus group sessions was communicated to the Sergeants in charge of each of the six COP teams and focus groups were scheduled at a time when most officers could attend. Officers from all six COP teams operating in CANCITY during the pandemic (n = 39; 65% of CPOs) participated in the study. Sample demographics are presented in Table 3. Most of the officers who attended the sessions were male (n = 32) with significant job experience (M = 7 years for the service). All CPOs had worked in patrol prior to working as a CPO. The demographics of

Table 3 Demographics

Communities	*Gender*		*Years of service*	
	Male	*Female*	*Mean*	*Range*
1	9	2	9	4–15
2	5	0	9	6–17
3	4	2	12	6–22
4	5	1	10	6.5–16
5	4	2	7	3–12
6	5	0	11	5–21
Total	32	7		

the sample of officers who participated in the focus groups is very similar to demographics of the total sample of CPOs.

Data Collection

We used a focus group methodology in this study. Focus groups involve assembling a group of people (in this case CPOs who had worked together during the pandemic) who are guided via a facilitator to provide feedback on a clearly defined topic (Morgan, 1997). This qualitative research methodology was selected for use in this study because it encourages candid responses, allows participants to 'piggyback' off each other's ideas, leverages the team's collective experiences, and makes it possible for researchers to go beyond the numbers and gain insights that would be harder to gather using a survey methodology (Morgan, 1997). It is also important to acknowledge that CPOs have many demands on their time and a focus group methodology proved to be a very efficient way to collect information from a substantive group of people.

The focus groups lasted between 1 and 2.5 hours and were facilitated by one of the two lead researchers on the project (the second and third authors). Between five and 12 officers attended each of the focus groups. Several questions were used to guide the discussion. Responses to the following questions are reported in this paper: (1) In your view, what is the role of a CPO? (2) How has the pandemic impacted your ability to carry out your community policing role? (3) During the pandemic, did you learn any lessons that you can apply to being a good CPO when the pandemic is over? and, (4) What is one thing you would want your service to know about your experience working as a CPO during the pandemic?

Data Analysis

Detailed notes were taken by members of the research team during the focus group sessions (two note takers per session). These two sets of notes were merged and cleaned. This process resulted in text that represented what was said in each of the six focus groups. We used content analysis (Berg, 2007), to code the data. Content coding is a systematic approach to qualitative data analysis that systematically allocates data into content categories that represent the ideas, patterns, or themes that occur in the text. Relationships between categories are then identified. A main strength of this approach is that it provides a structured method for quantifying focus group data (Berg, 2007).

The analysis was conducted by one member of our research team (the first author) to ensure reliability of the coding process and validated by one other member of the team (the second author). The following steps were followed in all cases. The coder began by reading the notes several times to develop familiarity with the data and to identify nascent themes. Concepts of meaning were identified within the text and given a label (i.e., a code) that represented the meaning of the concept that had been identified. Codes were sorted into categories to provide structure to the data. The codes were reviewed by the second author and any necessary changes were incorporated into the coding scheme. Frequencies of categories were calculated (each focus group was considered a separate case). In the Results sections below, we present the findings from this analysis for each of the four different questions of relevance to this study. Direct quotes from officers are included to help the reader appreciate what we heard during these sessions.

Results

The CPO Role

We first asked officers how they define their role as a CPO. There was a high degree of consensus within our sample on how they defined their role, with all officers agreeing that they were to be a co-producer of public safety and build relationships with the community. Officers also emphasized the importance of differentiating their role from the role of patrol officer.

Co-producing Public Safety

CPOs saw their role as co-producing public safety by working with community members ('people in the community have our work numbers'), to identify problems ('we need to identify major issues within the community because every community is different'), bringing in resources, and coordinating the response ('investigate complaints while coordinating with specialty units'), to solve crime problems ('this team has effectively dealt with two problem addresses by knowing people one-on-one in the areas').

Relationship Building

Officers emphasized that co-producing public safety requires them to proactively engage in activities which enable them to develop positive relationships with community stakeholders. CPOs emphasized the importance of establishing a presence ('you're out there and you have to talk to everyone'), that is positive ('a constant familiar face in the community'), and consistent ('it takes 3–4 months to build rapport with community') to repair relationships broken by reactive policing. Officers highlighted examples of compassion and trust developed in both directions from these activities. One officer stated: 'Because of the relationships they become people, you understand why they are where they are. Yeah, they've done some things but they're still a person behind all that.' Another officer provided the following description:

> 'This one guy was at an extreme, he didn't like us. He would yell at us from his balcony for talking to someone in the parking lot ... we engaged with him over multiple events and now our relationship is completely different ... now he comes out and says hi to us.'

Relationship building requires differentiating our role from those working in patrol. The COP teams noted the importance of differentiating themselves from patrol officers as the communities were deeply dissatisfied with the reactive model of policing. They felt the CPO's job was to provide a service to the community ('so they feel like we are there to help them') that patrol officers could not ('that's the difference between us and patrol, you're already there when stuff is happening ... they're more likely to tell you stuff'). They attribute the time they spend in communities as the key differentiator that allows them to establish trust ('they refused to speak to patrol. But spilt the beans to us'). One CPO elaborated on this idea as follows:

> There was a well-known drug dealer in the area that our officers built a relationship with. We made efforts to communicate with her without penalizing her for her crimes. Then one day she came and turned in stolen laptops. That's a way to measure success. It's hard to put it on paper but people are letting us in.

Impact of the Pandemic on the CPO Role

Next, we asked officers how the pandemic impacted their ability to carry out their role as they defined it. In the focus groups, officers talked about how the pandemic and subsequent actions taken by municipal, provincial, and federal governments negatively impacted their ability to deliver on the two key role responsibilities of the CPO: to co-produce public safety and to build positive relationships within the community.

Negatively Impacted Ability to Co-produce Public Safety

Officers in all six teams shared examples of how the pandemic, in general, impacted their ability to co-produce public safety. Officers felt that community concerns had shifted from crime and social disorder to how best to minimize the risk of COVID-19 transmission and protect vulnerable groups within the area. These findings are consistent with data showing that active cases were higher in the communities where CPOs were assigned. Understanding and respecting these concerns discouraged officers from entering establishments and talking to people which, in turn, made it harder for them to engage with the community and develop positive relationships.

Officers also highlighted how lockdowns, social distancing measures, and isolation periods impacted their ability to address community concerns. CPOs continued to make arrests during the pandemic, but reduced jail capacity and backlogs in the court system meant that criminals were quickly released back into the community where they would re-offend. CPOs were frustrated with this turn of events, stating that all they can do is disrupt crime, but ultimately crime can't be stopped. As one officer stated: 'theft is pretty much legal now, the courts are just throwing them out … it didn't take long for repeat offenders to realize they wouldn't go to jail.' According to the CPOs, this situation negatively impacted community members' perceptions of them. Specifically, re-offences were blamed on CPOs and community members accused them of not doing their job. Inability to address crime problems was exacerbated by government mandated isolation periods. As front-line employees, officers were frequently exposed to the virus and losing officers to isolation periods reduced capacity and gave them less community coverage ('entire areas of the community are being ignored').

Negatively Impacted Relationship Building

Second, all groups indicated that their usual strategies to engage with the community were no longer effective. During lockdowns, many community events were cancelled which limited opportunities to engage with the public. One officer observed that: 'There used to be rec nights. You could drop in at all these events (bingo, dart night, etc.). Now we can't as they are cancelled.' Another officer explained:

> We used to attend community functions … this was very good for relationship building. We would talk to youth at these events … without them feeling like they were 'snitching.' This built a level of comfort with youth, so that when we saw them in the street, we could talk to them … because of lockdown … we lost the opportunity to connect with youth in a comfortable manner.

Events that were not cancelled were moved to virtual platforms which officers felt was an ineffective way to build relationships ('COP doesn't work virtual. It has to be in person'), especially during the initial contact with community members.

Finally, CPOs felt the mask mandate hindered relationship building by making it harder for them to read facial expressions and interpret how community members were reacting to them. Many officers indicated they felt faceless when they had their masks on noting that people either didn't recognize them or thought they looked more intimidating. The following comment summarizes what we heard from officers:

'It is hard to build relationships with community stakeholders while maintaining social distancing, wearing masks, etc. We tried holding events in gyms, but everyone stood far apart, were masked and shouting, not conducive at all to relationship building.'

Impacted Our Ability to Differentiate Our Role from Those Working in Patrol

In five of the focus groups, officers indicated that government actions meant that CPOs and patrol officers engaged in essentially the same types of activities. They felt that this negatively impacted community members' perceptions of them. Specifically, they mentioned that during the pandemic CPOs were expected to take on enforcement activities. Such activities were at odds with what the CPOs were expected to do, making it hard for the community to distinguish between CPOs and patrol officers. As one officer noted:

> Then they brought up this order that we are going to check people. People are coming to us like what the heck. It really scared people. It was really hard for us ... That was a big set-back for us with the community ... they thought we were picking on them or racial profiling.

Impact of Social Movements Following the Murder of George Floyd

While we asked our focus group participants to talk about how the pandemic had impacted their ability to fulfill their role, we note that without prompting, all six groups also talked about how the negative impacts of the pandemic on their ability to co-produce public safety and to build positive relationships was exacerbated by social movements following the murder of George Floyd in March of 2020.

CPOs shared that community members accepted and perpetuated biases they saw in the media, interfered with their ability to do their job ('random people walk by, harass us, film us'), and became unwilling to collaborate. Officers talked about how members of the community, particularly racialized individuals, started to believe that the publicized incidents of the misuse of force by police officers was representative of all police, including CPO's ('people believe they have to hate you because of your role ... they are far, far away from the point of wanting to build a relationship'). Other CPOs spoke about how relationships in the racialized communities where they served were breaking down: 'how are we going to build these bridges, and resolve the whole culture of anti-police if you don't want us there.'

Lessons Learned That Can Be Applied Post-Pandemic

In the focus groups, officers shared things about the role of CPOs that they either learned because of, or that were reinforced by, their experience policing during the pandemic. Specifically, our findings provide support for the idea that the pandemic taught officers that they are adaptable, reinforced, in their minds, the value of COP (as compared with the reactive model of policing), and emphasized how important it was for the service to continue to invest in COP initiatives.

CPOs Are Adaptable

CPOs emphasized that when the activities that worked to fulfill their role pre-pandemic no longer worked during the pandemic, they worked as a team to overcome challenges and find new ways to serve the community. They explained that the communities they serve were hit hard during the pandemic, which created ('new opportunities') to help ('we had the time to deliver food to people in need in the community').

The CPOs also realized the value of empathy in working with the community to identify pandemic-related problems. One team shared a story of how they addressed a problem through empathy and teamwork:

> We met this lady who came up from the States and was being targeted for where she was from ... She was living at the motel with her two kids in one room ... her son is autistic. It was a really bad situation for her. We got her in touch with housing ... even got furniture donated for her for her house and on New Year's Day we all went and helped her move in. We went from meeting this woman, talking to her, seeing what she needed, and acting on it.

The Value of COP Compared with the Reactive Model of Policing

The CPOs we spoke to shared that, to them, the pandemic reinforced the value of proactive approaches to policing. Officers highlighted the importance of smiling to enable positive interactions with the public ('a smile or facial expression can de-escalate a situation'), a practice that was lost during mask mandates. The impact of smiling was reinforced during a re-opening period in CANCITY: 'it was good to take masks off outside yesterday … people commented that they were happy to see us smile, not wearing masks.'

They also learned the value of conversations for fostering police-community relationships. For example, officers shared that having conversations with community members who are causing problems, as opposed to reprimanding them, allows them to empathize with the individual. One officer explained an example of this:

> The harshest punishment is not always the right one, sometimes a conversation is more impactful. For example, if people are in a space they are not supposed to be, simply talking to them about why they are there can be better … maybe they just needed to get out of their house.

Many officers stated that the need for CPOs to differentiate themselves from patrol became increasingly important throughout the pandemic. Officers who were expected to take on enforcement activities actively tried to emphasize differences between them and patrol ('show that we are more than just enforcement'), and continued to implement a proactive approach by engaging with individuals and showing them respect ('I let them know at every opportunity that I have to be present, and I put it on them to invite me in'). During the focus groups the officers emphasized how the need for CPOs to encourage positive relationships between the police and the community became particularly important following the murder of George Floyd and community backlash against police. The CPOs noted that they had observed that by opening a dialogue between themselves and community members they were able to differentiate themselves from patrol officers ('they didn't want us in there anymore … we had to go and explain that he [the officers involved in the George Floyd incidence] didn't reflect us … we had to build back our trust').

COP Requires Integrated Resourcing

Finally, four teams stated that they would like their service to know that if they are going to adopt a COP model, the service must resource it appropriately. As CPOs, they felt that they were doing important work ('we are having an impact') in the communities they serve but were frustrated because in their experience, proactive policing requires a multi-pronged approach (e.g., police, social services, city resources, etc.) and they simply did not have the resources they needed to do the job the way it should be done ('we want to do more, just give us the tools and resources'). Officers shared that this lack of resources was impacting their ability to deliver on their key role responsibilities because they could not solve crime problems that mattered to the community, which made it difficult for community members to differentiate them from the reactive model they were burned by in the past. For example, one police officer stated:

> 'They say we have access to city resources, but that's not true. We don't have the city resources available to come and help the people who need them. I call these services, and get told they'll get back to me, but they never do. Getting support from city resources was supposed to be part of the COP vision, but we are not getting the collaboration we need.'

Discussion

Studying the implementation of COP in the context of the COVID-19 pandemic supported the COP's theoretical assumptions that relationship building and the establishment of trust are key to the success of this type of policing. Perhaps more importantly, our study also shed light on how fragile police-community relationships and trust can be during real-world implementations of COP, especially when the context is sub-optimal for delivering on the central tenants of the model.

CPOs in our sample defined their role in a way that is consistent with the literature. Of note, all COP teams we spoke to felt that their

Table 4 Differentiations between COP and reactive models of policing made by CPOs

	COP	*Reactive*
Presence	*Dedicated presence*	*Response*
	Friendly (approachable)	Intimidating
Interactions	Unbiased (fair)	Biased
	Trustworthy	Untrustworthy
	Compassionate	Controlling
	Community focused	Enforcement focused
Community perceptions	CPOs are a reliable presence dedicated to solving community problems	Patrol officers respond when there is an issue but do not follow-up.
	CPOs deliver sustainable solutions to community problems.	Patrol delivers temporary fixes to community problems.

role was very different from that performed by patrol officers and that COP is needed to repair police-community relationships and establish trust (see Table 4). These insights were driven by the fact that government responses to the pandemic made it very hard for CPOs to differentiate themselves from patrol officers and, according to the CPOs in our focus groups, this meant that community members started to perceive CPO programs as no different from the reactive model of policing they were dissatisfied with. This frustrated the CPOs who reported that the positive relationships they had worked hard to establish (particularly in racialized communities) had broken down during the pandemic and that trust in the police had similarly declined.

Although these findings are predominantly negative, it is important to note that CPOs in our sample appeared to adapt remarkably well to the pandemic and their experiences may help future CPOs navigate complex situations. Based on our data, CPOs learned important lessons about COP that allowed them to adapt to the pandemic as individuals and as teams. Officers talked about how the pandemic reinforced the fact that empathy is a key part of the CPO's job and how important it was for them to differentiate themselves from patrol officers to address negative perceptions of police and maintain positive community relationships. These findings emphasize how important positive relationships driven by empathy are to the ultimate success of CPO programs.

Also important is the extent to which the officers we talked to emphasized how successful implementation of COP initiatives requires adequate resourcing and police service support. The need for adequate resourcing was made especially clear in the extreme context we investing ated where old problems were exacerbated, and new ones were created. According to many of the CPOs in our focus groups, resourcing for the COP teams in CANCITY was not adequate. These officers felt that the lack of adequate resourcing was making it very difficult, if not impossible, for them to effectively address important community issues. While adequate resourcing from the police service was seen as critically important, the CPOs also felt that the city needed to provide additional resources to support people who were homeless and in poor mental health. They talked about how CPOs on their own could not solve many of the social issues they encountered within the communities they served and spoke of the need for more funding to support a broader social services ecosystem that would help them to meet their mandate; a mandate they felt passionate about. According to the CPOs in our study, it is through this more coordinated, collaborative approach that disorder will be meaningfully reduced, and root causes of crime will be effectively managed.

Beyond adequate resourcing, our data shows the importance of police service support for COP activities. CPOs in our sample who were expected to take on enforcement activities during the pandemic gave evidence that this tarnished the relationships they had dedicated time to building (this was compounded by social movements in response to police violence in the media). Both community members and CPOs in CANCITY do not see enforcement activities as aligned with the COP model.

Many of the issues that CPOs in our sample faced, such as dealing with mental health and social disorder issues, are widespread in the current context of policing and are expected to continue post-pandemic (Jones, 2020). If police services and communities can work through these issues, this will likely support the successful implementation of COP in a way that allows this model of police to deliver on the outcomes we desire and have come to expect from the model.

Study Limitations and Future Research Directions

Although our focus groups unveiled several important findings related to the impact of the COVID-19 pandemic on COP in CANCITY, and on the role that key factors play in delivering effective COP services to communities, our study is not without limitations. Two limitations in particular warrant further discussion. First, given the methodology we employed, we cannot determine whether our findings generalize to other settings that have been impacted by the COVID-19 pandemic. The degree to which they do will depend on how closely the COP initiatives in other contexts are like the initiative we examined, and how similar the community contexts are to the neighbourhoods we examined (e.g., in terms of demographics, socioeconomic challenges, and relations with the local police service). We believe, however, that our study sheds light on some of the key building blocks that underlie successful implementations of COP initiatives (i.e., adequate resources, differentiation of CPO and patrol officer roles, the importance of empathy and the development of positive social relationships between police and community members), and that key findings from this study will be valuable in other policing jurisdictions. Future studies should continue to explore these findings in diverse contexts.

Second, the results from the present study do not speak to the effectiveness of the COP teams that have been implemented in CANCITY, only to the experiences of the officers on these teams. While the CPOs in our focus groups believe that COP does allow them to provide more effective policing to the communities they serve and leads to the sorts of positive outcomes often reported in the research literature (e.g., better police-community relations), we provide no data demonstrating that these things are true. Future research in CANCITY will have to empirically examine the effectiveness of the COP teams before this determination can be made. Ideally, this would take the form of a randomized controlled trial comparing communities that do and do not have assigned COP teams, but if this is not possible, pre-post comparisons can be made in relevant communities to evaluate the impact of the teams.

Conclusion

Our examination of COP in an extreme context supports the key assumptions on which the model is based and provides a greater understanding of how the context in which COP is implemented challenges CPOs to deliver the benefits we have come to expect from the model for police, police services, and communities. The extreme context of the COVID-19 pandemic taught us that the community issues CPOs in our sample regularly face (e.g., high rates of mental illness, crime, and social disorder) were exacerbated by the context of the communities they served during the pandemic (e.g., restrictions on social activities, negative perceptions of police following publicized instances of police misuse of force) as well as the context of the CANCITY police service (e.g., a lack of resourcing to support COP and the re-assignment of COP activities that were not in line with the model), which made it difficult for CPOs to carry out their roles.

CPOs in our sample provided some important lessons they learned in this context and believe these lessons would improve their performance in the future. Namely, CPOs need to dedicate time and effort to implementing programs in a way that makes their value clear to community members so that they can get the buy-in necessary for relationships and trust to develop. For the officers we engaged with, this involved establishing positive relationships with community members driven by empathy for their situations and differentiating themselves from traditional reactive models of policing that they feel their communities are dissatisfied with. It would be beneficial for future researchers to look further into how diverse contexts influence the implementation of COP and if the lessons provided here transfer to different contexts.

Disclosure Statement

No potential conflict of interest was reported by the authors.

Funding

This work was supported by the Social Science and Humanities Research Council Partnership under Grant number 111933; Mitacs under grant number IT16354

Discussion Questions

1. What steps did the researchers take to improve reliability?
2. In what ways did the interviewed officers believe that COVID-19 impacted their COP work?
3. What are the reasons why these findings lack generalizability?

References

Alexander, D. C., & Ekici, N. (2020). Survey: COVID-19's impact on LE operations. www.police1.com/coronavirus-covid-19/articles/survey-covid-19s-impact-on-le-operations-JmGm4beDhdAHhrE5/

Ashby, M. J. (2020). Changes in police calls for service during the early months of the 2020 coronavirus pandemic. *Policing: A Journal of Policy and Practice*, *14*(3), 1–19. http://doi.org/10.1093/police/paaa037

Berg, B. L. (2007). *Qualitative research methods for the social sciences* (6th ed.). Pearson.

Braga, A. A., Papachristos, A. V., & Hureau, D. M. (2014). The effects of hot spots policing on crime: An updated systematic review and meta-analysis. *Justice Quarterly*, *31*(4), 633–663. https://doi.org/10.1080/07418825.2012.673632

Compeau, S., & Duxbury, L. (2021). *Police well-being in times of COVID-19*. Report prepared for the Canadian Police Association, Carleton University. https://newsroom.carleton.ca/wp-content/uploads/PoliceCOVIDSurveyReportRCMPV1-Final.pdf

Cordner, G. W. (1997). Community policing: Elements and effects. In R. G. Dunham & G. P. Alpert (Eds.), *Critical issues in policing: Contemporary readings* (Vol. 3, pp. 451–468).

Cordner, G. W. (1998). Problem-oriented policing vs. zero tolerance. In S. T., O'Connor & A. C. Grant (Eds.), *Problem-oriented policing: Crime-specific patterns, critical issues, and making POP work*. Police Executive Research Forum.

CTV News Ottawa. (2021, March 11). Interactive Timeline: 365 Days of COVID-19 in Ottawa. https://ottawa.ctvnews.ca/specials/interactive-timeline-365-days-of-covid-19-in-ottawa

Dias Felix, A., & Hilgers, T. (2020). Community oriented policing theory and practice: Global policy diffusion or local appropriation? *Policing and Society*, 1–9. https://doi.org/10.1080/10439463.2020.1776280

Drew, J. M., & Martin, S. (2021). Policing during a global health pandemic: Exploring the stress and well-being of police and their families. *Journal of Community Safety and Well-Being*, *6*(3), 104–111. https://doi.org/10.35502/jcswb.195

Eve, R. A., Rodeheaver, D. G., Eve, S. B., Hockenberger, M., Perez, R., Burton, K., & Walker, S. L. (2003). Community-oriented policing in a multicultural milieu: The case of loitering and disorderly conduct in East Arlington, Texas. *International Journal of Police Science & Management*, *5*(4), 245–264. http://do.org/.10.1350/ijps.5.4.245.24930

Ghaemmaghami, A., Inkpen, R., Charman, S., Ilett, C., Bennett, S., Smith, P., & Newiss, G. (2021). Responding to the public during a pandemic: Perceptions of 'satisfactory' and 'unsatisfactory' policing. *Policing: A Journal of Policy and Practice*, *15*(4), 2310–2328. https://doi.org/10.1093/police/paab058

Gill, C., Weisburd, D., Telep, C. W., Vitter, Z., & Bennett, T. (2014). Community-oriented policing to reduce crime, disorder and fear and increase satisfaction and legitimacy among citizens: A systematic review. *Journal of Experimental Criminology*, *10*(4), 399–428. https://doi.org/10.1007/s11292-014-9210-y

Gill, C., Weisburd, D., Telep, C., Vitter, Z., & Bennett, T. (2017). Protocol: Community-oriented policing to reduce crime, disorder, and fear and improve legitimacy and satisfaction with police: A systematic review. *Campbell Systematic Reviews, 13*(1), 1–30. https://doi.org/10.1002/cl2.174

Greene, J. R. (2000). Community policing in America: Changing the nature, structure, and function of the police. *Criminal Justice, 3*(3), 290–370. www.ncjrs.gov/Criminal_Justice2000/Vol_3/03g.Pdf?Q=Understanding-Community-Policing

Hällgren, M., Rouleau, L., & De Rond, M. (2018). A matter of life or death: How extreme context research matters for management and organization studies. *Academy of Management Annals, 12*(1), 111–153. https://doi.org/10.5465/annals.2016.0017

Hawdon, J., & Ryan, J. (2003). Police-resident interactions and satisfaction with police: An empirical test of community policing assertions. *Criminal Justice Policy Review, 14*(1), 55–74. https://doi.org/10.1177/0887403402250919

Jones, D. J. (2020). The potential impacts of pandemic policing on police legitimacy: Planning past the COVID-19 crisis. *Policing: A Journal of Policy and Practice, 14*(3), 579–586. https://doi.org/10.1093/police/paaa026

Kelling, G. L., Pate, A. M., Dieckman, D., & Brown, C. (1974). *The Kansas City patrol experiment: Summary version*. Police Foundation.

Laufs, J., & Waseem, Z. (2020). Policing in pandemics: A systematic review and best practices for police response to COVID-19. *International Journal of Disaster Risk Reduction, 51*, 101812. https://doi.org/10.1016/j.ijdrr.2020.101812

Lum, C., Koper, C. S., & Willis, J. (2017). Understanding the limits of technology's impact on police effectiveness. *Police Quarterly, 20*(2), 135–163. https://doi.org/10.1177/1098611116667279

Lum, C., Maupin, C., & Stoltz, M. (2020). The impact of COVID-19 on law enforcement agencies (Wave 2). Retrieved September 27, 2020b, from www.theiacp.org/sites/default/files/IACP_Covid_Impact_Wave2.pdf

Maskály, J., Ivković, S. K., & Neyroud, P. (2021). Policing the COVID-19 pandemic: Exploratory study of the types of organizational changes and police activities across the globe. *International Criminal Justice Review, 31*(3), 266–285. https://doi.org/10.1177/10575677211012807

Mastrofski, S. (2006). Critic community policing: A skeptical view. In D. Weisburd & A. Braga (Eds.), *Police innovation: Contrasting perspectives* (Cambridge studies in criminology) (pp. 44–74). Cambridge University Press. https://doi.org/10.1017/CBO9780511489334.003

Mazerolle, L., Bennett, S., Davis, J., Sargeant, E., & Manning, M. (2013). Procedural justice and police legitimacy: A systematic review of the research evidence. *Journal of Experimental Criminology, 9*(3), 245–274. https://doi.org/10.1007/s11292-013-9175-2

Meško, G. (2021). Police, policing and COVID-19 pandemic. *European Journal of Crime, Criminal Law and Criminal Justice, 29*(3–4), 183–188. https://doi.org/10.1163/15718174-29030001

Morgan, D. L. (1997). *Focus groups as qualitative research*. (2nd ed.). Sage. https://doi.org/10.4135/9781412984287

Neyroud, P. (2017). Managing the police through a time of change. In *Transformations of policing* (pp. 213–224). Routledge.

Neyroud, P. (2021). Globalizing evidence-based policing: Case studies of community policing, reform, and diversion. In *The globalization of evidence-based policing* (pp. 23–38). Routledge.

Pate, A., Willson, V., & Kelling, G. L. (1981). Reported crime in Newark and elizabeth and arrests in newark. In The police foundation (Eds.), *The Newark foot patrol experiment* (pp. 43–50). Police Foundation.

Peyton, K., Sierra-Arévalo, M., & Rand, D. G. (2019). A field experiment on community policing and police legitimacy. *Proceedings of the National Academy of sciences, 116*(40), 19894–19898.

Reisig, M. D. (2010). Community and problem-oriented policing. *Crime and Justice, 39*(1), 1–53. https://doi.org/10.1086/652384

Segrave, M., & Ratcliffe, J. (2004). *Community policing: A descriptive overview*. Australian Institute of Criminology. www.aic.gov.au/publications/archive/archive-168

Sherman, L. W. (1986). Policing communities: What works? *Crime and Justice, 8*, 343–386. https://doi.org/10.1086/449127

10 Field Research

One of the criticisms of survey research is that it can be weak on validity, since we are asking people about what they did in the past or what they would do in a hypothetical situation. Numerous factors impact the accuracy of the answers we will receive, including honesty, quality of respondent's memory, and concerns about social desirability. Trust in the researcher may be another consideration, as we often ask people in criminal justice to self-report sensitive matters, some of which even involve illegal behavior. We might be able to get a better, more complete, understanding of individuals' circumstances and their behavior through field research. Not only is field research beneficial when we want to learn about individual and group behavior, but it can help us learn about the environment. Going out into the field allows us to see the layout of neighborhoods and streets and learn about how physical characteristics of spaces can make them more or less attractive to someone considering committing a crime.

This chapter covers field research, which addresses a wide range of data collection activities. Field research includes no-contact activities where researchers make note of buildings, traffic patterns, and landscaping, as well as make observations of people who are unaware they are being monitored. At the other end of the spectrum, fieldwork can involve some of the most extensive contact between researchers and participants, with researchers spending weeks, months, and even years immersing themselves in a group's culture. In between these two extremes are depth interviews, focus groups, and in-person survey dissemination, topics that were addressed in previous chapters. In this chapter, I will focus on two types of field research—participant observation and structured field observations.

Roles for Field Researchers

Gold (1958) discussed four different roles for researchers operating in the field (Figure 10.1). The extent of researcher interactions with informants varies a great deal in each of these. First, there is the **complete observer** who has no contact at all with research participants, and participants might not even notice that they are being observed. A complete observer might sit on a park bench near a picnic area and observe the number of people who use the available trash cans to dispose of their trash, how many pack up and take their waste away with them, and how many leave their litter in the park. The next type of field researcher is the **observer as participant**. Gold noted that this group does one-visit interviews with participants. The work of Wright and colleagues (1992) interviewing active residential burglars would be considered observer-as-participant research. While informants are clearly aware of the researchers' presence, neither party has extensive exposure to the other. Complete observers and observers as participants can serve various roles in the field, and as such some might be there to collect quantitative data, including the percentage of park-goers who litter, or qualitative data coming from interviews and observations.

DOI: 10.4324/9781003661511-10

Complete observer ----- Observer as participant ----- Participant as observer ----- Complete participant

Figure 10.1 Roles of field researchers, by level of interaction with informants

Source: Gold., R. L. (1958). Roles in sociological field observations. *Social Forces, 36,* 217–223.

The next two groups spend considerable amounts of time interacting with and participating in the lives of research participants and primarily collect qualitative data. **Participants as observers** reveal their identity and purpose to their informants but then participate in the daily lives of the group they are looking to study. A classic example of this is Bill Whyte's (1943) *Street Corner Society.* Whyte was a researcher at Harvard University who spent four years living and doing research in a low-income Italian American neighborhood in Boston. The individuals in the neighborhood with which he had the most frequent contact were aware of his identity and purpose. Given Whyte's constant presence in the neighborhood and his skill at making individuals feel comfortable around him, he was able to gain a thorough understanding of the neighborhood's culture, to the point where informants were discussing criminal behavior and even recruiting Whyte to engage in some illegal activities. Finally, **complete participants** keep their true identity secret from informants (Gold, 1958). As you would expect, complete participation introduces ethical concerns, should only be used if there is no other way to collect the data, and the work should be carefully monitored by an Institutional Review Board. I will get into a more detailed discussion of ethical concerns in fieldwork later in this chapter. These last two roles, participant as observer and complete participant, are types of ethnographic fieldwork. Hammersly and Atkinson (1995) define ethnography as the researcher

> participating, overtly or covertly, in people's daily lives for an extended period of time, watching what happens, listening to what is said, asking questions—in fact, collecting whatever data are available to throw light on the issues that are the focus of the research (p. 1).

Ethnography is an approach to research that is very common in anthropology and sociology.

Qualitative Field Research

In Chapter 1, I briefly discussed the differences between qualitative and quantitative research. Whereas quantitative research designs require large sample sizes and work to draw generalizations from samples after conducting statistical analysis, qualitative work largely relies on interviews and observations of much smaller groups. Quantitative research gives us information about broad patterns and trends, but as Weisheit (2015) observed, "what it gains in breadth it loses in depth" (p. 191). Weisheit correctly noted that quantitative researchers who study drugs may amass an entire body of scholarship without ever actually having a conversation with someone who uses drugs. Rather than considering numbers and generalizing results to populations, qualitative research focuses more on learning as much as possible about small groups and even a few individuals. In these studies, which are smaller in scope but often take much more time to complete, the goal is to develop a deep understanding. Max Weber (Weber & Shils, 1949) referred to this as *Verstehen,* which means "understanding" in German. Ferrell (1998) defined ***Verstehen*** as

> a process of subjective interpretation on the part of the social researcher, a degree of sympathetic understanding between social researcher and subjects of study, whereby the researcher comes to share, in part, the situated meanings and experiences of those under scrutiny (p. 27).

Quantitative research rarely, if ever, involves a level of contact between researchers and participants where the researcher shares experiences to this extent. This level of understanding comes from extensive periods of time in the field, interacting with, and even participating in the activities of the individuals being studied. Qualitative research has been used in criminal justice primarily to study gangs, drug dealing and use, property crimes, and transmission of criminogenic values (Miller & Miller, 2015).

Qualitative research often begins by approaching research differently than projects with a quantitative orientation. As you know from earlier chapters, quantitative work is firmly situated in the deductive approach. Research using quantitative methods begins with the researcher developing a strong familiarity with the existing theory and literature, and from there one proceeds to generate hypotheses based on that previous knowledge. After that, data collection takes place. Inductive reasoning has a different starting point, with observations being the first step in the research process. This methodological shift is especially appropriate when the research goal is to learn about a new topic and/or generate new theories. Some researchers might even purposefully avoid exposure to relevant literature or theories so that they can consider their observations without any preconceived ideas.

Thomas Vander Ven (1998) wanted to study crime in a city he referred to as "Chronic Town," which had a reputation for being high in crime. He described his experience of going into the field as frightening, not only because of the neighborhood's reputation but also because he struggled to make sense of what he was seeing. He initially had hopes of explaining his observations by using social disorganization theory, a popular criminological theory that explains why some neighborhoods have high crime rates while others do not. Eventually, he stopped trying to force the explanations of his observations with that one theory and just simply observed. Once he allowed himself to do that, he realized that his observations were better explained by a different perspective called labeling theory. This is an example of an inductive reasoning approach. Vander Ven used his observations to add to theory, and future researchers could then use his work to generate hypotheses for testing.

Glaser and Strauss (1967), in their classic work on theory in sociological research, warned of the same problem that Vander Ven experienced years before he entered "Chronic Town." Glaser and Strauss identified two problems that can arise when social scientists take a deductive approach to research. First, they might continue to force a fit between a theory and observations when it is time to write up the results. Second, once they decide on a theory to test, researchers might practice "exampling," whereby they work to find field examples to support the theory. The latter was precisely what Vander Ven found himself doing when he went into the field with the plan of using social disorganization as the basis of his research. Instead of using the deductive approach and starting with theory, Glaser and Strauss recommended that researchers take the inductive approach and generate their theories with data rather than collecting data and trying to make the findings fit existing theories. This is called grounded theory, because theory is generated right there on the ground through observations. Qualitative research that includes making observations and listening to informants explain phenomena in their own words is well suited for such theory generation.

Gaining Access for Research

Participant observation requires tremendous commitment on the part of the researcher, but it also requires individuals, groups, and organizations to grant the researcher access. Imagine if, suddenly, someone wanted to spend long periods of time following you around at work or hanging around and observing you and your friends all the time. It can be inconvenient at best and invasive at worst. If you and your friends are involved in illegal behavior, having a stranger observing what you are doing all the time can also be frightening, as you might suspect that the researcher is undercover law enforcement. Even if you are confident that the person is, in fact, a researcher, you and your friends would be justified in worrying whether that person will share information with the police.

The stakes may not be quite as high for people who work for organizations, such as courts, police, or corrections departments, but a researcher's presence is not always welcome. Staff and administrators may not want to have to deal with the inconvenience of having an outsider observing and asking questions. The larger concern is likely to be what will come of this research. Will it reveal that the agency is ineffective in achieving its goals? Will it shed light on unethical, or even illegal behavior among staff members? Concerns about illegal behavior are uncommon, as most agencies and their employees are law-abiding. The worry about an unflattering portrayal of the staff and the agency as a whole, however, is likely to be more widespread and even justified. Some people have had unpleasant experiences with researchers in the past, while others are just a bit paranoid about what might happen, especially if they have reason to distrust the researcher.

When thinking about gaining access, we need to take different approaches depending on the type of group we want to study. Obviously, we would want to approach a formal organization differently than we would a gang or a group of people who hang out in front of the local liquor store.

Organizations

Getting in touch with someone who can arrange for you to have access to a criminal justice or social service agency can be very challenging. Let's face it, no one is sitting around and hoping to get a call or a letter from a researcher. They have other things on their minds and a long list of things to do. So, how do you make your case for gaining access?

Maxfield and Babbie (2012) suggest finding a sponsor. If it is at all possible for you to do this, this is definitely the preferred way to approach an agency. A **sponsor** is someone known and respected by the agency contact, likely the director or administrator of the organization. The sponsor can give you valuable insight into which agencies to contact or avoid and which individuals within those agencies might be willing to assist you. Personally, I have two outstanding colleagues who have served this role for me several times. Both are retired criminal justice practitioners who were born and raised in the area (I moved here in my mid-20s for the job, so my roots in the community are not as deep). Between their personal and professional connections, they have been able to help my students and I gain access to agencies for various class projects and research activities. They always know which department or individual might be amenable to working with me or my students. Perhaps of equal value is that they have steered me away from agencies and individuals that I should avoid. If you don't personally know people who can help, it is quite possible that your professor does, so ask.

If you are very lucky, your professor or another well-connected contact will serve as a sponsor and contact the agency to vouch for you. It is more likely, though, that you will need to do the legwork yourself. You should reach out first in writing, through either a letter or an email. Be professional! I cannot stress enough how you should never, ever communicate with a professional contact or your professors the same way you do with your friends. It is a guaranteed way to ensure that you will never gain access to that agency. Your written communication should serve to introduce yourself, briefly explain the purpose of your research, and then explain what you would like from the agency. Maxfield and Babbie (2012) suggest ending it with a date and time when you will call them, along with a request that they let you know if they would prefer a different time. When you talk over the phone, you can elaborate a bit more on what you are hoping to do and, hopefully, schedule a date and time to start. If you are looking to do a one-shot interview with the administrator and/or get some data from the agency, you will not need the cooperation of too many people. If your work with the agency requires the cooperation of multiple staff members, you could be in for a challenge. Just because the director or administrator has agreed to work with you, there is no guarantee that goodwill is going to extend to the entire agency. I have personally experienced several instances where the upper administration has invited me into their agency to do research, yet I have run into resistance, and even a certain degree of sabotage, from civilian and sworn staff. You must handle this very carefully. First, consider how much of an obstacle that problematic behavior is to your work. If it is not a big deal, I would suggest just ignoring it. Also keep in mind whether you requested agency access or whether they invited you to work with them. If the latter, you can be more forthcoming with supervisors about the resistance you are experiencing. Your professor is an excellent resource, so I suggest scheduling a meeting with them to get advice.

Subcultures

Gaining access to a subculture is quite different and can be more difficult. How do you get a group of people, including those who are involved in criminal activity, to trust you? There are a few ways that people have succeeded. One is to find a gatekeeper, sometimes also referred to as a locator (Brougham et al., 2023), who is a well-known, respected, and trusted member of that subculture. In the sampling chapter, I briefly discussed the work of Wright and colleagues (1992), who sought to interview active residential burglars but without using police or corrections agency records as a sampling frame. Since few of us happen to have the contact information of active residential burglars saved in our phones, Wright et al. faced the dual hurdles of finding people and gaining their trust. They hired someone previously involved in criminal activity as a gatekeeper. This individual used to be involved in criminal activity in that area but had retired from that life after being shot and paralyzed. Now in a wheelchair, he was still well known and a respected member of the community. The gatekeeper identified some local people who were still “hustling” and some streetwise law-abiding individuals who knew lots of contacts. Once it was time to make contact with the potential research participants, the gatekeeper vouched for the researchers, made assurances that they were not affiliated with law enforcement, and promised that their interviews would remain confidential.

Phillippe Bourgois (2002) did not have a gatekeeper when he moved to Spanish Harlem, New York in the hopes of doing qualitative research. Once he decided that he would focus on the lives of crack dealers, he had to find a way to introduce himself and become accepted among a group of dealers. Gaining access to a group was not easy. He has fair skin, so the neighborhood residents initially thought he was either an undercover police officer or just another White individual who traveled to a non-White neighborhood in search of drugs. For the first three months, he worked to make himself visible around town and became friendly with some of his neighbors. He then asked a neighbor who was addicted to crack to introduce him to Primo, the man who owned the crack houses in the neighborhood (Primo was not his real name. Bourgois gave all his informants **pseudonyms** to protect their identity). Primo initially dismissed Bourgois as an undercover police officer, but after two more weeks of seeing Bourgois every day in the neighborhood, Primo invited him over for a drink. Bourgois was up-front from the beginning that he was a professor looking to write a book about the neighborhood. Primo and Bourgois wound up spending years together, as the drug dealer later admitted that he always wanted to “conversate” with someone from “drug free” White America.

Many field researchers lack contacts in the field and must find ways to get a foothold on their own. Polsky (1967) suggested that, when starting from scratch, the best way to approach individuals would be to connect with them at “play” instead of at “work.” Polsky grew up playing pool, so his favorite place to go to meet people actively involved in crime was the pool halls. He suggested that researchers play to their own strengths and knowledge, so if, for example, they like to play cards, finding out where there are some card games happening might be a good approach.

People who can hold their liquor might try bars. Polsky cautioned that, while the researcher may initially pose as just another bar patron or pool player, they should quickly explain who they are before they have too many conversations and develop connections. That serves to prevent potential informants from feeling betrayed. Additionally, Polsky suspected that most potential informants are likely to guess that the researcher is somehow different anyway, so the researcher might as well be forthcoming.

Bill Whyte (1943) was a pioneer in urban anthropology, and he spent three years living in a low-income Italian American neighborhood in Boston while conducting participant observation. He struggled to gain access, as he and his mentors lacked connections in the neighborhood that he selected for his study. Whyte made multiple attempts to gain access to the locals' social circles. First, he asked a housing agency for their sponsorship in exchange for his sharing of the research results. They agreed, so he started knocking on doors and asking residents questions about their living arrangements. Whyte eventually realized that this approach was rather invasive and was not helping him build the relationships that he needed for ethnographic research. His second attempt was quite comical. Whyte went into a bar, walked up to three people who were sitting together, and asked to join them. The male in the group promptly offered to toss Whyte down a flight of stairs. His third, successful attempt involved going to a settlement house and meeting with the social workers. Whyte explained his research objectives, and a helpful social worker offered to arrange a meeting with one of the locals, whom Whyte referred to as "Doc" in his book. Doc was amenable to working with Whyte and offered to take him around the neighborhood. This gave Whyte the "in" he needed.

Sandberg and Copes (2012) interviewed 15 ethnographers who studied drug use and dealing, and found that most gained access by going to where dealers and users hung out with the hopes of being seen and becoming a familiar face in the area. For example, Jacobs (1998) walked up and down the street in an area frequented by people dealing drugs every day. Locals initially assumed he was a police officer and would yell warnings to others on the street that they should disperse. What eventually helped him, ironically, was several incidents in which the police stopped, questioned, and searched him on the streets. Witnessing that made others feel confident that he was not actually working for law enforcement. Sandberg and Copes (2012) found that gaining access always took longer than researchers anticipated, with one person working for eight months before making the proper connections.

Issues Specific to Ethnographic Research

Sampling

Random sampling is not typically used for studies involving ethnographic work. Weisheit (2015) identified convenience sampling (also called availability sampling) and snowball sampling as two of the most frequently used methods for qualitative work. Researchers may utilize convenience sampling to select individuals or groups already known to them or to recruit participants via posters or ads. As discussed in Chapter 8, snowball sampling involves respondents identifying other possible research participants, so the sample grows, similar to a snowball being rolled on the ground. This is sometimes the only possible option, especially when subcultures and people involved in crime are the subjects of research.

During her participant observation study of drug-using club-goers, Perrone (2010) used a combination of convenience and snowball sampling. When she started the project, she selected her first club to observe because she had an acquaintance who went there and knew some of the other club-goers. When she arrived, she ran into another old acquaintance who, upon learning about her research plans, offered to take her to additional clubs and introduce her to more informants.

Mowder, Lutze, and Namgung (2018) were interested in learning about how undocumented women seek help after being involved in intimate partner violence. Undocumented individuals have an incentive to maintain a low profile, and they might hesitate to respond to a flyer or other advertisement recruiting them, as some government agencies have set up fake schools and other programs to conduct immigration stings. Mowder et al. initially recruited participants from shelters serving women getting out of abusive relationships that specifically cater to Spanish-speaking individuals and received referrals from victim assistance coordinators. After that, they continued to build their sample through word of mouth. Of course, selection bias is a problem inherent in snowball sampling, so we must always be mindful of the fact that we are unlikely to produce a representative sample this way. Ethnographic research, however, tends to be less concerned with finding a representative sample, as the goal is to fully appreciate and understand one specific subculture or group of individuals and not necessarily generalize findings to a larger population.

The Work's Impact on the Researcher

Working in the field is bound to have an impact on researchers' lives, with some projects requiring more of a commitment and sacrifice than others. The two more involved types of participant observation—participant as observer and as complete participant—take a level of commitment that is often well beyond what is required for most quantitative projects. This commitment can be thought of in four parts: time/money, personal cost, danger, and ethical dilemmas.

Time/Money

Whyte (1943) was able to move into a low-income section of Boston and live among the residents for years because he had a fellowship at Harvard University that paid for him to do so. Residing in that community, making observations, and conducting interviews became his full-time job.

Whyte is far from being the only researcher to consider it necessary to live among those he was studying. Bourgois (2002) made the same decision and moved his family to Spanish Harlem for the duration of his data collection on neighborhood crack dealers. Quantitative work generally does not involve such a dramatic commitment as moving to a location with a lower quality of life than the middle-class environment where college faculty usually live. The time commitment is also much more intense for this type of work. Ethnographers spend large portions of their time in the field. Even when they are at home or in their offices, they are often faced with hours of note-taking, trying to catalog everything that they saw and heard while in the field. Over the course of my career, I have done more quantitative work than qualitative. I took a qualitative research methods class in graduate school and loved it, but the time commitment and patience that is required proved to be too much for me. While the time commitment is difficult, what might be even more of a hurdle is finding funding to allow one to spend so much time observing and interviewing instead of earning money by teaching or working on other projects.

Personal Cost

I already noted that some of these researchers felt the need to uproot their entire lives, give up their middle-class lifestyles, and spend extraordinary amounts of time observing, interviewing, and taking notes. What might be just as difficult is the mental challenge of having to be two different people at the same time. Gold (1958) discussed constantly reminding oneself that the role is to observe and to make sure that one doesn't become too invested in the participant aspect of what is happening. Whyte (1943) recalled having to find a way to navigate the two different worlds in which he operated—life at Harvard as a research fellow and life on the streets of "Cornerville." He eventually chose to keep the two worlds separate, as he worried that his Harvard associates would unintentionally say things that would complicate his relationships with the "Cornerville" residents.

Ted Conover (2000), a reporter for the *New York Times,* entered a corrections officer academy and spent a full year working as an officer while not telling anyone that he was actually there to write a story about his experience. As he spent months working in a maximum security prison, he found himself growing bored at dinner parties with his intellectual friends. Conover began to resent their discussions of topics that he now considered trivial, because he believed he had bigger problems facing him at work. He also noticed that his relationships with his family changed, and he even put his hands on his child in anger, something he had never done before. Conover realized that his research role of being an officer was starting to consume him to the point that it was changing both his thoughts and behaviors while on and off duty.

What happened to Conover, and what at times happened to Whyte (1943) is that they both started to "go native," meaning that they started to identify with the people they were studying. As was evident with Conover, going native can cause a multitude of problems in one's personal life, but it can also have a negative impact on the research. Hammersly and Atkinson (1995) define **going native** as abandoning the task of analysis in "favor of the joys of participation" and bias arising from "over-rapport." This is problematic for a few reasons. From a professional standpoint, this interferes with the researcher's ability to notice what is happening, resulting in a failure to analyze events. When I think of going native, I always think of the saying "the last thing a fish would ever notice would be water." Whyte (1943) discussed struggling with this after spending a long time living in the field. He wrote,

> I had to balance familiarity with detachment, or else no insights would have come. There were fallow periods when I seemed to just be marking time. Whenever life flowed so smoothly that I was taking it for granted, I had to try to get outside of my participating self and struggle again to explain the things that seemed obvious (p. 357).

When we hang out in our own social circles, we rarely question why things are the way they are. We don't think to question why we might go to the same restaurant every Sunday for lunch, that large gatherings only occur at one person's house, or that spouses are only invited to certain events. We don't sit back and analyze whether the person who hosts the big events is the leader of the group or whether they are using those parties to somehow enhance her reputation among the circle of friends (Maybe some of us overthinkers contemplate these things, but we can't be objective about our own social groups). Most of us, overthinkers excluded, just go with the flow and don't analyze these things. Approaching a qualitative study by going with the flow and failing to analyze would be pointless, so one must always maintain some sense of detachment from the group being observed and their activities. Otherwise, as Whyte noted, the researcher will lose the ability to have insight. This is why experts on qualitative research strongly discourage people from researching groups to which they are close or are already a member. It is difficult enough to spend months or years with other groups and still maintain a certain level of detachment. It is just about impossible to do so if one is already a member of the group that is the subject of study.

The second problem with going native in the social sciences is that it can prompt us to engage in illegal and dangerous activities. Whyte (1943) got caught up in the excitement of a local election and illegally voted several times to try to help the candidate favored by the group he was studying. I should note here that voting illegally in the early 1940s was much easier than it is now, which is why Whyte never suffered any legal consequences for his behavior. Lyng (1998) worked as a pilot for a skydiving company while in graduate school and became interested in the extreme risk-taking behavior of skydivers who did drugs in the plane before jumping. Since his observations had to end at the point when they jumped out of the plane and he was left to land it, he quit his job and decided to spend more time with the group both in the air and on the ground. One characteristic of extreme risk-taking is that this group would intentionally do things to make an already dangerous activity even more treacherous. Jumping out of a plane was not risky enough, so the group took drugs and then jumped. Riding a motorcycle was too boring, so they would ride at high speeds while also under the influence of drugs or alcohol. Doing so is illegal in every state. Lyng became so enmeshed in this lifestyle that he took a curve at 120 miles per hour while under the influence, crashed his bike, and nearly killed himself. After having some time to reflect, Whyte regretted his ballot stuffing, realizing that he got caught up in the moment. Lyng certainly regretted becoming so involved in the culture of risk-takers that he stopped seeing the danger to himself and others.

Danger

Even if a researcher maintains a sense of detachment and avoids going native, the nature of ethnographic research in criminal justice presents risks to one's personal safety and legal status. Being an ethnographer can be like being a police officer in that significant amounts of time are filled with boredom, but then there are moments that are extremely frightening. Jacobs (1998) was robbed at gunpoint and then repeatedly harassed by a drug-dealing informant who felt that the researcher disrespected him. During their burglary study, Wright and colleagues' (1992) research staff were giving an informant a ride when he started to yell that he was going to shoot a person walking on the street. The informant repeatedly yelled at the driver to stop the car so he could show them how a drive-by happens. Instead, the driver increased his speed to prevent the shooting. Bourgois's (2002) decision to move himself and his family to Spanish Harlem for his research came at a price, as they witnessed several major crimes. These incidents included a deadly shotgun shooting and bombing as well as a machine-gunning of rival gang members, both of which Bourgois witnessed from his apartment window. He was also mugged while living in that neighborhood.

Ferrell (1998) and Inciardi (Inciardi & Pottieger, 1993) were arrested while doing fieldwork on graffiti artists and people who smoke crack respectively. Bourgois (2002) and Jacobs (1998) were repeatedly stopped, searched, and berated by the police. These incidents actually helped to strengthen the fieldworkers' reputations among the people the researchers were attempting to study, as it reinforced the fact that they were not working with law enforcement. While the police interaction helped them gain credibility with people in the neighborhood, legal trouble does come with significant costs, including legal fees paid to lawyers and the risk of developing a criminal record.

Perrone (2010) was frequently faced with unwanted sexual advances during her club-drug research. She often had to tell men that she was not interested in having sex, tell them to stop touching her, and remove their hands from her. Her concern about being sexually assaulted impacted her decisions about which events to attend.

Unfortunately, it is not uncommon for criminal justice field researchers to feel unsafe. Brougham, Uttley, and Haley (2023) surveyed researchers in sociology, criminal justice/criminology, and psychology about their experiences, and 41% reported experiencing some level of risk while in the field. It is essential for field researchers and their supervisors to proactively consider potential dangers and make plans to maximize safety. What can be done?

Brougham and colleagues (2023) suggested several steps, including becoming familiar with the physical environment prior to conducting observations or interviews. For example, if the observations will take place in a public housing high-rise, staff should be aware of all the exits. If possible, researchers might benefit from traveling together or having multiple researchers handle certain tasks to maintain safety. Researchers should always have their phones with them, and they should set designated check-in or return times with colleagues who can take action if the researcher fails to make contact. Additionally, researchers should learn as much as possible about the culture and environment that they are about to enter, dress appropriately, and work to establish rapport with those in the area. Earlier, I discussed the key role of having a gatekeeper. The gatekeeper or someone else in the subculture might help to serve as a protector who looks out for the researcher and helps to ensure safety. If the research involves paying informants, researchers should limit the amount of money they carry at any point in time to reduce the likelihood of becoming a target for robbery. Finally, it is important to consider the psychological safety of researchers. Having a mentor or colleague who understands field research can be a key tool for helping to process the stress of the job.

Ethical Dilemmas

One particularly difficult aspect of qualitative research is anticipating and responding to ethical dilemmas. Researchers who are not in the field are in a better position to respond to ethical problems, since they are more likely to have the time to consult with colleagues, mentors, and ethics boards. When researchers in the field are confronted with ethical dilemmas, they are often forced to respond immediately without the benefit of time to reflect or seek advice. Polsky (1967) recommended that researchers try to limit their exposure to such problems by being up-front with informants immediately about what they are and are not willing to witness and hear. Polsky was also resigned to the belief that, if the fieldwork involved people actively involved in crime, the field researcher was going to wind up also breaking the law at some point during the project.

> He need not be a "participant" observer and commit the criminal acts under study, yet he has to witness such acts or be taken into confidence about them and not blow the whistle. That is, the investigator has to decide that when necessary he will "obstruct justice" or have "guilty knowledge" or be an "accessory" before or after the fact, in the full legal sense of those terms. He will not be enabled to discern some vital aspects of criminal lifestyles and subcultures unless he (1) makes such a moral decision, (2) makes the criminals believe him, and (3) convinces them of his ability to act in accord with his decision (p. 124).

Even when researchers work to establish specific boundaries, they might not always be respected. Polsky (1967) said that his request to be shielded from certain crimes and discussions of them was respected most of the time, but not always. Toward the end of his fieldwork, Bourgois (2002) started being pressured by one of the most powerful drug dealers in the community to launder money. Luckily, his quick thinking helped him talk his way out of doing it without putting himself or his work in danger.

Should researchers engage in illegal behavior for the sake of research? I will first note my bias here. I am not a qualitative researcher, and most of the work that I've done throughout my career has started with a call to a police station or correctional agency to get their cooperation, because I generally do evaluation research. My point is that it is difficult for me to personally relate to this type of dilemma, so my immediate response would be that researchers should not break the law. I am sympathetic, however, to the fact that some minor law-breaking could go a very long way toward gaining trust. Researchers must understand and then be willing to accept the consequences of that. Personally, I would not be willing to get a criminal record for the sake of participant observation, but that is also because my clean record is something that I need to gain access to criminal justice agencies for my evaluation work.

Of course, there are ethnographers who do not depend on a clean criminal record as I do and either participated in some illegal behaviors as recreation even before their study or felt that the benefits of committing minor crimes for the sake of research outweighed the costs. Ethnographers studying drug use and drug dealers reported to Sandberg and Copes (2012) that their own drug use helped to signal to the potential research participants that they were not police or social workers. Adler (1993) only met her key informant for her drug dealing study because she used recreational drugs herself. Adler, her husband, and "Dave" were neighbors, started socializing, and spent many nights using marijuana and cocaine together. It was through those experiences that Dave began to trust her and eventually revealed that he was a dealer. Researchers who witnessed and/or participated in illegal activities, such as Polsky (1967), Ferrell (1998), and Adler (1993), argue that, from a methodological standpoint, obeying the law could act as a barrier to understanding the subculture. Ferrell (1998) suggests "criminological verstehen" can be best achieved in some instances by being there in the criminal moment, but urges that criminologists do this "as best they can within limits of patronal responsibility and professional identity" (p. 28). Both Ferrell (1998), with his graffiti research, and Lyng (1998), with extreme risk-taking research, noted that it was only after their informants witnessed their participation in these activities that they began to open up and explicitly discuss their own involvement.

What about witnessing criminal behavior? It is inevitable that, when one studies drug dealers or users, one will witness lots of drug dealing and using. When deciding what you can observe without notifying authorities, you should give this lots of thought and anticipate as many scenarios as possible before entering the field. Work with an experienced fieldworker or someone who is familiar with that setting. As Polsky (1967) suggests, you should then be clear about what you are and are not willing to witness while maintaining confidentiality. For example, if you are observing gang members, you should tell them that you do not want to hear about plans for assaulting or murdering anyone, nor do you want to be around for any of that. Sandberg and Copes (2012) surveyed ethnographers about the dilemmas they have faced with reporting issues to the police. Like Polsky, these researchers asked their informants to avoid talking about specific persons, using real names of individuals, or discussing future crimes. The researchers who did hear information about serious crimes, such as murders that already occurred, did not report the information to the police, because what they heard was so general that it would not have aided in any investigation. The general rule adopted by these ethnographers was that they would go to the police if they learned of any serious crimes that were in the planning stages or if children or other innocent "third parties" were at risk. Weisheit (2015) noted that, depending on the researchers' occupation and where they live, they may be mandated reporters. For example, as a college professor in New Jersey, I am a mandated reporter. If I witness or hear a credible report of child abuse or neglect, I am legally obligated to report it to the authorities, regardless of any promise of confidentiality that I made as part of my research. Of course, as a responsible researcher, I would want to anticipate this and warn the people I was about to interview if I thought that this subject might arise in our conversations.

What if the police approach you and ask for information? You likely promised confidentiality to all your participants. Priests and attorneys are legally shielded from having to give up information on their parishioners and clients, respectively. Most researchers have no such protections. I say most, because there are federal certificates of confidentiality, but these are rare. They are available for certain federal grants, such as those provided by the National Institutes of Health and the Department of Health and Human Services. Researchers who are doing work without federal funds can apply for such a certificate, but granting it is at the discretion of the federal agencies (National Institutes of Health, 2019). Weisheit (2015) recommends that researchers who lack these certificates give much thought in advance of their fieldwork to what they are willing to do if police or prosecutors request fieldnotes or testimony. Adler (1993) purposefully avoided all publicity and held back on publishing her ethnographic work on drug dealing until after she moved away from the area so that she would not come to the attention of local authorities while she was still doing data collection. Speaking of publishing findings, how do we avoid harming our participants by publishing stories about their criminal behavior? Researchers handle this by being vague about where they collected their data. This is why Vander Ven (2001) identified his research site as "Chronic Town" and Whyte (1943) called his location "Cornerville." Additionally, for fieldnotes, interview notes, and the actual publication of their work, researchers use pseudonyms rather than people's real names.

Another set of ethical issues arises when researchers choose to engage as a complete participant, otherwise called a covert participant. People who do research in a complete observer role may conceal their identity from those they are studying, but they also refrain from interacting with them, making deception unnecessary (Miller & Miller, 2015). Miller and Miller listed potential ethical problems associated with **covert participation**, including invasion of privacy, lack of informed consent, and potential exposure of unwitting research participants to danger. Is it advisable to do this? Polsky (1967), who studied hustlers at pool halls, argued against it. He wrote:

> In doing field research on criminals you damned well better not pretend to be "one of them," because they will test this claim out and one of two things will happen: either you will, as Sutherland and Cressy [famous criminological theorists] indicate, get sucked into "participant" observation of the sort you would rather not undertake, or you will be exposed, with still greater negative consequences. You must let the criminals know who you are; and if it is done properly, it does not sabotage the research (p. 110).

Other researchers argue that, in certain circumstances, covert work is simply the only way to research some very important topics. Goode (2015) recalled the backlash that Laud Humphreys (1970) received after doing complete observation of men having secret, anonymous sex with other men. Humphreys' university tried to revoke his degree and called his publisher to urge them not to publish the book. Despite that, *Tearoom Trade* won a prestigious research award. Goode noted that this and other classic sociological studies would now be considered unethical. Goode also used a modern-day example of Scientology, a group that has developed a reputation for fiercely attacking anyone who criticizes them. He argued that anyone wishing to do ethnographic research on Scientology would have to do it covertly, as they would otherwise put themselves at too great of a risk. When thinking about whether covert activities are necessary, this decision should be made on a case-by-case basis (Miller & Miller, 2015), and Goode (2015) noted the necessity of demonstrating that the benefits of covert research outweigh the risks. If there is any way that the work can be done without using covert tactics, researchers should explore that option. Adler (1993) was covert with some participants but honest with others about her identity and purpose. When she met people, she initially remained quiet about her intentions. She would then work to gain their trust by offering favors, such as loaning out her car and lending people her telephone. As she gained people's trust, she would either have those who already knew her identity approach them and vouch for her trustworthiness, or if she felt comfortable enough, she would have that conversation with the new potential participants herself.

If you recall the discussion of Institutional Review Boards (IRBs) from Chapter 3, you are probably wondering right now how some of these research practices would be received by ethics boards. Ever since the passage of the National Research Act in 1974, ethnographers have been concerned about their ability to collect data. Miller and Miller (2015) noted that IRBs' reluctance to approve research that proposes extensive contact with participants, and perhaps some deception, has impacted researchers' ability to collect data. Europe's ethical guidelines for research vary from location to location, and Sandberg and Copes (2012) found that many of the European ethnographers who did drug research did their work without clearing it with ethics boards. In the United States, drug researchers engaging in participant or complete observation recalled having difficulty convincing the IRBs that requesting signed consent forms would have a chilling effect on participant recruitment. There are numerous people encountered during field research whom the researcher never interviews and maybe never speaks with, so providing informed consent to each would be impractical (Goode, 2015; Sandberg & Copes, 2012). American IRBs have been criticized for serving more as a vehicle to prevent universities and members of the IRB themselves from being sued rather than understanding the difficulty of field research and weighing the risks and benefits of the work. The lack of flexibility has prompted some fieldworkers to be intentionally vague and leave out important details about their planned work in their IRB applications for the sake of getting approval, while others have skipped IRB approval entirely, foregoing the legal protection that they would otherwise receive from their universities (Sandberg & Copes, 2012). As was discussed in Chapter 3, failure to obtain IRB approval for research involving human subjects can lead to serious legal and career-threatening trouble for the researcher.

Goode (2015) recommended that, instead of attempting to apply rigid guidelines, many of which were written with medical research in mind, IRBs and investigators work together to develop protocols with the following principles in mind: no physical harm to participants; no coercion to participate in research; no sexual harassment; no acts that would constitute exploitation of participants; no serious felonious behavior by researchers; no behavior that will "spoil" the research site/population for future investigators; and making every effort to conceal the identity of the research participants.

Note-Taking for Qualitative Research

Another difficult aspect of participant and complete observation is recording what is happening. You are not really participating in the activities of the group if you have a notepad or your cell phone in your hands, jotting down notes about what is taking place. Time spent in the field can last hours at a time, and it is very hard to keep track of everything. Whyte (1943) used to make trips to the men's room to write a few notes before returning to the group. He would also work to make mental maps of rooms and try to remember which groups of people interacted with each other. As soon as he returned home, he would immediately draw the map and then finish taking his notes. Of course, in the 1940s, Whyte did not have a cell phone with a built-in camera. Then again, taking pictures likely would have made others in the room very suspicious, so while tempting, it probably would have been unwise to utilize such technology in that setting.

While in the field, some researchers use mnemonics to try to remember events that took place. **Mnemonic devices** are rhymes or other verbal tools used to help us remember things. When we were in grade school learning the colors of the rainbow, we were told to memorize ROYGBIV (red, orange, yellow, green, blue, indigo, violet) (Hagan, 2007; Miller, 1995). One of the reasons why qualitative research is so time-consuming is that those who do it spend hours and hours in the field, but when they get home, they are not even close to being finished with the day's work. Whatever short notes with a few keywords that they jotted down must now be expanded into detailed notes about what people said and did.

When it comes to conducting interviews, field researchers have mixed opinions about using recording devices (Sandberg & Copes, 2012). Some worry that audio recording or videotaping interviews will scare respondents, particularly those who are involved in illegal behavior. Polsky (1967) was of the belief that researchers should not seek to record interviews with people currently involved in crime. Adler (1993) did tape all depth interviews with informants who discussed how they entered and then progressed in the field of drug dealing. In addition to concerns about the comfort of respondents, qualitative researchers have identified some practical barriers to recording interviews, including the setting where the interview is being conducted. Some settings, such as bars and even parks, might be too noisy to make effective use of recording devices (Sandberg & Copes, 2012).

Structured Field Observations

This section addresses fieldwork that does not include participant or complete observation. Previous chapters of this book, such as Chapter 9, have provided information about the work of observers as participants who enter the field for the purpose of interviewing or otherwise surveying participants. Here, I would like to discuss the work of people who are complete observers. Through this type of work, we can conduct social as well as physical observations. For social observations, the act of researchers witnessing behavior addresses an important threat to validity found in survey research. With surveys, people can incorrectly recall or lie about how they handled a situation in the past, and for hypothetical questions about how they would handle something in the future, they may give us an inaccurate account of what they would do (Think of anyone in your life who talks tough but does not act that way in practice.). Field research largely eliminates that problem by allowing us to observe human behavior as it happens. I wrote "largely eliminates," because there is still the possibility of reactivity, or people changing their behavior because they become aware that they are being observed. When we are seeking to learn about the characteristics of places, we can get some of what we need through surveys (e.g., rates of household burglar alarm ownership, presence of CCTV cameras in convenience stores), but there are other features of the environment that would best be measured by trained researchers to ensure reliability.

Field observation can provide us with data that would otherwise be impossible to collect. We can do telephone interviews with crime victims about recent auto thefts or household burglaries, or send mail surveys to business owners to find out how many times in the past year their business has been robbed. Unfortunately, those surveys will not tell us much about the environment where the crime occurred. Knowing about a home's visibility from the road, the physical layout of the parking lot where the car was parked, or the design of the business that was robbed can tell us a lot about the crime and the chances of revictimization. A parking garage might have more thefts and incidences of vandalism than others in the same town because of a design flaw that would be evident upon observation. For example, a review of one parking garage with high rates of vandalism revealed that the side walls were easy to climb, providing convenient access to juveniles who were entering and exiting the garage without being seen by security (Poyner, 1997). Through interviews with people actively involved in crime, researchers know what makes certain homes and businesses attractive targets for crime. For example, convenience stores that lack visibility from the street are considered more attractive locations to target, as there is less of a chance of a robbery being detected while in progress (Hunter & Jeffrey, 1997). Researchers who are studying convenience store robberies would likely want to visit the stores to assess the visibility of the cashiers from the street to measure the target's attractiveness for robbery.

A colleague and I did field research to study locations in Atlantic City, New Jersey, that had repeat reports of auto theft either in 2004–2005 or 2006–2007. The local police department shared with us the dates of the reported thefts and the location where the car was parked. We did site visits to the 2004–2005 locations in the summer of 2006 and visited the 2006–2007 locations in the summer of 2008. At each location, we used a structured data collection form to collect information about the WALLS: Watchers (people present to serve as informal social control), Activity Nodes (locations that draw heavy use for legal and illegal activities), Location (landscaping and design features), Lighting, and Security Indexes (Levy & Tartaro, 2010). We visited each location both during the day and after sunset. While one researcher completed the data collection form, the other took photographs with a GPS camera. Data from the GPS camera were used to help map the theft locations. While we could have taken the addresses of the theft locations from the police data and mapped that information without going out into the field, there really was no other way to collect the data for the physical characteristics of each street. In this study, we used three different types of data collection—unpublished agency records, structured observation form, and photographs—two of which required our presence in the field.

One common criticism of crime prevention techniques is that they might displace crimes to another time or location. To measure that, Weisburd and colleagues (2006) worked with the Jersey City, New Jersey police department to observe neighborhoods targeted for police interventions as well as areas adjacent to the targeted neighborhoods. The research team measured crime and victimization several different ways over nine months, including over 6,000 20-minute social observations conducted by researchers. Researchers went to each randomly selected street segment and sat in their cars, or stood on the sidewalk if they did not have cars, for 20 minutes. Using a structured observation form, they noted any instances of drug activity, solicitation for sex work, public intoxication, fights, police presence, and loud music. Researchers also conducted physical observations of those same street segments during each wave of the project.

For structured observations, training is essential. If there are multiple field researchers collecting data, lack of rigorous training will likely produce problems with interrater reliability. I mentioned in Chapter 4 that I was one of the student field researchers on the Weisburd et al. (2006) project who conducted both social and physical observations. For the physical observations, my coworkers and I went into the neighborhoods and took note of the conditions before, during, and after the police interventions. This took a lot of preparation and continued reliability checks, as we all had to come to an agreement about what was "a little" bit of litter versus "a lot." Not only did we all undergo initial training, but we did reliability checks every day that we conducted observations. If observers were seeing things differently, we discussed it until we came to an agreement. Even if there is only one person conducting field observations, it is important that the individual rate items consistently each day.

Validity and Reliability of Field Research

How does field research compare to other types of inquiry with regard to validity and reliability? As I just noted, structured field observations, if handled properly, are generally high in reliability. They are also generally high in validity, but there is one issue that might have a detrimental effect on validity—reactivity. If you were about to attempt to break into a car, my guess would be that the first thing you would do is look around to see if anyone was watching. A researcher standing on the sidewalk or sitting in a car could prompt the would-be thief to either skip stealing that day or to go somewhere a little more private to do it. Somewhat surprisingly, a researcher's presence does not always inhibit criminal behavior. During data collection for the Weisburd et al. (2006) study, my field researcher colleagues and I spent so much time on the streets that the locals, including those involved in drug dealing and sex work, grew accustomed to us and learned that we were not calling the police to report what we observed each day. While we likely influenced some people's behavior through our presence, we were still able to capture numerous instances of illegal acts. Researchers did make every effort to blend in and act as though they were not actively watching people. While I was conducting a social observation from my car, a fight broke out about two feet away from my driver side window. I tried to act casually and uninterested. I had an old newspaper, so I picked it up and pretended to be reading it while two men yelled and even came to blows right next to me. While they apparently felt comfortable enough with my presence to fight, the pushing and shoving ended before anyone got hurt. What was interesting is that the aggressor then began talking to me to explain that the other man just cut off a school bus with his car. The fact that he felt compelled to justify his behavior is an example of reactivity, because at least one person clearly noticed my presence and felt that his actions needed to be put in the proper context.

A strength of ethnographic work is its high degree of validity. Researchers witness actions, including offending, rather than relying exclusively on recollections and interpretations of past attempts. By being in the field, researchers can get a very accurate picture of the actions and motivations of individuals. They can personally witness group dynamics and understand the context in decision-making. James Marquart (1986) did research on the culture of corrections officers and their legal and illegal activities on the job while working as a corrections officer. Marquart personally witnessed 30 incidents of officers physically punishing incarcerated individuals. It is very unlikely that he would have learned about much of what he was eventually able to report had he mailed officers surveys or even sat down and interviewed them, given the culture of silence found among corrections and police officers. Field researchers also have the advantage of observing and speaking to people in their natural setting, where they are most comfortable and most likely to act naturally.

Research that focuses on small samples, specific groups, and individual locations tends to be weak on generalizability. What Whyte (1943) learned while observing men and women in one small Italian American neighborhood in Boston is unlikely to be applicable to another neighborhood, even within the same city. As Maxfield and Babbie (2012) note,

> because field researchers get a full and in-depth view of their subject matter, they can reach an unusually comprehensive understanding. By its very comprehensiveness, however, this understanding is less generalizable than results based on rigorous sampling and standardized measurements (p. 213).

Marquart's (1986) observations of officer culture at a specific prison at one point in time in Texas have some lessons that are certainly applicable to other corrections settings, but we must also understand that prisons are closed institutions that can easily develop their own culture and practices that might not even be transferrable to other prisons within that state department of corrections. We could possibly generalize some findings regarding officer solidarity and willingness to protect each other. But we would also have to look at the Texas Department of Criminal Justice at that particular time, understand its peculiarities (They had a now-illegal Building Tender system where some of the most violent incarcerated persons were chosen to serve as quasi-guards and a first line of defense for the officers.), and appreciate the impact that their very unique security and discipline processes had on officer reactions to the incarcerated.

Reliability tends to be questionable with ethnographic research. Unlike research involving structured data collection tools, observations and unstructured/depth interviews inherent in qualitative work are subject to interpretation by researchers. Each researcher's life experiences, and even the criminological theories that they use to interpret what they see, will likely color their interpretations. We also must realize that people in the field may react to us one way and to other researchers differently based on our own backgrounds. Pawson and Kelly (2014) conducted participant observation of jam band and hip-hop concerts with the goal of understanding the role of marijuana consumption in the experience. In their limitations, they cautioned that the fact that they are White made it much easier for them to blend in at the jam band events and more difficult at hip-hop concerts. In other words, two African American researchers who conducted this same project might have had different experiences in the field and, therefore, generated different results.

Summary

In this chapter, I used Gold's (1958) four roles for field researchers—complete observer, observer as participant, participant as observer, and complete participant. Chapter 9 largely addressed observer as participant, so the focus of this chapter was the three remaining roles. Participant as observer and complete participant are characterized by extensive field presence and the researchers' involvement in the lives of the group under observation. Unlike quantitative research, which almost always approaches topics with a deductive approach to problems, qualitative research with participant observation or complete observer roles is more likely to approach issues using inductive reasoning. This type of research is more conducive to generating theories. Ethnographic work can also let us observe a group for so long and in such detail that we can gain a greater understating of a specific phenomenon than is possible with quantitative research.

One significant challenge to fieldwork is gaining access to the group or organization that we want to study. Ideally, we would be able to use our contacts to put us in touch with people and maybe even help to set up a meeting. If we do not have such resources, then we must work to gain access ourselves by sending an introductory letter or email and requesting a meeting. Subcultures may be much more difficult to access, given individuals' rightful suspicion that outsiders might be undercover law enforcement. Negotiating access to an organization or subculture is only one of several challenges faced by ethnographers. This work generally takes longer than quantitative studies, might require sacrifices such as spending long hours in dangerous areas and exposing oneself to victimization, and can pose ethical challenges that must be addressed without benefit of being able to seek advice from colleagues or supervisors. Covert participation, where the researcher is engaging in complete participation without revealing their true identity, presents additional ethical and safety dilemmas and should only be done if the work cannot be conducted otherwise and the benefits of going covert outweigh the risks and costs.

A very different type of field research that includes little to no contact with human research participants is complete observer work. There is great value in researchers going out to communities to personally see the environment and gauge its impact on contributing to or preventing crime. Researchers can bring field observation sheets with them, and they can also use still and video cameras to document characteristics, such as visibility, cleanliness, amount of foot and vehicle traffic, and security or law enforcement presence. This information can be used alone, or in combination with other types of data, to contribute to our understanding of crime and crime prevention.

Key Terms

Complete observer
Complete participant
Pseudonym
Mnemonic device
Observer as participant
Verstehen
Going native
Participant as observer
Sponsor
Covert participation

Discussion Questions

1. What are the four roles of researchers, according to Gold (1958), and how do they differ from each other?
2. Generally, how well does field research fare in terms of generating valid, reliable, and generalizable results?
3. What are the ethical concerns associated with covert research participation?
4. Why is going native problematic? What steps can researchers take to prevent that from occurring?
5. What types of sampling procedures are common in ethnographic research?

References

Adler, P. A. (1993). *Wheeling & dealing: An ethnography of upper-level drug dealing and smuggling community* (2nd ed.). Columbia University Press.
Bourgois, P. (2002). *In search of respect: Selling crack in El Barrio.* Cambridge University Press.

Brougham, P. L., Uttley, C. M., & Haley, T. M. (2023). Researcher safety: Studying social deviance or criminal behavior. *Journal of Criminal Justice Education, 34*(1), 53–70. https://doi.org/10.1080/10511253.2022.2137540
Conover, T. (2000). *New Jack: Guarding Sing Sing.* Random House.
Ferrell, J. (1998). Criminological verstehen. In. J. Ferrell & M. S. Hamm (Eds.), *Ethnography at the edge* (pp. 28–42). Northeastern University Press.
Glaser, B. G., & Strauss, A. (1967). *The discovery of grounded theory: Strategies for qualitative research.* Aldine Publishing Co.
Gold, R. L. (1958). Roles in sociological field observations. *Social Forces, 36,* 217–223.
Goode, E. (2015). Ethical issues in the qualitative study of deviance and crime. In H. J. Copes & M. Miller (Eds.), *The Routledge handbook of qualitative criminology* (pp. 49–59). Routledge.
Hagan, F. (2007). *Essentials of research methods in criminal justice and criminology* (2nd ed.). Pearson.
Hammersly, M., & Atkinson, P. (1995). *Ethnography*. ITP.
Humphreys, L. (1970). *Tearoom trade: Interpersonal sex in public places.* Aldine Publishing Company.
Hunter, R. D., & Jeffrey, C. R. (1997). Preventing convenience store robbery through environmental design. In R. V. Clarke (Ed.), *Situational crime prevention* (2nd ed, pp. 191–199). Harrow and Heston.
Inciardi, J. A., Lockwood, D., & Pottieger, A. E. (1993). *Women and crack cocaine.* Macmillan.
Jacobs, B. (1998). Researching crack dealers: Dilemmas and contradictions. In J. Ferrell & M. S. Hamm (Eds.), *Ethnography at the edge* (pp. 160–177). Northeastern University Press.
Levy, M. P., & Tartaro, C. (2010). Repeat victimization: A study of auto theft in Atlantic City using the W.A.L.L.S. variables to measure environmental indicators. *Criminal Justice Policy Review, 21*(3), 296–318. https://doi.org/10.1177/0887403409350190
Lyng, S. (1998). Dangerous methods: Risk taking and the research process. In J. Ferrell & M. S. Hamm (Eds.), *Ethnography at the edge* (pp. 221–251). Northeastern University Press.
Marquart, J. W. (1986). Prison guards and the use of physical coercion as a mechanism of prisoner control. *Criminology, 24*(2): 347–365.
Maxfield, M. G., & Babbie, E. (2012). *Basics of research methods for criminal justice and criminology* (3rd ed.). Thomson Wadsworth.
Miller, J. M., & Miller, H. V. (2015). Edge ethnography and naturalistic inquiry in criminology. In H. J. Copes & M. Miller (Eds.), *The Routledge handbook of qualitative criminology* (pp. 88–102). Routledge.
Miller, M. (1995). Covert participant observation: Reconsidering the leased used method. *Journalof Contemporary Criminal Justice, 11*(2), 97–105.
Mowder, D., Lutze, F., & Namgung, H. (2018). Ayúdame! Who can help me? the help-seeking decisions of battered undocumented Latinas. *Journal of Ethnicity in Criminal Justice, 16*(3), 205–224. https://doi.org/10.1080/15377938.2018.1498818
National Institutes of Health. (2019). *Certificates of confidentiality (CoC).* National Institutes of Health. https://grants.nih.gov/policy/humansubjects/coc.htm
Pawson, M., & Kelly, B. C. (2014). Consumption and community: The subcultural contexts of disparate marijuana practices in jam band and hip-hop scenes. *Deviant Behavior, 35,* 347–363.
Perrone, D. (2010). Gender and sexuality in the field: A female ethnographer's experience researching drug use in dance clubs. *Substance Use & Misuse, 45,* 717–735. https://doi.org/10.3109/10826081003595127
Polsky, N. (1967). *Hustlers, beats, and others.* Anchor Books.
Poyner, B. (1997). Situational crime prevention in two parking facilities. In R. V. Clarke (Ed.), *Situational crime prevention* (2nd ed, pp. 157–166). Harrow & Heston.
Sandberg, S., & Copes, H. (2012). Speaking with ethnographers: The challenges of researching drug dealers and offenders. *Journal of Drug Issues, 43,* 176–197. https://doi.org/10.1177/0022042612465275
Vander Ven, T. M. (2001). Fear of victimization and the interactional construction of harassment in a Latino neighborhood. In C. E. Pope., R. Lovell, & S. G. Brandl (Eds.), *Voices from the field* (pp. 141–159). Wadsworth Thompson Learning.
Weber, M., & Shils, E. (1949). *Max Weber on the methodology of the social sciences.* Free Press.
Weisburd, D., Wyckoff, L. A., Ready, J., Eck, J. J., Hinkle, J. C., & Gajewski, F. (2006). Does crime just move around the corner? A controlled study of spatial displacement and diffusion of crime control benefits. *Criminology, 44*(3), 549–592. https://doi.org/10.1111/j.1745-9125.2006.00057.x
Weisheit, R. A. (2015). Researching drug crime using qualitative methods. In H. J. Copes & M. Miller (Eds.), *The Routledge handbook of qualitative criminology* (pp. 191–203). Routledge.
Whyte, W. F. (1943). *Street corner society.* University of Chicago Press.
Wright, R., Decker, S. H., Redfern, A. K., & Smith, D. L. (1992). A snowball's chance in hell: Doing fieldwork with active residential burglars. *Journal of Research in Crime and Delinquency, 29,* 148–161. https://doi.org/10.1177/0022427892029002003

Reading 10.1 Evaluating Technologies to Identify Fentanyl and Adulterants in Street Drug Paraphernalia

The availability of fentanyl has contributed to record-setting numbers of opioid overdose deaths in the United States. Public health advocates seeking to reduce the harm caused by abuse of this drug have turned to technology for assistance. Santelices, Matsumoto, Boulad, and Stopka (2023) conducted field research at an agency that seeks to reduce the harm of drug use by providing services to people dealing with substance abuse. Their specific focus was on test strips that would inform users whether the drugs they planned to consume were laced with fentanyl. Given the sensitive nature of this topic, the researchers had to take precautions to make participants feel comfortable, and they also had to take steps to protect the identity of anyone involved in this research. The researchers used a combination of inductive and deductive strategies here. Fieldwork often lends itself to the inductive approach, but the researchers relied on their knowledge of the topic as well as field observations preceding the interviews to shape their interview guides.

Evaluating Technologies to Identify Fentanyl and Adulterants in Street Drug Paraphernalia: Qualitative Perspectives of Service Providers and Their Clientele

Claudia Santelices, Atsushi Matsumoto, Mathieu Boulad, and Thomas J. Stopka

Introduction

In the past two decades, opioid overdose has taken a devastating toll on public health in the United States, where more than 100,000 fatal overdoses, the highest number ever, were recorded in 2021 (CDC, 2021). Fentanyl, a short-acting opioid analgesic 50-100 times more potent than morphine, and fentanyl analogs have been identified as the main contributors to the rise in opioid-related morbidity and mortality rates (CDC, 2015; Department of Justice, 2016). Illicitly manufactured fentanyl and fentanyl analogs have appeared in the unregulated drug supply and have been sold for their heroin-like effect, often taken in combination with heroin or cocaine (Wilson et al., 2020), and other stimulants (Jenkins, 2021). As early as 2013, several states in the U.S., primarily those in the Northeast, began to report a rise in the total number of overdose deaths attributable to fentanyl and fentanyl analogs (CDC, 2015; Ciccarone, 2019; Fogger, 2019; Hedegaard, 2018; Twillman et al., 2020). In 2020, of 1,937 opioid-related overdose deaths in Massachusetts where a toxicology screen was also available, fentanyl was present in 92% of individuals (Massachusetts Department of Public Health, 2020).

To address this public health crisis, drug checking services designed to inform people who use drugs (PWUD) about the contents in their drug purchases began to be implemented. While some research has been conducted on the implementation of some of these devices to test and detect an array of drugs and safely trace drug compounds invisible to the naked eye, including fentanyl and other adulterants, little is known about the acceptability of the use of such devices among PWUD. Previous studies on fentanyl checking using Immunoassay Fentanyl Test Strips (FTS),

Fourier Transform Infrared Spectroscopy (FTIR) (Green et al., 2020; Sherman et al., 2019), or High Pressure Mass Spectrometry (HPMS) (Karch et al., 2021) indicate that in the presence of fentanyl-contaminated drugs, PWUDs tend to show interest and to see the effectiveness of drug checking devices in the mitigation of behaviors associated with higher risk of overdose. Several studies have confirmed a high acceptability of FTS use among the PWUD (Karamouzian et al., 2018; Long et al., 2020). For instance, Krieger (Krieger et al., 2018) found that more than 90% of PWUD participants in Rhode Island reported willingness to use FTS regardless of having had an overdose, indicating that this drug checking device is an acceptable harm reduction intervention.

The goal of the current study was to assess staff and client experiences with drug checking devices. We conducted qualitative interviews to assess implementation, use, acceptability, and effectiveness of drug paraphernalia checking at a harm reduction agency (HRA) in a Northeastern U.S. city. Our study builds upon a growing body of quantitative research studies on drug checking technologies utilized in the context of harm reduction services (Green et al., 2020; Sherman et al., 2019; Vandergrift & Gill, 2019; Zibbell et al., 2021) and provides an insider look at use of the HPMS device within a syringe services program (SSP) in the Northeast using qualitative methods.

Risk Environment Model

The conceptual framework of our study was informed by the risk environment framework (Rhodes, 2002, 2009). The framework promotes understanding of harm, and harm reduction contingent upon social context, comprising interactions between individuals and environments. In our study, the risk environment allows us to contextualize drug checking services within a wider social context comprised of social inequities, social and political institutions, criminalization, and stigma of people who use drugs (Wallace, 2021).

Methods

Study Site

Our study site was an SSP that provides a wide range of services to people who use drugs (PWUD) in a Northeastern U.S. city. At the time we conducted this study, this SSP was the only agency in the Northeastern U.S. that had a drug checking device on site. During our data collection period (May 2019 thru December 2020), two drug checking devices were incorporated in this SSP as part of the harm reduction package, both with the potential to expand drug checking capabilities: the hand-held high pressure mass spectrometer (HPMS, also known as MX908; MX908™, Boston MA) and the Fourier Transform Infrared Spectroscopy (FTIR, also known as Bruker Alpha II; Bruker Alpha™, Billerica, MA). Both devices were added to complement the Immunoassay fentanyl test strips (FTS; Rapid Response™, Canada) device already in use in this agency since 2018. In the current study we focus on the use of the HPMS primarily, and only tangentially on the FTIR, which was added toward the end of our data collection to address some of the deficiencies of the HPMS device.

Participant Recruitment

We conducted a total of 28 on-the-spot qualitative interviews with HRA staff members ($n = 10$, one was interviewed twice at different stages of HPMS implementation) and PWUDs ($n = 17$). For staff and clientele, recruitment was facilitated by rapport building through indirect participant observation, while the project ethnographer (CS) spent large blocks of time at the agency volunteering as interpreter for Spanish speaking clients, translating informational brochures and signs from English into Spanish, preparing safe injection kits, and joining staff on the SSP van during street outreach activities. Immersing herself by collaborating with harm reduction staff helped to facilitate rapport building with participants. To participate in on-the-spot interviews, clients and staff had to be at least 18 years of age. Clients also needed to self-identify as PWUD. An additional eligibility criterion for staff included being directly involved in any activity related to drug paraphernalia checking. Five SSP staff members were directly involved in conducting actual checking of drug supply samples whereas the remaining five undertook outreach-related tasks. On-the-spot interviews were conducted following receipt of verbal consent.

Data Collection

Data collection began with fieldnotes from ethnographic observation episodes and interactions with SSP staff and PWUD clientele. Fieldnotes were utilized to generate and refine interview guides. On-the-spot interviews with SSP staff and clients were designed to explore experiences with drug checking (perceived benefits and challenges); interest in future drug checking; suggestions for quality improvement and patient satisfaction. All interviews were conducted in a private space within the SSP and lasted between 20 and 45 min. All interviews with SSP staff were digitally recorded, and due to client concerns, all on-the-spot interviews with PWUD clientele, except for one, were not digitally recorded, but salient quotes and key findings were subsequently captured and accurately summarized.

Recorded interviews were transcribed verbatim, and transcripts were subsequently checked for clarity and accuracy, together with the written record from interviews with participants who refused to be audio-recorded.

Pseudonyms were used to protect the confidentiality of study participants. The study protocol was reviewed and approved by the Institutional Review Board at the [Blinded] University School of Medicine.

Data Analysis

We utilized standard thematic content analysis techniques (Braun & Clarke, 2006) and relied on deductive and inductive strategies to code our data. First, using fieldnotes from ethnographic observation and interview guides, we developed a preliminary codebook (*a priori codes*) broadly capturing the objectives of the study. Subsequently, through initial readings of transcripts the ethnographer and interviewer of the study (CS), and a trained research assistant refined preliminary ideas for codes until conceptual categories were exhausted. Preliminary codes were refined using iterative comparative methods to define limits and boundaries of conceptual categories. Seven codes and ten subcodes emerged from interviews with SSP staff and PWUDs. Once the code book was finalized, codes were noted in a table in Microsoft Excel and entered into NVivo 12, a qualitative data analysis program that sorts text based on researcher-assigned codes (QSR International Pty Ltd, 2020).

Following standard procedures, and to achieve reliability in coding, all transcripts and fieldnotes were double-coded, and coding team members met regularly to assess consistency in coding, discuss different interpretations and achieve resolution in final code applications. Next, we identified patterns in coded data, comparing salient themes and organizing them into overarching domains. The research team examined patterns within and across the transcripts and grouped similar responses along with illustrative quotations.

Results

On-the-Spot Interviews with Specimen Testing Staff

We identified two salient themes from the on-the-spot interviews with SSP staff and PWUD clients: 1) drug checking *implementation challenges, and 2) perceived benefits of HPMS capabilities.* We address each of these, in turn.

Drug Checking Implementation Challenges

External barriers (the law and the community at large). At the time of our study, interpretation of laws tied to the checking of drug residues varied by police jurisdiction and, as a result, SSPs could not be as open in promoting drug checking services without putting their entire program at risk. According to interviewed staff, local communities tended to perceive HPMS checking as a service that, contrary to helping people use drugs more safely and get real-time useful information about their drug supplies, might encourage them to seek more potent drugs and search for an even more powerful high. Given the inconsistent interpretation of the legality of drug checking services, most SSP staff described their role of drug checking providers as "a necessary evil." Both, uncertain legal interpretation and suspicions hampered outreach efforts and recruitment by limiting the number of street recruitment venues and restricting service advertisement. Staff relied on person-to-person promotion and word of mouth, as opposed to flyers to promote drug checking services. "Bringing the machine out [during outreach] is not happening right now, because of legal questions and the grey areas," mentioned a participant, who mentioned the following,

> It is far from illegal, but somebody could pick a bone if they wanted to. We don't want to make too big of a show with that because to the wrong person it could raise an eyebrow… (Joseph)

SSP staff concurred that massive advertisement of services could have yielded a much higher number of drug checking requests, which, in turn, could potentially have helped avoid a greater number of opioid-related overdoses and deaths, yet caution prevailed throughout the timeframe of our study.

Clients suspicion toward drug checking services. Early, during our data collection, outreach and recruitment were also hampered by clients' suspicion that drug checking services involved a concerted effort between the SSP and local police. Thus, at first, and despite some awareness of the extent to which fentanyl and fentanyl analogs had diffused into local underground drug markets increasing overdose risks among PWUD, clients reported trusting their drug providers, needing to exercise caution and wait, see, and hear from peers' experiences about the drug checking service. The following interview excerpts illustrate this point:

> I am from Pittsburg. Came here three weeks ago. I don't need to get my shit tested, but who knows, maybe down the road… I guess I'll see what others say about this. I don't want trouble…
>
> I'll just sit around and watch for now. But yeah, I hear you, there's so much shit out there. I lost two of my friends last week. It looks like we've been declared some kinda of war. Fentanyl is our number one enemy now. It's scary, honey.

Fear of becoming a new fentanyl-related fatality made some clients in our sample open to the idea of benefitting from drug checking. This interest increased gradually. "At first, I didn't think it was important, but now I am all for it. I don't want to die," said *Richard.* According to some staff, with time the SSP's long-lived reputation of "serving" and not judging or criminalizing this population, paid off.

Clients' expectations toward drug checking services. SSP staff found that clients inaccurately believed that the drug checking device would be able to identify the purity of checked specimens, and the quantity or proportion of substances present. In part, this misconception could have been the result of the staff's brief "sales pitch," which took place during outreach and recruitment. A more comprehensive explanation of what the drug checking device could and could not do was discussed when clients brought their empty bags for drug checking. As a staff member stated below, learning about the HPMS limitations disappointed some clients and slowed down further outreach and recruitment:

> My conversation with them begins: I have a machine now. I swab your empty bag and I tell you what's in there. It's a sales pitch… Then, the longer the conversation [goes like this]: yeah, unfortunately it's [the HPMS] not going to tell you everything that is in there but is going to tell you the most alarming things that pop up in

> the catalogue. That is really the real core part of the conversation to have, but that usually comes at the time of the testing [drug checking] rather than at the time of the sales pitch... They [clients] say Well that really sucks, but it's cool, I guess. Most people understand that some information is better than nothing... (Peter)

The limitations of the device capabilities, and the fact that there are many more "false positives/negatives" than HRA staff felt comfortable with, also added to the ambivalence of the drug checking implementation services.

HPMS device troubleshooting. Several technical challenges and malfunctions of the MX908 device were identified by SSP staff, which put the device out of commission for a period of time. Staff members indicated that solving these problems took more time than anticipated, especially when the device company's technical support didn't have immediate availability. Troubleshooting often occurred due to inconsistency in the quantity of trace specimens needed to test, or when the device got clogged due to testing larger residual samples of fine particles. Marijuana and methamphetamine were reported to clog the machine more often than any other known substances. The frustration during clogging incidents was eloquently illustrated in the following interview excerpt:

> ...So, you don't know exactly how careful you need to be with certain samples that can clog the machine... So, something that 100 percent appears visually not being methamphetamine, tested for meth! The problem with meth is that the machine only wants 30 or 60 nanograms, which is like billionths of a gram, and meth comes sometimes in like glass crystals, and sometimes somebody brings a tiny spec and that spec is probably like the size of a grain of sand, that's too much, that would clog the machine. So, how can we make it smaller?! Joseph

Following such experiences, cleaning of the HPMS device was found to take longer than expected, and a limited number of team members had experience with cleaning protocols or the patience to complete the protocols. Cleaning involved the time-consuming process of taking some parts of the device out and examining them meticulously. Sometimes, when not done properly the first time, the cleaning had to be repeated.

Perceived Benefits of HPMS Capabilities

Empowering PWUDs through knowledge. According to SSP staff, the checking of drug paraphernalia was extremely valuable, because it provided real answers that defied the faulty information or lack of information clients would typically get on the streets. Even though this information might not often translate into harm reduction behavior change (e.g., naloxone requests), it would, nonetheless, provide knowledge that had the potential to facilitate informed decisions, which could, in the end, prevent or decrease drug use-related risks among PWUD. Indeed, as a staff member reported, even though it had been the norm among SSP staff to not hold expectations of connecting PWUD to substance use treatment, results from drug checking helped some participants, even if temporarily, to shift toward less risky drug use patterns. Instances of clients spontaneously sharing their intention to shift from injecting to smoking or snorting upon receiving their drug checking results did not abound in our data but the reported cases where such intentionality was communicated, left room for optimism. In *Julia*'s words, facilitating positive change in behavior is, "the ultimate goal worthy of striving toward... respecting people's autonomy and giving them the option of knowing what's in their drug, [and] what they're going to put into their body is an important pursuit in and of itself." Prior to the appearance of drug checking technologies such as the HPMS, it was not in the realm of possibilities for PWUD to acquire such knowledge. This connoted an important shift. In *Sandra*'s words, "Outwardly, maybe doesn't look like behavior change, but it is, [because] if they are changing their thought patterns, that's changing behavior as well."

One such case is *Carlos*, a drug user and seller, for whom the HPMS became an "eye-opener." He mentioned that:

> The test showed [that] people use so many different things, like broken pills to stretch the drug out to make a profit, you know, or make it strong, or have the same side effects as dope. One of these things was methamphetamine. That was crazy, I never do that…

He went on to note the benefit of the drug checking device, because:

> …that way one knows the truth about what we are selling, and not what they believe is in their drug…

Enriching harm reduction through drug checking technology. In addition, using the devices for drug checking was also reported to have helped staff enrich outreach skills by engaging clients more. Thus, when reflecting on the importance of drug checking services, SSP staff described these as a catalyst that provided more time to engage, one-on-one with clients, inquire about client needs, learn about behaviors associated with higher risk of overdose, and encourage HIV testing, or substance use treatment. As the ethnographer of the study reported in her fieldnotes upon observing interactions between SSP staff and clients, a substantial number of conversations during drug checking encounters was around overdose prevention and the prevention of harm. In addition, SSP staff reported a steady increase in the use of naloxone among local PWUD who received positive results for fentanyl in association with drug checking. The increase in naloxone use was, in part, attributed to the imminent threat posed by fentanyl, which clients learned more about through the drug checking services. In *Daniel*'s words, the drug checking provided "a door for having a longer conversation and to engage people in services they were never interested in before." He continued,

> With the machine people are willing to stick around a little bit longer. It increases our outreach to people who do not use injection drugs, but people who are smoking meth or crack or use pills. Typically, we haven't had as many services to engage those kinds of people. It also helps us…people are coming more for HIV testing.

According to SSP staff, drug checking devices also empowered them with knowledge they didn't have before. For example, checking empty drug bags or other drug paraphernalia gave them great insight into what the drug landscape was, and thus, into the multiple perils their clients encounter in their daily lives. This knowledge was accentuated by the drug checking process, as SSP staff did research to try to better understand and explain test results to clients (e.g., the chemistry of the drugs).

During the first several months following implementation of drug checking services, the challenges posed by the HPMS device were only partially addressed by the manufacturing company, in advance of the arrival of the COVID-19 pandemic in March 2020, and a desktop Fourier Transform Infrared Spectrometer (FTIR) was added in July 2020 to enhance drug checking services. While the HPMS did not inspire great confidence among SSP staff, the arrival of the FTIR soon gained the reputation of a reliable confirmatory and complimentary technology. SSP staff described the FTIR as a "better piece of analytical machinery," with greater drug checking capabilities than the HPMS. Sometimes checking samples "accurately" meant "triple checking," which included checking with the HPMS, the FTIR, and FTS in succession. Thus, while the HPMS did not inspire great confidence among SSP staff, the FTIR allowed them to gain more confidence in the HPMS, and in some cases it validated existing concerns about it. In *Julia*'s words,

> Having access to the [FTIR] gave SSP staff the possibility to tell a little bit more what was cut into the drug that was sort of a buff or a cut or something innocuous that the machine wouldn't pick up on like something like lactose which is commonly cut into you know, like, the powder—I'm going to say powder heroin but really what I mean is like powder fentanyl because there's very little heroin, but people

> here still call it dope or heroin, even though they know that there's fentanyl in it. But there's a lot of weird stuff around that...

Thus, with additional technological drug checking options on hand, SSP staff and clientele reported an increase in comfort levels around drug checking.

During early 2020, before the COVID-19 pandemic hit locally, another wave of PWUD clients, unseen previously, started to frequent the SSP. Fieldnotes from participant observation episodes indicated that these "new" clients seemed curious about the HPMS device and the drug checking service. Other frequent clients appeared to be more comfortable with drug checking. Some clients claimed to purchase drugs for their own use and sell some occasionally. A staff member stated that since the advent of COVID-19, and not necessarily because of it, SSP clientele seemed to have shifted partially from clients who brought single empty drug bags for checking, to clients bringing bulk samples, including some that they might have sold to others. This shift might have been indicative of the presence of what *Julia* called "some kind of dealers" (or clients who carry out "small-time dealing") wanting to know the quality of their drug before selling it to their peers. Thus, in contrast to the pre-COVID-19 era, an increasingly common feature of drug checking included clients who appeared to be invested in making sure that they were not selling anything that could cause someone to overdose or have an adverse reaction. In *Sandra*'s words, "they are very diligent about bringing samples in and following up on test results."

Discussion

We present qualitative findings focused on implementation and use of the HPMS drug checking device with harm reduction staff members and SSP clients in a Northeastern U.S. city. Our study responded to the call from previous research to develop a better understanding of innovative strategies geared toward promoting harm reduction and prevention in the context of fentanyl-adulterated, street-acquired drug samples (Barratt et al., 2018; Goldman et al., 2019; Green et al., 2020; Krieger et al., 2018; Tupper et al., 2018). Our findings build upon previous research conducted on the use of fentanyl test strips (FTS), a precursor of the HPMS and FTIR technologies (Anderson et al., 2006; Barratt et al., 2018; Ciccarone et al., 2017; Green et al., 2020; Harper et al., 2017; Kennedy et al., 2018; Mars et al., 2016; Peiper et al., 2019; Tupper et al., 2018). We present evidence of the importance of the use of advanced drug checking technology that is capable of providing useful insights on local drug supplies, which could foster adoption of harm reduction strategies among PWUD. Our findings indicate that implementation of drug checking devices in harm reduction programs is not without challenges, but that it shows promise for increasing harm reduction conversations and opportunities between SSP staff and clients. We also found that, while it took time for clients to trust the use of drug checking devices, eventually many of them began to bring increasing numbers of specimens for drug checking.

Implementation and use of the HPMS device was not free of challenges and malfunctions, which often delayed drug checking opportunities, and initially increased suspicion and distrust of the drug checking devices and process. In concordance with what Carroll et al. (2017) reported, we also identified several drawbacks of the HPMS device, among these, the clogging of the equipment, and false positive test results, which were reported to hamper its implementation and use. In addition, and similar to what Carroll et al. (2017) found, the inconsistent interpretation of legality of drug checking services, together with clients' initial suspicion that such services were a set up to help local police carry out arrests, hampered and delayed outreach and recruitment efforts, and the possibility of making harm reduction available to a wider segment of the local PWUD population.

When working properly, we found that the device and the process of drug checking facilitated new levels of engagement with harm reduction clients, and more in-depth conversations about the risk of the drug supply and opportunities to engage clients in different harm reduction and disease prevention services. Our study confirms findings from previous research showing how the prevalence of fentanyl-adulterated street drug purchases generates an interest among PWUD in seeking drug checking services as an effective risk mitigation strategy (Barratt et al., 2018; Sherman et al., 2019). Furthermore, despite the abovementioned drawbacks, drug checking services, and the one-on-one encounters between SSP staff and PWUD clients that accompany them, was demonstrated to be a powerful tool to foster conversation and generate valuable knowledge (Ciccarone et al., 2017; Sherman et al., 2019). With the transition to the FTIR as the primary drug checking technology, SSP staff members became empowered with the acquired knowledge they did not have before: the complexity of the local drug landscape, the chemical compositions of purchased drugs, clients' information on their health and social well-being, their drug risk behaviors and intentionality to start practicing harm reduction. Staff found that drug checking services also enriched staff-client engagement, for a longer period (the time the drug checking lasts), facilitating more opportunities for wrap-around harm reduction services, such as naloxone distribution, HIV/HCV testing, and harm reduction education that SSPs provide (Heimer, 1998; Muncan et al., 2021; Tookes et al., 2020). Clients, on their part, acquired valuable information about the composition of their drug purchases, the perils of the underground drug market, and available information on social services they might need. A novel finding from our study is that it took time for clients to feel comfortable in availing themselves of drug checking services and our study allowed us to capture a range of experiences with the drug checking devices that are difficult to obtain in quantitative data and analyses.

In the midst of the COVID-19 pandemic, we also noted increasing interest in drug checking, an enhanced provision of test results through the use of the HPMS in conjunction with the FTIR device. We also report on the inclusion of PWUD, who shared selling part of their drugs to peers and, thus, seeking drug checking services to verify the quality of their drugs and make sure that, if sold, such drug would not cause someone to overdose or have an adverse reaction. This finding echos those from Long et al. (2020) and Betsos' (2021) in Canada, where "market safety" through drug checking technologies was of interest among PWUD involved with sales.

Finally, findings from our study contribute to evidence reported in national and international studies on the efficacy and acceptability of drug checking technologies. Our study shows that due to its margins of error, its malfunction and percentage of false/positive results, the use of HPMS in a harm reduction setting, like the one we studied, may not be the ideal drug checking technology. However, other drug checking technologies such as the FTIR in conjunction with the FTS seem to be a reasonable and innovative harm reduction response to the opioid overdose-related public health crisis (Carroll et al., 2017; Green et al., 2020). These findings are similar to those reported in recent studies assessing the feasibility and acceptability of take-home rapid FTS (Anderson et al., 2006; Harper et al., 2017; Kennedy et al., 2018; Krieger et al., 2018). Whether using the HPMS or the FTIR, drug checking services introduce in the minds of some PWUD the concept of product safety into the unregulated illicit drug supply. This may potentially facilitate important behavioral outcomes associated with the receipt of, or the anticipation of receiving a positive drug checking result signaling the presence of a potent adulterant. Once initial suspicions and distrust toward drug checking services dissipated, clients and HRA staff reported that positive drug checking results for fentanyl served as a motivational factor for positive change in overdose risk behavior.

Our findings should be considered in light of several limitations. First, we relied on brief on-the-spot interviews when in-depth interviews might have provided even more detailed insights, perceptions, and experiences. Given the novelty of the new device, and apprehension around its use, we believe this was the best way to learn about initial implementation and use experiences and perspectives among staff and clients, without disrupting services. Second, we were not able to record most of our on-the-spot interviews, given client concerns. Our interviews, however, were conducted by an anthropologist with more than 20 years of ethnographic and qualitative field research, ensuring that salient quotes and key findings were captured, expanded, and summarized accurately following interviews. Finally, we conducted this study during the year leading up to the COVID-19 pandemic. Harm reduction services and the drug use landscape changed drastically in March 2020, as service models changed to reduce COVID-19 transmission risk among staff and clients. This forced us to suspend our data collection involving clients more abruptly than anticipated, which left us with a smaller sample. However, through our 28 on-the-spot interviews, we achieved thematic saturation in both the staff and client interviews.

Conclusions

We present novel experiences among SSP staff and clients with a HPMS in a harm reduction agency in the Northeastern U.S. Our findings provide a glimpse into the successes and challenges regarding the drug checking device and related processes, as experienced by harm reduction staff and clients. We found that the device and drug checking process, while evoking initial suspicions and distrust, ultimately led to increased opportunities for engagement between harm reduction staff and clients, which had the potential to decrease risk behaviors and expand on health promotion services and successes in local drug using communities, thus indicating that the use of advanced drug checking technology in a harm reduction setting has the potential to become an acceptable harm reduction intervention in places severely hit by high rates of fentanyl-related overdose deaths.

Conflicts of Interest

The authors declare that there are no conflicts of interest.

Funding

The Kraft Foundation; Kraft Center for Community Health

Discussion Questions

1. What were the inclusion/exclusion criteria for research participation? How were the interview protocols similar or different for the staff and the clients?
2. How did COVID-19 impact both drug testing behavior and the study itself?
3. How did existing drug laws impact the implementation of the drug testing program?

References

Anderson, E. S., Wagstaff, D. A., Heckman, T. G., Winett, R. A., Roffman, R. A., Solomon, L. J., Cargill, V., Kelly, J. A., & Sikkema, K. J. (2006). Information-motivation-behavioral skills (IMB) model: Testing direct and mediated treatment effects on condom use among women in low-income housing. *Annals of Behavioral Medicine*, *31*(1), 70–79. https://doi.org/10.1207/s15324796abm3101_11

Barratt, M. J., Bruno, R., Ezard, N., & Ritter, A. (2018). Pill testing or drug checking in Australia: Acceptability of service design features: Designing a drug-checking service. *Drug and Alcohol Review*, *37*(2), 226–236. https://doi.org/10.1111/dar.12576

Braun, V., & Clarke, V. (2006). Using thematic analysis in psychology. *Qualitative Research in Psychology*, *3*(2), 77–101. https://doi.org/10.1191/1478088706qp063oa

Carroll, J. J., Marshall, B. D. L., Rich, J. D., & Green, T. C. (2017). Exposure to fentanyl-contaminated heroin and overdose risk among illicit opioid users in Rhode Island: A mixed methods study. *The International Journal on Drug Policy*, *46*, 136–145. https://doi.org/10.1016/j.drugpo.2017.05.023

Centers for Disease Control and Prevention. (2015, October 26). *Increases in fentanyl drug confiscations and fentanyl-related overdose fatalities: CDCHAN-00384*. Health Alert Network (HAN). https://emergency.cdc.gov/han/han00384.asp

Centers for Disease Control and Prevention, National Center for Health Statistics. (2021). *Drug overdose deaths in the U.S. top 100,000annually*. www.cdc.gov/nchs/pressroom/nchs_press_releases/2021/20211117.htm

Ciccarone, D. (2019). The triple wave epidemic: Supply and demand drivers of the US opioid overdose crisis. *International Journal of Drug Policy*, *71*, 183–188. https://doi.org/10.1016/j.drugpo.2019.01.010

Ciccarone, D., Ondocsin, J., & Mars, S. G. (2017). Heroin uncertainties: Exploring users' perceptions of fentanyl-adulterated and -substituted 'heroin. *The International Journal on Drug Policy*, *46*, 146–155. https://doi.org/10.1016/j.drugpo.2017.06.004

Department of Justice. (2016). *FY 2016 performance budget congressional submission*. www.justice.gov/file/338266/download

Fogger, S. A. (2019). Methamphetamine use: A new wave in the opioid crisis? *Journal of Addictions Nursing*, *30*(3), 219–223. https://doi.org/10.1097/JAN.0000000000000298

Goldman, J. E., Waye, K. M., Periera, K. A., Krieger, M. S., Yedinak, J. L., & Marshall, B. D. L. (2019). Perspectives on rapid fentanyl test strips as a harm reduction practice among young adults who use drugs: A qualitative study. *Harm Reduction Journal*, *16*(1), 3. https://doi.org/10.1186/s12954-018-0276-0

Green, T. C., Park, J. N., Gilbert, M., McKenzie, M., Struth, E., Lucas, R., Clarke, W., & Sherman, S. G. (2020). An assessment of the limits of detection, sensitivity and specificity of three devices for public health-based drug checking of fentanyl in street-acquired samples. *International Journal of Drug Policy*, *77*, 102661. https://doi.org/10.1016/j.drugpo.2020.102661

Harper, L., Powell, J., & Pijl, E. M. (2017). An overview of forensic drug testing methods and their suitability for harm reduction point-of-care services. *Harm Reduction Journal*, *14*(1), 52. https://doi.org/10.1186/s12954-017-0179-5

Hedegaard, H. (2018). Drug overdose deaths in the United States, 1999–2017. NCHS Data Brief, No. 329, November 2018.

Heimer, R. (1998). Syringe exchange programs: Lowering the transmission of syringe-borne diseases and beyond. *Public Health Reports (Washington, D.C.: 1974)*, *113*(Suppl 1), 67–74.

Jenkins, R. A. (2021). The fourth wave of the US opioid epidemic and its implications for the rural US: A federal perspective. *Preventive Medicine*, *152*(Pt 2), 106541. https://doi.org/10.1016/j.ypmed.2021.106541

Karamouzian, M., Dohoo, C., Forsting, S., McNeil, R., Kerr, T., & Lysyshyn, M. (2018). Evaluation of a fentanyl drug checking service for clients of a supervised injection facility, Vancouver, Canada. *Harm Reduction Journal*, *15*(1), 46. https://doi.org/10.1186/s12954-018-0252-8

Kennedy, M. C., Scheim, A., Rachlis, B., Mitra, S., Bardwell, G., Rourke, S., & Kerr, T. (2018). Willingness to use drug checking within future supervised injection services among people who inject drugs in a mid-sized Canadian city. *Drug and Alcohol Dependence*, *185*, 248–252. https://doi.org/10.1016/j.drugalcdep.2017.12.026

Krieger, M. S., Goedel, W. C., Buxton, J. A., Lysyshyn, M., Bernstein, E., Sherman, S. G., Rich, J. D., Hadland, S. E., Green, T. C., & Marshall, B. D. L. (2018). Use of rapid fentanyl test strips among young adults who use drugs. *The International Journal on Drug Policy*, *61*, 52–58. https://doi.org/10.1016/j.drugpo.2018.09.009

Krieger, M. S., Yedinak, J. L., Buxton, J. A., Lysyshyn, M., Bernstein, E., Rich, J. D., Green, T. C., Hadland, S. E., & Marshall, B. D. L. (2018). High willingness to use rapid fentanyl test strips among young adults who use drugs. *Harm Reduction Journal*, *15*(1), 7. https://doi.org/10.1186/s12954-018-0213-2

Long, V., Arredondo, J., Ti, L., Grant, C., DeBeck, K., Milloy, M.-J., Lysyshyn, M., Wood, E., Kerr, T., & Hayashi, K. (2020). Factors associated with drug checking service utilization among people who use drugs in a Canadian setting. *Harm Reduction Journal*, *17*(1), 100. https://doi.org/10.1186/s12954-020-00454-4

Mars, S. G., Bourgois, P., Karandinos, G., Montero, F., & Ciccarone, D. (2016). The textures of heroin: User perspectives on "black tar" and powder heroin in two U.S. cities. *Journal of Psychoactive Drugs*, *48*(4), 270–278. https://doi.org/10.1080/02791072.2016.1207826

Massachusetts Department of Public Health. (2020). *Data brief: Opioid-related overdose deaths among Massachusetts residents*. www.mass.gov/doc/opioid-related-overdose-deaths-among-ma-residents-november-2020/download

Muncan, B., Jordan, A. E., Perlman, D. C., Frank, D., Ompad, D. C., & Walters, S. M. (2021). Acceptability and effectiveness of hepatitis C care at syringe service programs for people who inject drugs in New York City. *Substance Use & Misuse*, *56*(5), 728–737. https://doi.org/10.1080/10826084.2021.1892142

Peiper, N. C., Clarke, S. D., Vincent, L. B., Ciccarone, D., Kral, A. H., & Zibbell, J. E. (2019). Fentanyl test strips as an opioid overdose prevention strategy: Findings from a syringe services program in the Southeastern United States. *The International Journal on Drug Policy*, *63*, 122–128. https://doi.org/10.1016/j.drugpo.2018.08.007

QSR International Pty Ltd. (2020). NVivo (released in March 2020), www.qsrinternational.com/nvivo-qualitative-data-analysis-software/home

Sherman, S. G., Morales, K. B., Park, J. N., McKenzie, M., Marshall, B. D. L., & Green, T. C. (2019). Acceptability of implementing community-based drug checking services for people who use drugs in three United States cities: Baltimore, Boston and Providence. *The International Journal on Drug Policy*, *68*, 46–53. https://doi.org/10.1016/j.drugpo.2019.03.003

Tookes, H., Bartholomew, T. S., Geary, S., Matthias, J., Poschman, K., Blackmore, C., Philip, C., Suarez, E., Forrest, D. W., Rodriguez, A. E., Kolber, M. A., Knaul, F., Colucci, L., & Spencer, E. (2020). Rapid identification and investigation of an HIV risk network among people who inject drugs – Miami, FL, 2018. *AIDS and Behavior*, *24*(1), 246–256. https://doi.org/10.1007/s10461-019-02680-9

Tupper, K. W., McCrae, K., Garber, I., Lysyshyn, M., & Wood, E. (2018). Initial results of a drug checking pilot program to detect fentanyl adulteration in a Canadian setting. *Drug and Alcohol Dependence*, *190*, 242–245. https://doi.org/10.1016/j.drugalcdep.2018.06.020

Twillman, R. K., Dawson, E., LaRue, L., Guevara, M. G., Whitley, P., & Huskey, A. (2020). Evaluation of trends of near-real-time urine drug test results for methamphetamine, cocaine, heroin, and fentanyl. *JAMA Network Open*, 3(1), e1918514–e1918514. https://doi.org/10.1001/jamanetworkopen.2019.18514

U.S. Department of Health and Human. (2015). Opioid abuse in the United States and Department of Health and Human Services actions to address opioid-drug-related overdoses and deaths. *Journal of Pain & Palliative Care Pharmacotherapy*, *29*(2), 133–139. https://doi.org/10.3109/15360288.2015.1037530

Vandergrift, G. W., & Gill, C. G. (2019). Paper spray mass spectrometry: A new drug checking tool for harm reduction in the opioid overdose crisis. *Journal of Mass Spectrometry: JMS*, *54*(9), 729–737. https://doi.org/10.1002/jms.4431

Welsh, E. (2002). Dealing with data: Using NVivo in the qualitative data analysis process. *Technology in the Qualitative Research Process*, *3*(2). https://search.proquest.com/docview/867759998?accountid=14434&rfr_id=info%3Axri/sid%3Aprimo

Wilson, N., Kariisa, M., Seth, P., Iv, H. S., & Davis, N. L. (2020). Drug and opioid-involved overdose deaths – United States, 2017–2018. *69*(11), 8.

Wilson, N., Kariisa, M., Seth, P., Smith, H., & Davis, N. L. (2020). Drug and opioid-involved overdose deaths- United States, 2017–2018. *MMWR. Morbidity and Mortality Weekly Report*, *69*(11), 290–297. https://doi.org/10.15585/mmwr.mm6911a4

Zibbell, J. E., Peiper, N. C., Duhart Clarke, S. E., Salazar, Z. R., Vincent, L. B., Kral, A. H., & Feinberg, J. (2021). Consumer discernment of fentanyl in illicit opioids confirmed by fentanyl test strips: Lessons from a syringe services program in North Carolina. *The International Journal on Drug Policy*, *93*, 103128. https://doi.org/10.1016/j.drug-po.2021.103128

Reading 10.2 Researcher Safety

Most of us go about our lives avoiding dangerous situations and, for the most part, I am the same way. I tend to avoid walking alone at night and mostly steer clear of high-crime areas. I have made exceptions to these life rules when I've taken on the role of criminal justice field researcher. I've sat in rooms alone with people convicted of serious crimes. I have hung out in very high crime neighborhoods by myself, sometimes in the middle of the night. I am one of many social scientists who have decided to take risks in the name of data collection. Researcher safety is an important topic that is not discussed enough, and that is why I was happy to read Brougham, Uttley, and Haley's (2023) article. This is a rare paper that focuses exclusively on researcher safety from the perspective of the researchers themselves. One very important theme of this article is the importance of planning ahead and anticipating what might go wrong before going into the field. Being able to calmly analyze potential problems before they happen allows us to come up with good safety plans so that all that is left is for us to put the plan into action should danger arise.

Researcher Safety: Studying Social Deviance or Criminal Behavior

Patricia L. Brougham, Clarissa M. Uttley, and Tammy M. Haley

Introduction

There is growing recognition of risk to researchers engaged in the study of social deviance and criminal behavior (Bloor, Fincham, & Sampson, 2007; Dickson-Swift et al., 2007; Johnson & Clarke, 2006; Kenyon & Hawker, 1999; Nikischer, 2019; Tang et al., 2020; Worley, Worley, & Wood, 2016). Some universities may require that researchers follow safety guidelines when conducting certain types of research. However, there are no universally established guidelines or protocols pertaining to researcher safety specifically for conducting research on social deviance or criminal behavior. As Kenyon and Hawker (1999) experienced when they were preparing for dissertation work, their institutions did not discuss matters of best practice for dealing with difficult circumstances they may encounter during fieldwork based social research. It is routinely left to each researcher to ensure their own safety. Reports continue to highlight the persistent need for self-reliance in promoting researcher safety despite the increased recognition of risk and ongoing lack of researcher preparedness for managing safety and self-care (Roguski & Tauri, 2013; Bloor, Fincham, & Sampson, 2010; Fenge et al., 2019). While some progress has been made to address the complex issue of researcher safety from an institutional perspective, challenges remain (Sluka, 2018).

An Institutional Review Board (IRB) or ethics committee is typically concerned only with the possibility of risk for participants (Domenech Rodríguez et al., 2017; Nilan, 2002; Webber & Brunger, 2018). Although some universities require a risk assessment with plans for managing physical risks, there are very few precautions or required planning to deal with issues of an emotional, legal, or personal/professional nature. The physical, psychological, and emotional aspects of encountering real or potential risk can impact a researcher long after they have finished the study (Fenge et al., 2019; Kloß, 2017; Nikischer, 2019). In addition to IRB or ethics committee guidelines, there is some professional advice or agency specific criteria available, however, these are not typically specific to dealing with deviant and criminal subjects or environments. For the individual looking for information on safety precautions, there is a growing body of narratives and reflexive accounts that provide suggestions to ensure safety.

In the past it was seen as taboo to reveal issues experienced while conducting research. Punch (1986) states, "the scientist has come to embody objectivity and detachment. Involvement in the field is viewed almost as contamination that has to be exorcised by an avoidance of reflection and an aseptic prose style" (p. 14). Normally only successful accounts would be reported and those would typically remove the researcher from the narrative. "Failures are rarely written up and analyzed, except via the academic grapevine, despite the fact that they can provide fruitful instructional material" (Punch, 1986, p. 14). According to Whyte (1981), it was as though "the academic world had imposed a conspiracy of silence" (p. 359).

> It was impossible to find realistic accounts that revealed the errors and confusions and the personal involvements that a field worker must experience. I decided to do my bit to fill this gap. In undertaking this task, it seemed to me important to be as honest about myself as I could possibly be. This meant not suppressing incidents that made me look foolish, like my abortive attempt to pick up a girl in a Scollay Square tavern, or my involvement in a federal crime (I voted four times in an election)—although in the latter case, several colleagues advised me against such a confession. I wrote as I did, not simply to cleanse my soul but, more importantly, to help future field workers understand that it is possible to make foolish errors and serious mistakes and still produce a valuable study (Whyte, 1981, p. 359).

Sharing of personal accounts of the research experience, such as Whyte's, has become more widely accepted (Doyle & McCarthy-Jones, 2017; Kloß, 2017; Nikischer, 2019). It is in such literature that we can learn about some of the issues facing researchers. However, Goldsmith (2003) claims that dealing with risks "has not received consideration by criminologists" (p. 104). Texts do not cover the risk involved in fieldwork (Goldsmith, 2003), nor do they fully explain role and role performance or the difficulties of managing roles while in the field (de Laine, 2000). Consistent with this finding, a sampling of current introductory textbooks used to support the teaching of research methods in Criminal Justice and Criminology was reviewed. In sharp contrast to the considerable focus on participant safety, the examination revealed little to no discussion of researcher safety when studying social deviance or criminal behavior. Given the changes in the way researchers share their experiences, more attention is currently drawn to risk and safety for social scientists. This is an opportune time to develop a better understanding of safety strategies that may better prepare the novice researcher as they embark on a venture into the realm of social deviance or criminal behavior.

Background

Risk is unpredictable and difficult to avoid (Wright et al., 1992). For example, Sharp and Kremer (2006) experienced unexpected difficulties during research as graduate students. "While we had both prepared for the possibility of routine problems encountered during fieldwork, neither of us thought about the possibility of experiencing harassment or intimidation from our subjects" (p. 321).

Another point to consider is that some researchers may not wish to eliminate risk. It may be counter-productive to eliminate all risk (Sluka, 2018 Webber & Brunger, 2018; Westmarland, 2000). It is important to be cautious, but danger and risk are essential ingredients in developing a complete understanding of the subject when conducting fieldwork. As Westmarland (2000) illustrates, experiencing the same risks as the subjects provides the researcher with an opportunity to understand the issue more clearly. If researchers take so many precautions as to create a completely safe environment, then they may lack insight, especially when conducting ethnographic research (Westmarland, 2000). This notion is logical. However, researchers should at least be aware of the possible risks they face in order to mentally, physically, and emotionally prepare themselves for the experience and to take precautions when they are able.

Dickson-Swift, James, Kippen, and Liamputtong (2008) "recommend that a set of guidelines be developed for use by qualitative researchers, supervisors, institutions, and granting bodies that are involved in sensitive research" (p. 142). Sampson and Thomas (2003) also suggest that steps be taken to minimize dangers. Some researchers have outlined such precautions for entering research (Belousov et al., 2007; Dickson-Swift et al., 2008; Kenyon & Hawker, 1999; Lee, 1995; Morris & Marquart, 2010; Paterson, Gregory, & Thorne, 1999; Peritore, 1990; Sharp & Kremer, 2006; Sluka, 1990; Williams et al., 2001). The Social Research Association (2001) also provides a code of practice for those who fund research, employ research managers, or conduct research. The SRA code includes safety guidelines for fieldwork-based research.

While the following suggestions for safety, compiled from the available literature, are focused on fieldworkers, it is possible that some of these suggestions would assist the non-fieldwork-based researcher as well. Though these steps may provide some protections, it is not known if they are the best precautions for all types of research. It should also be noted that there is no assurance that taking precautions will eliminate all forms of danger.

Conduct Risk Assessment

It is suggested that researchers complete a risk assessment before the start of research (Belousov et al., 2007; SRA 2001). Sluka (1990) recommends that the researcher conduct an evaluation to determine the extent and sources of danger prior to entering the field. A risk assessment can be a formal process or as simple as taking a little time to consider what types of risk the researcher may encounter. Sharp and Kremer (2006) suggests that researchers "discuss the possibility of sexual harassment or intimidation in the field and think about what types of behavior or situations are most likely to occur" (p. 326). Sluka (1990) stresses that the researcher should decide what risks they are prepared to accept.

Plan for the Unexpected

The need to terminate the research early may occur (Sluka, 1990). Researchers should develop knowledge of the working environment, geographical area, exit routes, and inform others of where they will be at all times (Kenyon & Hawker, 1999; Morris & Marquart, 2010; SRA, 2001). Sharp and Kremer (2006) stressed that all researchers should know that they can "end an interview if they feel uncomfortable or threatened" (p. 326). In this case, it is suggested that the researcher have a plan for getting out as quickly as possible. The researcher should visit the area prior to initiating the research project. This will provide an opportunity to become familiar with the area (Morris & Marquart, 2010; Sluka, 1990; SRA, 2001; Paterson et al., 1999) and plan an escape route if necessary (Paterson et al., 1999; SRA, 2001). It is also suggested that researchers carry a mobile phone (Kenyon & Hawker, 1999; Morris & Marquart, 2010; Sharp & Kremer, 2006; SRA, 2001). It is good practice to let friends or colleagues know the research schedule and a time to expect the researcher's return. Researchers should also make arrangements to contact someone at a designated time to report their status (Jamieson, 2000; Morris & Marquart, 2010; Sharp & Kremer, 2006; SRA, 2001). If the researcher doesn't call at the designated time, then the contact person will know that there is potentially something wrong and can take appropriate action.

Pay Attention to Style and Demeanor

It is recommended that the researcher pay attention to the style and demeanor of the area under study (Williams et al., 2001). The researcher should try to fit in by dressing in a style for the research environment, paying attention to customs of dress and language (Belousov et al., 2007; Peritore, 1990; Polsky, 1985; SRA, 2001; Williams et al., 2001). Individuals should be careful to present themselves as personable and stable. They should not appear to be a victim. It is further suggested that researchers have an awareness of body language, show respect for respondents, and develop a warm and honest manner in working with respondents (Kenyon & Hawker, 1999). Lack of knowledge about cultural differences may put the researcher at risk (Peritore, 1990). In addition, taking steps to become knowledgeable about cultural differences may reduce the potential risk to researchers. Goldsmith (2003), who has spent many years researching Colombian police, also suggests learning the language commonly used by the research participants. This will aid the researcher to build trust and rapport, as it allows for direct communication with subjects instead of relying on interpreters or linguistic technology aides.

Establish a Locator and Protector

The need for the researcher to establish a locator and protector is important for any fieldworker (Williams et al., 2001). A locator is someone within the community who can introduce the researcher and assist with making appropriate connections with potential research participants. The researcher needs to make sure that the locator is a well-respected and trusted individual. The researcher's acceptance in the community may depend on how people in the community perceive the locator. People in the community and potential research participants will associate the researcher with the locator. If the locator is not trustworthy, the community will not trust the researcher.

The locator can also function as the protector. Typically, once the researcher is established in the community, a protector will emerge. The protector is a person who helps to ensure the researcher is safe. As the researcher builds rapport and trust, different people will fill the role of protector at different times. This individual reminds people to be calm and hold things together when the researcher is present. If someone appears to give the researcher a hard time, the protector may step in to redirect or tell the individual to back off. Williams et al. (2001) found the role of protector to be especially important in conducting drug research. Inciardi (1993) also emphasized the need to have a protector when researching crack houses. Similarly, the SRA (2001) suggests that someone shadow or accompany the researcher on fieldwork assignments to ensure safety.

Develop a Network

Dickson-Swift et al. (2008) recommend professional supervision and "development of a structured mentoring program for novice researchers who are involved in sensitive projects, to ensure that they are provided with support in a timely and ongoing fashion" (p. 139). Developing a support network is critical for researchers, especially those engaging in research on sexuality (Peritore, 1990; Israel, 2006) or other sensitive issues (Dickson-Swift et al., 2008). Israel (2006) found that connecting with other professionals and professional organizations can be a source of support. "If researchers are not provided with opportunities to debrief, they risk the possibility that they will carry their research stories around with them, which may be detrimental to their emotional well-being" (Warr, 2004 in Dickson-Swift et al., 2008, p. 140). Someone with experience can assist the researcher with processing their emotions or devising a plan to deal with possible situations they may encounter. Wright et al. (1992) knew that they would be facing potentially dangerous situations when they entered research on residential burglars. Therefore, they contacted the police in the area to establish their presence as researchers and ensure that there would be no legal difficulties. The SRA (2001) also recommends contacting the police before beginning fieldwork based research that holds potential for risk.

Set Limits

Establishing limits ahead of time on what one is willing to discuss while conducting research can assist in ending conversations that may not be comfortable (Israel, 2006). The researcher must also decide what they are or are not willing to do or witness (Polsky & others, 1985). Polsky and others (1985) warns that on occasion a researcher may face unanticipated situations with no management plan. For example, the research subject may try to draw the researcher into the crime life. While one can plan dress, speech, and some basic behavioral responses, one cannot plan for every possibility. Deciding ahead of time where to draw the line would most likely benefit researchers.

Money Management

Sometimes money is offered as an incentive for interview participation. When researchers carry large amounts of money to pay interviewees, they could become the target for robbery. Lee (1995) suggests that researchers develop a strategy for dealing with ineligible individuals who wish to participate in the research because of a monetary incentive. Wright et al. (1992) made it very clear to their subjects that they did not carry more cash than necessary to pay the subjects for participation in the research. Such a strategy may prevent robbery.

Research Focus

The literature reviewed provided suggestions including conducting risk assessments, planning for the unexpected, paying attention to style and demeanor, establishing a locator and protector, developing a network, setting limits, and money management techniques. It is not known if any or all of the reviewed procedures are typically used by researchers or if the procedures used are considered to be successful. While there is much to be learned about the necessary precautions for all types of research, the focus of this research was to explore the utilization of precautions and their level of success specifically for researchers who have studied social deviance or criminal behavior.

Methods

As part of a study exploring risk to researchers, this research sought to fill the knowledge gap regarding safety for researchers by addressing the following research questions:

1. What safety precautions do researchers employ when engaging research on social deviance or criminal behavior?
2. What safety precautions do researchers judge to be the most useful to reduce or eliminate risks when researching social deviance or criminal behavior?

The target population for this study was social scientists who have conducted research on social deviance or criminal behavior. It must be recognized that risk comes in many forms, therefore, there is possibility for researchers collecting data by use of fieldwork or non-fieldwork based methods to experience risk. For this reason, the sample included researchers who have conducted fieldwork or non-fieldwork based research on social deviance or criminal behavior. In order to establish a list of potential participants, professionals in the fields of criminology and sociology were identified from membership lists for the American Society of Criminology (ASC), the Academy of Criminal Justice Sciences (ACJS), and the Midwest Sociological Society (MSS). These organizations were chosen because they spur further inquiry that advances our understanding of societal issues and they encourage members, including students, faculty and other professionals, to conduct research that is contributory. Therefore, within these membership lists, it was likely that a sample would be captured that would lead to a greater understanding of the issue. To prevent the possibility of multiple responses, available membership lists were combined, duplicates were removed, and the survey software was programmed to prevent repeat responses.

Because the focus of this research was to explore the topic of safety employed by those studying social deviance or criminal behavior, participants were asked to indicate if their research topics fell into the categories of social deviance or criminal behavior. Those who did not meet these criteria were excluded from the project.

As a large portion of the participants in this project were most likely employed in academia and accustomed to use of technology, an online survey was created for use in this endeavor. The survey queried respondents on types of safety precautions utilized to reduce or eliminate risk. The respondent was asked to consider any safety precautions they normally take before starting a research project. They were asked if they have used certain safety precautions as established by the literature review. For each safety precaution used, a Likert scale was available for them to indicate the level of success they felt the safety precaution provided (1–5, 1 = not successful, 5 = most successful). Scale reliability was α= .976. The respondents were also asked to provide advice about safety precautions to take before entering into a research project on deviance or crime. This question provided an open text box for a narrative response.

Results

Overall, 5,455 individuals were invited to participate in the survey. A total of 1,065 individuals accessed the online survey. There were 27 surveys with no answers given for any item. These 27 were excluded from analysis. The resulting response rate was 19%. Of the remaining 1,038 surveys, the final sample for analysis included 805 respondents who indicated that they have conducted research on social deviance or criminal behavior.

In the final sample (n = 805), 46.3% (n = 373) of those surveyed identified as male, 42.4% (n = 341) identified as female, and 11.3% (n = 91) did not provide a gender. Respondents identified their discipline as criminologists (68.8%; n = 473), *sociologists* (20.2%; n ¼ 145), or *other social scientists* (11%; n = 100) which included *psychologists*, *political scientists*, *victimologists*, and a combined role of *sociologist and criminologist*. The remaining 87 respondents (10.8%) did not provide a specific discipline. Participants reported engagement in a broad range of research foci including violence, white collar crime, gangs, counter culture, juvenile crime/delinquency, drug use, homelessness, marginalized populations, sexual offences/offenders, terrorism, prisons, and policing.

In this sample, 41% (n = 330) of respondents reported that they had experienced risk due to their involvement in research on social deviance or criminal behavior. Of those reporting research related risk, the large majority conducted fieldwork-based research (taking place outside of their home or normal place of business) with only 5.8% (n = 19) identifying exclusive engagement in non-fieldwork based research. A follow-up question asked if they had reported the risk they experienced, only 33% (n ¼ 109) indicated that they did report the risk event. They were also asked if they sought support for dealing with the experience of risk. Of those experiencing risk, 72.7% (n = 240) indicated that they did not seek support. Of the respondents who did seek support, almost 90% (n = 59) reported that the support was beneficial.

The majority of respondents (54.4%; n = 438) indicated that they do not believe that social scientists enter into research projects fully aware of risks that may await them, with more than half (53.9%; n = 434) indicating that they believe safety issues for researchers require more attention or awareness within the social sciences. Findings from this study that identify specific risks to researchers studying social deviance or criminal behavior are described elsewhere (Brougham & Uttley, 2017).

Safety Precautions

Respondents were asked if they utilize any type of safety precaution for research. About half of those surveyed (51.6%, n = 415) indicated that they use safety precautions. However, the use of safety precautions was reported by a slightly higher percentage (59.1%; n = 195) of researchers who also reported they had experienced research related risk. Little difference was noted in the selection of safety precautions between those who reported experiencing risk and those who did not experience risk. The types of safety precautions used by researchers who reported the experience of risk is provided in Figure 1.

The most frequently used safety precautions reported by researchers who reported the experience of risk were: consider or discuss possible safety issues (95.9%), dress for the environment

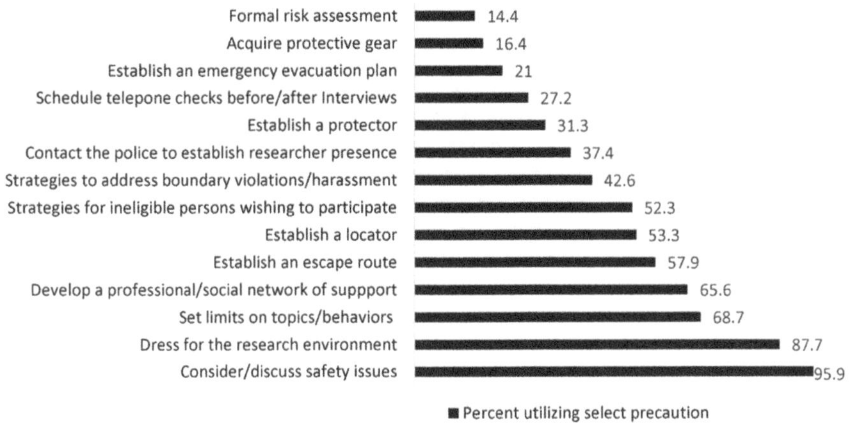

Figure 1 Use of select safety precautions by researchers who have experienced risk (n = 195).

(87.7%), set limits (68.7%), and develop a professional/social network of support (65.6%). The use of a formal risk assessment was the least commonly used safety precaution, reported by only 14% of these researchers. Under the category of other safety precautions, respondents provided several additional precautions they use for preventing risk while conducting research. Some general themes emerged from this category including: take preventative precautions, follow agency policies for safety, create safety plans, develop strategies or solutions for managing situations that may occur, and complete an IRB review.

Reduce or Eliminate Risks

Respondents were asked to rate the level of success they found for the safety precautions they have used. A Likert scale was used for this question allowing respondents to rate success on a scale of 1 = not successful at all for reducing risks to 5 = most successful at eliminating risks. Frequencies were reviewed for the rate of success given for the safety precautions identified in the previous section. The ratings of *not very successful* and *not successful at all* held little variation for all categories of safety precautions, therefore the results were collapsed to create three categories: not/not very successful, somewhat successful, most/very successful. The reported level of success for the safety precautions used by researchers who experienced risk is provided in Figure 2.

Three of the four most widely used safety precautions were found to be very successful or better for reducing or eliminating risk by the majority of respondents who had experienced risk. Specifically, consider or discuss possible safety issues received a rating of *most/very successful* from 60.3%; set limits received a rating of *most/very successful* from 70.4%; and develop a professional/social network of support was rated as *most/very successful* by 54.8% of those who had used the safety precaution. Despite being one of the most commonly used precautions, dressing specifically for the research environment was found to be *not/not very successful* by 10.9% of those using the precaution; with fewer than half (48.5%) rating this precaution as *most/very successful* in reducing or eliminating risk. Formal risk assessments, the least used safety precaution, was noted to be *most/or very successful* at reducing or eliminating risks by the majority of those using this method. Establishing a protector received proportionally higher ratings for success than other safety precautions with 80.3% of users rating this precaution as *most/very successful*. Overall, most safety precautions evaluated provided what was perceived to be at least some level of success for reducing risk with each precaution rated as *somewhat successful* or greater by at least 80% of users.

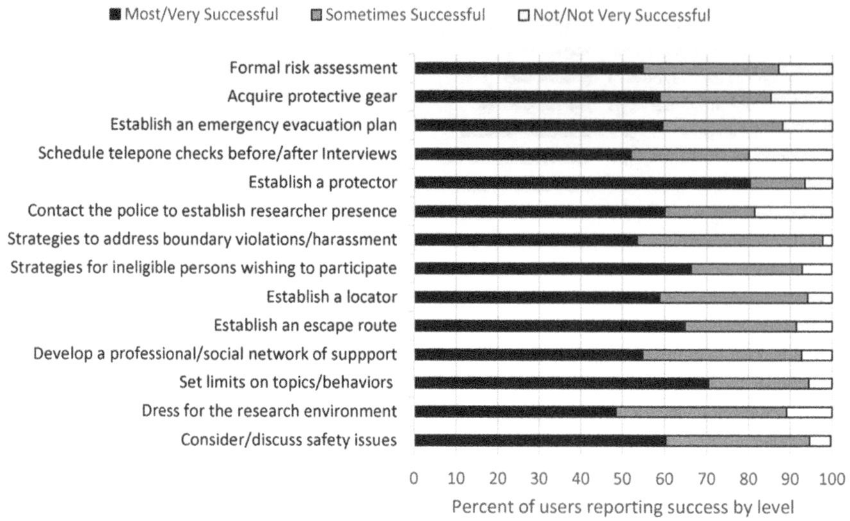

Figure 2 Reported success of select safety precautions used by researchers who have experienced risk

Words of Wisdom from Current Researchers

Respondents were given one open-ended question at the end of the survey. They were asked to give advice about safety precautions to take before entering into a research project on deviance or crime. Themes emerged from the narratives that support the findings above.

Many respondents recommended *talking to experienced researchers, police, and community organizers*. One respondent said:

> I have worked with enough agencies and practitioners to realize that social scientists are often clueless about what they are getting themselves into. My advice: (1) talk to people in agencies (e.g. police officers) that are familiar with the area of research you want to examine; (2) LISTEN to what these people have to say—they actually know more than we (researchers) think they know; (3) develop your safety plan and have one or more practitioners review it; and (4) FOLLOW YOUR PLAN to the letter—diverging from it is not an option.

Respondents also suggested getting to *know the area, subjects of interest, culture, custom, and laws of the area*. One respondent said, "Conduct a full analysis of your target region including Amnesty International reports, US embassy warnings, Police overviews, UN reports and local news before starting." Other respondents said:

> Meet repeatedly with different members of the community you are studying in order to gain a full understanding of the potential complications, objections or problems you may encounter. Relying solely on one source of information is ill-advised and limiting. The representatives should also come from different disciplines, i.e. police, church, social services, etc. as they are exposed to different challenges and issues.
>
> Knowing exactly what you are getting into before starting the project. That is, know the area and the potential dangers and take time to think about all of the crazy situations you may get involved in and have a plan for dealing with them. Also, don't assume CJ personnel (police officers, corrections officers, etc.) are going to look after your safety or will not put you in risky situations. Finally, lose the arrogant Ph.D. attitude and act and dress in a way that does not make you stand out or look like you think you are better than the people you are

> with (regardless whether they are offenders or CJ personnel).

Many respondents cautioned *care and respect* in the manner of interaction with subjects. Respondents pointed out that paying attention to demeanor and the wording of questions is important as they have an impact on the study participants. One respondent cautioned, "Be mindful that research questions can create risk." Another respondent suggested that researchers "reflect on his or her status (race, class, gender, education, etc.) and how that may or may not enhance or mitigate risks associated with the research."

Some suggested *meeting with a lawyer or preparing for legal risks*. It was also suggested that researchers *look at any possible shield laws* that might be useful. One respondent stated:

> Know the law (national/state/local); know EXACTLY what information you can collect and EFFECTIVELY protect; know the human subjects/ethnical issues thoroughly by talking at length with researchers experienced in the area of your research and what strategies they have ACTUALLY found effective. And, make sure you know what the position has been and is of those persons you will need to help you if the worse happens, especially university and research institute lawyers and administrators. What is their track record? Do they actually know the law and regs? Will they fight for you?

Some respondents included reminders of *ethical responsibilities*. One respondent said, "I would also recommend that the research proceed with common sense and remember that s/he is only part of the subject's life for a short time and should not impart her/his own values onto the situation."

Several respondents suggested *have some type of support, working in a team, or having a locator or gatekeeper*. One respondent offered, "Go with a partner. Be sure someone knows what you are doing, where you are going, with whom you will be meeting, and when you expect to return." Others recommended:

> Dress to fit in (but not excessively), contact the local police only if they are known to be of help, map out the area, get as much information about the area and the people as possible, and (MOST IMPORTANT) get a locator who can make introductions. Mine kept me from [people] who might have killed me.

Don't be afraid to voice concerns. The agencies I worked for were very experienced and had procedures in place to manage risk. We followed the facility's procedures, worked in teams, wore body alarms if necessary, and had prep and debrief meetings every time. Those were very valuable in managing any emotional stress. It helps to know that you aren't the only one who is nervous or concerned.

Most respondents made comments about *using common sense or listening to your instinct or gut*.

> If you are conducting observational research in a high crime area, then you should take the proper precautions and be cognizant of your surroundings. If you are conducting interviews with active offenders then you should do so in either a public place or if possible get them to come to your campus. Again, there are no special safety precautions that need to be taken other than those dictated by common sense. We are not chemists or nuclear scientists who work with substances that could kill us. We do not need safety gear, just a good head on our shoulders and to know when you may be in a potentially dangerous situation.

Many *suggested thinking about potential issues and make a plan for dealing with them* in the event they do occur. One respondent suggested that researchers "take necessary precautions seriously, follow protocol. You can be taken by surprise or find yourself in an unexpected situation faster than you would anticipate. Do not overrate your own abilities to handle risky situations."

Several respondents suggested *safety training* for the population and environment, as well, many suggested *preparation for emotional issues*. One respondent stated, "I would recommend a class or training on what to expect in terms of emotional harm for researchers engaging in fieldwork. My guess is that most risk that most of us face is emotional." One respondent, more specifically said, "If you experience a sexual assault, know that it was not your fault and talk to your colleagues about what happened." Others further emphasized the need for emotional support.

> Do not forget about emotional stress/trauma that may occur and merely focus on physical risk. In conducting research, you may hear about and/or experience things that are not necessarily pleasant and therefore may cause you as the researcher emotional stress. Have a game plan that includes professional help (e.g. therapy) to deal with this if it arises.
>
> Pay attention to self-care. Sometimes what we hear, even though it is expected, can negatively affect us. Attend to your emotions, pay attention to what you are feeling, and acknowledge the basis for your emotion. Do not be afraid to set up a process for dealing with emotional stress prior to your research—it only strengthens your commitment to your research as well as yourself.
>
> I would caution researchers to be aware that if you are exploring issues related to trauma to be aware of the effects that this type of research might have on you. It can be quite depressing, so make sure that you have someone who you can talk to about your own emotional response to trauma, especially when you know that, as researcher, you are powerless to do anything about it.

Most suggestions were directed at field research; however, not all risk happens in the field. Some responses were inclusive of other types of research.

> Even secondary data analysis conjures potentially troubling and dark thoughts/feelings. I say to my graduate students that they should avoid topics that will produce discomfort for them. There's no way to quantify what that means, nor should we assume that discomfort is experienced similarly by all for the same reasons. That's why a lot of anticipatory thinking is necessary.
>
> Don't underestimate the emotional toll certain topics can have. Also don't underestimate the difficulty you might have interacting with certain types of offenders, e.g. sex offenders, those who've abused their children, etc. Be aware that even if you're not specifically looking for potentially disturbing information like this, it may come up, sometimes without warning. This can happen during interviews, or when looking through case files, etc.

Some respondents emphasized the need to be *clear about your purpose*. One respondent said, "Make sure people are very clear on your intentions. Most every problem I encountered was due to people making wildly inaccurate assumptions about my intentions and motivations for being there and/or studying them." Another said, "Identification of status is paramount. During fieldwork, due to my clothing/protective gear (ballistic vest) most subjects assumed that I was a detective, which actually served to increase my risk in many situations."

Some respondents made suggestions for specific topics of study or for specific environments.

> If your research is done to achieve any effect in the (juvenile) justice system, be aware that practitioners (prosecutors, judges, police, juvenile court social workers) will see your activity as intrusion into their territory and their responses can be quite hostile, which on researcher's side causes a lot of discomfort and emotional pressure. You feel isolated and you need a lot of emotional support to balance these adversities. Precaution: be aware into whose territories you step and arm yourself with a lot of resiliency.
>
> If you are conducting research in prison, know the population you are dealing with and take safety precautions when interviewing these individuals. You might want to have an officer nearby, you might want to plan an escape route from the interview room, and you might want to know where the exits are

> in the prison. Also, the correctional staff may pressure you to disclose the specifics of your research. Be sure that you know your confidentiality statement and repeat it to anyone who asks about your research.

Many respondents encouraged consideration of *safety precautions be included in education.* One respondent said, "I think more researchers should write about their experiences doing research in order to teach others these safety skills. Also, more focus on this issue in graduate school education." Others said:

> I think every doctoral student needs to take a research ethics course that includes not only protection of research participants, but protection of self. When I teach my research course on violence, I spend one class on the risks that such controversial and sensitive research poses to the researcher him/herself. No one ever thinks of that. They go into the work because they are interested in it, but don't consider the possible ramifications on themselves in terms of their mental and physical safety and health. Even areas that might seem non-controversial could hold risks to the researchers, and students need to think those risks through and learn what they can do to minimize those risks.
>
> I think there should be more attention paid to the subject during training (we teach issues of ethics in research, we should also teach about safety in research). Also, I think that there could be institutional (but not IR, that is already a headache) or program-based efforts to make sure that researchers have reviewed a "safety plan" of sorts prior to beginning research. This would be the equivalent of asking the "could this harm participants?" question but about the research group and a plan to avoid or minimize the risks.

Some cautioned that researchers *beware of those in authority*. One respondent said, "If it's a real case, keep in mind that there are legal and political figures who may not want you to be digging or conducting research." Another said:

> Just be aware of yourself and those around you. Moreover, personal and physical risk can come just as easily from the authorities (i.e. police) as it can from those being policed. Police officers, for example, often take violent actions that can provoke a violent response. Depending on your positionality as a researcher (embedded with police, embedded with the policed), you may be in danger from either side directly, or from the tension inherent in the situation. But mostly, you're not—it's just a perception.

While many offered cautions, there was also a reoccurring sentiment well reflected by the statement, "don't let fear or minor risks stop you from going into the field and getting first-hand knowledge." Another respondent stated, "Don't go into the work blindly, but don't get so caught up in the potential danger that you allow it to dictate your evaluation/research/study." Many respondents pointed out that most of the time there is simply perceived risk, but no negative experience happens. One respondent said, "Think about the potential risks you may face beforehand, but also realize that most of the risks you think you will face are blown out of proportion." Another said:

> Don't worry about risks. Your job is to be bold and do great research. Figure out what it will take to do that. Then worry about risk to your SUBJECTS. After that, and after you have modified your research protocol to minimize any risks to your subjects, think about your own risks. They will most likely be minimal. Take them into account, then go do great work. Don't be paranoid. People who obsess about risk do not undertake important projects. Do important work; don't sit in an office dithering.

Discussion

While there is some professional advice or agency specific criteria available, there are no universally established guidelines on researcher safety specific for those studying social deviance or criminal behavior. Before this study there was limited knowledge as to the routine employment of safety precautions by researchers engaged in the study of social deviance or criminal behavior. Furthermore, it was not known if precautions utilized were perceived as successful at reducing or eliminating risks. From this study, it is known that researchers do employ a variety of safety precautions, including *considering or discussing possible safety issues, dressing for the environment, setting limits, and developing a professional/social network of support*. Also, many of the utilized safety precautions have been found to be successful for reducing or eliminating risks. This is beneficial information, especially for researchers new to the study of social deviance or criminal behavior. It is the novice researcher who could most benefit from exposure to safety protocols.

Although risk may present differently based on context or setting, evaluating the likelihood of risk when planning research should be routine. In this sample, four out of every ten respondents studying social deviance or criminal behavior indicated that they have experienced research related risk. While risk may be present in a variety of research methods, the overwhelming majority of those reporting the experience of research related risk in this sample engaged in fieldwork based research. Despite the relatively common occurrence of risk reported, only half of those conducting research identified the use of safety precautions with a slightly higher proportion of use noted among those reporting the experience of research related risk.

This information places emphasis on the need for safety awareness and safety considerations when entering research on social deviance or criminal behavior. Based on information provided by this work, it can be suggested that emphasis on the need for safety precautions, including strategies such as formal risk assessment, may be overlooked during initial research training. This notion is supported by the large number of respondents in this study who indicated their belief that social scientists enter into research projects without a full awareness of risks that may await them and that safety issues for researchers require more attention or awareness.

It is often assumed that students learn safety techniques while enrolled in research methods courses. This is simply not the case. It was suggested by many respondents that more emphasis on safety should be included in training or research methods courses. Without attention given to the topic of researcher safety, the experience of preventable risk may occur. However, some would argue that risk must be experienced and it is through the experience of risk that the young researcher comes to understand their topic of study.

The large number of respondents in this study who did not report events or seek assistance for dealing with risks they experienced is troubling. Decreasing stigma surrounding the occurrence of research related risk in formative research education is warranted. It is important for individuals who experience risk to seek help, especially in dealing with traumatic matters. Such encounters can cause issues in everyday life if not dealt with appropriately and in a timely manner. Experience of traumatic events "can lead to high levels of anxiety, depression, and perhaps even paranoia" (Worley et al., 2016, p. 304). The good news is that the vast majority of respondents in this study who did seek assistance found it to be beneficial.

The narratives provided by many respondents emphasized the need for more training/education on safety for researchers. Many of the narratives reflected the quantitative findings but provided more description. A great deal of emphasis was placed on the need for emotional preparation and support regardless of the type of research engaged, fieldwork or non-fieldwork. Two themes found throughout the narratives echoed that *most risk is perceived, but never experienced, and researchers shouldn't let the potential for risk stop them from engaging the research.*

Limitations

Generalizability of these findings to the greater population may be limited. However, because the recruited population conduct research on social deviance or criminal behavior, the results may also be generalizable to similar professionals. Response rate was also a concern as non-response bias contributes to limits on generalizability. To provide a broad overview of safety precautions utilized by researchers investigating social deviance or criminal behavior, both fieldwork and non-fieldwork researchers were included in this sample, with the specific type of research conducted identified with the reporting of risk. To more fully understand differences in the utilization of safety precautions between fieldwork and non-fieldwork based researchers and the temporal nature of risk experience and utilization of safety precautions, additional background information should be included in future research. Similarly, safety precautions may differ between those studying social deviance and criminal behavior. Investigation to more specifically identify these nuanced differences is needed. Despite these limitations, the information presented by this research holds value and may contribute to the greater conversation on the topic of risk and safety for researchers of crime and deviance.

Conclusions

This research was engaged with exploration in mind. The overarching goal was to discover safety precautions that are employed by researchers studying social deviance or criminal behavior and to identify what safety precautions are considered to be most successful at reducing or eliminating risks. While this information has been realized, there is still much to learn about researcher risk and safety. Future research endeavors on this topic could focus on safety aspects for specific areas of study that fall under the umbrella of social deviance or criminal behavior. A more narrow focus on safety aspects based on the type of methods employed, quantitative or qualitative, fieldwork or non-fieldwork, is needed. A survey of IRB and ethic committee requirements for safety is also suggested. This would provide a much better picture of the current state of safety measures required for those engaged in research.

It is recommended that all researchers be proactive in their preparations for research. The intention of this research was not to frighten or scare individuals away, but to better prepare them for entering research. As respondents expressed, it is good to be prepared for a risk that may never occur. Integration of the concept of risk at the undergraduate level with the initial introduction to research methods is suggested. Through awareness of safety precautions, novice researchers may be better prepared for entering into research projects that hold potential for risk. Experienced researchers may also find this information beneficial as they may enter new research projects that present possible risk not yet encountered. Some IRBs or ethics committees have established safety protocols that include researcher safety. Hopefully, more IRBs and ethics committees will move in this direction. It is also recommended that preparation for research include the utilization of safety precautions specific to the research environment. These safety precautions should include the establishment of support for dealing with emotional issues as well as ethical dilemmas that may arise during the course of research. Especially for new researchers, there should be support in place prior to beginning research on social deviance or criminal behavior. Mentoring of novice researchers by experienced researchers could prove to be most beneficial.

Disclosure Statement

We have no known conflict of interest to disclose.

Discussion Questions

1. What were the most frequently used safety precautions reported in Brougham et al.'s study, and how did they compare to the list of what researchers perceived as being particularly effective?

2. What are locators (gatekeepers) and protectors, and what role might they play in field research?
3. Based on your reading, what are some of the best tips that new researchers should consider when getting ready to do their first fieldwork assignments?

References

Belousov, K., Horlick-Jones, T., Bloor, M., Gilinskiy, Y., Golbert, V., Kostikovsky, Y., … Pentsov, D. (2007). Any port in a storm: Fieldwork difficulties in dangerous and crisis-ridden settings. *Qualitative Research*, *7*(2), 155–175. https://doi.org/10.1177/1468794107076019

Bloor, M., Fincham, B., & Sampson, H. (2007). *QUALITI (NCRM) commissioned inquiry into the risk to well-being of researchers in qualitative research.* www.cardiff.ac.uk/socsi/qualiti/CIReport.pdf

Bloor, M., Fincham, B., & Sampson, H. (2010). Unprepared for the worst: Risks of harm for qualitative researchers. *Methodological Innovations Online*, *5*(1), 45–55. https://doi.org/10.4256/mio.2010.0009

Brougham, P. L., & Uttley, C. M. (2017). Risk for researchers studying social deviance or criminal behavior. *Social Sciences*, *6*(4), 130. https://doi.org/10.3390/socsci6040130

de Laine, M. (2000). *Fieldwork, participation and practice: Ethics and dilemmas in qualitative research.* Sage Publications.

Dickson-Swift, V., James, E. L., Kippen, S., & Liamputtong, P. (2007). Doing sensitive research: What challenges do qualitative researchers face? *Qualitative Research*, *7*(3), 327–353. https://doi.org/10.1177/1468794107078515

Dickson-Swift, V., James, E. L., Kippen, S., & Liamputtong, P. (2008). Risk to researchers in qualitative research on sensitive topics: Issues and strategies. *Qualitative Health Research, 18*(1), 133–144.

Domenech Rodríguez, M. M., Corralejo, S. M., Vouvalis, N., & Mirly, A. K. (2017). Institutional review board: Ally not adversary. *Psi Chi Journal of Psychological Research*, *22*(2), 76–84. https://doi.org/10.24839/2325-7342.JN22.2.76

Doyle, C., & McCarthy-Jones, A. (2017). Researching in volatile environments and the importance of adaptive methods for junior researchers. *Qualitative Research Journal, 17*(4), 335–344. https://doi.org/10.1108/QRJ-03-2017-0005

Fenge, L. A., Oakley, L., Taylor, B., & Beer, S. (2019). The impact of sensitive research on the researcher: Preparedness and positionality. *International Journal of Qualitative Methods, 18,* 160940691989316. https://doi.org/10.1177/1609406919893161.

Goldsmith, A. (2003). Fear, fumbling and frustration: Reflections on doing criminological fieldwork in Columbia. *Criminal Justice*, *3*(1), 103–125. https://doi.org/10.1177/1466802503003001458

Inciardi, J. (1993). Appendix A: Some considerations on the methods, dangers, and ethics of crack-house research. In J. Inciardi, D. Lockwood, & A. E. Pottieger (Eds.), *Women and crack-cocaine* (pp. 147–157). Macmillan.

Israel, T. (2006). Studying sexuality: Strategies for surviving stigma. In J. Miller & R. Tewksbury (Eds.), *Research methods: A qualitative reader* (pp. 180–184). Prentice Hall.

Jamieson, J. (2000). Negotiating danger in fieldwork on crime. In G. Lee-Treweek & S. Linkogle (Eds.), *Danger in the field: Risk and ethics in social research* (pp. 61–71). Routledge.

Johnson, B., & Clarke, J. (2006). Collecting sensitive data: The impact on researchers. In J. Miller & R. Tewksbury (Eds.), *Research methods: A qualitative reader* (pp. 211–226). Prentice Hall.

Kenyon, E., & Hawker, S. (1999). 'Once would be enough': Some reflections on the issue of safety for lone researchers. *International Journal of Social Research Methodology*, *2*(4), 313–327. https://doi.org/10.1080/136455799294989

Kloß, S. T. (2017). Sexual (ized) harassment and ethnographic fieldwork: A silenced aspect of social research. *Ethnography, 18*(3), 396–414. https://doi.org/10.1177/1466138116641958

Lee, R. (1995). *Dangerous fieldwork.* Sage.

Morris, R. G., & Marquart, J. W. (2010). In the classroom and on the streets: How to teach qualitative field research to criminology/criminal justice graduate students. *Journal of Criminal Justice Education, 21*(4), 526–539. https://doi.org/10.1080/10511253.2010.516568

Nikischer, A. (2019). Vicarious trauma inside the academe: Understanding the impact of teaching, researching and writing violence. *Higher Education, 77*(5), 905–916. https://doi.org/10.1007/s10734-018-0308-4

Nilan, P. (2002). 'Dangerous fieldwork' re-examined: The question of researcher subject position. *Qualitative Research, 2*(3), 363–386. https://doi.org/10.1177/146879410200200305

Paterson, B., Gregory, D., & Thorne, S. (1999). A protocol for researcher safety. *Qualitative Health* Research, *9*(2), 259–269. https://doi.org/10.1177/104973299129121820

Peritore, N. P. (1990). Reflections on dangerous fieldwork. *The American Sociologist*, *21*(4), 359–372. https://doi.org/10.1007/BF02691846

Polsky, N. (1985). *Hustlers, beats and others*. University of Chicago.

Punch, M. (1986). *The politics and ethics of fieldwork*. Sage Publications.

Roguski, M., & Tauri, J. M. (2013). Key issues effecting field researcher safety: A reflexive commentary. *New Zealand Sociology*, *28*(1), 18–35.

Sampson, H., & Thomas, M. (2003). Risk and responsibility. *Qualitative Research*, *3*(2), 165–189. https://doi.org/10.1177/14687941030032002

Sharp, G., & Kremer, E. (2006). The safety dance: Confronting harassment, intimidation, and violence in the field. *Sociological Methodology*, *36*(1), 317–327. https://doi.org/10.1111/j.1467-9531.2006.00183.x

Sluka, J. A. (1990). Participant observation in violent social contexts. *Human Organization*, *49*(2), 114–126. https://doi.org/10.17730/humo.49.2.h033174683462676

Sluka, J. A. (2018). Too dangerous for fieldwork? The challenge of institutional risk-management in primary research on conflict, violence and 'terrorism'. *Contemporary Social Science*, *15*(2), 241–257. https://doi.org/10.1080/21582041.2018.1498534

Social Research Association. (2001). A code of practice for the safety of social researchers. http://the-sra.org.uk/wp-content/uploads/SRA-safety-code-of-practice.pdf

Tang, X., Cheung, M., Zhou, S., & Leung, P. (2020). The vulnerable researcher phenomenon. *Open Journal of Philosophy*, *10*(04), 511–527. https://doi.org/10.4236/ojpp.2020.104036

Webber, V., & Brunger, F. (2018). Assessing risk to researchers: Using the case of sexuality research to inform research ethics board guidelines. *Forum: Qualitative Social Research*, *19*(3). http://doi.org/10.17169/fqs-19.3.3062

Westmarland, L. (2000). Taking the flak. In G. Lee-Treweek & S. Linkogle (Eds.), *Danger in the field: Risk and ethics in social research* (pp. 26–42). Routledge.

Whyte, W. F. (1981). *Street corner society: The social structure of an Italian slum*. University of Chicago Press.

Williams, T., Dunlap, E., Johnson, B., & Hamid, A. (2001). Personal safety in dangerous places. In M. Miller & R. Tewksbury (Eds.), *Extreme methods: Innovative approaches to social science research* (pp. 216–238). Allyn & Bacon.

Worley, R. M., Worley, V. B., & Wood, B. A. (2016). 'There were ethical dilemmas all day long!': harrowing tales of ethnographic researchers in criminology and criminal justice. *Criminal Justice Studies*, *29*(4), 289–308. https://doi.org/10.1080/1478601X.2016.1237945

Wright, R., Decker, S., Redfern, A., & Smith, D. (1992). A snowball's chance in Hell: Doing fieldwork with active residential burglars. Journal of Research in Crime and Delinquency, 29(2), 148–161. https://doi.org/10.1177/0022427892029002003

11 Less Obtrusive Methods

Chapter 10 described work that involves time spent in the field and some of the most extensive contact between data collectors and participants found in any type of research. This chapter covers research that is just the opposite. The purpose of this chapter is to review unobtrusive, or at least less obtrusive, methods, meaning research that we can conduct with little to no contact with research participants or without going into the field. There are a few different techniques that we can use, including doing content analysis, gathering agency records, obtaining another researcher's dataset for secondary data analysis, conducting simulations, doing crime mapping, or doing systematic or meta-analyses.

Content Analysis

Kassarjian (1977) defined **content analysis** as the "scientific, objective, systematic, quantitative, and generalizable description of communications content" (p. 10). When performing content analysis, we examine communication or some type of social artifact and attempt to analyze its meaning. One of the earliest content analyses took place in World War II, when the US government funded research to analyze the content of enemy propaganda. Since then, content analysis has been used widely in the fields of social science and mass communications (Prassad, 2008). This type of research can help us understand types of communication and how the creators of a particular work seek to shape narratives. For example, how "true" are "true crime" books? These books might provide accurate depictions of a specific incident, but do the books give readers an understanding of what is typical of crime? As I mentioned in Chapter 2, researchers studied true crime books, as some members of the lay public use these books and documentaries to formulate their understanding of crime and the criminal justice system. Are these books helpful in educating the public? Durham and colleagues (1995) conducted a content analysis of true crime books and compared the books' content to national crime statistics. What they discovered is that these books largely describe atypical crimes, victims, and perpetrators. Whereas the typical murder in the United States involves an African American male perpetrator shooting an African American male victim, true crime books almost always described White people killing White victims, often with something other than a firearm.

Conducting a content analysis consists of long hours reading publications, viewing advertisements, and watching television shows. You should not think that this research is the same as sitting down and flipping through your favorite websites or magazines, nor is it similar to bingeing your favorite show with friends. Like the other research methods discussed throughout this book, content analysis follows the rules outlined in the scientific method. Specifically, Prasad (2008) identified three elements of content analysis. The first is objectivity. When doing this type of work, researchers develop and then follow explicit rules for selecting and reviewing materials. This will allow multiple researchers to obtain the same results from the same sets of documents, audio, or video messages. The second element is the systematic nature of content analysis. Before the start of data collection, we establish a strict set of inclusion and exclusion criteria for the

DOI: 10.4324/9781003661511-11

materials eligible for analysis. The third element is generalizability, as the results found here should be applicable to similar types of content. Adherence to these elements will greatly enhance the validity and reliability of the research.

Prasad (2008) identified six steps involved in content analysis. First, as with any study, we need to formulate a research question. Second, we identify a type of content to be the focus of our research. Once we do that, we can see how much content is available. It may be necessary at this point to develop a sampling procedure if there is too much material for us to review. Third, we operationalize our variables and put the definitions in writing to ensure consistency once data collection begins. Fourth is finalization of units of measurement. In this step, we get more specific about the type of content we are analyzing. We might have already decided on television commercials in step two, but what, exactly, about those commercials interests us? We might want to be so specific that we are looking for the presence of a specific word, phrase, or symbol, or we can look for themes of commercials. Other options would be looking at specific characteristics of news stories (e.g., where did it appear in the newspaper, what was the size or word count of the article), at entire articles (e.g., inclusion of terrorism research papers in criminal justice journals before and after 9/11), the characters of stories, or symbols. Prasad (2008) referred to this specific information as recording units or context units. Other, more common vocabulary for these are **manifest content** and **latent content**. Examples of recording units and manifest content are obvious, clearly measurable items. Manifest analysis "describes what the informants actually say, stays very close to the text, uses the words themselves, and describes the visible and obvious in the text" (Bengtsson, 2016, p. 10). In a manifest analysis, a researcher might view military recruiting commercials and then record the number of commercials that use the word "honor" or the number of commercials that show the American flag. Context units or latent content is more subtle and requires an analysis of the underlying meaning of the content (Bengtsson, 2016). For latent analysis, we might watch those same military recruitment commercials and, rather than count the number of times a word is used, we might analyze how the commercials appeal to viewers' sense of patriotism. For the fifth step of content analysis, we would develop a coding instrument, pilot test it, and if there are multiple coders, check for interrater reliability. If reliability is poor, we would consider making definitions more specific and provide additional training before proceeding with the full sample. The sixth and final step is data analysis. If the primary focus was on manifest content, the analysis will be quantitative, while analysis of latent content will be qualitative.

Do you always have to have the coding instrument ready to go before you start your research? While it would probably be ideal and save a little time, you could start reviewing material and then work to come up with a list of variables and codes. Fallik and colleagues (2024) studied the content of state hate crimes legislation. They collected all state statutes written during the 2016 legislative session and then conducted a type of analysis called subsumption. In other words, they started by reading the statutes to get a sense of what they contained. Next, the researchers worked to identify common themes and differences. Then, they began the coding process.

Examples of Content Analysis

A colleague and I were curious about state and federal corrections systems' suicide prevention and response policies. First, selecting our unit of analysis was rather easy, as we went with each department. Our second step was collecting the policies. We conducted internet searches and found policies for the Federal Bureau of Prisons and most of the state departments of corrections. For the states that did not have their policies posted on the internet, I reached out to them and requested that they share their policies with me. Document collection was a little tricky. Not every state has a policy with "suicide" in the title. Some states have larger department policies that have the suicide part embedded in there. Other states have very short suicide policies, but then issues related to suicide prevention and response are in additional state policies. For example, a state might have a suicide prevention policy, but suicide prevention training is addressed in a separate "training" policy, while rules regarding how to respond to a suicide are in a "death notification" document, and information about screening for suicidal ideation might be in the "screening and assessment" policy. Third, after collecting everything that we needed, we got to work on operationalizing our variables. To do so, we relied on previous literature and best practice documents published by professional organizations. Fourth, the decision about units of measurement was easy, as we wanted manifest content. Fifth, we made our coding sheet, consisting of a shared Google sheet. We coded each jurisdiction separately and then held weekly meetings to check for interrater reliability. When we finished that, we were ready for the sixth and final step of data analysis. We learned that the suicide prevention and response policies varied a great deal from state to state (Tartaro & Alas, 2024).

Secondary Data Analysis and Official Records

Secondary data analysis is the "reanalysis of data that were originally gathered or compiled for other purposes" (Hagan, 2007, p. 254). There are three broad categories of data that researchers might be able to obtain from organizations or even other researchers. First is raw data known as **primary data sources**. The other two are data that have already undergone some level of analysis by others, including agency reports/official records and datasets generated by other researchers. Both of these are known as **secondary data sources** (Hagan, 2007).

Secondary (Published) Agency Records and Primary (Raw) Data

One of the most frequently used sources of secondary data in criminal justice is the **Inter-university Consortium for Political and Social Research** (ICPSR). ICPSR is a collection of over 800 academic institutions and research organizations, and maintains a data archive of over 400,000 files pertaining to social and behavioral sciences. Specifically, ICPSR maintains 231 collections of data, including datasets in criminal justice, terrorism, and substance use collected by the Bureau of Justice Assistance, Bureau of Justice Statistics, National Institute of Justice, and National Institute on Drug Abuse, among several other agencies (ICPSR, 2026). You should also keep in mind that there are data offered by agencies outside of criminal justice that can still be very relevant to what we study. The US Census Bureau, for example, shares data on births, deaths, marriages, divorces, health information, and demographic characteristics of individuals by location. One of my research interests is suicide, and the Census Bureau offers yearly data on suicides among people living in a particular community. For suicides in prisons and jails, the Bureau of Justice Statistics publishes yearly figures for deaths in custody. One could construct a dataset to study suicides inside and outside of prison and jail just by visiting both agency websites.

Throughout this book, I have discussed several major criminal justice surveys, including the National Crime Victimization Survey, Monitoring the Future, and the National Youth Survey. All make their data available to people who wish to analyze it or combine their figures with other data sources to make new datasets.

Unpublished Agency Reports and Records

Just about every criminal justice and social service agency collects and maintains primary or raw data as part of their regular duties. In earlier chapters, I noted how the majority of law enforcement agencies in the United States participate in the NIBRS data collection efforts. Law enforcement, courts, and corrections agencies often also produce publicly available reports that are displayed on their web pages. Departments of corrections, for example, typically make available reports about the census of each facility, the racial and age breakdown of the incarcerated population, security classifications, programming, and sometimes even recidivism rates.

While organizations write reports and make some of them available to the public, that information typically represents a very small fraction of what they collect each year. Every agency collects data for various reasons. Since I used to work for a state department of corrections, I will use corrections as an example here. Anyone who has ever watched a prison documentary or movie knows that one vital corrections officer duty is counting people. When it is time to count, all other activities stop because the count is fundamental to the security of the institution and the surrounding communities. Officers report each cell block's count to supervisors, who add the numbers to confirm that the facility has accounted for all its residents. The counts are then sent to the central office to confirm that everyone in state custody is where they belong. In addition to the counts, staff make daily notes of every admission, release, transfer, trip to the hospital, furlough, and death. The same procedures apply to halfway houses. Halfway houses and work release staff must account for everyone at the facility, confirm that they arrived at their jobs, and then make sure that they returned to the facility at the end of their shifts. Then there are all the classification forms and risk assessments that are administered. Those data must be properly input and shared with the department's central office. What I mention here is the tip of the proverbial iceberg when it comes to data collection for a state department of corrections. Most of these data are never published or otherwise shared with the general public.

Non-published agency data are only available for research by agency staffers or outside researchers who are able to negotiate access to an agency and its files. If it is possible to get that access, the researcher must then either work with a staff member to retrieve the necessary data or be trained and get the proper access credentials to use the databases independently. A word of warning: you might be surprised at the condition of the files and/or the programs used to store them. Files going back a few decades might be in paper form. The more recent cases will be stored in databases, but some of the government-run systems are quite antiquated and are not at all user-friendly.

Maxfield and Babbie (2012) urge caution when using agency records, as they might better serve as measures of the organization's priorities than actual trends in criminal behavior. Let's consider recidivism data for people on parole. There are two ways that people on parole return to prison. The first is that they commit a new crime while on parole. The second is that they commit a technical violation, which is an act that is not a crime but is a violation of one's parole conditions. Examples of technical violations include violating curfew, associating with other people with criminal records, drinking alcohol, or even having alcohol in one's house. If a state reports that fewer individuals are being sent back to prison for technical violations, that can mean one of two things. The first option is that those being observed have changed their behavior and are abiding by their parole conditions. The second possibility is that the department has modified their supervision practices or adjusted their definition of what constitutes a violation worthy of reincarceration (Berman & Fox, 2016). When the California state government was ordered by the Supreme Court to reduce its prison population in 2011, one target of change was the parole system that sent 70% of people back to prison within three years of release. California then instituted an automated decision-making instrument to guide parole officers in making risk-based decisions (Berman & Fox, 2016). This means that reductions in parole violations leading to incarcerations after the introduction of this new system might have been more of a product of changes to parole officers' decision-making than a reflection of the behavior of those on parole. Still focusing on California, the state witnessed an overall reduction of recidivism, not only for technical violations but also for rearrests. While this was welcome news, and some of it has been attributable to the impact of more available rehabilitation programs, researchers noted that at least some of the decline could be traced to the reclassification of crimes. In 2014, California voters approved Proposition 47, which reclassified some nonviolent crimes, previously considered felonies, to misdemeanors. This change meant that, even when people committed new crimes, they were less likely to be sent back to prison for offenses that were newly classified misdemeanors (Bird et al., 2019). In other words, the state's decision to reclassify crimes likely explained at least some of California's reduced number of incarcerated persons, reincarceration rates, and even crime statistics. While some of the reductions might have been due to less crime, we also must consider the role that the state's change in priorities and reclassification of offenses had on its crime and offending statistics.

What about using official records to measure offending behavior rather than using self-reports? Official records, such as arrest, conviction, incarceration, or juvenile adjudication, are helpful in that they provide exact dates of when each part of criminal case processing occurred. With agency records, there is no worry about having to rely on someone's memory to recall age of first arrest or incarceration (Huizinga & Elliott, 1986). It is important to remember, though, that a good amount of offending occurs without the perpetrators being caught and, without an apprehension, there are simply no official records of the incident. Moffit and associates (2001) studied age of onset of criminal offending and compared research using official records to self-reports. Self-report research generally revealed that the onset of individuals' offending began three to five years prior to age of onset recorded in official records. Not only are official records devoid of information on crimes not known to the police, but Huizinga and Elliott also noted that available police data might lack some important details. There are details about offending that are not available through agency records, such as motive, level of planning, and others involved.

Example of Study Using Agency Records

For years, there has been a narrative that immigrants, particularly the undocumented, are criminals and present a major threat to our society. But what do crime statistics actually tell us? One of the most discussed states when it comes to immigration is Texas, since it shares a large border with Mexico. If illegal immigration were contributing to crime, we would certainly see it in Texas. Light, He, and Robey (2020) were given access to data from the Texas Department of Public Safety. Texas is an ideal setting for this kind of analysis of agency records since the state mandates that all jurisdictions share their criminal history data with the Department of Homeland Security, which then reports the immigration status of everyone in the database back to Texas. The researchers looked at who was arrested for violent, property, and drug crimes as well as traffic violations in Texas from 2012 through 2018. Undocumented individuals were significantly less likely than legal immigrants and even more unlikely than native-born people to have been arrested. A particularly interesting finding was that criminal involvement of undocumented individuals *decreased* around the same time that the national anti-immigration rhetoric increased in the mid-2010s.

Advantages and Disadvantages of Using Secondary Data and Agency Records

There are several advantages to using secondary data, one of which is convenience. I have a very fond memory of the first time I logged into ICPSR and downloaded a dataset. I wanted to study sentencing, and the Bureau of Justice Statistics had a dataset consisting of hundreds of cases and dozens of variables. Just two years earlier, I had spent a lot of time doing field research, including going into noisy jails, standing outside in below-freezing temperatures, staying out on the streets until 2 a.m., and sitting in lots of northern New Jersey traffic to get to where I needed to be to collect data. Because of that, I was particularly excited to sit in my climate-controlled office and download a sizable dataset that required no effort on my part to collect. What made it even more exciting was that, since my university is a member of the ICPSR consortium, the download was free.

An additional advantage is that secondary data provide access to many possibilities for research, and they often allow us to use data collected by very talented, sophisticated researchers. If the data were collected with individuals as the unit of analysis, the information is always de-identified, so there is no concern about needing to take precautions to protect human subjects. Another important advantage is that secondary data or agency records made available for public use have already been cleaned. That means that someone, or multiple people, already went through the dataset and checked for data entry errors. **Cleaning** a dataset is a very time-consuming, mind-numbing task, so being able to do research while skipping that step is a real advantage.

One significant drawback is that, because the data were collected for another purpose, what is there might not match your research needs. Data might not be at the appropriate unit of analysis. UCR and NIBRS data are collected at the city-level, but you might be looking to do research on crime in neighborhoods or even individual streets. Data on your topic might be available, but not for the location you are wishing to study. Since you played no role in the planning or collection of the data, there may be variables that are necessary for your work that are not included in the available data or datasets. If all the desired variables are available, they may not have been operationalized the way you would have preferred.

Another issue to consider is that, while you had no contact with any of the research participants, that may not be the case for the research team that collected the data. Some publicly available datasets are based on observations and surveys, meaning that there might have been contact between the research staff and the participants. That means that participants might have changed their behavior in reaction to being observed, or modified their survey responses out of concern for social desirability or a desire for privacy. In other words, secondary data are not always unobtrusive. Also, while you do not have to worry about harming anyone by reanalyzing de-identified data, it is possible that there were ethics violations during initial data collection (Rainbow, 2024).

When using existing datasets or agency records, you lack any control over the quality of data collection and handling. Most of the available data are good, but keep in mind that mistakes and manipulation do occur from time to time. Remember the examples that I provided in Chapter 5 of police manipulating UCR statistics to place their jurisdictions in a favorable light. Anyone who consulted UCR reports in the 1990s and then utilized Crime Index data from Philadelphia before the data manipulation was exposed used invalid data.

A final disadvantage applies only to unpublished agency records. The data that you obtain from an agency, such as police reports, may not be clean. There may be numerous errors that require you to spend hours, days, or even weeks sifting through to fix. It is not uncommon for researchers to get data from an agency that include dates of prison admission that predate the person's date of birth, misspelled names, and misnumbered prison or jail ID numbers. The latter two are problematic when it is necessary to access databases using incarcerated persons' names or identification numbers to collect additional information for the project.

Simulations

By now, we all know that survey responses may not capture individuals' true behavior, and that we can attempt to address this problem by observing people through fieldwork. Of course, there are two problems. First, the fieldworker's presence may alter the behavior of those being observed. The fieldworker sitting in a car or on a bench nearby might make the potential burglar think twice about breaking into a home at that time and place. One way around this is that we can tail a burglar who is willing to take us on a job, but this is where the second problem arises. The moral, legal, and ethical issues related to tailing people while they plan and then commit crimes make this an absolute "no." Criminologists struggle with the fact that we want to study lots of illegal behavior in progress that we cannot observe. There are also some also legal activities of interest that happen out of our view. One that immediately comes to mind is jury decision-making. No one besides jury members is allowed in the deliberation room for any reason.

One way to witness the aforementioned behaviors safely is to use **simulations** that mimic situations that we cannot necessarily observe ourselves. Simulations are not new to the social sciences. Two famous studies are the **Obedience to Authority Study** and the Stanford Prison Experiment, although both were criticized for their ethical treatment of participants. For a recap of the Stanford Prison Experiment, see Chapter 3. Following the Nazi atrocities in World War II, Stanley Milgram (1974) designed the Obedience to Authority Study, as he was interested the common defense of "I was just following orders" that Nazis used to justify torturing and murdering millions of people. He wanted to see how far people would be willing to go when someone in authority ordered them to harm another person. Of course, Milgram could not physically harm anyone, so he made research participants think that they were administering electric shocks to someone else. The research participant would be a "teacher" who would ask the "learner" to memorize and recite a series of words. If the learner was incorrect or failed to answer, the teacher would administer shocks of increasing intensity. Eventually, the learner would scream, beg for help, and then eventually he would be silent, suggesting that he passed out or even died. The research participants were unaware that the learner was a member of the research team who was not being harmed in any way. What Milgram did succeed in doing was getting a firsthand view of how far people would go when ordered to harm a stranger. It is unlikely that the findings would have been the same had he attempted to study this through a survey. Milgram was criticized for the psychological distress he caused the research participants who thought they might be seriously harming another individual, and it would be difficult to persuade a modern-day IRB to allow a complete replication of this project to proceed today.

Modern simulation techniques give us the ability to observe human behavior while taking fewer ethical risks. What if we could recreate Milgram's study, but with participants being informed that they would be working with a computerized "person" who would receive the shocks for poor performance? The immediate concern here is validity. If people know that they are interacting with a computer, will they react the same way as people who participated in the original Milgram study? Slater and colleagues (2006) sought to measure individuals' reactions when participating in Milgram's study, but with a computer "learner" who would get the shocks. Instead of being a real person, the computerized learner would either communicate with the research participant via text (no sight or sound) or appear on a computer screen in earshot and within view of the research participant. The participants who only had contact with the learner through text did not seem to be as emotionally or physically impacted by stress. They were less likely to withdraw from the study, less likely to report afterward that they were tempted to quit, and less likely to delay providing the shock after receiving an incorrect answer or no response. The researchers also tested skin conductance levels and skin conductance responses of the two groups and found significant differences, suggesting higher levels of stress among those who could see and hear the computerized learner. These results suggest that such simulations can mimic realistic scenarios and have high validity.

There have been studies where researchers have asked people involved in criminal activity about their decision-making, including how they choose houses or businesses to target and how they conduct burglaries and robberies, but we cannot then watch real burglaries take place. Nee et al. (2015) developed a simulation method to allow for observation in a legal and ethical way. First, the researchers were in a rare circumstance in that they had access to a building that they could decorate as a home. A small sample of people with a history of committing burglaries and a comparison group of graduate students entered the house individually using any entrance of their choosing, and they touched anything that they wished to steal. A short time later, each participant was asked to view a computer simulation of the same house. Now, their avatars were free to decide how to enter (using a mouse this time), and they then clicked on any item that they planned to "steal." Results indicated that both groups took similar approaches to the "burglaries" when they were faced with a real house and a simulated house. This suggests that studying simulated burglaries could provide valid information about offender decision-making. This is good news, because the vast majority of researchers cannot afford to get access to a building that they can hold on to for the purpose of simulating burglaries, but they can likely pay for computer software.

Van Gelder, Otte, and Luciano (2014) argue that virtual reality and other computer simulations hold great promise, as they allow for levels of interactivity and immersion that are not possible with surveys and vignettes. They do caution that there are potential validity issues, in that these simulations are artificial. The extent to which simulations are successful at mimicking real life depends on people's willingness to suspend disbelief and imagine being in the situation that is the subject of the simulation. Based on Slater et al.'s (2006) results simulating Milgram's study, it does appear that simulations are promising in that they can generate some of the stress and realism similar to previous studies conducted with humans. The Dutch National Police have had some success using virtual reality to simulate stressful scenarios for training purposes. While officers using the technology did experience stress during the scenarios, such training was hampered by the inability to integrate running and having to quickly put on protective gear. Those are typical elements of real policing-related emergencies that often enhance stress levels during training (Kleygrewe et al., 2024).

The aforementioned examples certainly include at least a little researcher-participant interaction. In that sense, these are not entirely unobtrusive measures. The interaction here is different, in that there are no ethical concerns about researchers encouraging and witnessing crimes, nor are they putting people in a position to harm (or think they are harming) others.

Crime Mapping

Crime mapping research may require researchers to venture out into the field, but it may not be necessary for every study. This technique is just as it sounds: We map locations of crimes or other items of interest with the intent of finding patterns. Crime mapping has been around for almost 200 years, with the earliest example involving the use of maps to assess the relationship between residents' education level and crime in France (Hunt, 2019). Of course, we have modernized since then and now use sophisticated software to generate and mark maps. Some modern theories of crime emphasize the importance of target location and site selection. The routine activities perspective suggests that crime is likely to occur if there is a convergence of a suitable target, a motivated person to commit the crime, and a lack of a capable guardian in time and space (Cohen & Felson, 1979). Brantingham and Brantingham (1981) discussed environmental criminology and argued that people generally travel to and from home, work, and play, and that they are likely to find criminal opportunities in those areas or en route to them. Research on crime and place has taught us that crime is not randomly distributed, so we can maximize criminal justice resources and reduce crime by targeting locations where crimes occur the most often (Weisburd, 2015).

Crime mapping can help us learn a lot about offending patterns. In the previous chapter, I discussed some fieldwork that I did with a colleague. After obtaining police reports on automobile thefts from the Atlantic City, New Jersey, police department, we visited each site to measure several environmental characteristics with the hope of learning which types of factors were common for areas with multiple thefts (Levy & Tartaro, 2010). Figure 11.1 shows a map from our analysis.

Today, many police departments use tactics that involve consideration of spatial distribution of crime, including problem-oriented-policing, hot spots policing, and Compstat (Hunt, 2019).

Predictive policing is a combination of existing police practices, including problem-oriented and intelligence-led policing, along with crime mapping to help police be more proactive in

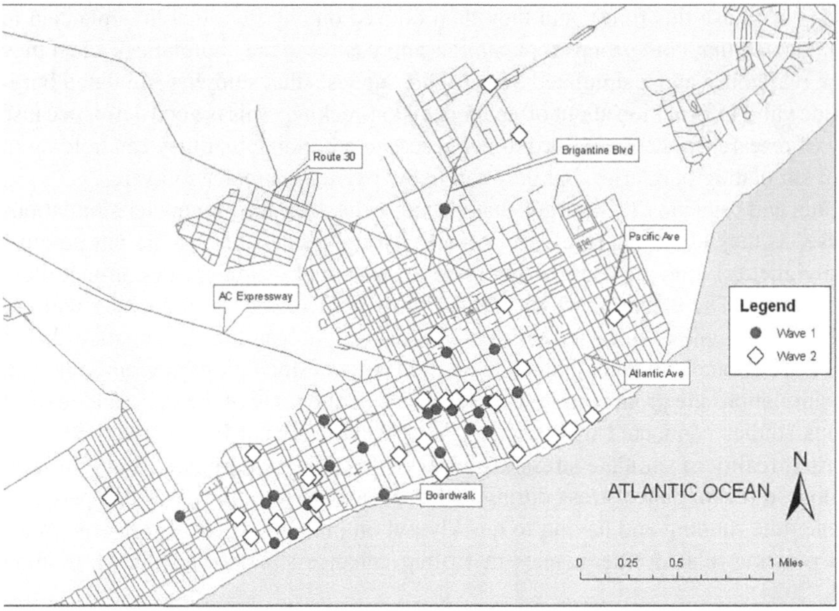

Figure 11.1 Map of auto thefts in Atlantic City, NJ, during two different waves of data collection

Source: Levy, M. P. & **Tartaro, C.** (2010). Repeat victimization: A study of auto theft in Atlantic City using the W.A.L.L.S. variables to measure environmental indicators. *Criminal Justice Policy Review*, 21(3), 296–318. DOI: 10.1177/0887403409350190

preventing crime. The National Institute of Justice defines **predictive policing** as "taking data from disparate sources, analyzing them and then using results to anticipate, prevent and respond more effectively to future crime" (Pearsall, 2010, p. 16). The goal is to anticipate crime spikes in local areas and then establish prevention plans. For example, Richmond, Virginia, had a problem with random gunfire on New Year's Eve. In the early 2000s, the police department mapped gunshot incidents from previous years so that they could anticipate the time and location of gunfire for the upcoming holiday. By using these data to focus enforcement on New Year's Eve 2003, they helped to reduce random gunfire by 50%. Kennedy, Kaplan, and Duwe (2022) used crime mapping techniques to study convenience store robberies. They worked with an urban police department to develop an officer deployment strategy for these locations, and this resulted in a 63% reduction of robberies in four months.

While police were the first branch of the criminal justice system to embrace crime mapping, the judiciary and corrections systems have also adopted mapping to both prevent crimes and better allocate resources. Specifically, corrections departments and probation and parole offices are using mapping to identify violence hot spots inside institutions, direct people on probation or parole to services available near their homes and jobs, and assign officers by geographic location (Karuppannan, 2005).

Crime mapping can be a very powerful tool to help us gain a better understanding of how various blocks and neighborhoods are viewed by people thinking about committing a crime. Of course, the process of conducting crime mapping is not always smooth, and there are issues that can make the work difficult and possibly unreliable. The mapping will only be as good as our data. To generate maps, analysts often rely on agency records, such as police calls for service or crime reports. By now, you should be well acquainted with the pitfalls of using police records. To quickly review, police crime data are better indicators of law enforcement priorities than actual incidents of crime in a particular jurisdiction. Police calls for service data are better in that they involve calls from residents and bystanders and lack the filtering that comes with police discretion at the scene or any other reclassifications of the incident that might occur. Boba (2001) cautioned that policy or law changes can result from our analysis, so we must be careful and fully understand all the nuances of the data. Finally, we must always remember that not all crimes are reported to the police, so reliance on official records will result in undercounting of several types of crime.

An additional potential data problem is the condition of the data. Criminal justice agencies might have data in formats that are not easily transferable to the analysts (Boba, 2001). As I mentioned earlier in this chapter, some of the government databases are quite antiquated and are not user-friendly, so it may be difficult for agencies to capture and then transfer data to researchers. Additionally, the data might be "dirty" and require a good deal of cleaning. Reports that include addresses must have the full addresses, with proper spelling, for that information to be input into software for mapping. If researchers get police reports that lack addresses (as many do) and instead just include landmarks, intersections, or nicknames for areas, the researchers will have to search for each address to input it into the mapping software. I learned this the hard way when working with a local police department along the Atlantic coast. This city has a long boardwalk, and instead of inputting addresses, officers would often just write "Boardwalk" or "wood" (since the boardwalk is made of wood planks). Researchers who plan to do crime mapping using agency data would be well advised to build in a good bit of "data cleaning" time into their research plans and to ask police supervisors to remind officers to use full addresses in their reports.

Systematic Review and Meta-analysis

One very frustrating part about reviewing available research is that there might be multiple studies, some of which find a positive relationship between X and Y, some of which report a negative relationship between the two variables, and then some that find no relationship between X and Y. For people interested in institutional corrections, this was the case for research on the association between prison and jail crowding and institutional violence. The common assumption has been that there is a positive relationship between the two, meaning that increased crowding is associated with increased violence. However, with different researchers reporting so many different findings, it was very difficult for corrections administrators and policymakers to make much sense of research. This is the problem that systematic reviews and meta-analyses are designed to address. Researchers who conduct systematic reviews and meta-analyses seek to learn, overall, what a large body of scholarship tells us about a particular topic. The two approaches differ in the extent of the statistical analysis that they conduct. **Systematic reviews** involve collection and summarization of empirical evidence that meets prespecified inclusion criteria, whereas a **meta-analysis** includes the work of a systematic review but applies statistical techniques to summarize the research findings (Centre for Cognitive Ageing and Cognitive Epidemiology, n.d.). Systematic reviews differ from literature reviews or reviews of research that you have probably already conducted for papers in other classes. What sets systematic reviews apart is the rigor and systematic approach to searching for and reviewing the existing literature (Joanna Briggs Institute, 2001). Returning to the issue of crowding in correctional facilities and violence, Franklin, Franklin, and Pratt (2006) conducted a meta-analysis on the existing crowding and violence research. They found that it was not crowding that predicted violence in prisons and jails but the concentration of certain types of people in institutions, specifically young males, that predicted violence.

If done properly, systematic reviews, and especially meta-analyses, can be very helpful in advancing our knowledge of criminal justice. Figure 11.2 shows a hierarchy of evidence pyramid that helps us understand how research designs are generally ranked. As you can see, systematic reviews and meta-analyses are at the top of the pyramid. These types of analyses are currently

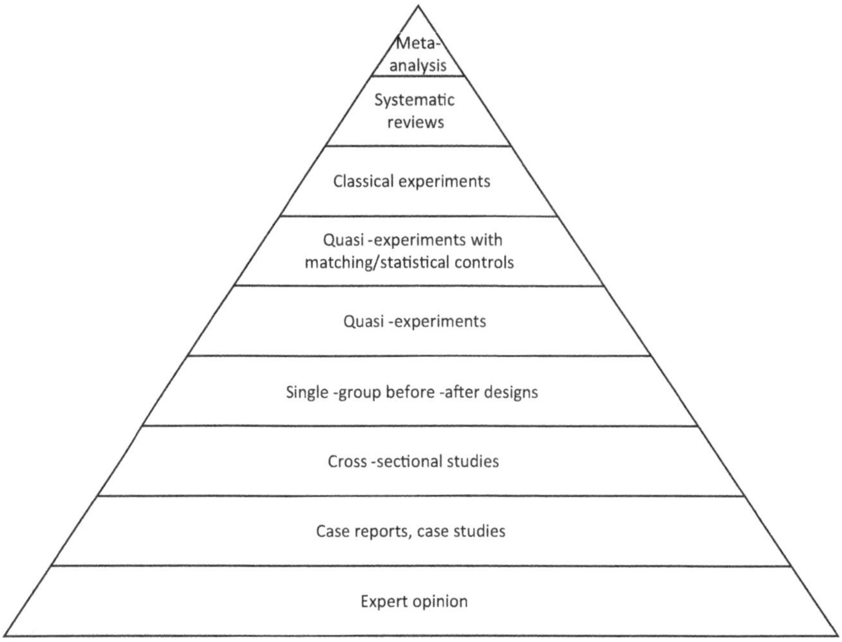

Figure 11.2 Research pyramid for social sciences

Source: Oxford Centre for Evidence-Based Medicine (2009). *Levels of Evidence.* Centre for Evidence-Based Medicine. www.cebm.ox.ac.uk/resources/levels-of-evidence/oxford-centre-for-evidence-based-medicine-levels-of-evidence-march-2009

being used to educate researchers, practitioners, and policymakers on what works and what does not in criminal justice.

There are several steps involved in systematic reviews and meta-analyses. As with all studies, the first step is to identify a research question. Second, researchers must decide on their inclusion and exclusion criteria that they will use to select studies for analysis. One criteria decision that needs to be made has to do with quality of the research design. As we have learned already, not all designs are created equal. A possible useful tool to consider during this step is the **Maryland Scientific Methods Scale** (SMS), which is a five-point scale, introduced by Farrington, Gottfredson, Sherman, and Welsh (2002), that measures the quality of research methodologies. Level 1 includes cross-sectional designs that might establish a correlation between a crime prevention program and crime reduction. Research falling into this category fails to address the question of time order between X and Y and to fails rule out many possible threats to internal validity. Level 2 includes studies that do establish time order between X and Y by measuring crime before and after the introduction of some sort of intervention. One-group before-after designs fall into this category, but they still leave open the possibility of several threats to internal validity. Level 3 studies are considered by many researchers, including the developers of the SMS, to be the minimum level that is adequate for drawing conclusions. These are studies that include both a before-after design and an experimental and comparison group. In other words, they are quasi-experiments. Because there is no random selection into the two groups, there is still the possibility of some threats to validity, such as regression to the mean and selection effects. Level 4 studies include quasi-experiments that also control for factors that could influence variation in the dependent variable. Finally, level 5 studies are classical experiments with a sufficiently large sample size of participants randomly assigned to experimental and control groups.

Braga, Schnell, and Welsh (2024) collected empirical research on types policing meant to combat disorder. Their goal was to compare community-oriented problem-solving approaches characterized by police working with the community to identify and address problems to aggressive order maintenance policing, where there is little cooperation with the community and police rely on increasing misdemeanor arrests, writing summonses, and stopping and questioning pedestrians. The researchers decided that the minimally acceptable research design for studies to be included in their analysis was quasi-experiments.

You might be wondering if it is necessary to be so selective with research designs when deciding on studies to be included in systematic reviews and meta-analyses. It is actually quite important. Less rigorous research designs are more likely to produce desirable outcomes than the more rigorous designs (Chin et al., 2023). In other words, research utilizing less rigorous designs is more likely to generate support for research hypotheses. While I am sure that none of us hold anything against researchers and want them to be happy, it is more important that the results they disseminate are accurate reflections of what is happening in the world.

The third step in this type of research is to conduct an exhaustive literature search and to document all the steps taken in that search. Before you start, you should decide on a series of key words and databases that you will use. Once you start the search and identify some studies for potential inclusion, you might also want to review the bibliographies of those studies to find more research for consideration. Fourth, once you have gathered an initial sample of studies, the next step is to do a preliminary review and read the abstracts of each article. Just reading the title and abstract will allow you to quickly disqualify a substantial number of articles. Fifth, once the sample size is smaller, that is the time to read all the studies carefully, coding the data that you will need for your analysis, and inputting that into a spreadsheet or statistical software package. Sixth, you are ready to do whatever type of analysis you plan to do. If it is a systematic review, the analysis might simply be tallying results of studies, also known as ballot counting.

Madson, Villarosa-Hurlcoker, Schumacher, Williams, and Gauthier (2019) conducted a systematic review of motivational interview training for substance use treatment professionals. They provided readers with summaries of the research, including the percentage of studies that were randomized control trials, the components of the treatment programs, and the percentages of each study that included various components (e.g., description of training methods, coaching and evaluation of motivational interviewing skills of participants).

I previously mentioned Braga et al.'s (2024) research on disorder policing. They had multiple criteria for study inclusion. First, studies had to evaluate a policing program that aimed to reduce crime through combating disorder in the communities. Examples of disorder were trash left on the street, abandoned buildings, visible drug dealing, visible solicitation for sex work, panhandling or loitering, and overgrown vegetation and graffiti. Second, police activities needed to include either community problem-oriented policing or aggressive order maintenance programs that were designed to address disorder. Third, as was noted earlier, all studies had to have a comparison or control group, and they needed to have a before-after component. In other words, only quasi- or classical experiments were included. Fourth, the units of analysis for each study had to be areas within a single city. Fifth, all outcome measures had to be recorded with official records, such as police incident reports, 911 calls, or arrests. These criteria ensured that Braga and colleagues were able to collect high-quality evaluations that took place within single cities and measured similar types of police interventions to address disorder. After analyzing 56 eligible studies, the researchers concluded that community-oriented problem-solving approaches are substantially better at reducing crime than aggressive order maintenance policing.

Of course, systematic reviews and meta-analyses are only as good as the studies that they include. The extent to which studies are screened for methodological rigor is important, as it could impact the validity and reliability of the results. A potential weakness of meta-analyses could result from overreliance on published studies. It should be of no surprise that published studies are the easiest to find. The problem is that there is the potential for publication bias. **Publication bias** is the tendency for studies that find support for the research hypothesis, or positive findings, to have a greater chance of being accepted for publication than studies that find no support (Joanna Briggs Institute, 2001). Mitchell, Wilson, and MacKenzie (2012) found that published studies of incarceration-based drug treatment programs included evaluations of programs that were more effective than those appearing in unpublished studies. Researchers should be aware of the potential for publication bias and try to include unpublished studies in their analysis. One way to find such work is to contact the authors who frequently publish on the topic of interest to ask for their assistance in identifying unpublished studies (Braga et al., 2015; 2024). Another technique is to search gray literature databases (Wong et al., 2019). **Gray literature** consists of work that has not been formally published in sources such as books or journals. Some university libraries maintain gray literature databases. The Rutgers University Don Gottfredson Library of Criminal Justice is one of them. Their gray literature database includes working papers, conference proceedings, technical reports, online dissertations, and government and agency reports (Rutgers University, n.d.). There are also statistical techniques that researchers can use to determine whether publication bias is impacting their results (Jalain et al., 2024; Pirelli, Gottdiener, & Zapf, 2011).

My description of systematic reviews and meta-analyses was very basic, and there is a lot more that goes into this type of work. If you are interested in learning more, the **Preferred Reporting Items for Systematic Reviews and Meta-Analyses (PRISMA)** statement is an excellent reference. Many systematic reviews and meta-analyses follow the PRISMA 27-item checklist that ensures researchers are transparent about how they conducted their reviews and what they found. PRISMA was originally written in 2009, but the statement was updated in 2020 to include guidance to reflect advances in research (Page et al., 2021).

Summary

In this chapter, I introduced several unobtrusive, or at least less obtrusive, ways to study crime. Content analysis gives us an opportunity to study how crime is portrayed in various types of media content, such as "true crime" documentaries, fictionalized crime shows, and newspaper articles. We can also use content analysis to study the media's reaction to types of crime, victims, and offenders. There is no human interaction necessary, as the steps involved in this research are aimed at setting up rules for a systematic identification of sources; collecting data through reading, listening, or watching; and then evaluating the material through a pre-identified analysis plan.

Secondary data analysis and analysis of agency records saves researchers from having to collect their own data. Instead, researchers obtain datasets created by others, use publicly available figures from government or private agencies, or access nonpublic agency records. Secondary analysis gives individual researchers access to data that they might not otherwise have the time or money to collect themselves. While datasets available for download from groups such as ICPSR are generally the product of high-quality work and are already cleaned, agency records might not be as user-friendly and might contain errors and, in rare instances, outright manipulation.

There are some activities that are difficult for us to observe due to their infrequency, the private nature of the actions, or ethical limitations of what researchers are permitted to do and witness. Simulations give us a way to make observations by creating scenarios in a safe laboratory setting. Researchers can simulate household burglaries, potentially fight-inducing scenarios in bars and restaurants, and jury deliberations. Validity is a potential problem, however, if participants lack full engagement and do not buy into the scenario.

Crime mapping has been a recognized tool for studying crime, public health problems, environmental disasters, and many other problems for centuries. Police were the first branch of the criminal justice system to appreciate and utilize mapping to investigate crime patterns and make apprehensions, but mapping is now being used in all branches of the system to track people and service usage patterns as well as to allocate resources.

Systematic reviews and meta-analyses are helping us learn about what works in criminal justice. These studies help us sift through large bodies of research and inform us about the trends in research on that topic. An important aspect of this research is that they take into consideration the methodological rigor of each of the individual studies included in their reviews.

Key Terms

Content analysis	Manifest content	Latent content
Secondary data analysis	Primary data sources	Secondary data sources
Inter-university Consortium for Political and Social Research (ICPSR)	Cleaning	Simulation
Obedience to Authority Study	Crime mapping	Predictive policing
Systematic review	Meta-analysis	Maryland Scientific Methods Scale (SMS)
Publication bias	Gray literature	Preferred Reporting Items for Systematic reviews and Meta-Analysis (PRISMA)

Discussion Questions

1. What are the advantages and disadvantages of conducting secondary data analysis?
2. What are the similarities and differences of systematic reviews and meta-analysis?
3. Explain the ways that content analysis of television or streaming shows differs from our regular viewing.
4. Why are simulations susceptible to threats to validity?

References

Bengtsson, M. (2016). How to plan and perform a qualitative study using content analysis. *NursingPlus Open, 2,* 8–14.

Berman, G., & Fox, A. (2016). *Trial and error in criminal justice reform: Learning from failure (revised edition).* The Urban Institute Press.

Bird, M., Goss, J., & Nguyen, V. (2019). *Recidivism of felony offenders in California.* Public Policy Institute of California.

Boba, R. (2001). *Introductory guide to crime analysis and mapping.* Office of Community Oriented Policing Services.

Braga, A. A., Schell, C., & Welsh, B. C. (2024). Disorder policing to reduce crime: An updated systematic review and meta-analysis. *Criminology & Public Policy, 23*(3), 745–775.

Braga, A. A., Welsh, B. C., & Schnell, C. (2015). Can policing disorder reduce crime? Asystematic review and meta-analysis. *Journal of Research in Crime and Delinquency, 52*(4), 567–588.https://doi.org/10.1177/0022427815576576

Brantingham, P. J., & Brantingham, P. L. (1981). *Environmental criminology.* Sage Publications.

Centre for Cognitive Ageing and Cognitive Epidemiology. (n.d.). *Systematic reviews and meta-analyses: A guide.* University of Edinburgh Centre for Cognitive Ageing and Cognitive Epidemiology.

Chin, J. M., Pickett, J. T., Vazire, S., & Holcombe, A. O. (2023). Questionable research practices and open science in quantitative criminology. *Journal of Quantitative Criminology, 39*(1), 21–51. https://doi.org/10.1007/s10940-021-09525-6

Cohen, L. E., & Felson, M. (1979). Social change and crime rate trends: A routine activity approach. *American Sociological Review, 44*(4): 588–608. https://doi.org/10.2307/2094589

Durham, A. M., Elrod, H. P., & Kinkade, P. T. (1995). Images of crime and justice: Murder and the "true crime" genre. *Journal of Criminal Justice, 23*(2), 143–152.

Fallik, S. W., Gardner, S. E., Remillard, A., Venuto, T., Atkin-Plunk, C. A., & Dobrin, A. (2024). Defining hate: A content analysis of state hate crime legislation in the United States of America. *Victims & Offenders, 19*(3), 371–394. https://doi.org/10.1080/15564886.2022.2140729

Farrington. D. P., Gottfredson, D. C., Sherman, L. W., & Welsh, B. C. (2002). The Maryland scientific methods scale. In L. W. Sherman, D. P. Farrington, B. C. Welsh, & D. L. MacKenzie (Eds.), *Evidence-based crime prevention* (pp. 13–22). Routledge.

Franklin, T. W., Franklin, C. A., & Pratt, T. C. (2006). Examining the empirical relationship between prison crowding and inmate misconduct: A meta-analysis of conflicting research results. *Journal of Criminal Justice, 34*(4), 401–412. https://doi.org/10.1016/j.jcrimjus.2006.05.006

Hagan, F. (2007). *Essentials of research methods in criminal justice and criminology* (2nd ed.). Pearson.

Huizinga, D., & Elliott, D. S. (1986). Reassessing the reliability and validity of self-report delinquency measures. *Journal of Quantitative Criminology, 2*(4), 293–327.

Hunt, J. (2019). *From crime mapping to crime forecasting: The evaluation of place-based policing.* National Institute of Justice.

Inter-university Consortium for Political and Social Research (2026). *About IPCSR.* Institute for Social Research. www.icpsr.umich.edu/sites/icpsr/about

Jalain, C. I., Lucas, P. A., & Higgins, G. E. (2024). Assessing the effectiveness of mental health courts in reducing recidivism: A systematic review with meta-analysis. *Justice Evaluation Journal, 7*(2), 212 – 230 https://doi/full/10.1080/24751979.2024.2373245

Joanna Briggs Institute for Evidence Based Nursing and Midwifery. (2001). *Changing practice: Evidence based practice information sheets for health professionals* (Supplement 1). Joanna Briggs Institute.

Karuppannan, J. (2005). Mapping and corrections management of offenders with geographic information systems. *Corrections Compendium, 30*(1), 1–10.

Kassarjian, H. H. (1977). Content analysis in consumer research. *Journal of Consumer Research, 4*, 8–17.

Kennedy, L. W., Caplan, J. M., & Drawve, G. (2022). Data-informed crime prevention at convenience stores in Atlantic City. *Police Practice and Research, 23*(2), 125–142. https://doi.org/10.1080/15614263.2021.1917399

Kleygrewe, L., Hutter, R. I. V., Koedijk, M., & Oudejans, R. R. D. (2024). Virtual reality training for police officers: A comparison of training responses in VR and real-life training. *Police Practice and Research, 25*(1), 18–37. https://doi.org/10.1080/15614263.2023.2176307

Levy, M. P., & Tartaro, C. (2010). Repeat victimization: A study of auto theft in Atlantic City using the W.A.L.L.S. variables to measure environmental indicators. *Criminal Justice Policy Review, 21*(3), 296–318. https://doi.org/10.1177/0887403409350190

Light, M. T., He, J., & Robey, J. P. (2020). Comparing crime rates between undocumented immigrants, legal immigrants, and native-born US citizens in Texas. *PNAS, 117*(51), 32340–32347. https://doi.org/10.1073/pnas.2014704117

Madson, M. B., Villarosa-Hurlocker, M. C., Schumacher, J. A., Williams, D. C., & Gauthier, J. M. (2019). Motivational interviewing training of substance use treatment professionals: A systematic review. *Substance Abuse, 40*(1), 43–51. https://doi.org/10.1080/08897077.2018.1475319

Maxfield, M. G., & Babbie, E. (2012). *Basics of research methods for criminal justice and criminology* (3rd ed.). Thomson Wadsworth.

Milgram, S. (1974). *Obedience to authority: An experimental view.* Harper.

Mitchell, O., Wilson, D. B., & MacKenzie, D. L. (2012). The effectiveness of incarceration-based drug treatment on criminal behavior: A systematic review. *Campbell Systematic Reviews, 18.* https://doi.org/10.4073/csr.2012.18

Moffitt, T., Caspi, A., Rutter, M., & Silva, P. A. (2001). *Sex differences in antisocial behavior.* Cambridge University Press.

Nee, C., White, M., Woolford, K., Pascu, T., Barker, L., & Wainwright, L. (2015). New methods for examining expertise in burglars in natural and simulated environments: Preliminary findings. *Psychology, Crime, & Law, 21*(5), 507–513.

Page, M. J., McKenzie, J. E., Bossuyt, P. M., Boutron, I., Hoffmann, T. C., Mulrow, C. D., Shamseer, L., Tetzlaff, J. M., Aki, E. A., Brennan, S. E., Chou, R., Glanville, J., Grimshaw, J. M., Hróbjartsson, A., Lalu, M. M., Li, T., Loder, E. L., Mayo-Wilson, E., McDonald, S. … Moher, D. (2021). The PRISMA 2020 statement: An updated guideline for reporting systematic reviews. *BMJ (Clinical Research ed.), 372*, n71. https://doi.org/10.1136/bmj.n71

Pearsall, B. (2010). Predictive policing: The future of law enforcement? *NIJ Journal, 266,* 16–19.

Pirelli, G., Gottdiener, W. H., & Zapf (2011). A meta-analytic review of competency to standtrial research. *Psychology, Public Policy, and Law, 17*(1), 1–53.

Prasad, B. D. (2008). Content analysis: A method in social science research. In D. K. Lal Das &V. Bhaskaran (Eds.), *Research Methods for Social Work* (pp. 173–193). Rawat Publications.
Rainbow, J. A. (2024). *Researching prisons.* Routledge.
Rutgers University. (n.d.). *Criminal justice library.* Rutgers University. http://library.law.rutgers.edu/criminal-justice-library
Slater, M., Antley, A., Davison, A., Swapp, D., Guger, C., Barker, C., Pistrang, N., & Sanchez-Vive, M. V. (2006). A virtual reprise of the Stanley Milgram obedience experiments. *PLoS One, 8*(1), e52–66. https://doi.org/10.1371/journal.pone.0052766
Tartaro, C., & Alas, E. (2024). Elements of state and federal prison suicide prevention and response policies. *Criminal Justice Policy Review, 35*(2), 85–110. https://doi.org/10.1177/08874034241227885
Van Gelder, J., Otte, M., & Luciano, E. C. (2014). Using virtual reality in criminological research. *Crime Science, 3*, 10–22. https://doi.org/10.1186/s40163-014-0010-5
Weisburd, D. (2015). The 2014 Sutherland address: The law of crime concentration and the criminology of place. *Criminology, 53*(2), 133–157.
Wong, J. S., Bouchard, J., Lee, C., & Gushue, K. (2019). Examining the effects of day reporting centers on recidivism: A meta-analysis. *Journal of Offender Rehabilitation, 58*(3), 240–260.

Reading 11.1 An Analysis of Motivating Factors in 1,725 Worldwide Cases of Mass Murder between 1900-2019

When researchers approach the topic of mass murderers and their psychological conditions and motivations, they have limited options for data collection. The UCR and NIBRS do not have many details about motivation or the perpetrators' psychiatric history, and the NCVS does not collect victimization data on murders. While it might have been possible for Brucato et al. (2023) to search for people convicted of mass murder in prison, gain permission to conduct interviews with them, and travel the country to visit them in prison, it is unlikely that it would have been financially feasible to do so. Also, we cannot interview suspects who died at the scene or were killed while being apprehended, so the interview option would require researchers to reduce their sample size by eliminating deceased individuals from their analysis. The best option was to use existing materials to do a content analysis on the killers' motivations and psychiatric conditions.

An Analysis of Motivating Factors in 1,725 Worldwide Cases of Mass Murder between 1900-2019

Gary Brucato, Hannah Hesson, Gabriella Dishy, Kathryn Lee, Tyler Pia, Faizan Syed, Alexandra Villalobos, R. Tyler Rogers, Thomas Corbeil, Michael H. Stone, Jeffrey A. Lieberman, Paul S. Appelbaum, and Ragy R. Girgis

Introduction

Mass murders, which we have previously defined as three or more individuals killed in one event in a single setting, without a cooling-off period (Brucato et al., 2021), have garnered great public and academic attention. This has particularly been true for those involving firearms and especially in the United States, where mass shootings have proved increasingly prevalent and deadly in the current millennium (Follman et al., 2020; Peterson & Densley, 2020). With an eye to how such tragic events might be prevented, there has been much focus on the question of what motivates these attacks, often examining the role of mental illness (McGinty et al., 2014; Parks et al., 2019). Sorely-needed research has been limited, however, in two notable respects: first, the proportion of mass-shooting events associated with mental illness varies widely across studies, depending, in part, on how *mental illness* is defined. Remarkably, Parks et al. (2019) noted mental illness rates ranging from 4.7% to 78% across studies of mass-shooters. In a previous report from our group (Brucato et al., 2021), examining mass murderers who employed any means, we provided separate rates of psychotic symptoms (11%), depressive symptoms (10%), personality disorders (5%), neurological conditions (1%), post-traumatic stress symptoms (<1%), bipolar disorder or mania symptoms (<1%), low I.Q. (<1%), autism spectrum disorder symptoms (<1%), anxiety disorder (excluding post-traumatic stress disorder) symptoms (<1%), and other psychiatric symptoms (<1%) among perpetrators. Psychotic symptoms (i.e. delusions, hallucinations and/or disorganized thought), though uncommon, overall, were found to be even less prevalent to a significant extent among mass shooters than among mass murderers who did not employ firearms.

A second limitation involves the challenge of how to optimally categorize the motivating factors precipitating mass murders, moving beyond frank psychiatric illness. Such efforts aim to gain insight into the complex ways in which mental state, personality structure, personal morality, culture, sociocultural factors, and life circumstances intersect among such individuals at the times of their attacks.

We sought to categorize our sample of 1,725 mass murders with the aim of better understanding the roles of severe mental illness, involving psychotic symptoms; criminal objectives; and other motivational factors (e.g. acute, severe emotional upset following adverse life events).

Methods

We examined 1,725 worldwide cases of mass murder, which occurred between 1900–2019, included in the Columbia Mass Murder Database (CMMD), based on extensive review of English-language databases of murderers and mass murderers publicly available in print and online. We used the Congressional definition of mass murder (i.e. three or more fatalities) (Douglas et al., 2012; Krouse & Richardson, 2015). We exclusively included *personal-cause* cases, excluding those associated with war, state- or group-sponsored terrorism, gang activity, or organized crime. We collected perpetrator names and incidents from academic, governmental/public (e.g. Everytown for Gun Safety (2020)), and lay/popular (e.g. Amok Fandom list) sources, though all information in our database was obtained from primary sources and reports. The methods involved in the creation of the database, including search terms, the databases and sources used, and how all data were coded, have previously been described in detail (Brucato et al., 2021). Note that the sample included 409 perpetrators who might be better categorized as *spree killers*, due to having killed two (three for CMMD analyses) or more people in more than one location or at more than one point in time, with no cooling-off period (which was defined as killing across one week or less) between murders. The database excluded 1,571 additional perpetrators who were considered for possible inclusion, but who committed two episodes of murder with any victim count more than seven days apart, irrespective of any connections between murders. Persons best termed *serial killers*, due to a cooling-off period between killings, which we defined as a week or more, would fall into this exclusionary category.

To identify motivating factors, the apparent motivations in the first 300 cases of mass murder prepared for the database were examined, based on two or more English-language media primary sources. The first step in this process utilized the motivating factors identified by two of the authors of the present article (G.B., M.H.S.) and their colleagues, in an unrelated study (Petreca et al., 2020). Their categories included *practical/secondary gain*, *excess emotionality*, *revenge*, *sadism*, *group-cause*, *sexual*, and *mental health-related/psychotic*. These motivational categories served as a basic framework for the current study. We modified and developed the categories empirically as cases were reviewed, and clear, overarching patterns emerged. The resulting categories we employed, which have been fully described and distinguished, with examples, in the Supplement, were: (1) *Self-Survival Objectives*; (2) *Criminal Objectives*; (3) *Personal Religious or Political Beliefs*; (4) *Psychosis or Other Severe Psychiatric Disturbance*; (5) *Severe Emotional Upset*, divided into the nine subcategories of: despair or extreme sadness over life event(s); disgruntled employee; disgruntled student; family/marital/custody dispute; overwhelming and impulsive anger; revenge for bullying; romantic rejection or loss/severe jealousy; social/peer rejection; or a specific non-romantic grudge; (6) *Psychopathic or Sadistic Traits*; (7) *Narcissistic Traits*; (8) *Schizoid-Autistic Detachment*; (9) *Disorganization-Motivated*, subdivided into cases involving psychosis, intellectual or cognitive impairment, or severe psychiatric disturbance, and those associated with drug or alcohol intoxication; and (10) *Unknown/No Determinable Motive*.

Based on this typology, as the full list of incidents included in the CMMD was amassed, the first (G.B.) and senior (R.G.) authors, a clinical psychologist and psychiatrist, respectively, divided the cases and reviewed available English-language sources for information regarding motivating factors. Each rater then reviewed the other's designations. Wherever there was disparity between the categories selected by the raters, cases were reviewed and discussed, until there was agreement regarding the most appropriate designations. Furthermore, for the following variables, a code of 'Yes' was only applied in cases wherein at least one primary source confirmed the presence of the variable (i.e. all others would be coded 'no'): completed suicide at the scene; perpetrator injured or killed at the scene; history of psychotic symptoms; history of non-psychotic psychiatric/neurologic symptoms; recreational drug use/alcohol misuse; and criminal history. See the Supplement for further details.

Analyses

We tallied descriptive statistics for all 1,725 offenders, including age, gender, and race. The frequencies of each motivational subtype were tabulated, as well as the various subcategories of emotionally-driven killings. We separately examined perpetrators who used firearms (i.e. mass-shooters) and those who did not (i.e. mass murderers of other types), and U.S.-based mass-shooters versus non-U.S.-based mass-shooters. Differences in demographics and clinical features between groups were examined using Pearson χ^2 tests for categorical variables (e.g. history of psychotic symptoms, gender), and two-sample t-tests for continuous variables. Statistical significance was evaluated at an alpha level of 0.05; as this is an exploratory analysis, alpha level was not adjusted for multiple comparisons. As such, p-values should be interpreted with caution. Data analyses were conducted using SAS 9.4 (Cary, NC, 2013).

Results

The raters' designations were in full accord for 1,699 (98.49%) of cases. The remaining 26 cases were assigned designations following review and consensus between the raters. Demographic features are as previously reported (Brucato et al., 2021, Table 1).

Table 1 Description of sample

Variable	*N*	*Frequency*	*%*
Gender	1725		
Male		1611	93.39
Female		106	6.14
Transgender		3	0.17
Unknown		5	0.29
Race	1725		
Caucasian		1038	60.17
African American		310	17.97
Asian/Pacific Islander		290	16.81
Native American/ First Nations		11	0.64
Mixed/More Than One Race		24	1.39
Other		4	0.23
Unknown		48	2.78
Ethnicity	1725		
Hispanic		152	8.81
Non-Hispanic		1496	86.72
Unknown		77	4.46
Age Category	1609		
9–19		158	9.82
20–29		564	35.05
30–39		466	28.96
40–49		276	17.15
50–59		108	6.71
60–75		37	2.30
Location	1725		
U.S.		1061	61.51
Canada		39	2.26
Mexico/Central America		12	0.70
Africa		47	2.72
Asia		259	15.01

Table 1 (Continued)

Variable	*N*	*Frequency*	*%*
Australia or New Zealand		45	2.61
Europe		214	12.41
South America		29	1.68
Mid-Travel between Regions		19	1.10
Fatalities	1725		
3 or 4		800	46.38
5 or 6		458	26.55
7–10		283	16.41
11–25		121	7.01
25–100		49	2.84
Over 100		14	0.81
Completed Suicide at Scene	1725		
No		1256	72.81
Yes		469	27.19
Perpetrator Injured or Killed at scene	1725		
No		1555	90.14
Non-Fatally Injured (by Others)		49	2.84
Accidentally Non-Fatally Injured (by Self)		17	0.99
Killed (by Others)		104	6.03
History of Psychotic Symptoms	1725		
No		1496	86.72
Yes		229	13.28
Non-Psychotic Psychiatric/ Neurologic Symptoms	1725		
No		1417	82.14
Yes		308	17.86
Recreational Drug Use/ Alcohol Misuse	1725		
No		1405	81.45
Yes		320	18.55
Criminal History	1725		
No		1372	79.54
Yes		353	20.46
Weapon	1725		
Non-Firearm		540	31.30
Firearm		1185	68.70
Categories of Motivating Factors	1725		
Self-Survival		16	0.93
Criminal Objectives		324	18.78
Religious or Political Beliefs		101	5.86
Psychosis/Other Severe Psychiatric Disturbance		98	5.68
Emotional Upset		998	57.86
Related to Psychopathic or Sadistic Traits		46	2.67
Related to Narcissistic Traits		10	0.58
Related to Schizoid/Autistic Detachment		10	0.58
Disorganization Related to Severe Psychiatric Disturbance		68	3.94
Disorganization Related to Drug or Alcohol Intoxication		25	1.45
No Motivation/ Category Determined		29	1.68
Sub Types of "Emotional Upset"	1725		
Type 1: Despair or extreme sadness over life event(s)		161	9.33
Type 2: Disgruntled employee		51	2.96
Type 3: Disgruntled student		8	0.46
Type 4: Family/ marital/custody dispute (non-impulsive in nature)		57	3.30

(Continued)

Table 1 (Continued)

Variable	*N*	*Frequency*	*%*
Type 5: Overwhelming, impulsive anger		266	15.42
Type 6: Revenge for bullying		22	1.28
Type 7: Romantic rejection or loss/ severe jealousy		204	11.83
Type 8: Social/ peer rejection (e.g. feeling isolated or unwanted, not necessarily involving bullying)		17	0.99
Type 9: Specific non-romantic grudge		212	12.29
Not applicable		727	42.14
Types – N/A excluded	998		
Type 1: Despair or extreme sadness over life event(s)		161	16.13
Type 2: Disgruntled employee		51	5.11
Type 3: Disgruntled student		8	0.80
Type 4: Family/ marital/custody dispute (non-impulsive in nature)		57	5.71
Type 5: Overwhelming, impulsive anger		266	26.65
Type 6: Revenge for bullying		22	2.20
Type 7: Romantic rejection or loss/ severe jealousy		204	20.44
Type 8: Social/ peer rejection (e.g. feeling isolated or unwanted, not necessarily involving bullying)		17	1.70
Type 9: Specific grudge		212	21.24

Raters were able to classify all but 29 (1.68%) mass murder incidents into one of the categories of motivating factors (see Table 1 and the Supplement for a full description of each category). Criminal objectives were identified in 324 (18.78%) events. Slightly more than half (998, 57.86%) of incidents were motivated by impulses related to severe affective upset, associated with sudden or pent-up emotionality related to adverse life events (i.e. 'severe emotional upset'). Most mass murderers assigned to this category were found to be driven by despair or extreme sadness over life events (161, 9.33% of overall events, 16.13% within the category); romantic rejection or loss, or severe jealousy (204, 11.83% of overall events, 20.44% within the category); some specific non-romantic grudge (212, 12.29% of overall events, 21.24% within the category); or explosive, overwhelming rage following some dispute (266, 15.42% of overall events, 26.65% within the category). Several motivational factors emerged as highly uncommon, including self-survival (16, 0.93%), religious or political beliefs (101, 5.86%), psychosis/other severe psychiatric disturbance (98, 5.68%), disorganization associated with severe psychiatric disturbance (68, 3.94%) or drug or alcohol intoxication (25, 1.45%), psychopathic or sadistic traits (46, 2.67%), narcissistic traits (10, 0.58%), and schizoid/autistic detachment (10, 0.58%).

When comparing categories of mass murders that involved firearms versus those that did not (Table 2), perpetrators were significantly more likely to use firearms when motivated by criminal objectives or extreme emotional upset ($p = 0.007$, $p = 0.010$, respectively). Mass

Table 2 Frequencies of motivating factors among firearm and non-firearm mass murders

Motivating Factor	*Non-Firearm (n=540)*		*Firearm (n=1185)*		*p**
	n	*%*	*n*	*%*	
Self-Survival	5	0.93	11	0.93	0.996
Criminal Objectives	81	15.00	243	20.51	**0.007**
Religious or Political Beliefs	30	5.56	71	5.99	0.721
Psychosis/Other Severe Psychiatric Disturbance	45	8.33	53	4.47	**0.001**
Emotional Upset	288	53.33	710	59.92	**0.010**
Sub Types of "Emotional Upset"					
Type 1: Despair or extreme sadness over life event(s)	62	21.53	99	13.94	**0.003**
Type 2: Disgruntled employee	9	3.13	42	5.92	0.070
Type 3: Disgruntled student	2	0.69	6	0.85	1.000
Type 4: Family/marital/custody dispute (non-impulsive in nature)	15	5.21	42	5.92	0.663
Type 5: Overwhelming, impulsive anger	75	26.04	191	26.90	0.781
Type 6: Revenge for bullying	3	1.04	19	2.68	0.152
Type 7: Romantic rejection or loss/severe jealousy	62	21.53	142	20.00	0.588
Type 8: Social/peer rejection (e.g. feeling isolated or unwanted, not necessarily involving bullying)	3	1.04	14	1.97	0.422
Type 9: Specific non-romantic grudge	57	19.79	155	21.83	0.475
Related to Psychopathic or Sadistic Traits	22	4.07	24	2.03	**0.014**
Related to Narcissistic Traits	4	0.74	6	0.51	0.515
Related to Schizoid/Autistic Detachment	5	0.93	5	0.42	0.201
Disorganization Related to Severe Psychiatric Disturbance	41	7.59	27	2.28	**<.001**
Disorganization Related to Drug or Alcohol Intoxication	10	1.85	15	1.27	0.345
Unknown/No Determinable Motive	9	1.67	20	1.69	0.975

*P-values are derived from chi-square tests comparing each row with the rest of the sample. For comparisons with any cell values<5, Fishers Exact Test is used.

murderers motivated by psychosis or other severe psychiatric disturbance ($p = 0.001$), psychopathic or sadistic traits ($p = 0.014$), and disorganization related to severe psychiatric disturbance ($p < 0.001$) were significantly more likely to employ methods other than firearms. Additionally, mass murderers were less likely to use firearms when driven by severe emotional upset, associated with despair or extreme sadness over life events ($p = 0.003$).

We separately examined mass-shooters which were carried out within and without the U.S. (see Table 3). Criminal objectives were common among U.S.-based mass shooters (213, 25.51%) but not among those from other geographic areas (30, 8.57%, $p < 0.001$). Conversely, religious or political beliefs were more commonly associated with non-U.S.-based mass shootings ($p < 0.001$). Again, extreme emotionality in the face of adverse life events emerged as the most common motivation for mass shootings irrespective of geographic location (482, 57.72% U.S.-based; 228, 65.14% non-U.S.-based). In terms of specific emotional grievances, despair over life events ($p = 0.023$) and family disputes ($p < 0.001$) were more common in the U.S. than elsewhere, while revenge for bullying was more common outside of the U.S.

Table 3 Frequencies of motivating factors among US-based mass-shooters versus non-US-based mass-shooters

Motivating Factor	*U.S.-Based (n=835)*		*Non-U.S.-Based (n=350)*		
	n	*%*	*n*	*%*	*p*
Self-Survival	7	0.84	4	1.14	0.740
Criminal Objectives	213	25.51	30	8.57	**<.001**
Religious or Political Beliefs	32	3.83	39	11.14	**<.001**
Psychosis/Other Severe Psychiatric Disturbance	40	4.79	13	3.71	0.414
Emotional Upset	482	57.72	228	65.14	**0.017**
Sub Types of "Emotional Upset"					
Type 1: Despair or extreme sadness over life event(s)	77	15.98	22	9.65	**0.023**
Type 2: Disgruntled employee	32	6.64	10	4.39	0.235
Type 3: Disgruntled student	4	0.83	2	0.88	1.000
Type 4: Family/marital/custody dispute (non-impulsive in nature)	38	7.88	4	1.75	**<.001**
Type 5: Overwhelming, impulsive anger	122	25.31	69	30.26	0.165
Type 6: Revenge for bullying	4	0.83	15	6.58	**<.001**
Type 7: Romantic rejection or loss/severe jealousy	102	21.16	40	17.54	0.260
Type 8: Social/peer rejection (e.g. feeling isolated or unwanted, not necessarily involving bullying)	10	2.07	4	1.75	1.000
Type 9: Specific non-romantic grudge	93	19.29	62	27.19	**0.017**
Related to Psychopathic or Sadistic Traits	17	2.04	7	2.00	0.968
Related to Narcissistic Traits	4	0.48	2	0.57	1.000
Related to Schizoid/Autistic Detachment	3	0.36	2	0.57	0.635
Disorganization Related to Severe Psychiatric Disturbance	16	1.92	11	3.14	0.197
Disorganization Related to Drug or Alcohol Intoxication	8	0.96	7	2.00	0.143
Unknown/No Determinable Motive	13	1.56	7	2.00	0.589

*P-values are derived from chi-square tests comparing each row with the rest of the sample. For comparisons with any cell values<5, Fishers Exact Test is used.

($p < 0.001$), as was a specific non-romantic grudge ($p = 0.017$). We again found the primary drivers to be despair or extreme sadness over life events (77, 15.98% U.S.-based; 22, 9.65% non-U.S.-based); romantic rejection or loss, or severe jealousy (102, 21.16%; 40, 17.54% non-U.S.-based); some specific non-romantic grudge (93, 19.29% U.S.-based; 62, 27.19% non-U.S.-based); or explosive, overwhelming rage following a dispute (122, 25.31% U.S.-based; 69, 30.26% non-U.S.-based).

Differences between motives involved in non-spree versus spree-type mass-shooters can be found in Supplementary Table 1.

Discussion

In the present study, we sought to examine motivating factors of mass murder with the goal of expanding on previously proposed systems in a number of critical ways. To increase the generalizability of findings, we examined a large dataset of 1,725 mass murder incidents and included worldwide cases spanning 1900–2019. We examined cases not only involving firearms, but also those carried out by any methods, permitting exploration of possibly distinct motivating factors between groups.

Motivational categories employed in the study were developed based upon previous work (Petreca et al., 2020) in conjunction with an examination of a subsample of 300 mass murderers, allowing data to define subtypes, rather than envisioning motivating factors in advance and attempting to fit all mass murders into them. Emphasis was placed upon whether offenders were seeking to obtain some specific secondary gain, including criminal objectives, with forethought; acting out of impulsive, overwhelming emotion in the wake of challenging life events and circumstances; acting as a part of longstanding personality drivers that were independent of circumstances; or whether there was simply no logic to a killer's actions, reflecting sheer disorganization. Finally, we distinguished between cases of serious mental illness, involving psychosis, in which the offender had a specific external aim which was idiosyncratically logical, but based upon a delusional premise, such as responding to what one believes is the voice of God, and cases in which there was only disorganized thought or behavior, sometimes associated with illicit substance use or alcohol misuse. The utility of the motivating factors we examined is supported by the excellent agreement between independent raters, who selected the same designations in 98.49% of cases and were able to arrive at consensus on the remaining 26 cases with discussion. Discordant designations almost uniformly arose in the context of cases in which more than one motivating factor seemed possible, and the system required selecting the one which predominated. Raters were able to identify motivations in all but 29 (1.68%) of mass murder incidents. Our hope is that the motivational categories we have presented will also allow for easy adaptation for future research, including further examinations of mass murder, but also studies of possible differences in motives between mass murderers and murderers who kill once or in a serial manner over time.

A lack of insight into the diverse situational and psychological factors which might precipitate mass shootings and other mass murder incidents have hampered efforts to develop policies and improved screening methods aimed at prevention. To date, efforts to understand specific drivers for these tragic events have involved establishing categories that might not encompass the full spectrum of motivating factors for perpetrating mass murder (Arluke et al., 2018; Dietz, 1986; Petee et al., 1997; Rocque & Duwe, 2018).

Among the general public and in media reports following mass murder events, the killings are sometimes misrepresented as uniformly involving severe psychopathology, characterized by psychotic symptoms and/or disorganized in nature, or as being perpetrated by individuals taking prescribed psychotropic medications (Hall et al., 2019; Knoll & Dietz, 2023). Empirical evidence suggests that, in reality, while severe mental illness is somewhat overrepresented among those who perpetrate mass shootings – the most common type of mass murder – it plays a significant role in only a small fraction of cases. As noted in our introduction, the impact of mental illness reported in a given study of mass shooters is very much dependent upon how that term is defined (Parks et al., 2019). In a previous report from the CMMD (Brucato et al., 2021), we observed lifetime psychotic symptoms among 11% of mass murderers, consistent with previous reports, including 18% who did not use firearms and 8% who did. Findings suggested that mental illness may, in many cases, be incidental to the motivations for the murders. In addition to an overemphasis on severe psychopathology among those who carry out such acts, the specific triggers that precipitate mass murder have been stereotyped in the public eye. It is commonly believed, for instance, that mass murders are often triggered by bullying; work- or school-related grievances; a desire for attention; or in the context of poor social connections.

Our findings regarding motivating factors were highly consistent in terms of frequencies, irrespective of whether we examined mass murderers of all types, mass-shooters versus those who employed other methods, or mass-shooters based within versus outside of the U.S., and were generally consistent with the literature (Dietz, 1986; Petee et al., 1997). In particular, criminal objectives, such as theft, killing individuals who might have served as witnesses to a crime or eliminating persons who impede some desired end, such as obtaining an inheritance, are common, especially in the U.S., as also reported by Petee et al. (1997). Most mass murder incidents, however, are impulsive in nature – a point that has implications for those seeking to prevent future mass murder by screening for persons potentially planning such attacks (Petee et al., 1997). These attacks are largely associated with either sudden emotionality or some 'last straw' event that precipitates expression of long pent-up affect, occurring in the wake of difficult life events or circumstances.

We found the most common triggers for such emotional reactions to be despair or extreme sadness over life events; romantic rejection or loss, or severe jealousy; some specific grudge; or explosive, overwhelming rage following a dispute. Inconsistent with popular stereotypes of mass murder triggers, we found mass murder driven by disorganized psychotic illness, attention-seeking, and upset specifically associated with workplace or school grievances to be uncommon. Our distinction between psychotic symptoms related to the commands of voices or firmly-held delusional beliefs versus disorganized psychosis helps to clarify that, when psychotic illness is a driver for mass murder, we would not expect such an individual to be openly bizarre or obviously impaired. Such an individual might be expected to be organized enough to conceal such delusional beliefs, for instance, during a psychiatric evaluation or when attempting to acquire a firearm, and to recognize the impact and meaning of murderous actions.

We fully recognize that one of the chief limitations of this study, and such work in general, is the uncertain validity of motivating factors drawn from media reports and court/police records – an unavoidable limitation of this type of work. We further acknowledge an underrepresentation of mass murders in non-English-speaking countries, which may have resulted in systematic overrepresentation of primarily English-speaking countries (see, e.g. the Early Warning Project's (2023) analysis of statistical risk for mass killings ranked by country).

The fact that the CMMD dataset spans more than a century introduces further potential limitations, such as possible changes in the prevalence of certain motivating factors or the attention given to some motivating factors over others in media reports. Additionally, we conducted multiple statistical tests to compare motivations between perpetrators who used firearms and those who did not, as well as those perpetrated within the U.S. and outside the U.S. Because of the exploratory nature of these analyses, we elected to report all results without correcting for multiple comparisons. We therefore recommend further investigation of observed associations.

Despite these potential limitations, the motivating factors described herein were empirically developed and categorized based on a dataset of 1,725 mass murders. There is presently no universally-accepted system for classifying motivating factors of mass murder. The key implication arising from our findings is that, rather than focusing on the role of mental illness in mass shootings, emphasis should be placed on criminal history and objectives, as well as a lack of emotional coping skills for dealing with life's challenges, associated with psychological challenges, but not severe mental illness. This information can be considered by law enforcement and policy-makers as they seek to develop and improve measures aimed at preventing

Disclosure Statement

R. Girgis acknowledges research support from Otsuka, Allergan/Forest, BioAvantex and Genentech as well as royalties and/or advances from books on mental health published by Wipf and Stock and Routledge/Taylor and Francis. He has consulted for Noble Insights and consults for law firms. Dr. Brucato receives royalties and/or advances from the books *The New Evil: Understanding the Emergence of Modern Violent Crime* from Rowman & Littlefield and *Understanding and Caring for People with Schizophrenia: Fifteen Clinical Cases* from Routledge/Taylor and Francis, as well as from a Boston College Connell School of Nursing

Innovation Grant. No other authors have disclosures. The sources of funding had no role in the study design; in the collection, analysis, and interpretation of data; in the writing of the report; and in the decision to submit the paper for publication. The corresponding author had full access to all the data in the study and had final responsibility for the decision to submit for publication. We were not paid to write this article by a pharmaceutical company or other agency.

Funding

The work was supported by the National Institute of Mental Health [R01 MH113861];New York State Office of Mental Hygiene Elizabeth K. Dollard Charitable Trust 272 G. BRUCATO ET AL.

Sources of Funding

The authors were supported by R01 MH113861 (RRG); New York State Office of Mental Hygiene; and the Elizabeth K. Dollard Charitable Trust.

Discussion Questions

1. What were the inclusion/exclusion criteria for the sample of spree killers? How did the researchers select the sample?
2. What motive categories did the authors use, and how did the researchers handle reviewing the materials and coding them?
3. How do Brucato et al.'s findings differ from our stereotypes of mass shooters?

References

Arluke, A., Lankford, A., & Madfis, E. (2018). Harming animals and massacring humans: Characteristics of public mass and active shooters who abused animals. *Behavioral Sciences & the Law*, *36*(6), 739–751. https://doi.org/10.1002/bsl.2385

Brucato, G., Appelbaum, P. S., Hesson, H., Shea, E. A., Dishy, G., Lee, K., Pia, T., Syed, F., Villalobos, A., Wall, M. M., Lieberman, J. A., & Girgis, R. R. (2021). Psychotic symptoms in mass shootings vs. mass murders not involving firearms: Findings from the Columbia Mass Murder Database. *Psychological Medicine*, *17*(15), 1–9. https://doi.org/10.1017/S0033291721000076

Dietz, P. E. (1986). Mass, serial and sensational homicides. *Bulletin of the New York Academy of Medicine*, *62*(5), 477–491.

Douglas, J. E., Burgess, A. W., Burgess, A. G., & Ressler, R. K. (2012). *Crime classification manual: A standard system for investigating and classifying violent crime* (3rd ed). Wiley.

Early Warning Project. (2023). "Ranking all countries: 2022–2023 statistical risk assessment for mass killing." https://earlywarningproject.ushmm.org/ranking-of-all-countries .

Everytown for Gun Safety. (2020). "Mass shootings in America: 2009–2020." https://everytown.org

Follman, M., Aronsen, G., & Pan, D. U. S. M. S. (2020). Data from mother Investigation. www.motherjones.com/politics/2012/12/mass-shootings-mother-jones-full – data/ [updated January 26, 2020].

Hall, R. C. W., Friedman, S. H., Sorrentino, R., Lapchenko, M., Marcus, A., & Ellis, R. (2019). The myth of school shooters and psychotropic medications. *Behavioral Sciences & the Law*, *37*(5), 540–558. https://doi.org/10.1002/bsl.2429

Knoll, J., IV, & Dietz, P. (2023). Mass violence and the complex spectrum of mental illness and mental functioning. *JAMA Psychiatry*, *80*(2), 186–188. https://doi.org/10.1001/jamapsychiatry.2022.4191

Krouse, W. J., & Richardson, D. J. (2015). *Mass murder with firearms: Incidents and victims, 1999–2013* (Vol. 2020). Congressional Research Service.

McGinty, E. E., Webster, D. W., & Barry, C. L. (2014). Gun policy and serious mental illness: Priorities for future research and policy. *Psychiatric Services*, *65*(1), 50–58. https://doi.org/10.1176/appi.ps.201300141

Parks, J., Bechtold, D., Shelp, F., Lieberman, J., & Coffey, S. (2019). *Mass violence in America: Causes, impacts and solutions*. National Council for Behavioral Health. www.thenationalcouncil.org/wp-content/uploads/2019/08/Mass-Violence-in-America_8-6-19.pdf?daf=375ateTbd56

Petee, T. A., Padgett, K. G., & York, T. S. (1997). Debunking the stereotype: An examination of mass murder in public places. *Homicide Studies*, *1*(4), 317–337. https://doi.org/10.1177/1088767997001004002

Peterson, J., & Densley, J. (2020). The violence project database of mass shootings in the United States, 1966–2020. www.theviolenceproject.org/ .

Petreca, V. G., Burgess, A. W., Stone, M. H., & Brucato, G. (2020). Dismemberment and mutilation: A data- driven exploration of patterns, motives, and styles. *Journal of Forensic Sciences*, *65*(3), 888–896. https://doi.org/10.1111/1556-4029.14274

Rocque, M., & Duwe, G. (2018). Rampage shootings: An historical, empirical, and theoretical overview. *Current Opinion in Psychology*, *19*, 28–33. https://doi.org/10.1016/j.copsyc.2017.03.025

Reading 11.2 New Methods for Examining Expertise in Burglars in Natural and Simulated Environments

This is one of the older articles included in this reader, but it is the one I always use to discuss simulations with my students. What are the ways that we can learn about the decision-making of people as they are committing crimes? We can survey people, but then we are only learning about what they say they would do. It is better to see them in action, making decisions in real time. Of course, the problem in our field is that it is unethical to know someone is about to commit a burglary and to sit by and watch them without calling the police. It is also potentially dangerous for the researchers, as they can be arrested or, worse, be killed by a homeowner or police officer coming upon the crime in progress. Nee and colleagues (2015) wanted to explore the use of simulation technology to allow them to watch a "burglary" in progress, but they naturally had concerns about validity. Would their participants approach the simulated house in the same way they would a real house? Nee et al. were lucky enough to have access to a real house, so they could compare how both students, playing the part of novice burglars, and people with a history of burglary entered, stole from, and exited both the real and simulated homes.

New Methods for Examining Expertise in Burglars in Natural and Simulated Environments: Preliminary Findings

Claire Nee, Martin White, Kirk Woolford, Tudor Pascu, Leon Barker, and Lucy Wainwright

Introduction

We are in the early stages of applying what is known about expert decision-making in mainstream cognitive psychology to offending behaviour. This is an avenue worth developing as understanding the implicit decision-making of offenders has important lessons for crime prevention and interventions with experienced offenders. It is difficult, both ethically and logistically, to observe offending behaviour in action and the testing of hypotheses has been limited to interview methods and rudimentary experiments using maps and slides, often with incarcerated prisoners. While useful, these reconstructive methods with relatively unrealistic contextual cues fall short of observing actual behaviour. To that end, we assessed two new methods which would bring us closer to empirically observing actual offending behaviour in relevant criminogenic contexts. We tested hypotheses emerging from previous experimental and interview studies with burglars by, for the first time, observing a small number of experienced burglars undertaking a mock burglary in a real house and comparing their responses to an inexperienced control group consisting of postgraduate students. Second, we tested the same hypotheses with the same participants in a simulated 'virtual' version of the house on a laptop computer. If viable, simulated environments would be far easier to use with large groups of offenders than using real environments and real offenders (as we indicate below) and would open up numerous avenues of scientific study, using a more ecologically valid method than simple face-to-face interviews.

Expertise can be defined as the characteristics, skills and knowledge in a particular domain that distinguish specialists in any field from those new to it (Ericsson, 2006). Through repeated exposure to environments experts build up more complex and interconnected cognitive schemas (Chase & Simon, 1973; Fiske & Taylor, 1991) allowing them to recognise salient cues more quickly and accurately (Shanteau, 1992). Regarding burglary, research has noted the instantaneous use of cues by burglars during target selection (Bernasco & Luykx, 2003; Clare, 2011; Nee & Meenaghan, 2006) and superior performance in relation to novices (householders, students, police officers and offenders without experience of burglary) in terms of speedier decision-making in relation to cues signifying greater value; better recognition memory for burglary-related cues; more efficient use of decision-making heuristics and more systematic routes taken by burglars (Garcia-Retamero & Dhami, 2009; Logie, Wright, & Decker, 1992; Nee & Taylor, 2000; Taylor & Nee, 1988; Wright, Logie, & Decker, 1995). Comparing skill levels within experienced and less-experienced burglars (Clare, 2011) has shown that practice increases competence in entering novel but familiar property types, suggesting more complex schemata in long-term memory.

Less work has been carried out examining behaviour once inside the property, and findings need to be empirically validated in a free-responding methodology such as those examined in the current experiment. Wright and Decker (1997) and Nee and Meenaghan (2006) reported offenders' use of automatic procedural scripts enabling efficient, high-yielding searches using routine and practised routes [similar to the 'route skeleton' heuristic noted in wayfinding expertise by Kuipers, Tecuci, and Stankiewicz (2003)]. Alongside the consistent finding that experienced burglars are more likely to enter at the rear of the property than novices the two studies above suggest that experienced burglars are also more likely to explore upstairs first and avoid bathrooms (Nee & Meenaghan, 2006; Wright & Decker, 1997).

Using these findings we put two free-responding methods to an empirical test. A small sample of experienced ex-burglars undertook mock burglaries in a real house and we compared their responses to students with no experience of offending. We hypothesised that burglars would search the house more efficiently than students (i.e., spending proportionately more time searching high value areas of the house) taking fewer, higher value items. We further expected that burglars compared to students would: navigate the house in a more systematic way using fewer routes; enter at the rear of the property; be unlikely to enter bathrooms; and be more likely to explore upstairs first. We then tested the same hypotheses using a virtual environment, aiming to replicate the findings of the mock burglary in the real house.

Method

Participants

Six male ex-offenders (henceforth burglars), aged between 25 and 33, with extensive experience of residential burglary were recruited. All had been active for at least five years resulting in several hundred burglaries per head. Six male, postgraduate students, screened to ensure no experience of offending,[1] aged 22–28, were recruited through advertisements and were used to control for experience of offending behaviour.

Challenges

Considerable challenges were associated with this project. First, obtaining the use of a typical residential house as householders were reluctant to allow ex-burglars into their houses. Negotiations with three police forces resulted in the use of a two-storey, residential property normally used as an interviewing suite for two days. Second, the recruitment of ex-offenders. After exhaustive advertising, ex-offenders were recruited from resettlement charities. Third, the time-consuming nature of each trial per participant (over 1 hour). These challenges combined resulted in small sample sizes.

Procedure

The real house comprised a kitchen, study, living room and toilet downstairs. Upstairs was an interview recording room set up like a music room and two rooms made to look like a teenage boy's and girl's bedroom. Typical items targeted by burglars (e.g. laptops, mobile phones and wallets) were placed in predictable places around the house (based on previous research). There was a small front garden and a driveway to the left of the house which led to the back garden and access to the back door.

A simple, navigable, 3D virtual simulation of the house was modelled on a laptop to represent the real house in a basic way (see Figure 1). Most items (including valuable or otherwise) could be stolen by clicking on the item to make it disappear, and these were positioned identically to that of the real house. The house could be entered by both the front and back door and was navigable using a mouse.

After giving informed consent participants were fitted with a head-mounted camera. They were asked to stand at the front gate of the property, to enter the property and to 'burgle' it in their own time by exploring the house and touching items that they would like to take, returning to the researcher once they had finished. Touching rather than removal of the items was chosen to reduce potential damage to items and to reduce testing time (as articles would have to be replaced in identical positions before each trial.

After completion, each participant was shown the video from the head-mounted camera and asked to 'talk through' their approach to the burglary which was audio-taped (rather than to 'think aloud' during the burglary which would increase cognitive load and would make the burglary unrealistic). Participants then undertook a filler task (spelling a list of words on the wall backwards) followed by the mock burglary in the simulated house on the laptop with identical instructions. They were seated at a desk in front of the laptop with a view of the simulated house from the street. They were given a quick demonstration of how to navigate the simulated environment in front of the house on the laptop using the mouse. They were told they could click on doors to open them and click on items to steal them. They were then positioned at the identical spot at the front gate in the virtual environment as in the real environment and asked to burgle the house in their own time, returning to the front gate when finished. They were only informed about this second burglary at this stage to reduce rehearsal from one burglary to the other. This mock burglary of the simulated house was again videoed using the head-mounted camera, and afterwards the participants were again shown their videos and interviewed. Half of each group began with the real life house followed by the simulation (described above) and the other half began with the simulation followed by the real house. Data regarding routes taken, time to commit the burglary, nature, number and value of items taken in each condition were coded and analysed.

Front view of house Rear view of house

Figure 1 Front and exterior examples of simulated house

Results

Exploration and Navigation of the Real House

As predicted, burglars spent significantly more time searching the higher value areas of the house (Mdn = 58%) as a proportion of total time than students (Mdn = 20%, $U < 0.0001$, $p = 0.005$, $r = .80$). Burglars spent most of their time in the valuable downstairs rooms, while students spent 20 seconds on average in all rooms equally. The strong effect size indicates the magnitude of the effect.

There was no significant difference between the groups in the overall number of items taken from the house but central tendencies were in the expected direction (Burglars: Mdn = 28.5, Range = 10; Students: Mdn = 34, Range = 30, $U = 17.5$, $p = .936$ ns). The spread of response was considerably wider for students indicating less honing of skill. However, the value of the items taken by burglars was higher and this difference approached statistical significance with a notable effect size ($U = 9$, $p = .074$, $r = .40$). The sample size is likely to have made the analysis underpowered and a larger sample may well have produced a statistically significant difference. The value of the burglars' haul was worth nearly £1000 more (Burglars: Mdn = £4875, Range = £850; Students: Mdn = £3945, Range = £3520) and again a markedly wider range was found in the student group. Students were unaware of the value of designer bags with cash, wallets and phones inside, and failed to notice leather jackets in the hallway. The upstairs recording room also divided groups. Burglars, suspicious of this more atypical room, spent little time here taking a total of five items. Students, oblivious to this, took 26 items.

Burglars navigated the house in a different way to students, all entering and exiting at the rear (all students doing so at the front door, (χ^2 (1), ($n = 12$) = 12.00, $p = 0.001$). Students were unaware that the front door was completely exposed to onlookers and were also unaware of the easy rear access. Once inside burglars focused on the high value[2] areas of bedrooms and downstairs rooms to the exclusion of the recording room and the bathroom, all of which students entered using a variety of routes, suggesting greater naivety and less script-like knowledge in students. As predicted, three out of six burglars began their search upstairs (all students started downstairs) and all six burglars chose one of only two routes (χ^2 (1), ($n = 12$) = 4.00, $p = 0.046$).

Exploration and Navigation of the Simulated House

Very similar findings were found in comparison to the real house in relation to: time spent in higher value areas ($U = 4$, $p = .038$, $r = .54$, Burglars: Mdn = 44%, Range = 20; Students: Mdn = 37%, Range = 25); overall number of items taken from the house ($U = 11.5$, $p = .831$ ns, Burglars: Mdn = 39, Range = 9; Students: Mdn=34, Range=12); and value of items ($U = 7$, $p = .071$, r = 42, Burglars: Mdn = £4120, Range = £940; Students: Mdn = £3477, Range = £1550). Larger ranges were again evident in the student group in relation to item choice and value and effect sizes were again impressive. Similarly, all burglars entered the simulated house at the rear, all students at the front (χ^2 (1), ($n = 12$) = 12.00, $p = 0.001$). Once inside, three out of five[3] burglars explored upstairs first entering high value bedrooms initially and all but one burglar took an identical route when upstairs (while students were notably haphazard with no pattern emerging). In contrast, all but one student explored downstairs first (χ^2 (1), ($n = 11$) = 7.60, $p = 0.006$). Burglars used a variety of routes to explore downstairs, but students were more consistent with four out of six following a living room, study, kitchen pattern.

Burglars unexpectedly spent a little more time overall (Mdn = 5.6 minutes, Range = 7 minutes) than students (Mdn = 3.8 minutes, Range = 5 minutes, $U = 12$, $p = 0.168$ ns) in the real house. This was likely because the burglars were more persistent than the students, resulting in more valuable burglaries. In the simulated house there was little difference in time spent overall between burglars (Mdn = 4 minutes, Range = 4.7

minutes) and students (Mdn = 4.25 minutes, Range = 6 minutes, $U = 14$, $p = 0.261$ ns). The basic modelling in the simulation made it a little too obvious which items to steal (though burglars still had a more profitable haul than students). These two unexpected findings have been useful in highlighting the importance of providing relatively rich and realistic environments in future work.

Discussion

As predicted burglars undertook more efficient burglaries, spending significantly more of their time (proportionately) in lucrative parts of the property, indicating domain-specific knowledge allowing for instant recognition of more valuable areas of each room, which resulted in taking fewer and higher value items. Regarding wayfinding, burglars stuck to a narrower range of routes, suggesting that automatic decision-making based on structural representations in memory were playing out (Chase & Simon, 1973; Fiske & Taylor, 1991). All-in-all, the much narrower distribution of response from burglars in almost all measures within this environment and the strong effect sizes supported the idea of a more discriminate, systematic and practised approach to the tasks at hand (Ericsson, Krampe, & Tesch-Römer, 1993).

Several limitations should be noted in relation to this exploratory study. The sample sizes were very small making the findings underpowered, and the study needs replicating with larger, more representative samples. Both environments were relatively impoverished in terms of the goods that would be available in a real burglary and items could only be touched or clicked on. The direction of the findings however, and the considerable magnitude of the effects associated with them, show real promise for the development of these methodologies.

These limitations acknowledged, empirical observation of the actual behaviour of albeit a small sample of offenders in comparison to non-offenders strongly supported previous interview and experimental data on expertise in offenders in both conditions indicating that these methods are likely to be able to distinguish levels of expertise and improve our understanding in the field.

Predictions made were generally borne out in both environments, representing proof in principle that these methods are both worth pursuing. Eliciting and observing actual behaviour in natural environments, even though somewhat staged, provided compelling evidence in a small sample of participants, of the predicted cognitions and actions emerging from mainstream psychological science. Observing data collection using this method suggested that there will be numerous new hypotheses generated by offenders through watching their unprompted behaviour for burglary and other types of less well-studied offending behaviour.

The finding that the simulated environment triggered almost identical behaviour in the participants was an important one. This method is a lot easier to undertake than recruiting ex-offenders to real environments and it will be worth examining whether the two methods continue to reveal the predicted differences between experts and non-experts if examined in a between-subjects design using larger sample and more matched control groups. If this is the case, a range of simulated environments can be created and used to study a wide range of offending behaviour with both incarcerated and active offenders. Simulated environments have been considered reliable methods for some time to train a variety of professionals such as surgeons, pilots and soldiers (see e.g. Gallagher et al., 2004) with accruing evidence that participants behave in the same way in real and virtual environments (Slater et al., 2013). Work has already been conducted on fear of crime (Park et al., 2012) and our exploratory work here shows that they are likely to have a notable part to play in our enhanced understanding offending behaviour.

Discussion Questions

1. Research participants had to do three different tasks to complete their participation in the study. What were the tasks, and in what order did they complete them?

2. What were the differences and similarities in the student versus burglar approaches to entering homes and stealing items?
3. What potential validity issues are present in this study?

Notes

1 This was established via email after potential participants responded to the advertisement. The importance of having no offending experience of any type was stressed and consequently four potential participants could not be used.
2 These were areas where higher value items were concentrated.
3 The laptop route failed to record for one burglar so n = 5 (it was noted that he had entered and exited at the rear).

References

Bernasco, W., & Luykx, F. (2003). Effects of attractiveness, opportunity, and accessibility to burglars on residential burglary rates of urban neighbourhoods. *Criminology*, *41*, 981–1002. https://doi.org/10.1111/j.1745-9125.2003.tb01011.x

Chase, W. G., & Simon, H. A. (1973). Perception in chess. *Cognitive Psychology*, *4*(1), 55–81. https://doi.org/10.1016/0010-0285(73)90004-2

Clare, J. (2011). Examination of systematic variations in burglars' domain-specific perceptual and procedural skills. *Psychology, Crime & Law*, *17*, 199–214.

Ericsson, K. A. (2006). An introduction to the Cambridge handbook of expertise and expert performance: Its development, organisation and content. In K. Ericsson, N. Charness, P. Feltovich, & R. Hoffman (Eds.), *The Cambridge handbook of expertise and expert performance* (pp. 3–20). Cambridge: Cambridge University Press.

Ericsson, K. A., Krampe, R. T., & Tesch-Römer, C. (1993). The role of deliberate practice in the acquisition of expert performance. *Psychological Review*, *100*, 363–406. https://doi.org/10.1037/0033-295X.100.3.363

Fiske, S. T., & Taylor, S. E. (1991). *Social cognition* (2nd ed.). McGraw-Hill.

Gallagher, A., Ritter, M., Champion, H., Higgins, H., Fried, M., Moses, G.,...Satava, G. (2004). Virtual reality simulation for the operating room proficiency-based training as a paradigm shift in surgical skills training. *Annals of Surgery*, *241*, 364–372.

Garcia-Retamero, R., & Dhami, M. K. (2009). Take-the-best in expert-novice decision strategies for residential burglary. *Psychonomic Bulletin & Review*, *16*, 163–169. https://doi.org/10.3758/PBR.16.1.163

Kuipers, B. J., Tecuci, D. G., & Stankiewicz, B. J. (2003). The skeleton in the cognitive map: A computational and empirical exploration. *Environment & Behavior*, *35*(1), 80–106.

Logie, R., Wright, R., & Decker, S. (1992). Recognition memory performance and residential Burglary. *Applied Cognitive Psychology*, *6*(2), 109–123. https://doi.org/10.1002/acp.2350060203

Nee, C., & Meenaghan, A. (2006). Expert decision-making in burglars. *British Journal of Criminology*, *46*, 935–949. https://doi.org/10.1093/bjc/azl013

Nee, C., & Taylor, M. (2000). Examining burglars' target selection: Interview, experiment, or ethnomethodology? *Psychology, Crime & Law*, *6*, 45–60. https://doi.org/10.1080/10683160008410831

Park, A., Clare, J., Spicer, V., Brantingham, P. L., Calvert, T., & Jenion, G. (2012). Examining context-specific perceptions of risk: Exploring the utility of 'human-in-the-loop' simulation models for criminology. *Journal of Experimental Criminology*, *8*(1), 29–47. https://doi.org/10.1007/s11292-011-9132-x

Shanteau, J. (1992). How much information does an expert use? Is it relevant? *Acta Psychologica*, *81*(1), 75–86. https://doi.org/10.1016/0001-6918(92)90012-3

Slater, M., Rovira, A., Southern, R., Swapp, D., Zhang, J. J., Campbell, C., & Levine, M. (2013). Bystander responses to a violent incident in an immersive virtual environment. *PLoS One*, *8*(1), e52766. https://doi.org/10.1371/journal.pone.0052766

Taylor, M., & Nee, C. (1988). The role of cues in simulated residential burglary. *British Journal of Criminology*, *28*, 396–402.

Wright, R., Logie, R. H., & Decker, S. H. (1995). Criminal expertise and offender decision making: An experimental study of the target selection process in residential burglary. *Journal of Research in Crime and Delinquency*, *32*(1), 39–53. https://doi.org/10.1177/0022427895032001002

Wright, R. T., & Decker, S. (1997). *Armed robbers in action: Stick-ups and street culture*. Northeastern University Press.

Reading 11.3 Assessing the Effectiveness of Mental Health Courts in Reducing Recidivism

There are many evaluations of criminal justice programs, and it can be frustrating when a few find that something is effective, while other evaluations find the opposite. What should researchers tell practitioners? We certainly should discuss the context in which some programs succeeded and others failed, and reading each of the individual program evaluations will supply us with that information. But if someone asks us "overall, is XYZ program effective?", meta-analyses help us provide an answer. Jalain, Lucas, and Higgins (2024) worked to address the question of whether mental health courts are successful at reducing recidivism.

Assessing the Effectiveness of Mental Health Courts in Reducing Recidivism: A Systematic Review with Meta-analysis

Caroline I. Jalain, Paul A. Lucas, and George E. Higgins

Introduction

Mental health courts (MHCs) are a type of treatment court based on the successful drug treatment court (DTC) model (Almquist & Dodd, 2009). The primary aim of MHC is to divert justice-involved individuals suffering from a mental illness away from incarceration and toward community-based rehabilitation. While MHCs vary by jurisdiction, the diversion of the court participant away from incarceration rests on the agreement the individual will abide by all court orders, including, but not limited to, attending court-monitored mental health treatment (Honegger, 2015). While slight variation exists between jurisdictions given their need to adapt to the unique needs of their communities, all treatment court ideology rests firmly on the use of therapeutic jurisprudence (TJ) and effective intervention (EI) (Lucas et al., 2023; Marlowe et al., 2016; Winick, 1997).

TJ, which is the use of the law and courts as a therapeutic agent, combined with EI, which calls for the use of evidence-based interventions to promote the best possible outcomes, ultimately informs the operation of MHCs through their adherence to the 10 Essential Elements of MHCs[1] (Shaffer, 2010; Wexler, 2000). In combination, these elements of the MHC model assist with the primary goal of reducing both the recidivism and incarceration of persons with mental illness through the improvement of mental health functioning for the participants within the court (Honegger, 2015). Additionally, MHCs aim to achieve the goal of reduced recidivism and the incarceration of persons with mental illness through the use of a specialized court docket which focuses primarily on justice-involved individuals diagnosed with a mental illness, voluntary agreement to participate within the court, required mental health treatment alongside any other court-ordered programming requirements, a graduated use of sanctions and incentives to incentivize compliance and punish non-compliance, and on-going judicial interactions through frequent status hearings (Almquist & Dodd, 2009; Canada et al., 2019; Steadman et al., 2001; Thompson et al., 2007).

The creation of MHCs was and is necessitated by the number of individuals incarcerated within the United States who have also been diagnosed with a mental illness. While it is difficult to determine the exact number of adults who are incarcerated and also have a mental health disorder, recent estimates are that 43%

of state and 23% of federal prisoners within the United States (US) have a history of a mental health problem with 14% of state and 8% of federal prisoners meeting the threshold for past 30-day serious psychological distress (Maruschak et al., 2021). These estimates highlight the fact that adults with serious psychiatric needs are overrepresented in the prison population compared to the general population. It should come as no surprise, then, that there are currently more than 490 MHCs operating within 39 states/territories (Devall et al., 2022).

Literature Review

Research has shown that mentally ill inmates serve longer sentences compared to other inmates (Bonfine et al., 2020). Despite the large number of individuals with mental illness in jails and prisons, many facilities are not equipped to provide mental health services and medication to this population (Schaefer & Stefancic, 2003; Wallace & Wang, 2020). This is mostly due to jail and prison overcrowding coupled with a lack of financial resources and trained personnel (Morris et al., 1997; Schaefer & Stefancic, 2003; Wallace & Wang, 2020). Thus, with a lack of treatment and services during their stay in jail or prison and the lack of services after leaving the correctional system, offenders with mental illnesses find themselves in a system of revolving doors where they are arrested, jailed, and eventually released back into the community to begin this cycle again due to the lack of resources needed to address their needs (Broner et al., 2004; Steadman et al., 1999; Trejo, 2018). Therefore, in an effort to slow or end the cycle of reoffending and decrease the number of adults with mental illnesses entering correctional institutions, MHCs have spread across the United States. Additionally, the proliferation of MHCs coincides with the rising public support for the use of balanced justice when considering the punishment of offenders.

Mental Health Court and Balanced Justice

MHCs were created in order to reduce recidivism among mentally ill offenders by addressing the underlying criminogenic factors contributing to the individual's involvement with the criminal justice system. These goals are accomplished through the use of TJ and EI, which call for combining pro-social rehabilitative treatment with frequent judicial interaction. Additionally, MHCs also aim to reduce the number of incoming court cases, which contribute to decreases in jail and prison overcrowding (Goldkamp & Irons-Guynn, 2000; Petrila et al., 2000). Furthermore, the MHC model falls within the realm of balanced justice, which aims to strike the balance between punishment and rehabilitation. Previous research has shown the public largely supports the balanced justice model for various types of offenses, including for those who suffer from a severe mental illness (SMI) (Applegate et al., 1997; Atkin-Plunk, 2020; Atkin-Plunk & Sloas, 2019; Cullen et al., 2000; Nagin et al., 2006; Sloas & Atkin-Plunk, 2019; Thielo et al., 2015, 2019; Weaver et al., 2018). Specifically, when examining factors relating to the public's support for balanced justice for mentally ill offenders, Atkin-Plunk (2020), building upon previous literature (see Mears et al., 2015), discovered support for the model, a promising sign for jurisdictions using or considering the MHC model.

The Ten Essential Elements of MHCs (see above) were tailored from the successful drug treatment court (DTC) model defined in the Department of Justice Publication *Defining Drug Courts: The Key Components* (United States Department of Justice, 1997). The 10 key components are: 1) substance abuse treatment; 2) a non-adversarial approach; 3) early screening and detection of drug court participants; 4) more access to community treatment options; 5) frequent monitoring and drug testing; 6) coordinated strategies to be implemented involving participant compliance; 7) ongoing judicial interaction with each participant; 8) evaluation of program goals and effectiveness; 9) continuing interdisciplinary education to promote effective drug court planning, implementation, and operation; and 10) forging partnerships with community providers and public agencies to generate local support. While all treatment courts are advised, through the use of best practices, to follow these key components, albeit with slight modifications for differing courts, the potential for substantial variation exists within each court's adherence to, and application of, these components (see Kaiser, 2020; Kaiser & Rhodes, 2019). Operating procedures, then, can vary between jurisdictions and are impacted by differing state laws (eg certain offenses in certain states cannot be considered for inclusion within certain treatment courts) and federal guidelines (eg, federal funding cannot be sought for DTCs if they include participants with violent charges). These variations between differing courts can make cross-comparison a difficult task. Thus, while individual courts can, and have been, empirically examined, claiming that the success of the MHC model as a whole must be done with careful consideration given to the variations in MHC operations and how and why each court selects its target population. While the adherence to the essential elements of MHCs is not the intent of the current examination and is beyond the scope of aims of this study, it must be presented to the reader in order to frame the importance of the current study; through highlighting the variation which exists between individual MHC adherence to these principles, using individual studies to illustrate the success of these types of treatment courts would be inadequate and justifies the current meta-analytical approach undertaken by the authors. Furthermore, despite previous research highlighting the effectiveness of the MHC model in reducing recidivism (Han & Redlich, 2016, 2018; Lowder et al., 2016), little attention has been paid to how this promotes the increasingly popular balanced justice approach to individuals suffering from SMI entering our criminal justice system. Answering the call from researchers such as Sloas and Larrea (2023), this article directly combines the examination of the effectiveness of the MHC model in reducing recidivism considering increasing public support for balanced justice, which is at the heart of the MHC approach. A common approach to remedying the difficulties of cross-comparing treatment courts has been to conduct meta-analyses using independent studies concerning a single theme, such as the type of court and outcome variables. As such, Lowder et al. (2018) conducted a systematic search of three databases and found 17 studies published between 2004 and 2015. Results from their study showed a small effect of MHC participation on recidivism compared to traditional criminal court processing.

As is with any criminal justice intervention, ongoing and rigorous assessment of their impact and effectiveness is needed and should be informed by the best available research evidence. Systematic reviews and meta-analyses aim to identify, summarize and evaluate findings of evidence-based research. Thus, given the support for the balanced justice model, which is in line with the Ten Essential Elements of MHCs as described above, the current study is a meta-analysis of independent research examining MHC program effectiveness in terms of reductions in participant recidivism. Our study replicates the study conducted by Lowder et al. (2018) with several modifications. First, the current study uses the new 2020 Preferred Reporting Items for Systematic reviews and Meta-Analyses (PRISMA) guidelines (Page et al., 2021). The title and abstract follow new PRISMA recommendations to include important information about the study. The methodology section below also highlights the noteworthy inclusions of new PRISMA guidelines into the research process. For instance, following the new PRISMA guidelines the methodology includes information about the full search strategy for all databases the authors had access to (as opposed to at least one database as the PRISMA 2009 guidelines recommended), an emphasis on the inclusion and exclusion criteria, key-words used in the search and reporting of how many reviewers screened each record retrieved, whether authors worked independently and details about tools used in the process (eg, the use of a*bstrackr)*. The methodology also includes statements about study characteristics and bias among studies contributing to the results and additional sensitivity analysis (Page et al., 2021). In addition to using the new PRISMA guidelines, the current study differs from Lowder et al.'s (2018) in that it was conducted in February 2023, providing the opportunity for newer research to be included in the analysis. Through our analysis, we hope to contribute to the growing body of knowledge surrounding MHCs and highlight their interconnectedness with balanced justice ideals.

Methodology

Criteria for Inclusion and Exclusion of Studies in the Review

To be eligible for inclusion in this systematic review, studies had to meet several criteria. First, we required an experimental or quasi-experimental design with a comparison group for evaluating the effects of MHCs. Following Mitchell et al.'s (2012) metaanalysis of drug courts and the recommended best practices by the National Drug Court Institute, we excluded evaluations that used program dropouts as the comparison group, as program dropouts are likely to have different baseline characteristics related to study outcomes than individuals who do not drop out (Heck, 2006; Mateyoke-Scrivner et al., 2004). In addition, MHCs were required to be on a docket separate from non-MHC cases and participation had to be voluntary. The MHCs were required to be focused on adults with at least one evaluation outcome being recidivism. Finally, to be included in the meta-analysis, studies needed to have reported sufficient information to compute an effect size.

The number of our selected studies is lower that Lowder et al (2018) and Fox et al. (2021) for several reasons. First, Fox et al. (2021) included MHC evaluations for both adults and juveniles which expanded their results. Moreover, Cross (2011) and Sarteschi et al. (2011) selected studies that included participants who were 17 and older (as opposed to the legal definition of the age at which a person gains the legal status of an adult, ie, 18 years of age in most states according to the Cornell Law School's, n.d.), which could have inflated the number of selected studies. We elected to focus on adults only which reduced the number of eligible studies.

Lowder et al. (2018) had three primary inclusion criteria: MHC for adults, recidivism being a dependent variable and a comparison group. Our inclusion criteria were more restrictive which led to more studies being excluded. Fox et al. (2021) also had three primary inclusion criteria: a quantitative evaluation of the effects of MHC on recidivism, the presence of effect sizes and published between 1997 and 2020 in a peer-reviewed outlet. Our inclusion and exclusion criteria included studies with an experimental or quasi-experimental design with a comparison group, we excluded program dropouts, selected studies which had a docket separate from non-MHC cases, where participation was voluntary, focused on adults, had one evaluation outcome being recidivism and reported sufficient information to compute effect sizes. Another difference worth noting, the current study used *abstrackr* to screen abstracts of selected studies. Using a machine learning tool to expedite the systematic review process and predict relevant articles could have led to articles being missed. As a result, our selected articles differed from articles selected by previous meta-analyses and Fox and colleagues' (2021) more recent meta-analysis. Nonetheless, while our list of articles may differ from previous meta-analyses, the number and quality of the selected articles allowed us to conduct analyses yielding significant results.

Search Strategy

Following the PRISMA guidelines for reporting inclusion criteria, publication bias assessment, and reporting results (Page et al., 2021), the first step for the search strategy included a computerized keyword search of bibliographic databases. Specifically, Criminal Justice Abstract, Cumulative Index of Nursing and Allied Health (CINAHL) with Full Text, PsycINFO, National Criminal Justice Reference Service (NCJRS), ProQuest Sociological Abstracts, Social Science Citation Index, Science Citation Index, Arts and Humanities Citation Index, PubMed, Nexis Uni, OpenDissertations, and ProQuest Dissertation and Theses databases

Table 1 Summary of Study Characteristics

Study	*n*	*Follow-up length (months)*	*Recidivism measures*	*Used court refusers within comparison group*	*Variables used to match treatment and control groups*
Aldigé Hiday et al. (2016)	2,190	24	Re-arrest	No	Charge (non-violent misdemeanors) and severity of mental illness
Anestis and Carbonell (2014)	792	12	Re-arrest	No	Age, gender, race, diagnosis, offense type, offense severity
Bagwell (2013)	1,727	12	Re-arrest resulting in incarceration	Yes	Gender, ethnicity, and age
Christy et al. (2005)	434	12	Re-arrest	No	Race, gender, age, and symptom severity
Cosden et al. (2005)	392	6	Re-arrest	No	Gender, race, mental health diagnosis
Dirks-Linhorst and Linhorst, 2012	2,308	12	Re-arrest	Yes	N/A
Ferguson et al. (2008)	872	12	Re-arrest	No	Gender, race, and age
Gallagher et al. (2018)	714	12	Re-arrest	No	Gender, race, substance use, mental health diagnosis, charge type, charge severity
Han and Redlich (2016)	1,482	6	Re-arrest	No	N/A
Hiday et al. (2013)	1,503	12	Re-arrest	No	Age, gender, race, illegal drug use, and number of prior arrests
Kubiak et al. (2015)	300	12	Re-arrest	Yes	Charge type (felony or non-violent)
Moore and Hiday (2006)	530	12	Re-arrest	No	Mental health diagnosis, charge, age race, gender, criminal history, prior incarceration, charge severity
Rossman et al. (2012, Site 1)	2,424	24	Re-arrest and conviction	No	Age, race, gender, prior criminal history, offense characteristics, and drug use
Rossman et al. (2012, Site 2)	935	24	Re-arrest and conviction	No	Age, race, gender, prior criminal history, offense characteristics, and drug use
Shaw (2019)	445	120	Re-arrest	Yes	Gender, age, race, initial offense level, prior criminal history, felony prior, violation on initial charge initial charge
Vangeem (2015)	379	36	Re-arrest	Yes	Gender, race, age, and mental health diagnosis

were included. The keywords used were as follows: ("mental health court*" OR "diversion program*" OR "problem solving court*") AND (recidivism OR evaluation OR "re-arrest" OR "re-conviction"). The last search was conducted in February 2023.

Eligible evaluations were also retrieved by carefully reviewing the reference sections of existing reviews of MHC evaluations as recommended by Lowder et al. (2018). All studies that appeared to be eligible for this study on a preliminary review of the title were retrieved and uploaded into the open-source web-based semi-automated abstract screening software *abstrackr* (2019). Since the evaluations of a*bstrackr* as a citation screening program came back positive (Gates et al., 2018; Wallace et al., 2012), we decided to use this free, open-source program to predict the likelihood of citations being relevant. Abstracts were then examined by two of the authors to determine potential eligibility. This step was facilitated by a structured screening guide. Both authors conducted a pilot test of 50 abstracts and achieved 92% agreement on the screening decisions. The authors then discussed discrepancies and potential issues before moving on to review the remaining studies. The screeners agreed on 97% of the 356 decisions made during this stage, and all disagreements were centered on whether the sample was eligible for review and were resolved successfully.

Criteria for Determination of Independent Studies

Eligible studies used a two-group design with a post-release outcome measure of recidivism. The two groups were a treatment group and a treatment as usual (TAU) comparison group participants who had their cases adjudicated through traditional courts and did not receive referrals to mental health services through the court. Matching variables used in the selected studies included age, race, gender/sex, prior arrest/prior criminal history, mental health diagnosis/symptom severity, and criminal charge.

Results

Description of Eligible Studies

Our search identified 1,588 total studies for review. Figure 1 represents a flow chart of the eligibility and study selection process.

After removing duplicates, 1,026 studies remained. After title screening, we found 421 potentially eligible studies. Studies were excluded because they evaluated MHCs for youths (as opposed to adults) or they evaluated a traditional court or treatment court that was not a mental health court (most of the studies excluded at this stage evaluated drug courts). Of the remaining 421 studies, the abstract screening excluded 378 studies because they did not meet the inclusion criteria. Studies either did not report MHC as an intervention, were not empirical, or did not report a MHC level participant outcome (ie, recidivism). Therefore, we retrieved 43 studies for full-text evaluation and examined their reference sections for potentially relevant studies. This strategy yielded an additional six studies. We conducted full-text screening on these 49 reports. Seven were not empirical studies about recidivism in MHCs. Three studies did not examine MHC. Seven studies did not measure recidivism. Six studies did not possess comparison groups and eleven studies were incomplete as they were missing crucial information to assess recidivism (ie, missing numbers on the number of people in either the treatment group or control group who had recidivated or not recidivated). The authors contacted authors of studies with missing data without success. Thus, the total number of studies for this meta-analysis was 15. These studies reported on 16 different MHC models (Rossman et al., 2012), reported on two MHC models.

Overall Mean Effects

A total of k = 15 studies were included in the analysis. The observed outcomes ranged from –1.4543 to 0.8673, with the majority of estimates being negative (80%). The estimated average e based on the random-effects model was (95% CI: –0.8749 to –0.2304, z = –3.3608,

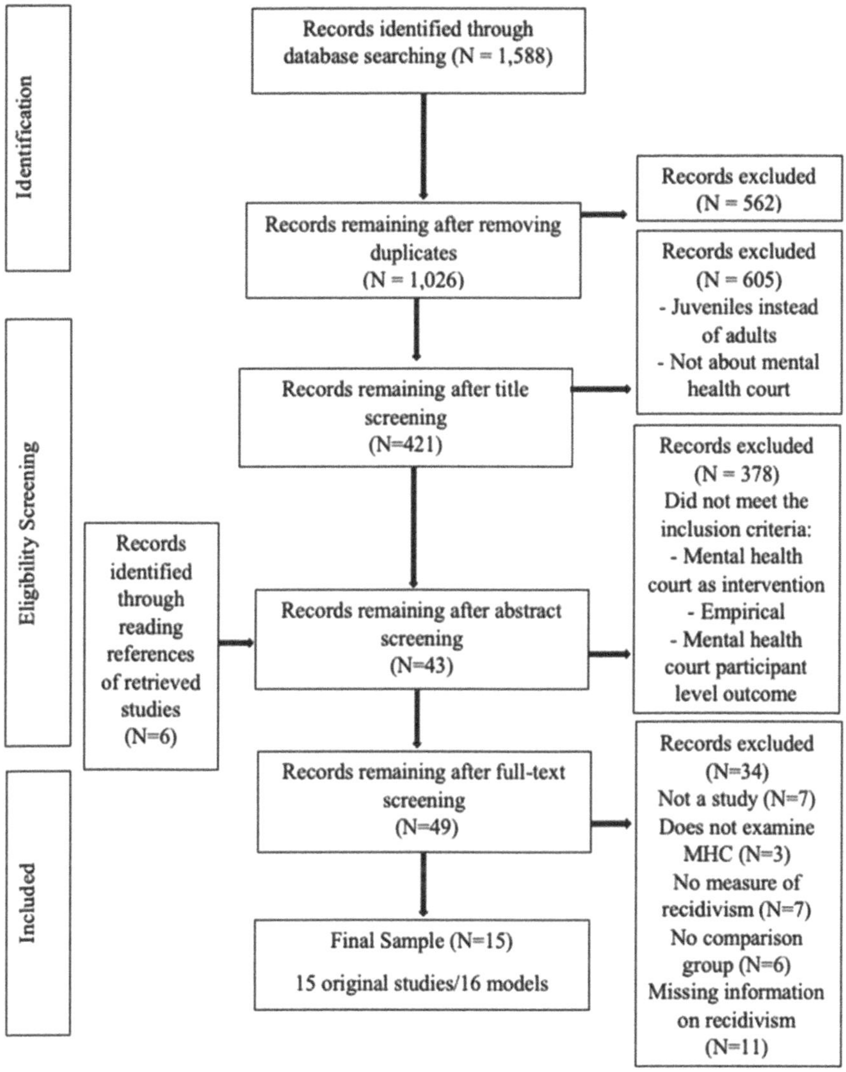

Figure 1 Flow chart of eligibility and study selection

p = .0008). This result indicates that the effect of mental health courts reduces recidivism. This was transformed to an odds ratio (OR = 0.5754; prediction interval = 0.1773 to 1.8676) indicating mental health courts resulted in a 42.46% decrease in recidivism. The prediction interval for the average odds ratio indicates studies showed as much as an 82.27% decrease in recidivism to an 86.76% increase in recidivism..

According to the Q-test, the true effect on recidivism appeared to be heterogeneous ($Q(14) = 133.5626, p < .0001, , I^2 = 88.\ 1392\%$). A 95% prediction interval for the true effect on recidivism was given by –1.7300 to 0.6247. Hence, although the average effect on recidivism was estimated to be negative, in some studies, the true effect on recidivism may in fact be positive.

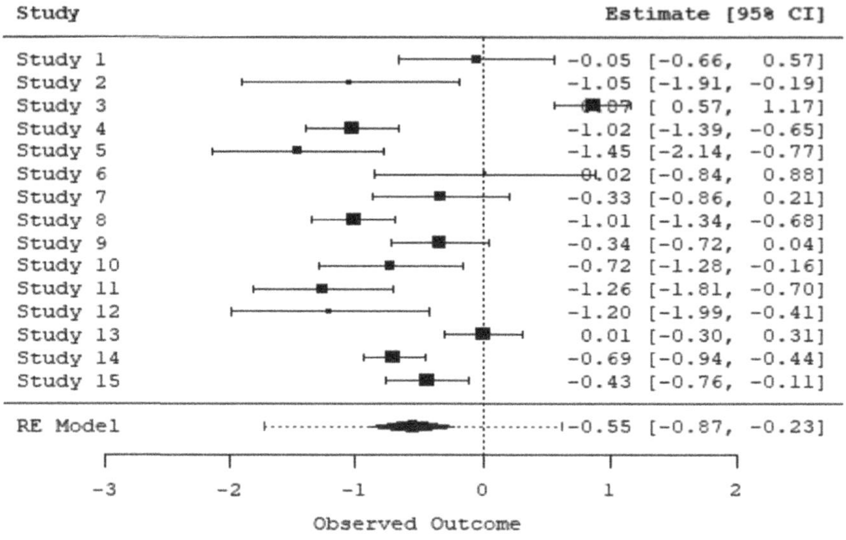

Figure 2 Confidence intervals for the reviewed studies.

Robustness of Findings to Methodological Weakness

Evaluations selected for this study were considered rigorous quasi-experiments because they used a subject-level key variable. Eight studies matched the comparison group with the treatment group on age, race/ethnicity, and sex/gender. One study only included gender and race but omitted age. Six studies matched using prior arrest/prior criminal history and/or current charge. Six studies included matching based on mental health diagnoses or symptom severity and two included drug use and/or substance use diagnoses.

While all studies used re-arrest as their recidivism outcome measure, some varied in that they also included violation resulting in incarceration and conviction as a measure of recidivism. We did not have enough studies to test this variation in measurement as a moderator. Additionally, studies varied in their follow-up length.

Several differences on important key features were noticed. Twelve studies had a measure of co-occurring disorders that would help explain offenders "criminality and recidivism." One study alluded to it but did not directly mention co-occurring disorders (Han & Redlich, 2016). Information about offense type was sparse across the studies. For three studies, the offense type could only be a misdemeanor (Aldigé Hiday et al., 2016; Christy et al., 2005; Hiday et al., 2013) while Ferguson et al. (2008), Gallagher et al. (2018), and Moore and Hiday (2006) reported that the MHCs allowed misdemeanors and violent offenses, but the degree and circumstances of the violence would be the determining factor of exclusion. Kubiak et al. (2015) reported non-violent felonies as their offense type while Anestis and Carbonell (2014) explained that the determination is done on a case-by-case basis.

Studies also varied on the length of treatment provided in MHCs. While all the evaluations included in this study provide evidence of the effectiveness of MHCS in reducing recidivism post-graduation, 10 studies did not specify how long treatment was. For Aldigé Hiday et al. (2016), treatment ranged from 4 to 6 months. Hiday et al. (2013) reported treatment length between 4 and 6 months, but the length of treatment could be extended to 7 or 8 months "if participants are making progress." Moore and Hiday (2006) reported treatment length from 6 to 12 months with a minimum of 6 months of treatment. Rossman et al. (2012) reported treatment lengths between 6 and 24 months for the MHC in the Bronx and 12 to 24 months for the MHC in Brooklyn.

Additional Sensitivity Analyses

Publication bias is one potential threat to the validity of our conclusions. Even though the evaluations included in this review were found in published, peer-reviewed journals and in unpublished outlets (eg, unpublished dissertations and government reports), we conducted several tests to help assess the possibility and extent of publication bias in our database of studies. We report several tests as a triangulation strategy in part because there are no very good tests of publication bias (see, for example, Vevea et al., 2019) and because the number of reports available to us (16) is on the low side of the minimum recommended for most publication bias assessments. The three publication tests are trim and fill (Duval & Tweedie, 2000), the rank test (Begg & Mazumdar, 1994), and the regression test (Egger et al., 1997).

The funnel plot from the trim and fill procedure suggested that there was one study "missing" to the right of the mean effect size (ie, in the direction in which we would expect publication bias to operate given that the mean effect size is negative). The trim and fill procedure inputs these missing effect sizes and adjusts the meta-analytic effect size and statistical significance test to incorporate the missing study effect sizes. We elected to keep the study because even though the existence of some publication bias is possible, it is not severe enough to undermine our overall conclusions about the magnitude and statistical significance of the MHC effect on recidivism.

Discussion

The purpose of this article was to determine if MHCs resulted in a reduction in recidivism. To examine this issue, our search, originally, yielded 421 studies, but based on exclusion criteria the number of studies was reduced to 15 studies that contained the proper information for our analysis.

The main result of this study confirms that MHCs do result in a reduction in recidivism. MHCs constitute a 42% reduction in recidivism. This is consistent with previous meta-analyses (Cross, 2011; Fox et al., 2021; Lowder et al., 2018; Sarteschi et al., 2011) further suggesting the robust nature of the results in the present study. As pointed out in the front-end of this manuscript, while previous research suggests that there exists homogeneity among key program-level characteristics regardless of type of treatment court (eg, drug treatment courts or mental health courts), future research must concern itself with within-group variation (see Kaiser, 2020; Kaiser & Rhodes, 2019). While the authors initially sought to address the issue of heterogeneity within the studies included within this meta-analysis, it simply was not possible to do so. While the initial analyses included a moderator analysis to determine what impact heterogeneity had on certain outcomes, given the limited sample size, the power was much too low. Given the low power, no meaningful interpretation of those results was possible (briefly discussed below and suggested for future researchers to pay attention to once the body of literature examining MHCs grows). Additionally, and considering our findings, practitioners and policymakers alike should take care to pay attention and implement the successful MHC model's connection with balanced justice and both its growing empirical and public support. Public and political support typically go hand-in-hand with criminal justice interventions. Therefore, by utilizing the public's support for balanced justice while promoting the MHC model through its empirically tested effectiveness may prove beneficial in aiding with both their creation within new jurisdictions as well as the sustainment of already established MHCs throughout the country. This point agrees with previous research (see Kaiser & Rhodes, 2019), which suggests that policymakers, researchers, and legal practitioners should emphasize the quality and consistency of treatment services and options delivered to certain types of treatment court participants. Given our justice system's struggle with the number of justice-involved individuals suffering with a SMI, and in conjunction with public support for the balanced justice model, the current study further enforces the need for MHCs and calls for policymakers to utilize these courts to alleviate the current overincarceration of individuals suffering from SMI.

While these results are important and advance MHC research, they must be consumed within the context of their limits. The first limitation is we made the decision to retain a study that may be an outlier. The outlier may be influencing the overall effect size and direction. Analyses, however, with and without the outlier were similar suggesting the outlier is not influencing the overall effect size and direction. The second limitation is the potential heterogeneity of the studies. This may be because some studies included refusers as the comparison group and some studies did not, which is an important distinction that future research should assess. The third limitation is the number of studies in our analysis. The number of studies in the analysis did not allow for a moderator type of analysis to determine the effect of studies containing refusers. In addition, the inability to perform a moderator type of analysis adds another limitation to our results. Our 42% reduction in recidivism may be time-dependent. We included studies with follow-up periods ranging from 6 months to 3 years. The studies we included with longer periods of recidivism may provide a greater opportunity for recidivism. The lack of uniformity in follow-up periods may influence the overall recidivism rate.[2] Future research should address the moderator issues by using a larger pool of studies with our inclusion and exclusion criteria to examine a moderator effect.

Conclusion

Over the past 30 years, the increasing number of different types of PSCs has led to an increased empirical examination of their effectiveness. While future meta-analyses with more studies not containing a potential outlier study and containing more heterogeneous studies and a product of different inclusion and exclusion criteria that examine a moderator effect are relevant, the results of the current study are substantive. In short, based on the inclusion and exclusion criteria of the present study, MHCs are effective. To clarify, MHCs produced more than a 40% reduction in recidivism. This result suggests the robust nature of MHCs and should become a potential judicial tool for working with individuals with mental illness and be endorsed both by their reductions in recidivism and alignment with the ideals of balanced justice.

Disclosure Statement

No potential conflict of interest was reported by the author(s).2

Discussion Questions

1. What were the inclusion and exclusion criteria for the studies included in the article?
2. Describe the steps in the authors' search strategy for identifying appropriate articles for their meta-analysis. Were there any drawbacks to how they conducted their search?
3. What did the researchers find in terms of the success of mental health courts? What information was this study unable to provide about mental health courts and the need for further study?

Notes

1 The Ten Essential Elements are as follows: 1) planning and administration; 2) target population; 3) timely participant identification and linkage to services; 4) terms of participation; 5) informed choice; 6) treatment supports and services; 7) confidentiality; 8) court team; 9) monitoring adherence to court requirements; and 10) sustainability.

2 We thank the anonymous reviewer who suggested the time variability issue in our results. In addition, we are appreciative of this reviewer's notion the outlier study may have a longer follow-up period influencing the recidivism rate. We did attempt to perform the moderator analysis, but we did not feel these results wouldn't be anything by tentative at best due to so few studies in our pool. They are available from the third author on request. In actuality, the outlier study has a follow-up period consistent with the majority of the other studies included in this study.

References

Abstrackr. (2019). http://abstrackr.cebm.brown.edu/

Aldigé Hiday, V., Ray, B., & Wales, H. (2016). Longer-term impacts of mental health courts: Recidivism two years after exit. *Psychiatric Services (Washington, D.C.)*, *67*(4), 378–383. https://doi.org/10.1176/appi.ps.201400569

Almquist, L., & Dodd, E. (2009). *Mental health courts: A guide to research informed policy and practice*. www.bja.gov/PublicationsCSGMHC_Research.pdf

American Psychiatric Association. (2022). New national poll cites wide support for mental health programs in jails and prisons. APA. www.psychiatry.org/News-room/News-Releases/Poll-Mental-Health-Jails-Prisons

Anestis, J. C., & Carbonell, J. L. (2014). Stopping the revolving door: Effectiveness of mental health court in reducing recidivism by mentally ill offenders. *Psychiatric Services*, *65*(9), 1105–1112. https://doi.org/10.1176/appi.ps.201300305

Applegate, B. K., Cullen, F. T., & Fisher, B. S. (1997). Public support for correctional treatment: The continuing appeal of the rehabilitative ideal. *The Prison Journal*, *77*(3), 237–258. https://doi.org/10.1177/0032855597077003002

Atkin-Plunk, C. A. (2020). Should all violent offenders be treated equally? Perceptions of punishment and rehabilitation for violent offenders with varying attributes. *Victims & Offenders*, *15*(2), 218–242. https://doi.org/10.1080/15564886.2019.1711277

Atkin-Plunk, C. A., & Sloas, L. B. (2019). Support for balanced justice and rehabilitation for justice-involved veterans. *Criminal Justice Review*, *44*(2), 165–182. https://doi.org/10.1177/0734016818793698

Begg, C. B., & Mazumdar, M. (1994). Operating characteristics of a rank correlation test for publication bias. *Biometrics*, *50*(4), 1088–1101. https://doi.org/10.2307/2533446

Bonfine, N., Wilson, A. B., & Munetz, M. R. (2020). Meeting the needs of justice-involved people with serious mental illness within community behavioral health systems. *Psychiatric Services (Washington, D.C.)*, *71*(4), 355–363. https://doi.org/10.1176/appi.ps.201900453

Broner, N., Lattimore, P. K., Cowell, A. J., & Schlenger, W. E. (2004). Effects of diversion on adults with co-occurring mental illness and substance use: Outcomes from a national multi-site study. *Behavioral Sciences & the Law*, *22*(4), 519–541. https://doi.org/10.1002/bsl.605

Burns, P. J., Hiday, V. A., & Ray, B. (2013). Effectiveness 2 years post-exit of a recently established mental health court. *American Behavioral Scientist*, *57*(2), 189–208. https://doi.org/10.1177/0002764212465416

Canada, K., Barrenger, S., & Ray, B. (2019). Bridging mental health and criminal justice systems: A systematic review of the impact of mental health courts on individuals and communities. *Psychology, Public Policy, and Law*, *25*(2), 73–91. https://doi.org/10.1037/law0000194

Christy, A., Poythress, N. G., Boothroyd, R. A., Petrila, J., & Mehra, S. (2005). Evaluating the efficiency and community safety goals of the Broward County mental health court. *Behavioral Sciences & the Law*, *23*(2), 227–243. https://doi.org/10.1002/bsl.647

Cochran, W. G. (1954). The combination of estimates from different experiments. *Biometrics*, *10*(1), 101–129. https://doi.org/10.2307/3001666

Cornell Law School. (n.d.). Legal age. In *Wex Legal Information Institute Dictionary*. www.law.cornell.edu/wex/legal_age#:~:text=This%20is%20the%20age%20at,age%20as%2018%20years%20old

Cosden, M., Ellens, J., Schnell, J., & Yamini-Diouf, Y. (2005). Efficacy of a mental health treatment court with assertive community treatment. *Behavioral Sciences & the Law*, *23*(2), 199–214. https://doi.org/10.1002/bsl.638

Costopoulos, J. S., & Wellman, B. L. (2017). The effectiveness of one mental health court: Overcoming criminal history. *Psychological Injury and Law*, *10*(3), 254–263. https://doi.org/10.1007/s12207-017-9290-x

Cross, B. (2011). Mental health courts effectiveness in reducing recidivism and improving clinical outcomes: A meta-analysis. [Master's thesis, University of South Florida]. https://digitalcommons.usf.edu/etd/3052

Cullen, F. T., Fisher, B. S., & Applegate, B. K. (2000). Public opinion about punishment and corrections. *Crime and Justice*, *27*, 1–79. https://doi.org/10.1086/652198

Devall, K., Lanier, C., & Baker, L. J. (2022). *Painting the current picture: A national report on treatment courts in the United States*. https://ndcrc.org/pcp/

Dirks-Linhorst, P. A., & Linhorst, D. M. (2012). Recidivism outcomes for suburban mental health court defendants. *American Journal of Criminal Justice*, *37*(1), 76–91. https://doi.org/10.1007/s12103-010-9092-0

Duval, S. J., & Tweedie, R. L. (2000). Trim and fill: A simple funnel-plot-based method of testing and adjusting for publication bias in meta-analysis. *Biometrics*, *56*(2), 455–463. https://doi.org/10.1111/j.0006-341x.2000.00455.x

Egger, M., Davey Smith, G., Schneider, M., & Minder, C. (1997). Bias in meta-analysis detected by a simple, graphical test. *BMJ (Clinical Research ed.)*, *315*(7109), 629–634. https://doi.org/10.1136/bmj.315.7109.629

Ferguson, A., Hornby, H., & Zeller, D. (2008). *Outcomes from the last frontier: An evaluation of the Anchorage Mental Health Court*. Alaska Mental Health Trust Authority.

Fox, B., Miley, L. N., Kortright, K. E., & Wetsman, R. J. (2021). Assessing the effect of mental health courts on adult and juvenile recidivism: A meta-analysis. *American Journal of Criminal Justice*,

46(4), 644–664. https://doi.org/10.1007/s12103-021-09629-6

Gallagher, A. E., Anestis, J. C., Gottfried, E. D., & Carbonell, J. L. (2018). The effectiveness of a mental health court in reducing recidivism in individuals with severe mental illness and comorbid substance use disorder. *Psychological Injury and Law*, *11*(2), 184–197. https://doi.org/10.1007/s12207-017-9307-5

Gates, A., Johnson, C., & Hartling, L. (2018). Technology-assisted title and abstract screening for systematic reviews: A retrospective evaluation of the Abstrackr machine learning tool. *Systematic Reviews*, *7*(1), 45. https://doi.org/10.1186/s13643-018-0707-8

Goldkamp, J., & Irons-Guynn, C. (2000). *Emerging judicial strategies for the mentally ill in the criminal caseload: Mental health courts in Fort Lauderdale, Seattle, San Bernardino, and Anchorage* (NCJ 182504). Bureau of Justice Assistance.

Han, W., & Redlich, A. (2018). Racial/ethnic disparities in community behavioral health service usage: A comparison of mental health court and traditional court defendants. *Criminal Justice and Behavior*, *45*(2), 173–194. https://doi.org/10.1177/0093854817739045

Han, W., & Redlich, A. D. (2016). The impact of community treatment on recidivism among mental health court participants. *Psychiatric Services (Washington, D.C.)*, *67*(4), 384–390. https://doi.org/10.1176/appi.ps.201500006

Heck, C. H. (2006). *Local drug court research: Navigating performance measures and process evaluations*. National Drug Court Institute.

Herinckx, H. A., Swart, S. C., Ama, S. M., Dolezal, C. D., & King, S. (2005). Rearrest and linkage to mental health services among clients of the Clark County mental health court program. *Psychiatric Services (Washington, D.C.)*, *56*(7), 853–857. https://doi.org/10.1176/appi.ps.56.7.853

Hiday, V. A., & Ray, B. (2010). Arrests two years after exiting a well-established mental health court. *Psychiatric Services (Washington, D.C.)*, *61*(5), 463–468. https://doi.org/10.1176/ps.2010.61.5.463

Hiday, V. A., Wales, H. W., & Ray, B. (2013). Effectiveness of a short-term mental health court: Criminal recidivism one-year post-exit. *Law and Human Behavior*, *37*(6), 401–411. https://doi.org/10.1037/lhb0000030

Higgins, J. P. T., & Thompson, S. G. (2002). Quantifying heterogeneity in a meta-analysis. *Statistics in Medicine*, *21*(11), 1539–1558. https://doi.org/10.1002/sim.1186

Honegger, L. N. (2015). Does the evidence support the case for mental health courts? A review of the literature. *Law and Human Behavior*, *39*(5), 478–488. https://doi.org/10.1037/lhb0000141

Kaiser, K. (2020). An evaluation of successful program completions across types of problem-solving courts. *Justice Evaluation Journal*, *3*(1), 54–68. https://doi.org/10.1080/24751979.2019.1679009

Kaiser, K., & Rhodes, K. (2019). A drug court by any other name? An analysis of problem-solving court programs. *Law and Human Behavior*, *43*(3), 278–289. https://doi.org/10.1037/lhb0000325

Kubiak, S., Roddy, J., Comartin, E., & Tillander, E. (2015). Cost analysis of long-term outcomes of an urban mental health court. *Evaluation and Program Planning*, *52*, 96–106. https://doi.org/10.1016/j.evalprogplan.2015.04.002

Lowder, E. M., Desmarais, S. L., & Baucom, D. J. (2016). Recidivism following mental health court exit: Between and within-group comparisons. *Law and Human Behavior*, *40*(2), 118–127. https://doi.org/10.1037/lhb0000168

Lowder, E. M., Rade, C. B., & Desmarais, S. L. (2018). Effectiveness of mental health courts in reducing recidivism: A meta-analysis. *Psychiatric Services (Washington, D.C.)*, *69*(1), 15–22. https://doi.org/10.1176/appi.ps.201700107

Lucas, P. A., Lucas, K. T., & Marcum, C. D. (2023). Best practices and beyond: Exploring the impact of the COVID-19 pandemic on treatment courts in a US southern state. *International Journal for Court Administration*, *14*(2), 11–32. https://doi.org/10.36745/ijca.476

Marlowe, D. B., Hardin, C. D., & Fox, C. L. (2016). Painting the current picture: A national report on drug courts and other problem-solving courts in the United States. *Technical Report*. National Drug Court Institute (NADCP). www.ndci.org/wp-content/uploads/2016/05/Painting-the-Current-Picture-2016.pdf

Maruschak, L. M., Bronson, J., & Alper, M. (2021). Indicators of mental health problems reported by prisoners. *Bureau of Justice Statistics*. https://bjs.ojp.gov/library/publications/indicators-mental-health-problems-reported-prisoners-survey-prison-inmates

Mateyoke-Scrivner, A., Webster, J. M., Staton, M., & Leukefeld, C. (2004). Treatment retention predictors in a rural state. *The American Journal of Drug and Alcohol Abuse*, *30*(3), 605–625. https://doi.org/10.1081/ada-200032304

McNiel, D. E., & Binder, R. L. (2007). Effectiveness of a mental health court in reducing criminal recidivism and violence. *The American Journal of Psychiatry*, *164*(9), 1395–1403. https://doi.org/10.1176/appi.ajp.2007.06101664

Mears, D. P., Pickett, J. T., & Mancini, C. (2015). Support for balanced juvenile justice: Assessing views about youth, rehabilitation, and punishment. *Journal of Quantitative Criminology*, *31*(3), 459–479. https://doi.org/10.1007/s10940-014-9234-5

Mitchell, O., Wilson, D. B., Eggers, A., & MacKenzie, D. L. (2012). Assessing the effectiveness of drug courts on recidivism: A meta-analytic review of traditional and non-traditional drug courts. *Journal of Criminal Justice*, *40*(1), 60–71. https://doi.org/10.1016/j.jcrimjus.2011.11.009

Moore, M. E., & Hiday, V. A. (2006). Mental health court outcomes: A comparison of re-arrest and re-arrest severity between mental health court and traditional court participants. *Law and Human Behavior*, *30*(6), 659–674. https://doi.org/10.1007/s10979-006-9061-9

Morris, S. M., Steadman, H. J., & Veysey, B. M. (1997). Mental health services in United States jails: A survey of innovative practices. *Criminal Justice and Behavior*, *24*(1), 3–19. https://doi.org/10.1177/0093854897024001001

Nagin, D. S., Piquero, A. R., Scott, E. S., & Steinberg, L. (2006). Public preferences for rehabilitation versus incarceration for juvenile offenders: Evidence from a contingent valuation. *Criminology & Public Policy*, *5*(4), 627–651. https://doi.org/10.1111/j.1745-9133.2006.00406.x

Page, M. J., McKenzie, J. E., Bossuyt, P. M., Boutron, I., Hoffmann, T. C., Mulrow, C. D., ... Moher, D. (2021). The PRISMA 2020 statement: An updated guideline for reporting systematic reviews. *BMJ (Clinical Research ed.)*, *372*, n71. https://doi.org/10.1136/bmj.n71

Petrila, J., Poythress, N. G., McGaha, A., & Boothroyd, R. A. (2001). Preliminary observations from an evaluation of the Broward County Mental Health Court. *Court Review*, *37*, 14–22.

R Core Team. (2020). *R: A language and environment for statistical computing*. R Foundation for Statistical Computing. www.R-project.org/

Riley, R. D., Higgins, J. P. T., & Deeks, J. J. (2011). Interpretation of random effects meta-analyses. *BMJ (Clinical Research ed.)*, *342*(feb10 2), d549–d549. https://doi.org/10.1136/bmj.d549

Rossman, S. B., Willison, J. B., Mallik-Kane, K., Kim, K., Debus-Sherrill, S., & Downey, P. M. (2012). *Criminal justice interventions for offenders with mental illness: Evaluation of mental health courts in Bronx and Brooklyn, New York*. Urban Institute. www.urban.org/publications/412603.html

Sarteschi, C. M., Vaughn, M. G., & Kim, K. (2011). Assessing the effectiveness of mental health courts: A quantitative review. *Journal of Criminal Justice*, *39*(1), 12–20. https://doi.org/10.1016/j.jcrimjus.2010.11.003

Schaefer, N., & Stefancic, A. (2003). Alternative to prison programs for the mentally ill offender. *Journal of Offender Rehabilitation*, *38*(2), 41–55. https://doi.org/10.1300/J076v38n02_03

Shaffer, D. K. (2010). Looking inside the black box of drug courts: A meta-analytic review. *Justice Quarterly*, *28*(3), 493–521. https://doi.org/10.1080/07418825.2010.525222

Shaw, D. (2019). *Predicting recidivism using survival analysis: Evidence from a mental health court*. (Dissertation). University of Akron.

Sloas, L. B., & Atkin-Plunk, C. A. (2019). Perceptions of balanced justice and rehabilitation for drug offenders. *Criminal Justice Policy Review*, *30*(7), 990–1009. https://doi.org/10.1177/0887403418762532

Sloas, L. B., & Larrea, M. (2023). Rethinking sanctioning for offenders with mental health issues: A balanced justice approach. *American Journal of Criminal Justice*, *48*(1), 51–64. https://doi.org/10.1007/s12103-021-09620-1

Steadman, H. J., Cocozza, J., & Veysey, B. (1999). Comparing outcomes for diverted and nondiverted jail detainees with mental illness. *Law and Human Behavior*, *23*(6), 615–627. https://doi.org/10.1023/a:1022385204967

Steadman, H. J., Davidson, S., & Brown, C. (2001). Law & psychiatry: Mental health courts: Their promise and unanswered questions. *Psychiatric Services (Washington, D.C.)*, *52*(4), 457–458. https://doi.org/10.1176/appi.ps.52.4.457

Steadman, H. J., Redlich, A., Callahan, L., Robbins, P. C., & Vesselinov, R. (2011). Effect of mental health courts on arrests and jail days: A multisite study. *Archives of General Psychiatry*, *68*(2), 167–172. https://doi.org/10.1001/archgenpsychiatry.2010.134

Sterne, J. A. C., & Egger, M. (2005). Regression methods to detect publication and other bias in meta-analysis. In H. R. Rothstein, A. J. Sutton, & M. Borenstein (Eds.), *Publication bias in metaanalysis: Prevention, assessment and adjustment* (pp. 99–110). Wiley.

Thielo, A. J., Cullen, F. T., Burton, A. L., Moon, M. M., & Burton, V. S., Jr. (2019). Prisons or problem-solving: Does the public support specialty courts? *Victims & Offenders*, *14*(3), 267–282. https://doi.org/10.1080/15564886.2019.1595243

Thielo, A. J., Cullen, F. T., Cohen, D. M., & Chouhy, C. (2015). Rehabilitation in a red state: Public support for correctional reform in Texas. *Criminology & Public Policy*, *15*(1), 137–170. https://doi.org/10.1111/1745-9133.12182

Thompson, M., Osher, F., & Tomasini-Joshi, D. (2007). *Improving responses to people with mental illnesses: The essential elements of a mental health court*. www.bja.gov/Publications/MHC_Essential_Elements.pdf

Trejo, M. (2018). The victimization of the misconceived: The mentally ill in the criminal justice system. *Research Journal of Justice Studies and Forensic Science*, *6*, 85–101.

Trood, M. D., Spivak, B. L., & Ogloff, J. R. P. (2021). A systematic review and meta-analysis of the effects of judicial supervision on recidivism and well-being factors of criminal offenders. *Journal of Criminal Justice*, *74*, 101796. https://doi.org/10.1016/j.jcrimjus.2021.101796

United States Department of Justice. (1997). *Defining drug courts: The key components*. Office of Justice Programs, Drug Courts Program Office.

VanGeem, S. (2015). *An evaluation of the Utah First District mental health court: Gauging the efficacy of diverting offenders suffering with serious mental illness*. (Doctoral dissertation). USF Tampa. ProQuest Dissertation & Theses Global.

Vevea, J. L., Coburn, K. M., & Sutton, A. (2019). Publication bias. In H. Cooper, L. V. Hedges, & J. C. Valentine, *Handbook of research synthesis and meta-analysis* (3rd ed.). Russell Sage Foundation.

Viechtbauer, W. (2005). Bias and efficiency of meta-analytic variance estimators in the random effects model. *Journal of Educational and Behavioral Statistics*, *30*(3), 261–293. https://doi.org/10.3102/10769986030003261

Viechtbauer, W. (2010). Conducting meta-analyses in R with the metafor package. *Journal of Statistical Software*, *36*(3), 1–48. https://doi.org/10.18637/jss.v036.i03

Viechtbauer, W., & Cheung, M. W.-L. (2010). Outlier and influence diagnostics for meta-analysis. *Research Synthesis Methods*, *1*(2), 112–125. https://doi.org/10.1002/jrsm.11

Wallace, B. C., Small, K., Brodley, C. E., Lau, J., & Trikalinos, T. A. (2012). Deploying an interactive machine learning system in an evidence-based practice center: Abstrackr. In *Proceedings of the ACM International Health Informatics Symposium* (pp. 819–824). ACM.

Wallace, D., & Wang, X. (2020). Does in-prison physical and mental health impact recidivism? *Population Health*, *11*, 1–16.

Weaver, C., Lee, J., Choi, H., Johnson, W. W., & Clements, C. (2018). Offenders living with mental illness: How are they perceived by future professionals? *Journal of Social Work*, *19*(1), 83–101. https://doi.org/10.1177/1468017318757383

Wexler, D. (2000). Therapeutic jurisprudence: An overview. *Thomas M. Cooley Law Review*, *17*, 125–134.

Winick, B. J. (1997). The jurisprudence of therapeutic jurisprudence. *Psychology, Public Policy, and Law*, *3*(1), 184–206. https://doi.org/10.1037/1076-8971.3.1.184

12 Policy Analysis and Program Evaluation

In this chapter, I will focus on the two different types of applied research: policy analysis and program evaluation. Specifically, this involves researching and recommending new programs and policies and then evaluating their effectiveness once implemented. Regardless of what part of the criminal justice system you like and what you plan to do when you finish school, it is likely that what is discussed in this chapter will be relevant to your career. Either you will be directly involved in this type of work, or people that you associate with will be doing it. That prediction might sound pretty far-fetched right now, especially if you anticipate going into a field with non-office jobs, such as law enforcement. Even if you do start out in the field, you should aim to work your way up the ranks. Law enforcement, corrections personnel, court administrators, victim-witness advocates, and just about every criminal justice and social service profession has people in the higher ranks making decisions all the time. They must analyze problems and propose new policies and programs. Then, they either evaluate the new system put into place or work alongside those who are called in to do the evaluation (like me!). If you just turned to your aunt, uncle, or grandparent who is a retired officer or case worker, and that person said that this is all nonsense because their jobs did not involve any policy or evaluation work, they aren't lying to you. What you must realize is that the field is changing, so things are different today. When your relatives entered the field, they did not need to have a college education to climb the career ladder, but you do now. It is now common for agencies to require their leaders to have master's degrees, which was something unheard of years ago. Our field is going to continue to move in the direction of relying on evidence-based policies, so this kind of work is going to be part of your future.

Policy analysis and program evaluation are two very different jobs that occur at different times in the life of a policy or program. Policy analysis, also known as problem analysis, is the process of identifying potential solutions to a current or anticipated problem. Program evaluation comes after policy analysis and involves studying how well the policy or program was implemented and whether it had the predicted impact.

Policy Analysis

It might be useful to first distinguish between programs, policies, and projects. Welsh and Harris (2013) define a **policy** as "a rule or set of rules or guidelines for how to make a decision" (p. 4). Policies may or may not lead to the development of programs and projects. A department of corrections, for example, can establish a policy that no one is to ever leave custody straight from isolation. With that announcement would come the need for the department to establish a new step-down program that would integrate people from isolation back into a more congregate setting within the prison for several months before they complete their sentences. A **program** is "a set of services aimed at achieving specific goals and objectives within specified individuals, groups, organizations, or communities" (Welsh & Harris, 2013, p. 5). So, the step-down program would work toward fulfilling the policy objective of acclimating people to social settings prior to release. **Projects** are smaller than programs and include a "time-limited set of services provided

DOI: 10.4324/9781003661511-12

to particular individuals, groups, organizations, communities, usually focused on a single need, problem, or issue" (Welsh & Harris, 2013, p. 5). A project within the larger step-down program might be offering 12 weekly one-hour anger management sessions to a group of 15 people.

In criminal justice, we are constantly working to develop new policies or modify existing ones. Ideally, these changes should be a product of careful consideration of the facts, with an eye on the impact that the proposed change might have on all constituents. We do this by trying to look into the future and predict possible outcomes. Patton and Sawicki (1993) noted that this type of work goes by many names, including ex ante, pre hoc, anticipatory, or prospective policy analysis.

Bardach and Patashnik (2023) identified eight steps to conduct policy analysis:

1. Verify and define the problem
2. Assemble evidence
3. Construct alternatives
4. Select criteria
5. Project outcomes
6. Confront trade-offs
7. Decide
8. Present the plan

The elements of policy analysis listed above make up a good formula for making a rational, evidence-based decision. Once analysts identify the problem and assemble evidence of a current or anticipated future problem, the next step is to consider our options. One possibility could be just staying the course and not changing the current trajectory. That can be used as a type of yardstick against which we can compare other ideas. After we identify alternatives, we need to list criteria that we will use to compare the viability of our options. Here, we might want to consider the potential effectiveness of addressing the problem, financial cost, political feasibility, ethical considerations, and administrative robustness of the plan. For ethical considerations, one thing that we must consider is how the proposed policy might differentially impact certain populations. **Administrative robustness** refers to how resilient the proposed policy would be when faced with poor implementation (Bardach & Patashnik, 2023). Next, we try to project the outcomes to predict how each of our policy alternatives might play out in the future. A good historical example of our failure to carefully consider the future impact of our decisions is the war on drugs policies of the 1980s and 1990s. These laws had disproportionately negative impacts on minority communities and pushed criminal justice expenditures to the point that counties, states, and the federal government could no longer afford to keep incarcerating people. When those laws were passed, there was little thought given to what the social or fiscal impacts would be. This is why some state governments now require fiscal or minority impact statements to accompany any punitive change to sentencing practices (Porter, 2021; Subramanian, Moreno, & Broomhead, 2014). Once we have those projections, we can compare our assembled evidence, consider how our policy alternatives rank on our selected evaluation criteria, select one, and then try to state our case to promote the proposed policy.

An unfortunate fact of life in criminal justice is that we do not always take this careful, logical approach to decision-making. Welsh and Harris (2013) discuss planned and unplanned change. **Planned change** is made more carefully and is likely to follow the aforementioned steps. **Unplanned change** occurs much more hastily and often without consideration of some important facts. Unplanned change and even ill-conceived planned change occur in criminal justice more often than they should. The reason for this goes back to something I mentioned in Chapter 1, and that is the belief among many that crime control is a "common sense" issue, so it is not necessary

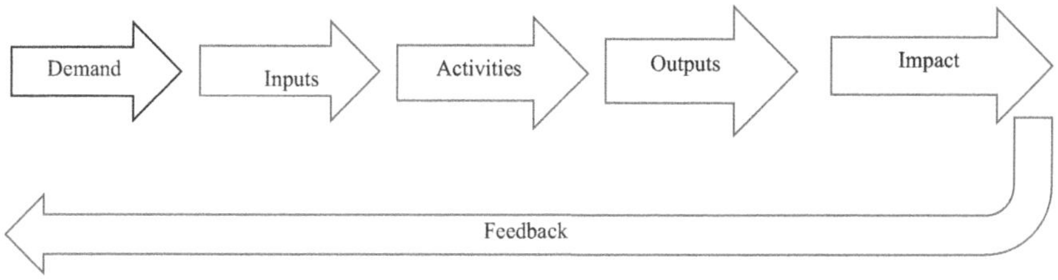

Figure 12.1 System Model
Source: Lineberry, R. L. (1977). *American Public Policy*. New York, NY: Harper Rowe. p. 43.

to consider research results or experts in the field when we make decisions. In criminal justice, there are numerous stakeholders, including criminal justice professionals, offenders, labor unions, politicians, special interest groups, corporations, and voters who have an interest in criminal justice policy. The result is that sometimes politicians will advocate for approaches that have been found not to work but that would still appeal to certain groups of constituents. Corporations, lobbyists, and even labor unions may push for policies that might not be effective but will provide job security and profits for the people they represent. The unfortunate result is that we often see policy analysis that does not conform to the appropriate steps, or it is done properly but is then ignored by decision-makers.

Regardless of how well we adhere to the steps of policy formulation, we introduce new or modified criminal justice policies at the national, state, county, local, agency, and department level all the time. Lineberry (1977), in his classic text on American public policy, presented the system model, shown in Figure 12.1. This model explains the policy implementation process.

The policy process begins with individuals or groups demanding action. The response to that demand results in some type of **input**, which could include money, personnel, or other resources that are to be used to address the demand. Next, we have **activities**, and those consist of whatever is done with the inputs. As a result of those activities, the new policy or program generates outputs. The **outputs** lead to some sort of **outcome** or **impact**, and hopefully a desirable one that addresses the original demand. As an example, we can consider bail reform efforts that are taking place throughout the country. The demand for these programs came from advocacy groups concerned about the racial disparities that exist in our pretrial detention practices, especially since pretrial detention has been found to be associated with worse sentencing outcomes (Donnelly & MacDonald, 2018; Tartaro & Sedelmaier, 2009). Even groups, such as fiscal conservatives who historically have been less concerned about the rights of defendants, became amenable to change due to the financial impact of incarceration on county and state budgets. That demand for change produced bail reform policies in some states and counties, with pretrial detention decisions being made based on risk assessment models that heavily weigh the seriousness of the current charge. The inputs for this new policy include resources to develop the risk assessment model and personnel to staff the pretrial services offices in the court and probation departments. Outputs include reduced jail populations and increased numbers of people released on recognizance or with pretrial supervision conditions. The outcome of bail reform is how much this is impacting the area's crime rates, the percentage of pretrial individuals who are failing to appear for court after release from jail, and the percentage of people subject to pretrial release who commit additional crimes while awaiting trial (See Figure 12.2).

There are several different types of desirable impacts and outcomes in criminal justice that we might want to measure. Some of the most obvious ones are numbers of crimes, crime rates, and recidivism statistics. Whenever the economy falters, cost saving becomes an especially important

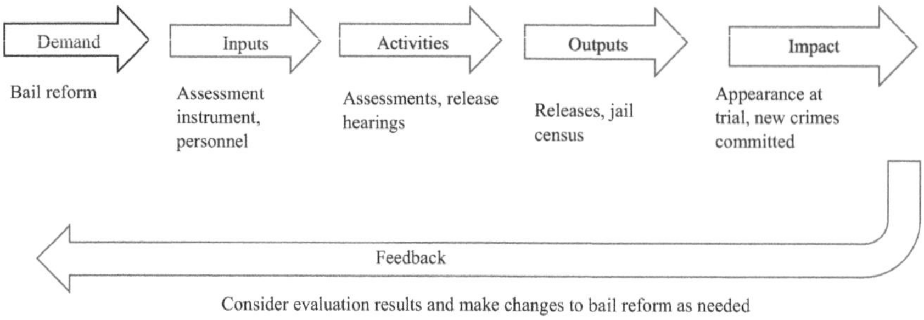

Figure 12.2 System Model applied to bail reform

Source: Lineberry, R. L. (1977). *American Public Policy*. New York, NY: Harper Rowe. p. 43.

outcome, as governments seek ways to manage operate with cheaper alternatives to incarceration. For juveniles, we might be interested in school attendance, suspensions, and graduation rates as outcomes.

Once we know about the impacts, we should provide feedback to influence what Lineberry (1977) calls tomorrow's inputs. Feedback is vital, as it allows us to consider keeping, modifying, or shutting down a new policy or program depending on its effectiveness. In New Jersey, police and prosecutor feedback following the initial months of bail reform implementation was used to modify the pretrial release procedure to make it easier to detain people charged with gun crimes, with eluding the police, with assault on a police officer, or with crimes related to child pornography (Office of the Attorney General, 2017). More recently, repeat auto theft was added to the list of charges that would prevent defendants from having the presumption of pretrial release (New Jersey, 2023). As officials observed the program in practice, they grew concerned about some of the types of offenders who were being released, and that feedback prompted changes. The next section will address how we evaluate programs to generate that feedback.

Evaluation Research

As you have probably already guessed, the purpose of evaluation research is to evaluate programs or policies to determine whether they are achieving their stated goals. Obviously, this occurs after the policy has been created. Earlier in this book, I mentioned that this falls into the category of applied research, since it has immediate policy and program implications. There are two types of evaluation research, each of which is equally valuable. First, there are process evaluations. **Process evaluations** involve studies of the implementation of the program. In other words, we would be studying what Lineberry (1977) referred to as inputs, activities, and outputs as shown in Figure 12.1. The question we ask ourselves at the outset of a process evaluation is whether the program was implemented as intended.

The second type of evaluation research is the **outcome or impact evaluation**. With this type of work, we are interested in the last part of Lineberry's (1977) system model—the impacts of our policy or program. With this, we look to establish a relationship, specifically a causal one, between the program's impact and the previous phases of the model, including the inputs, activities, and outputs. If the program is effective, the impact will be what the policymakers intended. If the impact evaluation reveals that the program was not effective, this is where the results of the process evaluation become really important. Due to funding and time restrictions, it is fairly common for researchers just to do outcome evaluations and skip the process evaluation. People are usually so anxious to get to the question of "did it work?" that they want to skip over the process issues and focus on the impacts. The problem is, without a process evaluation, we will not be able to answer the question of why the program failed.

With a process evaluation, we observe all the moving parts while the program is being implemented. We need to know the extent to which implementation matched what was planned. Think of it this way: you make a new recipe, and when you taste the finished product, it is just horrible. You should throw out that recipe, right? Not necessarily. First, you should read it again to make sure that you adhered to the directions. Did you leave out or substitute ingredients because you didn't have time to go to the store? Did you cook it on the right temperature for the correct amount of time? If it turns out that you did everything correctly and it was still terrible, then what you have is called **theory failure** (Suchman, 1969; Weiss, 1998) or a failure of concept (Berman & Fox, 2016). You carried out the plan (or policy or program) exactly how it was intended, yet it still failed. That means that the entire premise was flawed. Throw out the recipe, discontinue the program, or change the policy.

But what if you did not follow the recipe? The recipe called for flour, but you were out of that and figured that sugar looks like flour, so you used that instead. That is **implementation failure**, or a failure of the program due to lack of adherence to the program's plan. The recipe (theory) might be just fine, but we do not know for sure because you did not make the actual recipe. It is not yet time to scrap the recipe, program, or policy. Another way to think of a process evaluation is that it is a check on treatment integrity. **Treatment integrity** is the extent to which the program or policy was implemented as intended. If the program called for staff to be properly licensed and for everyone to undergo 40 hours of training before interacting with clients, yet only one employee was licensed and training lasted 20 hours, that program lacks treatment integrity.

The use of an outcome evaluation in the absence of a process evaluation is known as the **black box** approach to program evaluation (Duwe, 2013; Pawson & Tilley, 1997). Of course, it is nearly impossible to see inside a black box, so if you are asked to describe that box to someone, you would be very limited in what you would be able to say. Applied to research, the inputs, activities, and outputs are located inside the box, while the impacts and outcomes are on the outside. Evaluators who only do outcome evaluations will be unable to explain whether a program failed due to poor implementation, or whether it was executed correctly and still fell short of expectations. Conversely, if a program does well, it may be the result of an unexpected input or activity and not at all because the program was implemented correctly. At minimum, we should try to do **gray box evaluations** that would provide some indication of how the program was implemented. Ideally, the organization running the program and the researcher should work together to allow for a **clear box evaluation**, which is one where the researcher has complete access and a full view of how every aspect of the program is being implemented. Of course, this takes a lot of time and money, and that, combined with our interest in just finding out "did it work or not?" often results in us forgoing the process evaluation.

One great illustration of the importance of looking inside the box to see how a policy is being implemented can be found in Oselin et al.'s (2024) study of the California Fair Chance Act (CFCA). The CFCA was enacted in 2018 with the goal of mitigating the barriers to employment for people with criminal records. Two elements of the law were (1) banning the box on employment applications that asks people to disclose prior arrests and convictions, and (2) prohibiting public and private employers from conducting background checks on applicants until after a conditional offer of employment. The purpose was to allow people with criminal records the chance to impress the employer with their skills and demeanor so that can be weighed against anything that might come up in a background check later. By doing the background check after a *conditional* offer of employment, the employers would still retain their right to decline to hire someone if they believed the nature of that particular criminal record was disqualifying. Oselin et al. surveyed employers and found that 80% were continuing to seek information about candidates' backgrounds, either formally or informally, prior to conditional offers of employment. This information is important to know as we look at whether people with criminal records were more successful at finding employment after the CFCA became law in California. If it turns out that there was no increase in employment among people with criminal records after the passage of the CFCA, it could be because of the implementation problems uncovered by the researchers rather than the theory behind the program being problematic.

Issues Unique to Evaluation Research

Carol Weiss (1998) wrote extensively about evaluation research. She observed that researchers' experiences with applied research can be quite different from that involved in basic research. To start, the goal is different. For basic research, the objective is to produce knowledge with the hope of advancing the field. With program evaluation or applied research, we have a specific goal of helping an organization understand whether they are properly implementing a program and whether it is producing the desired outcomes. Applied research work tends to come with its own set of research questions built into the program. The program has a set of goals and objectives, and the evaluator is expected to compare "what is" to "what should be." So, if the curriculum is supposed to be 60 hours over a 12-week period, we need to compare that objective to what happened during implementation.

The researcher's obligation to examine the extent to which the program is being implemented as planned and producing positive outcomes has the potential to complicate the relationship between the researcher and practitioners. The arrival of researchers is not always met with enthusiasm, as practitioners can be fearful that the evaluation results will embarrass the organization and/or its employees and even put careers at risk. I have personally been involved in situations where staff members from the agency that hired me were uncooperative and even downright hostile. I was hired by a juvenile justice agency and was preparing to evaluate a cognitive-based intervention when all the course binders we were set to distribute to the clients "walked away" from a locked storage room that only the corrections officers could access. This theft of our materials forced us to delay the start of the program. During another evaluation, I drove 90 minutes to a secure facility on a Saturday to conduct an observation. I had been visiting that facility for weeks, but all my previous visits had been during times when high-ranking administrators were present. When I arrived that Saturday, the officer in the control room, who had previously met me and knew that his agency hired me to do this specific job, claimed he knew nothing of the project. That officer had previously been cooperative with the evaluation, but on a day when his supervisors were not present to correct him, he blocked my access to the facility. While most practitioners are cordial and professional, there are unfortunate incidents when staff try to derail evaluations, either out of a desire to derail the research or just because some people are mean-spirited.

Practitioners might also think that the research is a waste of time, as they doubt the researcher's ability to learn more about the program than the staff already know themselves. This can lead to friction and an unwillingness of the staff to cooperate with the evaluator. Staff might be reluctant to participate in interviews or help the researchers collect data, even if ordered to do so by supervisors. In some circumstances, they might even try to work against the researcher by concealing negative information or trying to mislead them to put themselves or the program in a more positive light. The researcher must engage in a balancing act. While we do not want to harm anyone, we have an obligation to provide the group funding the study with an honest evaluation, and we owe it to our profession to produce accurate work. The funding could be from a grant awarded by a private foundation or a government office. Funding can also come from the organization that is being evaluated, with the administrators deciding to request the evaluation.

One more unique aspect of evaluation research relates to the question of whether the results can be published. With evaluation research, the specific goal is to answer questions about one particular program, and since the researchers might be getting paid by the agency being evaluated, the agency might object to publishing the results. This is something that the researcher and the agency will have to negotiate. One possible work-around is that the researcher agrees to be vague about the agency that was subject to the evaluation. For example, the researcher can just state in the publication that the evaluation took place in a mid-Atlantic state and then not name the specific agency. Weiss (1998) remarked that, historically, evaluation research has not been published because some of the evaluations are of poor methodological quality. That is not necessarily due to a lack of effort and talent on the part of the evaluator. Instead, it is likely due to data restrictions that I will discuss in greater detail later in this chapter.

Designs for Evaluation Research

Evaluations can take place at various times. We can do a **formative evaluation**, which is conducted while the program is being implemented and helps to provide feedback to the designers so they can make improvements. This is essentially a process evaluation. **Summative evaluations** are conducted a bit later, such as after the program has been implemented, since the focus of summative evaluations is the program's outcomes. Weiss (1998) distinguished the purpose of these two types of evaluations as follows: Formative evaluations help improve the program as it is in its early stages of development, while summative work helps us decide whether to keep, modify, or discard the program.

The ideal plan is to conduct a summative or outcome evaluation with a classical experiment design. To review, classical experiments have three distinguishing characteristics: (1) the presence of an experimental and control group, (2) random assignment to the experimental and control groups, and (3) pre and post measurements. This design allows us to see how both groups, organizations, or geographic areas were at baseline, and then again after one is exposed to the experimental stimulus while the other is not. The random assignment increases our chances of having two groups that are similar in all respects except for the presence of the independent variable. If, after the posttest, we find a difference between the two groups on the variable of interest, we can confidently state that the independent variable contributed to that difference.

Unfortunately, it can be very difficult to conduct a classical experiment for several reasons, mostly having to do with the element of random assignment. There might be ethical concerns about withholding something potentially valuable from the control group. This issue is likely to arise when evaluating rehabilitation programs, including drug and mental health treatment. Another reason could be that it is simply impractical, given the way the program must be implemented. I have been involved in evaluations of programs in juvenile training schools where the determining factor of who would get the new curriculum versus treatment-as-usual (the control condition) was the housing unit where the students resided. Unfortunately, placement in housing units is not conducted randomly, as safety and security concerns outweigh the research goal of randomized assignment to the treatment condition. Due to the impracticality of randomization at times, researchers are often left with utilizing either a quasi-experiment or a one-group before-after design. If there is any way to come up with a comparison group, quasi-experiments are certainly preferable to any one-group design. As discussed in previous chapters, one-group designs leave us wondering what would have happened if time progressed without the introduction of the treatment stimulus. Would crime have decreased anyway? Would program participants have matured on their own and not recidivated? We can only answer those questions with either a control group, a matched comparison group, or a comparison group where we also use statistical controls to account for the differences between the two groups. As was mentioned earlier in Chapter 8, an additional possibility would be to use sophisticated statistical techniques to generate a synthetic control group.

Additional possibilities for evaluation research are cross-sectional or posttest-only designs with either one or two groups, but those should only be used if other options are unavailable. Without any pretest measures, we will have no way of knowing where the participants were at baseline. If I taught my students about ethics in criminal justice with the hope of making them better ethical decision-makers and then gave them a test at the end of the lesson that shows the students scored an 80%, what did I really learn from my evaluation? Maybe they picked up ethics lessons in a previous criminal justice course? The only way I would know if my teaching impacted the students would be if I had some sort of pretest to measure their knowledge *before* I began my instruction.

Should We Do the Evaluation?

Not every program should undergo an evaluation. There will be times when the program itself or the agency running it is just not at a state where an evaluation would be worthwhile. Before we commit time and energy to evaluating a program, we should first consider an evaluability assessment. Weiss (1998) defined **evaluability assessment** as "a systematic way to examine the program both theoretically and empirically to determine whether full evaluation of the program outcomes is warranted" (p. 73). In this process, we should consider how plausible it is that this program, with its current setup, would achieve its goals. There have been times when I have looked at programs and knew right away that they were being implemented in such a haphazard manner and so far removed from what constituted best practices that there was no way they could be effective. In those instances, I declined the opportunity to evaluate the programs. In one case, I quickly shared a few numbers with the director to illustrate my concerns and succeeded in getting the institution to discontinue the program in favor of something more evidence-based.

Weiss (1998) identified four circumstances where the evaluation would not be worthwhile. First, the program has few routines and little stability. If we do conduct the evaluation, by the time we are ready to share our findings, they will be outdated because the program will have changed since we evaluated it. Second, those involved in the program cannot agree on the program goals. There's a relevant saying: "If you don't know where you are going, you might not get there." If there are no clear program goals, how do we set up a plan to determine whether goals are being met? At best, the researcher could offer to do a process evaluation, but any outcome research would not be possible. Third, the program administrator of the organization sponsoring the research imposes strict limits on what the researcher can or cannot study. Of course, no agency is going to throw open their doors and give you access to every file that they have ever written, nor should they. The evaluation needs to have structure, but if it appears from the start that there are going to be efforts to steer the evaluation a certain way, it would be best to walk away. I was once offered an evaluation consulting job that would have provided me with three summers of pay, which is helpful since I don't get paid in July and August. When I sat with the agency to discuss the program and their evaluation needs, one of the staff members explained that they wanted the research done a certain way. While students were going to be receiving a curriculum over the period of an entire semester (either September through January or February through June), they wanted me hold off on the pretest and administer it on the last day immediately before the posttest. They remarked that their agency had been doing evaluations this way and were very pleased with the results. For the pretest, the facilitators asked students to think back to the start of the semester and answer the questions based on what knowledge they had back then. I explained that those results lacked validity since teenagers were unlikely to remember what they did or did not have stored in their brains four or five months earlier, and that the students were probably just filling out the surveys in a way that they knew would make the program look good. I told the staff that it would be unethical to knowingly design a problematic evaluation and that I would only do the work if I was granted the freedom to do it properly. Two days later, I was told that the agency had changed their mind about hiring me. While that was disappointing, I would rather lose that one opportunity in exchange for maintaining my integrity. Fourth, if there is not enough money or staff to do the evaluation, give very careful thought about moving forward. If it is something that really interests you and you can find the time to do it for little to no compensation, then that is okay. But, if the budget constraints are such that you would not be able to do a good job or get the supplies or assistance that you need, it is probably not worth doing.

Will the Results Be Used?

No one likes to waste time. Imagine if you found out that your professors weren't actually reading the papers you wrote. If you procrastinated and then tossed a bunch of words on a paper right before it was due, you might be relieved. If you put a lot of time and effort into what you did, though, you would want that work to mean something. One of the frustrating parts of being involved in evaluation research is that the evaluation might have been requested simply to fulfill a requirement. Criminal justice and human service agencies frequently apply for grants to fund new initiatives. The grants often come with a stipulation that some of the money must go toward an unbiased evaluation, usually conducted by an outside consultant. That means that doing the evaluation was not the agency's idea, and they might not even consider it necessary. So, they will comply for the sake of fulfilling the grant obligations, but the grant might not say anything about the agency's need to actually read and respond to the research findings. I was once called in to do an evaluation of a program offered by a state criminal justice agency, because their state department of education grant mandated that they hire an outside evaluator. As I did my work, I found out that the agency had already renewed the contract of the person who was facilitating the program, so regardless of my findings, the program was going to continue under the current leadership. My evaluation was not at all positive, and I think that, had the agency waited to read it before making any decisions, they might have gone in a different direction. Anyone who engages in evaluation research needs to be prepared to deal with the frustration and disappointment that comes with research findings being ignored, because it does happen from time to time.

Finding What Works in Criminal Justice

Thanks to evaluation research, we have a good idea of what works in criminal justice. I am happy to report that our discipline is beginning to follow the medical field's lead in adopting evidence-based practice. As noted in Chapter 1, evidence-based practice (EBP) involves our use of only criminal justice interventions that have been found by multiple, rigorous studies to be effective. Criminal justice has several top-flight graduate programs, think tanks, and advocacy groups that are active in promoting EBP in our field.

Part of an early effort to introduce evidence into criminal justice decision-making was the University of Maryland's 1998 publication *Preventing Crime: What Works, What Doesn't, What's Promising* (Sherman et al., 1998). Not only did this report present readers with examples of effective crime prevention strategies, it introduced the Maryland Scientific Methods Scale discussed in Chapter 11. The scale provides a rating system to evaluate the quality of research. For researchers conducting systematic reviews and meta-analyses, the scale helps them determine which studies to exclude from their analysis.

One group that is working to disseminate research on the effectiveness of programs is the Campbell Collaboration Crime and Justice Coordinating Group (CJCG). Their mission is to encourage production of systematic reviews using only high-quality research designs on topics including prevention and control of crime and delinquency, programs designed to improve the criminal justice system, and issues relating to police, courts, corrections, criminal law, and civil law (Campbell Collaboration, n.d.). The findings of these reviews can help to inform decision-makers of good policies and programs to utilize. For example, Anthony Braga (2007) conducted a systematic review of **hotspots policing**. This is a patrol technique that first requires departments to analyze their crime patterns. Departments that engage in such fact-finding typically learn that disproportionate numbers of crimes occur in just a small number of areas around town. Armed with that knowledge, police can then concentrate their enforcement efforts on those locations. Braga studied previously-completed classical and quasi-experiments of hotspot programs and found that seven of the nine studies reported substantial reductions in crime and disorder.

While the CJCG targets more academic readers than practitioners, other groups, such as the Community Oriented Policing Services (COPS), run by the National Institute of Justice, publish practitioner-friendly booklets on what works in policing (United States Department of Justice, n.d.). These publications summarize some of the best-practice research in a way that makes the information much more accessible to people who might not be interested in reading peer-reviewed research articles. For readers interested in drug treatment and recovery support services, the Substance Abuse and Mental Health Services Administration (SAMHSA) has its own website on EBP (SAMSHA, n.d.).

Communicating What Works to the Public

I have described how we can do research or find research that helps us understand what works. What do we need to do to spread the word so that information can be used to shape policy? I can think of four steps.

First, we need to support actual experts and work on getting their findings to the people who can use them, such as the practitioners and policymakers. This is an uphill battle in criminal justice. As I have noted throughout this book, criminal justice is a field where many people consider themselves proficient, regardless of their lack of knowledge. It is disheartening to turn on some news channels and see who they are consulting as "experts" in criminal justice. Where can we go to find experts? One group is working on that. The Crime and Justice Research Alliance (CJRA), works to connect criminal justice experts with the media, policymakers, and practitioners so that those groups can benefit from learning accurate information about some of the latest findings in criminal justice research. The CJRA experts are all vetted and must provide evidence that they have the qualifications to be considered experts in specific areas of criminal justice (CJRA, 2024).

Second, researchers have a responsibility to work on communicating their findings in venues and in language appropriate for the general public. How many members of the public, or even criminal justice professionals, read academic journals? I wish criminal justice practitioners would, but I am a realist. I have never seen any such journals lying around when I have visited police stations, prisons, jails, halfway houses, and correctional administrative offices. What I have seen lying around in these offices are practitioner-focused magazines, such as *American Jails* or *Corrections Today*, the official publications of the American Jail Association and the American Correctional Association respectively. The problem is that researchers and college professors get promoted by publishing in peer-reviewed academic journals, and these magazines are not peer-reviewed, nor are they considered prestigious in the academic world. What they do accomplish, however, is that they get our work into the hands of the people who can actually use the findings to shape policy. I regularly take my research and first publish it in peer-reviewed academic journals. I get the credit professionally, plus I have the peace of mind knowing that my work was vetted and deemed worthy of publication by people who could judge the steps I took to collect and analyze the data. Next, I make a short, easy-to-understand practitioner-friendly article that communicates my findings to a wider audience. I have gotten more inquiries about applying my findings in correctional facilities from these articles than I ever have from things I've written for academic audiences.

Third, and this is a hard one, we need to keep communicating the importance of replication rather than getting too excited about the finding of one or two studies. When we find some initial evidence that a new policy or program is effective, we need to resist the temptation to immediately place the "what works" tag on it and implement it across the country without doing careful replication. I noted in Chapter 6 that the rush to anoint Project HOPE as an effective tool in community corrections based on evaluations in only one jurisdiction resulted in nationwide adoption of a program that now appears to be ineffective (Cullen et al., 2018). We witnessed a similar situation in the 1980s when Sherman and Berk (1984) published a study finding that arrest of domestic violence perpetrators was an effective deterrent. Multiple replications of that work in other jurisdictions revealed that the relationship between arrest and future offending is more complicated than initially thought (Schmidt & Sherman, 1993; Weisz, 2001). Some programs will work in one location but not others for a variety of reasons, including the size of the jurisdiction, the quality and dedication of staff, and the dynamics between different organizations that need to come together for the initiative to succeed (Midgette & Reuter, 2024). In other words, we must understand the context in which some programs might or might not work (Pawson & Tilley, 1997). As someone who tends to be extremely impatient, I understand the desire to rush to make a decision, particularly when we are excited about an innovation that we think can help people. We are better off waiting for the replications, though, as we run the risk of expanding programs that are ultimately harmful. Researchers play a part in this. When they are speaking to the media and publicizing their work, they should ask that the article or interview include a statement that these findings really need to be tested in other locations before we opt for widespread adoption.

Fourth, we must not give up the fight against misinformation. Our field is one that has been hit particularly hard. The constant drumbeat leading up to the 2024 elections was that crime was out of control in the United States, and that it was not possible to walk in some of our cities without being robbed, raped, or murdered. Another talking point was that immigration was fueling this crime wave. What do the facts tell us about these two assertions? According to NIBRS statistics for January through March 2023 versus to January through March 2024, violent crime dropped by 15%. Rape was down 26%, robbery decreased by 18%, and aggravated assault decreased by 13%. The skeptic in you might think back to Chapter 6 and question whether the data were manipulated. Some who were pushing the crime increase narrative suggested that the statistics between 2020 and 2024 had been manipulated to manufacture a crime drop. Those assertions were found to be false (Robertson, 2024). Remember that murder statistics are the ones that are really, really difficult to manipulate, so let's look at murder statistics. Murders decreased by 26% between early 2023 and early 2024. So, crime was decreasing, yet over half of voters identified crime as one of their leading concerns two months before the 2024 election (Pew Research Center, 2024).

What about the assertion that immigration, particularly illegal immigration, is fueling this crime surge? We've already established that crime was not surging, but we can still look at immigration and crime. Researchers have looked at it multiple ways, even teasing out crime among people who are undocumented, and they have found either no link between immigration and crime or that immigrants (even the undocumented ones) are less likely to be perpetrators of crime than native-born individuals (Adelman et al., 2017; Green, 2016; Harris et al., 2023; Light et al., 2020; Mears, 2002; Sonnier & Haake, 2024). Should we build crime policy based on facts or myths? That is why experts need to continue not only to produce their research but to find ways to disseminate it in ways that people can hear it and understand.

Summary

The focus of this chapter was applied research, which seeks to answer rather specific questions about policy issues and the effectiveness of existing policies and programs. Policy analysis is a type of forward-looking work where analysts see a current problem, or one on the horizon, and identify policy alternatives. Analysts can then consider appropriate criteria to weigh the merits of each of the alternatives and then select one for recommendation. The criminal justice policy process is complicated by the presence of various stakeholders who are each promoting the interests of certain groups of constituents, and by the fact that there is historical precedent for crafting criminal justice policy hastily and without careful and rational analysis.

Once a new policy or program is implemented, evaluation research can give us insight into whether it is being executed properly and producing desirable outcomes. Research that documents program implementation and its fidelity to the original program proposal is called a process evaluation. Outcome or impact evaluations seek to answer the question "did the program work?" While process evaluations are frequently omitted to save time and money, they play a vital role in helping us put the outcome evaluation results in the proper context. Process evaluation data can tell us whether poor outcomes are a product of implementation failure or theory failure.

Evaluation research comes with a set of challenges that are different from what researchers engaging in basic research might experience. Evaluation researchers are almost certainly going to have to seek the cooperation of agency staff to complete the work. Navigating this relationship might be difficult at times, as some practitioners view researchers as threatening and/or disruptive. Even if the researcher is fortunate enough to forge a positive and cooperative relationship with the agency staff, departmental policies and program constraints might restrict the types of research designs that are feasible. Researchers also may not be at liberty to publish their findings. Researchers would be wise to conduct a short evaluability assessment before committing to participate in a program evaluation.

Our field is moving in the direction of adopting more programs based on evidence-based practice. EBP allows policymakers to root their decisions in sound research rather than emotion, political influence, or anecdotal information. This is an important step in discontinuing ineffective policies and programs and replacing them with initiatives that have been subject to rigorous evaluation and are backed by evidence of their effectiveness. Evaluation research makes identification of effective programs possible. While we are making progress, there are times when we still base crime policy decisions based on misinformation. It is important for criminal justice researchers to work on becoming effective communicators so that they can share knowledge of what works and what is ineffective with both decision-makers and the general public.

Key Terms

Policy	Program	Project
Administrative robustness	Planned change	Unplanned change
Inputs	Activities	Outputs
Outcomes/impacts	Process evaluation	Outcome/impact evaluation
Theory failure	Implementation failure	Treatment integrity
Black box evaluation	Gray box evaluation	Clear box evaluation
Formative evaluation	Summative evaluation	Evaluability assessment
Hotspots policing		

Discussion Questions

1. What are black box, gray box, and clear box evaluations? Why are these important in helping us understand program success or failure?
2. What should we look for when conducting an evaluability assessment?
3. What additional challenges do researchers have to face when doing applied research compared to basic research?
4. What are some reasons why we might make decisions in criminal justice that are not in line with evidence-based practice?

References

Adelman, R., Reid, L. W., Markle, G., Weiss, S., & Jaret, C. (2017). Urban crime rates and the changing face of immigration: Evidence across four decades. *Journal of Ethnicity in Criminal Justice*, *15*(1), 52–77. https://doi.org/10.1080/15377938.2016.1261057

Bardach, E., & Patashnik, E. M. (2023). *A practical guide for policy analysis* (7th ed.). Sage Publications.

Berman, G., & Fox, A. (2016). *Trial and error in criminal justice reform: Learning from failure* (revised edition). The Urban Institute Press.

Braga, A. (2007). The effects of hot spots policing on crime. *Campbell Systematic Reviews*, *1*, 1–36. https://doi.org/10.4073/csr.2007.1

Campbell Collaboration. (n.d). *Crime and justice.* Campbell Collaboration. www.campbellcollaboration.org/crime/

Criminal Justice Research Alliance. (2024). *About CJRA.* National Crime and Justice Alliance. https://crimeandjusticeresearchalliance.org/about/

Cullen, F. T., Pratt, T. C., Turanovic, J. J., & Butler, L. (2018). When bad news arrives: Project HOPE in a post-factual world. *Journal of Contemporary Criminal Justice, 34*(1), 13–34.

Donnelly, E. A., & MacDonald, J. M. (2018). The downstream effects of bail and pretrial detention on racial disparities in incarceration. *Journal of Criminal Law & Criminology, 108*, 775–814. https://scholarlycommons.law.northwestern.edu/jclc/vol108/iss4/4

Duwe, G. (2013). What's inside the "black box?" The importance of "gray box" evaluations for the "what works" movement. *Criminology & Public Policy, 12*(1), 145–152. https://doi.org/10.1111/1745-9133.12012

Green, D. (2016). The Trump hypothesis: Testing immigrant populations as a determinant of violent and drug-related crime in the United States. *Social Science Quarterly*, 97(3), 506 –524, https://doi.org/10.1111/ssqu/12300

Harris, C. T., Mutimer, A., & Thomas, S. (2023). From both near and far: Examining the diverse regions of origin for immigration and its relationship with crime across United States communities, 2015. *Justice Quarterly*, *40*(1), 51–74. https://doi.org/10.1080/07418825.2021.2013932

Light, M. T., He, J., & Robey, J. P. (2020). Comparing crime rates between undocumented immigrants, legal immigrants, and native-born US citizens in Texas. *PNAS, 117*(51), 32340–32347. https://doi.org/10.1073/pnas.2014704117

Lineberry, R. L. (1977). *American public policy.* Harper Rowe.

Mears, D. P. (2002). Immigration and crime: What's the connection? *Federal Sentencing Reporter*, *14*(5), 284–288. https://doi.org/10.1525/fsr.2002.14.5.284

Midgette, G., & Reuter, P. (2024). Diverting 911 calls: Lessons from early adopting urban jurisdictions. *Criminology & Public Policy, 23*(3), 777–799. https://doi.org/10.1111/1745-9133.12680

New Jersey. (2023). Governor Murphy toughens laws against auto theft. New Jersey's Governor's Office. www.nj.gov/governor/news/news/562023/approved/20230707a.shtml

Office of the Attorney General. (2017). *Attorney general strengthens bail reform directive to better ensure that dangerous and recidivist criminals are kept in jail pending trial.* New Jersey Office of the Attorney General.

Oselin, S. S., Ross, J. G. M., Wang, Q., & Kang, W. (2024). Fair chance act failures? Employers' hiring of people with criminal records. *Criminology & Public Policy, 23*, 361–390.

Patton, C. V., & Sawicki, D. S. (1993). *Basic methods of policy analysis and planning*. Prentice Hall.

Pawson, R., & Tilley, N. (1997). *Realistic evaluation.* Sage Publications.

Pew Research Center. (2024). *In tied presidential race, Harris and Trump have contrasting strengths, weaknesses: Issues and the 2024 election.* www.pewresearch.org/politics/2024/09/09/issues-and-the-2024-election/

Porter, N. D. (2021). Racial impact statements. *The Sentencing Project.* www.sentencingproject.org/reports/racial-impact-statements/

Robertson, L. (2024). Crime stats still show a decline since 2020. *Factcheck.org.* www.factcheck.org/2024/10/crime-stats-still-show-a-decline-since-2020/

Schmidt, J. D., & Sherman, L. W. (1993). Does arrest deter domestic violence. *American Behavioral Scientist, 36*, 601–609.

Sherman, L., & Berk, R. S. (1984). The specific deterrent effects of arrest for domestic assault. *American Sociological Review, 49*(2), 261–272.

Sherman, L. W., Gottfredson, D. C., MacKenzie, D. L., Eck, J., Reuter, P., & Bushway, S. D. (1998). *Preventing crime: What works, what doesn't, what's promising?* United States Department of Justice Office of Justice Programs.

Sonnier, O., & Haake, G. (2024). Trump's claims of a migrant crime wave are not supported by national data. *NBC News.* www.nbcnews.com/politics/2024-election/trumps-claims-migrant-crime-wave-are-not-supported-national-data-rcna140896

Subramanian, R., Moreno, R., & Broomhead, S. (2014). *Recalibrating justice: A review of 2013 state sentencing and corrections trends.* Vera Institute of Justice.

Substance Abuse and Mental Health Services Administration (SAMSHA). (n.d.). *Evidence-based practices resource center.* SAMSHA. www.samhsa.gov/libraries/evidence-based-practices-resource-center/emerging-practices

Suchman, E. A. (1969). Evaluating educational programs. *Urban Review, 3*(4), 15–17.

Tartaro, C., & Sedelmaier, C. (2009). A tale of two counties: The impact of pretrial detention on later court processing decisions. *Criminal Justice Studies: A Critical Journal of Crime, Law & Society, 22*(2), 203–221. https://doi.org/10.1080/14786010902975507

United States Department of Justice. (n.d.). *Community Oriented Policing Services (COPS).* United States Department of Justice. https://cops.usdoj.gov/

Weiss, C. H. (1998). *Evaluation* (2nd ed.). Simon & Schuster.

Weisz, A. (2001). *Spouse assault replication program: Studies of effectiveness of arrest on domestic violence.* National Online Resource Center on Violence Against Women. www.vav.net

Welsh, W. N., & Harris, P. W. (2013). *Criminal justice policy & planning* (4th ed.). Anderson Publishing.

Reading 12.1 Racial Differences in Drug Court Referral, Admission, and Graduation Rates

When we conduct program evaluations, we are often at the mercy of the organizations running the programs to provide data. Cheesman, Marlow, and Genthon (2023) used purposive sampling to target drug court programs that were collecting more data than others, but even after doing that, they still had to work around missing data. Despite that limitation, the researchers produced an informative evaluation about how drug courts operate and the extent to which there are racial disparities at various points of case processing. This is important work because most drug court evaluations focus exclusively on graduation and recidivism rates rather than benchmarks at the earlier stages of the programs. Their results are interesting and very concerning, as there appear to be racial differences at each stage for most of the drug courts studied. The authors do caution the readers, however, that they were only able to reveal that these disparities exist but, due to data limitations, could only speculate as to why.

Racial Differences in Drug Court Referral, Admission, and Graduation Rates: Findings from Two States and Eight Counties

Fred L. Cheesman II, Douglas B. Marlowe, and Kathryn J. Genthon

Introduction

Drug courts are special criminal court dockets that provide substance use treatment and other indicated services in lieu of prosecution or a sentence of incarceration for persons with substance use disorders charged with drug-related crimes (National Association of Drug Court Professionals [NADCP], 1997). The drug court judge leads a multidisciplinary team that best practice standards for drug courts recommend include a program coordinator, prosecuting attorney, defense attorney, probation or community supervision officer, treatment representatives, and law enforcement representative. Participants receive indicated treatment and social services, undergo random drug and alcohol testing, and attend frequent court hearings. During such hearings, the team reviews their progress in treatment and the judge may administer incentives (e.g., praise, reduced supervision requirements, token gifts), treatment adjustments, or sanctions (e.g., reprimands, increased supervision, brief jail detention) contingent on their performance. In pre-adjudication drug courts, graduates have their criminal charge(s) reduced or withdrawn and the arrest or conviction may be expunged from their legal record. Record expungement helps to avoid some of the negative collateral consequences of a criminal conviction, such as a loss of voting rights or access to subsidized housing or employment (Festinger et al., 2005). In post-adjudication drug courts, graduates avoid a sentence of incarceration and may reduce the length or conditions of their probation.

Meta-analyses and multisite studies conducted within the past decade determined that drug courts significantly reduced criminal recidivism—typically measured by re-arrest rates over at least 2 years—by an average of approximately 12%, with the most effective drug courts reducing recidivism by 50 to 85% (Carey et al., 2012; Mitchell et al., 2012; Trood et al., 2021). The Multisite Adult Drug Court Evaluation (MADCE), a national study of 23 adult drug courts, found that drug courts also significantly reduced illicit drug and alcohol use, improved participants' family relationships, and increased participants' access to needed financial and social services (Rossman et al., 2011).

Along with this evidence of effectiveness, drug courts are also often the last chance for criminal justice-involved persons with substance use disorders to avoid the criminogenic effects of incarceration. The accrual of these benefits through participation in drug court should not be influenced by race. The article that follows presents results that emerged from pilot-testing a tool for drug courts to assess inclusion and equity in their processes, the Equity and Inclusion Assessment Tool (EIAT). Cohorts of drug court referrals were tracked longitudinally to compare referral, admission, and graduation rates by race in two states and eight counties in diverse regions of the United States. We compared admission and graduation rates by race in each state or county using tests of the difference between independent proportions, displayed graphically with longitudinal state-level data. Based on our results, practice and policy recommendations are offered to improve measurement of cultural disparities in drug courts and the broader justice system and implement remedial strategies.

Racial Differences in Drug Courts

Drug court benefits have not accrued equally for all racial and ethnic groups. A study of more than 14,000 participants in 105 adult drug courts, culled from scores of quasi-experimental drug court evaluations, reported significantly lower average graduation rates for Black or African American participants (36%) and Hispanic or Latino/a participants (46%) compared with non-Hispanic White participants (53%) after accounting for other demographic variables that were associated with graduation rates, including participants' age, arrest history, employment status, educational attainment, and substance(s) used (Ho et al., 2018). Approximately two thirds of program evaluations have reported lower graduation rates for Black or Hispanic persons, whereas roughly one third reported no racial differences in graduation rates or higher graduation rates for Black participants (Ho et al., 2018; Marlowe, 2013).

Few studies have examined racial or ethnic differences in persons' initial access to drug courts. One statewide study in Vermont found that Black teens arrested for drug-related offenses were approximately 50% less likely than White teens to be referred to juvenile drug courts accounting for their age and severity of the arrest offense (Bellas, 2014); however, two evaluations of adult drug courts found no racial differences in referrals accounting for participants' age, ethnicity, marital status, and education (Morgan et al., 2016) or their age, gender, and indigenous ethnic minority status (Weinrath et al., 2018). A statewide study in Missouri found that Black persons referred to drug court were approximately 20% less likely than White persons to be admitted to the program after accounting for their assessed risk level and treatment needs (Yu & Dannerbeck, 2020). Similarly, an evaluation of a drug court in Milwaukee found that Black persons referred to the program were significantly less likely than White persons to be admitted accounting for their age, sex, assessed risk level, prior misdemeanor and felony charges, and primary substance used (Sheeran & Heideman, 2021). Beyond these isolated findings, little is known about whether there are pervasive racial or ethnic disparities in drug court referral or admission rates, and no published study has examined efforts to enhance equitable access to drug courts for all eligible persons.

In 2013, NADCP released the first volume of the *Adult Drug Court Best Practice Standards* (best practice standards). The best practice standards provide that drug courts should monitor their program at least annually for evidence of racial, ethnic, or other cultural disparities and adjust their eligibility criteria, assessment procedures and treatment services, as necessary, to eliminate disparities that are detected (NADCP, 2018 [text revision]). Among other strategies, compliance with the best practice standards requires drug courts to determine on an annual basis whether some cultural groups may encounter specific barriers or encumbrances hindering their access to or success in drug courts, implement remedial measures to resolve those barriers, and evaluate the success of the remedial efforts.

To assist drug courts in meeting their obligation to reduce unfair disparities, NADCP developed a suite of resources to help programs measure disparities, increase entry and engagement of various racial, ethnic, and other cultural groups, and apply culturally proficient practices to improve outcomes (NADCP, 2019). As part of these efforts, NADCP partnered with the National Center for State Courts (NCSC) to create a user-friendly tool designed to measure disparities by race, sex, ethnicity, gender identity, age, and sexual orientation. This tool, the *Equity and Inclusion Assessment Tool* or EIAT (Cheesman et al., 2019), examines proportional differences in referral, admission, and graduation rates between cultural groups as well as the reasons for non-entry or noncompletion, thus providing information to help drug courts develop effective remedial strategies.

Current Study

The current study reports data collected during pilot testing of the EIAT. We focus on racial differences in referral, admission, and graduation rates in a large sample of drug courts. These differences were examined retrospectively[1] using existing state or county administrative data compiled over intervals of up to 10 years, spanning roughly 2 to 5 years before and after NADCP issued the best practice standards. Ethnic and other cultural comparisons could not be performed because the jurisdictions did not record requisite information in a consistent or reliable manner. In addition, racial groups other than Black and White persons were represented infrequently in the pilot sites and could not be examined. Based on existing research, we had the following hypotheses:

1. Among persons arrested for drug offenses, White persons were referred more often to drug court than Black persons.
2. Among persons referred to drug court, White persons were admitted to the programs more often than Black persons.
3. Among persons admitted to drug court, White persons graduated from the programs more often than Black persons.
4. Racial differences in admission and graduation rates declined significantly over time as drug courts became better educated and prepared to address disparities.

To our knowledge, this is the first study to examine racial differences in drug court referral and admission rates in diverse regions of the United States, and the first to examine temporal patterns in admission and graduation rates over roughly a decade. By tracking referral cohorts longitudinally, from referral to exit from drug court, our study provides the most reliable estimates of referral, admission and successful completion rates by race in our pilot sites yet produced. We were unable to examine racial differences in the reasons for non-referral, non-admission or noncompletion of the programs because this information was not recorded by all jurisdictions included in this study. Future studies will examine the reasons why various cultural groups do not advance through successive stages of the drug court entry process, thus helping the field to identify indicated remedial strategies.

Method

Description of the EIAT

The EIAT examines drug court referral, admission, and completion rates and tracks referral cohorts as they advance or do not advance through these stages. To identify potential cultural differences in the probability of being referred to drug court, the EIAT compares the demographic characteristics of individuals arrested for drug court-eligible offenses to those of persons referred for possible admission to the program. Unfortunately, few jurisdictions collect sufficient information to determine which arrestees meet drug court eligibility criteria. For example, information is rarely available on whether arrestees have a substance use disorder making them potentially eligible for drug court. Many jurisdictions, out of necessity, use *drug abuse violations* as defined in the Uniform Crime Reporting (UCR) program (Federal Bureau of Investigation [FBI], 2017) as the best available proxy for estimating drug court-eligible charges. This UCR category includes drug crimes such as possession, sales, manufacturing, and possession with intent to distribute drugs; however, it excludes arrests for other drug court-eligible offenses (e.g., burglary or larceny committed to support a substance use disorder) and may include arrests for persons who are not eligible for drug court (e.g., drug dealing by a person who does not have a substance use disorder).

The EIAT provides more reliable estimates of admission and completion rates because the denominators (numbers of referrals and admissions) are more readily available. The number of referrals admitted to drug court is divided by the total number of referrals and compared by demographic characteristics of interest. These percentages indicate the probability that members of various demographic groups will be admitted to the program. Similarly, the number of persons graduating from drug court is divided by the number of persons admitted to the program and compared by demographic characteristics. If sample sizes are large enough, referral, admission, and completion rates are statistically contrasted between demographic groups to determine whether there are significant differences meriting remedial attention.

Study Sites

Two states and eight counties were purposefully selected for pilot testing of the EIAT because the jurisdictions were known by the research team to collect referral and admission data on their drug courts by race. The two states, one located in the southern region of the U.S. and the other in the midwestern region, provided aggregate state-level data and eight counties (four located in the same two states) provided county data. The eight counties are situated in the southern, midwestern, northeastern, and northern central regions of the U.S. and represent four urban, two sub-urban, and two rural communities. State-level analyses include 60 drug courts across both states in the first year examined, which increased to 166 drug courts by the last year as new programs were developed. County analyses represent one drug court serving each community.

Data Sources and Evaluation Intervals

Pilot sites back-filled data on referrals, admissions, and graduations into the EIAT (devoid of any subject-identifiable information) using information extracted from automated case-management systems maintained by local programs or state administrative offices of the courts. Three counties did not report any data on referrals and two counties did not report race data on admissions. Because referral rates were compared against arrest data, these analyses were performed for the most recent year for which arrest data were available. We obtained arrest data for the states from the UCR crime reporting program using the Bureau of Justice Statistics (BJS) *Arrest Data Analysis Tool*[2] and for the counties from their state Statistical Analysis Center (SAC).[3]

Time periods for examining admission and graduation rates varied considerably based on the availability of relevant information. Admission and graduation rates were available from the southern state for 2006-2015 (10 years) and from the midwestern state for 2010-2016 (7 years). For the counties, data for a single year (2016) was available for the midwestern suburban county and for six months (January – June of 2016) for the midwestern urban county. The northeastern urban county and one northern central rural county back-filled data on 100 randomly selected cases from 2016-2017. The remaining sites reported data spanning 2 to 10 years.

Results

Drug Court Referrals

Table 1 compares the number of persons referred to drug court per 1,000 drug arrests by race. Consistent with the first study hypothesis, Black persons were considerably less likely than White persons to be referred to drug court in five of the seven jurisdictions for which referral data were available. In contrast, Black persons were more likely to be referred to drug court in two of the seven sites. Across all sites, White persons were nearly twice as likely as Black persons to be referred to drug court.

Drug Court Admissions

Table 2 reports the percentages of persons referred to drug court who were admitted to the program. Consistent with the second study hypothesis, White persons were more likely to be admitted to drug court in seven of the eight jurisdictions for which admission data was available. State-level analyses reveal that White referrals were significantly more likely than Black referrals to be admitted to drug court in both the southern state (64% vs. 52%), $z = 11.95$, $p < .001$, and the midwestern state (58% vs. 31%), $z = 38.44$, $p < .001$.

Results were mixed at the county level but mostly reveal higher admission rates for White persons. White persons were significantly more likely to be admitted in the southern urban county (56% vs. 40%), $z = 7.07$, $p < .001$, and the northern central urban county (46% vs. 34%), $z = 2.011$, $p = .022$. In a third urban county in the northeast, White persons were relatively more likely to be admitted (24% vs. 19%); however, insufficient power (power = 24%) may have contributed to a nonsignificant difference. In one southern suburban county there was no racial difference in admission rates (both 60%). Finally, in both northern central rural counties White persons were considerably more likely to be admitted (29% vs. 18% and 74% vs. 24%); however, small numbers of Black persons precluded statistical analyses or contributed to low statistical power.

Table 1 Drug court referrals per 1,000 drug arrests by race

Jurisdiction		*Drug arrests*		*Drug court referrals*		*Referrals/1,000 drug arrests*	
State	*Year*	*White*	*Black*	*White*	*Black*	*White*	*Black*
Southern	2015	56,090	9,050	3,167	167	56	18
Midwestern	2016	33,003	9,828	2,941	1,494	89	152
Urban county							
Southern	2014	694	540	212	47	305	87
Northern central	2017	1,793	2,371	104	69	58	29
Northeastern	2017	2,410	7,721	n/a	n/a	n/a	n/a
Midwestern	2016	986	1,554	n/a	n/a	n/a	n/a
Suburban county							
Southern	2014	537	120	102	13	190	108
Midwestern	2016	184	87	n/a	n/a	n/a	n/a
Rural county							
Northern Central 1	2014	519	93	40	3	77	32
Northern Central 2	2017	855	181	12	4	14	22

Note. n/a: data not available on drug court referrals.

Table 2 Drug court admission and completion rates by race

Jurisdiction	*Time period*	*n referred*		*n (%) of referrals admitted*		*n (%) of admissions completed*	
		White	*Black*	*White*	*Black*	*White*	*Black*
State							
Southern	2006–2015	25,422	2,697	16,183 (64%)***	1,401 (52%)	6,333 (39%)***	433 (31%)
Midwestern	2010–2016	17,658	7,410	10,198 (58%)***	2,308 (31%)	5,302 (52%)***	899 (39%)
Urban county							
Southern	2006–2015	1,526	726	857 (56%)***	292 (40%)	276 (32%)[a]	84 (29%)
Northern Central	2016–2017	189	126	86 (46%)*[a]	43 (34%)	41 (48%)[a]	20 (47%)
Northeastern	2016–2017	41	54	10 (24%)[a]	10 (19%)	9 (90%)[a]	7 (70%)
Midwestern	Jan–Jun 2016	n/a	n/a	42 (n/a)	70 (n/a)	6 (14%)[a]	16 (23%)
Suburban county							
Southern	2006–2015	992	199	596 (60%)[a]	119 (60%)	240 (40%)***	27 (23%)
Midwestern	2016	n/a	n/a	84 (n/a)	23 (n/a)	48 (57%)*[a]	7 (30%)
Rural county							
Northern Central 1	2005–10; 2011–18	671	39	197 (29%)[a]	7 (18%)	146 (74%)[a]	5 (71%)
Northern Central 2	2016–2017	80	17	59 (74%)[b]	4 (24%)	20 (34%)[b]	0 (0%)

Note. n/a: data not available on drug court admissions. Significance tests of the difference between independent proportions are one-tailed.

*$p < .05$; **$p < .01$; ***$p < .001$.

a Statistical power < 80%.
b Insufficient cell size(s) for statistical comparison.

Drug Court Completions

The last column of Table 2 reports the percentages of persons admitted to drug court who completed the program. Support for the third study hypothesis is inconsistent but generally reveals higher completion rates for White participants in six of the ten jurisdictions. At the state level, White participants were significantly more likely than Black participants to complete drug court in both the southern state (39% vs. 31%), $z = 6.07$, $p < .001$, and the midwestern state (52% vs. 39%), $z = 11.31$, $p < .001$.

At the county level, White participants were significantly more likely to complete drug court in the southern suburban county (40% vs. 23%), $z = 3.62$, $p < .001$, and the midwestern suburban county (57% vs. 30%), $z = 2.27$, $p = .012$. White participants were relatively more likely to complete drug court in the northeastern urban county (90% vs. 70%); however, low statistical power (power = 31%) likely accounted for a nonsignificant difference. In one northern central rural county, White persons were also more likely to complete drug court (34% vs. 0%); however, low cell sizes precluded statistical analysis. In contrast, differences in completion rates were negligible in the northern central urban county (48% vs. 47%), a second northern central rural county (74% vs. 71%), and the southern urban county (32% vs. 29%). Finally, Black participants had a relatively *higher* completion rate in the midwestern urban county (23% vs. 14%); however, this difference was not statistically significant possibly because of insufficient power (power = 34%).

Longitudinal Trends in Admission and Completion Rates

Contrary to the fourth study hypothesis, longitudinal findings at the state level provide little assurance that drug courts in these states have taken adequate steps (as of 2015 or 2016) to address racial disparities. Figure 1 depicts admission rates by race from 2006 to 2015 in the southern state. White persons referred to drug court were significantly more likely to gain admission in every year examined, which is clearly evidenced by the fact that the 95% confidence intervals do not overlap in any year other than 2009 when they overlap minimally.

Figure 2 depicts completion rates by race in the southern state from 2006 to 2015. White persons admitted to drug court were significantly more likely than Black persons to complete the program from 2006 through 2010. Completion rates converged thereafter and were no longer significantly different other than in 2013. Unfortunately, this convergence is not attributable to increased completion rates for Black participants over time but rather to steadily lower completion rates for White persons.

Figure 3 depicts admission rates by race from 2010 to 2016 for the midwestern state. Black persons were significantly *more* likely than White persons to be admitted to drug court in 2010 and 2011. Admission rates for Black persons declined thereafter and were no longer significantly different in 2012 or 2013 and were significantly lower in 2014 through 2016.

Finally, Figure 4 depicts completion rates by race in the midwestern state. White persons admitted to drug court were significantly more likely than Black persons to graduate from the program in all years examined except 2012. This is clearly evidenced by the fact that the 95% confidence intervals do not overlap in any year other than 2012.

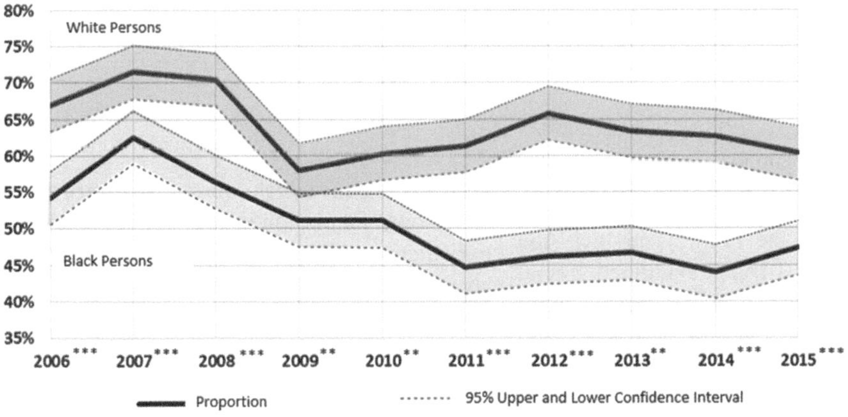

Figure 1 Percent of referrals admitted to drug court in a southern state by race and year

Note. Significance tests of the difference between independent proportions are one-tailed.

*$p < .05$. **$p < .01$. ***$p < .001$.

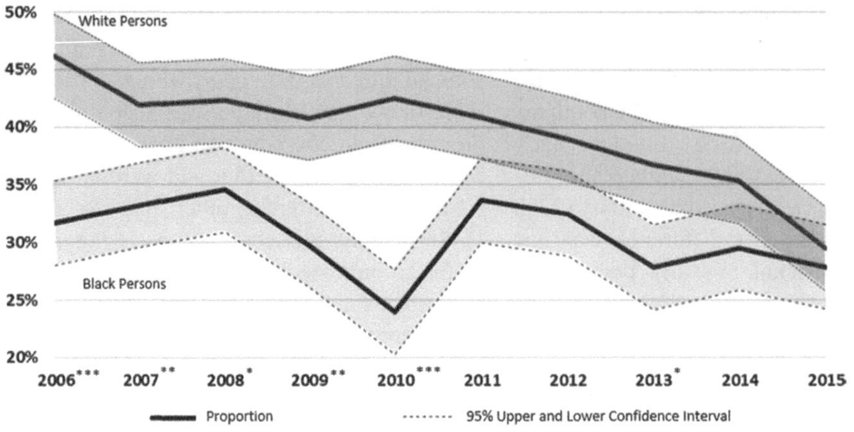

Figure 2 Percent of admissions completing drug court in a southern state by race and year

Note. Significance tests of the difference between independent proportions are one-tailed.

*$p < .05$. **$p < .01$. ***$p < .001$.

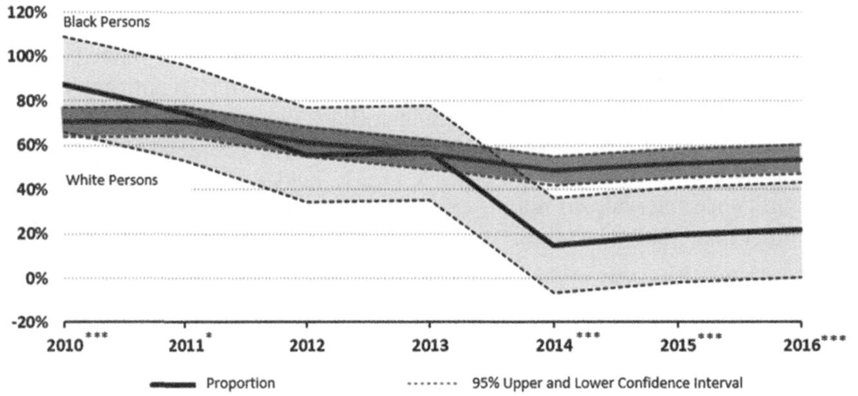

Figure 3 Percent of referrals admitted to drug court in a midwestern state by race and year.

Note. Significance tests of the difference between independent proportions are one-tailed.

*$p < .05$. **$p < .01$. ***$p < .001$.

Discussion

This pilot study of the Equity and Inclusion Assessment Tool (EIAT) examined racial differences in drug court referral, admission, and graduation rates in two states and eight counties located in diverse regions of the United States. Results reveal disturbing differences in most jurisdictions at each stage in drug court processing. Black persons who were arrested for drug offenses had lower referral rates to drug court in five of the seven jurisdictions for which referral data were available, lower admission rates in seven of the eight jurisdictions for which admission data was available, and lower graduation rates in six of the ten jurisdictions. These cascading impacts may contribute additively or multiplicatively to higher justice system involvement for Black persons, lesser access to needed treatment and social services, and poorer criminal justice and health outcomes. The findings offer a possible snapshot of systemic racial inequity

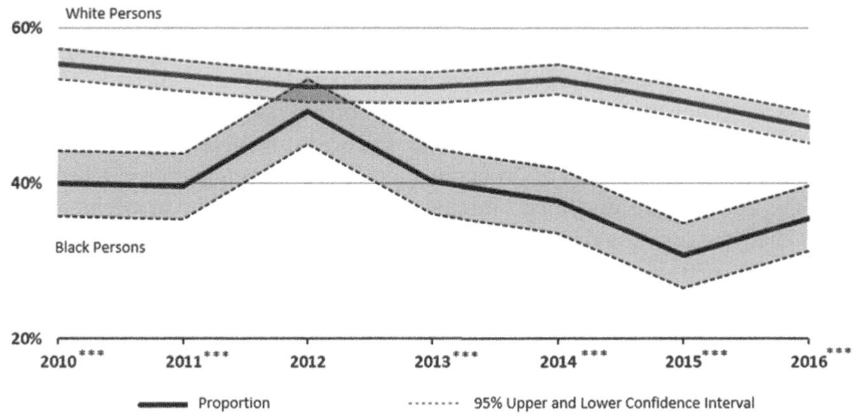

Figure 4 Percent of admissions completing drug court in a midwestern state by race and year

Note. Significance tests of the difference between independent proportions are one-tailed.

$*p < .05$. $**p < .01$. $***p < .001$.

and merit serious consideration and corrective measures by drug courts, other criminal justice professionals, and policy makers.

In two statewide analyses for which adequate longitudinal data were available, racial differences in admission and graduation rates persisted or worsened for up to a decade, suggesting that greater attention in recent years to racial equity by the drug court field may not be translating into effective remedial actions. Because the pilot sites were selected purposefully based on their ability to track referrals and provide information on participant demographics, they may be more data-driven and open to self-analysis than many programs. If so, then the disturbing differences and temporal trends reflected in this study could be widespread but not readily apparent to many drug courts. Considerable effort is required to train drug courts to use tools such as the EIAT to diagnose unfair disparities in their programs, identify indicated remedial strategies, and evaluate the success of their remedial efforts.

Drug Court Referrals

Consistent with the first study hypothesis, Black persons who were arrested for drug offenses were less likely than White persons to be referred to drug court in five of the seven sites for which referral data were available. On average, White persons were nearly twice as likely to be referred to drug court. Only a few studies have examined racial differences in drug court referral rates, with two program evaluations finding no differences in referrals to adult drug courts (Morgan et al., 2016; Weinrath et al., 2018) and one statewide study reporting fewer referrals for Black teens to juvenile drug courts (Bellas, 2014). The current findings add to this scant literature and raise concerns about potentially pervasive racial disparities in drug court referral practices.

No information is available to explain these discrepancies because none of the study sites reliably recorded the reasons persons were referred or not referred to drug court. Future research employing the EIAT with prospective samples of arrestees will hopefully shed light on this matter and help identify indicated remedial strategies. Black defendants may be, for example, less likely than White defendants to meet legal eligibility criteria for drug court. Federal funding restrictions and many state statutes or prosecutorial policies prohibit entry to drug court for persons with violent or drug-dealing charges or convictions, and Black individuals are more likely to have these exclusionary offenses in their criminal records (FBI, 2017; Mantha et al., 2021;

Sheeran & Heideman, 2021). These eligibility restrictions are not empirically justified and removing them may reduce unwarranted racial disparities. Persons with violence charges or histories typically perform as well or better than other participants in drug courts (Carey et al., 2012; Rossman et al., 2011; Saum & Hiller, 2008) as do persons charged with drug dealing offenses (Cissner et al., 2013)—assuming they have a substance use disorder. Although some studies have reported smaller effect sizes for participants with violence charges or histories (Mitchell et al., 2012; Shaffer, 2011), their outcomes were still comparable or favorable to those of persons with violence histories sentenced to other programs, especially incarceration.

Black defendants may also be less likely than White defendants to be informed about drug court in a timely and effective manner, making them less likely to accept referral offers. Unpublished findings from focus groups conducted with Black defendants in one state found that many were first informed about drug court after they had already served several weeks or months in pretrial detention (Janku, 2017). At that point, they were likely to be sentenced to time served if convicted of the index offense(s) and were uninterested in further involvement with the criminal justice system. They also objected to the way they were informed about drug court. Several participants reported that they first heard about drug court from a source they did not trust (typically the prosecutor), emphasis was placed on a long list of rules and obligations they had to obey and the punitive consequences that would ensue for infractions, and stigmatizing terms were often used in describing the program, such as *addicts*, *relapse*, or *dirty urines*. Retailers do not advertise their goods or services by emphasizing the negative features, predicting failure, and shaming potential customers. Learning to be better social marketers of drug court may enhance referral acceptances. Anecdotally, some drug courts have reported increased referrals of Black defendants by posting informational flyers and brochures at the jail and courthouse advertising the benefits of drug court and how to apply for admission (Janku, 2017). Outreach strategies such as these may alert defendants and their attorneys about drug court early in the case process before defendants have served undue time in pretrial detention and when they are more likely to accept referral offers.

Drug Court Admissions

Consistent with the second study hypothesis, Black persons referred to drug court were significantly less likely to be admitted in four of the eight sites for which admission data was available. They were also considerably less likely to be admitted in three additional sites; however, small sample sizes likely accounted for nonsignificant differences or precluded statistical comparisons.

As with referrals, no information is available to explain these discrepancies. Future studies using the EIAT with prospective samples of drug court referrals should investigate why Black persons may be less likely to be admitted to drug court and how to rectify those disparities. One factor may relate to suitability determinations. After confirming that a candidate meets formal eligibility criteria for the program ("paper eligibility"), some drug courts may screen referrals for their suitability for the program based on the team's subjective impressions of the person's attitude, motivation for change, or readiness for treatment (Belenko et al., 2011). Suitability determinations have been shown to have no impact on drug court graduation rates or post-program recidivism (Rossman et al., 2011). Intrinsic motivation for change and an optimistic attitude about recovery are not significant predictors of success at entry into drug court; however, they become important by the time of discharge to ensure that treatment gains are maintained after graduation (Cosden et al., 2006; Kirk, 2012). Studies also find that criminal justice professionals are more likely to attribute negative motivations and attitudes to persons from different cultural groups than their own in the absence of reliable supporting evidence (Casey et al., 2012). Because suitability determinations have the potential to exclude individuals from drug court for invalid reasons and may exacerbate racial or ethnic disparities as the result of implicit bias, the NADCP best practice standards provide that suitability determinations should be avoided, and entry procedures should be based on objective and empirically validated criteria.

Evidence further suggests that Black and Hispanic persons, particularly young adult males, may under-report mental health, substance use and trauma symptoms to criminal justice authorities, thus potentially disqualifying them from drug courts and other sorely needed treatment programs (Covington et al., 2011; Waters et al., 2018). Assessors in drug courts should be trained carefully on how to use effective interviewing and rapport-building techniques to boost disclosure of treatment needs, especially among young Black and Hispanic men. To encourage accurate self-reporting and protect participants' trial rights, use-immunity should attach to any disclosures made during an assessment. Candidates should be assured that information derived directly or indirectly from the assessment cannot be used to substantiate a criminal charge against them, bring new charges, or increase their sentence if convicted.

Drug Court Completions

Consistent with the third study hypothesis, Black participants were significantly less likely than White participants to graduate from drug court in four of the ten states and counties. They were considerably less likely to graduate in two additional counties; however, small samples likely accounted for nonsignificant differences or precluded statistical comparisons. Lower completion rates for Black participants are likely to contribute to disproportionate convictions for these individuals, higher incarceration rates, and negative collateral consequences stemming from a criminal record.

Notably, Black participants in the current study were more likely than White participants to graduate from drug court in one county and no appreciable differences were found in three additional counties. These favorable outcomes suggest that some drug courts may be more effective at avoiding disparities once participants are enrolled in their program and staff have greater control over the services that are delivered. Closer examination of drug courts producing equivalent benefits for Black participants may help to identify best practices to enhance racial equity.

Evidence suggests that Black participants may perceive less procedural fairness in drug courts relative to other participants (Atkin-Plunk et al., 2019), and White staff members have reported having a more difficult time developing a therapeutic alliance with Black participants (Connor, 2020). Cultural sensitivity and diversity training may help drug court staff develop more effective therapeutic alliances with participants from different cultures and recognize and resolve prejudicial thoughts or beliefs they may have but not be aware of. Studies in substance use treatment programs have found that culturally sensitive attitudes on the part of staff, especially program directors and supervisors, were among the strongest predictors of longer tenure and higher treatment completion rates for Black and Hispanic persons (Ely & Thomas, 2001; Guerrero, 2010; Guerrero & Andrews, 2011).

Many studies have found that Black drug court participants had significantly greater employment, educational, financial, and/or mental health needs than White participants (Dannerbeck et al., 2006; DeVall & Lanier, 2012; Gallagher, 2013a; Howard, 2016; McKean & Warren-Gordon, 2011), and in focus groups Black participants have commonly reported an increased need for educational, employment and mental health services (Cresswell & Deschenes, 2001; Gallagher, 2013b; Gallagher & Nordberg, 2016). Research is needed to determine whether augmenting interventions addressing these service needs reduces racial disparities. Greater employment and financial problems may also make it harder for Black participants to pay fines, treatment fees or transportation costs, which are often required to complete drug court. Adjustments to fee schedules and other costs may be required to eliminate racial inequities.

Finally, treatment quality may be a factor negatively affecting outcomes for Black and Hispanic participants. Many commonly administered substance-use treatments were designed for older, White, alcohol dependent persons, and they may not be suitable for younger Black individuals with divergent substance use profiles (Burlew et al., 2011). Black persons arrested for drug offenses are more likely than White persons to use marijuana as their primary drug of choice, and they may be less likely to meet diagnostic criteria for severe substance dependence (Guerrero et al., 2013; McElrath et al., 2016). Focus groups conducted in drug courts found that many Black participants felt the program was unsuited to their needs because they did not believe they had a substance use problem and resented being compelled to identify themselves as an "addict" or admit to being powerless over their drug use (Gallagher, 2013b; Gallagher & Nordberg, 2016). Drug courts may need to incorporate evidence-based treatments designed for persons engaged in problematic cannabis use who may not be clinically dependent, such as the treatments delivered in the Cannabis Youth Treatment (CYT) study (Dennis et al., 2004). With the recent reemergence of cocaine and methamphetamine use in some Black communities, they may also need to deliver treatments generally shown to be effective for treating stimulant addiction in drug courts, such as the Matrix Model (Marinelli-Casey et al., 2008). Two uncontrolled pilot studies reported that delivering services tailored specifically to participants' cultural backgrounds and experiences improved treatment retention and completion rates for young adult Black male drug court participants (Marlowe et al., 2018; Vito & Tewksbury, 1998). Further research is needed to replicate these preliminary findings in controlled trials and examine culturally proficient interventions designed for other racial, ethnic, or cultural groups.

Limitations and Directions for Future Research

Several design limitations may affect interpretation of the results from this study. As noted earlier, the sample was purposefully selected from jurisdictions known by the authors to collect data on drug court referrals and admissions. The findings cannot be assumed to be nationally representative of equity and inclusion in drug courts. Because these jurisdictions had sufficient wherewithal and concern for racial equity to record and share relevant information, disparities for Black persons could be worse in other programs.

Data elements and time intervals for analyses were limited by the availability of relevant information. Longitudinal analyses could only be performed at the state level for two jurisdictions and timely information for the longitudinal analyses was available only through 2015 or 2016. The most recent data for any analysis was from 2018. Racial differences might have improved in more recent years; however, for many communities this would have required major shifts in long-standing trends. Small sample sizes for some county-level analyses also raise questions about the reliability and generalizability of the findings, and nonsignificant differences in those analyses must be viewed cautiously because of low statistical power.

Importantly, this study does not include information on why racial differences may exist. None of the statewide data included the reasons why persons were not referred to drug court, why referrals were declined, or why participants were discharged unsuccessfully from the program. Some racial differences could have been warranted based on participants' risk or need profiles. For example, lower referral or admission rates for Black persons might have been justified if they had lower rates of substance use disorders. More research is needed to understand why differences exist and develop remedial strategies where such differences are unfair or unjustified. Future analyses of the EIAT pilot testing data may be able to develop preliminary findings on these issues using more limited data from individual courts that recorded the reasons for non-admission and unsuccessful discharge.

Finally, this study examined racial differences emerging from the point of referral to drug court. Research suggests that disparities occurring at earlier junctures in criminal case processing, such as differences in police surveillance and arrest practices or prosecutorial charging practices, may contribute progressively to poorer outcomes in later stages of case processing (Kutateladze et al., 2014). Future studies should examine racial differences in arrest and charging practices and determine how such practices may contribute to lower referral, admission, or graduation rates in drug courts.

Disclosure Statement

No potential conflict of interest was reported by the authors.

Funding

This research was supported by Grant G2099ONDCP02A from the Office of National Drug Control Policy (ONDCP) of the Executive Office of the President (EOP).

Discussion Questions

1. There were a few instances where the courts lacked data that the researchers wanted or lacked good sample sizes. What were those instances, and how does that impact our ability to interpret the results?
2. Why is it so difficult to measure how many individuals arrested in a jurisdiction are eligible for drug courts?
3. What did the authors' findings tell us about drug court referrals, admissions, completions, and race over the course of the study period?

References

Atkin-Plunk, C. A., Peck, J. H., & Armstrong, G. S. (2019). Do race and ethnicity matter? An examination of racial/ethnic differences in perceptions of procedural justice and recidivism among problem-solving court staff. *Race and Justice*, *9*(2), 151–179. https://doi.org/10.1177/2153368717691800

Belenko, S., Fabrikant, N., & Wolff, N. (2011). The long road to treatment: Models of screening and admission into drug courts. *Criminal Justice & Behavior*, *38*(12), 1222–1243.

Bellas, M. L. (2014). *Disproportionate minority contact assessment: Court and diversion referral decisions in Vermont's juvenile justice system.* Vermont Center for Justice Research. www.crgvt.org/uploads/5/2/2/2/52222091/dmc_assessment_2014.pdf

Brant, R. (2021). *Inference for proportions: Comparing two independent samples.* www.stat.ubc.ca/~rollin/stats/ssize/b2.html

Breitenbucher, P., Bermejo, R., Killian, C. M., Young, N. K., Duong, L., & DeCerchio, K. (2018). Exploring racial and ethnic disproportionalities and disparities in family treatment courts: Findings from the Regional Partnership Grant Program. *Journal for Advancing Justice*, *1*, 35–62.

Burlew, A. K., Weekes, J. C., Montgomery, L., Feaster, D. J., Robbins, M. S., Rosa, C. L., Ruglass, L. M., Venner, K. L., & Wu, L. (2011). Conducting research with racial/ethnic minorities: Methodological lessons from the NIDA clinical trials network. *American Journal of Drug & Alcohol Abuse*, *37*(5), 324–332.

Carey, S. M., Mackin, J. R., & Finigan, M. W. (2012). What works? The ten key components of drug court: Research-based best practices. *Drug Court Review*, *8*(1), 6–42.

Casey, P., Warren, R., Cheesman, F., & Elek, J. (2012). *Helping courts address implicit bias: Resources for education.* National Center for State Courts. https://ncsc.contentdm.oclc.org/digital/collection/accessfair/id/246/

Cheesman, F. L., Genthon, K., & Marlowe, D. B. (2019). From a performance measure to a performance evaluation tool: Conceptual development of the Equity and Inclusion Assessment Tool (EIAT). *Justice System Journal*, *40*(3), 259–266.

Cissner, A. B., Rempel, M., Franklin, A. W., Roman, J. K., Bieler, S., Cohen, R., & Cadoret, C. R. (2013). *A statewide evaluation of New York's adult drug courts: Identifying which policies work best.* Center for Court Innovation. www.bja.gov/Publications/CCI-UI-NYS_Adult_DC_Evaluation.pdf

Connor, T. A. (2020). Community courts & race: An examination of community court judges, staff, and racial dynamics. *Race and Justice*, *13*(2), 185–206.

Cosden, M., Basch, J. E., Campos, E., Greenwell, A., Barazani, S., & Walker, S. (2006). Effects of motivation and problem severity on court-based drug treatment. *Crime and Delinquency*, *52*(4), 599–618.

Covington, S. S., Griffin, D., & Dauer, R. (2011). *Helping men recover: A program for treating addiction – Special edition for use in the criminal justice system*. Jossey-Bass.

Cresswell, L. S., & Deschenes, E. P. (2001). Minority and nonminority perceptions of drug court program severity and effectiveness. *Journal of Drug Issues*, *31*(1), 259–291.

Dannerbeck, A., Harris, G., Sundet, P., & Lloyd, K. (2006). Understanding and responding to racial differences in drug court outcomes. *Journal of Ethnicity in Substance Abuse*, *5*, 1–22.

Dennis, M., Godley, S. H., Diamond, G., Tims, F. M., Babor, T., Donaldson, J., & Funk, R. (2004). The Cannabis Youth Treatment (CYT) study: Main findings from two randomized trials. *Journal of Substance Abuse Treatment*, *27*(3), 197–213.

DeVall, K. E., & Lanier, C. L. (2012). Successful completion: An examination of factors influencing drug court completion for white and nonwhite male participants. *Substance Use & Misuse*, *47*(10), 1106–1116.

Ely, R. J., & Thomas, D. A. (2001). The effects of diversity perspectives on work group processes and outcomes. *Administrative Science Quarterly*, *46*(2), 229–273.

Federal Bureau of Investigation [FBI]. (2017). *Crime in the United States*. U.S. Department of Justice. https://ucr.fbi.gov/crime-in-the-u.s/2017/crime-in-the-u.s.-2017

Festinger, D. S., DeMatteo, D. S., Marlowe, D. B., & Lee, P. A. (2005). Expungement of arrest records in drug court: Do clients know what they're missing? *Drug Court Review*, *5*(1), 1–21.

Gallagher, J. R. (2013a). Drug court graduation rates: Implications for policy advocacy and future research. *Alcoholism Treatment Quarterly*, *31*, 241–253.

Gallagher, J. R. (2013b). African American participants' views on racial disparities in drug court outcomes. *Journal of Social Work Practice in the Addictions*, *13*(2), 143–162.

Gallagher, J. R., & Nordberg, A. (2016). Comparing and contrasting White and African American participants' lived experiences in drug court. *Journal of Ethnicity in Criminal Justice*, *14*(2), 100–119. https://doi.org/10.1080/15377938.2015.1117999

Genthon, K., & Robinson, D. (2021). *Collecting race & ethnicity data: Courts statistics project data governance special topic*. National Center for State Courts. https://ncfsc-web.squiz.cloud/__data/assets/pdf_file/0018/42255/Race_Ethnicity_Data_Collection_2.pdf

Guerrero, E. (2010). Managerial capacity and adoption of culturally competent practices in outpatient substance abuse treatment organizations. *Journal of Substance Abuse Treatment*, *39*(4), 329–339.

Guerrero, E., & Andrews, C. M. (2011). Cultural competence in outpatient substance abuse treatment: Measurement and relationship to wait time and retention. *Drug & Alcohol Dependence*, *119*(1), 13–22.

Guerrero, E. G., Marsh, J. C., Duan, L., Oh, C., Perron, B., & Lee, B. (2013). Disparities in completion of substance abuse treatment between and within racial and ethnic groups. *Health Services Research*, *48*(4), 1450–1467.

Ho, T., Carey, S. M., & Malsch, A. M. (2018). Racial and gender disparities in treatment courts: Do they exist and is there anything we can do to change them? *Journal for Advancing Justice*, *1*, 5–34.

Howard, D. (2016). Race, neighborhood, and drug court graduation. *Justice Quarterly*, *33*(1), 159–184. www.tandfonline.com/doi/abs/10.1080/07418825.2014.908938

Janku, A. D. (2017). *Equity and inclusion in treatment courts* [Paper presentation]. Illinois Association of Problem-Solving Courts Annual Conference.

Kirk, J. N. (2012). *Assessing self determining attitudes and behaviors in court mandated treatment clients* [Doctoral dissertation]. Oklahoma State University. https://core.ac.uk/reader/215253102

Kutateladze, B. L., Andiloro, N. R., Johnson, B. D., & Spohn, C. C. (2014). Cumulative disadvantage: Examining racial and ethnic disparity in prosecution and sentencing. *Criminology*, *52*, 514–551. https://onlinelibrary.wiley.com/doi/pdf/10.1111/1745-9125.12047

Lowry, R. (2021). *The significance of the difference between two independent proportions*. VassarStats. http://vassarstats.net/propdiff_ind.html

Mantha, S., Nolan, M. L., Harcopos, A., & Paone, D. (2021). Racial disparities in criminal legal system involvement among New York City overdose decedents: Implications for diversion programs. *Drug and Alcohol Dependence*, *226*, 108867. https://doi.org/10.1016/j.drugalcdep.2021.108867

Marinelli-Casey, P., Gonzales, R., Hillhouse, M., Ang, A., Zweben, J., Cohen, J., Hora, P. F., & Rawson, R. A. (2008). Drug court treatment for methamphetamine dependence: Treatment response and posttreatment outcomes. *Journal of Substance Abuse Treatment*, *34*(2), 242–248.

Marlowe, D. B. (2013). Achieving racial and ethnic fairness in drug courts. *Court Review, 49*(1), 40–47.

Marlowe, D. B., Shannon, L. M., Ray, B., Turpin, D. P., Wheeler, G. A., Newell, J., & Lawson, S. G. (2018). Developing a culturally proficient intervention for young African American men in drug court: Examining feasibility and estimating an effect size for Habilitation Empowerment Accountability Therapy (HEAT). *Journal for Advancing Justice, 1*, 109–130. https://advancejustice.org/wp-content/uploads/2018/06/AJ-Journal.pdf

McElrath, K., Taylor, A., & Tran, K. K. (2016). Black-White disparities in criminal justice referrals to drug treatment: Addressing treatment need or expanding the diagnostic net? *Behavioral Sciences, 6*(4), 21. www.mdpi.com/2076-328X/6/4/21/htm

McKean, J., & Warren-Gordon, K. (2011). Racial differences in graduation rates from adult drug treatment courts. *Journal of Ethnicity in Criminal Justice, 9*, 41–55.

Mitchell, O., Wilson, D. B., Eggers, A., & MacKenzie, D. L. (2012). Assessing the effectiveness of drug courts on recidivism: A meta-analytic review of traditional and non-traditional drug courts. *Journal of Criminal Justice, 40*(1), 60–71.

Morgan, R. D., Mitchell, S. M., Thoen, M. A., Campion, K., Bolanos, A. D., Sustaita, M. A., & Henderson, S. (2016). Specialty courts: Who's in and are they working? *Psychological Services, 13*(3), 246–253.

National Association of Drug Court Professionals [NADCP]. (1997). *Defining drug courts: The key components*. Office of Justice Programs, U.S. Department of Justice. www.ndci.org/sites/default/files/nadcp/Key_Components.pdf

National Association of Drug Court Professionals [NADCP]. (2018). *Adult drug court best practice standards* (vol. I text revision). file:///C:/Users/Owner/Downloads/Adult-Drug-Court-Best-Practice-Standards-Volume-I-Text-Revision-December-2018.pdf

National Association of Drug Court Professionals [NADCP]. (2019). *Equity and inclusion toolkit*. www.ndci.org/resource/training/equity/

Office of National Drug Control Policy. (2021). *The Biden-Harris Administration's statement of drug policy priorities for year one*. Executive Office of the President. https://bidenwhitehouse.archives.gov/wp-content/uploads/2021/03/BidenHarris-Statement-of-Drug-Policy-Priorities-April-1.pdf

Rossman, S. B., Rempel, M., Roman, J. K., Zweig, J. M., Lindquist, C. H., Green, M., Downey, P. M., Yahner, J., Bahti, A. S., & Farole, D. J. (2011). *The multi-site adult drug court evaluation: The impact of drug courts* (Vol. 4). Urban Institute Justice Policy Center. www.ncjrs.gov/pdffiles1/nij/grants/237112.pdf

Saum, C. A., & Hiller, M. L. (2008). Should violent offenders be excluded from drug court participation? An examination of the recidivism of violent and nonviolent drug court participants. *Criminal Justice Review, 33*(3), 291–307.

Shaffer, D. K. (2011). Looking inside the black box of drug courts: A meta-analytic review. *Justice Quarterly, 28*(3), 493–521.

Sheeran, A. M., & Heideman, A. J. (2021). The effects of race and ethnicity on admission, graduation, and recidivism in the Milwaukee County Adult Drug Treatment Court. *Social Sciences, 10*, 261.

Trood, M. D., Spivak, B. L., & Ogloff, J. R. P. (2021). A systematic review and meta-analysis of the effects of judicial supervision on recidivism and well-being factors of criminal offenders. *Journal of Criminal Justice, 74*, 101796. https://doi.org/10.1016/j.jcrim-jus.2021.101796

Vito, G., & Tewksbury, R. (1998). The impact of treatment: The Jefferson County (Kentucky) Drug Court Program. *Federal Probation, 62*(2), 46–51.

Waters, N. L., Lee, C. G., Cochran, N., & Holt, K. (2018). Trauma treatment for men in recovery for substance use disorders: A randomized design within the Miami-Dade County Adult Drug Court. *Journal for Advancing Justice, 1*, 131–157.

Weinrath, M., Gorkoff, K., Watts, J., Smee, C., Allard, Z., Bellan, M., Lumsden, S., & Cattini, M. (2018). Accessing drug treatment courts: Do age, race or gender matter? *Australian & New Zealand Journal of Criminology, 51*(4), 619–637. https://doi.org/10.1177/0004865818757586

Yu, M., & Dannerbeck, A. (2020). Who is admitted into a drug treatment court? Comparing Caucasians and African Americans residing in a Midwest state. *Ewha Journal of Social Sciences, 36*(2), 133–162.

Reading 12.2 Superficial Adherence to EBP

In Chapter 12, you learned about the limits of black box evaluations. They can answer the question of whether a program had the desired impact, but if the answer is no, we will be left wondering what went wrong. In the field of corrections, research has come a long way in informing us about what works. The problem is that we know what works, and we might even write up a plan to implement a program based on the evidence, but there will always be the question of whether the program proceeded as planned. Fortunately, Borseth, Myer, and Makarios (2023) conducted both a process and outcome evaluation of the correctional halfway house they were studying. When the outcome evaluation did not produce the anticipated results, they were able to refer to their process evaluation to explain why.

Superficial Adherence to EBP: An Example of Low Fidelity to the RNR Model Using a Halfway House

Jenna L. Borseth, Andrew J. Myer, and Matthew D. Makarios

Introduction

The risk-need-responsivity (RNR) model of offender management has received steadfast empirical attention since it was introduced in the 1980s. Despite the nothing works (Martinson, 1974) mantra of the late 20th century, scholars have sought out identifying what works, for whom, and under what circumstances (Andrews et al., 1990; Cullen & Gilbert, 1982; Gendreau et al., 1996; Lipsey, 1999; Palmer, 1975). From an ever-growing body of research, the principles of effective intervention emerged, providing guidance to correctional practitioners on how to reduce recidivism. When boiled down, the principles seem straightforward – assess a person's risk, target those who are higher risk, refer clients to interventions based on their assessed criminogenic needs, and have those interventions use a cognitive-behavioral modality; however, the realities of the empirical research world and a practitioners' day-to-day world are rarely the same thing (Latessa et al., 2002). Furthermore, empirical research continues to expand upon the implementation of RNR practices (see, for example, Drawbridge et al., 2019).

The growing popularity of the principles of RNR have led to growths in research and assessment tools; however, the reality is that successfully implementing evidenced-based practices requires a lot of effort and many agencies struggle with fidelity (Lowenkamp et al., 2006). To illustrate, adherence to the risk principle requires (1) the development or purchase of an empirical risk tool, (2) training on administration and interpretation of the tool (see Holsinger et al., 2001), (3) staff buy in of the practice (La Vigne et al., 2008), (4) implementation and staff adherence to the tool (Bonta & Motiuk, 1987; Krauss, 2004; McCafferty, 2017; Wormith et al., 2012, 2015), and (5) reassessment and revalidation of the tool (Labrecque et al., 2014; Lloyd et al., 2020).

In short, adherence to the RNR model is not guaranteed simply by the purchase of a risk/need tool or by offering an intervention that is labeled as cognitive-behavioral; in fact, adherence to the RNR model can seem quite cumbersome to practitioners (Nagy, 2013). In addition, it is likely that a great deal of information can be gleaned from programs that struggle to implement RNR. This paper offers a case study of a correctional halfway house program that has attempted to implement the RNR model. Over time this program has adopted a risk tool and trained staff on programs that address specific criminogenic needs using a cognitive-behavioral intervention. Data were originally collected to conduct an outcome and process evaluation of the facility. However, the subsequent analyses suggest several lessons that can be learned from a surface-level adherence to EBP.

Literature Review

What Works?

Over 30 years of research on effective correctional intervention have led to an increased understanding of offender treatment (Andrews et al., 1990; Bonta & Andrews, 2007; Gendreau & Ross, 1987; Hannah-Mofatt, 2005; Makarios et al., 2014). These practices, referred to as the principles of effective intervention, have been shown to effectively guide treatment for a variety of offending populations, including men and women, adults and juveniles, as well as offenders served both within an institution and in the community (Andrews, Bonta, et al., 1990; Grieger & Hosser, 2014; Lowenkamp et al., 2006; Makarios et al., 2014; Vose et al., 2009). The versatile nature of the principles allows for them to be adopted into many different correctional programs. This section will review research on the four principles of effective intervention: risk, need, responsivity, and fidelity (Andrews et al., 1990; Bonta & Andrews, 2007; Hannah-Mofatt, 2005; Makarios et al., 2014).

Risk Principle

The risk principle states that programs should use an objective, empirical, and validated tool to assess an individual's likelihood of recidivating (Andrews et al., 1990; Bonta & Andrews, 2007; Hannah-Mofatt, 2005; Makarios et al., 2014). Risk assessment is the process of measuring the likelihood that an offender will re-offend. Over time, these assessments have developed and become more useful and accurate. Current versions not only measure risk but also allow correctional personnel to make informed sentencing, treatment, and release decisions (Andrews et al., 2006; Latessa & Lovins, 2010).

Once risk is determined using a validated risk assessment tool, the risk principle states that involvement in correctional interventions should be a function of the individual's risk level. Specifically, high-risk offenders should receive the most intensive services available, while moderate risk offenders receive less intense services. Low-risk offenders should avoid intensive interventions and avoid being mixed with higher risk offenders to stave off potential iatrogenic effects (Lowenkamp & Latessa, 2002). Ample research has suggested treatment services should be proportionate to the offenders' risk of reoffending (Bonta & Andrews, 2007; Lowenkamp & Latessa, 2005; Lowenkamp et al., 2006; Makarios et al., 2014; Sperber et al., 2013). However, despite these empirical findings, in practice risk is not always followed when placing offenders (Bonta & Motiuk, 1987).

While research has consistently demonstrated that targeting higher risk offenders produces the largest reductions in research, the literature has turned to inspection of how much intervention is required for each risk level. Sperber et al. (2013) contributed to this discussion with their study examining the impact that differing amounts of treatment have on the recidivism of people with varying risk levels. Overall, the study indicates that the amount of treatment that produces the largest change in recidivism does vary by a person's risk. For example, increasing the amount of treatment from 100–199 hours to more than 200 hours produces a significant decrease in recidivism for high-risk offenders but does not produce much of a decrease for moderate-risk offenders. However, dosage does not have a linear effect on recidivism; rather, there becomes a point where too high of a treatment dosage has adverse effects (Makarios et al., 2014). Cumulatively, this research indicates that effective dosage for offenders consists of little to no intervention for low-risk offenders, 100–150 hours for moderate risk, and a minimum of 200 hours for high-risk offenders (Makarios et al., 2014; Sperber et al., 2013).

Need Principle

The need principle is the second element of effective intervention for offenders (Bonta & Andrews, 2007). Criminogenic needs are dynamic characteristics of offenders that are statistically related to offending (Andrews & Bonta, 1998). They include antisocial attitudes, antisocial companions, antisocial personality, education/employment, leisure/recreation, family/marital, and drug/alcohol abuse (Andrews & Bonta, 1998). Changes in these criminogenic needs influence the probability that an offender will recidivate (Taxman & Caudy, 2015). In general, the need principle refers to the importance of focusing correctional treatment on addressing these crime producing needs (Bonta & Andrews, 2007). Research suggests that programs that focus on targeting criminogenic needs rather than non-criminogenic needs produce larger reductions in recidivism (Bonta & Andrews, 2007; Dowden & Andrews, 1999; Grieger & Hosser, 2014).

Therefore, decision-makers should rely on need assessment tools to aid them in matching individuals to treatment programs that focus on their specific needs. Simply having an assessment is not sufficient to meet the need principle. For example, in their study on criminogenic needs and dosage for juvenile offenders, Baglivio et al. (2018) report some inconsistencies with referrals based on criminogenic needs. In other words, offenders were not consistently placed into programming based on their top criminogenic needs. For instance, among their sample of 1,678 youth who had antisocial attitudes as a top need, 87.9% were placed into a service targeting antisocial attitudes; however, this service matching drops to 53.6% and 56.5%, respectively, for leisure/recreational time and family. This indicates that just because criminogenic needs are identified for a client does not mean that information is being consistently used to match those needs with appropriate services.

Responsivity Principle

The third element of effective intervention is the responsivity principle. Responsivity emphasizes the impact that various treatment approaches have on recidivism (Bonta & Andrews, 2007). The principle is comprised of two main components: specific responsivity and general responsivity. Specific responsivity refers to the consideration of personal sociological, biological, and personality factors that can impede treatment (Bonta & Andrews, 2007). These include factors such as cultural barriers, language barriers, or low motivation. General responsivity, on the other hand, states that programs should use a treatment modality that best adheres to the learning styles of offenders (Bonta & Andrews, 2007).

Research indicates that cognitive-behavioral therapy (CBT) is consistently one of the most effective strategies for teaching new behavioral skills among offenders (Hanson et al., 2002; Landenberger & Lipsey, 2005; Lipsey et al., 2001). A meta-analysis including 14 studies exemplifies this (Lipsey et al., 2001). The results of this analysis indicate that cognitive-behavioral programs produce a significant decrease in recidivism. Generally, these programs produce around a 30% reduction in recidivism compared to the control samples.

Fidelity

The final aspect of effective intervention is fidelity. The principle of fidelity refers to program integrity and whether programs are being implemented in the way they are intended. This is important because while research has indicated that programs that utilize the models of risk, need, and responsivity are more likely to reduce recidivism, administering an evidence-based program may not be effective if it is not correctly implemented (Barnoski, 2004). In addition, without proper implementation, it can be difficult to determine whether programs are effective in meeting their goals (P. Rossi et al., 1999). Therefore, program evaluations that fail to assess fidelity could determine an intervention to be unsuccessful when it is actually an issue of execution. Research provides strong support for the link between fidelity and program effectiveness

(Andrews & Dowden, 2005; Duwe & Clark, 2015; Lowenkamp, 2004; Lowenkamp et al., 2006; Myer & Makarios, 2017).

Programs can increase the likelihood of operating with higher fidelity by continually assessing the program through process evaluations (P. H. Rossi et al., 2004; Lowenkamp et al., 2006). These evaluations involve assessing program characteristics, such as the duration and dosage of treatment, characteristics of the offenders, and barriers to implementation. Ideally, process evaluations and outcome evaluations should go hand-in-hand. While outcome evaluations can provide insight into the program effectiveness, process evaluations can provide a look inside the Black Box and offer feedback to practitioners for improvement (Scarpitti et al., 1993).

Despite the overwhelming evidence and practices developed from RNR research, adherence to these practices remain inconsistent. Recently, fidelity adherence within correctional programs has been lower than it has been in a decade (Farringer et al., 2019). This indicates that many programs still have a long way to go to reach a high fidelity. The current study seeks to extend this conversation by identifying some lessons that can be learned from a halfway house facility that pays lip service to these practices.

Halfway Houses

Halfway houses are community-based correctional programs that offer residential-based programming. These programs consist of temporary housing for offenders in a community residential home, 24-h supervision, and transitional services to reintegrate offenders into the community (Caputo, 2004). Halfway house facilities can serve a variety of offenders ranging from released prisoners to those on probation. Therefore, halfway houses function as reentry and reintegration facilities as well treatment centers.

Literature suggests the impact of halfway houses on recidivism is mixed. While some studies suggest that halfway houses are effective in reducing and/or delaying arrest (Dowell et al., 1985; Hamilton & Campbell, 2014; Hartman et al., 1994), others indicate that they may have no effect on or increase recidivism (Bell et al., 2013; Latessa & Travis, 1991). The inconsistency in evaluation results lends one to examine the differences between effective and ineffective halfway houses. One way this has been examined is by assessing halfway house adherence to the RNR principles. The following section will examine research on effective intervention as well as how each principle of effective intervention can be utilized within a halfway house setting.

RNR and Halfway Houses

As noted above, the RNR model provides a broad framework that can be applied to a variety of forms of offender treatment; therefore, it is important to examine its effectiveness within the context of halfway houses specifically. The majority of this research has focused on the impacts of the risk principle within the context of these facilities (Bonta & Motiuk, 1987; Hamilton & Campbell, 2014; Lowenkamp & Latessa, 2002). One example of such is Lowenkamp and Latessa (2002) study on the impacts of the risk principle within community-based facilities and halfway houses. Their analysis of 22 halfway house programs provide support for the risk principle within the context of halfway house settings. Specifically, their results indicate that high-risk offenders who participate in these programs are significantly less likely to recidivate than high-risk offenders in the control group. However, this was opposite for low/moderate risk offenders. For low/moderate risk halfway house participant's recidivism was higher than the control group. This suggests that halfway houses may be most effective in treating high-risk offenders because they can offer more treatment dosage.

In addition to shortcomings with the risk principles, halfway houses can also struggle to adhere to the need principle. Some research indicates that treatment referrals are not consistently based on an offender's criminogenic needs (Lowenkamp & Latessa, 2002).

For instance, for vocational training referrals, 23.7% of offenders were identified as needing the service while only 7.6% of offenders received it. For other programs such as accommodations assistance, substance abuse counseling, and anger management, there were more offenders who received the services than there were offenders who were identified as having a need in the area.

In whole, the principles of effective intervention identify the need to assess existing programs. Therefore, the current study provides an examination of a Midwestern Halfway House (MHWH) that services offenders using the model of risk, need, and responsivity. Specifically, the study seeks to examine the effectiveness of the program as well as adherence to the RNR model. This is done by addressing two research questions. First, is the MHWH effective in reducing recidivism? Then, does the MHWH implement the RNR principles as they claim to? To address these, an outcome and process evaluation are used, respectively, through a quasi-experimental, matched case design. The following section will provide a brief overview of the facility and the steps they have taken to apply RNR within the facility.

Methodology

The Facility

The MHWH is a program that focuses on administering residential-based treatment services to offenders in the community through the application of the RNR model. The facility adopted the use of evidence-driven assessments to make offender recommendations. The Level of Service Inventory Revised (LSI-R (Andrews & Bonta, 1995)) is used for all clients to assess risk and need. In addition, they use the Texas Christian University Criminal Thinking Scales (TCU-CTS (Knight et al., 2006)), a self-administered survey, to assess cognitive functions related to criminal behavior such as coldheartedness, entitlement, and justification. Lastly, they use a tool developed by the American Society of Addiction Medicine (ASAM (Mee-Lee, 2013)) to assess a client's level of drug/alcohol addiction.

Collectively, these assessments are used by clients and their case managers to create a mutually agreed plan (MAP). In the plan, both parties come to mutual decisions regarding treatment placement based on the clients' needs. The plans include treatment referrals as well as individualized goals for any of the clients high-need areas. Referrals can be made to treatment programs targeting substance abuse (cognitive-behavioral substance group), antisocial attitudes, values, and beliefs and antisocial behavior (Thinking for a Change (Bush et al., 1997)), and employment (Employment Group). Once these plans are developed, clients and their case managers meet weekly to discuss progress, create new goals, and overcome barriers to achieving their goals.

In addition, the program also adopted cognitive-behavioral programming to further align with the RNR principles. The substance abuse group (SA) uses a cognitive-behavioral framework for offenders with a moderate to high need in substance abuse. At the MHWH, two levels of these groups are offered (level 2.1 and level 3.5). Level 2.1 is reserved for the clients who are nonresidential and is thus excluded from this study. Level 3.5 on the other hand offers intensive treatment for residential clients and consists of 20 hours of treatment per week for approximately 3 weeks. Case managers make the referrals to these programs based on whether or not the ASAM score indicates substance abuse issues. The MHWH also offers an aftercare program for offenders who require further intervention after completing SA. T4C also uses a cognitive-behavioral model but focuses on improving problem-solving skills, cognitive restructuring, and enhancing social skills (Bush et al., 1997).

Data

The primary source of data, for both portions of the study, is secondary data from the MHWH. The facility granted the research team permission to access their data for the sake of the current study. Collected information includes a variety of offender information including risk assessment scores, treatment attendance, length of stay, and demographics. In addition, information was also collected regarding staff procedures and referral criterion. All of the data was collected at the facility by one of the researchers. This information was supplemented by online public court record documents which were used to assess the recidivism variable.

It should be noted that it was not feasible for researchers to recover missing data from the system. Therefore, some participants are missing data on variables in the analyses. These cases are denoted by a "missing" column on any applicable tables.

Participants

The current study uses a sample of MHWH participants who received services at any point between January 1, 2015 and December 31, 2015. Most individuals served at MHWH are referred to by a probation agency while others enter from prison to receive reentry services. MHWH also provides outside care to some individuals in the community, such as veterans. To ensure the sample reflects individuals using the residential treatment aspect and criminal justice referral process of MHWH's services, any community-based participants were removed. This resulted in a final sample of 503 clients within the experimental group.

The comparison group is comprised of individuals who were under the supervision of a community supervision agency during the same time period (January 1, 2015 and December 31, 2015). Data for this group are secondary data that was initially collected during the day-to-day procedures of the community supervision agency. Due to some overlap with probation/parole clients being referred to MHWH services, all individuals who attended MHWH were removed from the list of community supervision clients as well as any duplicate cases. This resulted in an initial sample of 8,415 potential comparison group cases.

The comparison group was then matched using a fuzzy set, case-control matching procedure. The fuzzy set matching procedure allows the researcher to set thresholds for exact and non-exact matching. In essence, it allows for participants to be exact matches on some variables and not others. The current study was able to conduct exact matching on all but one variable: age. The matching parameters set are further discussed in the next paragraph.

MHWH participants were matched to the comparison group on five variables: gender, race, age, referral offense, and risk level. Gender was coded as a dichotomous variable so that males were matched to only males and females were matched to only females. Race was coded as a five-category variable (White, Hispanic, Native American, Black, and other) and used exact matching based on these groups. A similar process was done for the referral offense which was a six-category variable, with the categories being: violent offenses, sex offenses, property offenses, drug offenses, DUI offenses, and all other offenses. To match on age, a fuzzy set logic was used with a three-year restriction. This function allows MHWH participants to be matched to anyone who is up to three years older or three years younger. For example, an MHWH client who was 27 years old could be matched with any person who was 24–30 years old.

The last variable clients were matched on is risk level. The five categories of the LSI-R were collapsed into three categories to facilitate matching. The categories used for matching were low, moderate, and high. The low-risk group comprises the LSI-R categories of low and low/moderate. The LSI-R scores of moderate and moderate/high were merged to create the moderate risk category. The high-risk category then consists of the LSI-R high-risk scores.

Outcome Evaluation

In order to determine the impact that MHWH has on recidivism, recidivism data were collected. For the purposes of this study, recidivism was operationalized as a new conviction within two years of discharge. The two-year time period began at the time of release from the MHWH or probation. This allowed for a

Table 1 Matching demographics

Variable	*Treatment*		*Control*		*Test Statistic*
	n	%	*n*	%	
Gender					
Male	363	72.2	363	72.2	$\chi^2 = 0.00$
Female	140	27.8	140	27.8	p = 1.00
Referral Offense					
Violent	66	13.1	66	13.1	$\chi^2 = 0.00$
Sex Offense	9	1.8	9	1.8	p = 1.00
Property	82	16.3	82	16.3	
Drug Offense	246	48.9	246	48.9	
DUI	49	9.7	49	9.7	
Other	51	10.1	51	10.1	
Race/Ethnicity					
White	337	67.0	337	67	$\chi^2 = 0.00$
Native American	120	23.9	120	23.9	p = 1.00
African American	21	4.2	21	4.2	
Hispanic	24	4.8	24	4.8	
Other	1	0.2	1	0.2	
Age (n = 1,489)					
18–20	26	5.2	22	4.4	t = -0.60
21–30	202	40.2	208	41.4	p = .952
31–40	173	34.4	173	34.4	
41–50	69	13.7	67	13.3	
51–60	24	4.8	24	4.8	
61+	9	1.8	9	1.8	
Mean (S.D.)	33.32 (10.0)		33.29 (10.0)		
Min-Max		18–70	18–70		
LSI-R					
Low	70	13.9	70	13.9	$\chi^2 = 0.00$
Moderate	343	68.2	343	68.2	p = 1.00
High	90	17.9	90	17.9	

two-year follow-up for participants in both groups. Recidivism was measured as a dichotomous variable as a yes or no. All recidivism information was collected through the public court record websites. The outcome evaluation also includes a measure for discharge status. It is expected that clients who fail to complete the program may display different outcomes. Therefore, a dichotomous measure of discharge status (successful or unsuccessful) is included.

Process Evaluation

The process evaluation requires several variables to determine adherence to the MHWH policies and the principles of effective intervention. This was done by examining adherence to several factors relating to the risk and need of offenders. Information for the process portion of the evaluation, like the outcome evaluation, come from secondary MHWH data. The facility records data on treatment attendance, treatment notes, risk and need scores, as well as a variety of other information. This data was supplemented with training materials from the facility. Of this, most relevant are the guidelines for which case managers use to make referrals. The variables used for this portion of the study are further discussed below.

Since offender risk level is already examined within the outcome evaluation, the main indicator used to assess adherence to risk is dosage, or treatment hours given. Treatment hours include the total number of hours that an offender at the MHWH was involved in a treatment program. The facility tracks attendance at within all treatment programs as well as the duration of each treatment session. This information was recorded using an ordinal scale: 0–99 hours, 100–149 hours, or 150–199 hours. No client received 200 or more hours of treatment.

To assess adherence to need, the study also includes a measure for appropriate treatment placements. This was done for two of the primary treatment programs offered at the facility: Thinking for a Change and Substance Abuse group. These criteria from the MHWH were used to place offenders into two categories: those who have criterion (and thus should receive treatment) and those who do not. The criterion the facility uses for Thinking for a Change include an LSI-R score of 30 or more and at least two elevated areas on the TCU-CTS. This was replicated by the researchers. For the Substance Abuse Group, criterion for referrals is generally based on a client's ASAM score and whether or not the case manager deems substance abuse treatment to be necessary. The second criteria makes measuring referrals difficult as they differ among case managers. Therefore, new criterion was established. For the purposes of this study, criterion for the substance abuse program consists of an LSI-R score of moderate risk or higher and a history of chemical dependency.

Finally, treatment group completion is also included to assess adherence to the need principle. The need principle entails not only proper treatment referrals, but also attendance and completion. Treatment completion is assessed for two prominent treatment groups offered at the facility. These groups were chosen because they have a predetermined number of sessions required to complete the program. This includes 36 sessions for the SA group and 24 sessions for the T4C group. Completion is categorized into three groups: Completed 100%, Completed 50–99%, and Completed less than 50%.

Results

Outcome Evaluation Results

Analyses for the current study begin with the outcome evaluation. To match the two groups, matching was completed on five variables. The main goal of MHWH's programming is to reduce recidivism among the clients who receive services. To determine whether these rates are reduced, the sample from MHWH were compared to the matched group who did not receive the residential services. A chi-square test was conducted to compare the recidivism between the two groups. This information is provided in Table 2. Overall, the test indicates no significant difference in recidivism between the two groups; thus, those who attended the MHWH were no more or less likely to have a new charge within two years compared to those on supervision.

To further examine these results, supplemental analyses were conducted to account for factors that may influence recidivism. First, the discharge status of offenders receiving treatment at MHWH was examined. As presented in Table 3, these analyses indicate no significant differences. In other words, MHWH clients who were successfully discharged are not significantly more or less likely to recidivate than the comparison group. Research also suggests that MHWH may be more effective at treating high risk people than probation services, and less effective at treating low-risk individuals. To assess this, a chi-square test was conducted to examine if risk had any impact on recidivism between the two groups. These analyses reveal that there is no significant difference in recidivism between probation and MHWH

Table 2 Recidivism of clients

Variable	*Treatment*		*Comparison*		*Test Statistic*
	n	%	*n*	%	
Total Recidivism					
Yes	242	48.1	237	47.1	$\chi^2 = 0.100$
No	261	51.9	266	52.9	$p = .752$

Table 3 Recidivism broken down by discharge status and risk level

Variable	*Recidivism*	*Treatment*		*Comparison*		*Test Statistic*	
		n	%	*n*	%	χ^2	*p*
Discharge Status							
Successful	Yes	143	41.7	156	45.5	1.002	0.317
	No	200	58.3	187	54.5		
Unsuccessful	Yes	91	62.3	76	52.1	3.147	0.076
	No	55	37.7	70	47.9		
Missing		14		14			
Risk Level							
Low	Yes	17	24.3	16	22.9	0.040	0.842
	No	53	75.7	54	77.1		
Moderate	Yes	168	49.0	169	49.3	0.006	0.939
	No	175	51.0	174	50.7		
High	Yes	57	63.3	52	57.8	0.581	0.446
	No	33	36.7	38	42.2		

participants at any of the three risk levels. This information is presented in Table 3.

Process Evaluation Results

Evaluation of adherence to the principles of effective intervention begins with analyses regarding the risk principle. As noted previously, MHWH does use validated risk assessment tools to examine client risk; however, there are two central components to the risk principle: targeting higher risk clients and giving the appropriate treatment dosage based on an offender's risk. Table 3 indicates that targeting different risk levels failed to produce significant differences in outcome. To examine the second element of the risk principle, data were examined regarding the amount of intervention received by risk level.

As can be seen in Table 4, the majority of participants in the low, moderate, and high-risk categories received less than 100 hours of total treatment. In general, there appears to be a lack of variance in the amount of treatment being administered. Additionally, a higher percentage of low-risk clients (15.7%) received more intensive treatment than either moderate (9%) or high risk (5.6%) clients.

To further assess that the effects MHWH had when the dosage principle was followed,

Table 4 Treatment dosage by risk level for the treatment group

Variable	*Low Risk*		*Moderate Risk*		*High Risk*		*Test Statistic*	
	n	%	*n*	%	*n*	%	χ^2	*p*
Treatment Hours								
0–99 Hours	56	80.0	280	81.6	78	86.7	6.543	0.162
100–149 Hours	3	4.3	32	9.3	7	7.8		
150–199 Hours	11	15.7	31	9.0	5	5.6		

Table 5 Recidivism by treatment dosage and risk level

Variable	*Recidivism*	*Treatment*		*Comparison*		*Test Statistic*	
		n	%	*n*	%	χ^2	*p*
Low Risk							
0–99 Hours	Yes	15	26.8	15	26.8	0.000	1.000
	No	41	73.2	41	73.2		
100–149 Hours	Yes	1	33.3	0	0.0	1.200^	0.273
	No	2	66.7	3	100.0		
150–199 Hours	Yes	1	9.1	1	9.1	0.000	1.000
	No	10	90.9	10	90.9		
Moderate Risk							
0–99 Hours	Yes	138	49.3	138	49.3	0.000	1.000
	No	142	50.7	142	50.7		
100–149 Hours	Yes	19	59.4	19	59.4	0.000	1.000
	No	13	40.6	13	40.6		
150–199 Hours	Yes	11	35.5	12	38.7	0.069	0.793
	No	20	64.5	19	61.3		
High Risk							
0–99 Hours	Yes	47	60.3	46	59.0	0.027	0.870
	No	31	39.7	32	41.0		
100–149 Hours	Yes	5	71.4	4	57.1	0.311^	0.577
	No	2	28.6	3	42.9		
150–199 Hours	Yes	5	100.0	2	40.0	4.286^	0.038*
	No	0	0.0	3	60.0		

^multiple cells have an expected cell value below 5; results should be interpreted cautiously

a chi-square test was done to examine the combined impacts that risk, dosage, and treatment group has on recidivism. Table 5 provides these results. Based on these analyses, the only significant differences between the treatment and comparison group is with high-risk participants who received the most treatment (150–199 hours). These results indicate that the comparison group had lower recidivism rates among these clients than the treatment group.

Table 6 Offender placement by placement criteria

Variable	*n*	%
Thinking for a Change		
Attended & Had Criteria	14	4.6
Attended & Didn't meet	46	15.2
Didn't Attend & Had Criteria	50	16.6
Didn't Attend & Didn't meet	192	63.6
Missing	201	
Substance Abuse Group		
Attended & Had Criteria	118	27.0
Attended & Didn't meet	20	4.6
Didn't Attend & Had Criteria	235	53.8
Didn't Attend & Didn't meet	64	14.6
Missing	66	

Table 7 Rates of treatment group completion

Variable	*n*	%
Thinking for a Change	(n = 60)	
Completed 100% (24 Sessions)	52	86.7
Completed 50–99% (12–23 sessions)	0	0.0
Completed below 50% (<12 sessions)	8	13.3
Missing	0	0.0
Mean (SD) min-max	20.8 (7.6) 0–28	
Substance Abuse Group	(n = 138)	
Completed 100% (36 Sessions)	82	59.4
Completed 50–99% (18–35 sessions)	16	11.6
Completed below 50% (<18 sessions)	19	13.8
Missing	21	15.2
Mean (SD) minmax	29.92 (11.7) 039	

However, these results should be interpreted with caution due to low cell counts.

Analyses were also conducted to examine adherence to the need principle. To assess the needs principle, analyses focused on referrals and attendance for Thinking for a Change and Substance Abuse Treatment. Specifically, analyses examined the extent to which clients were properly referred to T4C and SA based on these guidelines. It should be noted that reporting of client TCU-CTS was inconsistent in the data. This resulted in many participants being unable to be classified as having met or not met criteria for T4C and them subsequently being excluded from analysis. These participants make up the "missing" row in Table 6.

For Thinking for a Change, 68.2% of clients were accurately placed. This consists of people who attended and met the criteria as well as people who did not attend and did not have criteria. That leaves 31.8% of clients who were inaccurately placed into Thinking for a Change or who were not placed into the program but met the criteria.

The pattern of these findings was different when examining the Substance Abuse Group. The most common placement outcome was for clients to have criteria and not attend. However, there were no clients who fell into the categories of attending and not meeting criteria, and not attending and meeting criteria. This is supplemented by examining rates of treatment program completion as well (presented in Table 7). Of the clients who attended the Substance Abuse Group, 59.4% completed all 36 sessions of the program. This is slightly higher for clients in Thinking for a Change (81.4%).

Further analyses were conducted to examine whether low program completion among referred clients contributes to the program's ineffectiveness. To examine the effects that program completion has on recidivism chi-square analyses were run. Due to low cell counts, the results presented in Table 8 should be interpreted with caution. Overall, they indicate that treatment completion did not influence lower recidivism rates. In fact, for the Substance Abuse Group, completion was associated with higher recidivism among the treatment group.

Table 8 Recidivism by substance abuse group and T4C completion for referred clients who met the criteria

Variable	*Recidivism*	*Treatment*		*Comparison*		*Test Statistic*	
		n	%	*n*	%	χ^2	*p*
Thinking for a Change							
Less than 50%	Yes	0	0.0	1	50.0	1.333	0.248
	No	2	100.0	1	50.0		
50–99%	Yes	–	–	–	–		
	No	–	–	–	–		
100%	Yes	6	50.0	7	58.3	0.168	0.682
	No	6	50.0	5	41.7		
Substance Abuse Group							
Less than 50%	Yes	8	50.0	10	62.5	0.508	0.476
	No	8	50.0	6	37.5		
50–99%	Yes	43	52.4	41	50.0	0.098	0.775
	No	39	47.6	41	50.0		
100%	Yes	5	71.4	1	14.3	4.667	0.031*^
	No	2	28.6	6	85.7		
Missing		13		13			

^Results should be interpreted with caution as four cells have an expected cell count less than 5

Conclusion

Discussion

Research on the principles of effective intervention has demonstrated key findings that contribute to successful reductions in recidivism. Programs that target the higher risk clients, refer clients to programs that target assessed criminogenic needs, and use a cognitive-behavioral modality during interventions have received the most empirical support. However, these findings are not always seamlessly applied in community settings.

The current study provides an examination of a halfway house program that adopted the RNR model for offender treatment. To begin, initial outcome analyses were conducted to examine whether these efforts were effective in reducing client recidivism. The results, however, indicate that the program does not significantly reduce recidivism when compared to matched probationers. Therefore, while the MHWH is implementing many of the recommendations covered in the RNR model (such as the use of actuarial risk assessment tools and evidence-based, cognitive-behavioral treatment programs), they are still failing to have an impact on client recidivism. These findings on their face, appear contrary to the decades of research which indicate that use of the RNR model can significantly reduce recidivism (Andrews et al., 1990; Gendreau & Ross, 1987; Makarios et al., 2014). Consequently, this study provides subsequent analyses to explore the programs adherence to this model. To do this, the principles of risk and need were broken down with an attempt to examine the degree to which each of these principles were followed.

This was done by first examining program adherence to risk. With regard to using actuarial assessment tools, the MHWH does administer the LSI-R on all incoming clients. This assessment, along with others, are conduced within two weeks of entry into the program and all of the information is stored within their computer system for case managers and treatment providers to access. However, despite the consistent implementation of risk assessments, this information should be used to screen offenders for the program to ensure that low-risk offenders are not admitted into the program.

Since the LSI-R is not conducted before program admittance to screen out low-risk offenders, it was important to also assess the risk levels of participants within the program. Descriptive analyses on the risk scores of admitted clients reveal that the majority of clients fell within the moderate risk category (68.2%), followed by high (17. 9%) and low risk (13.9%). This indicates that the program is fairly successful in targeting moderate and high risk clients. However, the mixing of low, moderate, and high-risk clients into the same living quarters, recreational spaces, and treatment programs may undermine this adherence to the risk principle (Lowenkamp & Latessa, 2002).

The third aspect of risk focuses on treatment dosage. When examining the breakdown of dosage administered based on client risk, this MHWH failed to adequately adhere to the risk principle. Specifically, while high-risk clients are admitted into the program, there are no clients who meet or exceed 200 hours of treatment. Additionally, the program lacks any diversity in dosage based on risk. Table 4 illustrates that the majority of clients within every risk category are given between 0 and 99 hours of treatment. Overall, analyses on risk indicate a discrepancy between the stated program practices and their practices in actuality. While the program screens for offender risk using a validated risk assessment tool, stores those results to make treatment decisions, and tracks the treatment hours of participants, they still fall short of fully adhering to the risk principle.

Adherence to the need principle was also explored by examining the extent to which clients are properly referred based on their criminogenic needs. Treatment referrals within the MHWH are based on whether a client meets specific diagnostic criteria based on their intake assessments and interviews. The results reveal that referrals for treatment programs were often not based on the criminogenic needs for offenders. For instance, when examining the T4C program, 31.8% of clients were either referred to attend despite not meeting admittance criteria or did meet admittance criteria and were not referred to the program. Therefore, when referring clients to the T4C group, case managers deviate from these criteria in nearly a third of cases. This could be due to a lack of communication of the referral criteria or the result of an overreliance on professional overrides.

In addition to proper referrals, the need principle was also examined through treatment completion. This includes Thinking for a Change and SA. Initial analyses of these programs demonstrate some variability in treatment completion. For example, while 81.4% of clients in Thinking for a Change completed the program, far fewer completed the SA group (59.4%). This could be due in part to the differences in group length. Since SA requires more sessions, clients may exit the program or be revoked from the program before completion.

Prior analyses and risk and need foreshadow the outcomes for these treatment groups. In large, the results indicate that the programs have no significant impact on recidivism. The one exception to this is that participants who completed all of the SA program were significantly more likely to recidivate than their matched counterparts; however, this group had very low cell counts and as a result may be misrepresentative. This is likely the result of the issues observed with the risk (mixing low and high-risk offenders and improper dosage) and need principles (improper referrals); however, it could also indicate issues with the fidclity of the treatment groups. While the current study does not explore whether these programs were administered properly, these results do emphasize the importance of examining program implementation.

Limitations

It should be noted that this study has several limitations. First, there were some limitations with the data since the study utilizes data previously collected by the halfway house. One issue with this is missing data. For example, when assessing treatment attendance, a large number of participants were missing data. Within the program data management system, there was a notable underreporting of CTU-CTS and chemical dependency measures. These disparities in the collected data could influence the outcomes of this study. In addition, this data also relies on the accuracy of the reporting by staff. When examining referrals to Thinking for a Change, only 64 participants met criteria for referral. It is unknown whether these low criteria are an accurate reflection of the clients being serviced or indicative of an assessment issue. Finally, using secondary data also limited the degree to which compliance with the RNR model could be assessed. This is particularly relevant with regard assessing proper implementation of risk assessments and treatment groups.

Another limitation of the current study is generalizability. The current study sought to focus on participants who were enrolled in and living in the halfway house facility. Therefore, there is a smaller sample of individuals who reside in the community and receive day services at the facility who are not represented in the sample. The results of this study do not represent these participants and should not be generalized to them. In addition, all of the data come from one halfway house program. There are many halfway house programs across the United States that accept different clients, provide different treatment programs, and in other ways operate under a different model. While the current study provides an example of problems that can arise when implementing the RNR model into halfway houses, more research is still needed to understand the degree to which these issues exist. Finally, a few of the analyses suffered from poor sample sizes. Due to the low numbers of high-risk clients in the facility, some tests have low sample sizes and should be interpreted with caution.

Lessons Learned

The current study serves to demonstrate the existing gap between research and practitioners. In doing so, it provides suggestions on how implementation of the RNR model can be improved. The facility examined here has adopted an evidence-based model for offender rehabilitation. They have adopted validated risk assessment tools, evidence-based programming, guidelines to structure treatment referrals, and have created a database to assess their progress. Nevertheless, reductions in recidivism are still not significant. Overall, the process evaluation reveals several lessons that can be learned from improper adherence to RNR.

First Lesson: Implementing an assessment tool is different than using an assessment tool. It is recommended that the halfway house apply the information gained from the risk assessment by screening out low-risk offenders. While the majority of offenders serviced in the program are primarily moderate and high risk, 70 clients, or around 14%, are still low risk. Since the program does not have the facilities necessary to separate these varying risk groups while in the program, it is advised they not accept low-risk clients. This will both reserve treatment services for higher risk offenders and avoid mixing high- and low-risk clients. This is a small additional step since the facility already implements risk assessment.

Second Lesson: Individualized case plans do not equate to individualized treatment. Despite each case manager making individual treatment plans for offenders, there is little variance in the amount of treatment being given. Analyses revealed that the majority of low, moderate, and high-risk offenders were receiving less than 100 hours of treatment. This is less than half of the dosage that high-risk offenders should be getting. One way this could be handled is by creating an additional place in treatment plans to track dosage. In addition, the program could outsource treatment services to other community treatment facilities to expand the number of treatments available.

Third Lesson: Willingness to change and evaluation can go a long way. If it were not for the facility seeking an evaluation, these problems may have gone undetected. While on their face the RNR principles seem straightforward, in practice they require a lot of effort. It should be expected that many programs will struggle with proper implementation of RNR but it is the role of researchers to help bridge this gap and offer suggestions for improvement.

Disclosure Statement

No potential conflict of interest was reported by the authors.

Funding

There is no funding to report for the following project.

Discussion Questions

1. The researchers were unable to arrange to have participants randomly assigned to either the halfway house or community supervision. How did they work to address this obstacle for the outcome evaluation?
2. How did the process evaluation help the researchers understand the results of their outcome evaluation?
3. On paper, the halfway house was supposed to be adhering to the Risk-Need-Responsivity model of treatments. In what ways did the actual program implementation deviate from that plan?

References

Andrews, D. A., & Bonta, J. (1995). *The level of service inventory-revised*. Multi-Health Systems.

Andrews, D. A., & Bonta, J. (1998). Classification of treatment: The risk principles, the need principle, and the responsivity principle. In *The psychology of criminal conduct* (pp. 242–245).

Andrews, D. A., Bonta, J., & Hoge, R. D. (1990). Classification for effective rehabilitation: Rediscovering psychology. *Criminal Justice and Behavior*, *17*(1), 19–52. https://doi.org/10.1177/0093854890017001004

Andrews, D. A., Bonta, J., & Wormith, J. S. (2006). The recent past and near future of risk and/or need assessment. *Crime and Delinquency*, *52*(5), 7–27. https://doi.org/10.1177/0011128705281756

Andrews, D. A., & Dowden, C. (2005). Managing correctional treatment for reduced recidivism: A meta-analytic review of program integrity. *Legal and Criminological Psychology*, *10*(2), 173–187. https://doi.org/10.1348/135532505X36723

Andrews, D. A., Zinger, I., Hoge, R. D., Bonta, J., Gendreau, P., & Cullen, F. T. (1990). Does correctional treatment work? A clinically relevant and psychologically informed meta-analysis. *Criminology*, *28*(3), 369–404. https://doi.org/10.1111/j.1745-9125.1990.tb01330.x

Baglivio, M. T., Wolff, K. T., Howell, J. C., Jackowski, K., & Greenwald, M. A. (2018). The search for the holy grail: Criminogenic needs matching, intervention dosage, and subsequent recidivism among serious juvenile offenders in residential placement. *Journal of Criminal Justice*, *55*, 46–57. https://doi.org/10.1016/j.jcrimjus.2018.02.001

Barnoski, R. (2004). *Assessing risk for re-offense: Validating the Washington State juvenile court assessment appendices*. Washington State Institute for Public Policy.

Bell, N., Bucklen, K. B., Nakamura, K., Tomkiel, J., Santore, A., Russel, L., & Orth, R. (2013). Pennsylvania Department of Corrections recidivism report 2013. Pennsylvania Department of Corrections.

Bonta, J., & Andrews, D. A. (2007). Risk-need-responsivity model for offender assessment and rehabilitation. *Rehabilitation*, *6*(1), 1–22.

Bonta, J., & Motiuk, L. L. (1987). The diversion of incarcerated offenders to correctional halfway houses. *Journal of Research in Crime and Delinquency*, *24*(4), 302–323. https://doi.org/10.1177/0022427887024004006

Bush, J., Glick, B., & Taymans, J. (1997). *Thinking for a change*. National Institute of Corrections, United States Department of Justice.

Caputo, G. A. (2004). *Intermediate sanctions in corrections* (No. 4). University of North Texas Press.

Cullen, F. T., & Gilbert, K. E. (1982). *Reaffirming rehabilitation*. Anderson.

Dowden, C., & Andrews, D. A. (1999). What works in young offender treatment: A meta-analysis. *Forum on Corrections Research*, *11*(2), 21–24.

Dowell, D. A., Klein, C., & Krichmar, C. (1985). Evaluation of a halfway house for women. *Journal of Criminal Justice*, *13*(3), 217–226. https://doi.org/10.1016/0047-2352(85)90100-X

Drawbridge, D. C., Todorovic, K., Winters, G. M., & Vincent, G. M. (2019). Implementation of risk-need-responsivity principles into probation case planning. *Law and Human Behavior*, *43*(5), 455. https://doi.org/10.1037/lhb0000351

Duwe, G., & Clark, V. (2015). Importance of program integrity: Outcome evaluation of a gender-responsive, cognitive-behavioral program for female offenders. *Criminology and Public Policy*, *14*(2), 301–328. https://doi.org/10.1111/1745-9133.12123

Farringer, A. J., Duriez, S. A., Manchak, S. M., & Sullivan, C. C. (2019). Adherence to "what works": Examining trends across 14 years of correctional program assessment. *Corrections*, 1–19. https://doi.org/10.1080/23774657.2019.1659193

Gendreau, P. (1996). The principles of effective intervention with offenders. In A. T. Harland (Ed.), *Choosing correctional options that work: Defining the demand and evaluating the supply* (pp. 117–130). Sage Publications.

Gendreau, P., Little, T., & Goggin, C. (1996). A meta-analysis of the predictors of adult offender recidivism: What works. *Criminology*, *34*(4), 575–608. https://doi.org/10.1111/j.1745-9125.1996.tb01220.x

Gendreau, P., & Ross, R. R. (1987). Revivification of rehabilitation: Evidence from the 1980's. *Justice Quarterly*, *4*(3), 349–408. https://doi.org/10.1080/07418828700089411

Grieger, L., & Hosser, D. (2014). Which risk factors are really predictive? An analysis of Andrews and Bonta's "central eight" risk factors for recidivism in German youth correctional facility inmates. *Criminal Justice and Behavior*, *41*(5), 613–634. https://doi.org/10.1177/0093854813511432

Hamilton, Z. K., & Campbell, C. M. (2014). Uncommonly observed: The impact of new jersey's halfway house system. *Criminal Justice and Behavior*, *41*(11), 1354–1375. https://doi.org/10.1177/0093854814546132

Hannah-Mofatt, K. (2005). Criminogenic needs and the transformative risk subject. *Punishment and Society*, *7*(1), 29–51. https://doi.org/10.1177/1462474505048132

Hanson, R. K., Gordon, A., Harris, A. J., Marques, J. K., Murphy, W., Quinsey, V. L., & Seto, M. C. (2002). First report of the collaborative outcome data project on the effectiveness of psychological treatment for sex offenders. *Sexual Abuse: A Journal of Research and Treatment*, *14*(2), 169–194. https://doi.org/10.1177/107906320201400207

Hartman, D. J., Friday, P. C., & Minor, K. I. (1994). Residential probation: A seven-year follow-up study of halfway house discharges. *Journal of Criminal Justice*, *22*(6), 503–515. https://doi.org/10.1016/0047-2352(94)90092-2

Holsinger, A. M., Lurigio, A. J., & Latessa, E. J. (2001). Practitioner's guide to understanding the basis of assessing offender risk. *Federal Probation*, *46*, 47.

Knight, K., Garner, B. R., Simpson, D. D., Morey, J. T., & Flynn, P. M. (2006). An assessment for criminal thinking. *Crime & Delinquency*, *52*(1), 159–177. https://doi.org/10.1177/0011128705281749

Krauss, D. A. (2004). Adjusting risk of recidivism: Do judicial departures worsen or improve recidivism prediction under the federal sentencing guidelines? *Behavioral Sciences and the Law*, *22*(6), 731–750. https://doi.org/10.1002/bsl.609

La Vigne, N., Daviews, E., Palmer, T., & Halberstadt, R. (2008). *Release planning for successful reentry: A guide for corrections, service providers, and community groups*. Urban Institute Justice Policy Center.

Labrecque, R. M., Smith, P., Lovins, B. K., & Latessa, E. J. (2014). The importance of reassessment: How changes in the LSI-R risk score can improve the prediction of recidivism. *Journal of Offender Rehabilitation*, *53*(2), 116–128. https://doi.org/10.1080/10509674.2013.868389

Landenberger, N. A., & Lipsey, M. W. (2005). The positive effects of cognitive—behavioral programs for offenders: A meta-analysis of factors associated with effective treatment. *Journal of Experimental Criminology*, *1*(4), 451–476. https://doi.org/10.1007/s11292-005-3541-7

Latessa, E. J., Cullen, F. T., & Gendreau, P. (2002). Beyond correctional quackery-professionalism and the possibility of effective treatment. *Federal Probation*, *66*, 43–49.

Latessa, E. J., & Lovins, B. (2010). The role of offender risk assessment: A policy maker guide. *Victims and Offenders*, *5*(3), 203–219. https://doi.org/10.1080/15564886.2010.485900

Latessa, E. J., & Travis, L. F., III. (1991). Halfway house or probation: A comparison of alternative dispositions. *Journal of Crime and Justice*, *14*(1), 53–75. https://doi.org/10.1080/0735648X.1991.9721426

Lipsey, M. W. (1999). Can intervention rehabilitate serious delinquents? *The Annals of the American Academy of Political and Social Science*, *564*(1), 142–166. https://doi.org/10.1177/000271629956400109

Lipsey, M. W., Chapman, G. L., & Landenberger, N. A. (2001). Cognitive-Behavioral programs for offenders. *The Annals of the American Academy of Political and Social Science*, *578*(1), 144–157. https://doi.org/10.1177/000271620157800109

Lloyd, C. D., Hanson, R. K., Richards, D. K., & Serin, R. C. (2020). Reassessment improves prediction of criminal recidivism: A prospective study of 3,421 individuals in New Zealand. *Psychological Assessment*, *32*(6), 568. https://doi.org/10.1037/pas0000813

Lowenkamp, C. T. (2004). *Correctional program integrity and treatment effectiveness: A multi-site, program level analysis* [Doctoral dissertation, University of Cincinnati].

Lowenkamp, C. T., & Latessa, E. J. (2002). *Evaluation of Ohio's community based correctional facilities and halfway house programs: Final Report.*

Unpublished Technical Report: University of Cincinnati.

Lowenkamp, C. T., & Latessa, E. J. (2005). Increasing the effectiveness of correctional programming through the risk principle: Identifying offenders for residential placement. *Criminology and Public Policy*, *4*(2), 263–290. https://doi.org/10.1111/j.1745-9133.2005.00021.x

Lowenkamp, C. T., Latessa, E. J., & Holsinger, A. M. (2006). The risk principle in action: What have we learned from 13,676 offenders and 97 correctional programs? *Crime and Delinquency*, *52*(1), 77–93. https://doi.org/10.1177/0011128705281747

Lowenkamp, C. T., Latessa, E. J., & Smith, P. (2006). Does correctional program quality really matter? The impact of adhering to the principles of effective intervention. *Criminology and Public Policy*, *5*(3), 575–594. https://doi.org/10.1111/j.1745-9133.2006.00388.x

Makarios, M., Sperber, K. G., & Latessa, E. J. (2014). Treatment dosage and the risk principle: A refinement and extension. *Journal of Offender Rehabilitation*, *53*(5), 334–350. https://doi.org/10.1080/10509674.2014.922157

Martinson, R. (1974). What Works?—Questions and answers about prison reform. *The Public Interest*, *35*, 22–54.

McCafferty, J. T. (2017). Professional discretion and the predictive validity of a juvenile risk assessment instrument: Exploring the overlooked principle of effective correctional classification. *Youth Violence and Juvenile Justice*, *15*(2), 103–118. https://doi.org/10.1177/1541204015622255

Mee-Lee, D. (2013). *The ASAM criteria: Treatment criteria for addictive, substance-related, and cooccurring conditions* (3rd ed.). Change Companies.

Myer, A. J., & Makarios, M. D. (2017). Understanding the impact of a dui court through treatment integrity: A mixed-methods approach. *Journal of Offender Rehabilitation*, *56*(4), 252–276. https://doi.org/10.1080/10509674.2017.1306007

Nagy, G. (2013). Moving implementation of evidence-based practice forward: A practitioner's view. *Justice Research and Policy*, *15*(1), 159–176. https://doi.org/10.3818/JRP.15.1.2013.159

Palmer, T. (1975). Martinson revisited. *Journal of Research in Crime and Delinquency*, *12*(2), 133–152. https://doi.org/10.1177/002242787501200206

Rossi, P., Freeman, H., & Lipsey, M. (1999). The social context of evaluation. In *Evaluation: A systematic approach* (pp. 397–416).

Rossi, P. H., Lipsey, M. W., & Freeman, H. E. (2004). *Evaluation: A systematic approach*. SAGE Publications.

Scarpitti, F., Inciardi, J., & Pottieger, A. (1993). Process evaluation techniques for corrections-based drug treatment programs. *Journal of Offender Rehabilitation*, *19*(3), 71–79. https://doi.org/10.1300/J076v19n03_04

Sperber, K. G., Latessa, E. J., & Makarios, M. D. (2013). Examining the interaction between level of risk and dosage of treatment. *Criminal Justice and Behavior*, *40*(3), 338–348. https://doi.org/10.1177/0093854812467942

Taxman, F. S., & Caudy, M. S. (2015). Risk tells us who, but not what or how: Empirical assessment of the complexity of criminogenic needs to inform correctional programming. *Criminology and Public Policy*, *14*(1), 71–103. https://doi.org/10.1111/1745-9133.12116

Vose, B., Lowenkamp, C. T., Smith, P., & Cullen, F. T. (2009). Gender and the predictive validity of the LSI-R: A study of parolees and probationers. *Journal of Contemporary Criminal Justice*, *25*(4), 49–471. https://doi.org/10.1177/1043986209344797

Wormith, J. S., Hogg, S., & Guzzo, L. (2012). The predictive validity of a general risk/needs assessment inventory on sexual offender recidivism and an exploration of the professional override. *Criminal Justice and Behavior*, *39*(12), 1511–1538. https://doi.org/10.1177/0093854812455741

Wormith, J. S., Hogg, S. M., & Guzzo, L. (2015). The predictive validity of the LS/CMI with aboriginal offenders in Canada. *Criminal Justice and Behavior*, *42*(5), 481–508. https://doi.org/10.1177/0093854814552843

Zhang, J. (2016). Testing the predictive validity of the LSI-R using a sample of young male offenders on probation in Guangzhou, China. *International Journal of Offender Therapy and Comparative Criminology*, *60*(4), 456–468. https://doi.org/10.1177/0306624X14557471

Glossary

Accelerated/intensive longitudinal design: A type of research design that involves frequent measurements of multiple cohorts.

Accidental sampling: See convenience sampling.

Activities: The third part of the system model of the policy process. Inputs are turned into outputs through activities. The combination of inputs, activities, and outputs produces impacts/outcomes.

Administrative robustness: The extent to which a program can remain successful in the face of poor implementation.

Aggregates: A group or collection of items.

Anecdotal evidence: Evidence collected informally and largely based on personal experience.

Anonymity: The identity of the research participant is not known to anyone, including the researcher. It is not possible to link the research participants' responses to any of the data.

Applied research: Research that deals with a specific policy or program question. Includes program evaluation and policy analysis.

Arrestee Drug Abuse Monitoring (ADAM): Originally called Drug Use Forecasting. Researchers interviewed newly arrested individuals and asked them to self-report drug use and provide a urine sample. ADAM I data were collected from 1997 to 2003, while ADAM II data were collected from 2007 to 2014.

Attribute: A characteristic that describes something.

Attrition bias: Nonrandom loss of research participants over the course of a longitudinal study in ways that result in a non-representative sample. Also known as mortality.

Basic research: Research conducted with the goal of contributing to academic knowledge and advancing science. Also called pure research or scientific research.

***Belmont Report*:** Report published by the U.S. Department of Health, Education, and Welfare in 1979. The report provided ethical guidelines for research involving human subjects, including three principles: respect for persons, beneficence, and justice.

Beneficence: A principle of the Belmont Report that requires researchers to maximize benefits to human participants in research while minimizing any possible harms.

Black box evaluation: A program evaluation that includes only the study of the program's impacts or outcomes.

Blind peer review: A process of reviewing research for publication that involves experts in the field reading manuscripts without knowing the identities of the authors.

Bounding: A technique used in panel studies to reduce telescoping. Researchers conduct a baseline interview, and then during the follow-up interview, the initial interview is used as a temporal reference point.

Cambridge Study in Delinquent Development: Prospective longitudinal design of delinquency including interviews of over 400 boys born in the early 1950s. The study began in the early 1960s, when most of the boys were eight or nine years old.

Causation: One event, specifically the independent variable, causes a particular outcome or impact on the dependent variable. To establish causation, one must demonstrate a relationship between the independent and dependent variables, that the independent variable precedes the dependent variable in time, and that all other possible relevant variables are explained away.

Certificate of Confidentiality (CoC): Certificate available through the U.S. National Institute of Health or the Department of Health and Human Services that allows researchers to protect the privacy of research participants. Researchers are prohibited from disclosing the identities or sensitive information of research participants to anyone outside of the research project without their consent. This certificate is available for research funded through the NIH or DHSS grants or for selected studies related to the NIH or DHSS but not funded through them.

Classical experiment: A research design characterized by three elements: (1) an experimental and control group, (2) random selection into the experimental and control group, and (3) at least one pretest and posttest measure for each group. This is commonly known as the gold standard in research design.

Cleaning: Preparing data for analysis by correcting mistakes, removing duplicates, and properly formatting the data.

Clear box evaluation: A type of program evaluation that involves both a full process evaluation and an outcome/impact evaluation. This is more informative than gray box and black box evaluations.

Close-ended questions: Survey items where the answer options are provided for the respondent to select.

Coding: Assignment of numerical values to items to facilitate data analysis.

Cohort study: A prospective longitudinal design that involves tracking individuals who are part of the same group, such as the same class in school or the same age.

Communities that Care Youth Survey: A panel study with repeated surveys of over 4,000 students, starting in the fifth grade. The goal is to assess risk and protective factors associated with substance abuse.

Comparison group: A group monitored as part of research for comparison purposes. Individuals, groups, or organizations are nonrandomly assigned to this group to compare to the experimental group being exposed to the independent variable. Researchers can then contrast the performance of the experimental group (exposed to the independent variable) to the comparison groups (not exposed to the independent variable) on the outcome of interest (dependent variable). Used in quasi-experimental and some pre-experimental designs.

Compensatory equalization of treatment: A threat to internal validity that involves efforts to compensate for the control or comparison group's lack of exposure to the independent variable.

Compensatory rivalry: A threat to internal validity that involves members of the control or comparison groups trying to improve their performance to keep pace with or outperform the experimental group.

Complete observer: See covert participation

Complete participant: A field researcher role where the researcher participates in the daily lives of the individuals being studied while keeping his/her true identity a secret. Also known as covert observation.

Computer-assisted interviewing (CAI): Interview protocol involving the use of a computer for data collection.

Computer-assisted survey instruments (CASI): Interview protocol involving the use of a computer for data collection. Respondents can either take the survey independently on a device with the CASI software on it, or interviewers can read the questions while respondents key in their answers on the computer or tablet.

Computer-assisted telephone interviewing (CATI): Telephone interview protocol where the interviewer reads questions from a computer and types in the respondents' answers.

Concept: An abstract idea or conception.

Concurrent validity: A type of criterion validity. This is the extent to which a measure or set of measures produces the same outcome as another measure taken at the same time.

Confidence interval: Range of values in which the population parameter lies.

Confidence level: Probability that the population mean falls within a confidence interval.

Confidentiality: Researchers are aware of the participants' identity, but they agree to keep their research participation secret. While researchers will share the results of the research, they promise not to attribute any specific aspect of the data to an individual. If direct quotations are to be used, researchers will use a pseudonym instead of actual names.

Constant: Something that is not a variable.

Construct validity: The extent to which a measure or set of measures accurately reflects the theory and philosophy the concept aims to measure.

Content analysis: Objective, systematic, and generalizable description of communication content.

Content validity: The extent to which a measure or set of measures captures the full range of meaning of the concept.

Contingency question: Survey questions that are asked only if the respondent provides a certain answer to the previous question. People who respond that they have not been victims of crime over the past six months would be asked to skip questions specific to recent victimization.

Continuous variables: Variables with an infinite number of answer options.

Control group: A group monitored as part of research for comparison purposes. Individuals, groups, or organizations are randomly assigned to this group to compare to the experimental group being exposed to the independent variable. Researchers can then contrast the performance of the experimental group (exposed to the independent variable) to the comparison groups (not exposed to the independent variable) on the outcome of interest (dependent variable). Control groups are an element of experimental research designs.

Control variable: A variable that is not the primary focus of research. Multivariate statistical analysis can account for the possible influence of control variables by holding them constant, allowing us to look at the relationship between X and Y independent of their influence.

Convenience sampling: Nonprobability sampling plan that is based on what is convenient for the researcher. This technique allows anyone willing and able to participate in the study to be involved. Also known as accidental sampling.

Correlation: A mutual relationship or association between two things.

Counterbalanced design: A research design that allows for the testing of the sequence of interventions. Each group would experience interventions (X, or the experimental stimuli) in a different order to learn their potential impact on the dependent variable.

Covert participation: A type of participant observation where research subjects are not informed of the researcher's true identity or purpose. Also known as complete participant.

Creaming: Selecting only those most likely to succeed for a sample in a program evaluation.

Crime clock: Visual depiction of how often crime occurs. Crime clocks have been found to be inaccurate due to their failure to account for population changes.

Crime mapping: Use of mapping software to analyze crime incidents.

Criterion validity: The extent to which a measure or group of measures predicts the outcome of another measure. Types of criterion validity are concurrent and predictive validity.

Crossover design: Experimental design that uses a program waitlist as the control group before eventually transitioning them into the experimental group.

Cross-sectional design: A study involving observations/data collection at a single point in time.

Dark figure of crime: Crimes not known to the police.

Declaration of Helsinki: Statement developed by the World Medical Association that outlines ethical principles for medical research involving human subjects.

Deductive reasoning: Method of inquiry where researchers start with what is already known, in the form of existing research and theories, then use that information do make predictions (hypotheses), followed by data collection. Deductive reasoning moves from more general ideas to examination of more specific issues.

Demoralization: A threat to internal validity where the control or comparison group experiences reduced morale or productivity due to its awareness that it is not receiving the experimental stimulus.

Dependent variable: The outcome or effect variable. Researchers hypothesize that changes in the independent variable will impact the dependent variable. Also known as "Y" or "DV."

Depth interview: Long interviews used in qualitative research. Researchers often approach these interviews with a topic list but no specific questions to be asked.

Diffusion of treatment: A threat to internal validity where the experimental stimulus is applied to the comparison or control group in addition to the experimental group. Also called contamination.

Dimension: One particular aspect of a concept.

Discrete variables: Variables with a finite number of answer options.

Disproportionate stratified sampling: A type of proportionate sampling where the population is first stratified into categories of interest (e.g., race), and then random samples are taken from each group, but disproportionately to provide some groups greater representation in the sample.

Ecological fallacy: Drawing conclusions about individuals based on research findings from a larger unit of analysis.

Empirical evidence: Information acquired through systematic observation and experimentation.

Equal probability selection method (EPSM): Sampling procedures that provide all members of the population an equal probability of being selected, typically achieved through random sampling.

Equivalent groups posttest-only design: An experimental design that involves random selection into either the treatment or the control group and then measurement of the dependent variable after the experimental group has been exposed to the independent variable.

Evaluability assessment: A systematic way to examine a program to determine whether a full evaluation is warranted.

Evidence-based practice (EBP): The use of methodologically rigorous research to inform decisions about which programs are effective and which should be discarded.

Exception fallacy: Generalizing findings from a few individuals or an exceptional circumstance to large groups. Also known as individualistic fallacy.

Exhaustive: Providing enough answer options for survey items that allows for every participant to truthfully and accurately answer the question.

Experimental group: The group in research that will be exposed to the experimental stimulus.

External validity: The likelihood of being able to replicate research findings in another time or place. A type of generalizability.

Face validity: The extent to which, by appearance, measures are accurately capturing what they intend to measure.

Factorial design: An experimental design that allows for comparison of multiple treatments. Also includes random assignment to groups and pre- and posttest measures.

Focus group: Type of in-person guided discussion, typically involving 8 to 15 people.

Forgiving introduction: A technique used to introduce self-report survey questions about socially undesirable, or even illegal, behavior by first assuring respondents that others have engaged in such behavior.

Formative evaluation: Program evaluation conducted while the program is being implemented with the goal of providing the implementation team feedback.

Gatekeeper: A known and well-respected member of a subculture who is willing to introduce researchers to informants and vouch for them.

Generalizability: The extent to which research results based on a sample are applicable to the population.

Going native: Ethnographers becoming too familiar with the group they are studying to the point that they start to identify with the study group.

Gray box evaluation: A type of program evaluation that involves an outcome/impact evaluation plus a partial process evaluation. This is more informative than a black box evaluation but less informative than clear box.

Gray literature: Unpublished research.

Grounded theory: Development of theory based on gathered data.

Hawthorne Effect: A threat to external validity that involves improved performance of individuals who realize that they are being observed. Named after the Hawthorne Plant where it was first noted.

Historicism: Belief that all historical and social events are unique and warrant chronicling.

History: A threat to internal validity that involves an event outside the study contributing to changes in the dependent variable.

Hotspots policing: Policing technique that starts with geographic analysis to identify locations experiencing disproportionate amounts of crime or calls for service and then conducting saturation patrols of those areas.

Hypothesis: Prediction of a relationship between variables.

Illusion of knowledge: Mistaken belief that we know more about a topic than we actually do.

Impact evaluation: See outcome evaluation.

Implementation failure: Failure of a program due to lack of adherence to the program's plan.

Incident: A single event.

Independent variable: The predictor or cause thought to impact the value of the dependent variable. Also known as "X," "IV," experimental stimulus, or treatment.

Index: A measures constructed by summing other items on a survey or data collection tool.

Individualistic fallacy: See exception fallacy.

Inductive reasoning: Method of inquiry beginning with specific observations and then moving to more general concepts, such as theory development.

Informed Consent: Agreement of individuals to participate in research after they have been fully informed of the elements of the study. Elements generally include the purpose, length of research participation, any potential risks or rewards, and the voluntary nature of participation.

Inputs: The second part of the system model of the policy process including resources allocated to address some type of demand.

Institutional Review Board (IRB): A formal board with the responsibility of reviewing and monitoring research involving human subjects. IRBs are tasked with ensuring that researchers are providing potential human research participants with necessary protections.

Instrumentation: A threat to internal validity that involves changes to data collection strategies for the same variables over time.

Inter-rater reliability: A measure of reliability across data collectors.

Interrupted time-series: A type of quasi-experiment with several data collection points over time before and after the introduction of the independent variable.

Interrupted time series with non-equivalent comparison group: A type of quasi-experiment with several data collection points over time, a non-equivalent comparison group, and the introduction of the independent variable as the "interruption" that occurs after several data collection waves.

Interrupted time series with treatment removal: A type of quasi-experiment with several data collection points over time and the introduction, and then removal, of the treatment stimulus, otherwise known as the independent variable.

Inter-university Consortium for Political and Social Research (ICPSR): A consortium of academic institutions and research organizations that maintains a data archive of over 350,000 files pertaining to social and behavioral sciences.

Interval level: A level of measurement with equal distance between the items.

Justice: One of three principles of the *Belmont Report*. Requires that the benefits and burdens of research be evenly distributed among research participants.

Kansas City Preventive Patrol Experiment: A study conducted in Kansas City in the early 1970s where neighborhoods were randomly assigned to receive intensive police patrols, regular numbers of patrols, or only visits from the police if they needed to respond to a call for service. The researchers found no difference in crime rates between the three areas.

Latent Content: Underlying meaning of content. Also known as context units.

Lehigh Longitudinal Study: A panel design that followed children and their parents to collect data on child abuse and children's exposure to domestic violence.

Likert scale: A scale, usually five to seven points, that allows respondents to indicate their level of satisfaction or agreement.

Longitudinal design: A type of research design with repeated measurements/observations over time.

Manifest content: Obvious, clearly measurable items. Also known as recording units.

Maryland Scientific Methods Scale (SMS): Measures research on methodological vigor on a five-point scale.

Matching: A technique used in research designs with non-equivalent groups to pair individuals from treatment and comparison groups on theoretically-relevant variables.

Matrix: A set of close-ended survey items where the same set of answer options appear in the columns, while the survey questions or statements are listed in the rows.

Maturation: A threat to internal validity where the change observed in study participants is a result of individual maturation rather than the treatment stimulus.

Meta-analysis: A systematic review of research that also involves statistical analysis of the studies' results.

Mnemonic device: Rhyme or other verbal tool used to aid memory.

Monitoring the Future (MTF): Cohort design study, sponsored by the National Institute of Drug Abuse, that surveys adolescents to learn about their drug and alcohol use and attitudes.

Mortality: A threat to internal validity that involves research participants withdrawing from the research before completion. Also known as attrition.

Multiple treatment interference: A type of threat to external validity that involves the inability of researchers to identify which, of multiple treatments, is producing a change in the dependent variable.

Multistage cluster sampling: A probability sampling technique that involves researchers dividing a location into segments and then taking random samples from each of those areas.

Mutually exclusive: Two events that cannot occur at the same time. For survey construction, this means that only one answer option will be an appropriate answer for each respondent.

National Crime Victimization Survey (NCVS): Longitudinal Panel Design of U.S. households conducted by the United States Census Bureau to measure victimization. All members of the household aged 12 and older are surveyed about their victimization experiences every six months for 3.5 years.

National Incident Based Reporting System (NIBRS): An incident-based, FBI-sponsored crime reporting system intended to replace the UCR. NIBRS provides crime data from participating federal, state, county, local, college/university, and tribal law enforcement agencies.

National Youth Survey (NYS): Longitudinal design of self-reported delinquent behavior of juveniles 11 to 17 years of age.

Nominal level: A level of measurement that places items into categories with no rank order.

Nonprobability sampling: Sampling techniques that violate the equal probability selection method.

Null hypothesis: A prediction of no relationship between the independent and dependent variables.

Nuremberg Code: Set of ethical principles written following the Nuremberg trial of Nazi war criminals. It includes 10 rules for protecting human subjects involved in research.

Obedience to Authority Study: An experiment conducted by Stanley Milgram to study human behavior. Participants were given the role of teacher and told to review vocabulary words with a person identified as a learner. If the learner did not recite the correct words, a man in charge of the laboratory would order the teacher to administer a shock to the learner. The teachers were unaware that they were not actually shocking anyone.

Observer as participant: A role for field researchers where the researchers do one-visit interviews with participants.

One-group before-after design: A pre-experimental design that includes observations of a sample before and after the introduction of the independent variable.

One-group posttest-only design: A pre-experimental design that lacks a comparison group and a pretest measurement. Researchers observe a sample after exposure to the independent variable.

Open-ended questions: Survey questions that require the respondents to answer using their own words.

Operationalization: Defining concepts to make them more specific, resulting in measurable variables.

Ordinal level: A level of measurement that rank orders the items.

Outcome evaluation: A type of evaluation research that studies outcomes produced by the program's inputs, activities, and outputs. Also known as an impact evaluation.

Outcomes: The fifth part of the system model of the policy process. Outcomes (or impacts) are the product of the policy's inputs, activities, and outputs.

Outputs: The fourth part of the system model of the policy process. Outputs are the product of inputs and activities and lead to outcomes.

Panel study: A longitudinal design that involves data collection from the same individuals at least twice.

Participant as observer: A fieldwork role where researchers perform participant observation by partaking in the daily lives of those being studied while making one's identity and purpose known.

Peer-review: A quality-control process used by many research and academic publications that involves manuscripts undergoing a review by experts in the field who will determine whether the document should be published. Peer-reviewed journals are considered the best outlet for research.

Philadelphia Birth Cohort Study: Cohort study of nearly 10,000 boys born in Philadelphia in 1945. Researchers tracked the boys from their 10th birthdays through their 18th birthdays and measured their involvement in delinquent behavior. Notable results included the finding that 6 percent of the cohort was responsible for over half of the group's offending and that the juveniles did not specialize in any particular type of criminal activity.

Plagiarism: Passing off someone else's work as one's own.

Planned change: Policy changes in response to a problem or perceived problem, often characterized by careful research and analysis.

Policy: Rule or set of rules or guidelines for how to make a decision.

Policy analysis: Process of researching and identifying potential solutions to a current or anticipated problem. Also called problem analysis.

Population parameter: Summary description of a variable in the population.

Positivism: Approach to research common in the natural sciences that prioritizes using the scientific method.

Power: The probability of correctly rejecting the null hypothesis. Power can be increased by increasing the sample size.

Predatory journals: Publications that prioritize self-interest at the expense of scholarship and quality. These journals often publish articles, for a fee, without concern for quality control.

Predictive policing: A combination of policing tactics, including problem-oriented policing, intelligence-led policing, and crime mapping, to allow police to analyze data and prevent crime.

Predictive validity: A type of criterion validity concerning the extent to which a measure or a set of measures predicts an outcome.

Pre-experimental design: A research design that lacks two of the three elements of the classical experiment. These designs lack randomization of participants into experimental and control groups. They may also lack pretest measures and/or a nonrandomly selected comparison group.

Prevalence: Number or proportion of unique individuals impacted by something, such as crime victimization.

Primary data sources: Raw data that researchers make available to other researchers for analysis.

Probability sampling: Sampling methods that are conducted using the Equal Probability Selection Method (EPSM).

Process evaluation: A type of evaluation research that involves studying program implementation.

Program: Set of services aimed at achieving specific goals and objectives within specified individuals, groups, organizations, or communities.

Program evaluation: Type of applied research that studies the extent to which a program was implemented as planned, and produced the desired outcomes. Includes process and outcome/impact evaluations.

Project: Time-limited set of services provided to individuals, groups organizations, and communities, and usually focus on a single need, problem, or issue.

Proofs: Mathematical procedure demonstrating that stated assumptions logically guarantee a conclusion.

Propensity score matching (PSM): Statistical technique that matches comparison group participants to experimental group members on variables relevant to the specific research project.

Proportionate stratified sampling: A type of probability sampling where the population is first stratified by some characteristic of interest, and then proportionate random samples are selected from each stratum.

Prospective design: A type of longitudinal design where researchers collect data at baseline and then follow participants for additional data collection to observe changes over time.

Pseudonym: A fictitious name given to a research participant to protect their identify.

Publication bias: Tendency for studies finding support for the research hypothesis to have a greater chance of being published.

Purposive sampling: A nonprobability sampling plan that is based on the judgment and knowledge of the researcher.

Quackery: Application of interventions that are not based on knowledge of effective programs for reducing crime or changing behavior of people involved in crime.

Quasi-experiment: A research design that is missing one of the characteristics of a classical experiment. Includes quasi-experiments with non-equivalent groups and time-series designs.

Quota sampling: A nonprobability sampling plan where the researcher selects proportions of individuals based on a characteristic of interest (e.g., race).

Randomized response technique (RRT): An approach to asking participants sensitive questions where the participant flips a coin and, based on the results, responds to one of two questions. The data collector records the answer but is unaware of which question was asked. The goal is to give the respondent a degree of privacy while participating in the interview.

Ratio level: A level of measurement with equal distance between the items. Similar to interval level but has a definite zero.

Reactivity: A research participant's change in behavior as a response to being observed.

Reliability: The consistency or stability of a measure or set of measures.

Replication: Repeating a study at a different time and/or place to see if the findings match earlier research results.

Research hypothesis: A prediction of a relationship between an independent and dependent variable.

Respect for persons: One of three principles of the *Belmont Report*. Requires that research participants be treated as autonomous agents who can make decisions for themselves free of coercion.

Respondent-driven sampling: A type of nonprobability snowball sampling. Researchers try to limit the amount of sample bias by increasing the number of initial informants and limiting the number of referrals from each informant.

Retrospective design: A research design that measures past behavior by asking participants to recall events or by researchers collecting data memorializing past events.

Rival causal factors: Variables other than the independent variable that impacts the value of the dependent variable. Also known as "Z" or threats to internal validity.

Sample: A subset of a population.

Sample bias: See selection bias.

Sample statistic: Summary description of a variable in the sample.

Sampling error: The discrepancy between a sample and the population.

Sampling frame: A comprehensive list of all members of a population from which a sample is to be selected.

Satisficing: Research respondents seeking to provide what they believe to be a satisfactory answer to a survey question without expending cognitive effort.

Scale: Ordered survey responses that allow researchers to increase the level of measurement from nominal to ordinal or possibly interval or ratio. Examples of scales are items from 1 to 5 with 1 = strongly disagree and 5 = strongly agree, or rating interest in an event from 1 = definitely will not go to 10 = definitely will go.

Scientific method: A blueprint for a way of doing empirical research that involves hypothesis formulation and testing, systematic observation, and precise measurements.

Scientism: An extreme form of positivism that suggests only concepts that can be measured are worth studying.

Secondary data analysis: Reanalysis of data that were originally gathered for other purposes.

Secondary data sources: Data that have already been analyzed and reported but then are used by other researchers for secondary data analysis.

Selection-maturation interaction: A threat to internal validity that involves the combination of selection bias in sample selection and differential maturation.

Selection (sample) bias: A threat to both internal and external validity that involves selection of nonequivalent groups.

Semi-structured survey: Surveys that contain a combination of close-ended and open-ended questions.

Series victimization: Crimes that are similar in type but occur with frequency.

Skip logic: Computerized survey programming that moves the respondent to the next appropriate question based on their response to a contingency question.

Simple random sampling: A type of probability sampling that involves selecting subjects at random, usually by "picking out of a hat" or using a random number generator.

Simulation: Attempted replication of real-life scenarios in a laboratory setting.

Snowball sampling: A nonprobability sampling method that involves researchers increasing their sample size by getting referrals from research participants.

Solomon four-group design: An experimental design including randomized assignment of participants into four groups. Group one is an experimental group that receives the pre- and posttest and is exposed to the independent variable. Group two gets the pre- and posttest but is not exposed to the independent variable. Group three is exposed to the independent variable and receives a posttest but not a pretest. Group four receives only the posttest.

Split-half method: A test of reliability that involves measuring the same construct on one survey by splitting the questions measuring that construct in half and then testing them for consistency.

Sponsor: A person or organization that can help researchers make connections with organizations they wish to study.

Spurious relationship: A relationship between the independent and dependent variables that is not genuine, because both are related to an additional variable, known as a rival causal factor (Z).

Stanford Prison Experiment: A simulation of prison conditions that occurred in the basement of an academic building at Stanford University. College-age males were randomly selected to act either as prisoners or guards. The two-week study ended after six days.

Statistical conclusion validity: A type of threat to internal validity that is the extent to which researchers are able to determine whether two variables are related.

Statistical regression: A threat to internal validity that involves those research participants with extreme scores regressing to the mean independent of the influence of the treatment stimulus.

Stratified random sampling: A probability sampling technique that involves dividing the population into different strata that are of interest to the study. After that division, the researchers take random samples from each stratum.

Structured survey: Surveys with close-ended questions or items where respondents choose from available answer options.

Summative evaluation: Program evaluation conducted after the program has been implemented and focuses on program outcomes.

Systematic random sampling: A probability sampling technique that involves selecting the nth (5th, 10th, etc.) element of the population.

Systematic review: Collection and summarization of empirical evidence that meets pre-specified inclusion criteria.

***Tearoom Trade*:** Controversial book published by Laud Humphreys in the 1970s. Humphreys did covert observation of males engaging in secret homosexual activities and then tracked them to their homes so that he could survey the men and their families under the guise of doing social health research.

Telescoping: Placement of an incident into an incorrect time span when asked to recall events.

Testing effects: A threat to internal validity that involves the pretest sensitizing of participants to the purpose of the study. This enhanced awareness then impacts the value of the dependent variable.

Test-retest method: A reliability check that involves surveying individuals and then surveying them again on some of the same variables to check for consistency of responses.

Theory: Attempt to construct a plausible explanation of reality.

Theory failure: Program failure due to flaws in the theory behind the program.

Threats to internal validity: Factors other than the independent variable that might explain variation in the dependent variable.

Time-series: A type of longitudinal design that involves numerous data collection points, typically collected at equal time intervals.

Treatment integrity: The extent to which the program or policy was implemented as intended.

Trend study: A type of longitudinal design that tracks specific characteristics of a population over time.

Triangulation: Using multiple measures and/or sources of information to measure the same concept.

Two-group posttest-only design: A non-equivalent groups design where posttest measures are taken after the experimental group is exposed to the independent variable.

Uniform Crime Report (UCR): Nationwide program with 18,000 participating police departments with that published crime data from states, counties, cities, colleges and universities, tribal areas, and federal law enforcement departments.

Unit of analysis: Who or what is being studied.

Unit of observation: Items or individuals from which researchers collect data with the goal of learning about the study's unit of analysis. In some studies, the unit of observation and the unit of analysis are the same.

Unplanned change: Policy changes that occur quickly, in reaction to a problem or perceived problem, with little consideration of consequences.

Unstructured survey: Surveys consisting of open-ended questions or items that respondents answer using their own words.

Validity: The extent to which an item or set of items accurately measures what it is intended to measure.

Variable: A measurable concept that varies from case to case.

***Verstehen*:** Means "understanding" in German. In the social sciences, it refers to ethnographers achieving a level of understanding of the culture they are studying.

Victimization rate: Number of victimizations over the number of persons in the population multiplied by a constant (such as 1,000). Rates allow us to compare statistics over time and across different populations.

Victimless crimes: Crimes that lack a clear victim, including sex work, drug dealing, and gambling.

Index

For Product Safety Concerns and Information please contact our EU representative GPSR@taylorandfrancis.com Taylor & Francis Verlag GmbH, Kaufingerstraße 24, 80331 München, Germany